JOHN DEWEY

THE MIDDLE WORKS, 1899–1924

Volume 5: 1908

Edited by Jo Ann Boydston
Associate Textual Editor, Paul F. Kolojeski
With an Introduction by Charles L. Stevenson

Carbondale and Edwardsville
SOUTHERN ILLINOIS UNIVERSITY PRESS
London and Amsterdam
FEFFER & SIMONS, INC.

CENTER FOR EDITIONS OF
AMERICAN AUTHORS
AN APPROVED TEXT
MODERN LANGUAGE
ASSOCIATION OF AMERICA

®

Editorial expenses for this edition have been met in part by grants from the National Endowment for the Humanities. Publishing expenses have been met in part by grants from the John Dewey Foundation, Mr. Corliss Lamont, and the National Endowment for the Humanities.

Library of Congress Cataloging in Publication Data
Dewey, John, 1859–1952.
     The middle works, 1899–1924.

     Vol. 5 has introd. by Charles L. Stevenson.
     Includes bibliographies and indexes.
     CONTENTS: v. 1. 1899–1901.—v. 2. 1902–1903.—v. 3.
1903–1906.—v. 4. 1907–1909.—v. 5. 1908.
     1. Dewey, John, 1859–1952. 2. Education—Philosophy.
I. Title.
LB875.D34 1976 370.1'092'4 76–7231
ISBN 0–8093–0834–7 (v. 5)

The Middle Works, 1899–1924

Advisory Board

Editor's Note: The Preface and Introduction to *Ethics* were written jointly by John Dewey and James H. Tufts. Chapters 2–9 and 22–26 were written by Tufts. The remaining chapters were written by Dewey.

CONTENTS

nomic Order (Continued), 480; Appendix
to Chapter 25, 505; 26 The Family, 510

INTRODUCTION

By Charles L. Stevenson

I

The first edition of the Dewey and Tufts *Ethics* was published in 1908, and became widely used as a classroom text. In 1932 it gave place to a revised edition, of which only Part I, written by Tufts and concerned with the history of moral opinions and practices, reappeared in what was recognizably its old form, though even there there were changes. Part II, written by Dewey and concerned with theory and analysis, was greatly changed; and Part III, written by Tufts (save for the first two chapters) and concerned with relatively specific problems "of the present," was brought up to date. In effect, then, the authors collaborated on two related but distinct books, one of them written when Dewey was in his late forties and Tufts in his middle forties, and the other written when Dewey was in his early seventies and Tufts in his late sixties. In the present volume only the *Ethics* of 1908 is republished. The *Ethics* of 1932 is scheduled for republication in a later volume.

It is not surprising that Dewey and Tufts should have wished to collaborate. They were colleagues at the University of Michigan for two years, beginning in 1889, and colleagues at the University of Chicago for ten years, beginning in 1894. At Chicago—where Tufts specialized in ethics and where Dewey, though busy with his pioneering work in the Department of Pedagogy, found time to teach several courses on ethics—the two men were closely associated with George H. Mead, James R. Angell, Addison W. Moore, and Edward S. Ames, with whom they developed convergent, practically minded views. As charter members of a school of thought that had become widely known, and had been described by William James as a "real" school with "real" thought,[1] Dewey

---

1. See James's letter to F. C. S. Schiller, dated 15 November 1903, published in R. B. Perry, *The Thought and Character of William James*, 2 vols. (Boston: Little, Brown and Co., 1935), 2:501.

and Tufts could not easily let their professional relationship
come to an end; so in spite of the fact that after 1904 they
were no longer colleagues, Dewey having gone to Columbia
while Tufts remained at Chicago, they managed to plan and
complete a book in which each of them had a special task, but
in which each "contributed suggestions and criticisms of the
work of the other" (p. 6).

Dewey had long been interested in presenting his conception of ethics in the form of a textbook—though a decidedly opinionated textbook that might also have been called
a treatise. His earlier *Outlines of a Critical Theory of Ethics*
(1891) was such a text,[2] but soon impressed him as being
somewhat unsatisfactory. He described it as having "received
a little of what is called 'favorable comment' as well as more
or less of the reverse," and added, "The present perceptual
structure is . . . such a weighty thing . . . that I don't
anticipate any success for the book."[3] And he could scarcely
have anticipated a greater success from his subsequent *The
Study of Ethics* (1894), which he called "a syllabus," prepared "primarily for the use and guidance of my own students."[4] For some years, accordingly, Dewey's approach to
ethics was likely to be known only from his relatively short,
early papers. The *Ethics* of 1908 enabled him to preserve and
enrich the content of those papers, with recollections of his
earlier texts, and to expound his position in a more systematic
manner. It was the work of a man surrounded by more ideas
than he could express with clarity; but even so it succeeded
in disclosing the practical insights by which he was constantly guided.

I need not greatly apologize, I trust, for speaking of the
insights by which Dewey was "constantly" guided, in spite of
the many years over which his views developed. He was born
just a year before Abraham Lincoln was elected president.
Students of philosophy were then reading Schopenhauer's
third and final version of *The World as Will and Idea*, though

---

2. *The Early Works of John Dewey, 1882–1898*, ed. Jo Ann Boydston
   (Carbondale: Southern Illinois University Press, 1969), 3:237–
   388.
3. Dewey to James, 10 May 1891. Perry, *William James*, 2:517.
4. *Early Works* 4:221.

those who were abolitionists might have preferred John
Stuart Mill's newly published essay *On Liberty*. He died in
the year when Dwight Eisenhower succeeded Harry Truman
to the presidency. Students of philosophy were then reading
Richard Hare's newly published *The Language of Morals*.
One might suppose that his approach to ethics, during that
long period, was subject to many changes. But if we look for
abrupt changes, as distinct from changes that arise from
growth, we shall find them only at the very beginning of his
career. He was to lose, to be sure, much of his early interest
in Hegel. And he was to lose an early interest in (orthodox)
religion, of the sort that led him, in 1887, to say that "whatever exiles theology makes ethics an expatriate."[5] But a
change to typically Deweyan views was not long in coming.
In 1891 he said that our moral ideas need to be "reinforced
and reconstructed by larger inquiries into the reality of
human relationships"[6]—a theme that reappeared, with elaborate development, not only in the *Ethics* of 1908 but in all of
Dewey's subsequent writings on ethics. Much the same can
be said of his aim to promote an "emancipation and enlightenment of individual judgment," rather than to inculcate "a
ready-made system" (p. 4). That was the avowed aim of Part
II of the *Ethics* of 1908; and it not only reappeared in the
Ethics of 1932 but also looked back to a paper that Dewey
wrote in 1893, where he said (perhaps with exaggerated
emphasis) that "the question is not what to do, *but how to
decide what to do*."[7] In some of his later works, particularly
in *Human Nature and Conduct* and in *The Quest for Certainty*, Dewey strengthened his ethical views by providing
them with a broader background; but his characteristic insights developed at a much earlier date.

II

    In commenting on the *Ethics* (referring to the unrevised
version unless I indicate to the contrary) I shall confine my

5. "Ethics and Physical Science," *Early Works* 1:209.
6. "Moral Theory and Practice," *Early Works* 3:103.
7. "Teaching Ethics in the High School," *Early Works* 4:56.

attention to Part II, and even there shall select only the topics
that I consider of central importance. I shall try to round out
Dewey's discussion of those topics, my purpose being interpretive rather than critical.

Chapter 10, which is the first of those in Part II, begins
by asking three questions that belong to a "theoretical analysis of reflective morality" (p. 187). They can perhaps be
called "meta-ethical" questions, though it must be remembered that "meta-ethical" is a recent term that had no place
in Dewey's vocabulary. They are concerned with (1) the connection between ethics and conduct, (2) the meaning of the
ethical terms, and (3) the "basis" on which the ethical terms
are applied "to their appropriate objects in conduct." Let me
begin by singling out the third of these questions for special
attention.

The term "basis," given its full context, can be taken as
referring to a *method*: the question asks about the sort of
reasoning or inquiry that will enable a man to reach ethical
opinions in a manner that is thoughtful, as distinct from a
manner that discloses only a thoughtless impulse, or a
thoughtless conformity to custom. Since Dewey's aim was to
emancipate and enlighten "individual" judgment, an emphasis on method was central to his work. He wanted his readers
to develop opinions of their own, subject to his *partial*
guidance. Being convinced that their opinions, if thoughtful,
will change with changing conditions and growing knowledge
(with regard not only to means but also to ends), he let his
partial guidance take the form of a methodology—an analysis
of the general type of reasoning or inquiry that he considered "appropriate" to ethics.

It can be argued, and not implausibly, that Dewey's
methodology was colored by a broad evaluation of his own:
he often disclosed a leaning toward a self-realization ethics,
coupled with a psychological conviction that self-realization
will include a predominating interest in the welfare of society. But however that may be (and I shall discuss the matter
later) it remains the case that an interest in method pervaded
a great deal of what he said, both in the *Ethics* and elsewhere.

Dewey's position on methodology, though half implied
by his claim that ethical problems arise from conflicting at-

titudes, and rather more than half implied by his criticisms
of traditional writers, becomes explicit in Chapter 16, from
which I quote the following passage—a passage introduced
by the caption, "Deliberation as Dramatic Rehearsal."

> [We are reasonable when we] estimate the import or sig-
> nificance of any present desire or impulse by forecasting what it
> would come or amount to if carried out. . . . Every foreseen re-
> sult at once stirs our present affections, our likes and dislikes, our
> desires and aversions. There is developed a running commentary
> which stamps values at once as good or evil. . . . [So] Delibera-
> tion is actually an imaginative rehearsal of various courses of
> conduct. We give way, *in our mind*, to some impulse; we try, *in
> our mind*, some plan. Following its career through various steps,
> we find ourselves in imagination in the presence of the conse-
> quences that would follow; and as we then like and approve, or
> dislike and disapprove, these consequences, we find the original
> impulse or plan good or bad. . . . The imagining . . . furnishes
> an opportunity for many impulses which at first are not in evi-
> dence at all, to get under way . . . [and thus establishes a] prob-
> ability that the capacity of self which is really needed and appro-
> priate will be brought into action (pp. 292 and 293).

It will be evident that the dramatic rehearsal (as I shall here-
after call it) provided a *method* for reaching evaluative
opinions—a method of *reasoning*, since it required an individual to foresee consequences. Dewey was not merely pointing out the possibility of such a method; he was taking it to
exemplify the only sort of reasoning that had a place in
ethics. It will also be evident that the dramatic rehearsal had
much to do with an individual's likes and dislikes. He emphasized that aspect of it by adding that the foreseen consequences, if they "were conceived *merely as remote*," would be
"as barren of influence upon behavior as the mathematical
speculations of a disembodied angel" (p. 292). As he put it
in a monograph written more than thirty years later, a
reflective ethics does not require the head to supercede the
heart, but simply requires the two to "work together."[8]

Note that Dewey's concepts, throughout the quoted passage, are entirely congenial to an empirical psychology (for
the term "imagination" is not, I trust, to be taken to imply

---

8. *Theory of Valuation* (Chicago: University of Chicago Press,
1939), p. 65.

that we invariably think in images). The reasoning in question is not dependent on a Kantian faculty of Practical Reason; it is just ordinary reasoning in a practical context. And the stamping of values is not done by a unique moral sense, or by an intuited, indefinable quality; it is done by various attitudes that reinforce or counteract one another, and are "brought into action" whenever reason discloses their varied objects.

Dewey mentioned the dramatic rehearsal only in connection with a man's plans about his own future conduct; but it can readily be extended to other cases. Suppose, for instance, that a man who has done something in the past is deciding whether or not he took the best course that was open to him. He can then enter into a retrospective rehearsal (so to speak) about what would have occurred if he had acted in alternative ways; and his evaluative decision, after he had surveyed both the actual consequences and the consequences that would alternatively have arisen (making allowances for what he was in a position to know at that earlier time), will again bear the stamp of his desires or aversions. Or suppose that a man is considering the conduct of other men. He can then survey the consequences of *their* conduct, again letting his desires and aversions stamp values—though the other men, as a result of their dramatic rehearsals, may reach opinions that, initially at least, are not the same as his.

Dewey's methodology manifestly looked back to the British empiricists, whose work on ethics, followed by a period when philosophical interests had shifted to Kant and Hegel, was in danger of being neglected. Hobbes's account of *deliberation*, if dissociated from its emphasis on desires for power, was of a sort that Dewey could very nearly have accepted.[9] Hume's account of reason in ethics, with its mis-

_____

9. The following passage occurs in Hobbes's *Leviathan*, pt. 1, chap. 6. "When in the mind of man, appetites, and aversions, hopes, and fears, concerning one and the same thing, arise alternately; and divers good and evil consequences of the doing, or omitting the thing propounded, come successively into our thoughts; so that sometimes we have an appetite to it; sometimes an aversion from it; sometimes hope to be able to do it; sometimes despair, or fear to attempt it; the whole sum of desires, aversion, hopes and fears continued till the thing be either done, or thought impossible, is that we call DELIBERATION. . . . So that he who hath by experience, or reason, the greatest and surest prospect

leading reference to the slave of the passions, needed only a Dewey-like revision that replaced "slave" by "way of organizing."[10] And Mill's account of ethics as a speculative "art," as given in the concluding chapter of his *System of Logic*, provided Dewey's work with a decidedly provocative background.[11] But having taken much from the history of philosophy, Dewey had something to give it in return. His most important claim was very much his own—the claim, namely, that the dramatic rehearsal, when accepted as central to the methodology of ethics, requires the means-ends distinction to be more carefully analyzed, and in a manner that eliminates the possibility, in a practical ethics, of taking any end as "fixed." Nor did Dewey use "fixed" in an unintelligible sense. For stated otherwise his claim was this: a man who takes the dramatic rehearsal in full seriousness, and who is deciding whether or not to accept a proposed end as worth pursuing, will find that he cannot safely reach his decision without reflecting upon

(1) the available means of obtaining the proposed end,

(2) the additional effects that would attend a use of those means, and

(3) the effects that the proposed end would have in its turn.

Accordingly, the man's reflections will grow with his growing experience and growing knowledge of the sciences; and his judgments, *with regard to ends no less than to means*, will be subject to the revisions that attend that growth.

---

of consequences, deliberates best himself; and is able when he will, to give the best counsel unto others." Thomas Hobbes, *Leviathan*, ed. Michael Oakeshott (New York: Collier-Macmillan, Collier Books, 1967), pp. 53–55.

10. See Hume's *Treatise of Human Nature*, pt. 3, sec. 3, [ed. T. H. Green and T. H. Grose, 2 vols., (London: Longmans, Green, and Co., 1898)], and Dewey's quotation from it in the present volume, p. 214.

11. John Stuart Mill, *A System of Logic Ratiocinative and Inductive*, ed. J. M. Robson (Toronto: University of Toronto Press, 1974), bk. 6, chap. 12. Mill's "art" provided for a selective organization of the sciences that connected ends with means, but recognized some other-than-scientific method (whose nature remained unspecified) for establishing ultimate ends. Dewey, in *The Study of Ethics* (*Early Works* 4:226), referred to Mill's chapter, suggesting that it makes too little of science. The question, "Is ethics a science or an art?" was much discussed in texts that were used prior to the appearance of the *Ethics*.

Let me continue, then, by turning to the topic of means and ends. I shall not thereby be departing from the dramatic rehearsal, but shall simply be completing my discussion of it.

III

The need of a reflective and scientifically oriented revision of ends is among the themes that recur in Dewey. It was touched upon in his first text,[12] and much discussed in his later works[13] (where the term "ends" usually gave place to "ends in view"). It needs more attention than I can here give to it;[14] but perhaps I can clarify a cryptic but important sentence that occurs in Chapter 10 of the *Ethics*—a sentence that reads: "Many questions about ends are in reality questions about means" (p. 194).

Dewey was combatting an all too tempting assumption. The assumption is that ethical judgments can be organized around some one end, E, where

(a) E and only E has intrinsic value, and
(b) anything else is good or right just to the extent that it is a means to E, and is bad or wrong just to the extent that it hinders E (or leads to the opposite of it).

Perhaps no philosopher has ventured to accept the assumption in this unqualified form;[15] but some, perhaps inad-

12. *Early Works* 3:261–388. See also "The Superstition of Necessity," *Early Works* 4:29–32.
13. See in particular chap. 6 of *Human Nature and Conduct* (New York: Henry Holt and Co., 1932), and chap. 11 of the *Ethics* of 1932 (New York: Henry Holt and Co.), and chap. 6 (entitled "The Continuum of Ends-Means") of *Theory of Valuation*.
14. I have said a little more about the topic in "Reflections on John Dewey's Ethics," in *Proceedings of the Aristotelian Society* 62 (1961–62): 77–98, and republished as Essay VI in my *Facts and Values* (New Haven: Yale University Press, 1963). And I have dealt with a similar topic in chap. 8 of my *Ethics and Language* (New Haven: Yale University Press, 1944), which was greatly influenced by Dewey. What I there called a focal aim is in essentials a particularly strong Deweyan end in view, though I discussed it with attention to ethical arguments rather than to ethical deliberations, taking the arguments to be deliberations "writ large."
15. For instance, the first chapter of Aristotle's *Nicomachean Ethics* (2d ed., trans. F. H. Peters [London: Kegan Paul, Trench and Co., 1884]), and the first chapter of Mill's *Utilitarianism* (*Dis-*

vertently, have developed their views *as if* they were accepting it. For it is not atypical of philosophers, in seeking to establish the nature of "the" desirable end, to neglect an inquiry into its causes and effects. Their neglect suggests, at least, that they are taking their proposed end to correspond to the above E. The causes of the E (and thus the means to it) are presumably neglected because they are taken to borrow their value from the E alone, and thus are taken to raise questions that become of ethical interest only *after* the nature of the E has been established. And the effects of the E are presumably neglected because they are taken to be incapable of increasing or decreasing its value, having no intrinsic value (positive or negative) of their own.

But Dewey, in letting ethical methodology center on the dramatic rehearsal, and in taking into account the nature of human attitudes, moved entirely away from such an assumption. He thought that an end, when accepted by a reflective individual, *could not* be E-like. Let me spell out his reasons, which he was content to imply rather than to make explicit.

In the dramatic rehearsal, it will be remembered, an individual's attitudes stamp values on foreseen consequences. But so long as the individual is human his attitudes will never stamp a consequence as the *only* one that has intrinsic value, and thus will never stamp any end as an E. On the contrary, they will stamp each of a great number of the consequences as having this or that degree of intrinsic value (positive or negative) *along with* this or that degree of extrinsic value. So when a reflective individual is evaluating a proposed end he will do so, in part at least, by considering the loss or gain in intrinsic value that will attend the means of obtaining the end, and the loss or gain in intrinsic value that will attend its further effects. His considerations will sometimes lead him to be more confident in accepting the proposed end: the means to it may prove to bring with them much else that his attitudes stamp with a positive, intrinsic value; and various effects of the end itself may also prove to be of that sort. But

---

sertations and Discussions: Political, Philosophical, and Historical [New York: Henry Holt and Co., 1874], 3:300–391), defended the assumption *with* qualifications.

at other times his considerations may lead him to modify his proposed end, or abandon it altogether: the only available means to it may prove to bring with them much else that his attitudes stamp with a negative, intrinsic value; and various effects of the proposed end itself may also prove to be of that sort.

In sum: a reflective individual will never grant to an end a full monopoly, so to speak, on intrinsic value. So before accepting a proposed end he will ask himself questions about the value of its causes and effects; and many of those questions (as Dewey put it) will be "in reality questions about means." And what a vast store of scientific knowledge he must have (as Dewey might alternatively have put it) if he is to escape academic theories that purport to "specialize" on ends, and is to develop ethical conclusions that provide a genuine guidance to his practical life!

Dewey was in no way denying, of course, that a man will often decide to accept an end as being of great importance—of such great importance that in *many* cases he will take it to justify the means of obtaining it. On reflection, perhaps a man will take social welfare to be such an end. Typically, however, he will take it to be an end that is reinforced by its consequences: he will take it, for instance, to be also a means to the welfare of his own family, and will count the latter higher than the welfare of any other group of similar size. Without that reinforcement he will feel that it justifies relatively few of the means of obtaining it, particularly when those means are costly to himself. Can we demand more of him than that?

The relation of such a view to "fixed" ends will be obvious. The causes and effects of a proposed end will vary with the circumstances; so any reflections on the desirability of accepting or rejecting it will tend, similarly, to vary with the circumstances. It is therefore stultifying, according to Dewey, to seek an end that can be established once and for all, and particularly stultifying to seek an end while claiming that an inquiry into the sciences can be left until later. At *no* time can an ethical discussion, when reflective, look away from the sciences.

In opposing fixed ends, let me add, Dewey was not implying that ends are to be accepted half-heartedly. A seeming implication of that sort arises from another unwarranted assumption, to the effect that a man will be half-hearted, in accepting an end, until his dramatic rehearsal has placed it in its *complete* .causal milieu. That assumption does indeed envisage half-heartedness—even with regard to Dewey-like ends that are adopted under given conditions and relatively to given means—since the dramatic rehearsal, concerned with an unlimited future, cannot reach completion. But what a man is likely to do, in following Dewey, is to carry out the dramatic rehearsal as far as his knowledge and time permit, thereafter abiding by his attitude-stamped judgment until he finds, as he may or may not, that further knowledge requires him to alter it. If he then *acts* in accordance with his judgment he can be expected to acknowledge the possibility of his having subsequent regrets; but that possibility will not, relatively to his evidence, be a probability. Meanwhile he will have the confidence of realizing that he has been as reasonable as his circumstances permit. A half-hearted judgment or act, as he sees it, will be likely to cause a more serious regret than a judgment or act that is confident.

Dewey himself, in writing on education (in particular), accepted many ends—ends that were connected with means, of course, and were accordingly subject to growth or alteration in the course of a dramatic rehearsal. His sustained rehearsal kept close, in his opinion, to the conditions that confronted him; and he intended his experimental school at Chicago, with its "progressive" education, to carry it further by yielding further knowledge. The fact that he accepted his ends with confidence, and indeed with zeal, was wholly compatible with his refusal to take them as fixed.

IV

Let me now turn to a further question—the second of those initially asked in Chapter 10 of the *Ethics*, and concerned with the *meaning* of the ethical terms. Dewey's answer, had he clearly given it, would have done much to illuminate his views: it would have established the extent, if

any, to which he was prepared to compromise with a straightforward naturalism. But in the *Ethics*, as elsewhere in his
writings, he never came wholly to grips with the question.
He was content with such a remark as this: "the right as the
rational good means that which is harmonious with all the
capacities and desires of the self, that which expands them
into a cooperative whole" (p. 285). But in what sense are we
to take the term "means" in that context? Is the remark a
definition of "right" or is it a judgment that merely uses
"right"?

In discussing the matter, accordingly, I shall give a
definition that seems to fit in with Dewey's work (acknowl-
edging that I am reading between the lines) and shall consider whether it is interpretively acceptable. It runs as
follows:[16]

(A) "X is right," when said by a given speaker, means that a
dramatic rehearsal based on scientifically true propositions,
if the speaker were to carry it out completely, would lead
him to have a predominating favor of X.

Let me immediately turn to my comments, stating them in
numbered order.

(1) The definition refers to a value-stamping favor that
would attend a *complete* dramatic rehearsal, even though no
actual rehearsal (being concerned with an unlimited future)
will ever be complete. But that, in my opinion, is Dewey-like.
Note that if the definition were weakened, specifying no more
than a "rather long" dramatic rehearsal, then a speaker's
judgment, after such a rehearsal had been carried out, would
need no further revision; whereas Dewey implied that the
possible need of further revision must always be taken into
account. He said, for instance, that "there is no act so intelligent that its actual consequences do not run beyond its
foreseen ones" (p. 239). Similarly, there is no judgment so

16. My definition strengthens one that is suggested by Sidney Hook,
who writes: " 'X is valuable,' for Dewey, may roughly be analyzed as 'I will choose or approve of *x* after reflection on the
relevant consequences of my choice.' " See p. 210 of his article,
"The Desirable and Emotive in Dewey's Ethics," in *John Dewey:
Philosopher of Science and Freedom, A Symposium*, ed. Sidney
Hook (New York: Barnes and Noble, 1967), pp. 194–216.

reflective that it is closed (save by lack of time, etc.) to further reflection.[17]

(2) The definition serves to suggest, at least, a point that is again Dewey-like: a speaker, being at a given time somewhat well convinced that X is right, will *at that same time* have a tentative (but not half-hearted) value-stamping favor of X. The latter, immediate favor, it is true, may imperfectly predominate over some contrary desire of the speaker that "tempts" him; but perhaps the speaker will then acknowledge his tendency to moral weakness. Or is moral weakness neglected in Dewey's writings? Not always, as is evident from such a remark as this: "The good whose claim to be good depends mainly on projection of remote considerations, may be theoretically recognized and yet the direct appeal to the particular agent at the particular time be feeble and pallid" (p. 305). Dewey also spoke, however, of the need for an individual to "regulate the formation of his desires and purposes so that the present and the permanent good, the good in desire and in reflection, will coincide" (p. 251).

(3) The definition explains why Dewey related ethics to all the sciences, rather than just to the science of psychology. When a speaker says that X is right he is saying, in part, that if he were to *believe* certain propositions—namely, those that would attend a complete dramatic rehearsal—he would have a predominating favor of X. To that extent he is making an assertion that belongs to psychology. But he is saying more than that: he is restricting the beliefs in question to *true* beliefs. And in determining their truth (i.e., in identi-

17. I venture to let the definiens of my definition include a subjunctive conditional with an impossible antecedent, even though in current studies of logic it is sometimes contended that *all* such conditionals are vacuously true. That contention is counterintuitive, and I would expect it to give place, eventually, to a more intuitive analysis. Thus the statement, "If Hobbes had succeeded in squaring the circle he would have been even more famous than he was" seems to me to have a better claim to truth than the statement, "If Hobbes had succeeded in squaring the circle he would have been less famous than he was." The impossible antecedent introduced in my definition is particularly innocuous when it serves the purpose that I assign to it—when it serves, like a Kantian regulative concept, as a reminder that reflection, however long and careful it may be, could always be continued at greater length and with greater care.

fying them) he would have to appeal to the various sciences. Of the multitude of beliefs that can enter into a dramatic rehearsal only some are likely to have a truth that can be established by psychology, and the others can be established as true (when they are true) only by an appeal to economics, biology, physics, and so on.

Let me expand my remark. A man's forecasts, when he evaluates X, are rarely *about* his attitudes. They are forecasts that he calls to mind because they are likely to *make a difference* to his attitudes. When he believes that X will cause Y, Y being something that he in fact favors, he *finds* that his favor of X increases; and when he believes that X will cause Z, Z being something that he in fact disfavors, he *finds* that his favor of X decreases. His attitudes then provide a "running commentary" on his beliefs, as distinct from constituting their subject-matter. But it is also the case that the occurrence of those beliefs, when verified, together with the attitudes that are found to attend them, provide scientific evidence (by extrapolation) for a more complicated belief. The latter is actually *about* an attitude, being the man's decision-prompting belief that his attitude to X would be favorable (or unfavorable) if he were to carry out a dramatic rehearsal, based on scientific truths, to its completion. It is this more complicated belief that my proposed definition emphasizes. But note that it is not, in practice, separable from the less complicated beliefs whose occurrence helps to provide it with evidence—beliefs that are of many sorts, and which are developed by the various sciences rather than by just one science.

(4) The definition says nothing, and designedly says nothing, about the use of ethical judgments in commending or reproving, in spite of the remarks that begin Chapter 19 of the *Ethics*. In that chapter Dewey was explicit in affirming that judgments can "react into the character of the agent upon whom they are directed" and thus "are part of the process of forming" that character (p. 359). He added that "commendation is of the nature of a reward calculated to confirm the person in the right course of action," and that "reprobation is of the nature of punishment, fitted to dissuade the agent from the wrong course" (p. 359). He would

have been more convincing had he replaced "right course of action" by "right course of action according to those who are doing the commending," with a corresponding alteration for "wrong course." But the quotations are of interest in showing that Dewey was not insensitive to what has since been called the emotive or prescriptive force of ethical judgments, or their special illocutionary force. Nor was he wholly forgetting a remark made by Mill—that moralists "do not express themselves in the indicative, but [rather] in the imperative mood, or in periphrases equivalent to it."[18] Having mentioned these aspects of the judgments, however, Dewey was thereafter content to pass over them. His aim, as I interpret him, was to exclude them from the meaning of ethical judgments, or to include them only insofar as they prod another person into rehearsing his plans more fully. That is to say, Dewey wanted to distill from an ethical judgment only those aspects of it that bear on a *reflective* guidance of attitudes. He rejected the residue, after the distillation, because he suspected it of leading *away* from reflective guidance. My proposed definition is worded accordingly: for the purpose of interpreting (though not of endorsing) Dewey's views I state it in purely cognitive terms.[19]

18. Mill, *System of Logic*, bk. 6, chap. 12, sec. 1. In sec. 6 of the same chapter Mill wrote: "The propositions now spoken of [namely, ethical propositions] do not assert that anything is, but enjoin or recommend that something should be. They are a class by themselves. A proposition of which the predicate is expressed by the words *ought* or *should be*, is generically different from one which is expressed by *is*, or *will be*." Cf. note 11 above.
19. Dewey devoted one of his very last papers ("Ethical Subject-Matter and Language," *Journal of Philosophy* 42 [1945]: 701–12) to a discussion of my *Ethics and Language*. He said little in criticism of many of my views (as was to be expected, since I had borrowed so heavily from him) but strongly objected to my emphasis on an extra-cognitive element in the *meaning* of ethical sentences, insisting that their content was wholly "predictive." "There can be no doubt," he wrote, "that sentences *claiming* to be ethical often use an extra-cognitive 'emotive' factor to influence conduct" (pp. 702–3, n.3); but he added that "those sentences are by just that much deprived of the properties sentences should have in order to be genuinely *ethical*" (p. 709). Had I answered his paper (as regrettably I did not) I would have pointed out that I was taking ethical sentences just as I found them in common use, regardless of whether their use was "genuinely" ethical, and regardless (accordingly) of whether they were supported by reasons. I handled reasons separately rather than (save by an allowance for "persuasive" definitions) build them

V

My comments have all been to the effect that my proposed definition is Dewey-like. Let me add a further comment that *may* prove to be of the same sort, though it will require a more extended discussion.

It will be evident that the definition — (A), page xx — specifies that a speaker's judgment always refers in part to himself. An equivalent definition could be stated thus:

(B) "X is right" has the same meaning as "A dramatic rehearsal based on scientifically true propositions, if I were to carry it out completely, would lead me to favor X."

It must be understood, of course, that "I" and "me" refer to the person who *says* that X is right. So the definition suggests that "right" enables a person to reveal a part of his "hypothetical autobiography." Now Dewey did indeed say that "judgments express the character of the one who utters them" (p. 359). And yet it may fairly be asked whether he made as much of "I" and "me" as the definition suggests. I can best introduce my (somewhat hesitant) answer to that question by commenting on an example.

Suppose that X is an action taken by a public official. Suppose that Mr. A claims that X is right, whereas Mr. B claims that it is not right. (As I have remarked on page xiv, the dramatic rehearsal or its equivalent can be used by men who are evaluating an act that is not their own.) And suppose further that there are individual differences between Mr. A and Mr. B that would persist even if each man were to complete his dramatic rehearsal in a way that was scientifically correct: the former would have a predominating favor of X on the basis of such a rehearsal and the latter would not. These suppositions are not impossible; and they seem to call the interpretive plausibility of my proposed definition into question, for the reason that follows.

---

into the very meaning of ethical sentences; and in handling them separately I was much closer, I think, to Dewey's view than he supposed.

I suspect that Dewey's view, with regard to *meaning*, was much the same in 1945 as it was in 1908—though that, of course, could be questioned.

If Mr. A and Mr. B are using "right" in any ordinary sense, or in any sense close enough to an ordinary sense to be of ethical interest, they are manifestly disagreeing about the value of X. But if they are using "right" in the defined sense, they are expressing views that are logically compatible. That is to say, each man is then making an assertion about what *his* attitudes would be under certain hypothetical circumstances; and since their individual differences may be of the sort just supposed, each of them may be making an assertion that is true.[20] So if I continue to ascribe my definition to Dewey I must accept one or the other of these alternatives: either

   (a) Dewey was so greatly diverting "right" from an ordinary sense that he deprived it of its ethical interest; or

   (b) Dewey implied, and in a way that remained of ethical interest, that it is possible for men to disagree about what is right even though their judgments are logically compatible.

But both alternatives, initially at least, seem foreign to a sympathetic reconstruction of Dewey's views. So perhaps he had in mind some definition *other* than my proposed one.

And yet I can think of no other definition that is more Dewey-like. So I shall retain my proposed definition (for interpretive purposes), and venture to argue that Dewey was content with alternative (b)—though content with it only because he made an assumption that served, in his opinion, to render it innocuous.

It must first be noted that Mr. A and Mr. B—granted that they are using "right" in the defined sense that I am considering, and granted, by (2) of page xxi, that their hypothetical remarks about their attitudes generate corresponding attitudes at the time that they are speaking—can be said to be disagreeing in a wholly familiar sense. As I have elsewhere put it[21] they are disagreeing in attitude rather than in

20. See G. E. Moore, *Ethics* (New York: Henry Holt and Co., 1912), pp. 91–93. Moore does not, however, make any explicit reference to Dewey.
21. See Essay 1 of my *Facts and Values,* or chap. 1 of my *Ethics and Language.*

belief: they are disclosing their diverging attitudes to the same X, neither being content (presumably) with the divergence. So in ascribing to Dewey my proposed definition I am saying nothing that would have *prevented* him from accepting alternative (b). Dewey used neither the term "disagreement in attitude" nor any equivalent term; but like a multitude of other men he must certainly have been aware, intuitively, of the sort of disagreement to which the term refers. The only point that requires discussion, then, is whether or not his part of the *Ethics* was colored by that awareness.

He showed no signs, it is true, of having provided a *welcome* place for cases like that of Mr. A and Mr. B. Such cases, where even a full use of science would leave an ethical disagreement (in attitude) unresolved, threaten to deprive ethical judgments of rational tests that are intersubjective. The intersubjectivity in question is of the sort commonly ascribed to the methods of the sciences, which Dewey wanted for ethics as well.

But the case of Mr. A and Mr. B is simply one that I have imagined. Do such cases ever arise in actual life? It is possible (though precarious) to assume that they do not.

Bearing that in mind I venture to ascribe to Dewey the following view: he recognized, implicitly, the logical possibility of scientifically unresolvable disagreements in attitude, along with the logical possibility that men, even if wholly rational, would continue to judge and act in opposition to one another rather than in accord with one another; but he went on, in the interest of making the most of scientific reasoning, to assume that such disagreements will not in fact arise. In other words, he believed (or "willed to believe") that men who have opposing attitudes would no longer have them, but instead would let their predominating attitudes stamp the same things with the same values, *if* they could complete their dramatic rehearsals. And that gave him reason to hope, at least, that their merely sustained, rather than completed, dramatic rehearsals would have the same effect. Relative to that assumption he ascribed to ethical methodology an intersubjectivity of its own, not far distant from that of the sciences.

In good measure, my interpretation is suggested by a *postulate* that Dewey introduced into his *Outlines of a Critical Theory of Ethics*,[22] and which, in spite of its early date, he *may* have taken for granted throughout his subsequent writings. Having there said that the postulate is one that moral theory must take on "faith"—unless it can subsequently be justified "by metaphysics"—he proceeded to state it (himself using the capital letters) in this way:

IN THE REALIZATION OF INDIVIDUALITY THERE IS FOUND ALSO THE NEEDED REALIZATION OF SOME COMMUNITY OF PERSONS OF WHICH THE INDIVIDUAL IS A MEMBER; AND, CONVERSELY, THE AGENT WHO DULY SATISFIES THE COMMUNITY IN WHICH HE SHARES, BY THAT SAME CONDUCT SATISFIES HIMSELF.

He then went on to hint that the size of the community of persons in question is large enough to foreshadow "the moral order of the world." And just a little later he said that the postulate has much the same relation to ethics that the principle of the uniformity of nature has to the sciences.

In the context of the *Outlines* the postulate can be taken, and perhaps should be taken, to be primarily of normative interest—an effort to defend an ethics of self-realization from the charge of being anti-social. But when combined with the dramatic rehearsal (not developed in the *Outlines*) it also becomes of methodological interest. If each man, in making use of the dramatic rehearsal, is also enabling others in his community to move toward a realization of their individuality, then we may expect men who are fully reflective, and fully possessed of the relevant scientific truths, to agree in attitude and to reach the same judgments. Should the postulate hold true only within small communities the result would not be congenial to Dewey's methodology: it would open the possibility of scientifically irresolvable ethical issues between those in different communities. But as I have remarked, Dewey hinted at a faith in the moral order "of the world."[23]

22. *Early Works* 3:322.
23. My interpretation presses Dewey's postulate toward an assumption made by Hume. For Hume assumed that "the notion of morals implies some sentiment common to all mankind, which recommends the same object to general approbation"—though

What happens, it may be asked, when the whole of a community cannot be "satisfied," and when men disagree about which group within it is to have priorities? Perhaps Dewey assumed that even that situation, among reflective individuals, would be only temporary; or perhaps he assumed that in such cases there would at least be an inclination to tolerance and compromise (again, among reflective individuals) that would prevent serious discord.

Did Dewey's postulate, which was emphasized *only* in his text of 1891, reappear with reduced emphasis, or with modifications, seventeen years later, when he was writing his portion of the *Ethics*? Perhaps so, though the word "perhaps" is essential to an interpretation that is properly cautious. But in the *Ethics* he did indeed pause to make such remarks as these: "The number of persons who after facing the entire situation, would still be anti-social enough deliberately to sacrifice the welfare of others is probably small" (p. 234), and "It is not so much that [a selfish man,] *after* thinking of the effects upon others . . . declines to give these thoughts any weight, as that he habitually fails to think at all, or to think in a vivid and complete way, of the interests of others" (pp. 234–35). Those remarks manifestly weaken the postulate: they seem to be making a qualified psychological generalization, and not to be introducing a postulate that can perhaps be justified "by metaphysics." And again, their methodological implications are somewhat veiled. But they are sufficient to suggest that Dewey was still bearing his earlier postulate in mind.

And in his chapter entitled "Social Organization and the Individual" Dewey wrote that a "distinctly *personal* morality . . . is simply the means of *social* reconstruction" (p. 387). The social reconstruction, I trust, can arise only when a personal morality, acting as a prod to the deliberation of others,

---

"much reason" must precede in order to give the approbation "a proper discernment of its object." (*An Inquiry Concerning the Principles of Morals*; in the Selby-Bigge edition of *Hume's Enquiries*, Oxford, 2d ed., 1902, pp. 272 and 173.) But Dewey did not restrict value-stamping attitudes to approbation (or disapprobation), whereas Hume did, contrasting approbation with "self-love." Presumably, Dewey's postulate was based on a faith that self-love would always lose out in a conflict with approbation, granted full reflection and knowledge.

becomes *shared*—that being the practical possibility with which Dewey's postulate was concerned.

In his later writings, moreover, Dewey was fond of drawing an analogy between ethics and engineering, pointing out that "technological" evaluations in the latter field, which "state the proper courses of action to be adopted," are quite evidently "grounded" in science.[24] Now these technological evaluations—concerned, say, with the *prima facie* desirability of using steel in bridge-building—arise from desires that are widely shared: they are not likely to occasion any disagreement in attitude that a knowledge of science will fail to dispel. Dewey's analogy suggests that he was generalizing such a view by extending it to moral evaluations, though with the understanding that the latter could be "grounded" not on some one science but only on the sciences taken together. It is not easy to accept the generalized view; but Dewey, recalling his "faith" in his early postulate, may have been content, and without further explanation, to accept the view in accordance with something rather like that faith.

My interpretation goes well beyond anything that Dewey *plainly* said; but that, in any interpretation of Dewey, is inevitable. He was a rich but often unclear thinker, whose views hang together only when rounded out. So along with my proposed definition (p. xx or p. xxiv) I venture to ascribe to him a continued faith in some variant of his early postulate, hoping to round out his views in a way that best accounts for his efforts to relate ethics to the sciences.

But was Dewey naturalistic without compromise, taking ethics to be *identical* with a science? I think not. He indeed held that the sciences—sciences in the plural, and specially organized to guide attitudes—were alone capable of providing ethical judgments with a reasoned support. But he also held, if I interpret him correctly, that ethical reasoning leads to intersubjectively established conclusions (and thus to "moral order") only if a special postulate holds true, whereas in the sciences proper there is an intersubjectivity, in some usual and important sense of the term, that does not depend on that postulate.

24. *Theory of Valuation*, p. 22.

VI

I have been emphasizing what would now be called the meta-ethical aspects of Dewey's work; but as I have had occasion to remark, those aspects were colored by his leanings toward a self-realization theory—a theory that takes self-realization to be a *desirable* end, and thus extends beyond meta-ethics into normative ethics. Let me say a little more in the latter connection.

Had he been content to do so, Dewey could have withheld his normative conclusions. He could have stopped short with a purely methodological claim, to the effect that the only *intelligible* reasoning, in ethics, is of the sort found in the dramatic rehearsal. That would not have required him to say that people ought to make a persistent use of that reasoning. It would have permitted him to say, for instance, that most people (for all he knew) ought not be entrusted with a use of reasoning, and instead ought to be encouraged to follow the customs of their community. Or in going beyond his methodology he could have stopped short with a purely psychological claim, to the effect that a full use of reasoning would in fact lead an individual to realize himself. Again, that would not have required him to use "ought" or "desirable" in connection with self-realization. But Dewey was particularly unwilling to withhold his normative conclusions when they moralized about moralizing. Both implicitly and explicitly he claimed that people ought to trust their powers of reasoning, and that self-realization would be among the desirable consequences of their doing so.

In some measure Dewey's normative interest in self-realization was a continuation of his interest in methodology: he needed to defend his methodology from an objection. Did his emphasis on value-stamping attitudes leave a place for reason that was distressingly small? Some of his readers may have thought so; and rather than "face" such an "impoverished" methodology they may have insisted to themselves that there "must" be some Kant-like or Sidgwick-like alternative to it. So Dewey wanted (presumably) to show that his methodology need not be faced but should instead be welcomed. Having envisaged a world where it was systematically employed, he may have rehearsed its consequences on self-

realization, and the consequences of self-realization in their
turn; and finding that his attitudes stamped those consequences as good, he may have concluded (granted his postulate) that others too, on reflection, would consider them
good. It remains the case that a dramatic rehearsal, when
concerned with such a complicated topic, would have to be
worked out with more care than Dewey devoted to it. And
perhaps he was speaking with a more persuasive intent than
his aversion to an emotive or prescriptive use of words (see
my fourth point in Section IV, pp. xxii and xxiii) would suggest. Still, Dewey's stand on self-realization is of genuine
interest.

In Chapter 18, where Dewey was particularly explicit in
discussing self-realization, he referred to it as "the theory
which attempts to do justice to the one-sided truths [con-
cerned with self-abnegation, for instance, and self-assertion]
we have been engaged with" (p. 351). The word "attempts"
suggests that he was not uncritical of the usual forms of the
theory, having reservations that arose, I take it, from his
conviction that the theory can be stated "in such an exaggerated perspective that it becomes false" (p. 353). So let me
examine his reservations.

He insisted that self-realization is "not *the* end of a
moral act—that is, it is not the only end" (p. 353). Given
his general approach to ethics, that could very nearly have
gone without saying: he recognized no *one* end of any sort.
When he was discussing the self-realization theory, however,
which may easily suggest that each individual is to have just
one fixed end, his conception of many and mutable ends was
in need of special emphasis.

In the case mentioned just above—where one individual
envisions a world where *other* individuals are realizing themselves—the envisioned world will obviously be no more than
one among many ends. The individual who envisions it,
judging it to be desirable, will find that it is reinforced by
other ends to which he considers it (in its turn) to be a
means, or will subsequently find, perhaps, that under given
circumstances it stands in conflict with other ends, and can
be obtained only at a cost that he finds excessive. And so on,
as I have discussed in Section III.

There is a further case, however, that is of particular

interest. It is not implausible, initially, to suggest that an individual's *own* self-realization should have a special place among his ends. There can again be no thought of its being his only end, since the individual's self-realization itself (as I take Dewey to have conceived it) depends on a reinforcement and an absence of conflict among his *other* ends. But perhaps the individual's self-realization should be an end governing ends — a centralizing and fixed end of the second order to which all of his first order ends should be subordinate.

Dewey, however, repudiates such a suggestion. We must "give up the notion," he wrote, "that there is in voluntary acts a thought of the self as the end for the sake of which the act is performed." Rather, "our original instincts are such that their objects do as *matter of result* conduce primarily to the well-being and advantage of the self" (p. 341). He pointed out, moreover, that an individual's potentialities are often poorly known to him, for "there is no way of discovering the nature of the self except in terms of objective ends which fulfill its capacities, and there is no *way* of realizing the self except as it is forgotten in devotion to these objective ends" (p. 352). So an individual's self-realization need not be the sole or even the main end toward which he is motivated, and, moreover, an individual who tries to take it as such will not only find that he is stultified by it but will also find (having still to "discover" its nature) that he has a not always workable conception of it.

There is a certain similarity, though amid differences, between Dewey's criticism of psychological hedonism (see p. 246) and his reservations about self-realization. Just as an individual's pleasure can arise from the attainment of what he desires but is not therefore the only object of his desire, so his self-realization can arise from the attainment of his reflectively established ends ("as matter of result") but is not therefore his only end.

And yet Dewey would scarcely have called attention to self-realization if he had expected his readers to be *wholly* forgetful of it. So I take his position to have been essentially this: he thought that an individual should on occasion look back on his past to consider the degree to which he was

realizing himself, feeling encouraged when he found that
degree to be high; but he also thought that an individual,
in the course of making any given practical decision, should
let his self-realization lie only in the extreme periphery of
his attention, and should direct his foveal attention, unself-
consciously, to the environmental and social situation which
he is seeking to alter, or to which he is seeking to adjust
himself.

It must not be forgotten that Dewey saw (or postulated)
a close connection between the self-realization of an individual and the needs of society. So what I have called his
leanings toward a self-realization ethics might also be called
his leanings toward a modified but still not unrecognizable
form of utilitarianism, stated in a way that let "social pleasure" give place to "social welfare." It is essential to speak of
Dewey's *leanings* to this or that broad normative conclusion,
to avoid the wholly incorrect implication that he was defending just one, all-embracing and fixed end.

VII

My aim, as previously indicated, has been to select only
a few topics from the *Ethics*, and to discuss them interpretively rather than critically.

Had I turned to further topics I could profitably have
examined Dewey's remarks about traditional writers, along
with his many suggestions about the psychological background of ethics and about what is now called the philosophy
of mind. But perhaps I can be pardoned for neglecting those
topics. Dewey there speaks well for himself, whereas the
topics I have selected are in particular need of being rounded
out and clarified. And perhaps I can also be pardoned for
withholding (save for a few implications) my criticisms,
which would have extended my introductory comments beyond their proper length.

Let me conclude, then, with these remarks: The reader
will not find the *Ethics* a meticulous work. It derives its force
not from an analytical skill but rather from a practical wisdom that repeatedly triumphs over an analytical clumsiness.

But perhaps it is necessary to point out, in our present "age of analysis," that practical wisdom is a philosophical virtue. Throughout the *Ethics* Dewey was stimulating and provocative. Always intent upon "a moral idealism [that] will rest upon a more secure and extensive natural foundation than that of the past" (p. 337), he insisted that ethics must constantly be nourished by a contact with the sciences, and by a concern with the changing problems of daily life. His influence has been great, and shows every promise of being enduring.

Ethics

Preface

The significance of this text in Ethics lies in its effort to awaken a vital conviction of the genuine reality of moral problems and the value of reflective thought in dealing with them. To this purpose are subordinated the presentation in Part I of historic material; the discussion in Part II of the different types of theoretical interpretation, and the consideration, in Part III, of some typical social and economic problems which characterize the present.

Experience shows that the student of morals has difficulty in getting the field objectively and definitely before him so that its problems strike him as real problems. Conduct is so intimate that it is not easy to analyze. It is so important that to a large extent the perspective for regarding it has been unconsciously fixed by early training. The historical method of approach has proved in the classroom experience of the authors an effective method of meeting these difficulties. To follow the moral life through typical epochs of its development enables students to realize what is involved in their own habitual standpoints; it also presents a concrete body of subject-matter which serves as material of analysis and discussion.

The classic conceptions of moral theory are of remarkable importance in illuminating the obscure places of the moral life and in giving the student clues which will enable him to explore it for himself. But there is always danger of either dogmatism or a sense of unreality when students are introduced abruptly to the theoretical ideas. Instead of serving as tools for understanding the moral facts, the ideas are likely to become substitutes for the facts. When they are proffered ready-made, their theoretical acuteness and cleverness may be admired, but their practical soundness and applicability are suspected. The historical introduction permits the student to be present, as it were, at the social situations in which the intellectual instruments were forged. He appreciates their relevancy to the conditions which provoked them, and he is encouraged to try them on simple problems before attempting the complex problems of the present. By assisting in their gradual development he gains confidence in the ideas and in his power to use them.

In the second part, devoted more specifically to the analysis and criticism of the leading conceptions of moral theory, the aim accordingly has not been to instill the notions of a school nor to inculcate a ready-made system, but to show the development of theories out of the problems and experience of every-day conduct, and to suggest how these theories may be fruitfully applied in practical exigencies. Aspects of the moral life have been so thoroughly examined that it is possible to present certain principles in the confidence that they will meet general acceptance. Rationalism and hedonism, for example, have contributed toward a scientific statement of the elements of conduct, even though they have failed as self-enclosed and final systems. After the discussions of Kant and Mill, Sidgwick and Green, Martineau and Spencer, it is possible to affirm that there is a place in the moral life for reason and a place for happiness,—a place for duty and a place for valuation. Theories are treated not as incompatible rival systems which must be accepted or rejected *en bloc*, but as more or less adequate methods of surveying the problems of conduct. This mode of approach facilitates the scientific estimation and determination of the part played by various factors in the complexity of moral life. The student is put in a position to judge the problems of conduct for himself. This emancipation and enlightenment of individual judgment is the chief aim of the theoretical portion.

In a considerable part of the field, particularly in the political and economic portions of Part III, no definitive treatment is as yet possible. Nevertheless, it is highly desirable to introduce the student to the examination of these unsettled questions. When the whole civilized world is giving its energies to the meaning and value of justice and democracy, it is intolerably academic that those interested in ethics should have to be content with conceptions already worked out, which therefore relate to what is least doubtful in conduct rather than to questions now urgent. Moreover, the advantages of considering theory and practice in direct relation to each other are mutual. On the one hand, as against the *a priori* claims of both individualism and social-ism, the need of the hour seems to us to be the application of methods of more deliberate analysis and experiment. The extreme conservative may deprecate any scrutiny of the present order; the ardent radical may be impatient of the critical and seemingly tardy processes of the investigator; but those who have considered well the conquest which man is making of the world of nature cannot forbear the con-viction that the cruder method of trial and error and the time-honored method of prejudice and partisan controversy need not longer completely dominate the regulation of the life of society. They hope for a larger application of the scientific method to the problems of human welfare and progress. Conversely, a science which takes part in the actual work of promoting moral order and moral progress must receive a valuable reflex influence of stimulus and of test. To consider morality in the making as well as to dwell upon values already established should make the science more vital. And whatever the effect upon the subject-matter, the student can hardly appreciate the full force of his materials and methods as long as they are kept aloof from the ques-tions which are occupying the minds of his contemporaries.

Teachers who are limited in time will doubtless prefer to make their own selections of material, but the following suggestions present one possible line of choice. In Part I, of the three chapters dealing with the Hebrew, Greek, and mod-ern developments, any one may be taken as furnishing an illustration of the method; and certain portions of Chapter 9 may be found more detailed in analysis than is necessary for the beginner. In Part II, Chapters 11–12 may be omitted without losing the thread of the argument. In Part III, any one of the specific topics—*viz.*, the political state, the eco-nomic order, the family—may be considered apart from the others. Some teachers may prefer to take Parts in their entirety. In this case, any two may be chosen.

As to the respective shares of the work for which the

authors are severally responsible, while each has contributed suggestions and criticisms to the work of the other in sufficient degree to make the book throughout a joint work, Part I has been written by Mr. Tufts, Part II by Mr. Dewey, and in Part III, Chapters 20 and 21 are by Mr. Dewey, Chapters 22–26 by Mr. Tufts.

It need scarcely be said that no attempt has been made in the bibliographies to be exhaustive. When the dates of publication of the work cited are given, the plan has been in general to give, in the case of current literature, the date of the latest edition, and in the case of some classical treatises the date of original publication.

In conclusion, the authors desire to express their indebtedness to their colleagues and friends Dr. Wright, Mr. Talbert, and Mr. Eastman, who have aided in the reading of the proof and with other suggestions.

1. INTRODUCTION

§ 1. Definition and Method

Provisional Definition.—The place for an accurate definition of a subject is at the end of an inquiry rather than at the beginning, but a brief definition will serve to mark out the field. Ethics is the science that deals with conduct, in so far as this is considered as right or wrong, good or bad. A single term for conduct so considered is "moral conduct," or the "moral life." Another way of stating the same thing is to say that Ethics aims to give a systematic account of our judgments about conduct, in so far as these estimate it from the standpoint of right or wrong, good or bad.

Ethical and Moral.—The terms "ethics" and "ethical" are derived from a Greek word *ethos* which originally meant customs, usages, especially those belonging to some group as distinguished from another, and later came to mean disposition, character. They are thus like the Latin word "moral," from *mores*, or the German *sittlich*, from *Sitten*. As we shall see, it was in customs, "ethos," "mores," that the moral or ethical began to appear. For customs were not merely habitual ways of acting; they were ways approved by the group or society. To act contrary to the customs of the group brought severe disapproval. This might not be formulated in precisely our terms—right and wrong, good and bad, —but the attitude was the same in essence. The terms ethical and moral as applied to the conduct of to-day imply of course a far more complex and advanced type of life than the old words "ethos" and "mores," just as economics deals with a more complex problem than "the management of a household," but the terms have a distinct value if they suggest the way in which the moral life had its beginning.

Two Aspects of Conduct.—To give a scientific account of judgments about conduct, means to find the principles which are the basis of these judgments. Conduct or the moral life has two obvious aspects. On the one hand it is a life of purpose. It implies thought and feeling, ideals and motives, valuation and choice. These are processes to be studied by psychological methods. On the other hand, conduct has its outward side. It has relations to nature, and especially to human society. Moral life is called out or stimulated by certain necessities of individual and social existence. As Protagoras put it, in mythical form, the gods gave men a sense of justice and of reverence, in order to enable them to unite for mutual preservation.[1] And in turn the moral life aims to modify or transform both natural and social environments, to build a "kingdom of man" which shall be also an ideal social order—a "kingdom of God." These relations to nature and society are studied by the biological and social sciences. Sociology, economics, politics, law, and jurisprudence deal particularly with this aspect of conduct. Ethics must employ their methods and results for this aspect of its problem, as it employs psychology for the examination of conduct on its inner side.

The Specific Problem of Ethics.—But ethics is not merely the sum of these various sciences. It has a problem of its own which is created by just this twofold aspect of life and conduct. It has to relate these two sides. It has to study the inner process *as determined by the outer conditions or as changing these outer conditions,* and the outward behavior or institution *as determined by the inner purpose, or as affecting the inner life.* To study choice and purpose is psychology; to study choice as affected by the rights of others and to judge it as right or wrong by this standard is ethics. Or again, to study a corporation may be economics, or sociology, or law; to study its activities as resulting from the purposes of persons or as affecting the welfare of persons, and to judge its acts as good or bad from such a point of view, is ethics.

Genetic Study.—When we deal with any process of life it is found to be a great aid for understanding the present conditions if we trace the history of the process and see how

1. Plato, Protagoras, § 320 ff.

present conditions have come about. And in the case of morality there are four reasons in particular for examining earlier stages. The first is that we may begin our study with a simpler material. Moral life at present is extremely complex. Professional, civic, domestic, philanthropic, ecclesiastical, and social obligations claim adjustment. Interests in wealth, in knowledge, in power, in friendship, in social welfare, make demand for recognition in fixing upon what is good. It is desirable to consider first a simpler problem. In the second place, this complex moral life is like the human body in that it contains "rudiments" and "survivals." Some of our present standards and ideals were formed at one period in the past, and some at another. Some of these apply to present conditions and some do not. Some are at variance with others. Many apparent conflicts in moral judgments are explained when we discover how the judgments came to be formed in the first instance. We cannot easily understand the moral life of to-day except in the light of earlier morality. The third reason is that we may get a more objective material for study. Our moral life is so intimate a part of ourselves that it is hard to observe impartially. Its characteristics escape notice because they are so familiar. When we travel we find the customs, laws, and moral standards of other peoples standing out as "peculiar." Until we have been led by some such means to compare our own conduct with that of others it probably does not occur to us that our own standards are also peculiar, and hence in need of explanation. It is as difficult scientifically as it is personally "to see ourselves as others see us." It is doubtless true that to see ourselves merely as others see us would not be enough. Complete moral analysis requires us to take into our reckoning motives and purposes which may perhaps be undiscoverable by the "others." But it is a great aid to this completer analysis if we can sharpen our vision and awaken our attention by a comparative study. A fourth reason for a genetic study is that it emphasizes the dynamic, progressive character of morality. Merely to examine the present may easily give the impression that the moral life is not a life, a moving process, something still in the making—but a changeless structure. There is moral progress as well as a moral order. This may be discovered by an analysis of the very nature of moral conduct, but it stands out more clearly and impressively if we trace the actual development in history. Before attempting our analysis of the present moral consciousness and its judgments, we shall therefore give an outline of the earlier stages and simpler phases.

Theory and Practice.—Finally, if we can discover ethical principles these ought to give some guidance for the unsolved problems of life which continually present themselves for decision. Whatever may be true for other sciences it would seem that ethics at least ought to have some practical value. "In this theatre of man's life it is reserved for God and the Angels to be lookers on." Man must act; and he must act well or ill, rightly or wrongly. If he has reflected, has considered his conduct in the light of the general principles of human order and progress, he ought to be able to act more intelligently and freely, to achieve the satisfaction that always attends on scientific as compared with uncritical or rule-of-thumb practice. Socrates gave the classic statement for the study of conduct when he said, "A life unexamined, uncriticized, is not worthy of man."

§ 2. *Criterion of the Moral*

It is not proposed to attempt at this point an accurate or minute statement of what is implied in moral conduct, as this is the task of Part II. But for the purposes of tracing in Part I the beginnings of morality, it is desirable to have a sort of rough chart to indicate to the student what to look for in the earlier stages of his exploration, and to enable him to keep his bearings on the way.

Certain of the characteristics of the moral may be seen in a cross-section, a statement of the elements in moral conduct at a given time. Other characteristics come out more clearly by comparing later with earlier stages. We give first a cross-section.

I. Characteristics of the Moral Life in Cross-section.— In this cross-section the first main division is suggested by the fact that we sometimes give our attention to *what* is done or intended, and sometimes to *how* or *why* the act is done. These divisions may turn out to be less absolute than they seem, but common life uses them and moral theories have often selected the one or the other as the important aspect. When we are told to seek peace, tell the truth, or aim at the greatest happiness of the greatest number, we are charged to do or intend some definite act. When we are urged to be conscientious or pure in heart the emphasis is on a kind of attitude that might go with a variety of acts. A newspaper advocates a good measure. So far, so good. But people may ask, what is the motive in this? and if this is believed to be merely selfish, they do not credit the newspaper with having genuine interest in reform. On the other hand, sincerity alone is not enough. If a man advocates frankly and sincerely a scheme for enriching himself at the public expense we condemn him. We say his very frankness shows his utter disregard for others. One of the great moral philosophers has indeed said that to act rationally is all that is necessary, but he at once goes on to claim that this implies treating every man as an end and not merely a means, and this calls for a particular kind of action. Hence we may assume for the present purpose a general agreement that our moral judgments take into account both what is done or intended, and how or why the act is done. These two aspects are sometimes called the "matter" and the "form," or the "content" and the "attitude." We shall use the simpler terms, the What and the How.

The "What" as a Criterion.—If we neglect for the moment the How and think of the What, we find two main standpoints employed in judging: one is that of "higher" and "lower" within the man's own self; the other is his treatment of others.

The distinction between a higher and lower self has many guises. We speak of a man as "a slave to his appetites," of another as possessed by greed for money, of another as insatiately ambitious. Over against these passions we hear the praise of scientific pursuits, of culture, of art, of friendship, of meditation, or of religion. We are bidden to think of things σεμνά, nobly serious. A life of the spirit is set off against the life of the flesh, the finer against the coarser, the nobler against the baser. However misguided the forms in which this has been interpreted, there is no doubt as to the reality of the conflicting impulses which give rise to the dualism. The source is obvious. Man would not be here if self-preservation and self-assertion and sex instinct were not strongly rooted in his system. These may easily become dominant passions. But just as certainly, man cannot be all that he may be unless he controls these impulses and passions by other motives. He has first to create for himself a new world of ideal interests before he finds his best life. The appetites and instincts may be "natural," in the sense that they are the beginning; the mental and spiritual life is "natural," as Aristotle puts it, in the sense that man's full nature is developed only in such a life.

The other aspect of the What, the treatment of others, need not detain us. Justice, kindness, the conduct of the Golden Rule are the right and good. Injustice, cruelty, selfishness are the wrong and the bad.

Analysis of the How: the Right and the Good.—We have used right and good as though they might be used interchangeably in speaking of conduct. Perhaps this may in the end prove to be true. If an act is right, then the hero or the saint may believe that it is also good; if an act is good in the fullest sense, then it will commend itself as right. But right and good evidently approach conduct from two different points of view. These might have been noted when speaking of the content or the What, but they are more important in considering the How.

It is evident that when we speak of conduct as *right* we think of it as before a judge. We bring the act to a standard, and measure the act. We think too of this standard as a "moral law" which we "ought" to obey. We respect its authority and hold ourselves responsible. The standard is conceived as a control over our impulses and desires. The man who recognizes such a law and is anxious to find and to do his duty, we call conscientious; as governing his impulses, he has self-control; as squaring his conduct strictly by his standard, he is upright and reliable.

If I think of "*good*," I am approaching conduct from the standpoint of value. I am thinking of what is desirable. This too is a standard, but it is a standard regarded as an end to be sought rather than as a law. I am to "choose" it and identify myself with it, rather than to control myself by it. It is an "ideal." The conscientious man, viewed from this standpoint, would seek to discover the true good, to value his ends, to form ideals, instead of following impulse or accepting any seeming good without careful consideration. In so far as impulses are directed by ideals the thoroughly good man will be straightforward, "sincere": that is, he will not be moved to do the good act by fear of punishment, or by bribery, just as the upright man will be "governed by a sense of duty," of "respect for principles."

Summary of the Characteristics of the Moral.—To sum up the main characteristics of the moral life viewed in cross-section, or when in full activity, we may state them as follows:

On the side of the "what," there are two aspects:

(a) The dominance of "higher," ideal interests of knowledge, art, freedom, rights, and the "life of the spirit."

(b) Regard for others, under its various aspects of justice, sympathy, and benevolence.

On the side of the "how" the important aspects are:

(a) The recognition of some standard, which may arise either as a control in the guise of "right" and "law," or as measure of value in the form of an ideal to be followed or good to be approved.

(b) A sense of duty and respect for the law; sincere love of the good.

(a) and (b) of this latter division are both included under the "conscientious" attitude.

2. *The Moral as a Growth.*—The psychologists distinguish *three stages* in conduct: (a) Instinctive activity. (b) Attention; the stage of conscious direction or control of action by imagery; of deliberation, desire, and choice. (c) Habit; the stage of unconscious activity along lines set by previous action. Consciousness thus "occupies a curious middle-ground between hereditary reflex and automatic activities upon the one hand and acquired habitual activities upon the other." Where the original equipment of instincts fails to meet some new situation, when there are stimulations for

which the system has no ready-made response, consciousness appears. It selects from the various responses those which suit the purpose, and when these responses have become themselves automatic, habitual, consciousness "betakes itself elsewhere to points where habitual accommodatory movements are as yet wanting and needed."[2] To apply this to the moral development we need only to add that this process repeats itself over and over. The starting-point for each later repetition is not the hereditary instinct, but the habits which have been formed. For the habits formed at one age of the individual's life, or at one stage of race development, prove inadequate for more complex situations. The child leaves home, the savage tribe changes to agricultural life, and the old habits no longer meet the need. Attention is again demanded. There is deliberation, struggle, effort. If the result is successful new habits are formed, but upon a higher level. For the new habits, the new character, embody more intelligence. The first stage, purely instinctive action, we do not call moral conduct. It is of course not *im*moral; it is merely *un*moral. The second stage shows morality in the making. It includes the process of transition from impulse, through desire, to will. It involves the stress of conflicting interests, the processes of deliberation and valuation, and the final act of choice. It will be illustrated in our treatment of race development by the change from early group life and customs to the more conscious moral life of higher civilization. The third stage, well-organized character, is the goal of the process. But it is evidently only a relative point. A good man has built up a set of habits; a good society has established certain laws and moral codes. But unless the man or society is in a changeless world with no new conditions there will be new problems. And this means that however good the habit was for its time and purpose there must be new choices and new valuations. A character that would run automatically in every case would be pretty nearly a mechanism. It is therefore the second stage of this process that is the stage of active moral consciousness. It is upon this that we focus our attention.

2. Angell, *Psychology*, p. 59.

Moral growth from the first on through the second stage may be described as a process in which man becomes more *rational*, more *social*, and finally more *moral*. We examine briefly each of these aspects.

The Rationalizing or Idealizing Process.—The first need of the organism is to live and grow. The first instincts and impulses are therefore for food, self-defense, and other immediate necessities. Primitive men eat, sleep, fight, build shelters, and give food and protection to their offspring. The "rationalizing" process will mean at first greater use of intelligence to satisfy these same wants. It will show itself in skilled occupations, in industry and trade, in the utilizing of all resources to further man's power and happiness. But to rationalize conduct is also to introduce new ends. It not only enables man to get what he wants; it changes the kind of objects that he wants. This shows itself externally in what man makes and in how he occupies himself. He must of course have food and shelter. But he makes temples and statues and poems. He makes myths and theories of the world. He carries on great enterprises in commerce or government, not so much to gratify desires for bodily wants as to experience the growth of power. He creates a family life which is raised to a higher level by art and religion. He does not live by bread only, but builds up gradually a life of reason. Psychologically this means that whereas at the beginning we want what our body calls for, we soon come to want things which the mind takes an interest in. As we form by memory, imagination, and reason a more continuous, permanent, highly-organized self, we require a far more permanent and ideal kind of good to satisfy us. This gives rise to the contrast between the material and ideal selves, or in another form, between "the world" and "the spirit."

The Socializing Process.—The "socializing" side of the process of development stands for an increased capacity to enter into relations with other human beings. Like the growth of reason it is both a means and an end. It has its roots in certain instincts—sex, gregariousness, parental instincts— and in the necessities of mutual support and protection. But the associations thus formed imply a great variety of activities which call out new powers and set up new ends.

Language is one of the first of these activities and a first step toward more complete socialization. Cooperation, in all kinds of enterprises, interchange of services and goods, participation in social arts, associations for various purposes, institutions of blood, family, government, and religion, all add enormously to the individual's power. On the other hand, as he enters into these relations and becomes a "member" of all these bodies he inevitably undergoes a transformation in his interests. Psychologically the process is one of building up a "social" self. Imitation and suggestion, sympathy and affection, common purpose and common interest, are the aids in building such a self. As the various instincts, emotions, and purposes are more definitely organized into such a unit, it becomes possible to set off the interests of others against those interests that centre in my more individual good. Conscious egoism and altruism become possible. And in a way that will be explained, the interests of self and others are raised to the plane of rights and justice.

What is Needed to Make Conduct Moral.—All this is not yet moral progress in the fullest sense. The progress to more rational and more social conduct is the indispensable condition of the moral, but not the whole story. What is needed is that the more rational and social conduct should itself be valued as good, and so be chosen and sought; or in terms of control, that the law which society or reason prescribes should be consciously thought of as right, used as a standard, and respected as binding. This gives the contrast between the higher and lower, as a conscious aim, not merely as a matter of taste. It raises the collision between self and others to the basis of personal rights and justice, of deliberate selfishness or benevolence. Finally it gives the basis for such organization of the social and rational choices that the progress already gained may be permanently secured, while the attention, the struggle between duty and inclination, the conscious choice, move forward to a new issue. Aristotle made these points clear:

But the virtues are not in this point analogous to the arts. The products of art have their excellence in themselves, and so it is enough if when produced they are of a certain quality; but in the case of the virtues, a man is not said to act justly or temperately (or like a just or temperate man) if what he does merely be of a certain sort—he must also be in a certain state of mind when he does it: i.e., first of all, he must know what he is doing; secondly, he must choose it, and choose it for itself; and, thirdly, his act must be the expression of a formed and stable character.

Summary of the Characteristics of the Moral as Growth. —The full cycle has three stages:

(a) Instinctive or habitual action.

(b) Action under the stress of attention, with conscious intervention and reconstruction.

(c) Organization of consciously directed conduct into habits and a self of a higher order: Character.

The advance from (a) to and through (b) has three aspects:

(a) It is a rationalizing and idealizing process. Reason is both a means to secure other ends, and an element in determining what shall be sought.

(b) It is a socializing process. Society both strengthens and transforms the individual.

(c) It is a process in which finally conduct itself is made the conscious object of reflection, valuation, and criticism. In this the definitely moral conceptions of right and duty, good and virtue appear.

§ 3. *Divisions of the Treatment*

PART I, after a preliminary presentation of certain important aspects of group life, will first trace the process of moral development in its general outlines, and then give specific illustrations of the process taken from the life of Israel, of Greece, and of modern civilization.

PART II will analyze conduct or the moral life on its inner, personal side. After distinguishing more carefully what is meant by moral action, and noting some typical ways in which the moral life has been viewed by ethical theory, it will examine the meaning of right and good, of duty and virtue, and seek to discover the principles underlying moral judgments and moral conduct.

PART III will study conduct as action in society. But instead of a general survey, attention will be centered upon three phases of conduct which are of especial interest and importance. Political rights and duties, the production, distribution, and ownership of wealth, and finally the relations of domestic and family life, all present unsettled problems. These challenge the student to make a careful examination, for he must take some attitude as citizen on the issues involved.

Literature

The literature on specific topics will be found at the beginning of each Part, and at the close of the several chapters. We indicate here some of the more useful manuals and recent representative works, and add some specific references on the scope and methods of ethics. Baldwin's *Dictionary of Philosophy and Psychology* has selected lists (see especially articles, "Ethical Theories," "Ethics," "Worth") and general lists (Vol. III). Runze, *Ethik*, 1891, has good bibliographies.

ELEMENTARY TEXTS: Mackenzie, *Manual of Ethics*, 4th ed., 1900; Muirhead, *Elements of Ethics*, 1892; Seth, *A Study of Ethical Principles*, 6th ed., 1902; Thilly, *Introduction to Ethics*, 1900.

REPRESENTATIVE BOOKS AND TREATISES IN ENGLISH: Green, *Prolegomena to Ethics*, 1883 (Idealism); Martineau, *Types of Ethical Theory*, 1885; 3d ed., 1891 (Intuitionism); Sidgwick's *Methods of Ethics*, 1874; 6th ed., 1901 (Union of Intuitionist and Utilitarian Positions with careful analysis of common sense); Spencer, *The Principles of Ethics*, 1892–93 (Evolution); Stephen's *Science of Ethics*, 1882. The comprehensive work of Paulsen (*System der Ethik*, 1889, 5th ed., 1900) has been translated by Thilly, 1899; that of Wundt (*Ethik*, 1886, 3d ed., 1903), by Titchener, Gulliver, and Washburn, 1897–1901. Among the more recent contributions, either to the whole field or to specific parts, may be noted: Alexander, *Moral Order and Progress*, 1889; 2d ed., 1891; Dewey, *Outlines of Ethics*, 1891 [*The Early Works of John Dewey* 3:237–388], and *The Study of Ethics: A Syllabus*, 1894 [*Early Works* 4:219–362]; Fite, *An Introductory Study of Ethics*, 1903; Höffding, *Ethik* (German tr.), 1888; Janet, *The Theory of Morals* (Eng. tr.), 1884; Ladd, *The Philosophy of Conduct*, 1902; Mezes, *Ethics: Descriptive and Explanatory*, 1901; Moore, *Principia Ethica*, 1903; Palmer, *The Field of Ethics*, 1901, *The Nature of Goodness*, 1903; Taylor, *The Problem of Conduct*,

1901,; Rashdall, *The Theory of Good and Evil*, 1907; Bowne, *The Principles of Ethics*, 1892; Rickaby, *Moral Philosophy*, 1888.

HISTORIES OF ETHICS: Sidgwick, *History of Ethics*, 3d ed., 1892; Albee, *A History of English Utilitarianism*, 1902; Stephen, *The Utilitarians*, 1900; Martineau, *Types of Ethical Theory*; Whewell, *Lectures on the History of Moral Philosophy in England*, 1852, 1862; Köstlin, *Geschichte der Ethik*, Vol. I, Part I, 1887 (ancient theories); Jodl, *Geschichte der Ethik*, 2 vols., 1882–89 (modern); Wundt, *Ethik*, Vol. II; the histories of philosophy by Windelband, Höffding, Erdmann, Ueberweg, Falckenberg.

SCOPE AND METHOD OF ETHICS: See the opening chapters in nearly all the works cited above, especially Palmer (*Field of Ethics*), Moore, Stephen, Spencer, Paulsen, and Wundt (*Facts of the Moral Life*); see also Ritchie, *Philosophical Studies*, 1905, pp. 264–91; Wallace, *Lectures and Essays on Natural Theology and Ethics*, 1898, pp. 194 ff.; Dewey, *Logical Conditions of a Scientific Treatment of Morality* (University of Chicago Decennial Publications, 1903) [*The Middle Works of John Dewey* 3:3–39]; Stuart, *The Logic of Self-Realization*, in University of California Publications in Philosophy, I, 1904; Small, *The Significance of Sociology for Ethics*, 1902; Hadley, Articles on Economic Theory in Baldwin's *Dictionary*.

RELATION OF THEORY TO LIFE: Green, *Prolegomena*, Book IV; Dewey, *International Journal of Ethics*, Vol. I, 1891, pp. 186–203 [*Early Works* 3:93–109]; James, same journal, Vol. I, 330–54; Mackenzie, same journal, Vol. IV, 1894, pp. 160–73.

Part I   The Beginnings and Growth of Morality

General Literature for Part I

Hobhouse, *Morals in Evolution*, 2 vols., 1906.

Westermarck, *The Origin and Development of Moral Ideas*, Vol. I, 1906.

Sutherland, *The Origin and Growth of· Moral Instinct*, 2 vols., 1898.

Wundt, *Facts of the Moral Life*, 1897; also *Ethik*, 3d ed., 1903, Vol. I, pp. 280–523.

Paulsen, *A System of Ethics*, 1899, Book I.

Sumner, *Folkways*, 1906.

Bergemann, *Ethik als Kulturphilosophie*, 1904.

Mezes, *Ethics: Descriptive and Explanatory*, Part I.

Dewey, "The Evolutionary Method as Applied to Morality," *Philosophical Review*, XI, 1902, pp. 107–24, 353–71.

Adam Smith, *Theory of Moral Sentiments*, 1892.

Baldwin, *Social and Ethical Interpretations*, 1902.

Taylor, *The Problem of Conduct*, 1901, chap. iii.

Spencer, *Data of Ethics*, 1879; *Psychology*, 1872, Part IX, chs. v–viii.

Ihering, *Der Zweck im Recht*, 3d ed., 1893.

Steinthal, *Allgemeine Ethik*, 1885.

2. EARLY GROUP LIFE

To understand the origin and growth of moral life, it is essential to understand primitive society. And while there is much that is uncertain, there is one fact of capital importance which stands out clearly. This is *the dominant influence of group life*. It is not asserted that all peoples have had precisely the same type of groups, or the same degree of group solidarity. It is beyond question that the ancestors of modern civilized races lived under the general types of group life which will be outlined, and that these types or their survivals are found among the great mass of peoples to-day.

§ 1. *Typical Facts of Group Life*

Consider the following incident as related by Dr. Gray:

A Chinese aided by his wife flogged his mother. The imperial order not only commanded that the criminals should be put to death; it further directed that the head of the clan should be put to death, that the immediate neighbors each receive eighty blows and be sent into exile; that the head or representatives of the graduates of the first degree (or B.A.) among whom the male offender ranked should be flogged and exiled; that the grand-uncle, the uncle, and two elder brothers should be put to death; that the prefect and the rulers should for a time be deprived of their rank; that on the face of the mother of the female offender four Chinese characters expressive of neglect of duty towards her daughter should be tattooed, and that she be exiled to a distant province; that the father of the female offender, a bachelor of arts, should not be allowed to take any higher literary degrees, and that he be flogged and exiled; that the son of the offenders should receive another name, and that the lands of the offender for a time remain fallow. (J. H. Gray, *China*, Vol. I, pp. 237 f.)

Put beside this the story of Achan:

Achan had taken for his own possession certain articles from the spoil of Jericho which had been set apart or "devoted" to Jehovah. Israel then suffered a defeat in battle. When Achan's act became known, "Joshua and all Israel with him took Achan, the son of Zerah, and the mantle, and the wedge of gold, and his sons and his daughters, and his oxen, and his asses, and his sheep, and his tent, and all that he had. . . . And all Israel stoned him with stones; and they burned them with fire and stoned them with stones." (Joshua vii: 24–25.)

The converse of these situations is brought out in the regulations of the Kumi, a Japanese local institution comprising five or more households:

As members of a Kumi we will cultivate friendly feelings even more than with our relatives, and will promote each other's happiness as well as share each other's grief. If there is an unprincipled or lawless person in a Kumi, we shall all share the responsibility for him. (Simmons and Wigmore, *Transactions, Asiatic Society of Japan*, Vol. XIX, pp. 177 f.)

For another aspect of the group take Caesar's description of landholding among the Germans:

No one possesses privately a definite extent of land; no one has limited fields of his own; but every year the magistrates and chiefs distribute the land to the clans and the kindred groups (*gentibus cognationibusque hominum*) and to those (*other* groups) who live together. (*De Bello Gallico*, VI, § 22.)

Of the Greeks, our intellectual ancestors, as well as fellow Aryans, it is stated that in Attica, even to a late period, the land remained to a large degree in possession of ideal persons, gods, phylae (tribes) or phratries, kinships, political communities. Even when the superficies of the land might be regarded as private, mines were reserved as public.[1] The basis on which these kinship groups rested is thus stated by Grote:[2]

All these phratric and gentile associations, the larger as well as the smaller, were founded upon the same principles and tendencies of the Grecian mind—a coalescence of the idea of worship with that of ancestry, or of communion in certain special religious rites with communion of blood, real or supposed. . . . The god or hero, to whom the assembled members offered their sacrifices, was conceived as the primitive ancestor to whom they owed their origin.

1. Wilamowitz-Moellendorff, *Aristoteles und Athen*, II, pp. 47, 93.
2. G. Grote, *History of Greece*, Vol. III, p. 55.

Coulanges gives a similar statement as to the ancient family group:[3]

> The members of the ancient family were united by something more powerful than birth, affection, or physical strength; this was the religion of the sacred fire, and of dead ancestors. This caused the family to form a single body both in this life and in the next.

Finally, the following passage on clanship among the Kafirs brings out two points: (1) That such a group life implies feelings and ideas of a distinctive sort; and (2) that it has a strength rooted in the very necessities of life.

> A Kafir feels that the "frame that binds him in" extends to the clan. The sense of solidarity of the family in Europe is thin and feeble compared to the full-blooded sense of corporate union of the Kafir clan. The claims of the clan entirely swamp the rights of the individual. The system of tribal solidarity, which has worked so well in its smoothness that it might satisfy the utmost dreams of the socialist, is a standing proof of the sense of corporate union of the clan. In olden days a man did not have any feeling of personal injury when a chief made him work for white men and then told him to give all, or nearly all of his wages to his chief; the money was kept within the clan, and what was the good of the clan was the good of the individual and *vice versa*. The striking thing about this unity of the clan is that it was not a thought-out plan imposed from without by legislation upon an unwilling people, but it was a *felt-out* plan which arose spontaneously along the line of least resistance. If one member of the clan suffered, all the members suffered, not in sentimental phraseology, but in real fact. (Dudley Kidd, *Savage Childhood*, pp. 74 f.)

The above passages refer to Aryan, Semitic, Mongolian, and Kafir peoples. They could be matched by similar statements concerning nearly every people. They suggest a way of living, and a view of life very different from that of the American or of most Europeans.[4] The American or European belongs to groups of various kinds, but he "joins" most of them. He of course is born into a family, but he does not stay in it all his life unless he pleases. And he may choose his

---

3. Fustel de Coulanges, *The Ancient City*, p. 51.
4. Russian mirs, South Slavonian "joint" families, Corsican clans with their vendettas, and tribes in the Caucasus still have the group interest strong, and the feuds of the mountaineers in some of the border states illustrate family solidarity.

own occupation, residence, wife, political party, religion, social club, or even national allegiance. He may own or sell his own house, give or bequeath his property, and is responsible generally speaking for no one's acts but his own. This makes him an "individual" in a much fuller sense than he would be if all these relations were settled for him. On the other hand, the member of such groups as are referred to in our examples above, has all, or nearly all, his relations fixed when he is born into a certain clan or family group. This settles his occupation, dwelling, gods, and politics. If it doesn't decide upon his wife, it at least usually fixes the group from which she must be taken. His conditions, in the words of Maine, are thus of "status," not of "contract." This makes a vast difference in his whole attitude. It will help to bring out more clearly by contrast the character of present morality, as well as to see moral life in the making, if we examine more carefully this group life. We shall find, as brought out in the passages already quoted, that the most important type of group is at once a kindred or family, an economic, a political, a religious, and a moral unit. First, however, we notice briefly the most important types of groups.

§ 2. Kinship and Household Groups

1. The Kinship Group.—The kinship group is a body of persons who conceive of themselves as sprung from one ancestor, and hence as having in their veins one blood. It does not matter for our study whether each group has actually sprung from a single ancestor. It is highly probable that the contingencies of food-supply or of war may have been an original cause for the constitution of the group, wholly or in part. But this is of no consequence for our purpose. The important point is that the members of the group regard themselves as of one stock. In some cases the ancestor is believed to have been an animal. Then we have the so-called totem group, which is found among North American Indians, Africans, and Australians, and was perhaps the early form of Semitic groups. In other cases, some hero or even some god is named as the ancestor. In any case the essential part of the theory remains the same: namely, that one blood circulates in all the members, and hence that the life of each is a part of the common life of the group. There are then no degrees of kindred. This group, it should be noted, is not the same as the family, for in the family, as a rule, husband and wife are of different kinship groups, and continue their several kinship relations. Among some peoples marriage ceremonies, indeed, symbolize the admission of the wife into the husband's kinship, and in this case the family becomes a kinship group, but this is by no means universally the case.

The feeling that one is first and foremost a member of a group, rather than an individual, is furthered among certain kin groups by a scheme of class relationship. According to this system, instead of having one definite person whom I, and I alone, regard and address as father or mother, grandfather, uncle, brother, sister, I call any one of a given group or class of persons mother, grandfather, brother, sister. And any one else who is in the same class with me calls the same persons, mother, grandfather, brother, or sister.[5] The simplest form of such a class system is that found among the Hawaiians. Here there are five classes based upon the generations corresponding to what we call grandparents, parents, brothers and sisters, children, and grandchildren, but the words used to designate them do not imply any such specific parentage as do these words with us. Bearing this in mind, we may say that every one in the first class is equally grandparent to every one in the third; every one in the third is equally brother or sister to every other in the third, equally father or mother to every one in the fourth, and so on. In Australia the classes are more numerous and the relation-

5. "In all the tribes with whom we are acquainted all the terms coincide without any exception in the recognition of relationships, all of which are dependent on the existence of a classificatory system, the fundamental idea of which is that the women of certain groups marry the men of others. Each tribe has one term applied indiscriminately to the man or woman whom he actually marries and to all whom he might lawfully marry, that is, who belong to the right group: One term to his actual mother and to all the women whom his father might lawfully have married."—Spencer and Gillen, *Native Tribes of Central Australia*, p. 57.

ships far more intricate and complicated, but this does not, as might be supposed, render the bond relatively unimportant; on the contrary, his relationship to every other class is "one of the most important points with which each individual must be acquainted"; it determines marital relations, food distribution, salutations, and general conduct to an extraordinary degree. A kinship group was known as "tribe" or "family" (English translation) among the Israelites; as genos, phratria, and phyle among the Greeks, gens and curia among the Romans; clan in Scotland; sept in Ireland; Sippe in Germany.

2. *The Family or Household Group.*—Two kinds of families may be noted as significant for our purpose. In the *maternal family* the woman remains among her own kin, and the children are naturally reckoned as belonging to the mother's kin. The husband and father is more or less a guest or outsider. In a blood feud he would have to side with his own clan and against that of his wife if his clan quarreled with hers. Clan and family are thus seen to be distinct. In the *paternal*, which easily becomes the *patriarchal* family the wife leaves her relatives to live in her husband's house and among his kin. She might then, as at Rome, abjure her own kindred and be formally adopted into her husband's gens or clan. The Greek myth of Orestes is an illustration of the clashing of these two conceptions of father kin and mother kin, and Hamlet's sparing of his mother under similar circumstances, shows a more modern point of view.

It is evident that with the prevalence of the paternal type of family, clan and household ties will mutually strengthen each other. This will make an important difference in the father's relation to the children, and gives a much firmer basis for ancestral religion. But in many respects the environing atmosphere, the pressure and support, the group sympathy and group tradition, are essentially similar. The important thing is that every person is a member of a kindred, and likewise, of some family group, and that he thinks, feels, and acts accordingly.[6]

6. The fact that primitive man is at once an individual and a member of a group—that he has as it were two personalities or selves, an individual self and a clan-self, or "tribal-self," as

§ 3. *The Kinship and Family Groups Are Also Economic and Industrial Units*

1. The Land and the Group.—In land, as a rule, no individual ownership in the modern sense was recognized. Among hunting and pastoral peoples there was, of course, no "ownership" by any group in the strict sense of modern law. But none the less, the group, large or small, had its fairly well-defined territory within which it hunted and fished; in the pastoral life it had its pasture range and its wells of water. With agriculture a more definite sense of possession arose. But possession was by the tribe or gens or household, not by the individual:

> The land belonged to the clan, and the clan was settled upon the land. A man was thus not a member of the clan, because he lived upon, or even owned, the land; but he lived upon the land, and had interests in it, because he was a member of the clan.[7]

Greek and German customs were quoted at the outset. Among the Celts the laws of ancient Ireland show a transitional stage. "The land of the tribe consisted of two distinct allotments, the 'fechfine' or tribeland, and the 'orta' or inheritance land. This latter belonged as individual property to the men of the chieftain groups."[8] The Hindoo joint-family

---

Clifford called it,—is not merely a psychologist's way of stating things. The Kafir people, according to their most recent student, Mr. Dudley Kidd, have two distinct words to express these two selves. They call one the *idhlozi* and other the *itongo*. "The *idhlozi* is the individual and personal spirit born with each child —something fresh and unique which is never shared with any one else—while the *itongo* is the ancestral and corporate spirit which is not personal but tribal, or a thing of the clan, the possession of which is obtained not by birth but by certain initiatory rites. The *idhlozi* is personal and inalienable, for it is wrapped up with the man's personality, and at death it lives near the grave, or goes into the snake or totem of the clan; but the *itongo* is of the clan, and haunts the living-hut; at death it returns to the tribal *amatongo* (ancestral spirits). A man's share in this clan-spirit (*itongo*) is lost when he becomes a Christian, or when he is in any way unfaithful to the interests of the clan, but a man never loses his *idhlozi* any more than he ever loses his individuality."—Kidd, *Savage Childhood*, pp. 14 f.

7. Hearn, *The Aryan Household*, p. 212.
8. McLennan, *Studies in Ancient History*, p. 381.

and the house-community of the Southern Slavonians are
present examples of group ownership. They are joint in food,
worship, and estate. They have a common home, a common
table. Maxims of the Slavs express their appreciation of
community life: "The common household waxes rich"; "The
more bees in the hive, the heavier it weighs." One difficulty
in the English administration of Ireland has been this
radical difference between the modern Englishman's individualistic conception of property and the Irishman's
more primitive conception of group or clan ownership.
Whether rightly or not, the Irish tenant refuses to regard
himself as merely a tenant. He considers himself as a member of a family or group which formerly owned the land,
and he does not admit the justice, even though he cannot
disprove the legality, of an alienation of the group possession. For such a clan or household as we have described is
not merely equivalent to the persons who compose it at a
given time. Its property belongs to the ancestors and to the
posterity as well as to the present possessors; and hence in
some groups which admit an individual possession or use
during life, no right of devise or inheritance is permitted.
The property reverts at death to the whole gens or clan. In
other cases a child may inherit, but in default of such an
heir the property passes to the common possession. The
right to bequeath property to the church was long a point on
which civil law and canon law were at variance. The relations of the primitive clan or household group to land were
therefore decidedly adapted to keep the individual's good
bound up with the good of the group.

2. *Movable Goods.* — In the case of movable goods, such
as tools, weapons, cattle, the practice is not uniform. When
the goods are the product of the individual's own skill or
prowess they are usually his. Tools, weapons, slaves or
women captured, products of some special craft or skill,
are thus usually private. But when the group acts as a unit
the product is usually shared. The buffalo and salmon and
large game were thus for the whole Indian group which
hunted or fished together; and in like manner the maize
which was tended by the women belonged to the household
in common. Slavic and Indian house communities at the

present day have a common interest in the household property. Even women and children among some tribes are regarded as the property of the group.

§ 4. *The Kinship and Family Groups Were Political Bodies*

In a modern family the parents exercise a certain degree of control over the children, but this is limited in several respects. No parent is allowed to put a child to death, or to permit him to grow up in ignorance. On the other hand, the parent is not allowed to protect the child from arrest if a serious injury has been done by him. The *State*, through its laws and officers, is regarded by us as the highest authority in a certain great sphere of action. It must settle conflicting claims and protect life and property; in the opinion of many it must organize the life of its members where the cooperation of every member is necessary for some common good. In early group life there may or may not be some political body over and above the clan or family, but in any case the *kin or family is itself a sort of political State*. Not a State in the sense that the political powers are deliberately separated from personal, religious, and family ties; men gained a new conception of authority and rose to a higher level of possibilities when they consciously separated and defined government and laws from the undifferentiated whole of a religious and kindred group. But yet this primitive group was after all a State, not a mob, or a voluntary society, or a mere family; for (1) it was a more or less permanently organized body; (2) it exercised control over its members which they regarded as rightful authority, not as mere force; (3) it was not limited by any higher authority, and acted more or less effectively for the interest of the whole. The representatives of this political aspect of the group may be chiefs or sachems, a council of elders, or, as in Rome, the House Father, whose *patria potestas* marks the extreme development of the patriarchal family.

The control exercised by the group over individual

members assumes various forms among the different peoples. The more important aspects are a right over life and bodily freedom, in some cases extending to power of putting to death, maiming, chastising, deciding whether newly born children shall be preserved or not; the right of betrothal, which includes control over the marriage portion received for its women; and the right to administer property of the kin in behalf of the kin as a whole. It is probable that among all these various forms of control, the control over the marriage relations of women has been most persistent. One reason for this control may have been the fact that the group was bound to resent injuries of a member of the group who had been married to another. Hence this responsibility seemed naturally to involve the right of decision as to her marriage.

It is Membership in the Group Which Gives the Individual Whatever Rights He Has.—According to present conceptions this is still largely true of legal rights. A State may allow a citizen of another country to own land, to sue in its courts, and will usually give him a certain amount of protection, but the first-named rights are apt to be limited, and it is only a few years since Chief Justice Taney's dictum stated the existing legal theory of the United States to be that the negro "had no rights which the white man was bound to respect." Even where legal theory does not recognize race or other distinctions, it is often hard in practice for an alien to get justice. In primitive clan or family groups this principle is in full force. Justice is a privilege which falls to a man as belonging to some group—not otherwise. The member of the clan or the household or the village community has a claim, but the stranger has no standing. He may be treated kindly, as a guest, but he cannot demand "justice" at the hands of any group but his own. In this conception of rights within the group we have the prototype of modern civil law. The dealing of clan with clan is a matter of war or negotiation, not of law; and the clanless man is an "outlaw" in fact as well as in name.

Joint responsibility and mutual support, as shown in the blood feud, was a natural consequence of this fusion of political and kindred relations. In modern life States treat each other as wholes in certain respects. If some member of a savage tribe assaults a citizen of one of the civilized nations, the injured party invokes the help of his government. A demand is usually made that the guilty party be delivered up for trial and punishment. If he is not forthcoming a "punitive expedition" is organized against the whole tribe; guilty and innocent suffer alike. Or in lieu of exterminating the offending tribe, in part or completely, the nation of the injured man may accept an indemnity in money or land from the offender's tribe. Recent dealings between British and Africans, Germans and Africans, France and Morocco, the United States and the Filipinos, the Powers and China, illustrate this. The State protects its own members against other States, and avenges them upon other States. Each opposes a united body to the other. The same principle carried out through private citizens as public agents, and applied to towns, is seen in the practice which prevailed in the Middle Ages. "When merchants of one country had been defrauded by those of another, or found it impossible to collect a debt from them, the former country issued letters of marque and reprisal, authorizing the plunder of any citizens of the offending town until satisfaction should be obtained." Transfer the situation to the early clan or tribe, and this solidarity is increased because each member is related to the rest by blood, as well as by national unity. The Arabs do not say "The blood of M. or N. has been spilt," naming the man; they say, "Our blood has been spilt."[9] The whole group, therefore, feels injured and regards every man in the offender's kin as more or less responsible. The next of kin, the "avenger of blood," stands first in duty and privilege, but the rest are all involved in greater or less degree.

Within the group each member will be treated more or less fully as an individual. If he takes his kinsman's wife or his kinsman's game he will be dealt with by the authorities or by the public opinion of his group. He will not indeed be put to death if he kills his kinsman, but he will be hated, and may be driven out. "Since the living kin is not killed

9. Robertson Smith, *Kinship and Marriage in Early Arabia*, p. 23.

for the sake of the dead kin, everybody will hate to see him."[10]

When now a smaller group, like a family, is at the same time a part of a larger group like a phratry or a tribe, we have the phase of solidarity which is so puzzling to the modern. We hold to solidarity in war or between nations; but with a few exceptions[11] we have replaced it by individual responsibility of adults for debts and crimes so far as the civil law has jurisdiction. In earlier times the higher group or authority treated the smaller as a unit. Achan's family all perished with him. The Chinese sense of justice recognized a series of degrees in responsibility dependent on nearness of kin or of residence, or of occupation. The Welsh system held kinsmen as far as second cousins responsible for insult or injury short of homicide, and as far as fifth cousins (seventh degree of descent) for the payment in case of homicide. "The mutual responsibility of kinsmen for *saraad* and *galanas* (the Wergild of the Germans), graduated according to nearness of kin to the murdered man and to the criminal, reveals more clearly than anything else the extent to which the individual was bound by innumerable meshes to his fixed place in the tribal community."[12]

§ 5. *The Kinship or Household Group Was a Religious Unit*

The kinship or household group determined largely both the ideas and the cultus of primitive religion; conversely religion gave completeness, value, and sacredness to the group life. Kinship with unseen powers or persons was the fundamental religious idea. The kinship group as a religious body *simply extended the kin to include invisible as well as visible members.* The essential feature of religion is not unseen beings who are feared, or cajoled, or controlled by magic. It is rather *kindred* unseen beings, who may be feared, but who are also reverenced and loved. The kinship

---

10. Cited from the Gwentian Code. Seebohm, *The Tribal System in Wales*, p. 104.
11. E.g., certain joint responsibilities of husband and wife.
12. Seebohm, *The Tribal System in Wales*, pp. 103 f.

may be physical or spiritual, but however conceived it makes gods and worshippers members of one group.[13]

1. *Totem Groups.*—In totem groups, the prevailing conception is that one blood circulates in all the members of the group and that the ancestor of the whole group is some object of nature, such as sun or moon, plant or animal. Perhaps the most interesting and intelligible account of the relation between the animal ancestor and the members of the group is that which has recently been discovered in certain Australian tribes who believe that every child, at its birth, is the reincarnation of some previous member of the group, and that these ancestors were an actual transformation of animals and plants, or of water, fire, wind, sun, moon, or stars. Such totem groups cherish that animal which they believe to be their ancestor and ordinarily will not kill it or use it for food. The various ceremonies of religious initiation are intended to impress upon the younger members of the group the sacredness of this kindred bond which unites them to each other and to their totem. The beginnings of decorative art frequently express the importance of the symbol, and the totem is felt to be as distinctly a member of the group as is any of the human members.

2. *Ancestral Religion.*—At a somewhat higher stage of civilization, and usually in connection with the patriarchal households or groups in which kinship is reckoned through the male line, the invisible members of the group are the *departed ancestors*. This ancestor worship is a power to-day in China and Japan, and in the tribes of the Caucasus. The ancient Semites, Romans, Teutons, Celts, Hindoos, all had their kindred gods of the household. The Roman genius, lares, penates, and manes, perhaps the Hebrew teraphim,— prized by Laban and Rachel, kept by David, valued in the time of Hosea,—were loved and honored side by side with other deities. Sometimes the nature deities, such as Zeus or

13. "From the earliest times, religion, as distinct from magic or sorcery, addresses itself to kindred and friendly beings, who may indeed be angry with their people for a time, but are always placable except to the enemies of their worshippers or to renegade members of the community. It is not with a vague fear of unknown powers, but with a loving reverence for known gods who are knit to their worshippers by strong bonds of kinship, that religion in the only true sense of the word begins."— Robertson Smith, *Religion of the Semites*, p. 54.

Jupiter, were incorporated with the kinship or family gods. The Greek Hestia and Roman Vesta symbolized the sacredness of the hearth. The kinship tie thus determined for every member of the group his religion.

Religion Completes the Group.—Conversely, this bond of union with unseen, yet ever present and powerful kindred spirits completed the group and gave to it its highest authority, its fullest value, its deepest sacredness. If the unseen kin are nature beings, they symbolize for man his dependence upon nature and his kinship in some vague fashion with the cosmic forces. If the gods are the departed ancestors, they are then conceived as still potent, like Father Anchises, to protect and guide the fortunes of their offspring. The wisdom, courage, and affection, as well as the power of the great heroes of the group, live on. The fact that the gods are unseen enhances tremendously their supposed power. The visible members of the group may be strong, but their strength can be measured. The living elders may be wise, yet they are not far beyond the rest of the group. But the invisible beings cannot be measured. The long-departed ancestor may have inconceivable age and wisdom. The imagination has free scope to magnify his power and invest him with all the ideal values it can conceive. The religious bond is, therefore, fitted to be the bearer, as the religious object is the embodiment in concrete form, of the higher standards of the group, and to furnish the sanction for their enforcement or adoption.

§ 6. *Groups or Classes on the Basis of Age and Sex*

While the kindred and family groups are by far the most important for early morality, other groupings are significant. The division by ages is widespread. The simplest scheme gives three classes: (1) children, (2) young men and maidens, (3) married persons. Puberty forms the bound between the first and second; marriage that between, the second and third. Distinct modes of dress and ornament, frequently also different residences and standards of conduct, belong to these several classes. Of groups on the basis of sex, the *men's clubs* are especially worthy of note. They flourish now chiefly in the islands of the Pacific, but there are indications, such as the common meals of the Spartans, of a wide spread among European peoples in early times. The fundamental idea[14] seems to be that of a common house for the unmarried young men, where they eat, sleep, and pass their time, whereas the women, children, and married men sleep and eat in the family dwelling. But in most cases all the men resort to the clubhouse by day. Strangers may be entertained there. It thus forms a sort of general centre for the men's activities, and for the men's conversation. As such, it is an important agency for forming and expressing public opinion, and for impressing upon the young men just entering the house the standards of the older members. Further, in some cases these houses become the centre of rites to the dead, and thus add the impressiveness of religious significance to their other activities.

Finally, *secret societies* may be mentioned as a sub-division of sex groups, for among primitive peoples such societies are confined in almost all cases to the men. They seem in many cases to have grown out of the age classes already described. The transition from childhood to manhood, mysterious in itself, was invested with further mysteries by the old men who conducted the ceremonies of initiation. Masks were worn, or the skulls of deceased ancestors were employed, to give additional mystery and sanctity. The increased power gained by secrecy would often be itself sufficient to form a motive for such organization, especially where they had some end in view not approved by the dominant authorities. Sometimes they exercise strict authority over their members, and assume judicial and punitive functions, as in the Vehm of the Middle Ages. Sometimes they become merely leagues of enemies to society.

§ 7. *Moral Significance of the Kindred and Other Groups*

The moral in this early stage is not to be looked for as something distinct from the political, religious, kindred, and

14. Schurtz, *Altersklassen und Männerbünde.*

sympathetic aspects of the clan, family, and other groups. The question rather is, *How far are these very political, religious, and other aspects implicitly moral*? If by moral we mean a conscious testing of conduct by an inner and self-imposed standard, if we mean a freely chosen as contrasted with a habitual or customary standard, then evidently we have the moral only in germ. For the standards are group standards, rather than those of individual conscience; they operate largely through habit rather than through choice. Nevertheless they are not set for the individual by outsiders. They are set by a group *of which he is a member.* They are enforced by a group of which he is a member. Conduct is praised or blamed, punished or rewarded by the group of which he is a member. Property is administered, industry is carried on, wars and feuds prosecuted for the common good. What the group does, each member joins in doing. It is a reciprocal matter: A helps enforce a rule or impose a service on B; he cannot help feeling it fair when the same rule is applied to himself. He has to "play the game," and usually he expects to play it as a matter of course. Each member, therefore, is practicing certain acts, standing in certain relations, maintaining certain attitudes, just because he is one of the group which does these things and maintains these standards. And he does not act in common with the group without sharing in the group emotions. It is a grotesque perversion to conceive the restraints of gods and chiefs as purely external terrors. The primitive group could enter into the spirit implied in the words of the Athenian chorus, which required of an alien upon adoption

> To loathe whate'er our state does hateful hold,
> To reverence what it loves.[15]

The gregarious instinct may be the most elemental of the impulses which bind the group together, but it is reenforced by sympathies and sentiments growing out of common life, common work, common danger, common religion. The morality is already implicit, it needs only to become conscious. The standards are embodied in the old men or the

15. Sophocles, *Oedipus at Colonus.*

gods; the rational good is in the inherited wisdom; the respect for sex, for property rights, and for the common good, is embodied in the system—but it is there. Nor are the union and control a wholly objective affair. "The corporate union was not a pretty religious fancy with which to please the mind, but was so truly felt that it formed an excellent basis from which the altruistic sentiment might start. Gross selfishness was curbed, and the turbulent passions were restrained by an impulse which the man felt welling up within him, instinctive and unbidden. Clannish camaraderie was thus of immense value to the native races."[16]

16. Kidd, *Savage Childhood*, pp. 74 f.

Literature

The works of Hobhouse, Sumner, Westermarck contain copious references to the original sources. Among the most valuable are:

FOR SAVAGE PEOPLE: Waitz, *Anthropologie der Naturvölker*, 1859–72; Tylor, *Primitive Culture*, 1903; Spencer and Gillen, *The Native Tribes of Central Australia*, 1899, and *The Northern Tribes of Central Australia*, 1904; Fison and Howitt, *Kamilaroi and Kurnai*, 1880; Howitt, *The Native Tribes of South-East Australia*, 1904; N. Thomas, *Kinship Organizations and Group Marriage in Australia*, 1906; Morgan, *Houses and House-Life of the American Aborigines*, 1881, *League of the Iroquois*, 1851, *Systems of Consanguinity*, Smithsonian Contributions, 1870, *Ancient Society*, 1877. Many papers in the *Reports of the Bureau of Ethnology*, especially by Powell in 1st, 1879–80; Dorsey in 3d, 1881–82; Mindeleff in 15th, 1893–94.

FOR INDIA, CHINA, AND JAPAN: Lyall, *Asiatic Studies, Religious and Social*, 1882; Gray, *China*, 1878; Smith, *Chinese Characteristics*, 1894, *Village Life in China*, 1899; Nitobé, *Bushido*, 1905; L. Hearn, *Japan*, 1904.

FOR SEMITIC AND INDO-GERMANIC PEOPLES: W. R. Smith, *Kinship and Marriage in Early Arabia*, 1885, *The Religion of the Semites*, 1894; W. Hearn, *The Aryan Household*, 1879; Fustel de Coulanges, *The Ancient City*, 1874; Seebohm, *The Tribal System in Wales*, 1895, and *Tribal Custom in Anglo-Saxon Law*, 1902; Krauss, *Sitte und Brauch der Südslaven*, 1885.

GENERAL: Grosse, *Die Formen der Familie und die Formen der Wirthschaft*, 1896; Starcke, *The Primitive Family*, 1889;

Maine, *Ancient Law*, 1885; McLennan, *Studies in Ancient History*, 1886; Rivers, "On the Origin of the Classificatory System of Relationships," in *Anthropological Essays*, presented to E. B. Tylor, 1907; Ratzel, *History of Mankind*, 1896–98; Kovalevsky, *Tableau des origines et de l'evolution de la famille et de la propriété*, 1890; Giddings, *Principles of Sociology*, 1896, pp. 157–68, 256–98; Thomas, "Sex and Primitive Social Control" in *Sex and Society*, 1907; Webster, *Primitive Secret Societies*, 1908; Simmel, "The Sociology of Secrecy and of Secret Societies," *American Journal of Sociology*, Vol. XI, 1906, pp. 441–98. See also the references at close of Chapters 6, 7.

3. THE RATIONALIZING AND SOCIALIZING AGENCIES IN EARLY SOCIETY

§ 1. Three Levels of Conduct

A young man may enter a profession thinking of it only as a means of support. But the work requires foresight and persistence; it broadens his interests; it develops his character. Like Saul, he has gone to search for asses, he has found a kingdom. Or he may marry on the basis of emotional attraction. But the sympathies evoked, the cooperation made necessary, are refining and enlarging his life. Both these cases illustrate agencies which are moral in their results, although not carried on from a consciously moral purpose.

Suppose, however, that children are born into the family. Then the parent consciously sets about controlling their conduct, and in exercising authority almost inevitably feels the need of some standard other than caprice or selfishness. Suppose that in business the partners differ as to their shares in the profits, then the question of fairness is raised; and if one partner defaults, the question of guilt. Or suppose the business encounters a law which forbids certain operations, the problem of justice will come to consciousness. Such situations as these are evidently in the moral sphere in a sense in which those of the preceding paragraph are not. They demand some kind of judgment, some approval or disapproval. As Aristotle says, it is not enough to do the acts; it is necessary to do them in a certain way,—not merely to get the result, but to intend it. The result must be thought of as in some sense good or right; its opposite as in some sense bad or wrong.

But notice that the judgments in these cases may follow either of two methods: (1) The parent or business man may teach his child, or practice in business, what tradition or the accepted standard calls for; or (2) he may consider and examine the principles and motives involved. Action by the first method is undoubtedly moral, in one sense. It is judging according to a standard, though it takes the standard for granted. Action by the second method is moral in a more complete sense. It examines the standard as well. The one is the method of "customary" morality, the other that of reflective morality, or of conscience in the proper sense.

The Three Levels and Their Motives.—We may distinguish then three levels of conduct.

1. Conduct arising from instincts and fundamental needs. To satisfy these needs certain conduct is necessary, and this in itself involves ways of acting which are more or less rational and social. The conduct may be *in accordance with* moral laws, though not directed by moral judgments. We consider this level in the present chapter.

2. Conduct regulated by *standards of society*, for some more or less conscious end involving the social welfare. The level of custom, which is treated in Chapter 4.

3. Conduct regulated by a standard which is both social and rational, which is examined and criticized. The level of conscience. Progress toward this level is outlined in Chapters 5 to 8.

The motives in these levels will show a similar scale. In (1) the motives are external to the end gained. The man seeks food, or position, or glory, or sex gratification; he is forced to practice sobriety, industry, courage, gentleness. In (2) the motive is to seek some good which is social, but the man acts for the group mainly because he is *of* the group, and does not conceive his own good as distinct from that of the group. His acts are only in part guided by intelligence; they are in part due to habit or accident. (3) In full morality a man not only intends his acts definitely, he also values them as what he can do "with all his heart." He does them *because* they are right and good. He chooses them freely and intelligently. Our study of moral development will consider successively these three levels. They all exist in present morality. Only the first two are found in savage life. If (1) existed alone it was before the group life, which is our starting-point in this study. We return now to our consideration of group life, and note the actual forces which are at work. We wish to discover the process by which the first and second levels prepare the way for the third.

The Necessary Activities of Existence Start the Process.
—The prime necessities, if the individual is to survive, are
for food, shelter, defense against enemies. If the stock is
to survive, there must be also reproduction and parental
care. Further, it is an advantage in the struggle if the
individual can master and acquire, can outstrip rivals, and
can join forces with others of his kind for common ends.
To satisfy these needs we find men in group life engaged
in work, in war or blood feuds, in games and festal activities,
in parental care. They are getting food and booty, making
tools and houses, conquering or enslaving their enemies, protecting the young, winning trophies, and finding emotional
excitement in contests, dances, and songs. These all help in
the struggle for existence. But the workmen, warriors, sing-
ers, parents, are getting more. They are forming certain
elements of character which, if not necessarily moral in
themselves, are yet indispensable requisites for full morality.
We may say therefore that nature is doing this part of moral
evolution, without the aid of conscious intention on man's
part. To use the terms of Chapter 1, we may call this a
rationalizing and socializing process, though not a conscious
moral process. We notice some of the more important
agencies that are operative.

§ 2. *Rationalizing Agencies*

1. Work.—The earlier forms of occupation, hunting and
fishing, call for active intelligence, although the activity is
sustained to a great degree by the immediate interest or
thrill of excitement, which makes them a recreation to the
civilized man. Quickness of perception, alertness of mind
and body, and in some cases, physical daring, are the
qualities most needed. But in the pastoral life, and still more
with the beginning of agriculture and commerce, the man
who succeeds must have foresight and continuity of purpose.
He must control impulse by reason. He must organize
those habits which are the basis of character, instead of
yielding to the attractions of various pleasures which might
lead him from the main purpose. To a certain extent the
primitive communism acted to prevent the individual from

feeling the full force of improvidence. Even if he does not secure a supply of game, or have a large enough flock to provide for the necessities of himself and his immediate family, the group does not necessarily permit him to starve. The law "Whatsoever a man soweth that shall he also reap" does not press upon him with such relentless grasp as in the modern individualistic struggle for existence. Nevertheless it would be an entirely mistaken view of primitive group life to suppose that it is entirely a lazy man's paradise, or happy-go-lucky existence. The varying economic conditions are important here as measuring the amount of forethought and care required. It is the shepherd Jacob whose craft outwits Esau the hunter; and while the sympathy of the modern may be with Esau, he must remember that forethought like other valuable weapons may be used in a social as well as a selfish fashion. The early Greek appreciation of craft is probably expressed in their deification of theft and deception in Hermes. Agriculture and commerce, still more than preceding types of occupation, demand thoughtfulness and the long look ahead.

The *differentiation of labor* has been a powerful influence for increasing the range of mental life and stimulating its development. If all do the same thing, all are much alike, and inevitably remain on a low level. But when the needs of men induce different kinds of work, slumbering capacities are aroused and new ones are called into being. The most deeply-rooted differentiation of labor is that between the sexes. The woman performs the work within or near the dwelling, the man hunts or tends the flocks or ranges abroad. This probably tends to accentuate further certain organic differences. Among the men, group life in its simplest phases has little differentiation except "for counsel" or "for war." But with metal working and agricultural life the field widens. At first the specializing is largely by families rather than by individual choice. Castes of workmen may take the place of mere kinship ties. Later on the rules of caste in turn become a hindrance to individuality and must be broken down if the individual is to emerge to full self-direction.

2. *The Arts and Crafts.*—Aside from their influence as work, the arts and crafts have a distinctly elevating and re-

fining effect. The textiles, pottery, and skilfully made tools and weapons; the huts or houses when artistically constructed; the so-called free or fine arts of dance and music, of color and design—all have this common element: they give some visible or audible embodiment for order or form. The artist or craftsman must make definite his idea in order to work it out in cloth or clay, in wood or stone, in dance or song. When thus embodied, it is preserved, at least for a time. It is part of the daily environment of the society. Those who see or hear are having constantly suggested to them ideas and values which bring more meaning into life and elevate its interests. Moreover, the order, the rational plan or arrangement which is embodied in all well-wrought objects, as well as in the fine arts in the narrow sense, deserves emphasis. Plato and Schiller have seen in this a valuable preparation for morality. To govern action by law is moral, but it is too much to expect this of the savage and the child as a conscious principle where the law opposes impulse. In art as in play there is direct interest and pleasure in the act, but in art there is also order or law. In conforming to this order the savage, or the child, is in training for the more conscious control where the law, instead of favoring, may thwart or oppose impulse and desire.

3. *War.*—War and the contests in games were serving to work out characteristics which received also a definite social reenforcement: namely, courage and efficiency, a sense of power, a consciousness of achievement. All these, like craft, may be used for unmoral or even immoral ends, but they are also highly important as factors in an effective moral personality.

§ 3. *Socializing Agencies*

Cooperation and Mutual Aid.[1]—Aside from their effects in promoting intelligence, courage, and ideality of life, industry, art, and war have a common factor by which they all

---

1. Kropotkin, *Mutual Aid: A Factor of Evolution*; Bagehot, *Physics and Politics*.

contribute powerfully to the social basis of morality. They all require cooperation. They are socializing as well as rationalizing agencies. Mutual aid is the foundation of success. "Woe to him who stands alone, e'en though his platter be never so full," runs the Slav proverb. "He that belongs to no community is like unto one without a hand." Those clans or groups which can work together, and fight together, are stronger in the struggle against nature and other men. The common activities of art have value in making this community of action more possible. Cooperation implies a common end. It means that each is interested in the success of all. This common end forms then a controlling rule of action, and the mutual interest means sympathy. Cooperation is therefore one of nature's most effective agencies for a social standard and a social feeling.

1. Cooperation in Industry.—In industry, while there was not in primitive life the extensive exchange of goods which expresses the interdependence of modern men, there was yet much concerted work, and there was a great degree of community of property. In groups which lived by hunting or fishing, for instance, although certain kinds of game might be pursued by the individual hunter, the great buffalo and deer hunts were organized by the tribe as a whole. "A hunting bonfire was kindled every morning at daybreak at which each brave must appear and report. The man who failed to do this before the party set out on the day's hunt was harassed by ridicule."[2] Salmon fishery was also conducted as a joint undertaking. Large game in Africa is hunted in a similar fashion, and the product of the chase is not for the individual but for the group. In the pastoral life the care of the flocks and herds necessitates at least some sort of cooperation to protect these flocks from the attacks of wild beasts and from the more dreaded forays of human robbers. This requires a considerable body of men, and the journeying about in company, the sharing together of watch and ward, the common interest in the increase of flocks and herds, continually strengthens the bonds between the dwellers in tents.

2. Eastman, *Indian Boyhood.*

In the agricultural stage there are still certain forces at work which promote the family or tribal unity, although here we begin to find the forces which make for individuality at work until they result in individual ownership and individual property. Just as at the pastoral stage, so in this, the cattle and the growing grain must be protected from attacks by man and beast. It is only the group which can afford such protection, and accordingly we find the Lowland farmer always at the mercy of the Highland clan.

2. *Cooperation in War.*—War and the blood feud, however divisive between groups, were none the less potent as uniting factors within the several groups. The members must not only unite or be wiped out, when the actual contest was on, but the whole scheme of mutual help in defense or in avenging injuries and insults made constant demand upon fellow feeling, and sacrifice for the good of all. To gain more land for the group, to acquire booty for the group, to revenge a slight done to some member of the group, were constant causes for war. Now although any individual might be the gainer, yet the chances were that he would himself suffer even though the group should win. In the case of blood revenge particularly, most of the group were not individually interested. Their resentment was a "sympathetic resentment," and one author has regarded this as perhaps the most fundamental of the sources of moral emotion. It was because the tribal blood had been shed, or the women of the clan insulted, that the group as a whole reacted, and in the clash of battle with opposing groups, was closer knit together.

> Ally thyself with whom thou wilt in peace, yet know
> In war must every man be foe who is not kin.

"Comrades in arms" by the very act of fighting together have a common cause, and by the mutual help and protection given and received become, for the time at least, one in will and one in heart. Ulysses counsels Agamemnon to marshal his Greeks, clan by clan and "brotherhood (phratry) by brotherhood," that thus brother may support and stimulate brother more effectively; but the effect is reciprocal, and it is indeed very probable that the unity of blood which is believed to be the tie binding together the members of the group, is often an afterthought or pious fiction designed to account for the unity which was really due originally to the stress of common struggle.

3. *Art as Socializing Agency.*—Cooperation and sympathy are fostered by the activities of art. Some of these activities are spontaneous, but most of them serve some definite social end and are frequently organized for the definite purpose of increasing the unity and sympathy of the group. The hunting dance or the war dance represents, in dramatic form, all the processes of the hunt or fight, but it would be a mistake to suppose that this takes place purely for dramatic purposes. The dance and celebration after the chase or battle may give to the whole tribe the opportunity to repeat in vivid imagination the triumphs of the successful hunter or warrior, and thus to feel the thrill of victory and exult in common over the fallen prey. The dance which takes place before the event is designed to give magical power to the hunter or warrior. Every detail is performed with the most exact care and the whole tribe is thus enabled to share in the work of preparation.

In the act of song the same uniting force is present. To sing with another involves a contagious sympathy, in perhaps a higher degree than is the case with any other art. There is, in the first place, as in the dance, a unity of rhythm. Rhythm is based upon cooperation and, in turn, immensely strengthens the possibility of cooperation. In the bas-reliefs upon the Egyptian monuments representing the work of a large number of men who are moving a stone, we find the sculptured figure of a man who is beating the time for the combined efforts. Whether all rhythm has come from the necessities of common action or whether it has a physiological basis sufficient to account for the effect which rhythmic action produces, in any case when a company of people begin to work or dance or sing in rhythmic movement, their efficiency and their pleasure are immensely increased. In addition to the effect of rhythm we have also in the case of song the effect of unity of pitch and of melody, and the members of the tribe or clan, like those who to-day sing the Marseillaise or chant the great anthems of the church, feel in the strongest degree their mutual sympathy and support. For this reason, the Corroborees of the Australian, the sacred festivals of Israel, the Mysteries and public festivals of the Greeks, in short, among all peoples, the common gatherings of the tribe for patriotic or religious purposes, have been attended with dance and song. In many cases these carry the members on to a pitch of enthusiasm where they are ready to die for the common cause.

Melodic and rhythmic sound is a unifying force simply by reason of form, and some of the simpler songs seem to have little else to commend them, but at very early periods there is not merely the song but the recital, in more or less rhythmic or literary form, of the history of the tribe and the deeds of the ancestors. This adds still another to the unifying forces of the dance and song. The kindred group, as they hear the recital, live over together the history of the group, thrill with pride at its glories, suffer at its defeats; every member feels that the clan's history is his history and the clan's blood his blood.

§ 4. *Family Life as an Idealizing and Socializing Agency*

Family life, so far as it is merely on the basis of instinct, takes its place with other agencies favored by natural selection which make for more rational and social existence. Various instincts are more or less at work. The sex instinct brings the man and the woman together. The instinct of jealousy, and the property or possessing instinct, may foster exclusive and permanent relations. The parental instinct and affection bind the parents together and thus contribute to the formation of the social group described in the preceding chapter. Considering now the more immediate relations of husband and wife, parents and children, rather than the more general group relations, we call attention to some of the most obvious aspects, leaving fuller treatment for Part III. The idealizing influences of the sex instinct, when this is subject to the general influences found in group life, is familiar. Lyric song is a higher form of its manifestation, but even a mute lover may be stimulated to fine thoughts or brave deeds. Courtship further implies an adaptation, an effort to please, which is a strong socializing force. If "all the world loves a lover," it must be because the lover is on the whole a· likable rôle. But other forces come in. Sex love is intense, but so far as it is purely instinctive it may be transitory. Family life needed more permanence than sex attraction could provide, and before the powerful sanctions of religion, society, and morals were sufficient to secure permanence, it is probable that the property interest of the husband was largely effective in building up a family life, requiring fidelity to the married relation on the part of the wife.

But the most far-reaching of the forces at work in the family has been the parental instinct and affection with its consequences upon both parents and children. It contributes probably more than any other naturally selected agency to the development of the race in sympathy; it shares with work in the development of responsibility. It is indeed one of the great incentives to industry throughout the higher species of animals as well as in human life. The value of parental care in the struggle for existence is impressively presented by Sutherland.[3] Whereas the fishes which exercise no care for their eggs preserve their species only by producing these in enormous numbers, certain species which care for them maintain their existence by producing relatively few. Many species produce hundreds of thousands or even millions of eggs. The stickleback, which constructs a nest and guards the young for a few days, is one of the most numerous of fishes, but it lays only from twenty to ninety eggs. Birds and mammals with increased parental care produce few young. Not only is parental care a valuable asset, it is an absolute necessity for the production of the higher species. "In the fierce competition of the animated forms of earth, the loftier type, with its prolonged nervous growth, and consequently augmented period of helplessness, can never arise but with concomitant increases of parental care." Only as the emotional tendency has kept pace with the nerve

3. Sutherland, *The Origin and Growth of Moral Instinct*, chs. ii–v.

development has the human race been possible. The very refinements in the organism which make the adult a victor would render the infant a victim if it were without an abundance of loving assistance.[4]

Whether, as has been supposed by some, the parental care has also been the most effective force in keeping the parents together through a lengthened infancy, or whether other factors have been more effective in this particular, there is no need to enlarge upon the wide-reaching moral values of parental affection. It is the atmosphere in which the child begins his experience. So far as any environment can affect him, this is a constant influence for sympathy and kindness. And upon the parents themselves its transforming power, in making life serious, in overcoming selfishness, in projecting thought and hope on into the future, cannot be measured. The moral order and progress of the world might conceivably spare some of the agencies which man has devised; it could not spare this.

§ 5. *Moral Interpretation of This First Level*

On this first level we are evidently dealing with forces and conduct, not as moral in purpose, but as valuable in result. They make a more rational, ideal, and social life, and this is the necessary basis for more conscious control and valuation of conduct. The forces are biological or sociological or psychological. They are not that particular kind of psychological activities which we call moral in the proper sense, for this implies not only getting a good result but aiming at it. Some of the activities, such as those of song and dance, or the simpler acts of maternal care, have a large instinctive element. We cannot call these moral *in so far as* they are purely instinctive. Others imply a large amount of intelligence, as, for example, the operations of agriculture and the various crafts. These have purpose, such as to satisfy hunger, or to forge a weapon against an enemy. But the end is one set up by our physical or instinctive nature. So

4. Sutherland, *Origin and Growth*, p. 99.

long as this is merely *accepted* as an end, and not compared with others, valued, and *chosen*, it is not properly moral.

The same is true of emotions. There are certain emotions on the instinctive level. Such are parental love in its most elemental form, sympathy as mere contagious feeling, anger, or resentment. So far as these are at this lowest level, so far as they signify simply a bodily thrill, they have no claim to proper moral value. They are tremendously important as the source from which strong motive forces of benevolence, intelligent parental care, and an ardent energy against evil may draw warmth and fire.

Finally, even the cooperation, the mutual aid, which men give, so far as it is called out purely by common danger, or common advantage, is not in the moral sphere in so far as it is instinctive, or merely give and take. To be genuinely moral there must be some thought of the danger as touching others and *therefore* requiring our aid; of the advantage as being common and *therefore* enlisting our help.

But even although these processes are not consciously moral they are nevertheless fundamental. The activities necessary for existence, and the emotions so intimately bound up with them, are the "cosmic roots" of the moral life. And often in the higher stages of culture, when the codes and instruction of morality and society fail to secure right conduct, these elementary agencies of work, cooperation, and family life assert their power. Society and morality take up the direction of the process and carry it further, but they must always rely largely on these primary activities to afford the basis for intelligent, reliable, and sympathetic conduct.

Literature

Bagehot, *Physics and Politics*, 1890; Bücher, *Industrial Evolution*, Eng. tr., 1901, *Arbeit und Rythmus*, 3d ed., 1901; Schurtz, *Urgeschichte der Kultur*, 1900; Fiske, *Cosmic Philosophy*, Vol. II; "The Cosmic Roots of Love and Self-Sacrifice" in *Through Nature to God*, 1899; Dewey, "Interpretation of Savage Mind," *Psychological Review*, Vol. IX, 1902, pp. 217–30; Durkheim, *De la division du travail social*, 1893; P. Kropotkin, *Mutual Aid: A Factor of Evolution*, 1902; Ross, *Foundations of Sociology*,

1905, Chap. VII; Baldwin, Article "Socionomic Forces" in his *Dictionary of Philosophy and Psychology*; Giddings, *Inductive Sociology*, 1901; Small, *General Sociology*, 1905; Tarde, *Les lois de l'imitation*, 1895; W. I. Thomas, *Sex and Society*, 1907, pp. 55–172; Gummere, *The Beginnings of Poetry*, 1901; Hirn, *The Origins of Art*, 1900.

4. GROUP MORALITY—CUSTOMS OR MORES

We have seen how the natural forces of instinct lead to activities which elevate men and knit them together. We consider next the means which society uses for these purposes, and the kind of conduct which goes along with the early forms of society's agencies. The organization of early society is that of group life, and so far as the individual is merged in the group the type of conduct may be called "group morality." Inasmuch as the agencies by which the group controls its members are largely those of custom, the morality may be called also "customary morality." Such conduct is what we called at the opening of the previous chapter "the second level." It is "ethical" or "moral" in the sense of conforming to the *ethos* or *mores* of the group.

§1. Meaning, Authority, and Origin of Customs

Meaning of Customs or Mores.—Wherever we find groups of men living as outlined in Chapter 2, we find that there are certain ways of acting which are common to the group—"folkways." Some of these may be due merely to the fact that the members are born of the same stock, just as all ducks swim. But a large part of human conduct, in savage as truly as in civilized life, is not merely instinctive. There are *approved* ways of acting, common to a group, and handed down from generation to generation. Such approved ways of doing and acting are customs, or to use the Latin term, which Professor Sumner thinks brings out more clearly this factor of approval, they are *mores*.[1] They are habits—but they are more. They imply the judgment of the group that they are to be followed. The welfare of the group is regarded as in some sense imbedded in them. If any one acts contrary to them he

1. Sumner, *Folkways*.

is made to feel the group's disapproval. The young are carefully trained to observe them. At times of special importance, they are rehearsed with special solemnity.

Authority Behind the Mores.—The old men, or the priests, or medicine men, or chiefs, or old women, may be the especial guardians of these customs. They may modify details, or add new customs, or invent explanations for old ones. But the authority back of them is the group in the full sense. Not the group composed merely of visible and living members, but the larger group which includes the dead, and the kindred totemic or ancestral gods. Nor is it the group considered as a collection of individual persons. It is rather in a vague way the whole mental and social world. The fact that most of the customs have no known date or origin makes them seem a part of the nature of things. Indeed there is more than a mere analogy between the primitive regard for custom and that respect for "Nature" which from the Stoics to Spencer has sought a moral standard in living "according to nature." And there is this much in favor of taking the world of custom as the standard: the beings of this system are like the person who is expected to behave like them; its rules are the ways in which his own kin have lived and prospered, and not primarily the laws of cosmic forces, plants, and animals.

Origin of Customs; Luck.—The origin of customs is to be sought in several concurrent factors. There are in the first place the activities induced by the great primitive needs and instincts. Some ways of acting succeed; some fail. Man not only establishes habits of acting in the successful ways; he remembers his failures. He hands successful ways down with his approval; he condemns those that fail.

This attitude is reenforced by the views about good luck and bad luck. Primitive man—and civilized man—is not ruled by a purely rational theory of success and failure. "One might use the best known means with the greatest care, yet fail of the result. On the other hand, one might get a great result with no effort at all. One might also incur a calamity without any fault of his own."[2] "Grimm gives more than a

2. Sumner, *Folkways*, p. 6.

thousand ancient German apothegms, dicta, and proverbs about 'luck.'"[3] Both good and bad fortune are attributed to the unseen powers, hence a case of bad luck is not thought of as a mere chance. If the ship that sailed Friday meets a storm, or one of thirteen falls sick, the inference is that this is sure to happen again. And at this point the conception of the group welfare as bound up with the acts of every member, comes in to make individual conformity a matter for group concern—to make conduct a matter of mores and not merely a private affair. One most important, if not the most important, object of early legislation was the enforcement of lucky rites to prevent the individual from doing what might bring ill luck on all the tribe. For the conception always was that the ill luck does not attach itself simply to the doer, but may fall upon any member of the group. "The act of one member is conceived to make all the tribe impious, to offend its particular god, to expose all the tribe to penalties from heaven. When the street statues of Hermes were mutilated, all the Athenians were frightened and furious; they thought they should all be ruined because some one had mutilated a god's image and so offended him."[4] "The children were reproved for cutting and burning embers, on the ground that this might be the cause for the accidental cutting of some member of the family."[5] In the third place, besides these sources of custom, in the usefulness or lucky character of certain acts, there is also the more immediate reaction of individuals or groups to certain ways of acting according "as things jump with the feelings or displease them."[6] An act of daring is applauded, whether useful or not. The individual judgment is caught up, repeated, and plays its part in the formation of group opinion. "Individual impulse and social tradition are thus the two poles between which we move." Or there may even be a more conscious discussion analogous to the action of legislatures or philosophic discussion. The old men among the Australians deliberate carefully as to

3. Sumner, *Folkways*, p. 11.
4. Bagehot, *Physics and Politics*, p. 103.
5. Eastman, *Indian Boyhood*, p. 31.
6. Hobhouse, *Morals in Evolution*, Vol. I, p. 16. Hume pointed out this twofold basis of approval.

each step of the initiation ceremonies. They make customs to be handed down.

§ 2. *Means of Enforcing Customs*

The most general means for enforcing customs are public opinion, taboos, ritual or ceremony, and physical force.

Public approval uses both language and form to express its judgments. Its praise is likely to be emphasized by some form of art. The songs that greet the returning victor, the decorations, costumes, and tattoos for those who are honored, serve to voice the general sentiment. On the other hand ridicule or contempt is a sufficient penalty to enforce compliance with many customs that may be personally irksome. It is very largely the ridicule of the men's house which enforces certain customs among the men of peoples which have that institution. It is the ridicule or scorn of both men and women which forbids the Indian to marry before he has proved his manhood by some notable deed of prowess in war or chase.

Taboos.—Taboos are perhaps not so much a means for enforcing custom, as they are themselves customs invested with peculiar and awful sanction. They prohibit or ban any contact with certain persons or objects under penalty of danger from unseen beings. Any events supposed to indicate the activity of spirits, such as birth and death, are likely to be sanctified by taboos. The danger is contagious; if a Polynesian chief is taboo, the ordinary man fears even to touch his footprints. But the taboos are not all based on mere dread of the unseen.

They include such acts as have been found by experience to produce unwelcome results.—The primitive taboos correspond to the fact that the life of man is environed by perils: His food quest must be limited by shunning poisonous plants. His appetite must be restrained from excess. His physical strength and health must be guarded from dangers. The taboos carry on the accumulated wisdom of generations which has almost always been purchased by pain, loss, disease, and death. Other taboos contain inhibitions of what will be injurious to the group. The laws about the sexes, about property, about war, and about ghosts, have this

character. They always include some social philosophy. (Sumner,
Folkways, pp. 33 f.)

They may be used with conscious purpose. In order to
have a supply of cocoanuts for a religious festival the head
men may place a taboo upon the young cocoanuts to prevent
them from being consumed before they are fully ripe. The
conception works in certain respects to supply the purpose
which is later subserved by ideas of property. But it serves
also as a powerful agency to maintain respect for the authority of the group.

Ritual.—As taboo is the great negative guardian of customs, ritual is the great positive agent. It works by forming
habits, and operates through associations formed by actually
doing certain acts, usually under conditions which appeal to
the emotions. The charm of music and of orderly movement,
the impressiveness of ordered masses in processions, the awe
of mystery, all contribute to stamp in the meaning and value.
Praise or blame encourages or inhibits; ritual secures the
actual doing and at the same time gives a value to the doing.
It is employed by civilized peoples more in the case of military or athletic drill, or in training children to observe forms
of etiquette, so that these may become "second nature." Certain religious bodies also use its agency. But in primitive life
it is widely and effectively used to insure for educational,
political, and domestic customs obedience to the group standards, which among us it secures to the codes of the army, or
to those of social etiquette. Examples of its elaborate and
impressive use will be given below under educational ceremonies.

Physical Force.—When neither group opinion, nor taboo, nor ritual secures conformity, there is always in the
background physical force. The chiefs are generally men of
strength whose word may not be lightly disregarded. Sometimes, as among the Sioux, the older braves constitute a sort
of police. Between different clans the blood feud is the accepted method of enforcing custom, unless a substitute, the
wergeld, is provided. For homicide within a clan the remaining members may drive the slayer out, and whoever meets
such a Cain may slay him. If a man murdered his chief of

kindred among the ancient Welsh he was banished and "it was required of every one of every sex and age within hearing of the horn to follow that exile and to keep up the barking of dogs, to the time of his putting to sea, until he shall have passed three score hours out of sight."[7] It should be borne in mind, however, that physical pains, either actual or dreaded, would go but a little way toward maintaining authority in any such group as we have regarded as typical. Absolutism, with all its cruel methods of enforcing terror, needs a more highly organized system. In primitive groups the great majority support the authority of the group as a matter of course, and uphold it as a sacred duty when it is challenged. Physical coercion is not the rule but the exception.

§ 3. *Conditions Which Bring Out The Importance of Group Standards and Render Group Control Conscious*

Although customs or mores have in them an element of social approval which makes them vehicles of moral judgment, they tend in many cases to sink to the level of mere habits. The reason—such as it was—for their original force —is forgotten. They become, like many of our forms of etiquette, mere conventions. There are, however, certain conditions which centre attention upon their importance and lift them to the level of conscious agencies. These conditions may be grouped under three heads. (1) The education of the younger, immature members of the group and their preparation for full membership. (2) The constraint and restraint of refractory members and the adjustment of conflicting interests. (3) Occasions which involve some notable danger or crisis and therefore call for the greatest attention to secure the favor of the gods and avert disaster.

1. Educational Customs.—Among the most striking and significant of these are the initiation ceremonies which are so widely observed among primitive peoples. They are held

7. Seebohm, *The Tribal System in Wales*, p. 59.

with the purpose of inducting boys into the privileges of manhood and into the full life of the group. They are calculated at every step to impress upon the initiate his own ignorance and helplessness in contrast with the wisdom and power of the group; and as the mystery with which they are conducted imposes reverence for the elders and the authorities of the group, so the recital of the traditions and performances of the tribe, the long series of ritual acts, common participation in the mystic dance and song and decorations, serve to reenforce the ties that bind the tribe.

Initiation into the full privileges of manhood among the tribes of Central Australia, for instance, includes three sets of ceremonies which occupy weeks, and even months, for their completion. The first set, called "throwing up in the air," is performed for the boy when he has reached the age of from ten to twelve. In connection with being thrown up in the air by certain prescribed members of his tribe, he is decorated with various totem emblems and afterward the septum of his nose is bored for the insertion of the nose-bone. At a period some three or four years later a larger and more formidable series of ceremonies is undertaken, lasting for ten days. A screen of bushes is built, behind which the boy is kept during the whole period, unless he is brought out on the ceremonial ground to witness some performance. During this whole period of ten days, he is forbidden to speak except in answer to questions. He is decorated with various totem emblems, for which every detail is prescribed by the council of the tribal fathers and tribal elder brothers. He is charged to obey every command and never to tell any woman or boy what he may see. The sense that something out of the ordinary is to happen to him helps to impress him strongly with a feeling of the deep importance of compliance with the tribal rules, and further still, with a strong sense of the superiority of the older men who know and are familiar with the mysterious rites of which he is about to learn the meaning for the first time. At intervals he watches symbolic performances of men decorated like various totem animals, who represent the doings of the animal ancestors of the clan; he hears mysterious sounds of the so-called bull-roarers, which are supposed by the women and uninitiated to be due to unseen spirits; and the whole ends with the operation which symbolizes his induction into young manhood. But even this is not all; when the young man has reached the age of discretion, when it is felt that he can fully comprehend the traditions of the tribe, at the age of from twenty to twenty-five, a still more impressive series of ceremonies is conducted, which in the instance reported lasted from September to January. This period was filled up with dances, "corroborees," and inspection of the churinga or sacred emblems—stones or sticks which were supposed to be the dwellings of ancestral spirits and which are carefully preserved in the tribe, guarded from the sight of women and boys, but known individually to the elders as the sacred dwelling-place of father or grandfather. As these were shown and passed around, great solemnity was manifest and the relatives sometimes wept at the sight of the sacred object. Ceremonies imitating various totem animals, frequently of the most elaborate sort, were also performed. The young men were told the traditions of the past history of the tribe, and at the close of the recital they felt added reverence for the old men who had been their instructors, a sense of pride in the possession of this mysterious knowledge, and a deeper unity because of what they now have in common. One is at a loss whether to wonder most at the possibility of the whole tribe devoting itself for three months to these elaborate functions of initiation, or at the marvelous adaptability of such ceremonies to train the young into an attitude of docility and reverence. A tribe that can enforce such a process is not likely to be wanting in one side, at least, of the moral consciousness, namely, reverence for authority and regard for the social welfare.[8]

2. *Law and Justice.*—The occasions for some control over refractory members will constantly arise, even though the conflict between group and individual may need no physical sanctions to enforce the authority of the group over its members. The economic motive frequently prompts an individual to leave the tribe or the joint family. There was a constant tendency, Eastman states, among his people,

8. The account is based on Spencer and Gillen, *Native Tribes of Central Australia*, chs. vii–ix.

when on a hunting expedition in the enemy's country, to
break up into smaller parties to obtain food more easily and
freely. The police did all they could to keep in check those
parties who were intent on stealing away. Another illustration of the same tendency is stated by Maine with reference
to the joint families of the South Slavonians:

> The adventurous and energetic member of the brotherhood
> is always rebelling against its natural communism. He goes
> abroad and makes his fortune, and as strenuously resists the
> demands of his relatives to bring it into the common account. Or
> perhaps he thinks that his share of the common stock would be
> more profitably employed by him as capital in a mercantile
> venture. In either case he becomes a dissatisfied member or a
> declared enemy of the brotherhood.[9]

Or covetousness might lead to violation of the ban, as
with Achan. Sex impulse may lead a man to seek for his wife
a woman not in the lawful group. Or, as one of the most
dangerous offenses possible, a member of the group may be
supposed to practice witchcraft. This is to use invisible
powers in a selfish manner, and has been feared and punished by almost all peoples.

In all these cases it is of course no abstract theory of
crime which leads the community to react; it is self-preservation. The tribe must be kept together for protection against
enemies. Achan's sin is felt to be the cause of defeat. The
violation of sex taboos may ruin the clan. The sorcerer may
cause disease, or inflict torture and death, or bring a pestilence or famine upon the whole group. None the less all such
cases bring to consciousness one aspect of moral authority,
the social control over the individual.

And it is a *social* control—not an exercise of brute force
or a mere terrorizing by ghosts. For the chief or judge generally wins his authority by his powerful service to his tribes-
men. A Gideon or Barak or Ehud or Jephthah judged Israel
because he had delivered them. "Three things, if possessed
by a man, make him fit to be a chief of kindred: That he
should speak on behalf of his kin and be listened to, that he
should fight on behalf of his kin and be feared, and that he

9. Maine, *Early Law and Custom*, p. 264.

should be security on behalf of his kin and be accepted."[10] If, as is often the case, the king or judge or chief regards himself as acting by divine right, the authority is still *within the group*. It is the group judging itself.

In its *standards* this primitive court is naturally on the level of customary morality, of which it is an agent. There is usually neither the conception of a general principle of justice (our Common Law), nor of a positive law enacted as the express will of the people. At first the judge or ruler may not act by any fixed law except that of upholding the customs. Each decision is then a special case. A step in advance is found when the heads or elders or priests of the tribe decide cases, not independently of all others, but in accordance with certain precedents or customs. A legal tradition is thus established, which, however imperfect, is likely to be more impartial than the arbitrary caprice of the moment, influenced as such special decisions are likely to be by the rank or power of the parties concerned.[11] A law of precedents or tradition is thus the normal method at this level. The progress toward a more rational standard belongs under the next chapter, but it is interesting to note that even at an early age the myths show a conception of a divine judge who is righteous, and a divine judgment which is ideal. Rhadamanthus is an embodiment of the demand for justice which human collisions and decisions awakened.

The conscious authority of the group is also evoked in the case of feuds or disputes between its members. The case of the blood feud, indeed, might well be treated as belonging under war and international law rather than as a case of private conflict. For so far as the members of the victim's clan are concerned, it is a case of war. It is a patriotic duty of every kinsman to avenge the shed blood. The groups concerned were smaller than modern nations which go to war for similar reasons, but the principle is the same. The chief difference in favor of modern international wars is that since the groups are larger they do not fight so often and require a more serious consideration of the possibility of peaceable

10. Welsh Triads, cited by Seebohm, *The Tribal System in Wales,* p. 72.
11. Post, *Grundlagen des Rechts,* pp. 45 ff.

adjustment. Orestes and Hamlet feel it a sacred duty to avenge their fathers' murders.

But the case is not simply that of clan against clan. For the smaller group of kin, who are bound to avenge, are nearly always part of a larger group. And the larger group may at once recognize the duty of vengeance and also the need of keeping it within bounds, or of substituting other practices. The larger group may see in the murder a pollution, dangerous to all;[12] the blood which "cries from the ground"[13] renders the ground "unclean" and the curse of gods or the spirits of the dead may work woe upon the whole region. But an unending blood feud is likewise an evil. And if the injured kin can be appeased by less than blood in return, so much the better. Hence the wergeld, or indemnity, a custom which persisted among the Irish until late, and seemed to the English judges a scandalous procedure.

For lesser offenses a sort of regulated duel is sometimes allowed. For example, among the Australians the incident is related of the treatment of a man who had eloped with his neighbor's wife. When the recreant parties returned the old men considered what should be done, and finally arranged the following penalty. The offender stood and called out to the injured husband, "I stole your woman; come and growl." The husband then proceeded to throw a spear at him from a distance, and afterwards to attack him with a knife, although he did not attempt to wound him in a vital part. The offender was allowed to evade injury, though not to resent the attack. Finally the old men said, "Enough." A curious form of private agencies for securing justice is also found in the Japanese custom of hara-kiri, according to which an injured man kills himself before the door of his offender, in order that he may bring public odium upon the man who has injured him. An Indian custom of Dharna is of similar significance, though less violent. The creditor fasts before the door of the debtor until he either is paid, or dies of starvation. It may be that he thinks that his double or spirit will haunt the cruel debtor who has thus permitted ,him

12. Deuteronomy 21:1–9; Numbers 35:33–34.
13. Genesis 4:10–12; Job 16:18.

to starve to death, but it also has the effect of bringing public opinion to bear.

In all these cases of kindred feuds there is little personal responsibility, and likewise little distinction between the accidental and intentional. These facts are brought out in the opening quotations in Chapter 2. The important thing for the student to observe is that like our present practices in international affairs they show a *grade* of morality, a limited social unity, whether it is called kinship feeling or patriotism; complete morality is not possible so long as there is no complete way of settling disputes by justice instead of force.[14]

3. *Occasions Which Involve Some Special Danger or Crisis.*—Such occasions call for the greatest attention to secure success or avoid disaster. Under this head we note as typical (a) the occasions of birth, marriage, death; (b) seed time and harvest, or other seasons important for the maintenance of the group; (c) war; (d) hospitality.

(a) *Birth and Death Customs.*—The entrance of a new life into the world and the disappearance of the animating breath (*spiritus, anima, psyche*), might well impress man with the mysteries of his world. Whether the newborn infant is regarded as a reincarnation of an ancestral spirit as with the Australians, or as a new creation from the spirit world as with the Kafirs, it is a time of danger. The mother must be "purified,"[15] the child, and in some cases the father, must be carefully guarded. The elaborate customs show the group judgment of the importance of the occasion. And the rites for the dead are yet more impressive. For as a rule the savage has no thought of an entire extinction of the person. The dead lives on in some mode, shadowy and vague, perhaps, but he is still potent, still a member of the group, present at the tomb or the hearth. The preparation of the body for burial or other disposition, the ceremonies of interment or of the pyre, the wailing, and mourning costumes, the provision of

---

14. On the subject of early justice Westermarck, *The Origin and Development of the Moral Ideas*, Vol. I, ch. vii ff.; Hobhouse, *Morals in Evolution*, Vol. I, ch. ii; Pollock and Maitland, *History of English Law*.
15. Leviticus, 12.

food and weapons, or of the favorite horse or wife, to be with the dead in the unseen world, the perpetual homage paid— all these are eloquent. The event, as often as it occurs, appeals by both sympathy and awe to the common feeling, and brings to consciousness the unity of the group and the control exercised by its judgments.

The regulations for marriage are scarcely less important; indeed, they are often seemingly the most important of the customs. The phrases "marriage by capture" and "marriage by purchase," are quite misleading if they give the impression that in early culture any man may have any woman. It is an almost universal part of the clan system that the man must marry out of his own clan or totem (exogamy), and it is frequently specified exactly into what other clan he must marry. Among some the regulations are minute as to which of the age classes, as well as to which of the kin groups, a man of specific group must choose from. The courtship may follow different rules from ours, and the relation of the sexes in certain respects may seem so loose as to shock the student, but the regulation is in many respects stricter than with us, and punishment of its violation often severer. There can be no doubt of the meaning of the control, however mistaken some of its features. Whether the regulations for exogamy, which provides so effectually for avoiding incest, are reenforced by an instinctive element of aversion to sex relations with intimates, is uncertain; in any case, they are enforced by the strongest taboos. Nor does primitive society stop with the negative side. The actual marriage is invested with the social values and religious sanctions which raise the relation to a higher level. Art, in garments and ornament, in dance and epithalamium, lends ideal values. The sacred meal at the encircled hearth secures the participation of the kindred gods.

(b) *Certain Days or Seasons Important for the Industrial Life.*—Seed time and harvest, the winter and summer solstices, the return of spring, are of the highest importance to agricultural and pastoral peoples, and are widely observed with solemn rites. Where the rain is the centre of anxiety, a whole ritual may arise in connection with it, as among the Zuñi Indians. Ceremonies lasting days, involving the preparation of special symbols of clouds and lightning, and the participation of numerous secret fraternities, constrain the attention of all. Moreover, this constraint of need, working through the conception of what the gods require, enforces some very positive moral attitudes:

A Zuñi must speak with one tongue (sincerely) in order to have his prayers received by the gods, and unless his prayers are accepted no rains will come, which means starvation. He must be gentle, and he must speak and act with kindness to all, for the gods care not for those whose lips speak harshly. He must observe continence four days previous to, and four days following, the sending of breath prayers through the spiritual essence of plume offerings, and thus their passions are brought under control. (Mrs. M. C. Stevenson in 23d Report, *Bureau of Ethnology*.)

Phases of the moon give other sacred days. Sabbaths which originally are negative—the forbidding of labor—may become later the bearers of positive social and spiritual value. In any case, all these festivals bring the group authority to consciousness, and by their ritual promote the intimate group sympathy and consciousness of a common end.

(c) *War.*—War as a special crisis always brings out the significance and importance of certain customs. The deliberations, the magic, the war paint which precede, the obedience compelled by it to chiefs, the extraordinary powers exercised by the chief or heads at such crises, the sense of danger which strains the attention, all insure attention. No carelessness is permitted. Defeat is interpreted as a symbol of divine anger because of a violated law or custom. Victory brings all together to celebrate the glory of the clan and to mourn in common the warriors slain in the common cause. Excellence here may be so conspicuous in its service, or in the admiration it calls out, as to become a general term for what the group approves. So the *aretē* of the Greeks became their general term, and the Latin *virtus*, if not so clearly military, was yet largely military in its early coloring. The "spirit of Jehovah," the symbol of divine approval and so of group approval, was believed to be with Samson and Jephthah in their deeds of prowess in Israel's behalf.

(d) *Hospitality.*—To the modern man who travels without fear and receives guests as a matter of almost daily

practice, it may seem strained to include hospitality along
with unusual or critical events. But the ceremonies observed
and the importance attached to its rites, show that hospitality was a matter of great significance; its customs were
among the most sacred. "But as for us," says Ulysses to the
Cyclops,

we have lighted here, and come to these thy knees, if perchance
they will give us a stranger's gift, or make any present, as is the
due of strangers. Nay, lord, have regard to the gods, for we are
thy suppliants, and Zeus is the avenger of suppliants and
sojourners, Zeus, the god of the stranger, who fareth in the
company of reverend strangers.

The duty of hospitality is one of the most widely recognized. Westermarck has brought together a series of maxims
from a great variety of races which show this forcibly.[16] Indians, Kalmucks, Greeks, Romans, Teutons, Arabs, Africans,
Ainos, and other peoples are drawn upon and tell the same
story. The stranger is to be respected sacredly. His person
must be guarded from insult even if the honor of the daughter of the house must be sacrificed.[17] "Jehovah preserveth the
sojourners," and they are grouped with the fatherless and
the widow in Israel's law.[18] The Romans had their *dii hospi-
tales* and the "duties toward a guest were even more strin-
gent than those toward a relative"—*primum tutelae, deinde
hospiti, deinde clienti, tum cognato, postea affini.*[19] "He who
has a spark of caution in him," says Plato, "will do his best to
pass through life without sinning against the stranger." And
there is no doubt that this sanctity of the guest's person was
not due to pure kindness. The whole conduct of group life
is opposed to a general spirit of consideration for those outside. The word "guest" is akin to *hostis*, from which comes
"hostile." The stranger or the guest was looked upon rather
as a being who was specially potent. He was a "live wire."
He might be a medium of blessing, or he might be a medium
of hurt. But it was highly important to fail in no duty toward
him. The definite possibility of entertaining angels unawares

16. "The Influence of Magic on Social Relationships" in *Sociological
    Papers*, II, 1906. Cf. also Morgan, *House-Life*.
17. Genesis 19:8; Judges 19:23, 24.
18. Psalms 146:9; Deuteronomy 24:14–22.
19. Gellius, in Westermarck, *Origin and Development*, p. 155.

might not be always present to consciousness, but there seems reason to believe that the possibility of good luck or bad luck as attending on a visitor was generally believed in. It is also plausible that the importance attached to sharing a meal, or to bodily contact, is based on magical ideas of the way in which blessing or curse may be communicated. To cross a threshold or touch a tent-rope or to eat "salt," gives a sacred claim. In the right of asylum, the refugee takes advantage of his contact with the god. He lays hold of the altar and assumes that the god will protect him. The whole practice of hospitality is thus the converse of the custom of blood revenge. They are alike sacred—or rather the duty of hospitality may protect even the man whom the host is bound to pursue. But, whereas the one makes for group solidarity by acts of exclusive and hostile character, the other tends to set aside temporarily the division between the "we-group" and the "others-group." Under the sanction of religion it keeps open a way of communication which trade and other social interchange will widen. It adds to family and the men's house a powerful agency in maintaining at least the possibility of humaneness and sympathy.

§ 4. *Values and Defects of Customary Morality*

These have been suggested, in the main, in the description of the nature of custom and its regulation of conduct. We may, however, summarize them as a preparation for the next stage of morality.

1. *The Forming of Standards.*—There is a standard, a "good," a "right," which is to some degree rational and to some degree social. We have seen that custom rests in part on rational conceptions of welfare. It is really nothing against this that a large element of luck enters into the idea of welfare. For this means merely that the actual conditions of welfare are not understood. The next generation may be able to point out as equally absurd our present ignorance about health and disease. The members of the group embodied in custom what they thought to be important; they were approving some acts and forbidding or condemning others; they

were using the elders, and the wisdom of all the past, in order to govern life. So far, then, they were acting morally. They were also, to a degree, using a rational and social standard when they made custom binding on all, and conceived its origin as immemorial. When further they conceived it as approved by the gods, they gave it all the value they knew how to put into it.

The standards and valuations of custom are, however, only partly rational. Many customs are irrational; some are injurious. But in them all the habitual is a large, if not the largest, factor. And this is often strong enough to resist any attempt at rational testing. Dr. Arthur Smith tells us of the advantage it would be in certain parts of China to build a door on the south side of the house in order to get the breeze in hot weather. The simple and sufficient answer to such a suggestion is, "We don't build doors on the south side."

An additional weakness in the character of such irrational, or partly rational standards, is the misplaced energy they involve. What is merely trivial is made as important and impressive as what has real significance. Tithing mint, anise, and cummin is quite likely to involve neglect of the weightier matters of the law. Moral life requires men to estimate the value of acts. If the irrelevant or the petty is made important, it not only prevents a high level of value for the really important act, it loads up conduct with burdens which keep it back; it introduces elements which must be got rid of later, often with heavy loss of what is genuinely valuable. When there are so many ways of offending the gods and when these turn so often upon mere observance of routine or formula, it may require much subsequent time and energy to make amends. The morals get an expiatory character.

2. *The Motives.*—In the motives to which it appeals, custom is able to make a far better showing than earlier writers, like Herbert Spencer, gave it credit for. It doubtless employs fear in its taboos; it doubtless enlists the passion of resentment in its blood feuds. Even these are modified by a social environment. For the fear of violating a taboo is in part the fear of bringing bad luck on the whole group, and not merely on the violator. We have, therefore, a quasi-social fear, not a purely instinctive reaction. The same is true in

perhaps a stronger degree of the resentments. The blood revenge is in a majority of cases not a personal but a group
affair. It is undertaken at personal risk and for others' interest—or rather for a common interest. The resentment is
thus a *"sympathetic resentment."*[20] Regarded as a mere reaction for self-preservation this instinctive-emotional process
is unmoral. As a mere desire to produce pain it would be immoral. But so far as it implies an attitude of reacting from a
general point of view and to aid others, it is moral. Aside
from the passions of fear and resentment, however, there is
a wide range of motives enlisted. Filial and parental affection, some degree of affection between the sexes over and
above sex passion, respect for the aged and the beings who
embody ideals however crude, loyalty to fellow clansmen,—
all these are not only fostered but actually secured by the
primitive group. But the motives which imply reflection—
reverence for duty as the imperious law of a larger life, sincere love of what is good for its own sake—cannot be brought
to full consciousness until there is a more definite conception of a moral authority, a more definite contrast between
the one great good and the partial or temporary satisfactions.
The development of these conceptions requires a growth in
individuality; it requires conflicts between authority and
liberty, and those collisions between private interests and the
public welfare which a higher civilization affords.

3. *The Content.*—When we consider the "what" of
group and customary morality we note at once that the factors which make for the idealizing and expansion of interests
are less in evidence than those which make for a common
and social interest and satisfaction. There is indeed, as we
have noted, opportunity for memory and fancy. The traditions of the past, the myths, the cultus, the folk songs—these
keep up a mental life which is as genuinely valued as the
more physical activities. But as the mode of life in question
does not evoke the more abstractly rational activities—reasoning, selecting, choosing—in the highest degree, the ideals
lack reach and power. It needs the incentives described in

---

20. Westermarck regards this as one of the fundamental elements
in the beginnings of morality.

the following chapters to call out a true life of the spirit. The social aspects of the "what," on the other hand, are well rooted in group morality. It is unnecessary to repeat what has been dwelt upon in the present and preceding chapters so fully. We point out now that while the standard is social, it is unconsciously rather than consciously social. Or perhaps better: it is a standard of society but not a standard which each member deliberately makes his own. He takes it as a matter of course. He is in the clan, "with the gang"; he thinks and acts accordingly. He cannot begin to be as selfish as a modern individualist; he simply hasn't the imagery to conceive such an exclusive good, nor the tools with which to carry it out. But he cannot be as broadly social either. He may not be able to sink so low as the civilized miser, or debauchee, or criminal, but neither can he conceive or build up the character which implies facing opposition. The moral hero achieves full stature only when he pits himself against others, when he recognizes evil and fights it, when he "overcomes the world."

4. *Organization of Character.*—In the organization of stable character the morality of custom is strong on one side. The group trains its members to act in the ways it approves and afterwards holds them by all the agencies in its power. It forms habits and enforces them. Its weakness is that the element of habit is so large, that of freedom so small. It holds up the average man; it holds back the man who might forge ahead. It is an anchor, and a drag.

Literature

Much of the literature at the close of Chapters 2 and 3, particularly the works of Spencer and Gillen and Schurtz, belongs here also. Schoolcraft, *Indian Tribes*, 1851–57; Eastman, *Indian Boyhood*, 1902. Papers on various cults of North American Indians in reports of the *Bureau of Ethnology*, by Stevenson, 8th, 1886–87; Dorsey, 11th, 1889–90; Fewkes, 15th, 1893–94, 21st, 1899–1900; Fletcher, 22d, 1900–01; Stevenson, 23d, 1901–02; Kidd, *Savage Childhood*, 1906, *The Essential Kafir*, 1904; Skeat, *Malay Magic*, 1900; N. W. Thomas, general editor of Series, *The Native Races of the British Empire*, 1906–07; Barton, *A Sketch of Semitic Origins*, 1902; Harrison, *Prolegomena to the Study of*

Greek Religion, 1903; Reinach, *Cultes, mythes et religions*, 3 vols., 1905–08; Frazer, *The Golden Bough*, 3 vols., 1900; Marett, "Is Taboo Negative Magic?" in *Anthropological Essays*, presented to E. B. Tylor, 1907; Crawley, *The Mystic Rose*, 1902; Spencer, *Sociology*, 1876–96; Clifford, "On the Scientific Basis of Morals" in *Lectures and Essays*, 1886; Maine, *Early History of Institutions*, 1888, *Early Law and Custom*, 1886; Post, *Die Grundlagen des Rechts und die Grundzüge seiner Entwickelungsgeschichte*, 1884, *Ethnologische Jurisprudenz*, 1894–95; Pollock and Maitland, *History of English Law*, 1895; Steinmetz, *Ethnologische Studien zur ersten Entwicklung der Strafe*, 1894.

5. FROM CUSTOM TO CONSCIENCE; FROM GROUP MORALITY TO PERSONAL MORALITY

§ 1. Contrast and Collision

1. *What the Third Level Means.*—Complete morality is reached only when the individual recognizes the right or chooses the good freely, devotes himself heartily to its fulfillment, and seeks a progressive social development in which every member of society shall share. The group morality with its agencies of custom set up a standard, but one that was corporate rather than personal. It approved and disapproved, that is it had an idea of good, but this did not mean a good that was personally valued. It enlisted its members, but it was by drill, by pleasure and pain, and by habit, rather than by fully voluntary action. It secured steadiness by habit and social pressure, rather than by choices built into character. It maintained community of feeling and action, but of the unconscious rather than the definitely social type. Finally it was rather fitted to maintain a fixed order than to promote and safeguard progress. Advance then must (1) substitute some rational method of setting up standards and forming values, in place of habitual passive acceptance; (2) secure voluntary and personal choice and interest, instead of unconscious identification with the group welfare, or instinctive and habitual response to group needs; (3) encourage at the same time individual development and the demand that all shall share in this development—the worth and happiness of the person and of *every* person.

2. *Collisions Involved.*—Such an advance brings to consciousness two collisions. The oppositions were there before, but they were not felt as oppositions. So long as the man was fully with his group, or satisfied with the custom, he would make no revolt. When the movement begins the collisions are felt. These collisions are:

(1) The collision between the authority and interests of

the group, and the independence and private interests of the individual.

(2) The collision between order and progress, between habit and reconstruction or reformation.

It is evident that there is a close connection between these two collisions; in fact, the second becomes in practice a form of the first. For we saw in the last chapter that custom is really backed and enforced by the group, and its merely habitual parts are as strongly supported as those parts which have a more rational basis. It would perhaps be conceivable that a people should move on all together, working out a higher civilization in which free thought should keep full reverence for social values, in which political liberty should keep even pace with the development of government, in which self-interest should be accompanied by regard for the welfare of others, just as it may be possible for a child to grow into full morality without a period of "storm and stress." But this is not usual. Progress has generally cost struggle. And the first phase of this struggle is opposition between the individual and the group. The self-assertive instincts and impulses were present in group life, but they were in part undeveloped because they had not enough stimulus to call them out. A man could not develop his impulse for possession to its full extent if there was little or nothing for him to possess. In part they were not developed because the group held them back, and the conditions of living and fighting favored those groups which did keep them back. Nevertheless they were present in some degree, always contending against the more social forces. Indeed what makes the opposition between group and individual so strong and so continuous is that both the social and the individual are rooted in human nature. They constitute what Kant calls the *unsocial sociableness* of man. "Man cannot get on with his fellows and he cannot do without them."

Individualism.—The assertion by the individual of his own opinions and beliefs, his own independence and interests, as over against group standards, authority, and interests, is known as individualism. It is evident that such assertion will always mark a new level of conduct. Action must now be personal and voluntary. It is also evident that it may be either better or worse than the level of custom and group life. The first effect is likely to be, in appearance at least, a change for the worse. The old restraints are tossed aside; "creeds outworn" no longer steady or direct; the strong or the crafty individual comes to the fore and exploits his fellows. Every man does what is "right in his own eyes." The age of the Sophists in Greece, of the Renaissance in Italy, of the Enlightenment and Romantic movement in western Europe, and of the industrial revolution in recent times illustrate different phases of individualism. A people, as well as an individual, may "go to pieces" in its reaction against social authority and custom. But such one-sided individualism is almost certain to call out prophets of a new order; "organic filaments" of new structures appear; family, industry, the state, are organized anew and upon more voluntary basis. Those who accept the new conditions and assume responsibility with their freedom, who direct their choices by reason instead of passion, who "aim at justice and kindness" as well as at happiness, become moral persons and gain thereby new worth and dignity. While, then, the general movement is on the whole a movement of individualism, it demands just as necessarily, if there is to be moral progress, a *reconstructed individual*—a person who is individual in choice, in feeling, in responsibility, and at the same time social in what he regards as good, in his sympathies, and in his purposes. Otherwise individualism means progress toward the immoral.

§ 2. *Sociological Agencies in the Transition*

The agencies which bring about the change from customary and group morality to conscious and personal morality are varied. Just as character is developed in the child and young man by various means, sometimes by success, sometimes by adversity or loss of a parent, sometimes by slow increase in knowledge, and sometimes by a sudden right-about-face with a strong emotional basis, so it is with peoples. Some, like the Japanese at the present, are brought into sudden contact with the whole set of commercial and military forces from without. Among others, as with the Greeks, a fermentation starts within, along intellectual, economic, political, and religious lines. Or again, national calamities may upset all the old values, as with the Hebrews. But we may note four typical agencies which are usually more or less active.

1. Economic Forces.—The action of economic forces in breaking up the early kinship group or joint family may be noticed in the history of many peoples. The clan flourishes in such conditions of hunting life or of simple agriculture as were found among Australians and Indians, or among the Celts in Ireland and the Scottish Highlands. It cannot survive when a more advanced state of agriculture prevails. A certain amount of individualism will appear wherever the advantage for the individual lies in separate industry and private ownership. If buffalo was to be hunted it was better to pool issues, but for smaller game the skillful or persistent huntsman or shepherd will think he can gain more by working for himself. This is intensified when agriculture and commerce take the place of earlier modes of life. The farmer has to work so hard and long, his goal is so far in the future, that differences of character show themselves much more strongly. Hunting and fishing are so exciting, and the reward is so near, that even a man who is not very industrious will do his part. But in agriculture only the hard and patient worker gets a reward and he does not like to share it with the lazy, or even with the weaker. Commerce, bargaining, likewise puts a great premium on individual shrewdness. And for a long time commerce was conducted on a relatively individual basis. Caravans of traders journeyed together for mutual protection but there was not any such organization as later obtained, and each individual could display his own cunning or ability. Moreover commerce leads to the comparison of custom, to interchange of ideas as well as goods. All this tends to break down the sanctity of customs peculiar to a given group. The trader as well as the guest may overstep the barriers set up by kin. The early Greek colonists, among whom a great individualistic movement began, were the traders of their day. The parts of Europe where most survives of primitive group life are those little touched by modern commerce.

But we get a broader view of economic influences if we consider the methods of organizing industry which have successively prevailed. In early society, and likewise in the earlier period of modern civilization, the family was a great economic unit. Many or most of the industries could be advantageously carried on in the household. As in the cases cited above (p. 62) the stronger or adventurous member would be constantly trying to strike out for himself. This process of constant readjustment is, however, far less thoroughgoing in its effects on mores than the three great methods of securing a broader organization of industry. In primitive society large enterprises had to be carried on by the cooperation of the group. Forced labor as used by the Oriental civilizations substituted a method by which greater works like the pyramids or temples could be built, but it brought with it the overthrow of much of the old group sympathies and mutual aid. In Greece and Rome slavery did the drudgery and left the citizens free to cultivate art, letters, and government. It gave opportunity and scope for the few. Men of power and genius arose, and at the same time all the negative forces of individualism asserted themselves. In modern times capitalism is the method for organizing industry and trade. It proves more effective than forced labor or slavery in securing combination of forces and in exploiting natural resources. It likewise gives extraordinary opportunities for the rise of men of organizing genius. The careers of "captains of industry" are more fascinating than those of old-time conquerors because they involve more complex situations, and can utilize the discoveries and labors of more men. But modern capitalism has been as destructive to the morality of the Middle Ages, or even of a hundred years ago, as was forced labor or slavery to the group life and mores which they destroyed.

2. *The Progress of Science and the Arts.*—The effect of the progress of science and intelligence upon the mores is direct. Comparisons of the customs of one people with those of another bring out differences, and arouse questions as to the reasons for such diversity. And we have seen that there is more or less in the customs for which no reason can be given. Even if there was one originally it has been forgotten.

Or again, increasing knowledge of weather and seasons, of plants and animals, of sickness and disease, discredits many of the taboos and ceremonials which the cruder beliefs had regarded as essential to welfare. Certain elements of ritual may survive under the protection of "mysteries," but the more enlightened portion of the community keeps aloof. Instead of the mores with their large infusion of the accidental, the habitual, and the impulsive, increasing intelligence demands some rational rule of life.

And science joins with the various industrial and fine arts to create a new set of interests for the individual. Any good piece of workmanship, any work of art however simple, is twice blest. It blesses him that makes and him that uses or enjoys. The division of labor, begun in group life, is carried further. Craftsmen and artists develop increasing individuality as they construct temples or palaces, fashion statues or pottery, or sing of gods and heroes. Their minds grow with what they do. Side by side with the aspect of art which makes it a bond of society is the aspect which so frequently makes the skilled workman the critic, and the artist a law to himself. In the next place note the effect on those who can use and enjoy the products of the arts. A new world of satisfaction and happiness is opened which each person can enter for himself. In cruder conditions there was not much out of which to build up happiness. Food, labor, rest, the thrill of hunt or contest, the passion of sex, the pride in children — these made up the interests of primitive life. Further means of enjoyment were found chiefly in society of the kin, or in the men's house. But as the arts advanced the individual could have made for him a fine house and elaborate clothing. Metal, wood, and clay minister to increasing wants. A permanent and stately tomb makes the future more definite. The ability to hand down wealth in durable form places a premium on its acquirement. Ambition has more stuff to work with. A more definite, assertive self is gradually built up. "Good" comes to have added meaning with every new want that awakes. The individual is not satisfied any longer to take the group's valuation. He wants to get his own good in his own way. And it will often seem to him that he can get his own good most easily and surely either by keeping out of the common life or by using his fellow men to his own advantage. Men of culture have frequently shown their selfishness in the first way; men of wealth in the second. An aristocracy of culture, or birth, or wealth may come to regard the whole process of civilization as properly ministering to the wants of the select few. Nearly every people which has developed the arts and sciences has developed also an aristocracy. In the ancient world slavery was a part of the process. In modern times other forms of exploitation may serve the purpose better. Individualism, released from the ties which bound up the good of one with the good of all, tends to become exclusive and selfish; civilization with all its opportunities for increasing happiness and increasing life has its moral risks and indirectly, at least, its moral evils.

These evils may appear as the gratification of sense and appetite and thus may be opposed to the higher life of the spirit, which needs no outer objects or luxuries. Or they may appear as rooted in selfishness, in the desire for gratifying the exclusive self of material interests or ambition, as over against sympathy, justice, and kindness, which mark a broadly human and social life. In both cases serious men have sought to overcome by some form of "self-denial" the evils that attend on civilization, even if they are not due to it.

3. *Military Forces.*—The kinship group is a protection so long as it has to contend only with similar groups. The headlong valor and tribal loyalty of German or Scottish clans may even win conflicts with more disciplined troops of Rome or England. But permanent success demands higher organization than the old clans and tribes permitted. Organization means authority, and a single directing, controlling commander or king. As Egypt, Assyria, Phoenicia show their strength the clans of Israel cry, "Nay, but we will have a king over us; that we may also be like all the nations; and that our king may judge us, and go out before us, and fight our battles."[1] Wars afford the opportunity for the strong and unscrupulous leader to assert himself. Like commerce they may tend also to spread culture and thus break down barriers of ancient custom. The conquests of Babylon and Alexander,

1. 1 Sam. 8:19–20.

the Crusades and the French Revolution, are instances of the power of military forces to destroy old customs and give individualism new scope. In most cases, it is true, it is only the leader or "tyrant" who gets the advantage. He uses the whole machinery of society for his own elevation. Nevertheless custom and group unity are broken for all. Respect for law must be built new from the foundation.

4. *Religious Forces.*—While in general religion is a conservative agency, it is also true that a new religion or a new departure in religion has often exercised a powerful influence on moral development. The very fact that religion is so intimately bound up with all the group mores and ideals, makes a change in religion bear directly on old standards of life. The collision between old and new is likely to be fundamental and sharp. A conception of God may carry with it a view of what conduct is pleasing to him. A doctrine as to the future may require a certain mode of life. A cultus may approve or condemn certain relations between the sexes. Conflicting religions may then force a moral attitude in weighing their claims. The contests between Jehovah and Baal, between Orphic cults and the public Greek religion, between Judaism and Christianity, Christianity and Roman civilization, Christianity and Germanic religion, Catholicism and Protestantism, have brought out moral issues. We shall notice this factor especially in Chapters 6 and 8.

§ 3. *The Psychological Agencies*

The psychological forces which tend toward individualism have been already stated to be the self-assertive instincts and impulses. They are all variations of the effort of the living being first to preserve itself and then to rise to more complicated life by entering into more complex relations and mastering its environment. Spinoza's "*sui esse conservare*," Schopenhauer's "will to live," Nietzsche's "will to power," the Hebrew's passionate ideal of "life," and Tennyson's "More life, and fuller" express in varying degree the meaning of this elemental bent and process. Growing intelligence adds to its strength by giving greater capacity to control. Starting with organic needs, this developing life process may find satisfactions in the physical world in the increasing power and mastery over nature gained by the explorer or the hunter, the discoverer, the craftsman, or the artist. It is when it enters the world of persons that it displays a peculiar intensity that marks the passions of individualism *par excellence*. We note four of these tendencies toward self-assertion.

1. Sex.—The sex instinct and emotion occupies a peculiar position in this respect. On the one hand it is a powerful socializing agency. It brings the sexes together and is thus fundamental to the family. But on the other hand it is constantly rebelling against the limits and conventions established by the social group for its regulation. The statutes against illicit relations, from the codes of Hammurabi and Moses to the latest efforts for stricter divorce, attest the collision between the individual's inclination and the will of the group. Repeatedly some passion of sex has broken over all social, legal, and religious sanctions. It has thus been a favorite theme of tragedy from the Greeks to Ibsen. It finds another fitting medium in the romance. It has called into existence and maintains in every large city an outcast colony of wretched creatures, and the evils which attend are not limited in their results to those who knowingly take the risks. It has worked repeated changes in the structure of the family authorized by society. Its value and proper regulation were points at issue in that wide-reaching change of mores attendant upon the Reformation, and apparently equilibrium has not yet been reached.

2. The Demand for Possession and Private Property. —In the primitive group we have seen that there might be private property in tools or weapons, in cattle or slaves. There was little private property in land under the maternal clan; and indeed in any case, so long as the arts were undeveloped, private property had necessary limits. The demand for private property is a natural attendant upon individual modes of industry. As we have said, it was a common principle that what the group produced was owned by the group, and what the individual made or captured was treated as his. When individual industry came to count for more, the individual claimed more and more as private possession.

The change from the maternal clan to the paternal family or household was a reenforcement to the individual control of property. The father could hand down his cattle or his house to his son. The joint family of India is indeed a type of a paternal system. Nevertheless the tendency is much stronger to insist on individual property where the father's goods pass to his son than where they go to his sister's children.

The chiefs or rulers were likely to gain the right of private property first. Among certain families of the South Slavs to-day, the head has his individual eating utensils, the rest share. Among many people the chiefs have cattle which they can dispose of as they will; the rest have simply their share of the kin's goods. The old Brehon laws of Ireland show this stage.

But however it comes about, the very meaning of property is, in the first place, exclusion of others from some thing which I have. It is therefore in so far necessarily opposed to group unity, opposed to any such simple solidarity of life as we find in group morality. As the American Indian accepts land in severalty, the old group life, the tribal restraints and supports, the group custom and moral unity that went with it, are gone. He must find a new basis or go to pieces.

3. *Struggles for Mastery or Liberty.*—In most cases these cannot be separated from economic struggles. Masters and slaves were in economic as well as personal relations, and nearly all class contests on a large scale have had at least one economic root, whatever their other sources. But the economic is not their only root. There have been wars for glory or for liberty as well as for territory or booty or slaves. As the struggle for existence has bred into the race the instinct of self-defense with its emotion of anger, the instinct to rivalry and mastery, and the corresponding aversion to being ruled, so the progress of society shows trials of strength between man and man, kin and kin, tribe and tribe. And while, as stated in the preceding chapter, the cooperation made necessary in war or feud is a uniting force, there is another side to the story. Contests between individuals show who is master; contests between groups tend to bring forward leaders. And while such masterful men may serve the

group they are quite as likely to find an interest in opposing
group customs. They assert an independence of the group,
or a mastery over it, quite incompatible with the solidarity of
the kinship clan, although the patriarchal type of household
under a strong head may be quite possible. There comes to be
one code for rich and another for poor, one for Patricians
and another for Plebs, one for baron and another for peasant,
one for gentry and another for the common folk. For a time
this may be accepted patiently. But when once the rich become arrogant, the feudal lord insolent, the bitter truth is
faced that the customs have become mere conventions. They
no longer hold. All the old ties are cast off. The demand for
freedom and equality rises, and the collision between authority and liberty is on.

Or the contest may be for intellectual liberty—for free
thought and free speech. It is sometimes considered that
such liberty meets its strongest opponent in the religious or
ecclesiastical organization. There is no doubt a conservative
tendency in religion. As we have pointed out, religion is the
great conservator of group values and group standards. Its
ritual is most elaborate, its taboos most sacred. Intellectual
criticism tends to undermine what is outgrown or merely
habitual here as elsewhere. Rationalism or free thought has
set itself in frequent opposition likewise to what has been
claimed to be "above reason." Nevertheless it would be absurd to attribute all the individualism to science and all the
conservatism to religion. Scientific dogmas and "idols" are
hard to displace. Schools are about as conservative as
churches. And on the other hand the struggle for religious
liberty has usually been carried on not by the irreligious but
by the religious. The prophet Amos found himself opposed
by the religious organization of his day when he urged social
righteousness, and the history of the noble army of martyrs
is a record of appeal to individual conscience, or to an immediate personal relation to God, as over against the formal,
the traditional, the organized religious customs and doctrines
of their age. The struggle for religious toleration and religious liberty takes its place side by side with the struggles
for intellectual and political liberty in the chapters of individualism.

4. *The Desire for Honor, or Social Esteem.* — James, in his psychology of the self, calls the recognition which a man gets from his mates his "social self." "We are not only gregarious animals, liking to be in sight of our fellows, but we have an innate ·propensity to get ourselves noticed, and noticed favorably by our kind. No more fiendish punishment could be devised, were such a thing physically possible, than that one should be turned loose in society and remain absolutely unnoticed by all the members thereof."[2] From such a punishment "the cruelest bodily tortures would be a relief; for this would make us feel that however bad might be our plight, we had not sunk to such depth as to be unworthy of attention at all."[3] Honor or fame is a name for one of the various "social selves" which a man may build up. It stands for what those of a given group may think or say of him. It has a place and a large place in group life. Precedence, salutations, decorations in costume and bodily ornament, praises in song for the brave, the strong, the cunning, the powerful, with ridicule for the coward or the weakling are all at work. But with the primitive group the difference between men of the group is kept within bounds. When more definite organization of groups for military or civil purposes begins, when the feudal chief gathers his retainers and begins to rise above the rest of the community in strength, finally when the progress of the arts gives greater means for display, the desire for recognition has immensely greater scope. It is increased by the instinct of emulation; it often results in envy and jealousies. It becomes then a powerful factor in stimulating individualism.

But while desires for honor and fame provoke individualism, they carry with them, like desires for property and power, elements that make for reconstruction of the social on a higher level. For honor implies some common sentiment to which the individual can make appeal. Group members praise or blame what accords with their feeling or desire, but they do not act as individuals merely, praising what pleases them as individuals. They react more or less completely from the group point of view; they honor the man

2. James, *Psychology*, Vol. I, ch. x.
3. James, *Psychology*, Vol. I, pp. 293 f.

who embodies the group-ideal of courage, or other admirable
and respected qualities. And here comes the motive which
operates to force a better ideal than mere desire of praise.
No group honors the man who is definitely seeking merely its
applause rather than its approval—at least not after it has
found him out. The force of public opinion is therefore calculated to elicit a desire to be *worthy* of honor, as well as to
be honored. This means a desire to act as a true social individual, for it is only the true member of the group,—true
clansman,—true patriot,—true martyr,—who appeals to the
other members when they judge as members, and not sel-
fishly. When now the group whose approval is sought is
small, we have class standards, with all the provincialism,
narrowness, and prejudice that belong to them. As the honor-
seeker is merely after the opinion of his class, he is bound
to be only partly social. So long as he is with his kin, or his
set, or his "gang," or his "party," or his "union," or his "country"—regardless of any wider appeal—he is bound to be imperfectly rational and social in his conduct. The great possibilities of the desire for honor, and of the desire to be
worthy of honor, lie then in the constant extension of the
range. The martyr, the seeker for truth, the reformer, the
neglected artist, looks for honor from posterity; if misjudged
or neglected, he appeals to mankind. He is thus forming for
himself an ideal standard. And if he embodies this ideal
standard in a personal, highest possible judging companion,
his desire to be worthy of approval takes a religious form.
He seeks "the honor that is from God." Though "the inner-
most of the empirical selves of a man is a self of the *social*
sort, it yet can find its only adequate *socius* in an ideal
world."[4]

The moral value of these three forces of individualism
was finely stated by Kant:

The means which nature uses to bring about the development of all the capacities she has given man is their *antagonism*
in society, in so far as this antagonism becomes in the end a
cause of social order. Men have an inclination to *associate* themselves, for in a social state they feel themselves more completely
men: i.e., they are conscious of the development of their natural

4. James, *Psychology*, Vol. I, p. 316.

capacities. But they have also a great propensity to *isolate* themselves, for they find in themselves at the same time this unsocial
characteristic: each wishes to direct everything solely according
to his own notion, and hence expects resistance, just as he knows
that he is inclined to resist others. It is just this resistance which
awakens all man's powers; this brings him to overcome his
propensity to indolence, and drives him through the lust for
honor, power, or wealth to win for himself a rank among his
fellowmen. Man's will is for concord, but nature knows better
what is good for the species, and she wills discord. He would
like a life of comfort and pleasure; nature wills that he be
dragged out of idleness and inactive content, and plunged into
labor and trouble in order that he may find out the means of
extricating himself from his difficulties. The natural impulses
which prompt this effort, the sources of unsociableness and of
the mutual conflict from which so many evils spring, are then
spurs to a more complete development of man's powers.[5]

We have spoken of the "forces" which tend to break
down the old unity of the group and bring about new organization. But of course these forces are not impersonal.
Sometimes they seem to act like the ocean tide, pushing
silently in, and only now and then sending a wave a little
higher than its fellows. Frequently, however, some great
personality stands out preeminent, either as critic of the
old or builder of the new. The prophets were stoned because
they condemned the present; the next generation was ready
to build their sepulchers. Socrates is the classic example of
the great man who perishes in seeking to find a rational
basis to replace that of custom. Indeed, this conflict—on the
one hand, the rigid system of tradition and corporate union
hallowed by all the sanctions of religion and public opinion;
upon the other, the individual making appeal to reason, or
to his conscience, or to a "higher law"—is the tragedy of
history.

§ 4. Positive Reconstruction

It must not be supposed that the moral process stops
at the points indicated under the several divisions of this

5. Kant, "Idea of a Universal History from a Cosmopolitical Point
of View."

last section. As already stated, if the people really works out
a higher type of conscious and personal morality, it means
not only a more powerful individual, but a reconstructed individual and a reconstructed society. It means not only the
disintegration of the old kinship or family group, which is
an economic, political, and religious unity as well. It means
the construction of a new basis for the family; new moral
principles for business; a distinct political state with new
means for government, new conceptions of authority and
liberty; finally, a national or universal religion. And the individual must on this higher level choose all these voluntarily.
More than this: as he chooses in the presence of the new
conflicting ends presented by individualism, he sets up or
adopts a standard for himself. He thinks definitely of what is
"good" and "right." As he recognizes its claim, he is responsible as well as free. As he identifies himself heartily
with it, he becomes sincerely and genuinely moral. Reverence, duty, and love for what is good become the quickening
emotions. Thoughtfulness, self-control, aspiration toward an
ideal, courageous venturing in its achievement, kindness and
justice, become the dominant temper, or at least are recognized as the temper that should be dominant. The conception
of moral character and moral personality is brought to consciousness. The development of the Hebrews and Greeks will
show how these positive values emerge.

Literature

Kant's Principles of Politics, tr. by Hastie, 1891, especially
the essay "Idea of a Universal History from a Cosmopolitical
Point of View"; Hegel, *Philosophy of History*, tr. by Sibree, 1881;
Darwin, *The Descent of Man*, 1871; Schurman, *The Ethical Import of Darwinism*, 1888; Seth, "The Evolution of Morality," *Mind*,
XIV, 1889, pp. 27–49; Williams, *A Review of Systems of Ethics
Founded on the Theory of Evolution*, 1893; Harris, *Moral Evolution*, 1896; Tufts, "On Moral Evolution," in *Studies in Philosophy
and Psychology* (Garman Commemorative Volume), 1906; Iher-
ing, *Der Kampf um's Recht*; Simcox, *Natural Law*, 1877; Sorley,
Ethics of Naturalism, 1885.

6. THE HEBREW MORAL DEVELOPMENT

§ 1. General Character and Determining Principles

1. *The Hebrew and the Greek.* — The general character of the Hebrew moral development may be brought out by a contrast with that of the Greeks.[1] While many phases are common, there is yet a difference in emphasis and focus. There were political and economic forces at work in Israel, and religious forces in Greece. Nevertheless, the moral life in one people kept close to the religious, and in the other found independent channels. Conscientious conduct for the Hebrew centered in doing the will of God; for the Greek, in finding rational standards of good. For the Hebrew, righteousness was the typical theme; for the Greek, the ideal lay rather in measure and harmony. For the Greek, wisdom or insight was the chief virtue; for the Hebrew, the fear of the Lord was the beginning of wisdom. The social ideal of the Hebrews was the kingdom of God; of the Greeks, a political State. If we distinguish in conscience two aspects, thoughtfulness in discovering what to do and hearty desire to do the right when found, then the Greeks emphasize the former, the Hebrews the latter. Intellect plays a larger part with the Greek; emotion and the voluntary aspect of will with the Hebrew. Feeling plays its part with the Greeks largely as an aesthetic demand for measure and harmony; with the Hebrews it is chiefly prominent in motivation, where it is an element in what is called "the heart," or it functions in appreciation of acts performed, as the joy or sorrow felt when God approves or condemns. Both peoples are interesting for our study, not only as illustrating different kinds of moral development, but also as contributing largely to the moral consciousness of western peoples to-day.

1. Arnold, "Hebraism and Hellenism," in *Culture and Anarchy,* ch. iv.

2. *The Early Morality.*—The accounts of the tribal life
and customs in the early period after the settlement in
Canaan, show the main features of group life which are
already familiar to us. Clan or kinship loyalty was strong on
both its good and its defective sides. There were fidelity, a
jeoparding of lives unto death, honor for group heroes, joint
responsibility, and blood revenge. There were respect for hospitality and regulation of marriage, though not according to
later standards. A rough measure of justice was recognized
in "as I have done, so God hath requited me." But there was
no public authority to restrain the wrongdoer, except when
a particularly revolting brutality shocked public sentiment.
Festivals and sacrificial meals united the members of the
family or clan more closely to each other and to their god.
Vows must be kept inviolable even if they involved human
sacrifice. The interests and ends of life were simple. The
satisfaction of bodily wants, the love of kin and above all of
children, the desire to be in right relation of favor and harmony with the unseen deity who protected from enemies and
sent fruitful seasons,—these made their chief good. The line
of their progress from these rude beginnings to a lofty moral
ideal lay through religion. But the religious conceptions were
directly related to political, social, and economic conditions;
hence, both aspects must be briefly characterized.

3. *Political Development.*—The political development
(a) built up a national unity which worked to break down
old group units, (b) strengthened military ambition and
race pride, (c) stimulated the prophets to their highest conceptions of the divine majesty and universality, but, finally
when the national power and hope were shattered, (d) compelled the most thoroughgoing reconstruction of all the
values, ideals, and meaning of life. It is not possible or necessary to trace this process in detail, but we may point out
here the general effect of the political development in bringing into clearer consciousness the conceptions of authority
and law which were important factors in Hebrew morality.
The earlier patriarchal head of the clan or family exercised
certain political power, but there was no explicit recognition
of this. Government by the "elders" or by the heads of the
household makes no clear distinction between the common

kinship and the political and legal authority of the sovereign. The "judges," whose rule preceded the kingdom, were military deliverers who owed their authority to personal powers rather than to a definite provision. To establish an organized political community, a kingdom, was then to bring into clearer recognition this element of authority which was merely implicit in the tribal organization. It allowed a more distinctly voluntary relationship to be differentiated from the involuntary relationship of kinship, or the personal relationship of the hero. While, therefore, in the formation of the kingdom the earlier prophets saw only a rejection of God, the later prophets saw in it the symbol of a higher type of relation between God and people. It was given religious sanction and the king was regarded as the son of Jehovah. It was thus ready to serve as the scheme or setting for the moral unity and order of a people.

4. *The Economic Factors.*—The organization and growing prosperity of the political power were attended by economic and social changes. The simple agricultural life of the early period had not caused entire loss of clan organization and customs. But the growth of trade and commerce under Solomon and later kings brought in wealth and shifted the centre of power and influence from country to city. Wealth and luxury had their usual results. Clashing interests asserted their strength. Economic and social individualism destroyed the old group solidarity. At the times of the prophets Amos, Hosea, Isaiah, there were classes of rich and poor. Greed had asserted itself in rulers, judges, priests, and "regular" prophets. Oppression, land monopoly, bribery, extortion, stirred moral indignation. The fact that these were practiced by the most zealous observers of ritual and guardians of religion roused in the great reformers a demand for a change in religion itself. Not sacrifices but justice is the need of the hour and the demand of God.

§ 2. *Religious Agencies*

The interaction between the religious and the moral education of the Hebrews was so intimate that it is difficult to distinguish the two, but we may abstract certain concep-

tions or motives in Israel's religion which were especially
significant. The general conception was that of the close
personal relation between god and people. Israel should
have no other god; Jehovah—at least this was the earlier
thought—would have no other people. He had loved and
chosen Israel; Israel in gratitude, as well as in hope and
fear, must love and obey Jehovah. Priests maintained his
cultus; prophets brought new commands according to the
requirements of the hour; the king represented his sovereignty and justice; the course of events exhibited his purpose.
Each of these elements served to provoke or elicit moral
reflection or moral conduct.

   1. *The "Covenant" Relation was a Moral Conception.*—
The usual religious conception is that of some blood or kin
relation between people and deity. This has the same potential meaning and value as that of the other relations of
group life outlined in Chapter 2. But it is rather a natural
than a "moral"—i.e., conscious and voluntary—tie. To conceive of the relation between god and people as due to voluntary choice, is to introduce a powerful agency toward making
morality conscious. Whatever the origin of the idea, the
significant fact is that the religious and moral leaders present the relation of Israel to Jehovah as based on a covenant.
On the one hand, Jehovah protects, preserves, and prospers;
on the other, Israel is to obey his laws and serve no other
gods. This conception of mutual obligation is presented at
the opening of the "Ten Commandments," and to this covenant relation the prophets again and again make appeal.
The obligation to obey the law is not "This is the custom," or
"Our fathers did so"; it is placed on the ground that the
people has voluntarily accepted Jehovah as its god and lawgiver.

   The meaning of this covenant and the symbols by which
it was conceived, changed with the advance of the social
relationships of the people. At first Jehovah was "Lord of
Hosts," protector in war, and giver of prosperity, and the
early conceptions of the duty of the people seemed to include human sacrifice, at least in extreme cases. But with
later prophets we find the social and family relationship of
husband and father brought increasingly into use. Whether

by personal experience or by more general reflection, we find Hosea interpreting the relationship between God and his people in both of these family conceptions. The disloyalty of the people takes on the more intimate taint of a wife's unfaithfulness, and, conversely, in contrast to the concepts of other religions, the people may call Jehovah "my husband" and no longer "my master" (Baal). The change from status to contract is thus, in Israel's religion, fruitful with many moral results.

2. *The Conception of a Personal Lawgiver.* — The conception of a personal lawgiver raises conduct from the level of custom to the level of conscious morality. So long as a child follows certain ways by imitation or suggestion, he does not necessarily attach any moral meaning to them. But if the parent expressly commands or prohibits, it becomes a matter of obedience or disobedience. Choice becomes necessary. Character takes the place of innocence. So Jehovah's law compelled obedience or rebellion. Customs were either forbidden or enjoined. In either case they ceased to be merely customs. In the law of Israel the whole body of observances in private life, in ceremonial, and in legal forms, is introduced with a "Thus saith the Lord." We know that other Semitic people observed the Sabbath, practiced circumcision, distinguished clean from unclean beasts, and respected the taboos of birth and death. Whether in Israel all these observances were old customs given new authority by statute, or were customs taken from other peoples under the authority of the laws of Jehovah, is immaterial. The ethical significance of the law is that these various observances, instead of being treated merely as customs, are regarded as personal commands of a personal deity.

This makes a vital difference in the view taken of the violation of these observances. When a man violates a custom he fails to do the correct thing. He misses the mark.[2] But when the observance is a personal command, its violation is a personal disobedience; it is rebellion; it is an act of will. The evil which follows is no longer bad luck; it is punishment. Now punishment must be either right or wrong, moral

2. The Hebrew and Greek words for sin both mean "to miss."

or immoral. It can never be merely non-moral. Hence the
very conception of sin as a personal offense, and of ill as a
personal punishment, forces a moral standard. In its crudest
form this may take the god's commands as right simply because he utters them, and assume that the sufferer is guilty
merely because he suffers. We find this in the penitential
psalms of the Babylonians. These express the deepest conviction of sin and the utmost desire to please the god, but
when we try to discover what the penitent has done that
wakens such remorse within him, we find that he seems
merely to feel that in some way he has failed to please God,
no matter how. He experiences misfortune, whether of disease, or ill-luck, or defeat, and is sure that this must be due
to some offense. He does not know what this may be. It may
have been that he has failed to repeat a formula in the right
manner; it is all one. He feels guilty and even exaggerates
his own guilt in view of the punishment which has befallen
him. Job's three friends apply the same logic to his case.[3]

But side by side with the conception that the laws of
Jehovah must be obeyed because they were his commands,
there was another doctrine which was but an extension of
the theory that the people had freely accepted their ruler.
This was that Jehovah's commands were not arbitrary. They
were right; they could be placed before the people for their
approval; they were "life"; "the judge of all the earth" would
"do right." We have here a striking illustration of the principle that moral standards, at first embodied in persons,
slowly work free, so that persons are judged by them.

3. *The Cultus as Morally Symbolical.* — The elaborate
cultus carried on by the priests, symbolized, however imperfectly, certain moral ideas. The solicitous care for cere-

3. The general function of punishment as bringing home to the individual the consciousness of guilt and thus awakening the
   action of conscience, has an illustration in Shakespere's conception of the prayer of Henry Vth before the battle of Agin-
   court. In ordinary life the bluff King Harry devotes little time to
   meditation upon his own sin or that of his father, but on the
   eve of possible calamity the old crime rises fresh before 'him.
   Stimulated by the thought of an actual penalty to be imposed
   by a recognized authority, he cried: "Not to-day, O Lord! Oh,
   not to-day! Think not upon the fault my father made in com-
   passing the crown."

monial "purity" might have no direct moral value; the contamination from contact with birth or death or certain
animals might be a very external sort of "uncleanness."
Nevertheless, they emphasized in the most forcible manner
a constant control over conduct by a standard which was set
by a divine law. The "holiness" of the priests, as set apart to
special service of Jehovah, emphasized the seriousness of
their work; and further, it contributed to that distinction between spiritual and material, between higher and lower,
which is a part of moral life. Moreover, while part of this
value inheres in all ritual, the contrast between Jehovah's
worship and that of other deities challenged moral attention.
The gods of the land, the various Baals, were worshipped
"upon every high hill and under every green tree." As gods
of fertility, they were symbolized by the emblems of sex,
and great freedom prevailed at their festivals. At certain
shrines men and women gave themselves for the service of
the god. The first-born children were not infrequently sacrificed.[4] These festivals and shrines seem to have been adopted
more or less fully by Israel from the Canaanites, but the
prophets have an utterly different idea of Jehovah's worship. The god of Sinai rejects utterly such practices. License
and drunkenness are not, as the cultus of Baal and Astarte
implied, the proper symbols of life and deity. The sensual
cannot fitly symbolize the spiritual.

Moreover, one part of the cultus, the "sin offering,"
directly implied transgression and the need of forgiveness.
The "sins" might themselves be ceremonial rather than
moral, and the method of removing them might be external—
especially the process of putting the sins upon a scapegoat
which should "bear upon him all their iniquities into a soli-
tary land,"—nevertheless, the solemn confession, and the
shedding of the blood which was the "life," could not but
remind of responsibility and deepen reflection. The need of
atonement and reconciliation, thus impressed, symbolized
the moral process of reconstructing, of putting away a lower
past, and readjusting life to meet an ideal.

4. Recent excavations are held to confirm the prophets on this
(Marti, *Religion of the Old Testament*, pp. 78 ff.).

4. The Prophets as a Moral Force.—The prophets were by far the most significant moral agency in Israel's religion. In the first place, they came to the people bearing a message from a living source of authority, intended for the immediate situation. They brought a present command for a present duty. "Thou art the man," of Nathan to David, "Hast thou killed, and also taken possession?" of Elijah to Ahab, had personal occasions. But the great sermons of Amos, Isaiah, Jeremiah, were no less for the hour. A licentious festival, an Assyrian invasion, an Egyptian embassy, a plague of locusts, an impending captivity—these inspire demand for repentance, warnings of destruction, promises of salvation. The prophet was thus the "living fountain." The divine will as coming through him "was still, so to speak, fluid, and not congealed into institutions."

In the second place, the prophets seized upon the inward purpose and social conduct of man as the all-important issues; cultus, sacrifice, are unimportant. "I hate, I despise your feasts, and I will take no delight in your solemn assemblies," cries Amos in Jehovah's name, "But let justice roll down as waters and righteousness as a mighty stream." "I have had enough of the burnt offerings of rams, and the fat of fed beasts," proclaims Isaiah, "new moons, and sabbaths, the calling of assemblies,—I cannot away with iniquity and the solemn meeting." You need not ceremonial, but moral, purity. "Wash you, make you clean; put away the evil of your doings;—seek justice, relieve the oppressed, judge the fatherless, plead for the widow." Micah's "Shall I give my first-born for my transgression, the fruit of my body for the sin of my soul?" seized upon the difference once for all between the physical and the moral; a completely ethical standpoint is gained in his summary of religious duty: "What doth God require of thee, but to do justly, and to love mercy, and to walk humbly with thy God?" And the New Testament analogue marks the true ethical valuation of all the external religious manifestations, even of the cruder forms of prophecy itself. Gifts, mysteries, knowledge, or the "body to be burned"—there is a more excellent way than these. For all these are "in part." Their value is but temporary and relative. The values that abide, that stand criticism, are that staking of oneself upon the truth and worth of one's ideal which is faith; that aspiration and forward look which is hope; that sum of all social charity, sympathy, justice, and active helpfulness, which is love. "But the greatest of these is love."

5. *The Religious View of the Kingdom Gave the Setting for a Social Ideal.*—Jehovah was the king of his people. The human ruler in Jerusalem was his representative. The kingdom of Israel was under divine care and had on the other hand a serious purpose. The expansion and glory of the kingdom under Solomon showed the divine favor. Division and calamity were not mere misfortunes, or the victory of greater armies; they were divine rebukes. Only in righteousness and justice could the nation survive. On the other hand, the confidence in Jehovah's love for Israel guaranteed that he would never forsake his people. He would purify them and redeem them even from the grave. He would establish a kingdom of law and peace, "an everlasting kingdom that should not be destroyed." Politics in Israel had a moral goal.

6. *Religion Gave the Problem of Evil a Moral Significance.*—The Greek treatment of the problem of evil is found in the great tragedies. An ancestral curse follows down successive generations, dealing woe to all the unhappy house. For the victims there seems to be nothing but to suffer. The necessity of destiny makes the catastrophe sublime, but also hopeless. Ibsen's *Ghosts* is conceived in a similar spirit. There is a tremendous moral lesson in it for the fathers, but for the children only horror. The Greek and the Scandinavian are doubtless interpreting one phase of human life—its continuity and dependence upon cosmical nature. But the Hebrew was not content with this. His confidence in a divine government of the world forced him to seek some moral value, some purpose in the event. The search led along one path to a readjustment of values; it led by another path to a new view of social interdependence.

The book of Job gives the deepest study of the first of these problems. The old view had been that virtue and happiness always went together. Prosperity meant divine favor, and therefore it must be the good. Adversity meant divine punishment; it showed wrongdoing and was itself an evil.

When calamity comes upon Job, his friends assume it to be
a sure proof of his wickedness. He had himself held the same
view, and since he refuses to admit his wickedness and
"holds fast to his integrity," it confounds all his philosophy
of life and of God. It compels a "reversal and revaluation of
all values." If he could only meet God face to face and have
it out with him he believes there would be some solution. But
come what may, he will not sell his soul for happiness. To
"repent," as his friends urge, in order that he may be again
on good terms with God, would mean for him to call sin
what he believes to be righteousness. And he will not lie in
this way. God is doubtless stronger, and if he pursues his
victim relentlessly, may convict him. But be this as it may,
Job will not let go his fundamental consciousness of right
and wrong. His "moral self" is the one anchor that holds, is
the supreme value of life.

> As God liveth, who hath taken away my right,
> And the Almighty who hath vexed my soul;
> Surely my lips shall not speak unrighteousness.
> Till I die, I will not put away my integrity from me,
> My righteousness I hold fast, and will not let it go.[5]

Another suggestion of the book is that evil comes to prove
man's sincerity: "Does Job serve God for naught?" and from
that standpoint the answer is, Yes; he does. "There is a disinterested love of God."[6] In this setting, also, the experience
of suffering produces a shifting of values from the extrinsic
to the internal.

The other treatment of the problem of suffering is found
in the latter half of Isaiah. It finds an interpretation of the
problem by a deeper view of social interdependence, in which
the old tribal solidarity is given, as it were, a transfigured
meaning. The individualistic interpretation of suffering was
that it meant personal guilt. "We did esteem him stricken of
God." This breaks down. The suffering servant is not wicked.
He is suffering for others—in some sense. "He hath borne our
griefs and carried our sorrows." The conception here reached
of an interrelation which involves that the suffering of the

5. Job 27:1–6.
6. Genung, *The Epic of the Inner Life.*

good may be due to the sin or the suffering of others, and that the assumption of this burden marks the higher type of ethical relation, is one of the finest products of Israel's religion. As made central in the Christian conception of the Cross, it has furnished one of the great elements in the modern social consciousness.

§ 3. *The Moral Conceptions Attained*

The moral conceptions which were thus worked out may now be brought together for convenient summary under the two heads of the "How" and the "What" indicated in our introductory chapter. Under the first we specify the conceptions resulting (1) from recognition of a standard of right, and an ideal of good, (2) from free choice of this ideal. Under the What we indicate the content of the ideal on both its personal and its social sides.

1. *Righteousness and Sin.*—Righteousness and sin were not exact or contradictory opposites. The righteous man was not necessarily sinless. Nevertheless, the consciousness of sin, like a dark background, brought out more emphatically the conception of righteousness. This conception had its two aspects, derived from the civil and the religious spheres of life—spheres which were not separate for the Hebrew. On the one hand, the just or righteous respected the moral order in human society. The unrighteous was unjust, extortionate, cruel. He did not respect the rights of others. On the other hand, the righteous man was in "right" relation to God. This right relation might be tested by the divine law; but as God was conceived as a living person, loving his people, "forgiving iniquity, transgression, and sin," it might also be measured by an essential harmony of spirit with the divine will. There was the "righteousness of the law," and the "righteousness of faith." The first implies complete obedience; the second implies that in spite of transgressions there is room for atonement[7] or reconciliation. As the first means ethically the testing of conduct by a moral standard, a

---

7. See *Atonement in Literature and Life*, by Charles A. Dinsmore, Boston, 1906.

"moral law," so the second stands for the thought that character is rather a matter of spirit and of constant reconstruction than of exact conformity once for all to a hard and fast rule. Specific acts may fail to conform, but the life is more than a series of specific acts. The measurement of conduct by the law has its value to quicken a sense of shortcoming, but alone it may also lead either to self-righteous complacency or to despair. The possibility of new adjustment, of renewal, of "a new birth," means liberation and life. As such it may be contrasted with the Buddhist doctrine of Karma, the causality from which there is no escape but by the extinction of desire.

"Sin" had likewise its various aspects. It stood for missing the mark, for violating the rules of clean and unclean; but it stood also for personal disobedience to the divine will, for violation of the moral order of Israel. In this latter sense, as identified by the prophets with social unrighteousness, it is a significant ethical conception. It brings out the point that evil and wrongdoing are not merely individual matters, not merely failures; they offend against a law which is above the private self, against a moral order which has its rightful demands upon us.

2. *Personal Responsibility.*—The transition from group to individual responsibility was thoroughly worked out by the prophets, even if they were not able to carry full popular assent. In early days the whole kin was treated as guilty for the offense of the kinsman. Achan's case has already been cited; and in the case of Korah, Dathan, and Abiram, "Their wives and their sons and their little ones" were all treated alike.[8] In like manner, the family of the righteous man shared in the divine favor. The later prophets pronounced a radical change. The proverb, "The fathers have eaten sour grapes and the children's teeth are set on edge," is no more to be used, declares Ezekiel, speaking for Jehovah. "The soul that sinneth, it shall die; the son shall not bear the iniquity of the father, neither shall the father bear the iniquity of the son"; and it is especially interesting to note that the Lord is represented as pleading with the people that this is fair, while the people say, "Wherefore doth not the son bear the

8. Numbers 16; Joshua 7.

iniquity of the father?" The solidarity of the family resisted the individualism of the prophetic conception, and five hundred years after Ezekiel the traces of the older conception still lingered in the question, "Who did sin, this man or his parents, that he was born blind?"[9] For another aspect of responsibility, viz., intent, as distinct from accidental action,[10] we have certain transitional steps shown in the interesting "cities of refuge"[11] for the accidental homicide in which he might be safe from the avenger of blood, provided he was swift enough of foot to reach a city of refuge before he was caught. But the fullest development in the ethics of responsibility along this line seemed to take the form described under the next head.

3. *Sincerity, and Purity of Motive.*—The Hebrew had a philosophy of conduct which made it chiefly a matter of "wisdom" and "folly," but the favorite term of prophet and psalmist to symbolize the central principle was rather "the heart." This term stood for the voluntary disposition, especially in its inner springs of emotions and sentiments, affections and passions. The Greek was inclined to look askance at this side of life, to regard the emotions as perturbations of the soul, and to seek their control by reason, or even their repression or elimination. The Hebrew found a more positive value in the emotional side of conduct, and at the same time worked out the conception of a sincere and thoroughgoing interest as lying at the very root of all right life. The religious influence was as elsewhere the important agency. "Man looketh on the outward appearance, but Jehovah looketh on the heart," "If I regard iniquity in my heart, Jehovah will not hear me," are characteristic expressions. A divine vision, which penetrates to the deepest springs of purpose and feeling, will not tolerate pretense. Nor will it be satisfied with

9. John 9:2.
10. Hammurabi's code showed a disregard of intent which would make surgery a dangerous profession: "If a physician operate on a man for a severe wound with a bronze lancet and cause the man's death; or open an abscess [in the eye] of a man with a bronze lancet and destroy the man's eye, they shall cut off his fingers." Early German and English law is just as naïve. If a weapon was left to be repaired at a smith's and was then caught up or stolen and used to do harm, the original owner was held responsible.
11. Numbers 35; Deuteronomy 19; Joshua 20.

anything less than entire devotion: the Israelite must serve
Jehovah with all his heart. Outer conformity is not enough:
"Rend your heart and not your garments." It is the "pure in
heart" who have the beatific vision. Not external contacts,
or ceremonial "uncleanness," on which earlier ritual had insisted, defile the man, but rather what proceeds from the
heart. For the heart is the source of evil thoughts and evil
deeds.[12] And conversely, the interests, the emotions, and
enthusiasms which make up the man's deepest self do not
spring forth in a vacuum; they go with the steadfast purpose
and bent, with the self of achievement. "Where your treasure
is, there will your heart be also."

Purity of motive in a full moral consciousness means
not only (formal) sincerity, but sincere love of good and
right. This was not stated by the Hebrew in abstract terms,
but in the personal language of love to God. In early days
there had been more or less of external motives in the appeals of the law and the prophets. Fear of punishment, hope
of reward, blessings in basket and store, curses in land and
field, were used to induce fidelity. But some of the prophets
sought a deeper view, which seems to have been reached in
the bitterness of human experience. Hosea's wife had for-
saken him, and should not the love of people to Jehovah be
as personal and sincere as that of wife to husband? She had
said, "I will go after my lovers *that give me my bread and
my water, my wood and my flax, my oil and my drink.*"[13] Is
not serving God for hire a form of prostitution?[14] The calamities of the nation tested the disinterestedness of its fidelity.
They were the challenge of the Adversary, "Doth Job fear
God for naught?" And a remnant at least attested that
fidelity did not depend on rewards. The moral maxim that
virtue is its own reward is put in personal terms by the
prophet after the exile:

> For though the fig tree shall not blossom, neither shall fruit
> be in the vines; the labor of the olive shall fail, and the fields
> shall yield no meat; the flock shall be cut off from the fold, and
> there shall be no herd in the stalls: Yet I will rejoice in the
> Lord, I will joy in the God of my salvation.[15]

12. Mark 7:1-23.
13. Hosea 2:5.
14. H. P. Smith, *Old Testament History*, p. 222.
15. Habakkuk 3:17-18.

4. *The Conception of "Life" as an Ideal.* — The content of Israel's moral ideal on its individual side was expressed by the term "Life." All the blessings that the leader of Israel could offer his people were summarized in the phrase, "I have set before you life and death; wherefore choose life." The same final standard of value appears in the question of Jesus, "What shall it profit a man to gain the whole world and lose his own life?" When we inquire what life meant, so far as the early sources give us data for judgment, we must infer it to have been measured largely in terms of material comfort and prosperity, accompanied by the satisfaction of standing in right relations to the god and ruler. This latter element was so closely united with the first that it was practically identical with it. If the people were prosperous they might assume that they were right; if they suffered they were surely wrong. Good and evil were, therefore, in this stage, measured largely in terms of pleasure and pain. The end to be sought and the ideal to be kept in mind was that of long and prosperous life — "in her right hand length of days, in her left hand riches and honor." Intellectual and aesthetic interests were not prized as such. The knowledge which was valued was the wisdom for the conduct of life, of which the beginning and crown was "the fear of the Lord." The art which was valued was sacred song or poetry. But the ideal values which came to bulk most in the expanding conception of "life" were those of personal relation. Family ties, always strong among Oriental peoples, gained in purity. Love between the sexes was refined and idealized.[16] National feeling took on added dignity, because of the consciousness of a divine mission. Above all, personal union with God, as voiced in the psalms and prophets, became the desire. He, and not his gifts, was the supreme good. He was the "fountain of life." His likeness would satisfy. In his light the faithful would see light.

But even more significant than any specific content put into the term "life," was *what was involved in the idea itself.* The legalists had attempted to define conduct by a code, but there was an inherent vitality in the ideal of life, which refused to be measured or bounded. The "words of eternal life,"

16. The Song of Songs.

which began the new moral movement of Christianity, had
perhaps little definite content to the fishermen, and it is not
easy to say just what they meant in moral terms to the writer
of the Fourth Gospel who uses the phrase so often. With
Paul, life as the realm of the spirit gets definition as it
stands over against the "death" of sin and lust. But with all
writers of Old or New Testament, whatever content it had,
life meant above all the suggestion of something beyond, the
gleam and dynamic power of a future not yet understood. It
meant to Paul a progress which was governed not by law or
"rudiments," but by freedom. Such a life would set itself new
and higher standards; the laws and customs that had obtained were felt to be outgrown. The significance of early
Christianity as a moral movement, aside from its elements of
personal devotion and social unity to be noticed below, was
the spirit of movement, the sense of newly forming horizons
beyond the old, the conviction that as sons of God its followers had boundless possibilities, that they were not the
children of the bond woman, but of the free.

5. *The Social Ideal of Justice, Love, and Peace.*—We
have seen how this ideal was framed in the setting of a kingdom of God. At first national, it became universal, and with
a fraternity which the world is far from having realized, it
was to know "neither Jew nor Greek, bond nor free." At first
military, it took on with seer and psalmist the form of a reign
of peace and justice. After the fierce and crude powers typi-
fied by the lion and the bear and the leopard had passed, the
seer saw a kingdom represented by a human form. Such a
kingdom it was that should not pass away. Such was the
kingdom "not of this world" which Jesus presented as his
message. Membership in this moral kingdom was for the
poor in spirit, the pure in heart, the merciful, the peace-
makers, the hungerers after righteousness. Greatness in this
moral community was to depend on service, not on power.
The king should not fail till he had "set justice in the earth."
He should "deliver the needy, and the poor."

Certain features of this ideal order have since found
embodiment in social and political structures; certain features remain for the future. Certain periods in history have
transferred the ideal entirely to another world, regarding

human society as hopelessly given over to evil. Such theories find a morality possible only by renouncing society. The Hebrews presented rather the ideal of a moral order on earth, of a control of all life by right, of a realization of good, and of a completeness of life. It was an ideal not dreamed out in ecstatic visions of pure fancy, but worked out in struggle and suffering, in confidence that moral efforts are not hopeless or destined to defeat. The ideal order is to be made real. The divine kingdom is to come, the divine will to be done *"on earth* as it is in heaven."

Literature

The works of W. R. Smith (*Religion of the Semites*) and Barton (*A Sketch of Semitic Origins*) already mentioned. Schultz, *Old Testament Theology*, tr. 1892; Marti, *Religion of the Old Testament*, tr. 1907; Budde, *Religion of Israel to the Exile*, 1898–99; H. P. Smith, *Old Testament History*, 1903; W. R. Smith, *The Prophets of Israel*, 1895; Bruce, *Ethics of the Old Testament*, 1895; Peake, *Problem of Suffering in the Old Testament*, 1904; Royce, "The Problem of Job" in *Studies of Good and Evil*, 1898; Pratt, *The Psychology of Religious Belief*, 1907, ch. v; Harnack, *What Is Christianity?* tr. 1901; Cone, *Rich and Poor in the New Testament*, 1902; Pfleiderer, *Primitive Christianity*, tr. 1906; Matthews, *The Social Teaching of Jesus*, 1897; Wendt, *The Teaching of Jesus*, 1892–99; Pfleiderer, *Paulinism*, 1873; Cone, *Paul, The Man, the Missionary, and the Teacher*, 1898; Beyschlag, *New Testament Theology*, tr. 1895; The *Encyclopedia Biblica*, The *Jewish Encyclopedia*, and Hastings's *Dictionary*, have numerous valuable articles.

§ 1. The Fundamental Notes

Convention versus Nature.—The Hebrew moral life was
developed under the relation, first of the people, then of the
individuals, to God,—a relation at once of union and of conflict. It was out of the relation of the individual to social
traditions and political order that the Greek came to full
consciousness of moral law on the one hand, and a moral
personality on the other. And just as in Jewish life the law
and the prophets (or, later, the "law and the gospel") stood
for the conflicting forces, so in Greek life the opposition between the authority of the group, embodied in custom and
institutions, on the one hand, and the urging claims of developing personality, manifest in both intelligence and desire, on the other, found expression in contrasted terms. The
authority of the group embodied in customs and institutions,
came to be regarded by the radicals as relatively external,
artificial, and rigid. It was dubbed "convention," or "institution" (*thesis*, what is set up). The rapidly developing intelligence challenged the merely customary and traditional;
the increasing individuality challenged the superior authority of the group, especially when this manifested itself apparently in a government of force. Personal intelligence and
personal feeling asserted a more elemental claim, felt themselves rooted in a more original source, and called this source
"nature" (*physis*). Social tradition and authority, individual
reason and feeling, thus confronted each other as "convention" and "nature." It was a struggle which has its analogy
in the development of many a young man or young woman
who is emerging from parental control to self-direction. But
in Greek life more distinctly than elsewhere we see the steps
of the process as a civic and not merely an individual development. Aeschylus, Sophocles, and Euripides presented

this conflict of the individual with law or destiny as the great, oft-repeated tragedy of human life. Aristophanes mocked with bitter satire the "new" views. Socrates, Plato, Aristotle, Cynics, Cyrenaics, Epicureans, and Stoics took part in the theoretical discussions.

Measure.—The fundamental note of all Greek life, before, during, and after this development, was *Measure, Order, Proportion.* This note found expression in religion, science, art, and conduct. Among their gods, the Greeks set Moira, "Destiny," and Themis, "Custom," "Law," "Right." They found order in the universe, which on this account they called the "cosmos." They expressed it in their arts, especially in architecture, sculpture, the choral dance, and the more highly developed tragedy or lyric: "And all life is full of them [of form and measure]," says Plato,

as well as every constructive and creative art. And surely the art of the painter and every other creative and constructive art are full of them,—weaving, embroidery, architecture, and every kind of manufacture; also nature, animal and vegetable,—in all of them there is grace or the absence of grace; and if our youth are to do their work in life, must they not make these graces and harmonies their perpetual aim?

The best people, the "gentlemen," were styled kaloikagathoi—"fair and good." The motto at the Delphic shrine was, "Nothing in excess." Insolent disregard of propriety, "hybris," was the quality most denounced by the early moralizing poets. Tityus, Tantalus, and Sisyphus, the three special subjects of divine punishment, suffered the penalty of insatiate desire, or limits overstepped. And after criticism and individualism had done their work, Plato's conception of justice, Aristotle's doctrine of the "mean," the Stoic maxim of "life according to nature," have but discovered a deeper significance for the fundamental law of Greek life.

The Good and the Just.—The conceptions of the Good and the Just are developed from the two notes just presented. The motive for challenge to established institutions was the awakening desire of the individual to seek his own good, and to live his own life. Commerce was bringing a great variety of rewards to the shrewd merchant and a great variety of goods to evoke and gratify wants. Slavery set free the citizen from the need of manual labor and gave him leisure to cultivate his tastes. The forces of individualism, described in Chapter 5, were all at work to bring the process and object of desire to consciousness. Moreover, the term "good" was also in use to mark the popular ideal. It was applied to what we should call the "successful" men of the day. In present life our term "good" has become so definitely moral that probably most young persons would hesitate to say that they have it as their ideal to become good, although few would hesitate to say that they wish to be capable and successful. For social and political recognition seems to be based rather on achievement of striking results than upon what is technically called "goodness." But in Greece moral goodness was not used to designate "character" as contrasted with "results." The "good man" was like the "good lawyer" or "good athlete" or "good soldier," the man who was efficient and conspicuous. It was in the process which we are to trace that the ambiguities and deeper meanings of the term came to definition.

The terms Just and Justice were not of course merely synonyms for order and measure. They had likewise the social significance coming from the courts and the assembly. They stood for the control side of life, as Good stood for its aspect of valuation and desire. But as compared with the Hebrew conception of righteousness, they meant much less a conformity to a law divine or human which had been already set up as standard, and much more, an ordering, a regulating, a harmonizing. The rational element of measure or order was more prominent than the personal note of authority. Hence we shall find Plato passing easily back and forth between justice or order in the individual and justice or order in the State. On the other hand, the radicals of the day could seize upon the legal usage and declare that Justice or the Law was purely a matter of self-interest or class interest.

§ 2. Intellectual Forces of Individualism

The Scientific Spirit.—The older standards were embodied in religious and political ideas and institutions; the agency which was to disentangle and bring into clear consciousness the standards *as such*, was the scientific spirit, the knowledge and reflection of an intellectual people at a period of extraordinarily rapid development. The commercial life, the free intercourse with other peoples and civilizations, especially in the colonies, the absence of any generally dominating political authority, the architectural problems suggested by a beauty-loving people,—all promoted alertness and flexibility of mind.

In a concrete form, this rational character had already found expression in the quality of Greek art. Reference has already been made to the formal side of Greek art, with its embodiment of rhythm and measure; the subject-matter shows the same element. The Greek world, as contrasted with the barbarian world, was conceived by the Greek as the realm of light contrasted with darkness; the national God, Apollo, embodied this ideal of light and reason, and his fitting symbol was the sun. The great Pan-Athenaic procession, as reproduced in the Parthenon frieze, celebrated the triumph of Greek light and intelligence over barbarian darkness. Athena, goddess of wisdom, was a fitting guardian of the most Greek of all Greek cities. Greek tragedy, beginning in hymns of worship, soon passed over into a portrayal of the all-controlling laws of life, as these are brought into stronger relief by a tragic collision with human agents.

It was, however, in the realm of science that this intellectual genius found field for expression in a clearly conscious manner. Almost all our sciences were originated by the Greeks, and they were particularly successful in those which called for abstract thinking in the highest degree. Euclid's geometry and Aristotle's logic are conspicuous illustrations of this ability. The most general conceptions of natural science: e.g., the conception of the atom and the whole materialistic theory of the universe; the conception of evolution, meaning by this the process of change according to an all-controlling law; the conception of natural selection, according to which those organisms survive which are fitted for their environment,—all these were the product of the keen intelligence of the Greeks. Nor was their scientific ability expended upon external nature alone. The conception of history as more than a series of events, the comparative method in the study of political systems, the analysis of

literary and artistic effects, attest the same clarity of mind
and the same eager search for the most general laws of
every aspect of experience.

Science and Religion.—When, now, this scientific mind
began to consider the practical guidance of life, the older
political and religious controls presented serious difficulty.
The gods were supposed to reward the good and punish the
evil,[1] but how could this be reconciled with their practices?
Aeschylus attempted a purifying and elevating of the divine
ideal, similar to that which Israel's conception underwent in
the work of the prophets. He magnified the dignity and
providential government of Zeus, which, though dark, is yet
just and certain. But the great obstacle was that the earlier
and cruder conceptions of the gods had been fixed in literary
form; the tales of Cronos's impiety to Uranos, of Zeus' deceitful messenger and marital unfaithfulness, of Aphrodite's
amours, and Hermes' gift of theft, were all written in Hesiod
and Homer. The cruder conceptions of the gods had thus
become too firmly fixed in the popular imagination to be
capable of becoming the bearers of advancing ethical ideals,
and so not merely the irreverent scoffer, but the serious
tragedian, Euripides, and the religious idealist, Plato, do not
hesitate to challenge boldly the older conceptions, or to demand a revision of all this literature before it comes into the
hands of the young.

Social Standards.—The social standards of propriety
and honorable conduct were likewise brought in question by
advancing intelligence. The word which summed up the early
Greek idea of the best type was *Kalokagathos*. This word was
very nearly the equivalent of our English word "gentleman."
It combined the elements of birth, ability, and refinement,
but in the earlier usage the emphasis was upon the fact of
birth, even as our terms "generous," "noble," "gentle," orig-

1. Cf. Xenophon's account of the impressive appeal of Clearchus:
"For, first and greatest, the oaths which we have sworn by the
gods forbid us to be enemies to each other. Whoever is conscious
of having transgressed these,—him I could never deem happy.
For if one were at war with the gods, I know not with what
swiftness he might flee so as to escape, or into what darkness he
might run, or into what stronghold he might retreat and find
refuge. For all things are everywhere subject to the gods, and
the gods rule all everywhere with equity."—Xenophon, *Anabasis*,
II, ch. v.

inally referred to membership in a "gens." Socrates investigated the current estimates and found that the people who were generally regarded as the "respectable," or, as we should say, the "best" people of Athens, were not necessarily either "fine" or "good" in person or character; the term had come to be one of "convention," without basis in reason. Plato goes still further and with a direct application of the rational standard to the current estimates, pokes fun at the conventional judgment of what constitutes the respectable gentleman.

When they sing the praises of family and say that some one is a gentleman because he has had seven generations of wealthy ancestors, he [the philosopher] thinks that their sentiments only betray the dullness and narrowness of vision of those who utter them, and who are not educated enough to look at the whole, nor to consider that every man has had thousands and thousands of progenitors, and among them have been rich and poor, kings and slaves, Hellenes and barbarians, many times over. And when some one boasts of a catalogue of twenty-five ancestors, and goes back to Heracles, the son of Amphitryon, he cannot understand his poverty of ideas. Why is he unable to calculate that Amphitryon had a twenty-fifth ancestor, who might have been anybody, and was such as fortune made him, and he had a fiftieth, and so on? He is amused at the notion that he cannot do a sum, and thinks that a little arithmetic would have got rid of his senseless vanity.

The type of life that is really noble or fine and good is to be found in the seeker for true beauty and goodness. External beauty of form and appearance has its value in kindling the desire for the higher forms of beauty,—beauty of mind, of institutions and laws, of science,—until finally the conception of the true beauty is reached. This true beauty, as distinct from the particular beauties, and true good, as distinct from seeming or partial good, are discovered only by the "philosopher," the seeker for wisdom.

Popular Morals.—Nor did the more positively recognized types of moral excellence fare better. As recognized in common life, they were courage, prudence or moderation, holiness or a certain respect for the serious things of life, and justice; but none of these, Plato argues, is really an independent excellence, apart from conscious and intelligent action. Courage, for example, is not really courage unless one knows and foresees the danger in all its strength; otherwise there is merely reckless bravery. Prudence or moderation, to be really excellent, must be measured by wisdom. Even justice cannot be regarded as at bottom distinct from wisdom, the true measure of all the relations of life.

Science and the Laws.—The political control was likewise involved in question by the same forces of intelligence which had challenged the religious authority. The frequent changes of government, and the more or less arbitrary measures that were oftentimes adopted, were adapted to awaken doubt as to the absolute right and authority of the laws. The despot who gained control in many a Greek city was not bound by ties of blood to all members of the community, nor did he govern in accordance with the ancestral traditions of the tribe. The political authority frequently clashed with the instincts and traditions of family and kinship. Under such circumstances, the political authority was likely to be challenged and its constraining power stretched to the breaking point. So in the *Antigone* of Sophocles, the command of the ruler is opposed to the "higher law" of kinship and nature. The law of man is not the law of nature or of God. To disobey this conventional law of man is to be guilty of "holiest crime." The old standards, both of religion and of political life, crumbled before the analysis of the developing intelligence, and the demand for some standard could be met only by the intelligence itself. To question the old must inevitably seem irreverent and anarchical. Some questioned merely to doubt; others, and of these Socrates was the leader, questioned in order to find a firmer basis, a more authoritative standard. But naturally the popular mind did not distinguish between these two classes of questioners, and so Socrates perished, not merely as the victim of unjust popular calumny, but as the victim of the tragedy of moral progress, of the change from the established to the new.

§ 3. *Commercial and Political Individualism*

A further line of development joined forces with this growth of intelligence, to emphasize the problem of moral control, and to set the individual with his standards over against the objective standards of society. This was the rapidly growing consciousness of individual goods and interests. The commercial life, with its possibilities of individual property, the rapid changes of political life, with the rise of individuals to power and privilege, the increasing opportunities which a high civilization brought both men and women for personal enjoyment and gratification of rapidly increasing wants, all tended to make the individual seek his own good, and to shift the emphasis of life from the question, What is proper, or honorable? to the question, What is *good* —good for *me*?

Class Interests.—The conviction that the authority of government and law was largely dictated by the very considerations of private interests which they were supposed to overrule and eliminate, made the situation more acute. For the Greek States were no longer groups with common interests. The growth of capital, the corresponding eagerness for gain, the formation of distinct classes, each intent on its interests, supplanted the older, more homogeneous State. "The whole development of the political life of the Hellenic republics depended ultimately on the decision of the question, which of the different social classes—the capitalistic minority, the middle class, or the poor—should obtain the dominant place." Aristotle defines an oligarchy as a State governed in the interest of the rich; a democracy, as a State governed in the interest of the poor. Another contemporary writer explains a democracy as consulting the interests of the democrats, the "lower classes," and considers this a matter of course, "for if the rich had the say, they would do what was good for themselves but not for the multitude." Naturally such dominance by classes called out vigorous criticisms upon the laws and standards so established. The aristocratic minority inveighed against "custom" or conventions which would tame the strong to the level of the weak. Nature demands rather the "survival of the fittest," i.e., of the strong. The enlightened spectator of the game of government, on the other hand, declares that all laws are made in the interest of ruling classes. The reader of current criticisms on laws and courts will see how close is the parallel to present complaints.

We have to-day the same two classes: One inveighs against governmental interference with the right to combine, to contract, and in general to get from the earth or from men, women, and children all that superior power and shrewdness can possibly extract. The other complains that legislatures are owned by wealth, that judges are appointed from corporation lawyers, that common law is a survival of ancient aristocratic status, and that for these reasons labor can get no justice.

Let us first hear the plea for inequality:

> Custom and nature are generally at variance with one another; . . . for by the rule of nature, that only is the more disgraceful which is the greater evil; as, for example, to suffer injustice; but by the rule of custom, to do evil is the more disgraceful. For this suffering of injustice is not the part of a man, but of a slave, who indeed had better die than live; for when he is wronged and trampled upon, he is unable to help himself or any other about whom he cares. The reason, as I conceive, is that the makers of laws are the many weak; and they make laws and distribute praises and censures with a view to themselves and their own interests; and they terrify the mightier sort of men, and those who are able to get the better of them, in order that they may not get the better of them; and they say that dishonesty is shameful and unjust; meanwhile, when they speak of injustice, they desire to have more than their neighbors, for knowing their own inferiority, they are only too glad of equality. And therefore, this seeking to have more than the many is conventionally said to be shameful and unjust, and is called injustice, whereas nature herself intimates that it is just for the better to have more than the worse, the more powerful than the weaker; and in many ways she shows, among men as well as among animals, and indeed among whole cities and races, that justice consists in the superior ruling over and having more than the inferior. For on what principle of justice did Xerxes invade Hellas, or his father the Scythians? (not to speak of numberless other examples). They, I conceive, act according to nature; yes, and according to the law of nature; not perhaps, according to that artificial law which we frame and fashion, taking the best and strongest of us from their youth upwards, and taming them like young lions, and charming them with the sound of the voice, saying to them that with equality they must be content, and that this is the honorable and the just. But if there were a man who had sufficient force, he would shake off and break through and escape from all this; he would trample under foot all our formulas and spells and charms, and all our

laws, sinning against nature; the slave would rise in rebellion and be lord over us, and the light of natural justice would shine forth. And this I take to be the lesson of Pindar, in the poem in which he says that

"Law is the King of all, mortals as well as immortals!"

This, as he says:

"Makes might to be right, and does violence with exalted hand; as I infer from the deeds of Heracles, for without buying them——"

I do not remember the exact words, but the meaning is, that he carried off the oxen of Geryon without buying them, and without their being given to him by Geryon, according to the law of natural right, and that the oxen and other possessions of the weaker and inferior properly belong to the stronger and superior. (Plato, *Gorgias*, §§ 482–84.)

The essence of this view is, therefore, that might is right, and that no legislation or conventional code ought to stand in the way of the free assertion of genius and power. It is similar to the teaching of Nietzsche in recent times.

But the other side had its complaint also. The laws are made by the "shepherds" of the people, as Homer called them. But who is now so simple as to suppose that the "shepherds" fatten or tend the sheep with a view to the good of the sheep, and not to their own good? All laws and governments really exist for the interest of the ruling class.[2] They rest upon convention or "institution," not upon "nature."

Why Obey Laws? — And if laws and social codes are but class legislation, conventional, why obey them? The older Greek life had felt the motives described in Chapter IV, though it had embodied them in symbolism and imagery. The Nemesis that followed the guilty, the Erinyes, or avenging goddesses, were the personified wrath of outraged law; *aidōs*, respect or reverence, *aischyne*, regard for public opinion, were the inner feelings. But with the advancing tide of intellectual criticism and individual interest, these sanctions were discredited; feelings of personal enjoyment demanded recognition, and the moralists at first appealed to this. "Parents and tutors are always telling their sons and their wards that they are to be just; but only not for the sake

2. Plato, *Republic*, I, § 343.

of justice, but for the sake of character and reputation." But if the only reason for justice is reputation, there might seem to be no sufficient reason for taking the thorny path, if there be an easier. Will not the youth say, in the words of Pindar:

"Can I by justice, or by crooked ways of deceit, ascend a loftier tower which may be a fortress to me all my days?"[3]

And if I decide that the crooked way is the easier, why shall I not follow it? My party, or my "union," or my lawyer will stand by and see me through:

But I hear some one exclaiming that the concealment of wickedness is often difficult; to which I answer, Nothing great is easy. Nevertheless, the argument indicates this, if we would be happy, to be the path along which we should proceed. With a view to concealment we will establish secret brotherhoods and political clubs. And there are professors of rhetoric who teach the art of persuading courts and assemblies; and so, partly by persuasion and partly by force, I shall make unlawful gains and not be punished. Still I hear a voice saying that the gods cannot be deceived, neither can they be compelled. But what if there are no gods? or, suppose them to have no care of human things, why in either case should we mind about concealment?[4]

Besides, the greatest prizes, not only in material goods, but even in the line of reputation, seemed to fall to the individualist if he could only act on a sufficiently large scale. He could then be both prosperous and "respectable." If he could steal the government, or, in modern phrase, bribe a legislature to elect him to Congress, pass special legislation, or grant a franchise, he could not merely escape punishment, but be honored by his fellows.

I am speaking of injustice on a large scale, in which the advantage of the unjust is most apparent, and my meaning will be most clearly seen in that highest form of injustice, the perpetrator of which is the happiest of men, as the sufferers of these who refuse to do injustice are the most miserable—I mean tyranny which by fraud and force takes away the property of others, not retail but wholesale; comprehending in one things sacred as well as profane, private and public, for any one of

3. Plato, *Republic*, II, § 365.
4. Plato, *Republic*, II, § 365.

which acts of wrong, if he were detected perpetrating them singly, he would be punished and incur great dishonor; for they who are guilty of any of these crimes in single instances are called robbers of temples and man-stealers and burglars and swindlers and thieves. But when a man has taken away the money of the citizens and made slaves of them, then instead of these dishonorable names, he is called happy and blessed, not only by the citizens but by all who hear of his having achieved the consummation of injustice. For injustice is censured because the censurers are afraid of suffering, and not from any fear which they have of doing injustice. And thus, as I have shown, Socrates, injustice, when on a sufficient scale, has more strength and freedom and mastery than justice; and, as I said at first, justice is the interest of the stronger, whereas injustice is a man's own profit and interest.[5]

§ 4. *Individualism and Ethical Theory*

The Question Formulated.—The outcome of this first movement was thus twofold: (a) It forced the questions, "What is just?" "What is good?" into clear and definite consciousness. The very necessity of comparison and of getting a *general standard*, forced the inquirer to disentangle the concepts previously embodied in customs and laws. But when the essence was thus found and freed, or disembodied, as it were, the custom seemed lifeless, merely "convention," and the essence often quite opposed to the form. (b) It emphasized the *personal interest*, the affective or emotional side of conduct, and made the moral problem take the form, "What is the good?"

Furthermore, two positive theses have been established by the very forces which have been active in disintegrating the old status. If custom no longer suffices, then reason must set the standard; if society cannot prescribe the good to the individual, then the individual must find some method of defining and seeking it for himself unless he is to make shipwreck of his whole venture.

We may bring both aspects of the problem under the conception of "nature," as opposed to convention or institu-

---

5. Plato, *Republic*, I, § 343 f.

tion. Convention is indeed outgrown, nature is the imperious authority. But granting that nature is rightful master, is "nature" to be sought in the primitive beginnings, or in the fullest development? in a life of isolation, or in a life of society? in the desires and passions, or in reason and a harmonious life?

Or, stating the same problem otherwise: granting that reason must fix the measure, and the individual must define and seek the good for himself, is the good to be found in isolation, or is it to be sought in human society with its bonds of family, friendship, and justice? Is the end to be pleasure, found in the gratification of desires, irrespective of their quality, and is it the business of reason merely to measure one gratification with another and get the most? or is wisdom itself a good, and is it better to satisfy certain impulses rather than others? i.e., shall reason form the standard as well as apply it?

These contrasting solutions of the problem of life may be stated then under the two pairs of antitheses: (1) The Individual *versus* the Social; (2) The Immediate Satisfaction *versus* an Ideal Standard, at once higher and more permanent.

Typical Solutions.—Poets, radicals, sensualists, individualists of no philosophic school, as well as the historic philosophic schools, contributed to the discussion and solution of these problems. All sought the "natural" life; but it is noteworthy that all the philosophic schools claimed Socrates as their master, and all sought to justify their answers by reason, all made the wise man the ideal. The Cynics and Cyrenaics, Stoics and Epicureans, Plato and Aristotle represent the various philosophic answers to these alternatives. Cynics and Cyrenaics both answer (1) by individualism, but diverge on (2), the Cynics placing emphasis on independence from wants, the Cyrenaics on gratification of wants. Stoics and Epicureans represent broader and more social development of the same principles, the Stoics seeking a cosmopolitan state, the Epicureans a community of friends; the Stoics emphasizing reason or wisdom as the only good; the Epicureans finding for wisdom a field in the selection of refined pleasures. Plato and Aristotle, with varying emphasis but essential agreement, insist (1) that the good of man is found in fulfilling completely his highest possible functions, which is possible only in society; (2) that wisdom is not merely to apply a standard but to form one; that while neither reason alone nor feeling alone is enough for life, yet that pleasure is rather for life than life for pleasure. Finally, Plato, Aristotle and the Stoics, as well as the tragic poets, contribute successively to the formation of an ideal of responsible character.

Early Individualistic Theories.—Cynics and Cyrenaics were alike individualists. Society, they held, is artificial. Its so-called goods, on the one hand, and its restrictions on the other, are to be rejected unless they favor the individual's happiness. Independence was the mark of wisdom among the Cynics; Antisthenes, proud of the holes in his garment; Diogenes, dwelling in his tent or sleeping in the street, scoffing at the current "conventions" of decency, asking from Alexander only that he would get out of his sunshine—are the characteristic figures. The "state of nature" was opposed to the State. Only the primitive wants were recognized as natural. "Art and science, family and native land, were indifferent. Wealth and refinement, fame and honor, seemed as superfluous as those enjoyments of the senses which went beyond the satisfaction of the natural wants of hunger and sex."

The Cyrenaics, or hedonists (*hēdonē*, pleasure), gave a different turn to wisdom. The good is pleasure, and wisdom is found in that prudence which selects the purest and most intense. Hence, if this is the good, why should a man trouble himself about social standards or social obligations? "The hedonists gladly shared the refinement of enjoyment which civilization brought with it; they found it convenient and permissible that the intelligent man should enjoy the honey which others prepared; but no feeling of duty or thankfulness bound them to the civilization whose fruits they enjoyed. Sacrifice for others, patriotism, and devotion to a general object, Theodorus declared to be a form of foolishness which it did not become the wise man to share."[6]

6. Windelband, *History of Philosophy*, p. 86.

§ 5. *The Deeper View of Nature and the Good; of the Individual and the Social Order*

Value of a State.—Plato and Aristotle take up boldly the challenge of individualism. It may indeed be granted that existing states are too often ruled by classes. There are oligarchies in which the soldier or the rich control for their own interests; there are tyrannies in which the despot is greed and force personified; there are democracies (Plato was an aristocrat) in which the mob bears rule, and those who flatter and feed its passions are in authority. But all these do but serve to bring out more clearly the conception of a true State, in which the rule is by the wisest and best and is not for the interest of a class, but for the welfare of all. Even as it was, the State of Athens in Plato's day—except when it condemned a Socrates—meant completeness and freedom of life. It represented not merely a police force to protect the individual, but stood for the complete organization of all the life which needs cooperation and mutual support. The State provided instruction for the mind and training for the body. It surrounded the citizen with an atmosphere of beauty and provided in the tragedy and comedy opportunities for every citizen to consider the larger significance of life or to join in the contagious sympathy of mirth. In festivals and solemn processions it brought the citizen into unity of religious feeling. To be an Athenian citizen meant to share in all the higher possibilities which life afforded. Interpreting this life, Aristotle proclaims that it is not in isolation, but in the State, that "the goal of full independence may be said to be first attained."

The Natural.—Aristotle goes directly to the heart of the problem as to what is natural by asserting that nature is not to be found in the crude beginning, but rather in the complete development. "The nature of anything, e.g., of a man, a horse, or a house, may be defined to be its condition when the process of production is complete." Hence the State "in which alone completeness of life is attained" is in the highest sense natural:

The object proposed or the complete development of a thing is its highest good; but independence which is first attained in the State is a complete development or the highest good and is therefore natural.

For as the State was formed to make life possible, so it exists to make life good.

Thus we see that the State is a natural institution, that man is naturally a political animal and that one who is not a citizen of any State, if the cause of his isolation be natural and not accidental, is either a superhuman being or low in the scale of human civilization, as he stands alone like a "blot" on the backgammon board. The "clanless, lawless, heartless man," so bitterly described by Homer, is a case in point, for he is naturally a citizen of no state and a lover of war.[7]

Nor does Aristotle stop here. With a profound insight into the relation of man to society, and the dependence of the individual upon the social body, a relation which modern social psychology has worked out in greater detail, Aristotle asserts that the State is not merely the goal of the individual's development, but the source of his life.

Again, in the order of nature the State is prior to the household or individual. For the whole must needs be prior to its part. For instance, if you take away the body which is the whole, there will not remain any such thing as a hand or foot, unless we use the same word in a different sense, as when we speak of a stone hand as a hand. For a hand separated from the body will be a disabled hand; whereas it is the faculty or function of a thing which makes it what it is, and therefore when things lose their function or faculty, it is not correct to call them the same things, but rather homonymous, i.e., different things having the same name. We see, then, the State is a natural institution, and also that it is prior to the individual. For if the individual as a separate unit is not independent, he must be a part and must bear the same relation to the State as the other parts to their wholes; and one who is incapable of association with others or is independent and has no need of such association, is no member of a State; in other words, he is either a brute or a God.[8]

And, moreover, when we look into the nature of the individual, we do not find him a being devoid of the sympathies and qualities which find their natural expression not only in the State, but in various social and friendly relations. There is "an impulse toward the life in common" (φιλία) which expresses itself in friendship, but which is

---

7. Aristotle, *Politics*, Book I, ii, Welldon's translation.
8. Aristotle, *Politics*, Book I, ii, Welldon's translation.

also so essential to that recognition of others called justice that we may say "it is the most just of all just things." There is also a unity of disposition and purpose (ὁμόνοια) which may be called "political friendship."[9]

Plato's Ideal State.—How then is the State constituted and governed which is to provide for man's full development, his complete good? Evidently two principles must control. In the first place, it must be so constituted that every man may develop in it the full capacities of his nature, and thereby serve at once the perfection of the State and his own completeness; and in the second place, the State or social whole must be ruled by those best fitted for this work. Not the soldier, nor the plutocrat, nor the artisan, but the man who knows, is the suitable ruler for our ideal community. The soldier may defend, the artisan may support, but the scientific or intelligent man should rule. And it is evident that in settling this principle, we have also answered our first problem; for the soldier and the artisan will find his full development by doing the work which he can do well, not by meddling with a task in which he must necessarily fail. In order to guard against the greed which was so characteristic of the governments of his day, Plato would provide that the rulers and warriors should have no private property, and not even private families. Their eye should be single to the good of the whole. When asked as to the practicability of a State governed by such disinterested rulers, and with such wisdom, he admits indeed its difficulty, but he stoutly demands its necessity:

Until philosophers are kings, or the kings and princes of this world have the spirit and power of philosophy, and political greatness and wisdom meet in one, and those commoner natures who pursue either to the exclusion of the other are compelled to stand aside, cities will never have rest from their evils,—no, nor the human race, as I believe,—and then only will this our State have a possibility of life and behold the light of day.[10]

And yet the question of the actual existence of a perfect State is not the question of supreme importance. For Plato has grasped the thought that man is controlled not only by

9. Aristotle, *Ethics*, Book VIII, i; Book IX, vi.
10. Plato, *Republic*, V, § 473.

what he sees, but by what he images as desirable. And if a man has once formed the image of an ideal State or city of this kind, in which justice prevails, and life reaches fuller and higher possibilities than it has yet attained, this is the main thing:

> In heaven, there is laid up a pattern of it, methinks, which he who desires may behold, and beholding, may set his own house in order. But whether such an one exists, or ever will exist in fact, is no matter: for he will live after the manner of that city, having nothing to do with any other.[11]

The Social as Law of Nature.—The social nature of man, thus vindicated by Plato and Aristotle, remained as the permanent possession of Greek thought. Even the Epicureans, who developed further the hedonistic theory of life, emphasized the values of friendship as among the choicest and most refined sources of pleasure. The Stoics, who in their independence of wants took up the tradition of the Cynics, were yet far from interpreting this as an independence of society. The disintegration of the Greek states made it impossible to find the social body in the old city-state, and so we find with the Stoics a certain cosmopolitanism. It is the highest glory of man to be a citizen not of Athens but of the universe,—not of the city of Cecrops, but of the city of Zeus. And through this conception the social nature of man was made the basis of a "natural law," which found its expression in the principles of Roman and modern jurisprudence.

Passion or Reason.—In answering the question as to the true nature of man, Plato and Aristotle found the suggestions likewise for the problem of individual good. For if the soldier as the seeker for fame and honor, the avaricious man embodying the desire for wealth, and still more, the tyrant personifying the unbridled expression of every lust and passion, are abhorrent, is it not easy to see that an orderly and harmonious development of impulses under the guidance and control of reason, is far better than that uncramped expression of desires and cravings for which some of the radical individualists and sensualists of the day

11. Plato, *Republic*, IX § 592.

werę clamoring? As representative of this class, hear Callicles:

"I plainly assert that he who would truly live ought to allow his desires to wax to the uttermost, and not to chastise them; but when they have grown to their greatest, he should have courage and intelligence to minister to them and to satisfy all his longings. And this I affirm to be natural justice and nobility." The temperate man is a fool. It is only in hungering and eating, in thirsting and drinking, in having all his desires about him, and gratifying every possible desire, that man lives happily.[12]

But even Callicles himself admits that there are certain men, the creatures of degraded desire, whose lives are not ideal, and hence that there must be some choice of pleasure. And carrying out in the individual life the thought above suggested by the State, Plato raises the question as to whether man, a complex being, with both noble and ignoble impulses, and with the capacity of controlling reason, can be said to make a wise choice if he lets the passions run riot and choke out wholly his rational nature:

Is not the noble that which subjects the beast to the man, or rather to the god in man; and the ignoble that which subjects the man to the beast? He can hardly avoid admitting this,—can he now? Not if he has any regard for my opinion. But, if he admits this, we may ask him another question: How would a man profit if he received gold and silver on the condition that he was to enslave the noblest part of him to the worst? Who can imagine that a man who sold his son or daughter into slavery for money, especially if he sold them into the hands of fierce and evil men, would be the gainer, however large might be the sum which he received? And will any one say that he is not a miserable caitiff who sells his own divine being to that which is most atheistical and detestable and has no pity? Eriphyle took the necklace as the price of her husband's life, but he is taking a bribe in order to compass a worse ruin.[13]

Necessity of a Standard for Pleasure.—If, for the moment, we rule out the question of what is noble or "kalon," and admit that the aim of life is to live pleasantly, or if, in other words, it is urged as above that justice is not profitable

---

12. Plato, *Gorgias*, § 491 ff.
13. Plato, *Republic*, IX, § 589 f.

and that hence he who would seek the highest good will seek it by some other than the thorny path, we must recognize that the decision as to which kind of pleasure is preferable will depend on the character of the man who judges:

> Then we may assume that there are three classes of men, —lovers of wisdom, lovers of ambition, lovers of gain? Exactly. And there are three kinds of pleasure, which are their several objects? Very true. Now, if you examine the three classes and ask of them in turn which of their lives is pleasantest, each of them will be found praising his own and deprecating that of others; the money-maker will contrast the vanity of honor or of learning with the solid advantages of gold and silver? True, he said. And the lover of honor,—what will be his opinion? Will he not think that the pleasure of riches is vulgar, while the pleasure of learning, which has no need of honor, he regards as all smoke and nonsense? True, he said. But may we not suppose, I said, that philosophy estimates other pleasures as nothing in comparison with knowing the truth, and in that abiding, ever learning, in the pursuit of truth, not far indeed from the heaven of pleasure? The other pleasures the philosopher disparages by calling them necessary, meaning that if there were no necessity for them, he would not have them. There ought to be no doubt about that, he replied. Since, then, the pleasure of each class and the life of each is in dispute, and the question is not which life is most honorable, or better or worse, but which is the more pleasant or painless,—how shall we know? I cannot tell, he said. Well, but what ought to be the criterion? Is any better than experience and wisdom and reason? There cannot be a better, he said. If wealth and gain were the criterion, then what the lover of gain praised and blamed would surely be the truest? Assuredly. Or if honor or victory or courage, in that case the ambitions or contentments would decide best? Clearly. But since experience and wisdom and reason are the judges, the inference of course is, that the truest pleasures are those which are approved by the lover of wisdom and reason.[14]

It is thus evident that even if we start out to find the good in pleasure, we need some kind of measuring art. We need a "standard for pleasure," and this standard can be found only in wisdom. And this forces us to maintain that wisdom is after all *the* good. Not merely intellectual attainment—a life of intellect without feeling would be just as

14. Plato, *Republic*, IX, § 581 f.

little a true human life as would the life of an oyster, which
has feeling with no intelligence. A life which includes
sciences and arts, and the pure pleasures of beauty, presided
over by wisdom and measure and symmetry,—this is Plato's
vision of the life of the individual, viewed from within.

Eudaimonism.—Aristotle's conception of the good is
fundamentally the same. It is a full development of man's
capacities, culminating in a rational and harmonious life.
If, says Aristotle, we are to find the ultimate good, we must
try to find, if possible, some one end which is pursued as an
end in itself, and never as a means to something else, and
the most general term for this final end is "eudaimonia," or
well-being, "for we also choose it for itself and never for the
sake of something else." What is the essence of well-being?
This, according to Aristotle, is to be found by asking what
is the function of man. The life of nutrition and growth
man has in common with the plants; the life of sense in
common with the animal. It is in the life of his rational
nature that we must find his especial function. "The good
of man is exercise of his faculties in accordance with their
appropriate excellence." External goods are valuable because
they may be instruments toward such full activity. Pleasure
is to be valued because it "perfects the activities, and therefore perfects life, which is the aim of human desire"—rather
than valued as an end in itself. No one would choose to live
on condition of having a child's intellect all his life, though
he were to enjoy in the highest possible degree all the
pleasures of a child.[15]

The "Mean."—The crowning importance of wisdom as
the rational measure of the ideal life is also illustrated in
Aristotle's theory of excellence (or virtue) as a "mean." This
phrase is somewhat ambiguous, for some passages would
seem to indicate that it is merely striking an average between
two kinds of excesses, and finding, as it were, a moderate
amount of feeling or action; but there is evidently involved
here just the old thought of measure, and "the mean is what
right reason prescribes." It is not every one who can find
the mean, but only he who has the requisite knowledge.

15. Aristotle, *Ethics*, Book X, ii–iv.

The supreme excellence or virtue is, therefore, the wisdom which can find the true standard for action.[16]

The Wise Man.—Finally the conception of virtue as wisdom is illustrated in the ideals of the three prominent schools in later Greek thought,—the Sceptics, Epicureans, and Stoics. The wise man among Sceptics is he who suspends judgment where it is impossible to be certain. The wise man among Epicureans is he who chooses the finest and surest and most lasting pleasures. The wise man among Stoics is he who overcomes his emotions. But in every case the ideal is expressed in the same phrase, "the wise man."

Man and the Cosmos.—We see thus how Greek thought, starting out to challenge all society's laws and standards and bring them to the bar of knowledge, has found a deeper value and higher validity in the true social and moral order. The appeal was to the Caesar of reason, and reason taken in its full significance carries us beyond the immediate and transient to the broader and more permanent good. Nor can reason in its search for good be content, urges Plato, with the superficial facts of life and society. He who would find and achieve his complete function, his full development, must broaden his horizon still further. As his own particular life is but a part of the ongoing of the larger world, whose forces act upon him, limit him, and determine his possibili-

---

16. Among the various types of excellence which Aristotle enumerates as exemplifying this principle, the quality of high-mindedness ($\mu\epsilon\gamma\alpha\lambda o\psi v\chi i a$) is preeminent, and may be taken as embodying the trait most prized in an Athenian gentleman. The high-minded man claims much and deserves much; lofty in his standard of honor and excellence he accepts tributes from good men as his just desert, but despises honor from ordinary men or on trivial grounds; good and evil fortune are alike of relatively small importance. He neither seeks nor fears danger; he is ready to confer favors and forget injuries, slow to ask favors or cry for help; fearless in his love and hatred, in his truth and his independence of conduct; "not easily moved to admiration, for nothing is great to him. He loves to possess beautiful things that bring no profit, rather than useful things that pay; for this is characteristic of the man whose resources are in himself. Further, the character of the high-minded man seems to require that his gait should be slow, his voice deep, his speech measured; for a man is not likely to be in a hurry when there are few things in which he is deeply interested, nor excited when he holds nothing to be of very great importance; and these are the causes of a high voice and rapid movements" (*Ethics*, Book IV, iii, 29–34).

ties, it becomes absolutely necessary to study not merely his own end and purpose, but the end and purpose of the universe. Human good requires us to know the larger good, *the* Good, in the full and complete sense. And this perfect Good which is, in truth, the very essence of the universe, is but another term for God, and Plato often uses the two as interchangeable terms.

So the "Nature" which Greek life was seeking gets its deepest signiffcance and reinterprets the old religious demand for unity of the life of man with the forces of the unseen. And the Stoic later, in his maxim "Follow Nature," gives more explicit recognition to the return of the circle. For the great work of Greek science had brought out into complete clearness the idea of Nature as a system of law. The universe is a rational universe, a cosmos, and man, as above all else a rational being, finds thus his kinship to the universe. To follow Nature, therefore, means to know the all-pervading law of Nature and submit to it in calm acceptance or resignation.

"All is harmonious to me that is harmonious to thee, O universe; all is fruit to me which thy seasons bring."[17]

§ 6. *The Conception of the Ideal*

Contrast of Actual and Ideal.—The two stages of Greek thought which we have sketched did more than to readjust Greek life to deeper views of the State and the individual; of the good and of nature. The very challenge and process brought into explicit consciousness a new feature of the moral life, which is fundamental to true moral consciousness, viz., the factor of contrast between the actual and the ideal. We have seen that the clash of one-sided interests and political institutions and, in the case of Plato, the tragic execution of Socrates, obliged Plato and Aristotle to admit that the actual State did not subserve the real purpose which they were forced to seek in social organization. Both Plato and Aristotle, therefore, draw the picture of a State that

17. Marcus Aurelius, *Thoughts*, IV, § 23.

should serve the complete purposes of human development. And again, in the individual life, both the conception of the development of man's highest possibilities and the conception of a measure or standard for the conflicting desires and purposes lead on to a conception which shall embody not merely the existing status but the goal of yet unrealized purpose.

The Ideal as the True Reality.—Various qualities and aspirations are embodied by Plato in this conception, and with characteristic Greek genius he has given to this conception of the ideal almost as concrete and definite a form as the Greek sculptor of Apollo gave to his ideal of light and clarity, or the sculptor of Aphrodite to the conception of grace. As contrasted with the flux of transient emotions, or the uncertain play of half-comprehended or futile goods, this ideal good is conceived as eternal, unchanging, ever the same. It is superhuman and divine. As contrasted with various particular and partial goods on which the sons of men fix their affections, it is the one universal good which is valid for all men everywhere and forever. In his effort to find suitable imagery for this conception, Plato was aided by the religious conceptions of the Orphic and Pythagorean societies, which had emphasized the preexistence and future existence of the soul, and its distinction from the body. In its previous life, said Plato, the soul has had visions of a beauty, a truth, and a goodness of which this life affords no adequate examples. And with this memory within it of what it has looked upon before, it judges the imperfect and finite goods of this present world and longs to fly away again and be with God. This thought of contrast between ideal and actual, to which Plato in some of his writings gave the turn of a contrast between soul and body, passed on with increased emphasis into Stoic and later Platonist schools, and furnished a philosophic basis for the dualism and asceticism which is found in Hellenistic and mediaeval morality.

Ethical Significance.—While the true ethical contrast between the actual and the ideal was thus shifted over into a metaphysical contrast between soul and body, or between what is fixed and what is changing, the fundamental thought is highly significant, for it merely symbolizes in objective form the characteristic of every moral judgment, viz., the testing and valuing of an act by some standard, and what is even more important, the forming of a standard by which to do the testing. Even Aristotle, who is frequently regarded as the mere describer of what is, rather than the idealistic portrayer of what ought to be, is no less insistent upon the significance of the ideal. In fact, his isolation of reflection or *theoria* from the civic virtues was used by the mediaeval church in its idealization of the "contemplative life." Like Plato, he conceives the ideal as a divine element in human nature:

> Nevertheless, instead of listening to those who advise us as men and mortals not to lift our thoughts above what is human and mortal, we ought rather, as far as possible, to put off our mortality and make every effort to live in the exercise of the highest of our faculties; for though it be but a small part of us, yet in power and value it far surpasses all the rest.[18]

§ 7. *The Conception of the Self;*
of Character and Responsibility

The Poets.—Out of the fierce competition of individual desires, the clashing of individual ambitions, the conflict between the individual and the state, and the deepening of the conception of the individual's "nature," emerged also another conception of fundamental importance for the more highly developed reflective moral life, viz., that of the moral personality, its character and its responsibility. We may trace the development of this conception through the poets, as well as in the philosophers. Aeschylus set man over against the gods, subject to their divine laws, but gave little play to human character or conscious self-direction. With Sophocles, the tragic situation was brought more directly into the field of human character, although the conception of destiny and the limitations marked thereby were still the dominant note. With Euripides, human emotions and character are brought into the foreground. Stout-heartedness, the high spirit that can endure in suffering or triumph in death, which shows

18. Aristotle, *Ethics*, Book X, vii, 8.

not merely in his heroes but in the women, Polyxena and Medea, Phaedra and Iphigenia, evinces the growing consciousness of the self—a consciousness which will find further development in the proud and self-sufficient endurance of the Stoic. In more directly ethical lines, we find increasing recognition of the self in the motives which are set up for human action, and in the view which is formed of human character. Conscience in the earlier poets and moralists, was largely a compound of Nemesis, the external messenger and symbol of divine penalty, on the one hand, and Aidos, the sense of respect or reverence for public opinion and for the higher authority of the gods, on the other. But already in the tragedians we find suggestions of a more intimate and personal conception. Pains sent by Zeus in dreams may lead the individual to meditate, and thus to better life. Neoptolemus, in Sophocles, says,

> All things are noisome when a man deserts
> His own true self and does what is not meet.

and Philoctetes replies,

> Have mercy on me, boy, by all the gods,
> And do not shame thyself by tricking me.

The whole *Antigone* of Sophocles is the struggle between obedience to the political rulers and obedience to the higher laws which as "laws of reverence" become virtually inner laws of duty:

> I know I please the souls I ought to please.

Plato.—Here, as in the formulation of his conception of the ideal, religious imagery helped Plato to find a more objective statement for the conception of a moral judgment and a moral character. In the final judgment of the soul after death, Plato sees the real self stripped bare of all external adornments of beauty, rank, power, or wealth, and standing as naked soul before the naked judge, to receive his just reward. And the very nature of this reward or penalty shows the deepening conception of the self, and of the intrinsic nature of moral character. The true penalty of injustice is not to be found in anything external, but in the very fact that the evildoers become base and wicked:

They do not know the penalty of injustice, which above all things they ought to know,—not stripes and death, as they suppose, which evil doers often escape, but a penalty which cannot be escaped.

THEOD. What is that?

Soc. There are two patterns set before them in nature; the one blessed and divine, the other godless and wretched; and they do not see, in their utter folly and infatuation, that they are growing like the one and unlike the other, by reason of their evil deeds; and the penalty is that they lead a life answering to the pattern which they resemble.[19]

The Stoics.—It is, however, in the Stoics that we find the conception of inner reflection reaching clearest expression. Seneca and Epictetus repeat again and again the thought that the conscience is of higher importance than any external judgment,—that its judgment is inevitable. In these various conceptions, we see attained the third stage of Adam Smith's description of the formation of conscience.[20] Man who read his duty at first in the judgments of his fellows, in the customs and laws and codes of honor, and in the religious precepts of the gods, has again come to find in gods and laws, in custom and authority, the true rational law of life; but it is now a law of self. Not a particular or individual self, but a self which embraces within it at once the human and the divine. The individual has become social and has recognized himself as such. The religious, social, and political judgments have become the judgments of man upon himself. "Duty," what is binding or necessary, takes its place as a definite moral conception.

===

Literature

Besides the writings of Plato (especially, the *Apology, Crito, Protagoras, Gorgias,* and *Republic*), Xenophon (*Memorabilia*), Aristotle (*Ethics, Politics*), Cicero (*On Ends, Laws, Duties; On the Nature of the Gods*), Epictetus, Seneca, M. Aurelius, Plutarch,

19. Plato, *Theaetetus,* § 176.
20. Smith held that we (1) approve or disapprove the conduct of others; (2) see ourselves as others see us, judging ourselves from their standpoint; (3) finally, form a true social standard, that of the "impartial spectator." This is an inner standard—conscience.

and the fragments of various Stoics, Epicureans, and Sceptics, the tragedies of Aeschylus, Sophocles, and Euripides, and the comedies of Aristophanes (especially the *Clouds*) afford valuable material.

All the histories of philosophy treat the theoretical side; among them may be mentioned Gomperz (*Greek Thinkers*, 1901–5); Zeller (*Socrates; Plato; Aristotle; Stoics, Epicureans, and Sceptics*); Windelband; Benn (*Philosophy of Greece*, 1898, chs. i, v).

On the Moral Consciousness: Schmidt, *Ethik der alten Griechen*, 1882. On the social conditions and theories: Pöhlmann, *Geschichte des antiken Kommunismus und Sozialismus*, 1893–1901; Döring, *Die Lehre des Sokrates als sociales Reformsystem*, 1895. On the religion: Farnell, *Cults of the Greek States*, 4 vols., 1899–1907; Rohde, *Psyche*, 1894.

On Political Conditions and Theory: Newman, Introduction to *Politics of Aristotle*, 1887; Bradley, "Aristotle's Conception of the State" in *Hellenica*; Wilamowitz-Moellendorff, *Aristoteles und Athen*, 1893.

On Nature and Law of Nature: Ritchie, *Natural Rights*, 1895; Burnet, *International Journal of Ethics*, VII, 1897, pp. 328–33; Hardy, *Begriff der Physis*, 1884; Voigt, *Die Lehre vom jus naturale*, 1856.

General: Denis, *Histoire des théoriés et des idées morales dans l'antiquité*, 1879; Taylor, *Ancient Ideals*, 1900; Caird, *Evolution of Theology in the Greek Philosophers*, 1904; Janet, *Histoire de la science politique dans ses rapports avec la morale*, 1887; Grote, *History of Greece*, 4th ed., 1872, *Plato and the Other Companions of Sokrates*, 1888.

8. THE MODERN PERIOD

The moral life of the modern western world differs from both Hebrew and Greek morality in one respect. The Hebrews and Greeks were pioneers. Their leaders had to meet new situations and shape new conceptions of righteousness and wisdom. Modern civilization and morality, on the other hand, received certain ideals and standards already worked out and established. These came to it partly through the literature of Hebrews, Greeks, and Latins, partly through Greek art and Roman civilization, but chiefly, perhaps, through two institutions: (1) Roman government and law embodied Stoic conceptions of a natural law of reason and of a world state, a universal rational society. This not only gave the groundwork of government and rights to the modern world; it was a constant influence for guiding and shaping ideas of authority and justice. (2) The Christian Church in its cathedrals, its cloisters, its ceremonials, its orders, and its doctrines had a most impressive system of standards, valuations, motives, sanctions, and prescriptions for action. These were not of Hebrew origin solely. Greek and Roman philosophy and political conceptions were fused with more primitive teaching and conduct. When the Germans conquered the Empire they accepted in large measure its institutions and its religion. Modern morality, like modern civilization, shows the mingled streams of Hebrew, Greek, Roman, and German or Celtic life. It contains also conceptions due to the peculiar industrial, scientific, and political development of modern times. Thus we have to-day such inherited standards as that of "the honor of a gentleman" side by side with the modern class standard of business honesty, and the labor union ideal of class solidarity. We have the aristocratic ideals of chivalry and charity side by side with more democratic standards of domestic and social justice. We find the Christian equal standard for the two sexes side by side with another which sets a high value on woman's chastity, but a trivial value on man's. We find a certain ideal of self-sacrifice side by side with an ideal of "success" as the only good. We cannot hope to disentangle all the threads that enter this variegated pattern, or rather collection of patterns, but we can point out certain features that at the same time illustrate certain general lines of development. We state first the general attitude and ideals of the Middle Ages, and then the three lines along which individualism has proceeded to the moral consciousness of to-day.

§ 1. The Mediaeval Ideals

The mediaeval attitude toward life was determined in part by the character of the Germanic tribes with their bold, barbaric strength and indomitable spirit, their clan and other group organizations, their customs or mores belonging to such a stock; and in part by the religious ideals presented in the church. The presence of these two factors was manifest in the strong contrasts everywhere present.

Associated with mail-clad knights whose trade is war and whose delight is to combat are the men whose sacred vocation forbids the use of force altogether. Through lands overspread with deeds of violence, the lonely wayfarer with the staff and badge of a pilgrim passes unarmed and in safety. In sight of castles, about whose walls fierce battles rage, are the church and the monastery, within the precincts of which quiet reigns and all violence is branded as sacrilege.[1]

The harsh clashes of the Venus music over against the solemn strains from the Pilgrim's Chorus in Tannhäuser might well symbolize not only the specific collision of the opera but the broader range of passions opposed to the religious controls and values in this mediaeval society.

The Group and Class Ideal.—The early Germans and Celts in general had the clan system, the group ideals, and group virtues which belonged to other Aryan peoples, but the very fact of the Germanic victories shows a military spirit

1. Fisher, *History of the Christian Church*, p. 227.

which included both personal heroism and good capacity for organization. Group loyalty was strong, and the group valuation of strength and courage was unbounded. A high value was also set on woman's chastity. These qualities, particularly the loyalty to the clan and its head, survived longest in Celtic peoples like the Scots and Irish who were not subjected to the forces of political organization. Every reader of Scott is familiar with the values and defects of the type; and the problems which it causes in modern democracy have been acutely described by Jane Addams.[2] Among the Germanic peoples, when the clan and tribal systems were followed by the more thoroughgoing demarcation of classes, free and serfs, lords and villains, chevalier or knight, and churl, the old Latin terms "gentle" and "vulgar" found a fitting application. The term "gentle" was indeed given in one of its usages the force of the kindred term "kind" to characterize the conduct appropriate within the kin, but in the compound "gentleman" it formed one of the most interesting conceptions of class morality. The "honor" of a gentleman was determined by what the class demanded. Above all else the gentleman must not show fear. He must be ready to fight at any instant to prove his courage. His word must not be doubted. This seems to have been on the ground that such doubt would be a refusal to take the man at his own estimate, rather than because of any superlative love of truth, for the approved way to prove the point at issue was by fighting, not by any investigation. But the class character appears in the provision that no insult from one of a lower class need be noticed. Homicide was not contrary to the character and honor of a gentleman. Nor did this require any such standard in sex relations as a "woman's honor" requires of a woman. In conduct toward others, the "courtesy" which expresses in ceremony and manner respect for personal dignity was a fine trait. It did not always prevent insolence toward inferiors, although there was in many cases the feeling, *noblesse oblige*. What was needed to make this ideal of gentleman a moral and not merely a class ideal,

2. Addams, *Democracy and Social Ethics*, pp. 222–77; *Newer Ideals of Peace*, ch. v.

was that it should base treatment of others on personal worth rather than on birth, or wealth, or race, and that it should not rate reputation for courage above the value of human life. This has been in part effected, but many traits of the old conception live on to-day.

The Ideal of the Church.—The ideal of life which the church presented contained two strongly contrasting elements, which have been frequently found in religion and are perhaps inevitably present. On the one hand, a spiritual religion implies that man in comparison with God is finite, weak, and sinful; he should therefore be of "a humble and contrite heart." On the other hand, as a child of God he partakes of the divine and is raised to infinite worth. On the one hand, the spiritual life is not of this world and must be sought in renouncing its pleasures and lusts; on the other hand, if God is really the supreme governor of the universe, then this world also ought to be subject to his rule. In the mediaeval view of life, the humility and withdrawal from the world were assigned to the individual; the sublimity and the ruling authority to the church. Ethically this distribution had somewhat the effect of group morality in that it minimized the individual and magnified the corporate body of which he was a part. Asceticism and humility go hand in hand with the power of the hierarchy. Individual poverty—wealth of the church; individual meekness and submission—unlimited power and authority in the church; these antitheses reflect the fact that the church was the heir both of a kingdom of God and of a Roman Empire. The humility showed itself in extreme form in the ascetic type of monasticism with its vows of poverty, chastity, and obedience. It was reflected in the art which took for its subjects the saints, conceived not individually, but typically and according to tradition and authority. Their thin attenuated figures showed the ideal prescribed. The same humility showed itself in the intellectual sphere in the preeminence given to faith as compared with reason, while the mystic losing himself in God showed yet another phase of individual renunciation. Even charity, with which the church sought to temper the hardship of the time, took a form which tended to maintain or even applaud the dependent attitude of the recipient. So far as life for

the individual had a positive value, this lay not in living
oneself out, but rather in the calm and the support afforded
by the church:

> A life in the church, for the church, through the church; a
> life which she blessed in mass at morning and sent to peaceful
> rest by the vesper hymn; a life which she supported by the con-
> stantly recurring stimulus of the sacraments, relieving it by con-
> fession, purifying it by penance, admonishing it by the presenta-
> tion of visible objects for contemplation and worship—this was
> the life which they of the Middle Ages conceived of as the right-
> ful life of man; it was the actual life of many, the ideal of all.[3]

On the other side, the church boldly asserted the right
and duty of the divine to control the world,—the religious
symbol of the modern proposition that conscience should
dominate political and business affairs. "No institution is
apart from the authority of the church," wrote Aegidius
Colonna. "No one can legitimately possess field or vine
except under its authority or by it. Heretics are not owners,
but unjustly occupy." Canossa symbolized the supremacy of
the spiritual over the temporal power, and there is a sublime
audacity, moral as well as political, in the famous Bull of
Boniface VIII, "We declare that every human creature is
subject to the Roman pontiff."

The church as a corporate society expressed also the
community of its members. It was indeed no mere collection
of individual believers. As a divine institution, the "body of
Christ on earth," it gave to its members rather than received
from them. It invested them with new worth, instead of
getting its own worth from them. Nevertheless, it was not an
absolute authority; it represented the union of all in a common fellowship, a common destiny, and a common cause
against the powers of evil.

The massive cathedrals which remain as the monuments of the ages of faith, are fitting symbols of these
aspects of mediaeval life. They dominate their cities archi-
tecturally, as the church dominated the life of the ages which
built them. They inspired within the worshipper, on the one
hand, a sense of finiteness in the presence of the sublime;

---

3. Bryce, *Holy Roman Empire*, p. 367.

on the other, an elevation of soul as he became conscious of union with a power and presence not his own. They awed the worshiping assembly and united it in a common service.

§ 2. *Main Lines of Modern Development*

We have seen that the mediaeval life had two sets of standards and values: one set by the tribal codes and the instinct of a warlike people; the other set by a church which required renunciation while it asserted control. Changes may be traced in both ideals. The group morality becomes refined and broadened. The church standards are affected in four ways: (a) The goods of the secular life, art, family, power, wealth, claim a place in the system of values. (b) Human authority asserts itself, at first in sovereign states with monarchs, then in the growth of civil liberty and political democracy. (c) Instead of faith, reason asserts itself as the agency for discovering the laws of nature and of life. (d) As the result of the greater dignity and worth of the individual which is worked out in all these lines, social virtue tends to lay less value on charity and more on social justice.

It must not be supposed that the movements to be outlined have resulted in the displacement or loss of the positive values in the religious ideal. The morality of to-day does not ignore spiritual values; it aims rather to use them to give fuller meaning to all experience. It does not abandon law in seeking freedom, or ignore duty because it is discovered by reason. Above all, it is seeking to bring about in more intimate fashion that supremacy of the moral order in all human relations for which the church was theoretically contending. And in recent times we are appreciating more thoroughly that the individual cannot attain a full moral life by himself. Only as he is a member of a moral society can he find scope and support for full development of will. In concrete phrase, it is just as necessary to improve the general social environment in which men, women, and children are to live, in order to make better individuals, as it is to improve the individuals in order to get a better society. This was a truth which the religious conception of salvation through the church taught in other terms.

To follow the development of the modern moral consciousness, we shall rely not so much on the formal writings of moral philosophers as on other sources. What men value most, and what they recognize as right, is shown in what they work for and fight for and in how they spend their leisure. This is reflected more immediately in their laws, their art and literature, their religion, and their educational institutions, although it finds ultimate expression in moral theories. The more concrete aspects are suggested in this chapter, the theories in Chapter 12.

§ 3. *The Old and New in the Beginnings of Individualism*

An interesting blending of the class ideal of the warrior and "gentleman" with the religious ideals of devotion to some spiritual service, and of protection to the weak, is afforded by *chivalry*. The knights show their faith by their deeds of heroism, not by renunciation. But they fight for the Holy Sepulcher, or for the weak and oppressed. Their investiture is almost as solemn as that of a priest. Honor and love appear as motives side by side with the quest of the Holy Grail. Chevalier Bayard is the gallant fighter for country, but he is also the passionate admirer of justice, the knight *sans peur et sans reproche*. Moreover, the literature which embodies the ideal exhibits not only feats of arms and religious symbolism. Parsifal is not a mere abstraction; he has life and character. "And who will deny," writes Francke,[4] "that in this character Wolfram has put before us, within the forms of chivalrous life, an immortal symbol of struggling, sinning, despairing, but finally redeemed, humanity?"

If chivalry represented in some degree a moralizing of the warrior class, the mendicant orders represented an effort to bring religion into secular life. The followers of St.

4. Francke, *Social Forces in German Literature*, p. 93.

Dominic and St. Francis were indeed ascetic, but instead of maintaining the separate life of the cloister they aimed to awaken a personal experience among the whole people. Further, the Dominicans adopted the methods and conceptions of Greek philosophy to support the doctrines of the church, instead of relying solely on faith. The Franciscans on their part devoted an ecstatic type of piety to deeds of charity and beneficence. They aimed to overcome the world rather than to withdraw from it. A bolder appeal to the individual, still within the sphere of religion, was made when Wyclif asserted the right of every instructed man to search the Bible for himself, and a strong demand for social justice found expression in Wyclif's teaching as well as in the vision of Piers Plowman.

In the political world the growing strength of the empire sought likewise a religious sanction in its claim of a divine right, independent of the church. The claims of the civic life find also increasing recognition with the spiritual teachers.

The State had been regarded by Augustine as a consequence of the fall of man, but it now comes to claim and receive a moral value: first, with Thomas Aquinas, as the institution in which man perfects his earthly nature and prepares for his higher destiny in the realm of grace; then, with Dante, as no longer subordinate to the church, but coordinate with it.

Finally, the rise of the universities shows a most significant appearance of the modern spirit under the old sanctions. The range of secular studies was limited and the subject-matter to be studied was chiefly the doctrine of the Fathers. The teachers who drew thousands of eager young men about them were clerics. But the very fact that dialectics—the art of reasoning—was the focus of interest, shows the dawn of a spirit of inquiry. Such a book as Abelard's *Sic et Non*, which marshaled the opposing views of the Fathers in "deadly parallel," was a challenge to tradition and an assertion of reason. And it is not without significance that the same bold thinker was the first of the mediaeval scholars to treat ethics again as a field by itself. The title *"Know Thyself"* suggests its method. The essence of the moral act is placed in the intent or resolve of the will; the criterion for judgment is agreement or disagreement with conscience.

§ 4. *Individualism in the Progress of Liberty and Democracy*

Rights.—It is not possible or necessary here to sketch the advance of political and civil liberty. Finding its agents sometimes in kings, sometimes in cities, sometimes in an aristocracy or a House of Commons, and sometimes in a popular uprising, it has also had as its defenders with the pen, Churchmen, Protestants, and freethinkers, lawyers, publicists, and philosophers. All that can be done here is to indicate briefly the moral significance of the movement. Some of its protagonists have been actuated by conscious moral purpose. They have fought with sword or pen not only in the conviction that their cause was just, but because they believed it just. At other times, a king has favored a city to weaken the power of the nobility, or the Commons have opposed the king because they objected to taxation. What makes the process significant morally is that, whatever the motives actuating those who have fought its battles with sword or pen, they have nearly always claimed to be fighting for "rights." They have professed the conviction that they are engaged in a just cause. They have thus made appeal to a moral standard, and in so far as they have sincerely sought to assert rights, they have been recognizing in some sense a social and rational standard; they have been building up a moral personality. Sometimes indeed the rights have been claimed as a matter of "possession" or of tradition. This is to place them on the basis of customary morality. But in such great crises as the English Revolutions of the seventeenth century, or the French and American Revolutions of the eighteenth, some deeper basis has been sought. A Milton, a Locke, a Rousseau, a Jefferson, has but voiced the sentiments of a people in formulating an explicitly moral principle. Sometimes this has taken the form of an appeal to God-given rights. All men are equal before God; why should one man assume to command another because of birth? In this sense the Puritans stood for liberty and democracy as part of their creed of life. But often the appeal to a moral principle borrowed the conceptions of Greek philosophy and Roman law, and spoke of "natural rights" or a "law of nature."[5]

Natural Rights.—This conception, as we have noted, had its origin in Greece in the appeal from custom or convention to Nature. At first an appeal to the natural impulses and wants, it became with the Stoics an appeal to the rational order of the universe. Roman jurists found in the idea of such a law of nature the rational basis for the law of society. Cicero had maintained that every man had its principles innate within him. It is obvious that here was a principle with great possibilities. The Roman law itself was most often used in the interest of absolutism, but the idea of a natural law, and so of a natural right more fundamental than any human dictate, proved a powerful instrument in the struggle for personal rights and equality. "All men naturally were born free," wrote Milton. "To understand political power right," wrote Locke, "and derive it from its original, we must consider what state all men are naturally in, and that is a state of perfect freedom to order their actions and dispose of their possessions and persons, as they think fit, within the bounds of the law of nature; without asking leave or depending on the will of any other man. A state also of equality, wherein all the power and jurisdiction is reciprocal." These doctrines found eloquent portrayal in Rousseau, and appear in the Declaration of Independence of 1776. Finally, the effort to find in nature some basis for independence and freedom is given a new turn by Herbert Spencer when he points to the instinct for liberty in animals as well as in human beings as the origin of the law of freedom.

By one of the paradoxes of history, the principle is now most often invoked in favor of "vested interests." "Natural" easily loses the force of an appeal to reason and to social good, and becomes merely an assertion of ancient usage, or precedent, or even a shelter for mere selfish interests. Natu-

5. Pp. 113 f., 118.

ral rights in property may be invoked to thwart efforts to protect life and health. Individualism has been so successful in asserting rights that it is now apt to forget that there are no rights morally except such as express the will of a good *member of society*. But in recognizing possible excesses we need not forget the value of the idea of rights as a weapon in the struggle in which the moral personality has gradually won its way. The other side of the story has been the growth of responsibility. The gain in freedom has not meant an increase in disorder; it has been marked rather by gain in peace and security, by an increasing respect for law, and an increasing stability of government. The external control of force has been replaced by the moral control of duty.

§ 5. *Individualism as Affected*
by the Development of Industry, Commerce,
and Art

The development of industry, commerce, and art affects the moral life in a variety of ways, of which three are of especial importance for our purpose.

(1) It gives new interests, and new opportunities for individual activity.

(2) This raises the question of *values*. Are all the activities good, and shall one satisfy whatever interest appeals to him, or are some better than others? — the old question of "kinds of happiness."

(3) It raises further the question of sharing and distribution. How far may one enjoy the goods of life in an exclusive way and how far is it his duty to share with others? Do society's present methods of industry, commerce, art, and education distribute these goods in a just manner?

The examination of these questions will be made in Part III. It is our purpose at this point merely to indicate the trend of the moral consciousness with regard to them.

1. The Increasing Power and Interests of the Individual. —Power for the mediaeval man could be sought in war or in the church; interests were correspondingly limited. The Crusades, contact, through them and later through commerce, with Arabian civilization, growing acquaintance with the literature and art of Greece and Rome, were effective agencies in stimulating the modern development. But when once started it needed but the opportunities of sufficient wealth and freedom to go on. Art and letters have depicted a variety and richness of experience which the ancient world did not feel. Shakespere, Rembrandt, Bunyan, Beethoven, Goethe, Balzac, Shelley, Byron, Hugo, Wagner, Ibsen, Thackeray, Eliot, Tolstoy, to name almost at random, reflect a wealth of interests and motives which show the range of the modern man. Commerce and the various lines of industry have opened new avenues for power. No one can see the palaces or dwellings of Venice or the old Flemish ports, or consider the enormous factories, shops, and office buildings of to-day, without a sense of the accession to human power over nature and over the activities of fellow men which trade and industry have brought with them. The use of money instead of a system of personal service—slavery or serfdom—has not only made it possible to have men's labor without owning the men, it has aided in a vastly more effective system than the older method allowed. The industrial revolution of the past century has had two causes: one the use of machinery; the other the combination of human labor which this makes possible. So far this has greatly increased the power of the few leaders, but not of the many. It is the present problem to make possible a larger opportunity for individual freedom and power.

2. *The Values of Art and Industry.*—Are all these wider interests and fuller powers good? The church ideal and the class ideal already described gave different answers. The class ideal of gentleman really expressed a form of self-assertion, of living out one's powers fully, and this readily welcomed the possibilities which art and its enjoyment afforded.[6] The gentleman of the Renaissance, the cavalier of England, the noblesse of France, were patrons of art and letters. The Romanticist urged that such free and full expression as art afforded was higher than morality with its control and limitation. The church admitted art in the service of

6. Tolstoy, *What Is Art?*

religion, but was chary of it as an individual activity. The Puritans were more rigorous. Partly because they associated its churchly use with what they regarded as "idolatry," partly as a protest against the license in manners which the freedom of art seemed to encourage, they frowned upon all forms of art except sacred literature or music. Their condemnation of the stage is still an element, though probably a lessening element, and it is not long since fiction was by many regarded with suspicion. On the whole, the modern moral consciousness accepts art as having a place in the moral life, although it by no means follows that art can be exempt from moral criticism as to its sincerity, healthfulness, and perspective.

In the case of industry the church ideal has prevailed. The class ideal of gentleman was distinctly opposed to industry, particularly manual labor. "Arms" or the Court was the proper profession. This was more or less bound up with the fact that in primitive conditions labor was mainly performed by women or by slaves. It was the business, the "virtue" of men to fight. So far as this class ideal was affected by the models of ancient culture, the prejudice was strengthened. The classic civilization rested on slave labor. The ideal of the gentleman of Athens was the free employment of leisure, not active enterprise. The church, on the other hand, maintained both the dignity and the moral value of labor. Not only the example of the Founder of Christianity and his early disciples, who were for the most part manual laborers, but the intrinsic moral value of work, already referred to, entered into the appraisal.[7] The Puritans, who have had a wide-reaching influence upon the standards of the middle and lower classes of England, and upon the northern and western portions of America, were insistent upon industry, not merely for the sake of its products,—they were frugal in their consumption,—but as expressing a type of character. Idleness and "shiftlessness" were not merely ineffective, they were sinful. "If any will not work, neither let him eat," commended itself thoroughly to this moral ideal. That the laborer brought something to the com-

7. P. 43.

mon weal, while the idler had to be supported, was a re-enforcement to the motives drawn from the relation of work to character. As the middle and lower classes became increasingly influential, the very fact that they were laborers and traders strengthened the religious ideal by a class motive. It was natural that a laboring class should regard labor as "honest," though from the history of the word such a collocation of terms as "honest labor" would once have been as absurd as "honest villain."[8] A further influence effective in America has been the fluidity of class distinctions in a new country. The "influence of the frontier" has been all on the side of the value of work and the reprobation of idleness. At least this is true for men. A certain tendency has been manifest to exempt women of the well-to-do classes from the necessity of labor, and even by training and social pressure to exclude them from the opportunity of work, and make of them a "leisure class," but this is not likely to establish itself as a permanent moral attitude. The woman will not be content to live in "The Doll's House" while the man is in the real work of the world.

3. *The Distribution of the Goods of Life.*—Mediaeval society made provision for both benevolence and justice. Charity, the highest of the virtues, had come to mean specifically the giving of goods. The monasteries relieved the poor and the infirm. Hospitals were established. The gentleman felt it to be not only a religious duty, but a tradition of his class to be liberal. To secure justice in the distribution of wealth, various restrictions were imposed. Goods were not to be sold for whatever they could bring, nor was money to be loaned at whatever rate of interest the borrower was willing to pay. Society aimed to find out by some means what was a "reasonable price" for products. In the case of manufactured goods this could be fixed by the opinion of fellow craftsmen. A "common estimation," where buyers and sellers met and bargained in an open market, could be trusted to give a fair value. A maximum limit was set for victuals in towns. Or, again, custom prescribed what should be the money equivalent for payments formerly made

8. See p. 164.

in kind, or in personal service.[9] Money-lending was under especial guard. To ask interest for the use of money, provided the principal was returned intact, seemed to be taking advantage of another's necessity. It was usury. Class morality added a different kind of restriction. As embodied in the laws, it bound the tenants to the soil and forbade the migration of laborers. The significant thing in the whole mediaeval attitude was that *society attempted to control business and industry by a moral standard.* It did not trust the individual to make his own bargains or to conduct his business as he pleased.

Modern Theory: Free Contract.—The distinctive feature of the modern development has been the tendency to abandon moral restrictions and to substitute a wage system, freedom of exchange, and free contract. It was maintained by the advocates of the new method that it was both more efficient and at least as just as the old. It was more efficient because it stimulated every one to make the best possible bargain. Surely every man is the most interested, and therefore the best promoter of his own welfare. And if each is getting the best results for himself, the good of the whole community will be secured. For—so ran the theory, when individualism had so far advanced—society is simply the aggregate of its members; the good of all is the sum of the goods of the members. The system also claimed to provide for justice between buyer and seller, capitalist and laborer, by the agencies noticed in the next paragraph.

Competition.—To prevent extortionate prices on the one hand, or unduly low prices or wages on the other, the reliance was on *competition* and the general principle of supply and demand. If a baker charges too high for his bread, others will set up shops and sell cheaper. If a money-lender asks too high interest, men will not borrow or will find a loan elsewhere. If a wage is too low, labor will go elsewhere; if too high, capital will not be able to find a profit and so will not employ labor—so runs the theory. Without analyzing the moral value of the theory at this point, we notice only that, so far as it assumes to secure

9. Cunningham, *An Essay on Western Civilization*, pp. 77 ff.

fair bargains and a just distribution, it assumes the parties to the free contract to be really free. This implies that they are upon nearly equal footing. In the days of hand work and small industries this was at least a plausible assumption. But a new face was placed upon the situation by the *industrial revolution*.

Problem Raised by the Industrial Revolution.—The introduction of machinery on a large scale near the end of the eighteenth century brought about a change which has had extraordinary economic, social, and moral effects. The revolution had two factors: (1) it used steam power instead of human muscle; (2) it made possible the greater subdivision of labor, and hence it made it profitable to organize large bodies of men under a single direction. Both these factors contributed to an enormous increase in productive power. But this increase made an overwhelming difference in the status of capitalist and laborer. Without discussing the question as to whether capital received more than a "fair" share of the increased profit, it was obvious that if one "Captain of Industry" were receiving even a small part of the profits earned by each of his thousand workmen, he would be immeasurably better off than any one of them. Like the mounted and armored knight of the Middle Ages, or the baron in his castle, he was more than a match for a multitude of poorly equipped footmen. There seemed to be in the nineteenth century an enormous disproportion between the shares of wealth which fell to capitalist and to laborer. If this was the result of "free contract," what further proof was necessary that "freedom" was a mere empty term—a name with no reality? For could it be supposed that a man would *freely* make an agreement to work harder and longer than any slave, receiving scarcely the bare necessities of existence, while the other party was to gain enormous wealth from the bargain?

The old class morality was not disturbed by such contrasts. Even the religious morality was apt to consider the distinction between rich and poor as divinely ordered, or else as insignificant compared with eternal destiny of weal or woe. But the individualistic movements have made it less easy to accept either the class morality or the religious interpretation. The latter lends itself equally well to a justification of disease because it is providentially permitted. Moreover, the old group morality and religious ideal had this in their favor: they recognized an obligation of the strong to the weak, of the group for every member, of master for servant. The cash basis seemed to banish all responsibility, and to assert the law of "each for himself" as the supreme law of life—except so far as individuals might mitigate suffering by voluntary kindness. Economic theory seemed to show that wages must always tend toward a starvation level.

Sympathy.—Such tendencies inevitably called out response from the sentiments of benevolence and sympathy. For the spread of civilization has certainly made man more sensitive to pain, more capable of sympathy and of entering by imagination into the situations of others. It is noteworthy that the same Adam Smith who argued so forcibly the cause of individualism in trade, made sympathy the basis of his moral system. Advance in sympathy has shown itself in the abolition of judicial torture, in prison reform, in the improved care of the insane and defective; in the increased provision for hospitals, and asylums, and in an innumerable multitude of organizations for relief of all sorts and conditions of men. Missions, aside from their distinctly ecclesiastical aims, represent devotion of human life and of wealth to the relief of sickness and wretchedness, and to the education of children in all lands. Sympathy has even extended to the animal world. And the notable fact in modern sympathy and kindness, as contrasted with the mediaeval type, is that the growth in individuality has demanded and evoked a higher kind of benevolence. Instead of fostering dependence and relieving wants, the best modern agencies aim to promote independence, to set the man upon his own feet and enable him to achieve self-respect. "Social settlements" have been strong factors in bringing about this change of attitude.

Justice.—Various movements looking toward greater justice in distribution have likewise been called out by the conditions since the industrial revolution. Naturally one reaction was to denounce the whole individualistic tendency as represented in the "cash-payment" basis. This found its most eloquent expositor in Carlyle. His *Past and Present* is a bitter indictment of a system "in which all working horses could be well fed, and innumerable workingmen should die starved"; of a *laissez-faire* theory which merely says "impossible" when asked to remedy evils supposedly due to "economic laws"; of a "Mammon Gospel" which transforms life into a mutual hostility, with its laws-of-war named "fair competition." The indictment is convincing, but the remedy proposed—a return to strong leaders with a reestablishment of personal relations—has rallied few to its support. Another reaction against individualistic selfishness has taken the form of communism. Numerous experiments have been made by voluntary associations to establish society on a moral basis by abolishing private property. "These new associations," said Owen, one of the most ardent and generous of social reformers, "can scarcely be formed before it will be discovered that by the most simple and easy regulations all the natural wants of human nature may be abundantly supplied; and the principle of selfishness will cease to exist for want of an adequate motive to produce it."

In contrast with these plans for a return to earlier conditions, the two most conspicuous tendencies in the thought of the past century have claimed to be advancing toward freedom and justice along the lines which we have just traced. The one, which we may call "individualistic" reform, has sought justice by giving free play to individual action. The other, socialism, has aimed to use the power of the State to secure more adequate justice and, as it believes, a more genuine freedom. The great reform movement in Great Britain during the nineteenth century emphasized free trade and free contracts. It sought the causes of injustice in the survival of some privilege or vested interest which prevents the full working of the principles of free contract and competition. Let every man "count as one"; make laws for "the greatest good of the greatest number." The trouble is not that there is too much individualism, but that there is too little. Tax reformers like Henry George have urged the same principle. If land is monopolized by a few who can levy a toll upon all the rest of society, how can justice obtain? The remedy for injustice is to be found in promoting greater freedom of industry and trade. Socialism on the other hand claims that individualism defeats itself; it results in tyranny, not freedom. The only way to secure freedom is through united action. The merits of some of these programs for social justice will be examined in Part III. They signify that the age is finding its moral problem set anew by the collision between material interests and social good. Greek civilization used the industry of the many to set free the higher life—art, government, science—of a few. The mediaeval ideal recognized the moral value of industry in relation to character. The modern conscience, resting back upon a higher appreciation of human dignity and worth, is seeking to work out a social and economic order that shall combine both the Greek and the mediaeval ideas. It will require work and secure freedom. These are necessary for the individual person. But it is beginning to be seen that these values cannot be divided so that one social class shall perform the labor and the other enjoy the freedom. The growth of democracy means that all members of society should share in the value and the service of work. It means that all should share according to capacity in the values of free life, of intelligence and culture. Can material goods be so produced and distributed as to promote this democratic ideal?

§ 6. The Individual and the Development of Intelligence

The development of intelligence in the modern world, as in Greece, has two sides: on the one hand, a working-free from the restrictions which theology or the State or other social authorities imposed; on the other hand, positive progress in knowledge of nature and of human life. Under its first aspect it is known as the growth of rationalism; under its second aspect, as the growth of science and education. We cannot separate the development into two periods, the one negative, the other positive, as was convenient in the case of Greece. The negative and the positive in the modern world have gone on contemporaneously, although the emphasis has sometimes been on one side and sometimes upon the other.

We may, however, indicate three periods as standing out with clearly defined characteristics.

(1) The Renaissance, in which the Greek spirit of scientific inquiry found a new birth; in which the discovery of new continents stimulated the imagination; and in which new and more fruitful methods of investigation were devised in mathematics and the natural sciences.

(2) The period of the Enlightenment, in which the negative aspect of the process reached its sharpest definition. The doctrines of revealed religion and natural religion were criticised from the standpoint of reason. Mysteries and superstition were alike rejected. General intelligence made rapid progress. It was the "Age of Reason."

(3) The Nineteenth Century, in which both the natural and social sciences underwent an extraordinary development. The doctrine of evolution has brought a new point of view for considering the organic world and human institutions. Education has come to be regarded as both the necessary condition for the safety of society and as the right of every human being; Science, in large measure set free from the need of fighting for its right to exist, is becoming constructive; it is assuming increasingly the duty of preserving human life and health, of utilizing and preserving natural resources, of directing political and economic affairs.

1. The Renaissance.—It would be giving a wrong impression to imply that there was no inquiry, no use of reason in the mediaeval world. The problems set by the inheritance of old-world religion and politics, forced themselves upon the builders of castles and cathedrals,[10] of law and of dogma. As indicated above, the universities were centres of discussion in which brilliant minds often challenged received opinions. Men like Roger Bacon sought to discover nature's secrets, and the great scholastics mastered Greek philosophy in the interest of defending the faith. But theological interest limited freedom and choice of theme. It was not until the expansion of the individual along the lines already traced—in political freedom, in the use of the arts, in the development of com-

---

10. The writer is indebted to his colleague Professor Mead for the significance of this for the beginnings of modern science.

merce—that the purely intellectual interest such as had once characterized Greece awoke. A new world of possibilities seemed dawning upon the Italian Galileo, the Frenchman Descartes, the Englishman Francis Bacon. The instruments of thought had been sharpened by the dialectics of the schools; now let them be used to analyze the world in which we live. Instead of merely observing nature Galileo applied the experimental method, putting definite questions to nature and thus preparing the way for a progress step by step toward a positive knowledge of nature's laws. Descartes found in mathematics a method of analysis which had never been appreciated before. What seemed the mysterious path of bodies in curved lines could be given a simple statement in his analytic geometry. Leibniz and Newton carried this method to triumphant results in the analysis of forces. Reason appeared able to discover and frame the laws of the universe—the "principles" of nature. Bacon, with less of positive contribution in method, sounded another note which was equally significant. The human mind is liable to be clouded and hindered in its activities by certain inveterate sources of error. Like deceitful images or obsessions the "idols" of the tribe, of the cave, of the market, and of the theatre—due to instinct or habit, to language or tradition—prevent the reason from doing its best work. It needs vigorous effort to free the mind from these idols. But this can be done. Let man turn from metaphysics and theology to nature and life; let him follow reason instead of instinct or prejudice. "Knowledge is power." Through it may rise above the kingdom of nature the "kingdom of man." In his *New Atlantis*, Bacon foresees a human society in which skill and invention and government shall all contribute to human welfare. These three notes, the experimental method, the power of rational analysis through mathematics, and the possibility of controlling nature in the interests of man, were characteristic of the period.

2. *The Enlightenment.*—A conflict of reason with authority went on side by side with the progress of science. Humanists and scientists had often set themselves against dogma and tradition. The Reformation was not in form an appeal to reason, but the clash of authorities stimulated men

to reasoning upon the respective claims of Catholic and Protestant. And in the eighteenth century, under the favoring influence of a broad toleration and a general growth of intelligence, the conflict of reason with dogma reached its culmination. The French call the period *"l'Illumination"* — the illumination of life and experience by the light of reason. The Germans call it the *Aufklärung*, "the clearing-up." What was to be cleared up? First, ignorance, which limits the range of man's power and infects him with fear of the unknown; then superstition, which is ignorance consecrated by wont and emotion; finally, dogma, which usually embodies irrational elements and seeks to force them upon the mind by the power of authority, not of truth. Nor was it merely a question of intellectual criticism. Voltaire saw that dogma was often responsible for cruelty. Ignorance meant belief in witchcraft and magic. From the dawn of civilization this had beset man's progress and quenched many of the brightest geniuses of the past. It was time to put an end once for all to the remnants of primitive credulity; it was time to be guided by the light of reason. The movement was not all negative. Using the same appeal to "nature," which had served so well as a rallying cry in the development of political rights, the protagonists of the movement spoke of a "natural light" which God had placed in man for his guidance—"the candle of the Lord set up by himself in men's minds, which it is impossible for the breath or power of man wholly to extinguish." A natural and rational religion should take the place of supposed revelation.

But the great achievement of the eighteenth century in the intellectual development of the individual was that the human mind came to realize the part it was itself playing in the whole realm of science and conduct. Man began to look within. Whether he called his work an *Essay concerning Human Understanding*, or a *Treatise of Human Nature*, or a *Theory of Moral Sentiments*, or a *Critique of Pure Reason*, the aim was to study human experience. For of a sudden it was dawning upon man that, if he was then living upon a higher level of knowledge and conduct than the animal or the savage, this must be due to the activity of the mind. It appeared that man, not satisfied with "nature," had gone on

to build a new world with institutions and morality, with art
and science. This was no creation of instinct or habit; nor
could it be explained in terms of sense, or feeling, or impulse
alone; it was the work of that more active, universal, and
creative type of intelligence which we call reason. Man, as
capable of such achievements in science and conduct, must
be regarded with new respect. As having political rights,
freedom, and responsibility, man has the dignity of a citizen,
sovereign as well as subject. As guiding and controlling his
own life and that of others by the power of ideas, not
of force, he has the dignity of a moral person, a moral
sovereignty. He does not merely take what nature brings; he
sets up ends of his own and gives them worth. In this, Kant
saw the supreme dignity of the human spirit.

3. *The Present Significance and Task of Scientific
Method.*—In the thought that man is able to form ends which
have value for all, to set up standards which all respect, and
thus to achieve worth and dignity in the estimation of his
fellows, the Individualism of the eighteenth century was already pointing beyond itself. For this meant that the individual attains his highest reach only as a member of a
moral society. But it is one thing to point out the need and
meaning of a moral society, it is another thing to bring such
a society into being. It has become evident during the past
century that this is the central problem for human reason to
solve. The various social sciences, economics, sociology,
political science, jurisprudence, social psychology, have either
come into being for the first time, or have been prosecuted
with new energy. Psychology has assumed new significance
as their instrument. Not that the scientific progress of the
century has seen its greatest triumphs in these fields. The
conspicuous successes have been rather in such sciences as
biology, or in the applications of science to engineering and
medicine. The social sciences have been occupied largely in
getting their problems stated and their methods defined. But
the discoveries and constructions of the nineteenth century
are none the less indispensable prerequisites for a moral
society. For the new conditions of city life, the new sources
of disease, the new dangers which attend every successive
step away from the life of the savage, demand all the re-

sources of the sciences.[11] And as the natural sciences overcome the technical difficulties which obstruct their work of aiding human welfare, the demand will be more insistent that the social sciences contribute their share toward enabling man to fulfill his moral life. Some of the specific demands will become more evident, as we study in subsequent chapters the present problems of political, economic, and family life.

Education.—The importance for the moral life of the modern development of science is paralleled by the significance of modern education. The universities date from the Middle Ages. The classical interest of humanism found its medium in the college or "grammar school." The invention of printing and the growth of commerce promoted elementary schools. Supposed necessities of popular government stimulated a general educational movement in the United States. Modern trade and industry have called out the technical school. Germany has educated for national defense and economic advance; England has concerned itself preeminently for the education of statesmen and administrators; and the United States for the education of voters. But, whatever the motive, education has been made so general as to constitute a new element in the modern consciousness and a new factor to be reckoned with. The moral right of every child to have an education, measured not by his parents' abilities, but by his own capacity, is gaining recognition. The

11. "Civilized man has proceeded so far in his interference with extra-human nature, has produced for himself and the living organisms associated with him such a special state of things by his rebellion against natural selection and his defiance of Nature's pre-human dispositions, that he must either go on and acquire firmer control of the conditions or perish miserably by the vengeance certain to fall on the half-hearted meddler in great affairs. . . . We may think of him as the heir to a vast and magnificent kingdom who has been finally educated so as to fit him to take possession of his property, and is at length left alone to do his best; he has wilfully abrogated, in many important respects, the laws of his Mother Nature by which the kingdom was hitherto governed; he has gained some power and advantage by so doing, but is threatened on every hand by dangers and disasters hitherto restrained: no retreat is possible —his only hope is to control, as he knows that he can, the sources of these dangers and disasters. They already make him wince: how long will he sit listening to the fairy-tales of his boyhood and shrink from manhood's task?"—Lankester, *The Kingdom of Man,* 1907, pp. 31 f.

moral value of a possession, which is not, like material goods, exclusive, but common, will be more appreciated when we have worked out a more social and democratic type of training.[12]

Theoretical Interpretation of this Period in Ethical Systems.—While the theoretical interpretation of this period is to be treated in Part II, we may point out here that the main lines of development which we have traced find expression in the two systems which have been most influential during the past century. These are the systems of Kant and of the Utilitarians. The political and certain aspects of the intellectual development are reflected in the system of Kant. He emphasized freedom, the power and authority of reason, human dignity, the supreme value of character, and the significance of a society in which every member is at once sovereign and subject. The Utilitarians represent the values brought out in the development of industry, education, and the arts. They claimed that the good is happiness, and happiness of the greatest number. The demands for individual satisfaction and for social distribution of goods are voiced in this system.

12. Dewey, *The School and Society.*

Literature

The histories of philosophy and of ethics give the theoretical side. In addition to those previously mentioned the works of Höffding, Falckenberg, and Fischer may be named. Stephen, *English Thought in the Eighteenth Century*, and *The English Utilitarians*; Fichte, "Characteristics of the Present Age" (in *Popular Works*, tr. by Smith); Stein, *Die sociale Frage im Lichte der Philosophie*, 1897; Comte, *Positive Philosophy*, tr. by Martineau, 1875, Book VI. Tufts and Thompson, *The Individual and His Relation to Society as Reflected in British Ethics*, 1896, 1904; Merz, *History of European Thought in the Nineteenth Century*, 1904; Robertson, *A Short History of Free Thought*, 1899; Bonar, *Philosophy and Political Economy in Some of Their Historical Relations*, 1893.

ON THE MEDIAEVAL AND RENAISSANCE ATTITUDE: Lecky, *History of European Morals*, 3d ed., 1877; Adams, *Civilization During the Middle Ages*, 1894; Rashdall, *The Universities of*

Europe in the Middle Ages, 1895; Eicken, *Geschichte und System der mittelalterlichen Weltanschauung,* 1887; Burckhardt, *The Civilization of the Renaissance in Italy,* 1892; Draper, *History of the Intellectual Development of Europe,* 1876.

ON THE INDUSTRIAL AND SOCIAL SIDE: Ashley, *English Economic History;* Cunningham, *Western Civilization in Its Economic Aspects,* 1898–1900, and *Growth of English Industry and Commerce,* 3d ed., 1896–1903; Hobson, *The Evolution of Modern Capitalism,* 1894; Traill, *Social England,* 1894–98; Rambaud, *Histoire de la civilisation française,* 1897–98; Held, *Zwei Bücher zur socialen Geschichte Englands,* 1881; Carlyle, *Past and Present;* Ziegler, *Die geistigen und socialen Strömungen des neunzehnten Jahrhunderts,* 1899.

ON THE POLITICAL AND JURAL DEVELOPMENT: Hadley, *Freedom and Responsibility in the Evolution of Democratic Government,* 1903; Pollock, *The Expansion of the Common Law,* 1904; Ritchie, *Natural Rights,* 1895, *Darwin and Hegel,* 1893, ch. vii; Dicey, *Lectures on the Relation Between Law and Public Opinion in England During the Nineteenth Century,* 1905.

ON THE LITERARY SIDE: Brandes, *Main Currents in Nineteenth Century Literature,* 1901–05; Francke, *Social Forces in German Literature,* 1896; Carriere, *Die Kunst im Zusammenhang der Culturentwickelung und die Ideale der Menschheit,* 3d ed., 1877–86.

9. A GENERAL COMPARISON OF CUSTOMARY AND REFLECTIVE MORALITY

To eat of the fruit of the tree of the knowledge of good and evil may result in ultimate gain. A more conscious and individualistic attitude may result in definite conceptions of duty and rights, of values and ideals. At the same time, as humanity's eyes have been opened and its wisdom increased, many forms of nakedness unknown in ruder conditions have been disclosed. With every increase of opportunity and efficiency for good there is a corresponding opportunity for evil. An immensely more complex environment gives scope for correspondingly more capable and subtle personalities. Some will react to the situation in such a way as to rise to a higher moral level, both in personal integrity and in public usefulness. Others will find in facilities for gratifying some appetite or passion a temptation too strong for their control and will become vicious, or will seize the chances to exploit others and become unjust in their acquirement and use of power and wealth. There will be a Nero as well as an Aurelius, a Caesar Borgia as well as a Savonarola, a Jeffreys as well as a Sidney, a Bentham, or a Howard. For an Eliot or a Livingston or an Armstrong, there are the exploiters of lower races; and for an Elizabeth Fry, the women who trade in the wretchedness of their kind. By the side of those who use great abilities and resources unselfishly are those who view indifferently the sacrifice of human health or life, and pay no heed to human misery. Such contrasts show that the "evolution of morality" is also an evolution of weakness, wretchedness, evil, and crime. They suggest some general comparisons between custom and reflective morality. They require from every age a renewed analysis of conduct and the social system. As a preliminary to such an analysis, we review in this chapter some of the general relations between the morality of custom and the morality of reflection.

§ 1. Elements of Agreement and Continuity

The moral life shows its continuity in two ways. First, the earlier type of group and customary morality persists in part; in the second place, when the moral is differentiated from the other spheres of life in which it was embedded, it does not have to find entirely new conceptions. It borrows its terms from the group life or from the various spheres, religious, political, aesthetic, economic, which separate out from the older group unity.

The following quotation from Grote will serve as a vivid restatement of the régime of custom:

This aggregate of beliefs and predispositions to believe, Ethical, Religious, Aesthetical, and Social, respecting what is true or false, probable or improbable, just or unjust, holy or unholy, honorable or base, respectable or contemptible, pure or impure, beautiful or ugly, decent or indecent, obligatory to do or obligatory to avoid, respecting the status and relations of each individual in the society, respecting even the admissible fashions of amusement and recreation—this is an established fact and condition of things, the real origin of which is for the most part unknown, but which each new member of the group is born to and finds subsisting. . . . It becomes a part of each person's nature, a standing habit of mind, or fixed set of mental tendencies, according to which particular experience is interpreted and particular persons appreciated. . . . The community hate, despise or deride any individual member who proclaims his dissent from their social creed. . . . Their hatred manifests itself in different ways . . . at the very least by exclusion from that amount of forbearance, good will and estimation without which the life of an individual becomes insupportable. . . . "Nomos (Law and Custom), king of all" (to borrow the phrase which Herodotus cites from Pindar) exercises plenary power, spiritual and temporal, over individual minds; moulding the emotions as well as the intellect, according to the local type . . . and reigning under the appearance of habitual, self-suggested tendencies.[1]

The important facts brought out are (1) the existence in a social group of certain habits not only of acting, but of feeling and believing about actions, of valuing or approving and disapproving. (2) The persistent forcing of these mental

1. G. Grote, *Plato and the Other Companions of Sokrates*, Vol. I, p. 249.

habitudes upon the attention of each new member of the group. The newcomer, whether by birth or adoption, is introduced into a social medium whose conditions and regulations he can no more escape than he can those of his physical environment. (3) Thus the mental and practical habits of the newly introduced individual are shaped. The current ways of esteeming and behaving in the community become a "standing habit" of his own mind; they finally reign as "habitual, self-suggested tendencies." Thus he becomes a full member of the social group, interested in the social fabric to which he belongs, and ready to do his part in maintaining it.

1. *Persistence of Group Morality.*—Comparing this state of affairs with what obtains to-day in civilized communities, we find certain obvious points of agreement. The social groups with which an individual comes in touch are now more numerous and more loosely formed. But everywhere there are customs not only of acting, but of thinking and feeling about acting. Each profession, each institution, has a *code* of which the individual has to take account. The nature of this code, unexpressed as well as formulated, is brought to the attention of the individual in countless ways; by the approval and disapproval of its public opinion; by his own failures and successes; by his own tendency to imitate what he sees about him, as well as by deliberate, intentional instruction.

In other words, group morality does not vanish in order that conscious and personal morality may take its place. Group and customary morality is still the morality of many of us most of the time, and of all of us for a good deal of the time. We do not any of us think out all of our standards, weigh independently our values, make all our choices in a rational manner, or form our characters by following a clearly conceived purpose. As children we all start in a family group. We continue in a school group and perhaps a church group. We enter an occupation group, and later, it may be, family, political, social, and neighborhood groups. In every one of these if we are members, we must to a certain degree accept standards that are given. We have to play according to the rules of the game. As children we do this unconsciously. We imitate, or follow suggestions; we are made to conform by all the agencies of group morality—group opinion, ritual, pleasure and pain, and even by taboos;[2] above all, we act as the others act, and cooperate more or less to a common end. We form habits which persist, many of them as long as we live. We accept many of the traditions without challenge. Even when we pass from the early family group to the new situations and surroundings which make us repeat more or less of the experience of the race, a large share of our conduct and of our judgments of others is determined by the influences of group and custom. And it is fortunate for progress that this is true. If every one had to start anew to frame all his ideals and make his laws, we should be in as melancholy a plight morally as we should be intellectually if we had to build each science anew. The fundamental safeguards which the group provides against individual impulse and passion, the condition of close association, interdependence and mutual sympathy which the group affords, the habituation to certain lines of conduct valued by the group— all this is a root on which the stem and flower of personal morality may grow. Individualism and intellectual activity, however necessary to man's progress, would give no morality did they not start out of this deeper level of common feeling and common destiny. The rational and personal agencies of the "third level" come not to destroy, but to fulfill the meaning of the forces and agencies of the first and second levels described in Chapters 3 and 4.

2. *The Moral Conceptions.*—The conceptions for the moral are nearly all taken from the group relations or from the jural and religious aspects, as these have been gradually brought to clearer consciousness. As already noted, the Greek term "ethical," the Latin "moral," the German "*sittlich*," suggest this—*ethos* meant the "sum of the characteristic usages, ideas, standards, and codes by which a group was

2. Nearly every railway journey or other occasion for observing family discipline discloses the prevalence of this agency of savage morality. "If you are not quiet I'll give you to the conductor," "the black man will get you," "Santa Claus will not give presents to naughty children." That persons who in many respects are kindly and decent should aim to cultivate morality by a system of deliberate lying and more or less brutal cruelty is one of the interesting phenomena of education. The savages who used taboos believed what they said.

differentiated and individualized in character from other groups."[3]

Some specific moral terms come directly from group relations. The "kind" man acts as one of the kin. When the ruling or privileged group is contrasted with the man of no family or of inferior birth, we get a large number of terms implying "superiority" or "inferiority" in birth, and so of general value. This may or may not be due to some inherent superiority of the upper class, but it means at least that the upper class has been most effectual in shaping language and standards of approval. So "noble" and "gentle" referred to birth before they had moral value; "duty" in modern usage seems to have been principally what was due to a superior. Many words for moral disapproval are very significant of class feeling. The "caitiff" was a captive, and the Italians have their general term for morally bad, "*cattivo*," from the same idea. The "villain" was a feudal tenant, the "black-guard" looked after the kettles, the "rascal" was one of the common herd, the "knave" was the servant; the "base" and "mean" were opposed to the gentle and noble. Another set of conceptions reflects the old group *approvals* or combines these with conceptions of birth. We have noted the twofold root of *kalokagathia* in Greek. "Honor" and "honesty" were what the group admired, and conversely "*aischros*" and "*turpe*" in Greek and Latin, like the English "disgraceful" or "shameful," were what the group condemned. "Virtue" was the manly excellence which called out the praise of a warlike time, while one of the Greek terms for morally bad originally meant cowardly, and our "scoundrel" has possibly the same origin. The "bad" was probably the weak or the womanish. The economic appears in "merit," what I have earned, and likewise in "duty" and "ought," what is due or owed—though duty seems to have made itself felt especially, as noted above, toward a superior. Forethought and skill in practical affairs provided the conception of "wisdom," which was highest of the virtues for the Greeks, and as "prudence" stood high in mediaeval systems. The conception of valuing and thus of forming some permanent standard of a better and a worse, is also aided, if not created, by economic exchange. It appears

3. Sumner, *Folkways*, p. 36.

in almost identical terms in Plato and the New Testament in the challenge, "What shall it profit a man if he gain the whole world and lose his own life?"[4] From the processes of fine or useful arts came probably the conceptions of measure, order, and harmony. A whole mode of considering the moral life is jural. "Moral law," "authority," "obligation," "responsibility," "justice," "righteousness," bring with them the associations of group control and of the more definitely organized government and law. Finally the last named terms bear also a religious imprint, and numerous conceptions of the moral come from that sphere or get their specific flavor from religious usage. The conceptions of the "soul" have contributed to the ideal of a good which is permanent, and which is made rather by personal companionship, than by sensuous gratification. "Purity" began as a magical and religious idea; it came to symbolize not only freedom from contamination but singleness of purpose. "Chastity" lends a religious sacredness to a virtue which had its roots largely in the conception of property. "Wicked" is from witch.

We have indeed certain conceptions drawn from individual experiences of instinct, or reflection. From the sense recoil from what was disgusting come such conceptions as "foul," and from kindred imagery of what suits eye or muscular sense come "straightforward," "upright," "steady." From the thinking process itself we have "conscience." This word in Greek and Latin was a general term for consciousness and suggests one of the distinctive, perhaps the most distinctive characteristic of the moral. For it implies a "conscious" thoughtful attitude, which operates not only in forming purposes, but in measuring and valuing action by the standards it approves. But it is evident that by far the larger part of our ethical terms are derived from social relations in the broad sense.

§ 2. *Elements of Contrast*

Differentiation of the Moral.—The most obvious difference between the present and the early attitude is that we

4. Plato's wording is given on p. 124.

now make a clear distinction between the moral aspect of behavior and other aspects such as the conventional, the political, the legal; while in customary morality all activities esteemed by society were put upon the same level and enforced with the same vigor. Matters which we should regard as purely matters of fashion or etiquette, or as modes of amusement, such as styles of wearing the hair, were imperative. To mutilate the body in a certain way was as exigent as to observe certain marriage customs; to refrain from speaking to the mother-in-law as binding as to obey the chieftain; not to step over the shadow of the chief was even more important than not to murder the member of another tribe. In general we make a clear distinction between "manners" and morals, while in customary morality manners *are* morals, as the very words "ethical," "moral" still testify.

When Grote speaks of "Ethical, Religious, Aesthetical, and Social" beliefs, the term "ethical" belongs with the other terms only from a modern standpoint. The characteristic thing about the condition of which he is speaking is that the "religious, aesthetical, and social" beliefs brought to bear upon the individual *constitute* the ethical. We make the distinction between them as naturally as the régime of custom failed to make it. Only by imagining a social set in which failure to observe punctiliously the fashions of the set as to the proper style of dress makes the person subject to a disparagement which influences his feelings and ideas as keenly *and in the same way* as conviction of moral delinquency, can we realize the frame of mind characteristic of the ethics of custom.

Observing versus Reflecting.—Customs may be "observed." Indeed, customary morality made goodness or rightness of character practically identical with observing the established order of social estimations in all departments. This word *observe* is significant: it means to note, or notice as matter of fact, by perception; and it means to yield allegiance, to conform to, in action.[5] The element of intelligence, of reason, is thus reduced to a minimum. The

5. "Recognition" has the same double sense. So has "acknowledgment," with greater emphasis upon rendering allegiance in action.

moral values are *there*, so to speak, palpably, tangibly; and the individual has only to use his mind enough to notice them. And since they are forced upon his notice by drastic and unrelaxing methods of discipline, little initiative is required for even the attitude of attention. But when the moral is something which is *in* customs and habits, rather than those customs themselves, the good and right do not stand out in so obvious and external fashion. Recognition now demands thought, reflection; the power of abstraction and generalization. A child may be shown in a pretty direct and physical fashion the difference between *meum* and *tuum* in its bearing upon his conduct: a fence may be pointed at which divides his yard from that of a neighbor and which draws as well the moral line between what is permissible and what is forbidden; a whipping may intensify the observation. But modern business knows also of "intangible" property— good will, reputation, credit. These, indeed, can be bought and sold but the detection of their existence and nature demands an intelligence which is more than perception. The greater number of duties and rights of which present morality consists are of just this type. They are relations, not just outward habits. Their acknowledgment requires accordingly something more than just to follow and reproduce existing customs. It involves power to see *why* certain habits are to be followed, what *makes* a thing good or bad. *Conscience* is thus substituted for *custom*; *principles* take the place of external *rules*.

This is what we mean by calling present morality reflective rather than customary. It is not that social customs have ceased to be, or even have been reduced in number. The exact contrary is the case. It is not that they have shrunk in importance, or that they have less significance for the individual's activity, or claim less of his attention. Again, the reverse is the case. But the individual has to grasp the *meaning* of these customs over and above the bare fact of their existence, and has to guide himself by their *meaning* and not by the mere fact noted.[6]

---

6. Logically, this means that intelligence works conceptually, not perceptually alone.

Custom is Static.—This difference introduces a second very important difference. In customary morality, there is no choice between being enmeshed in the net of social rules which control activity, and being an outlaw—one beyond the pale, whose hand is against every man's, and every man's against him. The extent to which social customs are regarded as of divine origin and are placed under the protection of the gods, i.e., the tendency of all sanctions to become religious and supernatural, is evidence of the binding force of institutions upon the individual. To violate them is impiety, sacrilege, and calls down the wrath of gods, as well as of men. The custom cannot be questioned. To inquire means uncertainty, and hence it is immoral, an attack upon the very foundations of the life of the group. The apparent exception, which after all exhibits the rule, is the case of great reforming heroes who demarcate epochs of history even in customary societies. Such individuals meet contemporary opposition and persecution; it is only by victory, by signal success over a rival faction at home, over plague and famine, or over an enemy abroad, that the hero is justified. Thereby it is proved that the gods are with him and sanction his changes —indeed that he is their own chosen instrument. Then the modified or new customs and institutions have all the binding sacredness and supernatural sanction of the old. It is not yet an outgrown story for the fathers to kill the prophets, and for the sons to build and adorn their tombs, and make them into shrines.

Reflection Discovers a Higher Law.—But in so far as the individual's activity is directed by his comprehension of the *meaning* of customs, not by his apprehension of their *existence*, so far the notion of moral progress or reform in social affairs becomes ethically important and greater moral responsibility is put upon the individual just as greater practical freedom is secured to him. For (a) the individual may set the meaning of a custom *against* its present form; or (b) he may find the meaning of some custom much more commanding in value than that of others, and yet find that its realization is hindered by the existence of these other customs of less moral importance. On the basis of such discrimination, the abolition or, at least, the modification of certain social habits is demanded. So far as this sort of situation frequently recurs, the individual (c) becomes more or less vaguely aware that he *must not accept the current standard* as justification of his own conduct, unless *it also* justify itself to his own moral intelligence. The fact that it exists gives it indeed a certain *prima facie* claim, but no ultimate moral warrant. Perhaps the custom is itself wrong—and the individual is responsible for bearing this possibility in mind.

Consequent Transformation of Custom.—Of course the plane of customary morality still persists; no wholesale divergence of reflective from customary morality exists. Practically, for example, many business men do not bother themselves about the morality of certain ways of doing business. Such and such is the custom of the trade, and if a man is going to do business at all he must follow its customs —or get out. Law, medicine, the ministry, journalism, family life, present, in considerable extent, the same phenomenon. Customary morality persists, almost as the core of present morality. But there is still a difference. A few, at least, are actively engaged in a moral criticism of the custom, in a demand for its transformation; and almost everybody is sufficiently affected by the discussions and agitations thus called out to have some lingering and uneasy idea of responsibility for his part in the maintenance of a questionable custom. The duty of some exercise of discriminating intelligence as to existing customs for the sake of improvement and progress, is thus a mark of reflective morality—of the régime of conscience as over against custom. In the morally more advanced members of contemporary society, the need of fostering a habit of examination and judgment, of keeping the mind open, sensitive, to the defects and the excellences of the existing social order is recognized as obligation. To reflect on one's own behavior in relation to the existing order is a standing habit of mind.

Deepening of Meaning.—While the materials and conceptions of more conscious morality are provided by the earlier stages, and taken from other spheres of life, we find that these conceptions naturally undergo a deepening of meaning when they are used to express the more intimate and personal attitude. Take, for example, the conceptions borrowed from the jural sphere. It is in the school of government and courts that man has learned to talk and think of right and law, of responsibility and justice. To make these moral instead of jural terms, the first thing that is needed is that we make the whole process an inward one. The person must himself set up a standard, recognize it as "law," judge his conduct by it, hold himself responsible to himself, and seek to do justice. It takes several persons to carry on these processes in the realm of government. Legislators, judges, jury, executive officers, all represent the State, organized society. That a single person can be himself lawgiver, judge, and jury, as well as claimant or defendant, shows that he is himself a complex being. He is a being of passions, appetites, and individual interests, but he is also a being who has a rational and social nature. As a member of society he not only feels his individual interest but recognizes social interests. As a rational being he not only feels the thrill of passion but responds to the authority of a law and obeys the voice of duty. Like a member of a democratic State he finds himself in the sphere of conduct, not only a subject but a sovereign, and feels the dignity of a *person*. A conscientious person is in so far one who has made the law of God or man an inward law of life—a "moral law." But the act of making the process inward makes possible a deepening of meaning. Governments and courts are necessarily limited in purview and fallible in decisions. They are sometimes too lenient, sometimes too severe. Conscience implies a knowledge of the whole act—purpose, motive, and deed. Its authority makes claim for absolute obedience. The laws of the State are felt to be binding just because they are believed to be, on the whole, right and just as measured by this moral court of appeal. When they conflict, the power may be with the political sovereign, but the man whose conscience is clear believes that he follows a "higher law." Much of the great literature of the world draws its interest from its portrayal of this fundamental fact of human experience. "Two things fill the mind with ever new and increasing admiration and awe, the oftener and the more steadily we reflect on them: the starry heavens above and the moral law within."

The conceptions taken from the economic sphere show similar deepening. In the economic world things are good or have value if people want them. It is in the experience of satisfying wants that man has learned the language of "good

and evil," and to compare one good with another; it is doubtless by the progress of science and the arts that objective
standards of more permanent, rational, and social "goods"
are provided. When this term is taken up to a higher level and
given moral meaning, two new factors appear. First the
individual begins to consider his various goods and values in
relation to each other and to his life as a whole. In the second
place, in thus comparing the various goods and the desires
they satisfy, he begins to realize that in some way he is
himself more than the mere sum of his natural instincts and
appetites. He finds that he can take an interest in certain
things, and is not merely passive. He *gives* value as well as
measures it. He feels that as such an active and organizing
judge and creator of value, he himself has a higher worth
than any of the particular things that gratify particular desires. "A man's life consisteth not in the abundance of the
things that he possesseth." "The life is more than meat." Or,
to use the phrase which will be explained later, moral good
implies purpose, character, "good will." In common language,
it implies being, and not merely having.

The term good where used in our judgments upon others
(as in a "good" man), may have a different history. As has
been noted, it may come from class feeling, or from the
praise we give to acts as they immediately please. It may be
akin to noble or fine or admirable. All such conceptions undergo a similar transformation as they pass from the sphere
of class or public opinion to become moral terms. As moral
they imply in the first place that we consider not merely outward acts, but inward purpose and character. They imply in
the second place that we who judge are ourselves acting not
as members of a class, not as merely emotional beings, but
as social and rational. Our moral judgments in this sense are
from a general, a universal standard; those of a class are
partial.

§ 3. *Opposition Between Individual and Social Aims and Standards*

Withdrawal from the Social Order.—The development
of reflection tends to set up a moral opposition between the

individual and society. Sometimes "conscience" goes beyond the need of criticizing, of discriminating, of interpreting social customs, of following their spirit rather than their letter; it takes the form of an assertion of a purely inner, personal morality, so distinct from the conditions of social life that the latter are conceived to be totally lacking in positive moral significance. The prescriptions of morality are thought to be revealed in conscience, as a faculty of pure intuition or revelation, receiving neither material nor warrant from social conditions. The distinction already spoken of between the moral and the economic, legal, or conventional, is conceived as a complete separation; customs and institutions are external, indifferent, irrelevant, or even hostile to the ideal and personally perceived demands of morality. Such a conception of morality is especially likely to arise in a period when through the clash of ways and standards of living, all customs, except those maintained by force and authority, are disintegrating or relaxing. Such a state existed in the early years of the Roman empire when, for the first time in history, local boundaries were systematically over-stepped; when the empire was a seething mixture of alien and unlike gods, beliefs, ideals, standards, practices. In the almost universal flux and confusion, *external* order was main-tained by the crystallized legislation and administration of Rome; but personal aims and modes of behavior had to be ascertained by the individual thrown back upon himself. Christian, Stoic, Epicurean, alike found the political order wholly external to the moral, or in chronic opposition to it. There was a withdrawal into the region of personal conscious-ness. In some cases the withdrawal was pushed to the point where men felt that they could be truly righteous only by going by themselves into the desert, to live as hermits; or by forming separate communities of those who agreed in their conceptions of life; mental and moral aloofness from prevail-ing social standards and habitudes was preached by all.

Individual Emancipation.—In other cases, what takes place is a consciousness of liberation; of assertion of personal rights and privileges, claims for new modes of activity and new kinds of enjoyment. The individual feels that he is his own end; that the impulses and capacities which he finds in himself are sacred, and afford the only genuine law for his behavior; that whatever restricts the full exercise of these personal powers and hampers the satisfaction of personal desires is coercive and morally abnormal. Existing social institutions may be practically necessary, but they are morally undesirable; they are to be used, or got around in the interests of personal gratifications. As some feel that social conditions are hostile to the realization of the highest moral *obligations*, so others feel that they are hostile to the full possession of their *rights*, of that to which they are properly entitled.

Eventual Transformation of Social Values and Aims. —In extreme cases, the individual may come to believe that, either on the basis of his true obligations or his true rights, the very principle of society is morally indifferent or even unworthy; that the moral life is eventually or intrinsically an individual matter, although it happens to be outwardly led under social conditions. But in the main the opposition is not to the social relations as such, but to existing institutions and customs as inadequate. Then the reaction of the individual against the existing social scheme, whether on the ground of ideals too high to be supported by it or on the ground of personal claims to which it does not afford free play, becomes a means to the reconstruction and transformation of social habits. In this way, *reflective morality is a mark of a progressive society, just as customary morality is of a stationary society.* Reflection on values is the method of their modification.

The monastic Christian in his outward withdrawal from social life, still maintained the conception of a perfected society, of a kingdom of God or Heaven to be established. This ideal became to some extent the working method for changing the existing order. The Stoics, who held in light esteem existing community ties, had the conception of a universal community, a cosmopolis, ruled by universal law, of which every rational being was a member and subject. This notion became operative to some extent in the development of judicial and administrative systems much more generalized and equitable than the purely local customs, laws, and standards which it swept away. The Epicurean had the ideal of friendship on the basis of which were formed groups of congenial associates held together neither by legal ties, nor by universal laws of reason, nor by unity of religious aspiration and belief, but by friendship and companionable intercourse. Thus were afforded other centres of social reconstruction.

§ 4. Effects upon the Individual Character

General Effects.—The characteristic differences which have been pointed out in the preceding section, when taken together with the specific conditions of change—liberty of action and thought, incentives to private acquisition, facilities for power and pleasure—enable us to understand the contrasts referred to at the opening of the chapter. We have, on the one hand, the inbred craving for power, for acquisition, for excitement, for gratification of sense and appetite, enhanced by what it feeds on. We have, on the other hand, the progressive differentiation of the moral, tearing the individual loose from the bonds of the external moral order and forcing him to stand on his own feet—or fall. Note how each of the points brought out in the preceding section operates.

(1) To separate out the moral as a distinct element from certain spheres of life, allows the less seriously minded and the less sympathetic individuals to live complacently a trivial or unscrupulous life. Fashion, "social duties," amusements, "culture" emptied of all earnest meaning, "business" and "politics" divorced from any humane or public considerations, may be regarded as justifiable vocations. A "gentleman" who no longer has the occupation of his fighting predecessors as an excuse for a distinct type of life, may find the support of a large leisure class in declining any useful service to the community and devoting himself to "sport"; a "lady" may be so engaged by the multifarious demands of "society" as never to notice what an utterly worthless round she follows.

(2) The fact that the morality of conscience requires reflection, progress, and a deeper meaning for its conception, makes it obvious why many fail to grasp any moral meaning at all. They fail to put forth the effort, or to break with habit. Under customary morality it was enough to "observe" and to

continue in the mores. It requires a higher degree of insight and a greater initiative to get any moral attitude at all when the forms have become mere forms and the habits mere habits. Hence when a change in personal environment or in general social and economic conditions comes, many fail to see the principles involved. They remain completely satisfied with the "old-fashioned virtues" or entrench themselves in the "righteousness" and "honesty" of a past generation. This habitual and "painless" morality will often mean a "virtue" or "righteousness" which involves no conflict with present conditions. A man who feels honest because he does not break contracts or defraud in old-fashioned ways, may be quite at ease about watering stock or adulterating goods. A society which abhors murder with iron and explosives in the form of daggers and bombs, may feel quite unconcerned about the preventable homicides by iron machinery, or by explosives used in coal mines.

(3) The conflict with society which reflective morality requires, works to thrust some below the general level, while it raises others above it. To criticize the general moral order may make a man a prophet, but it may also make him a Pharisee. Practical reaction may make reformers, but it is likely to make another set of men dissolute; to make them feel superior to the morality of "Philistines" and therefore exempt from social restraints.

Vices Incident to Reflective Stage.—The vices increase with civilization, partly because of increased opportunity, partly because of increased looseness in social restraint. There is a further element. When any activity of man is cut off from its original and natural relations and made the object of special attention and pursuit, the whole adjustment is thrown out of balance. What was before a useful function becomes pathological. The craving for excitement or stimulation is normal within certain limits. In the chase or the battle, in the venture of the explorer or the merchant, it functions as a healthy incentive. When isolated as an end in itself, taken out of the objective social situation, it becomes the spring of gambling or drunkenness. The instincts and emotions of sex, possessing power and interest necessitated by their place in the continuance of the race, become

when isolated the spring of passion or of obscenity or lubric-
ity. Avarice and gluttony illustrate the same law. The gladiatorial shows at Rome became base and cowardly when the
Romans were themselves no longer fighters.[7] Even the
aspiration for what is higher and better may become an
"otherworldliness" which leaves this world to its misery and
evil. Such a series of pictures as Balzac has given in his
Comédie Humaine, shows better than any labored description the possibilities of modern civilization.

There is, moreover, in civilized society a further most
demoralizing agency unknown to earlier life. As the vices
are specialized and pursued they become economic and political interests. Vast capital is invested in the business of
ministering to the vicious appetites. It is pecuniarily desirable that these appetites should be stimulated as greatly
as possible. It makes "business." The tribute levied by public
officials upon the illegal pursuits forms a vast fund for
carrying elections. The multitude engaged in the traffic or
dependent upon it for favors, can be relied upon to cast their
votes as a unit for men who will guarantee protection.

Relations to Fellow Men.—The motives and occasions
for selfishness and injustice have been indicated sufficiently
perhaps in preceding chapters. As the general process of
increasing individuality and reflection goes on, it is an increasingly easy matter to be indifferent or even unjust. When
all lead a common life it is easy to enter into the situation of
another, to appreciate his motives, his needs, and in general
to "put yourself in his place." The external nature of the
conduct makes it easy to hold all to a common standard. The
game must be shared; the property—so far as there is property—respected; the religious rites observed. But when standards become more inward the more intelligent or rigorous
may find sympathy less easy. When they attempt to be
"charitable" they may easily become condescending. The pure
will not soil their skirts by contact with the fallen. The "high-
minded citizen" refuses to mix in politics. The scholar thinks
the business man materialistic. The man of breeding, wealth,
and education finds the uneducated laborer lacking in cour-

7. Sumner, *Folkways,* p. 570.

tesy and refinement and argues that it is useless to waste sympathy upon the "masses." The class terms which have become moral terms are illustrations of this attitude. Finally, the moral process of building up freedom and right easily leads to a disposition to stand on rights and let other persons look out for themselves. Kant's doctrine, that since all morality is personal I can do nothing to promote my neighbor's perfection, is a *laissez faire* in ethics which he did not carry out, but it is a not unnatural corollary of reflective morality. "Am I my brother's keeper?" is much more likely to be the language of reflective, than of customary and group life.

Reconstructive Forces.—We have dwelt at length upon the disintegrating forces, not because civilization necessarily grows worse, but because, having pointed out in earlier chapters the positive advances, it becomes necessary to allude also to the other aspect of the process. Otherwise it might appear that there is no problem. If the evolution were supposed to be all in one direction there would be no seriousness in life. It is only in the pressure of constantly new difficulties and evils that moral character adds new fibre, and moral progress emerges. Individualism, self-seeking, and desire for property force the establishment of governments and courts which protect poor as well as rich. Luxury and ostentation have not only called out the asceticism which renounces the world and sees in all gratification of appetite an evil; they have brought into the fore the serious meaning of life; they have served to emphasize the demand for social justice. The countless voluntary associations for the relief of sickness, misfortune, and poverty; for aiding the defective, dependent, and criminal; for promoting numberless good causes—enlist a multitude in friendly cooperation. The rising demand for legislation to embody the new sentiments of justice is part of the process of reconstruction. And now when all the arts and goods of civilization are becoming more and more fully the work, not of any individual's labor or skill, but rather of the combined labor and intelligence of many, when life in cities is necessitating greater interdependence, finally when contrasts in conditions are brought more forcibly to notice by the very progress of knowledge and the means of knowledge,—the more thoroughly social use of all that civilization

produces becomes more insistent and compelling. It is not a
matter of sentiment but of necessity. If any one is disposed to
deny the claim, it becomes increasingly certain that Carlyle's
Irish widow will prove her sisterhood by infecting the denier
with fever;[8] that the ignorant, or criminal, or miserable will
jeopardize his happiness.

§ 5. Moral Differentiation and the Social Order

Two processes went on side by side in the movement we
have traced. (1) The primitive group, which was at once a
kinship or family, an economic, a political, a religious, an
educational, and a moral unit, was broken down and replaced by several distinct institutions, each with its own
special character. (2) The moral, which was so largely unreflective that it could be embodied in every custom and
observance, became more personal and subjective. The result
of this was either that the moral was now more consciously
and voluntarily *put into* the social relations, thereby raising
them all to a higher moral level, or that, failing such a
leavening of the distinct spheres of the social order, the latter
were emptied of moral value and lost moral restraints. We
notice very briefly certain illustrations of this, leaving a
fuller treatment for Part III.

The Family.—When the family was largely determined
by status, when it was an economic, a political, and a religious unit, it had a strong support. But the support was
largely external to the true purpose and meaning of the

8. "One of Dr. Alison's Scotch facts struck us much. A poor Irish
Widow, her husband having died in one of the Lanes of Edinburgh, went forth with her three children, bare of all resources,
to solicit help from the Charitable Establishments of that City.
At this Charitable Establishment and then at that she was refused; referred from one to the other, helped by none; till she
had exhausted them all; till her strength and heart failed her;
she sank down in typhus-fever; died, and infected her Lane with
fever, so that 'seventeen other persons' died of fever there in
consequence. . . . The forlorn Irish Widow applies to her fellow
creatures, as if saying, 'Behold I am sinking, bare of help; ye
must help me! I am your sister, bone of your bone; one God
made us; ye must help me.' They answer, 'No, impossible; thou
art no sister of ours.' But she proves her sisterhood; her typhus
fever kills *them*." (Carlyle, *Past and Present*, Book III, ch. ii.)

family. Only as these other elements were separated, and the family placed on a voluntary basis, could its true significance emerge. Affection and mutual supplementation of husband and wife, love and devotion to offspring, must stand the strains formerly distributed over several ties. The best types of family life which have resulted from this more moral basis are unquestionably far superior to the older form. At the same time the difficulties and perversion or subversion of the more voluntary type are manifest. When no personal attachment was sought or professed, or when marriage by purchase was the approved custom, the marriage contracted under these conditions might have all the value which the general state of intelligence and civilization allowed. When the essential feature which hallows the union has come to be recognized as a union of will and affection, then marriage without these, however "solemnized," almost inevitably means moral degradation. And if the consent of the parties is regarded as the basis of the tie, then it is difficult to make sure that this "consent" has within it enough of steadfast, well-considered purpose and of emotional depth to take the place of all the older sanctions and to secure permanent unions. The more complete responsibility for the children which has been gained by the separation of the family, has also proved susceptible of abuse as well as of service. For while savages have often practiced infanticide for economic reasons, it is doubtful if any savage family ever equaled the more refined selfishness and cruelty of the child labor which modern families have furnished and modern society has permitted.

The Economic and Industrial.—The economic lost powerful restraints when it became a separate activity divorced from family, religious, and, in the view of some, from moral considerations. It has worked out certain important moral necessities of its own. Honesty, the keeping of contracts, the steadiness and continuity of character fostered by economic relations, are important contributions. Modern business, for example, is the most effective agency in securing sobriety. It is far more efficient than "temperance societies." Other values of the economic and industrial process—the increase of production, the interchange of services and goods, the

new means of happiness afforded by the increase of wealth—
are obvious. On the other hand, the honesty required by
business is a most technical and peculiarly limited sort. It
does not interfere with adulteration of goods under certain
conditions, nor with corrupt bargains with public officials.
The measurement of values on a purely pecuniary basis
tends to release a large sphere of activity from any moral
restraints. The maxim "Business is business" may be made
the sanction for any kind of conduct not excluded by commercial standards. Unless there is a constant injection of
moral valuation and control, there is a tendency to subvert
all other ends and standards to the purely economic.

Law and Government.—To remove these functions from
the kinship group as such, is at once to bring the important
principles of authority and duty, and gradually of rights and
freedom, to consciousness. Only by such separation could the
universality and impartiality of law be established. And only
by universality can the judgment of the society as a whole be
guaranteed its execution as over against the variations in
intelligence and right purpose of individual rulers and judges.
Moreover, the separation of law from morality has likewise
its gain or loss. On the one hand, to separate off a definite
sphere of external acts to which alone physical constraints
or penalties may attach, is at once to free a great sphere of
inner thought and purpose and to enable purely psychical
values and restraints to attain far greater power in conduct.
Liberty of thought and religious belief, sincerity and thorough
responsibility, require such a separation. It is also to make
possible a general law which rises above the conscience of
the lower even if it does not always reach the level of the
most enlightened and just. To make a command a "universal law" is itself a steadying and elevating influence, and
it is only by a measure of abstraction from the individual,
inner aspect of conduct that this can be achieved. On the
other hand, the not infrequent contrast between law and
justice, the substitution of technicality for substantials, the
conservatism which made Voltaire characterize lawyers as
the "conservators of ancient barbarous usages," above all the
success with which law has been used to sanction or even
facilitate nearly every form of oppression, extortion, class

advantage, or even judicial murder, is a constant attestation of the twofold possibilities inherent in all institutions. Government in other functions exhibits similar possibilities. At first it was tyranny against which the subject had to defend himself. Now it is rather the use of political machinery for private gain. "Eternal vigilance" is the price not only of freedom, but of every moral value.

The Religious Life. — When freed from interdependence with kinship, economic, and political association, religion has an opportunity to become more personal and more universal. When a man's religious attitude is not fixed by birth, when worship is not so closely bound up with economic interests, when there is not only religious "toleration," but religious liberty, the significance of religion as a personal, spiritual relation comes to view. The kinship tie is sublimated into a conception of divine fatherhood. It becomes credible that Job does serve God "for naught." Faith and purity of heart are not secured by magistrates or laws.

And the universality of religion is no less a gain. So far as religion was of the group it tended to emphasize the boundary between Jew and Gentile, Greek and Barbarian, between the "we-group" and the "others-group." But when this group religion gave place to a more universal religion, the kingdom of Israel could give place to the kingdom of God; brotherhood could transcend family or national lines. In the fierce struggles of the Middle Ages the church was a powerful agency for restraining the powerful and softening the feuds of hostile clans and peoples. The "peace of God" was not only a symbol of a far-off ideal, but an actual relief. The universality might indeed be sought by force in a crusade of Christian against Moslem, or in the horror of a thirty years' war between Catholic and Protestant. But as the conception of religion as a spiritual relation becomes clearer, the tendency must inevitably be to disclose religion as essentially a unifying rather than a divisive and discordant force. If any religion becomes universal it will be because of its universal appeal. And so far as it does make universal appeal, like science, like art, it invites its followers.

The differentiation of the moral from the religious is often difficult to trace. For the religious has often been the agency through which certain of the characteristics of the moral have been brought about. The inward and voluntary aspect of the moral, as compared with the verdicts of law or public opinion, has been emphasized. But this is often developed by the religious conceptions of an all-seeing God, an all-wise judge. "Man looketh on the outer appearance, but the Lord looketh upon the heart" has its literary parallels in Xenophon and Plato and Shakespere. The distinction between higher and lower values has received its most impressive symbol in the conception of "another world," in which there is neither pain nor sin, but eternal blessedness and eternal life. Ideals of character, when embodied in divine persons, command love, reverence, and devotion in supreme degree. A society in which love and justice are the law of life has seemed more possible, more potent to inspire sacrifice and enthusiasm, when envisaged as the Kingdom of God. But in all these illustrations we have, not the religious as distinct from the moral, but the religious as modified by the moral and embodying the moral in concrete examples and imagery. We can see the two possible types of development, however, in the concrete instances of the Hebrews and the Greeks. In Israel religion was able to take up the moral ideals and become itself more completely ethical. The prophets of religion were at the same time the moral reformers. But in Greece, in spite of the efforts of some of the great poets, the religious conceptions for the most part remained set and hence became superstition, or emotional orgy, or ecstasy, while the moral found a distinct path of its own. Religion at present is confronting the problem of whether it will be able to take up into itself the newer ethical values—the scientific spirit which seeks truth, the enhanced value of human worth which demands higher types of social justice.

A brief characterization of the respective standpoints of religion and morality may be added, as they both aim to control and give value to human conduct. The religious has always implied some relation of man's life to unseen powers or to the cosmos. The relation may be the social relation of kin or friend or companion, the political of subject to a sovereign, the cosmic relation of dependence, or that of seeking in the divine completer meaning or more perfect fulfillment for what is fragmentary and imperfect. In its aspect of "faith" it holds all these ideals of power, wisdom, goodness, justice, to be real and effective. The moral, on the other hand, concerns itself, not with unseen beings or cosmic reality, but with human purposes and the relations of a man to his fellows. For religion, conscience may be the "voice of God"; for morality, it must be stated in terms of thought and feeling. The "moral law" must be viewed as a law which is capable of being approved, at least—and this implies that it may also be criticized—by the mind. The difference which religion states as a choice between "God and mammon," between heaven and earth, morality must state in terms of good and evil, right and wrong, ideal interests and natural appetites. Instead of regarding its standards as laws established once for all by a divine authority, morality seeks to reach *principles*. Instead of embodying its ideals in persons, the moral seeks to reshape them continually. It is for religion to hold that "God reigns," and therefore "All's right with the world." The moral as such must be continually overcoming evil, continually working out ideals into conduct, and changing the natural order into a more rational and social order.

Part II Theory of the Moral Life

General Literature for Part II

Among the works which have had the most influence upon the development of the theory of morals are: Plato, *Republic*, *Laws*, and Dialogues entitled *Protagoras* and *Gorgias*; Aristotle, *Ethics*; Cicero, *De finibus* and *De officiis*; Marcus Aurelius, *Meditations*; Epictetus, *Discourses*; Lucretius, *De Rerum Natura*; St. Thomas Aquinas (selected and translated by Rickaby under title of *Aquinas Ethicus*); Hobbes, *Leviathan*; Spinoza, *Ethics*; Shaftesbury, *Characteristics*, and "Inquiry Concerning Virtue"; Hutcheson, *System of Moral Philosophy*; Butler, *Sermons*; Hume, *Essays*, "Principles of Morals"; Adam Smith, *Theory of Moral Sentiments*; Bentham, *Principles of Morals and Legislation*; Kant, *Critique of Practical Reason*, and *Fundamental Principles of the Metaphysics of Ethics*; Comte, "Social Physics" (in his *Positive Philosophy*); Mill, *Utilitarianism*; Spencer, *Principles of Ethics*; Green, *Prolegomena to Ethics*; Sidgwick, *Methods of Ethics*; Selby-Bigge, *British Moralists*, 2 vols. (a convenient collection of selections). For contemporary treatises, and histories consult the literature referred to in the Introduction to this volume.

10. THE MORAL SITUATION

Object of Part Two and of Present Chapter.—From the history of morals, we turn to the theoretical analysis of reflective morality. We are concerned to discover (1) just what in conduct it is that we judge good and evil, right and wrong (conduct being a complicated thing); (2) what we mean by good and evil, right and wrong; (3) on what basis we apply these conceptions to their appropriate objects in conduct. But before we attempt these questions, we must detect and identify the *moral situation*, the situation in which considerations of good and evil, right and wrong, present themselves and are employed. For some situations we employ the ideas of true and false; of beautiful and ugly; of skillful and awkward; of economical and wasteful, etc. We may indeed apply the terms right and wrong to these same situations; but if so, it is to them in some other light. What then are the differentiating traits, the special earmarks, presented by the situation which we identify as distinctively moral? For we use the term moral in a broad sense to designate that which is either moral or immoral: i.e., right or wrong in the narrower sense. It is the moral situation in the broad sense as distinct from the non-moral, not from the immoral, that we are now concerned with.

The Moral Situation Involves Voluntary Activity.—It will be admitted on all hands that the moral situation is one which, whatever else it may or may not be, involves a voluntary factor. Some of the chief traits of voluntary activity we have already become acquainted with, as in the account by Aristotle, already noted (*ante,* pp. 16–17). The agent must know what he is about; he must have some idea of what he is doing; he must not be a somnambulist, or an imbecile, or insane, or an infant so immature as to have no idea of what he is doing. He must also have some wish, some desire, some preference in the matter. A man overpowered by superior force might be physically compelled by some ingenious device to shoot a gun at another, knowing what he was doing, but his act would not be voluntary because he had no choice in the matter, or rather because his preference was not to do the act which he is aware he is doing. But if he is ordered to kill another and told if he does not he will himself be killed, he has *some* will in the matter. He may do the deed, not because he likes it or wishes it in itself, but because he wishes to save his own life. The attendant circumstances may affect our judgment of the kind and degree of morality attaching to the act; but they do not take it entirely out of the moral sphere.[1] Aristotle says the act must also be the expression of a disposition (a habit or ἕξις), a more or less settled tendency on the part of the person. It must bear some relation to his character. Character is not, we may say, a third factor. It is making clear what is implied in deliberation and wish. There may be little deliberation in a child's act and little in an adult's, and yet we may regard the latter as much more voluntary than the child's. With the child, the thought is superficial and casual, because of the restricted stage of organization or growth reached (see p. 15): his act flows from organic instinct or from accidental circumstances—whim, caprice, and chance suggestion, or fancy. The adult's act may flow from habitual tendencies and be accompanied by an equally small amount of conscious reflection. But the tendencies themselves are the outcome of prior deliberations and choices which have finally got funded into more or less automatic habits. The child's act is to a slight extent the expression of character; the adult's to a large extent. In short, we mean by character whatever lies behind an act in the way of deliberation and desire, whether these processes be near-by or remote.

Not Everything Voluntary is Morally Judged.—A voluntary act may then be defined as one *which manifests character*, the test of its presence being the presence of desire and deliberation; these sometimes being present directly and

1. Aristotle illustrates by a man who throws his goods overboard in a storm at sea. He does not wish absolutely to lose his goods, but he prefers losing them to losing the ship or his own life: he wishes it *under the circumstances* and his act is so far voluntary.

immediately, sometimes indirectly and remotely through their effects upon the agent's standing habits. But we do not judge all voluntary activity from the moral standpoint. Some acts we judge from the standpoint of skill or awkwardness; others as amusing or boring; others as stupid or highly intelligent, and so on. We do not bring to bear the conceptions of right and wrong. And on the other hand, there are many things called good and bad which are not voluntary. Since what we are in search of must lie somewhere between these two limits, we may begin with cases of the latter sort.

(*1*) *Not Everything Judged Good or Right is Moral.*— We speak, for example, of an ill-wind; of a good engine; of a watch being wrong; or of a screw being set right. We speak of good and bad bread, money, or soil. That is, from the standpoint of value, we judge things as *means* to certain results in themselves desirable or undesirable. A "good" machine does efficiently the work for which it is designed; "bad" money does not subserve the ends which money is meant to promote; the watch that is wrong comes short of telling us time correctly. We have to use the notion of value and of contribution to value; that is a positive factor. But this contribution to valuable result is not, in inanimate objects, something meant or intended by the things themselves. If we thought the ill-wind had an idea of its own destructive effect and took pleasure in that idea, we should attribute moral quality to it—just as men did in early times, and so tried to influence its behavior in order to make it "good." Among things that promote favorable or unfavorable results a line is drawn between those which just do so as matter of fact, and those in which meaning so to do, or intention, plays a part.

(*2*) *Good in Animal Conduct.*—Let us now consider the case of good and bad animal conduct. We speak of a good watch-dog; of a bad saddle-horse, and the like. Moreover, we *train* the dog and the horse to the right or desired kind of action. We make, we repair the watch; but we do not *train* it. Training involves a new factor: enlistment of the animal's tendencies; of its own conscious attitudes and reactions. We pet, we reward by feeding, we punish and threaten. By these means we induce animals to exercise in ways that form the habits we want. We modify the animal's behavior by modifying its own impulses. But we do not give moral significance to the good and bad, for we are still thinking of means to ends. We do not suppose that we have succeeded in supplying the hunting dog, for example, with *ideas* that certain results are more excellent than others, so that henceforth he acts on the basis of his own discrimination of the less and the more valuable. We just induce certain habits by managing to make certain ways of acting *feel* more agreeable than do others. Thus James says: "Whether the dog has the notion of your being angry or of your property being valuable in any such abstract way as *we* have these notions, is more than doubtful. The conduct is more likely an impulsive result of a conspiracy of outward stimuli; the beast *feels like* acting so when these stimuli are present, though conscious of no definite reason why"[2] (*Psychology*, Vol. II, p. 350, note). Or putting it the other way: if the dog has an idea of the results of guarding the house, and is controlled in what he does by loyalty to this idea, by the satisfaction which he takes in it, then in calling the dog good we mean that in being good for a certain result, he is also morally good.

(3) *Non-moral Human Acts.*—There are also acts evoked by an idea of value in the results to be reached, which are not judged as coming within the moral sphere. "Conduct is three-fourths of life," but in some sense it is more: it is four-fourths. All conscious human life is concerned with ends, and with selecting, arranging, and employing the means, intellectual, emotional, and practical, involved in these ends. This makes *conduct*. But it does not follow that all conduct has *moral* import. "As currently conceived, stirring the fire, reading a newspaper, or eating a meal, are acts with which morality has no concern. Opening the window to air the room, putting on an overcoat when the weather is cold, are thought of as having no ethical significance. These, however, are all portions of conduct" (Spencer, *Principles of*

---

2. Of course, this is also true of a large part of human activity. But these are also the cases in which we do not ascribe moral value; or at least we do not except when we want to make the agent conscious of some reason why.

Ethics, Vol. I, p. 5). They all involve the idea of some result worth reaching, and the putting forth of energy to reach the result—of intelligently selected and adapted means. But this may leave the act morally indifferent—innocent.

Introduction of Moral Factor.—A further quotation from Spencer may introduce discussion of the needed moral qualification:

> As already said, a large part of the ordinary conduct is indifferent. Shall I walk to the waterfall to-day? or, shall I ramble along the sea-shore? Here the ends are ethically indifferent. If I go to the waterfall, shall I go over the moor or take the path through the wood? Here the means are ethically indifferent. . . . But if a friend who is with me has explored the sea-shore, but has not seen the waterfall, the choice of one or other end is no longer ethically indifferent. Again, if a probable result of making the one excursion rather than the other, is that I shall not be back in time to keep an appointment, or if taking the longer route entails this risk while the shorter does not, the decision in favour of one end or means acquires in another way an ethical character (Spencer, *Principles of Ethics*, Vol. I, pp. 5–6).

This illustration suggests two differing types of conduct; two differing ways in which activity is induced and guided by ideas of valuable results. In one case the end presents itself directly as desirable, and the question is only as to the steps or means of achieving this end. Here we have conduct which, although excited and directed by considerations of value, is still morally indifferent. Such is the condition of things *wherever one end is taken for granted by itself without any consideration of its relationship to other ends*. It is then a technical rather than a moral affair. It is a question of taste and of skill—of personal preference and of practical wisdom, or of economy, expediency. There are many different roads to most results, and the selection of this path rather than that, on the assumption that either path actually leads to the end, is an intellectual, aesthetic, or executive, rather than an ethical matter. I may happen to prefer a marine view to that of the uplands—that is an aesthetic interest. I may wish to utilize the time of the walk for thinking, and may find the moor path less distracting; here is a matter of intellectual economy. Or I may conclude that I shall best get the exercise I want by going to the water fall. Here it is a question of "prudence," of expediency, or practical wisdom. Let any one of the ends, aesthetic, intellectual, hygienic, stand alone and it is a fit and proper consideration. The moral issue does not arise. Or the various ends may be regarded as means to a further unquestioned end—say a walk with the maximum of combined aesthetic interest and physical exercise.

(4) *Criterion for Moral Factor.*—But let the value of one proposed end be felt to be really incompatible with that of another, let it be felt to be so opposed as to appeal to a different kind of interest and choice, in other words, to different kinds of disposition and agency, and we have a moral situation. This is what occurs when one way of traveling means self-indulgence; another, kindliness or keeping an engagement. There is no longer one end, nor two ends so homogeneous that they may be reconciled by both being used as means to some more general end of undisputed worth. We have alternative ends so heterogeneous that choice has to be made; an end has to be developed out of conflict. The problem now becomes what *is* really valuable. It is the *nature* of the valuable, of the desirable, that the individual has to pass upon.[3]

Suppose a person has unhesitatingly accepted an end, has acquiesced in some suggested purpose. Then, starting to realize it, he finds the affair not so simple. He is led to review the matter and to consider what really constitutes worth for him. The process of attainment calls for toil which is disagreeable, and imposes restraints and abandonments of accustomed enjoyments. An Indian boy, for example, thinks it desirable to be a good rider, a skillful shot, a sagacious scout. Then he "naturally," as we say, disposes of his time and energy so as to realize his purpose. But in trying to become a "brave," he finds that he has to submit to deprivation and hardship, to forego other enjoyments and undergo arduous toil. He finds that the end does not mean in actual realization what it meant in original contemplation —something that often happens, for, as Goldsmith said: "In

3. While we have employed Spencer's example, it should be noted that incompatibility of ends is not the criterion of the distinctively moral situation which Spencer himself employs.

the first place, we cook the dish to our own appetite; in the latter, nature cooks it for us."

This change in apparent worth raises a new question: Is the aim first set up of the value it seemed to be? Is it, after all, so important, so desirable? Are not other results, playing with other boys, convivial companionship, which are reached more easily and pleasantly, really more valuable? The labors and pains connected with the means employed to reach an end, have thrown another and incompatible end into consciousness. The individual no longer "naturally," but "morally," follows the selected end, whichever of the two it be, because it has been chosen after conscious valuation of competing aims.

Such competitions of values for the position of control of action are inevitable accompaniments of individual conduct, whether in civilized or in tribal life. A child, for example, finds that the fulfillment of an appetite of hunger is not only possible, but that it is desirable—that fulfillment brings, or is, satisfaction, not mere satiety. Later on, moved by the idea of this sort of value, he snatches at food. Then he is made aware of other sorts of values involved in the act performed—values incompatible with just the value at which he aimed. He brings down upon himself social disapproval and reproach. He is termed rude, unmannerly, greedy, selfish. He acted in accordance with an unhesitatingly accepted idea of value. But while reaching one result he accomplished also certain other results which he did not intend, results in the way of being thought ill of, results which are disagreeable: *negative values*. He is taught to raise the question of what, after all, in such cases is the *really* desirable or valuable. Before he is free to deliberate upon means, he has to form an estimate of the relative worth of various possible ends, and to be willing to forego one and select the other. The chapters on Hebrew and Greek moral development have shown this same process at work in the life of a people.

Summary and Definition.—If we sum up the three classes of instances thus far considered, we get the following defining traits of a moral situation, that is, of one which is an appropriate subject of determinations of right and wrong: Moral experience is (1) a matter of *conduct, be-*

havior; that is, of activities which are called out by *ideas of the worth, the desirability of results*. This evocation by an *idea* discriminates it from the so-called behavior of a pump, where there is no recognition of results; and from conduct attributed to the lower animals, where there are probably feelings and even dim imagery, but hardly ideas of the comparative desirability or value of various ends. Moral experience is (2) that kind of conduct in which there are ends so discrepant, so incompatible, as to require selection of one and rejection of the other. This perception of, and selection from, incompatible alternatives, discriminates moral experience from those cases of conduct which are called out and directed by ideas of value, but which do not necessitate passing upon the *real worth*, as we say, of the value selected. It is incompatibility of ends which necessitates consideration of the *true* worth of a given end; and such consideration it is which brings the experience into the moral sphere. Conduct as moral may thus be defined as *activity called forth and directed by ideas of value or worth, where the values concerned are so mutually incompatible as to require consideration and selection before an overt action is entered upon.*

End Finally at Issue.—Many questions about ends are in reality questions about means: the artist considers whether he will paint a landscape or a figure; this or that landscape, and so on. The general character of the end is unchanged: it is to paint. But let this end persist and be felt as desirable, as valuable; let at the same time an alternative end present itself as also desirable (say keeping an engagement), so that the individual does not find any way of adjusting and arranging them into a common scheme (like doing first one and then the other), and the person has a moral problem on his hands. Which shall he decide for, and why? The appeal is to himself; what does *he* really think the desirable end? What makes the supreme appeal to him? What sort of an agent, of a person, shall he be? This is the question finally at stake in any genuinely moral situation: What shall the agent *be*? What sort of a character shall he assume? On its face, the question is what he shall *do*, shall he act for this or that end. But the incompatibility of the ends forces the issue back into the question of the kinds of selfhood, of agency, involved in the respective ends. The distinctively moral situation is then one in which elements of value and control are bound up with the processes of deliberation and desire; and are bound up in a peculiar way: *viz.*, they decide what kind of a character shall control further desires and deliberations. When ends are genuinely incompatible, no common denominator can be found except by deciding what sort of character is most highly prized and shall be given supremacy.

The Moral and Indifferent Situations.—This criterion throws lights upon our earlier discussion of morally indifferent acts. Persons perform the greater bulk of their activities without any conscious reference to considerations of right and wrong, as any one may verify for himself by recollecting the general course of his activity on any ordinary day from the time he arises in the morning to the time he goes to bed at night. His deliberations and wants are mostly concerned with the ends involved in his regular vocation and recreations. But at any time the question of his character as concerned with what he is doing may arise for judgment. The person may later on realize that the type or kind of character which is to prevail in his further activity was involved in deeds which were performed without any such thought. He *then* judges them morally, approving or disapproving. On the other hand, a course of action which at the time presented a moral crisis even, may afterwards come to be followed as a matter of course. There is then no *fixed* line between the morally indifferent and the morally significant. Every act is *potential* subject-matter of moral judgment, for it strengthens or weakens some habit which influences whole classes of judgments.

Literature

There are comparatively few distinct analyses of the moral situation, the topic generally being treated as a running part of the theory of the author, or in connection with an account of character or conduct (see references at end of ch. 13). See, however, Mezes, *Ethics: Descriptive and Explanatory*, ch. ii; Martineau, *Types of Ethical Theory*, Vol. II, pp. 17–54; Spencer, *Principles of Ethics*, Vol. I; *Studies in Logical Theory*, Stuart, essay on Valuation as a Logical Process, pp. 237–41, 257–58, 273–75, 289–93; Dewey, *Logical Conditions of a Scientific Treatment of Morality*; Mead, "Philosophical Basis of Ethics," *International Journal of Ethics*, April, 1908; Fite, *Introductory Study of Ethics*, chs. ii, xviii, and xix.

We have identified in its framework and main outlines the sort of voluntary activity in which the problem of good and evil appears and in which the ideas of right and wrong are employed. This task, however, is only preliminary to theoretical analysis. For it throws no light upon just what we mean by good and bad; just what elements of complex voluntary behavior are termed right or wrong; or why they are so termed. It does not even indicate what must be discovered before such questions can be answered. It only sets forth the limits of the subject-matter within which such questions arise and in reference to which they must be answered. What are the distinctive problems which must be dealt with in the course of such a discussion?

Growth of Theory from Practical Problems.—Of one thing we may be sure. If inquiries are to have any substantial basis, if they are not to be wholly up in the air, the theorist must take his departure from the problems which men actually meet in their own conduct. He may define and refine these; he may divide and systematize; he may abstract the problems from their concrete contexts in individual lives; he may classify them when he has thus detached them; but if he gets away from them he is talking about something which his own brain has invented, not about moral realities. On the other hand, the perplexities and uncertainties of direct and personal behavior invite a more abstract and systematic impersonal treatment than that which they receive in the exigencies of their occurrence. The recognition of any end or authority going beyond what is embodied in existing customs, involves some appeal to thought, and moral theory makes this appeal more explicit and more complete. If a child asks why he should tell the truth, and is answered, "because you ought to and that is reason enough"; or, "because it will prove profitable for you to do so"; or, "because truth-telling is a condition of mutual communication and common aims," the answer implies a principle which requires only to be made explicit to be full-fledged theory. And when this principle is compared with those employed in other cases to see if they are mutually consistent, and if not, to find a still more fundamental reconciling principle, we have passed over the border into ethical system.

Types of Theoretical Problems.—The practical problems which a thoughtful and progressive individual must consider in his own conduct will, then, give the clue to the genuine problems of moral theory. The framework of one is an outline of the other. The man who does not satisfy himself with sheer conventional conformity to the customs, the *ethos*, of his class will find such problems as the following forced upon his attention: —(1) He must consider the *meaning* of habits which have been formed more or less unreflectively—by imitation, suggestion, and inculcation from others—and he must consider the meaning of those customs about him to which he is invited to conform till they have become personal habits. This problem of discovering the meaning of these habits and customs is the problem of stating what, after all, is *really* good, or worth while in conduct. (2) The one whose morality is of the reflective sort will be faced by the problem of moral advance, of progress beyond the level which has been reached by this more or less unreflective taking on of the habits and ideas of those about him, progress up to the level of his own reflective insight. Otherwise put, he has to face the problem of what is to be the place and rôle in his own conduct of ideals and principles generated not by custom but by deliberation and insight. (3) The individual must consider more consciously the relation between what is currently regarded as good by the social groups in which he is placed and in which he has to act, and that regarded as good by himself. The moment he ceases to accept conformity to custom as an adequate sanction of behavior, he is met by discrepancy between his personally conceived goods and those reigning in the customs about him. Now while this detachment makes possible the birth of higher and more ideal types of morality, and hence of systematic effort for social reform and advance, it also makes possible (as we have seen on the historical side, p.

175) a more generalized and deliberate selfishness: a less instinctive and more intentional pursuit of what the individual judges to be good *for himself* against what society exacts as good for itself. The same reflective attitude which generates the conscientious moral reformer may generate also a more deliberate and resolute anti-social egoism. In any case, the individual who has acquired the habit of moral reflection is conscious of a new problem—the relation of public good to individual good. In short, the individual who is thoughtfully serious and who aims to bring his habit of reflection to bear on his conduct, will have occasion (1) to search for the elements of good and bad, of positive and negative, value in the situations that confront him; (2) to consider the methods and principles by which he shall reach conclusions, and (3) to consider the relations between himself, his own capacities and satisfactions, and the ends and demands of the social situations in which he is placed.

The Corresponding Problems of Theory.—Theory will then have similar problems to deal with. (1) What is the Good, the end in any voluntary act? (2) How is this good known? Is it directly perceived, and if so, how? Or is it worked out through inquiry and reflection? And if so, how? (3) When the good is known, how is it *acknowledged*; how does it acquire authority? What is the place of *law*, of control, in the moral life? Why is it that some ends are attractive of themselves, while others present themselves as *duties*, as involving subordination of what is naturally attractive? (4) What is the place of selfhood in the moral process? And this question assumes two forms: (a) What is the relation of the good of the self to the good of others? (b) What is the difference between the morally good and the morally bad in the self? What are virtues and vices as dispositions of the self? These abstract and formal questions will become more concrete if we consider them briefly in the order of their development in the history of the moral theory.

Problem of Knowledge of Good Comes First in Theory. —The clash and overlapping of customs once so local as to be isolated, brought to Athenian moral philosophers the problem of discovering the underlying and final good to which all the conflicting values of customs might be referred for judgment. The movement initiated by Socrates was pre-

cisely the effort to find out what is the real good, the true
end, of all the various institutions, customs, and procedures
current among men. The explanation of conflict among
men's interests, and of lack of consistency and unity in any
given person's behavior, of the division of classes in the
state, of the diverse recommendations of different would-be
moral teachers, was that they were ignorant of their own
ends. Hence the fundamental precept is "Know thyself,"
one's own end, one's good and one's proper function. Different followers of Socrates gave very different accounts of
knowledge, and hence proposed very different final aims. But
they all agreed that the problem of knowing the good was
the central problem, and that if this were settled, action in
accord with good would follow of itself. Could it be imagined
that man could know his own good and yet not seek it? Ignorance of good is evil and the source of evil; insight into the
real good will clear up the confusion and partiality which
makes men pursue false ends and thus straighten out and
put in order conduct. Control would follow as a matter of
course from *knowledge* of the end. Such control would be
no matter of coercion or external restriction, but of subordination and organization of minor ends with reference to the
final end.

Problem of Motive Force.[1]—The problem of attaining
this knowledge was seen to be attended, however, by peculiar
obstructions and difficulties, the growing recognition of
which led to a shifting of the problem itself. The dilemma,
in brief, was this: The man who is already good will have no
difficulty in knowing the good both in general and in the
specific clothing under which it presents itself in particular
cases. But the one who does not yet know the good, does
not know *how* to know it. His ignorance, moreover, puts
positive obstacles in his way, for it leads him to delight in
superficial and transitory ends. This delight increases the
hold of these ends upon the agent; and thus it builds up an
habitual interest in them which renders it impossible for

---

1. On the *practical* side, this was always, as we have seen, the
prominent problem of Hebrew thought. But we are concerned
here with the statement of the problem by Plato and Aristotle
from the theoretical side.

the individual to get a glimpse of the final end, to say nothing of a clear and persisting view. *Only if the individual is habituated, exercised, practiced in good ends so as to take delight in them, while he is still so immature as to be incapable of really knowing how and why they are good, will he be capable of knowing the good when he is mature.* Pleasure in right ends and pain in wrong must operate as a motive force in order to give experience of the good, before knowledge can be attained and operate as the motor force.

Division of Problem.—But the exercise and training requisite to form the habits which make the individual rejoice in right activity before he knows how and why it is right, presuppose adults who already have knowledge of the good. They presuppose a social order capable not merely of giving theoretic instruction, but of habituating the young to right practices. But where shall such adults be found, and where is the social order so good that it is capable of right training of its own immature members? Hence the problem again shifts, breaking up into two parts. On the one hand, attention is fixed upon the irrational appetites, desires, and impulses, which hinder apprehension of the good; on the other, it is directed to the political laws and institutions which are capable of training the members of the State into a right manner of living. For the most part, these two problems went their own way independently of each other, a fact which resulted in the momentous breach between the inner and "spiritual," and the outer and "physical" aspects of behavior.

Problem of Control of Affections and Desires.—If it is the lively movements of natural appetites and desires which make the individual apprehend false goods as true ones, and which present obstacles to knowledge of the true good, the serious problem is evidently to check and so far as possible to abolish the power of desire to move the mind. Since it is anger, fear, hope, despair, sexual desire which make men regard particular things instead of the final end as good, the great thing is wholly to free attention and judgment from the influence of such passions. It may be impossible to prevent the passions; they are natural perturbations. But man can at least prevent his judgment of what is good or bad from being modified by them. The Stoic moral philosophers most emphasized the misleading influence of desire and passion, and set up the ideal of apathy (lack of passion) and "ataraxy" (absence of being stirred up). The other moral schools, the Sceptics and Epicureans, also made independence of mind from influence of passion the immediate and working end; the Sceptics because they emphasized the condition of mental detachment and non-committal, which is the state appropriate to doubt and uncertainty; the Epicureans because the pleasures of the mind are the only ones not at the mercy of external circumstances. Mental pleasures are equable, and hence are the only ones which do not bring reactions of depression, exhaustion, and subsequent pain. The problem of moral theory is now in effect, if not in name, that of *control*, of authority and subordination, of checking and restraining desire and passion.

Problem of Control of Private Interests by Law.—Such views could at the best, however, affect only a comparatively small number, the philosophers. For the great masses of men in the Roman Empire, the problem existed on the other line: by what laws and what administration of laws to direct the outward acts of men into right courses, courses at least sufficiently right so as to maintain outward peace and unity through the vast empire. In the Greek city-state, with its small number, the philosophers. For the great masses of men public affairs, it was possible to conceive an ideal of a common good which should bind all together. But in an Empire covering many languages, religions, local customs, varied and isolated occupations, a single system of administration and law exercised from a single central source could alone maintain the requisite harmony. The problems of legislations, codification, and administration were congenial to the Latin mind, and were forced by the actual circumstances. From the external side, then, as well as from the internal, the problem of control became dominant over that of value and the good.

Problem of Unification.—It was the province of the moral philosophers, of the theologians, of the church to attempt a fusion of these elements of inner and outer control. It was their aim to connect, to synthesize these factors into one commanding and comprehensive view of life. But the characteristic of their method was to suppose that the combination could be brought about, whether intellectually or practically, only upon a supernatural basis, and by supernatural resources. From the side of the natural constitution of both man and the State, the various elements of behavior are so hopelessly at war with one another that there is no health in them nor help from them. The appetites and desires are directed only upon carnal goods and form the dominant element in the person. Even when reason gets glimpses of the good, the good seen is narrow in scope and temporal in duration; and even then reason is powerless as an adequate motive. "We perceive the better and we follow the worse." Moreover, it is useless to seek aid from the habituation, the education, the discipline and restraint of human institutions. They themselves are corrupt. The product of man's lower nature cannot be capable of enlightening and improving that nature; at most it can only restrain outer action by appealing to fear. Only a divine revelation can make known man's true end; and only divine assistance, embodied in the ordinances and sacraments of the supernaturally founded and directed church, can bring this knowledge home to erring individuals so as to make it effectual. In theory the conception of the end, the good, was supreme; but man's true good is supernatural and hence can be achieved only by supernatural assistance and in the next world. In practice, therefore, the important thing for man in his present condition is implicit reliance upon and obedience to the requirements of the church. This represents on earth the divine sovereign, ultimate source of all moral law. In effect, the moral law became a net-work of ordinances, prescriptions, commands, rewards, penalties, penances, and remissions. The jural point of view was completely enthroned.[2] There was no problem; there was a final, because a supernatural, solution.

The Problems of Individuality and Citizenship.—With the Renaissance began the revolt against the jural view of life. A sense of the joys and delights which attend the free

2. The Ten Commandments, divided and subdivided into all their conceivable applications, and brought home through the confessional, were the specific basis.

and varied exercise of human capacities in this world was reborn. The first results were a demand for natural satisfaction; the next a profound reawakening of the antique civic and political consciousness. The first in its reaction against the Middle Ages was more individualistic than the Greek ideal, to which it was in some respects allied. The Greek had emphasized the notion of value, but had conceived this as generic, as the fulfillment of the essential nature of man as man. But with the moderns, satisfaction, the good, meant something direct, specific, personal; something the individual as an individual could lay hold of and possess. It was an individual right; it was final and inalienable. Nothing had a right to intervene or deprive the individual of it.

This extreme individualistic tendency was contemporaneous with a transfer of interest from the supernatural church-state over to the commercial, social, and political bodies with which the modern man found himself identified. The rise of the free cities, and more especially the development of national states, with the growth of commerce and exchange, opened to the individual a natural social whole. With this his connections were direct, in this he gained new outlets and joys, and yet it imposed upon him definite responsibilities and exacted of him specific burdens. If the individual had gained a new sense of himself as an individual, he also found himself enmeshed in national states of a power constantly increasing in range and intensity. The problem of the moral theorists was to reconcile these two tendencies, the individualistic and that of political centralization. For a time, the individual felt the social organization in which he was set to be, with whatever incidental inconveniences, upon the whole an outlet and reenforcement of prized personal powers. Hence in observing its conditions, he was securing the conditions of his own peace and tranquillity or even of his own freedom and achievement. But the balance was easily upset, and the problem of the relation of the individual and the social, the private and the public, was soon forced into prominence; a problem which in one form or other has been the central problem of modern ethical theory.

Individualistic Problem.—Only for a short time, during the first flush of new achievement and of hopeful adventure, did extreme individualism and social interests remain naïvely combined. The individualistic tendency found a convenient intellectual tool in a psychology which resolved the individual into an association or series of particular states of feeling and sensations; and the good into a like collection of pleasures also regarded as particular mental states. This psychological atomism made individuals as separate and disconnected as the sensations which constituted their selves were isolated and mutually exclusive. Social arrangements and institutions were, in theory, justifiable only as they could be shown to augment the sum of pleasurable states of feeling of individuals. And as, quite independent of any such precarious theory, the demand for reform of institutions became more and more imperative, the situation was packed by Rousseau into a formula that man was naturally both free and good, and that institutional life had enslaved and thereby depraved him. At the same time, there grew up an enthusiastic and optimistic faith in "Nature," in her kindly intentions for the happiness of humanity, and in her potency to draw it to perfection when artificial restrictions were once out of the way. Individuals, separate in themselves and in their respective goods, were thereby brought into a complete coincidence and harmony of interests. Nature's laws were such that if the individual obeyed them in seeking his own good he could not fail to further the happiness of others. While there developed in France (with original initiative from England) this view of the internal isolation and external harmony of men, a counterpart movement took place in Germany.

The Rationalistic Problem.—German thought inherited through both Roman law and the natural theology and ethics of the church, the conception that man's rational nature makes him sociable. Stoicism, with its materialistic idealism, had taught that all true laws are natural, while all laws of nature are diffusions and potencies of reason. As they bind things together in the world, so they bind men together in societies. Moral theory is "Natural Law" conceived in this sense. From the laws of reason, regarded as the laws of man's generic and hence sociable nature, all the principles of jurisprudence and of individual morals may be deduced. But man has also a sensuous nature, an appetitive nature

which is purely private and exclusive. Since reason is higher
than sense, the authority of the State is magnified. The
juristic point of view was reinstated, but with the important
change that the law was that of a social order which is the
realization of man's own rational being.[3] If the laws of the
State were criticized, the reply was that however unworthy
the civic regulations and however desirable their emendation,
still the State is the expression of the idea of reason, that is of
man in his true generic nature. Hence to attempt to overthrow the government is to attack the fundamental and objective conditions of moral or rational life. Without the
State, the particularistic, private side of man's nature would
have free sway to express itself. Man's true moral nature is
within. We are then left, from both the English-French and
the German sides, with the problem of the relation of the
individual and the social; of the relation of the inner and
outer, of the psychological structure of the person and the
social conditions and results of his behavior.

Literature

See the references on the scope and methods of ethics at
the end of ch. i, and also, Sorley, *Ethics of Naturalism*, ch. i, and
his *Recent Tendencies in Ethics*; Fite, *An Introductory Study of
Ethics*, ch. ii; Bowne, *Principles of Ethics*, ch. i; Seth, *Ethical
Principles*, "Introduction," ch. i; Martineau, *Types of Ethical
Theory*, Vol. I, Introduction; Hensel, "Problems of Ethics," in
Vol. I of *St. Louis Congress of Arts and Science*.

3. The idealistic philosophic movement beginning with Kant is in
   many important respects the outgrowth of the earlier *Naturrecht*
   of the moral philosophers from Grotius on.

§ 1. Typical Divisions of Theories

Problems and Theories.—We were concerned in the last chapter with the typical *problems* of moral theory. But it was evident that theories themselves developed and altered as now this, now that, problem was uppermost. To regard the question of how to know the good as the central problem of moral inquiry is already to have one type of theory; to consider the fundamental problem to be either the subordination or the satisfaction of desire is to have other types. A classification of types of theory is rendered difficult, a thoroughly satisfactory classification almost impossible, by the fact that the problems arrange themselves about separate principles leading to cross-divisions. All that we may expect to do is somewhat arbitrarily to select that principle which seems most likely to be useful in conducting inquiry.

(*1*) *Teleological and Jural.*—One of the fundamental divisions arises from taking either Value or Duty, Good or Right, as the fundamental idea. Ethics of the first type is concerned above all with *ends*; hence it is frequently called *teleological* theory (Greek τέλος, end). To the other type of theory, obligations, imperatives, commands, law, and authority, are the controlling ideas. By this emphasis, arise the *jural* theories (Latin, *jus*, law). At some point, of course, each theory has to deal with the factor emphasized by its rival. If we start with Law as central, the good resides in these acts which conform to its obligations. The good is obedience to law, submission to its moral authority. If we start from the Good, laws, rules, are concerned with the means of defining or achieving it.

(*2*) *Individual and Institutional.*—This fundamental division is at once cut across by another, arising from emphasizing the problem of the individual and the social. This

problem may become so urgent as to force into the background the conflict between teleological and jural theories,
while in any case it complicates and subdivides them. We
have individualistic and institutional types of theory. Consider, for example, the following representative quotations:
"No school can avoid taking for the ultimate moral aim a
desirable *state of feeling* called by whatever name—gratification, enjoyment, happiness. Pleasure somewhere, at some
time, *to some being or beings*, is an element of the conception"; and again, "the good is universally the pleasurable."[1]
And while the emphasis is here upon the good, the desirable,
the same type of statement, *as respects emphasis upon the
individual*, may be made from the side of duty. For example,
"it is the very essence of moral duty to be imposed by a man
on himself."[2] Contrast both of these statements with the
following: "What a man ought to do, or what duties he
should fulfil in order to be virtuous, is in an ethical community not hard to say. He has to do nothing except what
is presented, expressed, and recognized in his established
relations."[3] "The individual has his truth, real existence, and
ethical status only in being a member of the State. His particular satisfactions, activities, and way of life have in this
authenticated, substantive principle, their origin and result."[4]
And in another connection: "The striving for a morality of
one's own is futile and by its very nature impossible of attainment. In respect to morality the saying of one of the wisest
men of antiquity is the true one. To be moral is to live in
accord with the moral tradition of one's country."[5] Here
both the good and the law of the individual are placed on a
strictly institutional basis.

(3) *Empirical and Intuitional.*—Another cross-division
arises from consideration of the method of ascertaining and
determining the nature of moral distinctions: the method of

1. Spencer, *Principles of Ethics*, Vol. I, p. 46, and p. 30. (Italics
   not in original.)
2. Green, *Prolegomena to Ethics*, p. 354.
3. Hegel, *Philosophy of Right*, translated by Dyde, Part III, § 150
   (p. 159).
4. Hegel, *Philosophy of Right*, translated by Dyde, Part III, § 258
   (pp. 240–41).
5. Hegel, *Werke*, Vol. I, p. 389.

knowledge. From this standpoint, the distinction of ethical theories into the *empirical* (ἐμπειρικός) and the *intuitional* (Latin, *intueor*, to look at or upon) represents their most fundamental cleavage. One view makes knowledge of the good and the right dependent upon recollection of prior experiences and their conditions and effects. The other view makes it an immediate apprehension of the quality of an act or motive, a trait so intrinsic and characteristic it cannot escape being seen. While in general the empirical school has laid stress upon the consequences, the consequences to be searched for were considered as either individual or social. Some, like Hobbes, have held that it was directed upon law; to knowledge of the commands of the state. And similarly the direct perception or intuition of moral quality was by some thought to apply to recognition of differences of value, and by others to acknowledgment of law and authority, which again might be divine, social, or personal. This division cleaves straight across our other bases of classification. To describe a theory definitely, it would then be necessary to state just where it stood with reference to each possible combination or permutation of elements of all three divisions. Moreover, there are theories which attempt to find a deeper principle which will bridge the gulf between the two opposites.

Complexity of Subject-matter and Voluntary Activity.— This brief survey should at least warn us of the complexity of the attempt to discriminate types of theory, and put us on our guard against undue simplification. It may also serve to remind us that various types of theory are not arbitrary personal devices and constructions, but arise because, in the complexity of the subject-matter, one element or another is especially emphasized, and the other elements arranged in different perspectives. As a rule, all the elements are recognized in some form or other by all theories; but they are differently placed and accounted for. In any case, it is voluntary activity with which we are concerned. The problem of analyzing voluntary activity into its proper elements, and rightly arranging them, must coincide finally with the problem of the relation of good and law of control to each other, with the problem of the nature of moral knowledge, and

with that of the relation of the individual and social aspects
of conduct.

§ 2. *Division of Voluntary Activity into Inner and Outer*

The What and How of Activity.—Starting from the side
of the voluntary act, we find in it one distinction which when
forced into an extreme separation throws light upon all three
divisions in theory which have been noted. This is the relation between desire and deliberation as mental or private,
and the deed, the doing, as overt and public. Is there any
intrinsic moral connection between the *mental* and the *overt*
in activity? We may analyze an act which has been accomplished into two factors, one of which is said to exist within
the agent's own consciousness; while the other, the external
execution, carries the mental into operation, affects the
world, and is appreciable by others. Now on the face of the
matter, these two things, while capable of intellectual discrimination, are incapable of real separation. The "mental"
side, the desire and the deliberation, is for the sake of
determining what shall be *done*; the overt side is for the
sake of making real certain precedent mental processes,
which are partial and inadequate till carried into effect, and
which occur for the sake of that effect. The "inner" and
"outer" are really only the "how" and the "what" of activity,
neither being real or significant apart from the other. (See
ante, p. 11.)

Separation into Attitude and Consequences.—But under
the strain of various theories, this organic unity has been
denied; the inner and the outer side of activity have been
severed from one another. When thus divided, the "inner"
side is connected exclusively with the will, the disposition,
the character of the person; the "outer" side is connected
wholly with the consequences which flow from it, the changes
it brings about. Theories will then vary radically according
as the so-called inner or the so-called outer is selected as the
bearer and carrier of moral distinctions. One theory will
locate the moral quality of an act in that *from* which it issues; the other in that *into* which it issues.

The following quotations put the contrast in a nutshell, though unfortunately the exact meaning of the second is not very apparent apart from its context.

A motive is substantially nothing more than pleasure or pain operating in a certain manner. Now pleasure is in itself a good; nay, even setting aside immunity from pain, the only good. . . . It follows, therefore, immediately and incontestibly that there is no such thing as any sort of motive that is in itself a bad one. If motives are good or bad, it is only on account of their effects (Bentham, *Principles of Morals and Legislation,* ch. x, § 2).

Over against this, place the following from Kant:

Pure reason is practical of itself alone, and gives to man a universal law which we call the Moral Law. . . . If this law determines the will directly [without any reference to objects and to pleasure or pain] the action conformed to it is good in itself; a will whose principle always conforms to this law is good absolutely in every respect and is the supreme condition of all good.

If now we recur to the distinction between the "what" and the "how" of action in the light of these quotations, we get a striking result. "What" one does is to pay money, or speak words, or strike blows, and so on. The "how" of this action is the spirit, the temper in which it is done. One pays money with a hope of getting it back, or to avoid arrest for fraud, or because one wishes to discharge an obligation; one strikes in anger, or in self-defense, or in love of country, and so on. Now the view of Bentham says in effect that the "what" is significant, and that the "what" consists ultimately only of the pleasures it produces; the "how" is unimportant save as it incidentally affects resulting feelings. The view of Kant is that the moral core of every act is in its "how," that is in its spirit, its actuating motive; and that the law of reason is the only right motive. *What* is aimed at is a secondary and (except as determined by the inner spirit, the "how" of the action) an irrelevant matter. In short the separation of the mental and the overt aspects of an act has led to an equally complete separation of its initial spirit and motive from its final content and consequence. And in this separation, one type of theory, illustrated by Kant, takes its stand on the actuating source of the act; the other, that of Bentham, on its

outcome. For convenience, we shall frequently refer to these
types of theories as respectively the "attitude" and the "content"; the formal and the material; the disposition and the
consequences theory. The fundamental thing is that *both*
theories separate character and conduct, disposition and behavior; which of the two is most emphasized being a secondary matter.

Different Ways of Emphasizing Results.—There are,
however, different forms of the consequences or "content"
theory—as we shall, for convenience, term it. Some writers,
like Spencer as quoted, say the only consequences that are
good are simply pleasures, and that pleasures differ only in
intensity, being alike in everything but degree. Others say,
pleasure is the good, but pleasures differ in quality as well
as intensity and that a certain *kind* of pleasure is the morally
good. Others say that natural satisfaction is not found in
any one pleasure, or in any number of them, but in a more
permanent mood of experience, which is termed *happiness*.
Happiness is different from a pleasure or from a collection of
pleasures, in being an abiding consequence or result, which
is not destroyed even by the presence of pains (while a pain
ejects a pleasure). The pleasure view is called Hedonism;
the happiness view, Eudaimonism.[6]

Different Forms of the "Attitude" Theory.—The opposite
school of theory holds that the peculiar character of "moral"
good is precisely that it is *not* found in consequences of
action. In this negative feature of the definition many different writers agree; there is less harmony in the positive statement of just what the moral good is. It is an attribute or
disposition of character, or the self, not a trait of results
experienced, and in general such an attribute is called *Virtue.*
But there are as many differences of opinion as to what
constitutes virtue as there are on the other side as to what
pleasure and happiness are. In one view, it merges, in its
outcome at least, very closely with one form of eudaimonism.
If happiness be defined as the fulfillment of satisfaction of

6. The Greek words ἡδονή, pleasure, and εὐδαιμονία, happiness. The
   latter conception is due chiefly to Aristotle. Happiness is, however, a good translation only when taken very vaguely. The
   Greek term has a peculiar origin which influenced its meaning.

the characteristic functions of a human being, while a certain function, that of reason, is regarded as *the* characteristic human trait whose exercise is *the* virtue or supreme excellence, it becomes impossible to maintain any sharp line of distinction. Kant, however, attempted to cut under this union of happiness and virtue, which under the form of *perfectionism* has been attempted by many writers, by raising the question of *motivation*. Why does the person aim at perfection? Is it for the sake of the resulting happiness? Then we have only Hedonism. Is it because the moral law, the law of reason, requires it? Then we have law morally deeper than the end aimed at.

We may now consider the bearing of this discussion upon theories (1) of moral knowledge and (2) of moral authority.[7]

I. Characteristic Theories of Moral Knowledge.—(1) Those who set chief store by the goods naturally experienced, find that past experiences supply all the data required for moral knowledge. Pleasures and pains, satisfactions and miseries, are recurrent familiar experiences. All we have to do is to note them and their occasions (or, put the other way, to observe the tendency of some of our impulses and acts to bring pleasure as a consequence, of others to effect misery), and to make up our ends and aims accordingly. As a theory of moral knowledge, Hedonism is thus almost always allied with *empiricism*, understanding by empiricism the theory that particular past experiences furnish the method of all ideas and beliefs.

(2) The theory that the good is some type of virtuous character requires a special organ to give moral knowledge. Virtue is none the less the Good, even when it is not attained, when it is not experienced, that is, as we experience a pleasure. In any case, it is not good because it is experienced, but because it *is* virtue. Thus the "attitude" theory tends to connect itself with some form of Intuitionalism, Rationalism, or Transcendentalism, all of these terms meaning that there is something in knowledge going beyond the particular experiences. Intuitionalism holds there is a certain special

7. The differences as regards self and society will be considered in later chapters.

faculty which reveals truths beyond the scope of experience; Rationalism, that beside the particular elements of experience there are universal and necessary conceptions which regulate it; Transcendentalism, that within experience there is a factor derived from a source transcending experience.[8]

II. *Characteristic Theories of Moral Control.*—The result school tends to view authority, control, law, obligation from the standpoint of *means to an end*; the moralistic, or virtue, school to regard the idea of *law* as more fundamental than that of the good. From the first standpoint, the authority of a given rule lies in its power to regulate desires so that after all pleasures—or a maximum of them, and a minimum of pains—may be had. At bottom, it is a principle of expediency, of practical wisdom, of adjustment of means to end. Thus Hume said: "Reason is, and ought only to be, the slave of the passions"—that is, the principles and rules made known by reason are, at last, only instruments for securing the fullest satisfaction of desires. But according to the point of view of the other school, no satisfaction is *really* (i.e., morally) good unless it is acquired in accordance with a law existing independently of pleasurable satisfaction. Thus the good depends upon the law, not the law upon the desirable end.

§ 3. *General Interpretation of These Theories*

The Opposition in Ordinary Life.—To some extent, similar oppositions are latent in our ordinary moral convictions, without regard to theory. Indeed, we tend, at different times, to pass from one point of view to the other, without being aware of it. Thus, as against the identification of goodness with a *mere* attitude of will, we say, "It is not enough for a man to be good; he must be good for something." It is not enough to mean well; one must mean to do well; to excuse a man by saying "he *means* well," conveys a shade of depreciation. "Hell is paved with good intentions." Good "resolutions," in general, are ridiculed as not modifying overt action.

8. For similar reasons, the "content" theories tend to ally themselves with the positive sciences; the "attitude" theories with philosophy as distinct from sciences.

A tree is to be judged by its fruits. "Faith without works is dead." A man is said "to be too good for this world" when his motives are not effective. Sometimes we say, "So and so is a *good* man," meaning to say that that is about all that can be said for him—he does not count, or amount to anything, practically. The objection to identifying goodness with inefficiency also tends to render suspected a theory which seems to lead logically to such identification. More positively we dwell upon goodness as involving *service*; "love is the fulfilling of the law," and while love is a trait of character, it is one which takes immediate action in order to bring about certain definite consequences. We call a man Pharisaical who cherishes his own good character as an end distinct from the common good for which it may be serviceable.

On the other hand, indicating the supremacy of the voluntary attitude over consequences, we have, "What shall a man give in exchange for his soul?" "What shall it profit a man if he shall gain the whole world and lose his own life?" "Let us do evil that good may come, whose damnation is just." The deep-seated objection to the maxim that the end justifies the means is hard to account for, except upon the basis that it is possible to attain ends otherwise worthy and desirable at the expense of conduct which is immoral. Again, compare Shakespere's "There's nothing right or wrong, but thinking makes it so" with the Biblical "As a man thinketh in his heart, so is he." And finally we have such sayings as, "Take the will for the deed"; "His heart is in the right place"; *Pereat mundus, fiat justitia.*

Passing from this popular aspect of the matter, we find the following grounds for the "content" theory:

(*1*) *It Makes Morality Really Important.*—Would there be any use or sense in moral acts if they did not tend to promote welfare, individual and social? If theft uniformly resulted in great happiness and security of life, if truth-telling introduced confusion and inefficiency into men's relations, would we not consider the first a virtue, and the latter a vice?[9] So far as the identification of goodness with mere motive (apart from results effected by acts) reduces morality

9. "Suppose that picking a man's pocket excited in him joyful emotions, by brightening his prospects, would theft be counted among crimes?"—Spencer.

to nullity, there seems to be furnished a *reductio ad ab-surdum* of the theory that results are not the decisive thing.

(2) *It Makes Morality a Definite, Concrete Thing.* — Morality is found in consequences; and consequences are definite, observable facts which the individual can be made responsible for noting and for employing in the direction of his further behavior. The theory gives morality an objective, a tangible guarantee and sanction. Moreover, results are something objective, common to different individuals because outside them all. But the doctrine that goodness consists in motives formed by and within the individual without reference to obvious, overt results, makes goodness something vague or else whimsical and arbitrary. The latter view makes virtue either something unattainable, or else attained by merely cultivating certain internal states having no outward results at all, or even results that are socially harmful. It encourages fanaticism, moral crankiness, moral isolation or pride; obstinate persistence in a bad course in spite of its demonstrable evil results. It makes morality non-progressive, since by its assumption no amount of experience of consequences can throw any light upon essential moral elements.

(3) *The Content Theory Not Only Puts Morality Itself upon a Basis of Facts, but Also Puts the Theory of Morality upon a Solid Basis.* — We know what we mean by goodness and evil when we discuss them in terms of results achieved or missed, and can therefore discuss them intelligibly. We can formulate concrete ends and lay down rules for their attainment. Thus there can be a science of morals just as there can be a science of any body of observable facts having a common principle. But if morality depends upon purely subjective, personal motives, no objective observation and common interpretation are possible. We are thrown back upon the capricious individual *ipse dixit*, which by this theory is made final. Ethical theory is rendered impossible. Thus Bentham, who brings these charges (and others) against the "virtue" theory of goodness, says at the close of the preface to his *Principles of Morals and Legislation* (ed. of 1823):

Truths that form the basis of political and moral science are not to be discovered but by investigations as severe as mathematical ones, and beyond all comparison more intricate and extensive. . . . They are not to be forced into detached and general propositions, unincumbered with explanations and exceptions. They will not compress themselves into epigrams. They recoil from the tongue and the pen of the declaimer. They flourish not in the same soil with sentiment. They grow among thorns; and are not to be plucked, like daisies, by infants as they run. . . . There is no *King's Road* . . . to legislative, any more than to mathematic science.[10]

Arguments not unlike, however, may be adduced in favor of the attitude theory.

1. *It, and It Alone, Places Morality in the High and Authoritative Place Which by Right Characterizes It.*—Morality is not just a means of reaching other ends; it is an end in itself. To reduce virtue to a tool or instrumentality for securing pleasure is to prostitute and destroy it. Unsophisticated common sense is shocked at putting morality upon the same level with prudence, policy, and expediency. Morality is morality, just because it possesses an absolute authoritativeness which they lack.

2. *The Morally Good Must be Within the Power of the Individual to Achieve.*—The amount of pleasure and pain the individual experiences, his share of satisfaction, depends

10. Mill in his *Autobiography* has given a striking account of how this phase of Utilitarianism appealed to him. (See pp. 65–67 of London edition of 1874; see also his *Dissertations and Discussions*, Vol. I, Essay on Bentham, especially pp. 339 and ff.) Bentham "introduced into morals and politics those habits of thought, and modes of investigation, which are essential to the idea of science; and the absence of which made these departments of inquiry, as physics had been before Bacon, a field of interminable discussion, leading to no result. It was not his *opinions*, in short, but his *method*, that constituted the novelty and value of what he did. . . . Bentham's method may be shortly described as the method of *detail*. . . . Error lurks in generalities."

Mill finally says: "He has thus, it is not too much to say, for the first time introduced precision of thought in moral and political philosophy. Instead of taking up their opinions by intuition, or by ratiocination from premises adopted on a mere rough view, and couched in language so vague that it is impossible to say exactly whether they are true or false, philosophers are now forced to understand one another, to break down the generality of their propositions, and join a precise issue in every dispute. This is nothing less than a revolution in philosophy." In view of the character of the larger amount of discussions in moral and political philosophy still current, Mill perhaps took a too optimistic view of the extent to which this "revolution" had been accomplished.

upon outward circumstances which are beyond his control, and which accordingly have no moral significance. Only the beginning, the willing, of an act lies with the man; its conclusion, its outcome in the way of consequences, lies with the gods. Accident, misfortune, unfavorable circumstance, may shut the individual within a life of sickness, misery, and discomfort. They may deprive him of external goods; but they cannot modify the moral good, for that resides in the attitude with which one faces these conditions and results. Conditions hostile to prosperity may be only the means of calling forth virtues of bravery, patience, and amiability. Only consequences within character itself, the tendency of an act to form a habit or to cultivate a disposition, are really of moral significance.

3. *Motives Furnish a Settled and Workable Criterion by Which to Measure the Rightness or Wrongness of Specific Acts.*—Consequences are indefinitely varied; they are too much at the mercy of the unforeseen to serve as basis of measurement. One and the same act may turn out in a hundred different ways according to accidental circumstances. If the individual had to calculate consequences before entering upon action, he would engage in trying to solve a problem where each new term introduced more factors. No conclusion would ever be reached; or, if reached, would be so uncertain that the agent would be paralyzed by doubt. But since the motives are within the person's own breast, the problem of knowing the right is comparatively simple: the data for the judgment are always at hand and always accessible to the one who sincerely wishes to know the right.

Conclusion.—The fact that common life recognizes, under certain conditions, both theories as correct, and that substantially the same claims may be made for both, suggests that the controversy depends upon some underlying misapprehension. Their common error, as we shall attempt to show in the sequel, lies in trying to split a voluntary act which is single and entire into two unrelated parts, the one termed "inner," the other, "outer"; the one called "motive," the other, "end." A voluntary act is always a disposition, or habit of the agent *passing into an overt act*, which, so far as it can, produces certain consequences. A "mere" motive which does not do anything, which makes nothing different, is not a genuine motive at all, and hence is not a voluntary act. On the other hand, consequences which are not intended, which are not personally wanted and chosen and striven for, are no part of a voluntary act. *Neither the inner apart from the outer, nor the outer apart from the inner, has any voluntary or moral quality at all. The former is mere passing sentimentality or reverie; the latter is mere accident or luck.*

Tendency of Each Theory to Pass into the Other.—Hence each theory, realizing its own onesidedness, tends inevitably to make concessions, and to borrow factors from its competitor, and thus insensibly to bridge the gap between them. Consequences are emphasized, but only *foreseen* consequences; while to *foresee* is a mental act whose exercise depends upon character. It is disposition, interest, which leads an agent to estimate the consequences at their true worth; thus an upholder of the "content" theory ends by falling back upon the *attitude* taken in forecasting and weighing results. In like fashion, the representative of the motive theory dwells upon the tendency of the motive to bring about certain effects. The man with a truly benevolent disposition is not the one who indulges in indiscriminate charity, but the one who considers the effect of his gift upon its recipient and upon society. While lauding the motive as the sole bearer of moral worth, the motive is regarded as a force working towards the production of certain *results*. When the "content" theory recognizes disposition as an inherent factor in bringing about consequences, and the "attitude" theory views motives as forces tending to effect consequences, an approximation of each to the other has taken place which almost cancels the original opposition. It is realized that a complete view of the place of motive in a voluntary act will conceive motive as a motor force; as inspiring to action which will inevitably produce certain results unless this is prevented by superior external force. It is also realized that only *those* consequences are any part of voluntary behavior which are so congenial to character as to appeal to it as good and stir it to effort to realize them. *We may begin the analysis of a voluntary act at whichever end we please, but we are always carried to the other end in order to complete the analysis.* The so-called distinction between the "inner" and "outer" parts of an act is in reality a distinction between the *earlier* and the *later* period of its development.

In the following chapter we shall enter upon a direct discussion of the relation of conduct and character to one another; we shall then apply the results of the discussion, in successive chapters, to the problems already raised: The Nature of Good; of Knowledge; of Moral Authority; The Relation of the Self to Others and Society; The Characteristics of the Virtuous Self.

Literature

Many of the references in ch. 11 trench upon this ground. Compare, also, Lecky, *History of European Morals*, Vol. I, pp. 1–2, and 122–30; Sidgwick, *Methods of Ethics* (1901), pp. 6–11, 77–88 and 494–507; Wundt, *Ethics*, Vol. II, ch. iv; Mackenzie, *Manual of Ethics*, Book II, ch. ii; Murray, *Introduction to Ethics*, p. 143; Paulsen, *System of Ethics*, Introduction, and Book II, ch. i.

13. CONDUCT AND CHARACTER

Problem of Chapter.—We have endeavored in the preceding chapters (1) to identify the sort of situation in which the ideas of good and evil, right and wrong, in their moral sense, are employed; (2) to set forth the typical problems that arise in the analysis of this situation; and (3) to name and describe briefly the types of theory which have developed in the course of the history of the problems. We have now to return to the moral situation as described, and enter upon an independent analysis of it. We shall commence this analysis, as was indicated in the last chapter, by considering the question of the relation of attitude and consequences to each other in voluntary activity,—not that this is the only way to approach the problem, but that it is the way which brings out most clearly the points at issue among types of moral theory which since the early part of the nineteenth century have had the chief currency and influence. Accordingly the discussion will be introduced by a statement of the two most extreme doctrines that separate the "inner" and the "outer," the "psychical" and the "overt" aspects of activity: *viz.*, the Kantian, exclusively emphasizing the "how," the spirit, and motive of conduct; the Utilitarian, dwelling exclusively upon its "what," its effects and consequences. Our positive problem is, of course, by means of arraying these two extreme views against each other, to arrive at a statement of the mutual relations of attitude and act, motive and consequence, character and conduct.

We shall begin with Kant as a representative of the attitude theory.

§ 1. *The Good Will of Kant*

Kant says:

Nothing can possibly be conceived, in the world or out of it, which can be called Good without qualification, except a Good

Will. Intelligence, wit, judgment, and the other talents of the
mind, however they may be named, or courage, resolution, perseverance as qualities of temperament are individually good and
desirable in many respects; but these gifts of nature may also become extremely bad and mischievous, if the will which is to
make use of them and which, therefore, constitutes what is called
character, is not good. It is the same with the gifts of fortune.
Power, riches, honour, even health . . . inspire pride and often
presumption if there is not a Good Will to correct the influence
of these on the mind. Moderation of the affections and passions,
self-control and calm deliberation are not only good in many
respects, but even seem to constitute part of the intrinsic worth
of the person; but they are far from deserving to be called good
without qualification. . . . For without the principles of a good
will they may become extremely bad. The coolness of a villain
makes him both more dangerous and more abominable (Kant,
Theory of Ethics, tr. by Abbott, pp. 9–10).

Element of Truth in Statement.—There can be no doubt
that in some respects these ideas of Kant meet a welcome in
our ordinary convictions. Gifts of fortune, talents of mind,
qualities of temperament, are regarded as desirable, as good,
but we qualify the concession. We say they are good, if a
good use is made of them; but that, administered by a bad
character, they add to power for evil. Moreover, Kant's statement of the *intrinsic* goodness of the Good Will, "a jewel
which shines by its own light" (*Theory of Ethics*, p. 10),
awakens ready response in us. Some goods we regard as
means and conditions—health, wealth, business, and professional success. They afford moral opportunities and agencies,
but need not possess moral value in and of themselves; when
they become parts, as they may, of a moral good, it is because of their place and context. Personality, character, has
a dignity of its own, which forbids that it be considered a
simple means for the acquisition of other goods. The man
who makes his good character a simple tool for securing
political preferment, is, we should say, prostituting and so
destroying his own goodness.

Ambiguity of Statement.—The statement made by Kant,
however, is ambiguous and open to opposed interpretations.
The notion that the Good Will is good in and of itself may
be interpreted in two different ways: (i) We may hold, for
example, that honesty is good as a trait of will because it

tends inevitably to secure a desirable relationship among men; it removes obstructions between persons and keeps the ways of action clear and open. Every man can count upon straightforward action when all act from honesty; it secures for each singleness of aim and concentration of energy. (ii) But we may also mean that honesty is absolutely good as a trait of character just in and by itself, quite apart from any influence this trait of character has in securing and promoting desirable ends. In one case, we emphasize its goodness because it arranges for and tends towards certain results; in the other case, we ignore the factor of tendency toward results.

Kant's Interpretation of Goodness of Will is Formal.— Kant's further treatment leaves us in no doubt in which of these two senses he uses the term Good Will. He goes on (*Theory of Ethics*, p. 10):

A Good Will is good, not because of what it performs or effects, *not by its aptness for the attainment of some proposed end,* but simply by virtue of the volition; that is, it is good in itself. . . . Even if it should happen that, owing to the special disfavour of fortune, or the niggardly provision of a step-motherly nature, this will should wholly lack power to accomplish its purpose, if with its greatest efforts it should yet achieve nothing, and there should remain only the Good Will (not, to be sure, a mere wish, but the assuming of all means in our power), then, like a jewel, it would still shine by its own light as a thing which has its whole value in itself. Its fruitfulness or fruitlessness can neither add nor take away anything from this value.

And again he says:

An action . . . derives its moral worth not from the *purpose* which is to be attained by it, but from the maxim by which it is determined and therefore depends . . . merely on the principle of volition by which the action has taken place, without regard to any *object of desire.* . . . The purposes which we may have in view in our actions or their effect regarded as ends and springs of will cannot give the actions an unconditional or moral worth. . . . It cannot lie anywhere but in the principle of the Will, without regard to the ends which can be attained by the action (*Theory of Ethics*, p. 16).

Relation of Endeavor and Achievement to Will.—Here, also, we find a certain agreement with our every-day moral experience. It is undoubtedly true that in many cases we ascribe moral worth or goodness to acts without reference to the results actually attained by them; a man who tries to rescue a drowning child is not judged only on the basis of success. If he is prevented, because he is crippled, or because the current is too rapid for him, we do not refuse hearty moral approbation. We do not judge the goodness of the act or of the agent from the standpoint of its attained result, which here is failure. We regard the man as good because he proposed to himself a worthy end or aim, the rescue of another, even at the risk of harm to himself. We should agree with Kant in saying that the moral worth does not depend on the *realization* of the object of desire. But we should regard the worth of the man to consist precisely in the fact that, so far as he was concerned, he *aimed at a good result*. We do not rule out purpose, but we approve because the purpose was good. By will we mean tendencies, desires, and habits operating to realize results regarded as desirable. Will is not the *sole* condition of reaching a result—that is, of making the aim an actual fact. Circumstances need to co-operate to insure a successful issue; and if these fail, the best will in the world cannot secure the transformation of desire for an end into that end. We know that sometimes it is only by accident that the desirable end is not effected, but we also know that without the proper disposition it is only by accident that the results *are* achieved. Moreover, we know that our own attitude is not only an important condition of securing the results, but that it is the only condition *constantly* under our control. What we mean by calling it "ours" is precisely that it is that condition whose operation lies with us. Accordingly, it is the key and clue to the results, so far as they concern us. So far, given desire and endeavor, achievement is not necessary to volition.

"Meaning Well."—On the other hand, can a man justify himself on the ground that he "means well," if the "meaning well" does not *regulate the overt acts* that he performs, and hence the consequences that proceed from them? Are we not justified in suspecting a person's good faith when his good intentions uniformly bring suffering to others? If we do not question his good faith, do we not regard him

as needing moral enlightenment, and a change of disposition? We distinguish in our judgments of good between the fanatic and the thoroughly selfish man, but we do not carry this distinction to the point of approving the fanatic; of saying, "Let him alone; he means well, he has a good will, he is actuated by a sense of duty." On the contrary, we condemn his aims; and in so far we censure him for willingly entertaining and approving them. We may, indeed, approve of his character with respect to its sincerity, singleness of aim, and its thoroughness of effort, for such things, *taken by themselves*, or in the abstract, are good traits of character. We esteem them highly, however, just because they have so much to do with results; they are, *par excellence*, executive traits. But we do not approve of the man's whole character in approving these traits. There is something the matter with the man in whom good traits are put to a bad use. It is not true in such cases that we approve the *agent* but condemn his *acts*. We approve certain phases of conduct, and in so far regard the doer as praiseworthy; we condemn other features of acts, and in so far disapprove him.[1]

Overt Action Proves Will.—Again, under what circumstances do we actually "take the will for the deed"? When do we assume that so far as the will was concerned it did aim at the result and aimed at it thoroughly, without evasion and without reservation? Only when there is *some* action which testifies to the real presence of the motive and aim.[2] The man, in our earlier instance, must have made some effort to save the drowning child to justify either us or himself in believing that he *meant* to do it; that he had the right intent. The individual who habitually justifies himself (either to others or to himself) by insisting upon the rightness of his motives, lays himself open to a charge of self-deception, if not of deliberate hypocrisy, if there are no outward evidences of effort towards the realization of his pretended

---

1. When Kant says that the coolness of a villain makes him "more dangerous and more abominable," it is suggested that it is more abominable *because* it is more dangerous—surely a statement of the value of will in terms of the results it tends to effect.
2. Kant's distinction between a mere wish, and "assuming all the means in our power," appears to recognize this fact, but he does not apply the fact in his theory.

motive. A habitually careless child, when blamed for some disorder or disturbance, seeks to excuse himself by saying he "didn't mean to": i.e., he had no intention or aim; the results did not flow morally from him. We often reply, in effect, "that is just the trouble; you didn't mean at all; you ought to have meant *not* to do this." In other words, if you had thought about what you were doing you would not have done this and would not have brought about the undesirable results. With adults there is such a thing as culpable carelessness and blameworthy negligence. So far as the individual's conscious will was concerned, everything he deliberately intended may have been entirely praiseworthy; but we blame him because his character was such that the end appropriate to the circumstances did not occur to him. We do not disapprove when the failure to think of the right purpose is due to inexperience or to lack of intellectual development; but we do blame when the man does not employ his attained experience and intellectual capacity. Given these factors, if the right end is not thought of or is quickly dismissed, indisposition is the only remaining explanation. These two facts, that we require effort or evidence of sincerity of good will and that the character is disapproved for *not* entertaining certain aims, are sufficient to prove that we do not identify will and motive with something which has nothing to do with "aptness for attaining ends." Will or character *means intelligent forethought of ends and resolute endeavor to achieve them*. It cannot be conceived apart from *ends* purposed and desired.

§ 2. *The "Intention" of the Utilitarians*

Emphasis of Utilitarians upon Ends.—We are brought to the opposite type of moral theory, the utilitarian, which finds moral quality to reside in consequences, that is to say, in the ends achieved. To the utilitarians, motive means simply certain states of consciousness which happen to be uppermost in a man's mind as he acts. Not this subjective feeling existing only in the inner consciousness, but the external outcome, the objective change which is made in the common world, is what counts. If we can get the act done which produces the right sort of changes, which brings the right kind of result to the various persons concerned, it is irrelevant and misleading to bother with the private emotional state of the doer's mind. Murder would be none the less murder even if the consciousness of the killer were filled with the most maudlin sentiments of general philanthropy; the rescue of a drowning man would be none the less approvable even if we happened to know that the consciousness of the rescuer were irritable and grumpy while he was performing the deed. Acts, not feelings, count, and acts mean changes actually effected.[3]

Distinction of Intention from Motive.—The utilitarians make their point by distinguishing between intention and motive, attributing moral value exclusively to the former. According to them, intention is *what* a man means to do; motive is the personal frame of mind which indicates *why* he means to do it. Intention is the concrete aim, or purpose; the results which are foreseen and wanted. Motive is the state of mind which renders these consequences, rather than others, interesting and attractive. The following quotations are typical. Bentham says concerning motives:

> If they are good or bad, it is only on account of their effects: good, on account of their tendency to produce pleasure, or avert pain: bad, on account of their tendency to produce pain, or avert pleasure. Now the case is, that from one and the same motive, and from every kind of motive, may proceed actions that are good, others that are bad, and others that are indifferent.

Consequently the question of motive is totally irrelevant. He goes on to give a long series of illustrations, from which we select one:

> 1. A boy, in order to divert himself, reads an inspiring book; the motive is accounted, perhaps, a good one: at any rate, not a bad one. 2. He sets his top a spinning: the motive is deemed at any rate not a bad one. 3. He sets loose a mad ox among a crowd: his motive is now, perhaps, termed an abominable one. Yet in all three cases the motive may be the very same: it may be neither more nor less than curiosity.[4]

---

3. But, as we shall see, the utilitarians make finally a distinction between ends *achieved* and ends *attempted*.
4. Bentham, *Principles of Morals and Legislation*, ch. x, § 3.

Mill writes to the following effect:

The morality of the action depends entirely upon the *intention*
—that is, upon *what* the agent wills to do. But the motive,
that is, the feeling which made him will so to do, when it makes
no difference in the act, makes none in the morality.[5]

Now if motives were merely inert feelings or bare states
of consciousness happening to fill a person's mind apart
from his desires and his ideas, they certainly would not
modify his acts, and we should be compelled to admit the
correctness of this position. But Mill gives the whole case
away when he says that the motive which makes a man will
something, *"when it makes no difference in the act,"* makes
none in its morality. Every motive does make a difference in
the act; it makes precisely the difference between one act
and another. It is a contradiction in terms to speak of the
motive as that *which makes a man* will to do an act or intend
to effect certain consequences, and then speak of the motive
making no difference to the act! How can that which makes
an intention make no difference to it, and to the act which
proceeds from it?

Concrete Identity of Motive and Intention.—Ordinary
speech uses motive and intention interchangeably. It says,
indifferently, that a man's motive in writing a letter was to
warn the person addressed or was friendliness. According to
Bentham and Mill, only so-called states of consciousness in
which one feels friendly can be called motive; the object
aimed at, the warning of the person, is intention, not motive.
Again ordinary speech says either that a doctor's intention
was to relieve his patient, or that it was kind and proper,
although the act turned out badly. But the utilitarians would
insist that only the first usage is correct, the latter confound-
ing intent with motive. In general, such large terms as ambition, revenge, benevolence, patriotism, justice, avarice, are
used to signify both motives and aims; both dispositions *from*
which one acts and results *for* which one acts. It is the gist
of the following discussion that common speech is essentially
correct in this interchangeable use of intention and motive.

5. Mill, *Utilitarianism.*

The same set of real facts, *the entire voluntary act*, is pointed to by both terms.

Ambiguity in Term "Feelings."—There is a certain ambiguity in the term "feelings" as employed by Mill and Bentham. It may mean feelings apart from ideas, blind and vague mental states unenlightened by thought, propelling and impelling tendencies undirected by either memory or anticipation. Feelings then mean sheer instincts or impulses. In this sense, they are, as Bentham claims, without moral quality. But also in this sense there are no intentions with which motives may be contrasted. So far as an infant or an insane person is impelled by some blind impulsive tendency, he foresees nothing, has no object in view, means nothing, in his act; he acts without premeditation and intention. "Curiosity" of this sort may be the source of acts which are harmful or useful or indifferent. But no consequences were intelligently foreseen or deliberately wished for, and hence the acts in question lie wholly outside the scope of morals, even according to the utilitarian point of view. Morality is a matter of intent, and intent there was none.

Motive as Intelligent.—In some cases, then, motives have no moral quality whatsoever, and, *in these cases*, it is true that intention has no moral quality either, because there is none. Intention and motive are morally on the same level, not opposed to one another. But motive means not only blind feeling, that is, impulse without thought; it also means a tendency which is aware of its own probable outcome when carried into effect, and which is interested in the resulting effect. It is perhaps conceivable that a child should let loose a bull in a crowd from sheer innocent curiosity to see what would happen—just as he might pour acid on a stone. But if he were a normal child, the next time the impulse presented itself he would recall the previous result: the fright, the damage, the injury to life and limb, and would foresee that similar consequences are likely to happen if he again performs a like act. He now has what Bentham and Mill call an intention. Suppose he again lets loose the bull. Only verbally is motive now the same that it was before. In fact, curiosity is a very different thing. If the child is still immature and inexperienced and unimaginative, we might content ourselves with saying that his motive is egoistic amusement; but we may also say it is downright malevolence characteristic of a criminal. In no case should we call it curiosity. When foresight enters, intent, purpose enters also, and with it a change of motive from innocent, because blind, impulse, to deliberate, and hence to virtuous or blameworthy interest in effecting a certain result. Intention and motive are upon the same moral level. Intention is the *outcome* foreseen and wanted; motive, this outcome *as* foreseen and wanted. But the voluntary act, as such, is an *outcome, forethought and desired*, and hence attempted.

This discussion brings out the positive truth for which Bentham and Mill stand: *viz.*, that *the moral quality of any impulse or active tendency can be told only by observing the sort of consequences to which it leads in actual practice.* As against those who insist that there are certain feelings in human nature so sacred that they do not need to be measured or tested by noting the consequences which flow from them, so sacred that they justify an act *no matter what its results*, the utilitarians are right. It is true, as Bentham says, that if motives are good or bad it is on account of their effects. Hence we must be constantly considering the effects of our various half-impulsive, half-blind, half-conscious, half-unconscious motives, in order to find out what sort of things they are—whether to be approved and encouraged, or disapproved and checked.

Practical Importance of Defining Springs to Action by Results.—This truth is of practical as well as of theoretical significance. Many have been taught that certain emotions are inherently so good that they are absolutely the justification of certain acts, so that the individual is absolved from any attention whatsoever to results. Instance "charity," or "benevolence." The belief is engrained that the emotion of pity, of desire to relieve the sufferings of others, is intrinsically noble and elevating. Hence it has required much discussion and teaching to bring home, even partially, the evils of indiscriminate giving. The fact is that pity, sympathy, apart from forecast of specific results to be reached by acting upon it, is a mere psychological reaction, as much so as is shrinking from suffering, or as is a tendency to run away from danger; in this blind form it is devoid of any moral quality whatsoever. Hence to teach that the feeling is good in itself is to make its mere discharge an end in itself. This is to overlook the evil consequences in the way of fraud, laziness, inefficiency, parasitism produced in others, and of sentimentality, pride, self-complacency produced in the self. There is no doubt that the effect of some types of moral training is to induce the belief that an individual may develop goodness of character simply by cultivating and keeping uppermost in his consciousness certain types of feelings, irrespective of the objective results of the acts they lead to—one of the most dangerous forms of hypocrisy and of weakened moral fibre. The insistence of utilitarianism that we must become aware of the moral quality of our impulses and states of mind on the basis of the results they effect, and must control them—no matter how "good" they feel—by their results, is a fundamental truth of morals.

Existence and Influence of Idea of Consequences Depends upon Disposition.—But the converse is equally true. Behind every concrete purpose or aim, as idea or thought of results, lies something, some passion, instinct, impulse, habit, interest, which gives it a hold on the person, which gives it motor and impelling force; and which confers upon it the capacity to operate as motive, as spring to action. Otherwise, foreseen consequences would remain mere intellectual entities which thought might speculatively contemplate from afar, but which would never possess weight, influence, power to stir effort. But we must go further. Not only is some active tendency in the constitution of the man responsible for the motive power, whether attractive or otherwise, which foreseen consequences possess, but it is responsible for the fact that this rather than that consequence is suggested. A man of consistently amiable character will not be likely to have thoughts of cruelty to weigh and to dismiss; a man of greed will be likely to have thoughts of personal gain and acquisition constantly present to him. What an individual is interested in occurs to him; what he is indifferent to does not present itself in imagination or lightly slips away. Active tendencies, personal attitudes, are thus in the end the determining causes of our having certain intentions in mind, as

well as the causes of their active or moving influence. As
Bentham says, motives *make* intentions.

Influence of Interest on Ideas.—"Purpose is but the slave
of memory." We can anticipate this or that only as from past
experience we can construct it. But recall, re-membering
(rearticulation) is selective. We pick out certain past results,
certain formerly experienced results, and we ignore others.
Why? Because of our present interests. We are interested
in this or that, and accordingly it comes to mind and dwells
there; or it fails to appear in recollection, or if appearing, is
quickly dismissed. It is important that the things from the
past, which are relevant to our present activity, should come
promptly to mind and find fertile lodgment, and character
decides how this happens.

Says James:[6]

What constitutes the difficulty for a man laboring under an
unwise passion acting as if the passion were unwise? . . . The
difficulty is mental; it is that of getting the idea of the wise action to stay before our mind at all. When any strong emotional
state whatever is upon us the tendency is for no images but such
as are congruous with it to come up. If others by chance offer
themselves, they are instantly smothered and crowded out. . . .
By a sort of self-preserving instinct which our passion has, it
feels that these chill objects [the thoughts of what is disagreeable
to the passion] if they once but gain a lodgment, will work and
work until they have frozen the very vital spark from out of all
our mood. . . . Passion's cue accordingly is always and everywhere to prevent their still small voice from being heard at all.

This quotation refers to a strong passion. It is important
to note *that every interest, every emotion, of whatever nature
or strength, works in precisely the same way.* Upon this
hangs the entertaining of memories and ideas about things.
Hence interest is the central factor in the development of

6. James, *Psychology*, Vol. II, pp. 562–63. The whole passage, pp.
561–69, should be thoroughly familiar to every ethical student;
and should be compared with what is said in Vol. I, pp. 284–90,
about the selective tendency of feelings; and Vol. I, ch. xi, upon
attention, and Vol. I, pp. 515–22, upon discrimination.

Höffding, *Psychology* (translated), is also clear and explicit
with reference to the influence of our emotions upon our ideas.
(See especially pp. 298–307.) The development of this fact in
some of its aspects is one of the chief traits of the Ethics of
Spinoza.

any concrete intention, both as to what it is and as to what it is not—that is, what the aim would have been if the emotional attitude had been different. Given a certain emotional attitude, and the consequences which are pertinent to it are thought of, while other and equally probable consequences are ignored. A man of a truly kindly disposition is sensitive to, aware of, probable results on other people's welfare; a cautious person sees consequences with reference to his own standing; an avaricious man feels results in terms of the probable increase or decrease of his possessions; and so on. The intimate relation of interest and attention forms the inseparable tie of intention, *what* one will, to motive, *why* he so wills. When Bentham says that "Motives are the causes of intentions," he states the fact, and also reveals motive as the proper final object of moral judgment.

§ 3. *Conduct and Character*

The discussion enables us to place conduct and character in relation to each other. Mill, after the passage already quoted (see above, p. 228), to the effect that motive makes no difference to the morality of the act, says it

makes a great difference in our moral estimation of the *agent*, especially if it indicates a good or a bad habitual *disposition*—a bent of character from which useful, or from which hurtful, actions are likely to arise.

To like effect Bentham: "Is there nothing, then," he asks,[7]

about a man which can be termed good or bad, when, on such or such an occasion, he suffers himself to be governed by such and such a motive? Yes, certainly, his *disposition*. Now disposition is a kind of fictitious entity,[8] feigned for the convenience of discourse, in order to express what there is supposed to be *permanent* in a man's frame of mind, where, on such or such an occasion, he has been influenced by such or such a motive, to engage in an act, which, as it appeared to him, was of such or such a tendency.

7. Bentham, *Principles of Morals and Legislation*, ch. xi, § 1.
8. Bentham does not mean "unreal" by a fictitious entity. According to his logic, all general and abstract terms, all words designating relations rather than elements, are "fictitious entities."

He then goes on to say that disposition is good or bad according to its effects.

> A man is said to be of a mischievous[9] disposition, when by the influence of no matter what motives, he is *presumed* to be more apt to engage, or form intentions of engaging, in acts which are *apparently* of a pernicious tendency than in such as are apparently of a beneficial tendency: of a meritorious or beneficent disposition in the opposite case.[10]

And again:

> It is evident that the nature of a man's disposition must depend upon the nature of the motives he is apt to be influenced by; in other words, upon the degree of his sensibility to the force of such and such motives. For his disposition is, as it were, the sum of his intentions. . . . Now, intentions, like every thing else, are produced by the things that are their causes: *and the causes of intentions are motives*. If, on any occasion, a man forms either a good or a bad intention, it must be by the influence of some motive.[11]

Rôle of Character.—Here we have an explicit recognition of the fundamental rôle of character in the moral life; and also of why it is important. Character is that body of active tendencies and interests in the individual which make him open, ready, warm to certain aims, and callous, cold, blind to others, and which accordingly habitually tend to make him acutely aware of and favorable to certain sorts of consequences, and ignorant of or hostile to other consequences. A selfish man need not consciously think a great deal of himself, nor need he be one who, after deliberately weighing his own claims and others' claims, consciously and persistently chooses the former. The number of persons who after facing the entire situation, would still be anti-social enough deliberately to sacrifice the welfare of others is probably small. But a man will have a selfish and egoistic character who, irrespective of any such conscious balancing of his own and others' welfare, is habitually more accessible to the thought of those consequences which affect himself than he is to those which bear upon others. It is not so much

9. By mischievous he means pernicious, bad, vicious, or even depraved in extreme cases.
10. Bentham, *Principles of Morals and Legislation*, ch. xi, § 3.
11. Bentham, *Principles of Morals and Legislation*, ch. xi, §§ 27 and 28.

that *after* thinking of the effect upon others he declines to give these thoughts any weight, as that he habitually fails to think at all, or to think in a vivid and complete way, of the interests of others. As we say, he does not care; he does not consider, or regard, others.[12]

Partial and Complete Intent.—To Mill's statement that morality depends on intention not upon motive, a critic objected that on this basis a tyrant's act in saving a man from drowning would be good—the intent being rescue of life—although his motive was abominable, namely cruelty, for it was the reservation of the man for death by torture. Mill's reply is significant. Not so, he answered; there is in this case a difference of intention, not merely of motive. The rescue was not the whole act, but "only the necessary first step of an act." This answer will be found to apply to every act in which a superficial analysis would seem to make intent different in its moral significance from motive. Take into account the remote consequences in view as well as the near, and the seeming discrepancy disappears. The intent of rescuing a man and the motive of cruelty are both descriptions of the same act, the same moral reality; the difference lying not in the fact, but in the point of view from which it is named. Now there is in every one a tendency to fix in his mind only a part of the probable consequences of his deed; the part which is most innocent, upon which a favorable construction may most easily be put, or which is temporarily most agreeable to contemplate. Thus the person concentrates his thought, his forecast of consequences upon external and indifferent matters, upon distribution of commodities, increase of money or material resources, and upon positively valuable results, at the expense of other changes—changes for the worse in his disposition and in the well-being and freedom of others. Thus he causes to stand out in strong light all of those consequences of his activity which are

12. The fact that common moral experience, as embodied in common speech, uses such terms as "think of," "consider," "regard," "pay attention to" (in such expressions as "he is thoughtful of," "considerate of," "regardful of," "mindful of," "attentive to," the interests of others) in a way implying both the action of intelligence and of the affections, is the exact counterpart of the interchangeable use, already mentioned, of the terms intention and motive.

beneficial and right, and dismisses those of another nature to the dim recesses of consciousness, so they will not trouble him with scruples about the proper character of his act. Since consequences are usually more or less mixed, such half-conscious, half-unconscious, half-voluntary, half-instinctive selection easily becomes a habit. Then the individual excuses himself with reference to the actual bad results of his behavior on the ground that he "meant well," his "intention was good"! Common sense disposes of this evasion by recognizing the reality of "willing." We say a man is "willing" to have things happen when, in spite of the fact that in and of themselves they are objectionable and hence would not be willed in their isolation, they are consented to, because they are bound up with something else the person wants. And to be "willing" to have the harm follow is really to will it. *The agent intends or wills all those consequences which his prevailing motive or character makes him willing under the circumstances to accept or tolerate.*

Exactly the same point comes out from the side of motive. Motives are complex and "mixed"; ultimately the motive to an act is that *entire* character of an agent on account of which one alternative set of possible results appeals to him and stirs him. Such motives as pure benevolence, avarice, gratitude, revenge, are abstractions; we name the motive from the *general trend of the issue*, ignoring contributing and indirect causes. All *assigned* motives are more or less *post-mortem* affairs. No *actuating* motive is ever as simple as reflection afterwards makes it. But the justification of the simplification is that it brings to light some factor which needs further attention. No one can read his own motives, much less those of another, with perfect accuracy; —though the more sincere and transparent the character the more feasible is the reading. Motives which are active in the depths of character present themselves only obscurely and subconsciously. Now if one has been trained to think that motive apart from intention, apart from view of consequences flowing from an act, is the source and justification of its morality, a false and perverse turn is almost sure to be given to his judgment. Such a person fosters and keeps uppermost in the focus of his perceptions certain states of feeling, certain emotions which he has been taught are good; and then excuses his act, in face of bad consequences, on the ground that it sprang from a good motive. Selfish persons are always being "misunderstood." Thus a man of naturally buoyant and amiable disposition may unconsciously learn to cultivate superficially certain emotions of "good-feeling" to others, and yet act in ways which, judged by consequences that the man might have foreseen if he had chosen to, are utterly hostile to the interests of others. Such a man may feel indignant when accused of unjust or ungenerous behavior, and calling others to account for uncharitableness, bear witness in his own behalf that he never entertained any "feelings" of unkindness, or any "feelings" except those of benevolence, towards the individual in question.[13] Only the habit of reading "motives" in the light of persistent, thorough, and minute attention to the consequences which flow from them can save a man from such moral error.

§ 4. Morality of Acts and of Agents

Subjective and Objective Morality. —Finally we may discuss the point at issue with reference to the supposed distinction between subjective and objective morality—an agent may be good and his act bad or *vice-versa*. Both of the schools which place moral quality either in attitude or in content, in motive or intent independently of each other, agree in making a distinction between the morality of an act and the morality of the agent—between objective and subjective morality.[14] Thus, as we have seen, Mill says the motive

13. In short, the way an individual favors himself in reading his own motives is as much an evidence of his egoism as the way he favors himself in outward action. Criminals can almost always assign "good" motives.
14. "Formally" and "materially" good or bad are terms also employed to denote the same distinction. (See Sidgwick, *History of Ethics*, pp. 203–4; so Bowne, *Principles of Ethics*, pp. 39–40.) "The familiar distinction between the formal and the material rightness of action: The former depends upon the attitude of the agent's will toward his ideal of right; the latter depends upon the harmony of the act with the laws of reality and its resulting tendency to produce and promote well-being." Bowne holds that both are necessary, while formal rightness is ethically *more* important, though not all-important.

makes a difference in our moral estimate of its doer, even when it makes none in our judgment of his action. It is a common idea that certain acts are right no matter what the motive of the doer, even when done by one with a bad disposition in doing them. There can be no doubt that there is a serious difficulty in the facts themselves. Men actuated by a harsh and narrow desire for industrial power or for wealth produce social benefits, stimulate invention and progress, and raise the level of social life. Napoleon was doubtless moved by vanity and vainglory to an extent involving immense disregard of others' rights. And yet in jurisprudence, civil arrangements, and education he rendered immense social service. Again, the "conscientious man" is often guilty of bringing great evils upon society. His very conviction of his own rightness may only add to the intense vigor which he puts into his pernicious acts. Surely, we cannot approve the conduct, although we are not entitled morally to condemn the conscientious doer, who does "the best he knows" —or believes.

Moral Quality of Doer and Deed Proportionate.—If we rule out irrelevant considerations, we find that we never, without qualification, invert our moral judgments of doer and deed. So far as we regard Napoleon's actions as *morally* good (not merely as happening to effect certain desirable results) we give Napoleon credit for interest in bringing about those results, *and in so far forth*, call him good. Character, like conduct, is a highly complex thing. No human being is all good or all bad. Even if we were sure that Napoleon was an evil-minded man, our judgment is of him as evil *upon the whole*. Only if we suppose him to be bad and only bad all the time is there the opposition of evil character and good actions. We may believe that even in what Napoleon did in the way of legal and civic reform he was actuated by mixed motives —by vanity, love of greater, because more centralized, power, etc. But these interests in and of themselves could not have effected the results he accomplished. He must have had some insight into a better condition of affairs, and this insight evidences an interest in so far good. Moreover, so far as we judge Napoleon bad as to his character and motive in these acts, we are entitled to hold that the actions and also the outward results were also partially evil. That is, while to some extent, socially beneficial, they would have been still more so if Napoleon had been actuated by less self-centred considerations. If his character had been simpler, more sincere, more straightforward, then certain evil results, certain offsets to the good he accomplished, would not have occurred. The mixture of good and evil in the results and the mixture of good and evil in the motives are proportionate to each other. Such is the conclusion when we recognize the complexities of character and conduct, and do not allow ourselves to be imposed upon by a fictitious simplicity of analysis.

Summary.—The first quality which is the object of judgment primarily resides then in intention; in the consequences which are foreseen and desired. Ultimately it resides in that disposition or characteristics of a person which are responsible for his foreseeing and desiring just such consequences rather than others. The ground for judging an act on the basis of consequences not foreseen is that the powers of a man are not fixed, but capable of modification and redirection. It is only through taking into account in *subsequent* acts consequences of *prior* acts not intended in those prior acts that the agent learns the fuller significance of his own power and thus of himself. Every builder builds other than he knows, whether better or worse. In no case, can he foresee all the consequences of his acts.

In subsequent experience these results, mere by-products of the original volition, enter in. "Outer" and non-moral for the original act, they are within subsequent voluntary activity, because they influence desire and make foresight more accurate in detail and more extensive in range. This translation of consequences once wholly unforeseeable into consequences which have to be taken in account is at its maximum in the change of impulsive into intelligent action. But there is no act so intelligent that its actual consequences do not run beyond its foreseen ones, and thus necessitate a subsequent revision of intention. Thus the distinction of "inner" and "outer" is one involved in the *growth of character and conduct.* Only if character were not in process of change, only if conduct were a fixed because isolated thing, should we have that separation of the inner and the outer which underlies alike the Kantian and the utilitarian theories. In truth, there is no separation, but only a contrast of the different levels of desire and forethought of earlier and later activities. The great need of the moral agent is thus a character which will make him as open, as accessible as possible, to the recognition of the consequences of his behavior.

Literature

On CONDUCT AND CHARACTER in general, see Paulsen, *System of Ethics*, pp. 468–72; Mackenzie, *Manual of Ethics*, Book I, ch. iii; Spencer, *Principles of Ethics*, Part I, chs. i–viii; Green, *Prolegomena to Ethics*, pp. 110–17, 152–59; Alexander, *Moral Order and Progress* (1891), pp. 48–52; Stephen, *Science of Ethics*, ch. ii; Mezes, *Ethics*, ch. iv; Seth, *Ethical Principles*, "Introduction," ch. iii.

Upon MOTIVE AND INTENTION consult Bentham, *Principles of Morals and Legislation*, chs. viii and x; James Mill, *Analysis of Human Mind*, Vol. II, chs. xxii and xxv; Austin, *Jurisprudence*, Vol. I, Lectures xviii–xx; Green, *Prolegomena*, pp. 315–25; Alexander, *Moral Order and Progress* (1891), pp. 36–47; Westermarck, *Origin and Development of the Moral Ideas*, chs. viii, xi, and xiii; Ritchie, *International Journal of Ethics*, Vol. IV, pp. 89–94, and 229–38, where further references are given.

Upon FORMAL AND MATERIAL (or subjective and objective) RIGHTNESS see Sidgwick, *History of Ethics*, p. 203; Rickaby, *Moral Philosophy*, p. 3, pp. 33–40; Bowne, *Principles of Ethics*, pp. 39–40; Brown, *Philosophy of Mind*, Vol. III, p. 489 and pp. 499–500; Paulsen, *System of Ethics*, pp. 227–33; Green, *Prolegomena*, pp. 317–23; Sidgwick, *Methods of Ethics*, pp. 206–7.

14. HAPPINESS AND CONDUCT:
THE GOOD AND DESIRE

We have reached a conclusion as to our first inquiry (p. 187), and have decided that the appropriate subject-matter of moral judgment is the disposition of the person as manifested in the tendencies which cause certain consequences, rather than others, to be considered and esteemed — foreseen and desired. Disposition, motive, intent are then judged good or bad according to the consequences they tend to produce. But what are the consequences by which we determine anything to be good or bad? We turn from the locus or residence of the distinctions of good and bad to the nature of the distinctions themselves. What do good and bad mean as terms of voluntary behavior?

Happiness and Misery as the Good and Bad.—There is one answer to this question which is at once so simple and so comprehensive that it has always been professed by some representative ethical theory: the good is happiness, well-being, pleasure; the bad is misery, woe, pain.[1] The agreeableness or disagreeableness attending consequences differentiates them into good and bad; and it is because some deeds are found to lead to pleasure, while others lead to pain, that they are adjudged virtuous or vicious. In its modern form, this theory is known as utilitarianism. Bentham has given it a sweeping and clear formulation.

Nature has placed mankind under the governance of two sovereign masters, pain and pleasure. It is for them alone to point out what we ought to do as well as to determine what we shall do. On the one hand, the standard of right and wrong, on the other chain of causes and effects, are fastened to their throne. Strictly speaking nothing can be said to be good or bad but either in itself, which is the case only with pain or pleasure; or

1. Later we shall see reasons for discriminating between happiness and pleasure. But here we accept the standpoint of those who identify them.

on account of its effects, which is the case only with things that
are the cause or preventive of pain or pleasure.

Again:

By the principle of utility is meant that principle which approves
or disapproves of every action whatever according to the tendency
it appears to have to augment or diminish the happiness of the
party whose interests are in question.[2]

Once more:

The greatest happiness of all those whose interest is in question is
the right and proper, and the only right and proper and universally desirable end of human action.

Only on the basis of this principle do the words "right and wrong"
and "ought" have an intelligent meaning as applied to actions;
otherwise they have not.

This last statement need not mean, however, that all judgments of right and wrong are as matter of fact derived from
a consideration of the results of action in the way of pain
and pleasure, but that upon this ground alone *should* our
judgments be formed, since upon this basis alone can they
be justified.[3]

Axiomatic Identification of Good with Happiness. —The
principle that happiness is the ultimate aim of human action
and the ultimate standard of the moral value of that action
is generally regarded by the utilitarians as axiomatic and
not susceptible of proof. As Bentham says, "that which is
used to prove every thing else cannot itself be proved. A
chain of proofs must have their commencement somewhere."
So Bain says (*Moral Science*, p. 27), "Now there can be no
proof offered for the position that happiness is the proper
end of all human procedures, the criterion of all right conduct. It is an ultimate or final assumption to be tested by
reference to the individual judgments of mankind." Thus
also Mill (*Utilitarianism*): "The only proof capable of being

2. The context shows that this "party" may be either the individual, or a limited social group or the entire community. Even
   the pleasures and pains of animals, of the sentient creation
   generally, may come into the account.
3. These quotations are all taken from Bentham's *Principles of
   Morals and Legislation*; the first, third, fourth, and last from ch.
   i; the second from ch. xiii.

given that an object is visible is that people actually see it. In like manner the sole proof that it is possible to produce that any thing is desirable is that people do actually desire it."[4]

Extreme Opposition to Happiness Theory.—In striking contrast to this view of the self-evident character of happiness as the all-desirable, is the view of those to whom it is equally self-evident that to make pleasure the end of action is destructive of all morality. Carlyle is an interesting illustration of a violent reaction against utilitarianism. His more moderate characterization of it is "mechanical profit and loss" theory. It is "an upholstery and cookery conception of morals." It never gets above the level of considerations of comfort and expediency. More vehemently, it is a "pig philosophy" which regards the universe as a "swine trough" in which virtue is thought of as the attainment of the maximum possible quantity of "pig's wash." Again, apostrophizing man, he says: "Art thou nothing else than a Vulture that fliest through the Universe seeking after somewhat to eat; shrieking dolefully because carrion enough is not given thee?" Of the attempt to make general happiness the end, he says it proposes the problem of "Given a world of Knaves, to produce honesty from their united action," the term "knave" referring to the individualistic self-seeking character of pleasure and "honesty" to the social outcome desired. As a political theory, he thought that utilitarianism subordinated justice to benevolence, and in that light he referred to it as a "universal syllabub of philanthropic twaddle."

Ambiguity in Notion of Happiness.—If to some it is self-evident that happiness is the aim of action, and success in achieving it the test both of the act and the disposition from which it proceeds; while to others it is equally obvious that

4. With these statements may be compared Spencer, *Principles of Ethics*, Vol. I, pp. 30–32; Stephen, *Science of Ethics*, p. 42. Sidgwick, in his *Methods of Ethics* (1901), holds that the axiomatic character of happiness as an end proves that the position is not empirical but intuitional or *a priori*. Only as we base ourselves on certain ultimate deliverances of conscience can we be said to know that happiness is the desirable end and that the happiness of one is just as intrinsically desirable as the happiness of another. (See his *Methods of Ethics* (1901), Book III, chs. xiii and xiv.)

such a view means immorality or at least a base and sordid morality, it is reasonable to suppose that the "happiness" does not mean the same to both parties; that there is some fundamental ambiguity in the notion.

Source of Ambiguity.—The nature of this ambiguity may be inferred from the fact that Bentham himself—and in this he is typical of all the utilitarians—combines in his statement two aspects of happiness, or two views of pleasure. He says it is for pleasure and pain alone to *"point out what we ought to do,"* that they are the only basis upon which our judgments of right and wrong *ought* to be formed, or upon which they can be justified. Other things *may* be taken as pointing out what we ought to do; other standards of judgment—caprice, sympathy, dogma—are employed. But they are not the right and proper ones. Consideration of consequences of the act in the way of effect upon the happiness and misery of all concerned, furnishes the only proper way of regulating the formation of right ends. A certain happiness, that of results, is the standard. But this presupposes that in any case there is some end, and one which may be improper because not in accord with the standard. Yet this end also must be pleasure. Pleasure and pain "determine what we *shall* do," whether we act for the maximum of pleasures or not. The "chain of causes" as well as the "standard of right" is fastened to them. We act for pleasure, even when we do not act for the pleasures for which we ought to act. Pleasure or happiness thus appears in a double rôle. Only in the case of *right* ends, is it the same happiness which serves as a moving spring and as standard of judgment. In other cases, it is one pleasure which is the end in view, and another pleasure, one not in view, or at least not influencing action, which measures rightness. The essence, so to speak, of a wrong act is precisely that the pleasures which produce it are not these pleasures which measure its goodness; the agent is not moved to act by those pleasures and pains which as consequences settle its moral value, but by some pleasure or pain which happens to be strongly felt at the moment of action.

Two Sorts of Good.—Thus, even from Bentham's point of view, there is a difference between real and apparent happiness, between the good which moves to action and that which, being the standard, should move. If the end of *all* acts is happiness and yet we require a consideration of results to show us *what* happiness we are justified in seeking, then "happiness" is in a highly ambiguous position. While from one standpoint, it furnishes the standard of right and wrong; from another, it furnishes the moving spring of all wrong action; it is that which so solicits and tempts us that we fail to employ the right standard for the regulation of our action, and hence go astray. It seems to some (as to Carlyle) that this distinction is so fundamental that it is absurd to say that one and the same thing can be the standard of all right action and the moving spring of all wrong action. Hence they insist upon the fundamental opposition of virtue and happiness.

Moreover, from Bentham's own point of view, there is a difference between the good which *first* presents itself, which *first* stirs desire and solicits to action, and the good which being formed *after and upon the basis of consideration of consequences*, is the *right* good. In calling the latter the *right*, we mean that it has authority over the end which first appears; and hence has supreme claim over action. So it is again evident that we are using happiness in two quite different senses; so that if we call the first end that presents itself happiness, the right end will be something else; or if we call the consequences which measure the worth of the act happiness, then the first end ought to be called something else. If happiness is the *natural* end of all desire and endeavor, it is absurd to say that the same happiness ought to be the end. If all objects fall to the ground any way, we do not say they ought to fall. If all our acts are moved any way by pleasure and pain, this fact, just because it applies equally to all acts, throws no light upon the rightness or wrongness of any one of them. Or, on the other hand, if that for which we *should* act is a kind of happiness which involves full consideration of consequences, it is misleading to call that happiness from which we act "blindly" or without proper forethought.

If happiness is to be the same as the moral good, it must be after the right kind of happiness has been distinguished; namely, that which commends itself after adequate reflection. Our criticism of Bentham will be directed to show-

ing that, so far as he conceives of happiness as simply a sum
of pleasures alike in quality, but differing only in quantity,
he cannot make this distinction. As an early critic (Hazlitt)
of Bentham said: "Pleasure is that which is so in itself. Good
is that which approves itself on reflection, or the *idea* of
which is a source of satisfaction. All pleasure is not, therefore (morally speaking), equally a good; for all pleasure does
not equally bear reflecting upon." We shall further try to
show that the reason for Bentham's conceiving happiness as
simply a sum of pleasures is that he falls into the error
already discussed, of separating consequences from the
disposition and capacities or active tendencies of the agent.
And that, when we correct this error, the proper meaning of
happiness turns out to be the satisfaction, realization, or fulfillment of some *purpose and power of the agent.* Thus we
can distinguish between the false and unsatisfactory happiness found in the expression of a more or less isolated and
superficial tendency of the self, and the true or genuine good
found in the adequate fulfillment of a fundamental and fully
related capacity. We shall first take up the discussion under
the heads just brought out: I. Happiness *as the Natural End
or Object of Desire*; II. Happiness *as Standard of Judgment*;
III. *The Constitution of Happiness.*

§ 1. The Object of Desire

Hedonistic Theory of Desire.—That phase of utilitarianism which holds that the object of desire is pleasure, is
termed hedonism, or sometimes psychological hedonism to
distinguish it from ethical hedonism, the theory that pleasure
is the standard for judging acts. The fundamental fallacy
of psychological hedonism has been well stated by Green to
be "supposing that a desire can be aroused or created by the
anticipation of its own satisfaction"—i.e., in supposing that
the idea of the pleasure of exercise arouses desire for it, when
in fact the idea of exercise is pleasant only if there be already
some desire for it (Green, *Prolegomena to Ethics*, p. 168).
Given a desire already in existence, the idea of an object
which is thought of as satisfying that desire will always

arouse pleasure, or be thought of as pleasurable. But hedonism fails to consider the radical difference between an object's arousing pleasure, because it is regarded as satisfying desire, and the thought of a pleasure arousing a desire: — although the feeling of agreeableness may intensify the movement towards the object. A hungry man thinks of a beefsteak as that which would satisfy his appetite; his thought is at once clothed with an agreeable tone and the conscious force of the appetite is correspondingly intensified; the miser thinks of gold in a similar way; the benevolent of an act of charity, etc. But in each case the presence of the pleasurable element is dependent upon the thought of an object which is not pleasure—the beefsteak, the gold. The thought of the object *precedes* the pleasure and excites it because it is felt to promise the satisfaction of a desire.

Pleasure is the Felt Concomitant of Imagining a Desire Realized in Its Appropriate Object.—The object of desire is not pleasure, but some object is pleasurable because it is the congenial terminus of desire. The pleasure felt is a *present* pleasure, the pleasure which *now* accompanies the idea of the satisfied desire. It intensifies the desire in its present character, through opposition to the disagreeable tone of the experienced lack and want.

I. Pleasures and Original Appetites.—Biological instincts and appetites exist not for the sake of furnishing pleasure, but as activities needed to maintain life—the life of the individual and the species. Their adequate fulfillment is attended with pleasure. Such is the undoubted biological fact. Now if the animal be gifted with memory and anticipation, this complicates the process, but does not change its nature. The animal in feeling hungry may now consciously anticipate the getting of food and may feel pleasure in the idea of food. The pleasure henceforth attends not merely upon attained satisfaction of appetite, but also upon appetite prior to satisfaction, so far as that anticipates its future satisfaction. But desire is still for the object, for the food. If the desire is healthy, it will not depend for its origin upon the recollection of a prior pleasure; the animal does not happen to recall that it got pleasure from food and thus arouse a desire for more food. The desire springs up naturally

from the state of the organism. Only a jaded and unhealthy
appetite has to whip itself up by recalling previous pleasures.
But if there are many obstacles and discouragements in the
way of getting the object which satisfies want, the anticipation of pleasure in its fulfillment may normally intensify the
putting forth of energy, may give an extra reenforcement
to flagging effort. In this way, the anticipation of pleasure
has a normal place in the effective direction of activities. But
in any case, the desire and its own object are primary; the
pleasure is secondary.

2. *Pleasure and Acquired Desires.*—The same point
comes out even more clearly when we take into account the
so-called higher desires and sentiments—those which usually
enter into distinctively moral questions. In these cases it is
no longer a matter of the original instincts and appetites of
the organism. Their place is taken by acquired habits and
dispositions. The object of a benevolent desire is the supplying of another's lack, or the increase of his good. The pleasure
which accompanies the doing of a kindness to others is not
the object, for the individual thinks of the kindly act as
pleasure-giving only because he already has a benevolent
character which naturally expresses itself in amiable desires.
So far as he is not benevolent, the act will appear repulsive
rather than attractive to him; and if it is done, it will be not
from a benevolent desire, but from a cowardly or an avaricious desire, the pleasure in that case attending the thought
of some other objective consequence, such as escaping unpopularity. In like manner, the aim to behave honestly, or
to obey the civil law, or to love one's country, leads to
dwelling upon the acts and objects in which these desires and
intents may be fulfilled; and those objects which are thought
of as affording fulfillment are necessarily put in a favorable
and attractive light—they are regarded as sources of happiness. To a patriot the thought even of possible death may
arouse a glow of satisfaction as he thinks of this act as
strengthening his country's existence. But to suppose that
this attendant pleasure is the aim and object of desire is to
put the cart before the horse.

3. *Happiness and Desire.*—All men, then, may be said
to desire happiness. But this happiness is not dependent
upon prior experiences of pleasure, which, coming up in

memory, arouse desire and rivet attention upon themselves. To say that the desire of a man is for happiness is only to say that happiness comes in the fulfillment of desire, the desires arising on their own account as expressions of a state of lack or incompletion in which the person finds himself. Happiness thus conceived *is dependent upon the nature of desire and varies with it, while desire varies with the type of character*. If the desire is the desire of an honest man, then the prosperous execution of some honorable intent, the payment of a debt, the adequate termination of a trust, is conceived as happiness, as good. If it be the desire of a profligate, then entering upon the riotous course of living now made possible by inheritance of property is taken as happiness— the one consummation greatly to be wished. If we know what any person really finds desirable, what he stakes his happiness upon, we can read his nature. In happiness, as the anticipation of the satisfaction of desire, there is, therefore, no sure or unambiguous quality; for it may be a token of good or of bad character, according to the sort of object which appeals to the person. The present joy found in the idea of the completion of a purpose cannot be the object of desire, for we desire only things absent. But the joy is a mark of the congruity or harmony of the thought of the object, whatever it be—health, dissipation, miserliness, prodigality, conquest, helpfulness—with the character of the agent. It is an evidence of the moving force, the influence, the weight, of the conceived end; it registers the extent in which the end is not a mere intellectual abstraction, but is a *motive* (see p. 231). But the moral worth of this motive depends upon the character of the end in which the person finds his satisfaction.

4. *Confusion of Future and Present Pleasure.*—It is the confusion of *present* pleasure, attendant upon the thought of an object as satisfying desire, with the pleasure that *will come when the desire is satisfied*, that accounts for the persistence of the idea that pleasure is the object of desire. The fact that the object of desire is *now* pleasurable is distorted into the statement that we *seek* for an absent pleasure.[5]

5. This ambiguity affects the statement quoted from Bentham that pleasure and pain determine what we shall do. His implication is that pleasure as *object* of desire moves us; the fact is that *present* pleasure, aroused by the idea of some object, influences us.

A good illustration of the confusion is seen in the following quotation:

> The love of happiness must express the sole possible motive of Judas Iscariot and of his Master; it must explain the conduct of Stylites on his pillar or Tiberius at Capreæ or A Kempis in his cell or of Nelson in the cockpit of the Victory. It must be equally good for saints and martyrs, heroes, cowards, debauchees, ascetics, mystics, misers, prodigals, men, women and babes in arms (Leslie Stephen, *Science of Ethics*, p. 44).

This statement is true, as we have just seen, in the sense that different persons find different things good in accordance with their different characters or habitually dominant purposes; that each finds his happiness in whatever he most sets his affections upon. Where a man's heart is, there will his treasure be also, and where that is which a man regards as treasure, there also is the heart. A man's character is revealed by the objects which make him happy, whether anticipated or realized.

Our Ends are Our Happiness, Not a Means to It.—But the fallacy is in the words "love of happiness." They suggest that all alike are seeking for some one and the same thing, some one thing labeled "happiness," identical in all cases, differing in the way they look for it—that saints and martyrs, heroes and cowards, all have just the same objective goal in view—if they only knew it! In so far as it is true that there are certain fundamental conditions of the self which have to be satisfied in order that there shall be a *true self and a true satisfaction*, happiness is the same for all, and is the ultimate good of all. But this holds only of the *standard* of happiness which makes any particular conception of happiness right or wrong, not to the conceptions actually entertained. To say that all are consciously and deliberately after the same happiness is to pervert the facts. Happiness as standard means the genuine fulfillment of whatever is necessary to the development and integrity of the self. In this sense, it is what men *ought* to desire; it is what they do desire so far as they understand themselves and the conditions of their satisfaction. But as natural or psychological end, it means that in which a man happens at a given time to find delectation, depending upon his uppermost wishes and strongest habits.

Hence the objection which almost every one, including the hedonists, feels to the statement that happiness is the conscious aim of conduct. It suggests that the objects at which we ordinarily aim are not sought for themselves, but for some ulterior gratification to ourselves. In reality these ends, so far as they correspond to our capacity and intention, *are* our happiness. All men love happiness—yes, in the sense that, having desires, they are interested in the objects in which the desires may be realized, no matter whether they are worthy or degraded. No; if by this be meant that happiness is something other than and beyond the conditions in which the powers of the person are brought out, and made effective; no, or if it means that all love that which really will bring happiness.

Necessity for Standard.—As many sorts of character, so many sorts of things are regarded as satisfactory, as constitutive of good. Not all anticipations when realized are what they were expected to be. The good in prospect may be apples of Sodom, dust and ashes, in attainment. Hence some ends, some forms of happiness, are regarded as unworthy, not as "real" or "true." While they appeared to be happiness during the expectancy of desire, they are not approved as such in later reflection. Hence the demand for some standard good or happiness by which the individual may regulate the formation of his desires and purposes so that the present and the permanent good, the good in desire and in reflection, will coincide—so that the individual will find that to be satisfactory in his present view which will also permanently satisfy him. From happiness as a conceived good we turn to happiness as *rightly* conceived good; from happiness as result to happiness as standard. As before, we begin with the narrower utilitarian conception.

§2. *The Conception of Happiness as a Standard*

Utilitarian Method.—Hedonism means that pleasure is the end of human action, because the end of desire. Utilitarianism or universalistic hedonism holds that the pleasure of all affected is the standard for judging the worth of action,

—not that conduciveness to happiness is the sole measure actually employed by mankind for judging moral worth, but that it is the sole standard that should be employed. Many other tests may actually be used, sympathy, prejudice, convention, caprice, etc., but "utility" is the one which will enable a person to judge *truly* what is right or wrong in any proposed course of action. The method laid down by Bentham is as follows: Every proposed act is to be viewed with reference to its probable consequences in (a) *intensity* of pleasure and pains; (b) their duration; (c) their certainty or uncertainty; (d) their nearness or remoteness; (e) their fecundity—i.e., the tendency of a pleasure to be followed by others, or a pain by other pains; (f) their *purity*—i.e., the tendency of a pleasure to be followed by pains and *vice-versa*; (g) their extent, that is, the number or range of persons whose happiness is affected—with reference to whose pleasures and pains each one of the first six items ought also in strictness to be calculated! Then sum up all the pleasures which stand to the credit side of the account; add the pains which are the debit items, or liabilities, on the other; then take their algebraic sum, and "the balance of it on the side of pleasure will be the good tendency of the act upon the whole."

Circle in Method.—Bentham's argument depends wholly upon the possibility of both foreseeing and accurately measuring the amount of future pleasures and pains that will follow from the intention if it is carried into effect, and of being able to find their algebraic sum. Our examination will be directed to showing that we have here the same fallacy that we have just discussed; and that Bentham argues in a circle. For the argument purports to measure present disposition or intent by summing up future units of pleasure or pain; but there is no way of estimating amounts of future satisfaction, the relative intensity and weight of future possible pain and pleasure experiences, except upon the basis of present tendencies, the habitual aims and interests, of the person. (1) The only way to estimate the relative amount (bulk, intensity, etc.) of a future "lot" of pleasure or pain, is by seeing how agreeable to *present* disposition are certain anticipated consequences, themselves not pleasures or pains at all. (2) The only basis upon which we can be sure that there is a *right* estimate of future satisfactions, is that we already have a good character as a basis and organ for forming judgment.

(*1*) *How Pleasures and Pains are Measured.*—If we keep strictly to Bentham's own conception of pleasures as isolated entities, all just alike in quality, but differing in quantity—in the two dimensions of intensity and duration—the scheme he recommends is simply impossible. What does it mean to say that one pleasure, as an external and future fact, is equal to another? What practical sense is there in the notion that a pain may be found which is exactly equal to a pleasure, so that it may just offset it or reduce it to zero? How can one weigh the amount of pain in a jumping and long-continued toothache against, say, the pleasure of some charitable deed performed under conditions which may bring on the toothache? What relevancy has the quantitative comparison to a judgment of moral worth? How many units of pleasure are contained in the fulfillment of the intention to go to war for one's country? How many in the fulfillment of the intention to remain at home with one's family and secure profitable contracts from the government? How shall the pains involved in each set be detected and have their exact numerical force assigned them? How shall one set be measured over against the other? If a man is already a patriot, one set of consequences comes into view and has weight; if one is already a coward and a money-grubber, another set of consequences looms up and its value is measured on a rule of very different scale.

Present Congeniality to Character Measures Importance.—When we analyze what occurs, we find that this process of comparing future possible satisfactions, to see which is the greater, takes place on exactly the opposite basis from that set forth by Bentham. We do not compare results in the way of fixed amounts of pleasures and pains, but we compare *objective* results, changes to be effected in ourselves, in others, in the whole social situation; during this comparison desires and aversions take more definite form and strength, so that we find the idea of one result more agreeable, more harmonious, to our present character than another. *Then* we say it is more satisfying, it affords more pleasure than another. The satisfaction *now* aroused in the mind at the thought of getting even with an enemy may be stronger than the painfulness of the thought of the harm or loss that will come to him or than the thought of danger itself,—then the pleasures to follow from vengeance are esteemed more numerous, stronger, more lasting, etc., than those which would follow from abstinence. Or, to say that satisfactions are about equal means that we are *now* at a loss to choose between them. But we are not at a loss to choose because certain future pains and pleasures present themselves in and of themselves as fixed amounts irrespective of our own wishes, habits, and plans of life. Similarly we may speak of satisfactions being added to one another and the total sum increased; or of dissatisfaction coming in as offsets and reducing the amount of satisfaction. But this does not mean that pains and pleasures which we expect to arrive in the future are added and subtracted—what intelligible meaning can such a phrase possess? It means that as we think first of this result and then of another, the present happiness found in the anticipation of one is increased by the anticipation of the other; or that the results are so incompatible that the present satisfaction, instead of swelling and expanding as from one thought to another, is chilled and lessened. Thus we might find the thought of revenge sweet (and thus give a high valuation to the units of pleasure to result from it), but be checked by the thought of the meanness of the act, or of how we would feel if some one else, whose good opinion we highly esteem, should hear of it.

(2) *Congeniality to a Good Character the Right Measure.*—The net outcome of this discussion is that the practical value of our acts is defined to us at any given time by the satisfaction, or displeasure, we take in the ideas of changes we foresee in case the act takes place. The present happiness or distaste, depending upon the harmony between the idea in question and the character, defines for us the value of the future consequences: which is the reverse of saying that a calculation of future pains and pleasures determines for us the value of the act and character. But this applies to any end as it happens to arise, not to the end as we

ought to form it; we are still without a standard. What has been said applies to the criminal as well as to the saint; to the miser and the prodigal and the wisely generous alike. The idea of a certain result warms the heart of each, his heart being what it is. The assassin would not be one if the thought of a murder had not been entertained by him and if the thought had not been liked and welcomed—made at home. Only upon the supposition that character is already good can we trust judgment, first, to foresee all the consequences that should be foreseen; and, secondly, to respond to each foreseen consequence with the right emotional stamp of like and dislike, pleasure and pain. The Greeks said it is the object of a moral education to see that the individual finds his pleasure in the thought of noble ends and finds his pain in the contemplation of base ends. Again, as Aristotle said:

> The good man wills the real object of intent, but what the bad man desires may be anything; just as physically those in good condition want things that are wholesome, while the diseased may take anything to be healthful; for the good man judges correctly (*Ethics*, Book III, 4, 4).

And again: "The good man is apt to go right about pleasure, and the bad man is apt to go wrong" (Book II, 3, 7), and, finally, "It is only to the good man that the good presents itself as good, for vice perverts us and causes us to err about the principle of action" (Book VI, 12, 10).

Principle of Quality of Pleasure as Criterion.—Mill, still calling himself a utilitarian, reaches substantially the same result by (a) making the *quality* of pleasure, not its bulk or intensity, the standard; and (b) referring differences in quality to differences in the *characters* which experience them. "It is," he says, "quite compatible with the principle of utility to recognize the fact that some *kinds* of pleasure are more desirable and more valuable than others." "Human beings have faculties more elevated than the animal appetites, and, when once made conscious of them, do not regard any thing as happiness that does not include their gratification." The higher the capacity or faculty, the higher in quality the pleasure of its exercise and fulfillment, irrespective of bulk. But how do we know which faculty *is* higher, and hence what satisfaction is more valuable? By reference to the experience of the man who has had the best opportunity to exercise all the powers in question.

Few human creatures would consent to be changed into any of the lower animals, for a promise of the fullest allowance of a beast's pleasure; no intelligent human being would consent to be a fool, no instructed person would be an ignoramus, no person of feeling and conscience would be selfish and base, even though they should be persuaded that the fool, the dunce or the rascal is better satisfied with his lot than they are with theirs.

And again,

It is indisputable that the being whose capacities of enjoyment are low has the greatest chance of having them fully satisfied; and a highly endowed being will always feel that any happiness which he can look for, as the world is constituted, is imperfect. . . . It is better to be a human being dissatisfied than a pig satisfied; better to be a Socrates dissatisfied than a fool satisfied. And if the fool or the pig is of a different opinion, it is because he only knows his own side of the question. The other party to the comparison knows both sides.

The net result of our discussion is, then, (1) that happiness consists in the fulfillment in their appropriate objects (or the anticipation of such fulfillment) of the powers of the self manifested in desires, purposes, efforts; (2) true happiness consists in the satisfaction of those powers of the self which are of higher quality; (3) that the man of good character, the one in whom these high powers are already active, is the judge, in the concrete, of happiness and misery. We shall now discuss

§ 3. *The Constitution of Happiness*

Happiness consists in the agreement, whether anticipated or realized, of the objective conditions brought about by our endeavors with our desires and purposes. This conception of happiness is contrasted with the notion that it is a sum or collection of separate states of sensation or feeling.

1. *One View Separates, while the Other Connects, Pleasure and Objective Conditions.*—In one case, the agreeable

feeling is a kind of psychical entity, supposed to be capable of existence by itself and capable of abstraction from the objective end of action. The pleasant *thing* is one thing; the pleasure, another; or, rather, the *pleasant thing* must be analyzed into two independent elements, the pleasure as *feeling* and the *thing* with which it happens to be associated. It is the pleasure alone, *when dissociated*, which is the real end of conduct, an object being at best an external means of securing it. It is the pleasurable feeling which happens to be *associated* with food, with music, with a landscape, that makes it good; health, art, are not good in themselves. The other view holds that pleasure has no such existence by itself; that it is only a name for the *pleasant object*; that by pleasure is meant the agreement or congruity which exists between some capacity of the agent and some objective fact in which this capacity is realized. It expresses the way some object meets, fits into, responds to, an activity of the agent. To say that food is agreeable, means that food satisfies an organic function. Music is pleasant because by it certain capacities or demands of the person with respect to rhythm of hearing are fulfilled; a landscape is beautiful because it carries to fulfillment the visual possibilities of the spectator.

2. *Qualities of Pleasure Vary with Objects, and with Springs to Action.*—When happiness is conceived as an aggregate of states of feeling, these are regarded as homogeneous in quality, differing from one another only in intensity and duration. Their qualitative differences are not intrinsic, but are due to the different objects with which they are associated (as pleasures of hearing, or vision). Hence they disappear when the pleasure is taken by itself as an end. But if agreeableness is precisely the agreeableness or congruousness of some objective condition with some impulse, habit, or tendency of the agent, then, of course, pure pleasure is a myth. Any pleasure is qualitatively unique, being precisely the harmony of one set of conditions with its appropriate activity. The pleasure of eating is one thing; the pleasure of hearing music, another; the pleasure of an amiable act, another; the pleasure of drunkenness or of anger is still another. Hence the possibility of absolutely different moral values attaching to pleasures, according to the type or

aspect of character which they express. But if the good is only a sum of pleasures, any pleasure, so far as it goes, is as good as any other—the pleasure of malignity as good as the pleasure of kindliness, simply as pleasure. Accordingly Bentham said, the pleasure of push-pin (a game) is as good as that of poetry. And as he said again, since pleasure is the motive of every act, there is no motive which *in itself,* and as far as it goes, is not good—it is bad only if it turns out in the end to produce more pain than pleasure. The pleasure of malignant gossip is so far as it is pleasure a mitigation of the badness of the act. Not so, if happiness is the experience into which pleasures enter so far as the tendencies of character that produce them are approved of. An act may bring a pleasure and yet that pleasure be no part of happiness, but rather a blot and blemish. Such would be the case, for example, with the pleasure which one might take in an act of charity because one had thereby put himself in a position superior to that of the recipient. A good man who caught himself feeling pleasure from this phase of the act would not regard this pleasure as a further element of good attained, but as detracting from his happiness. A pleasure may be accepted or reacted against. So far as not acquiesced in it is, from the standpoint of happiness, positively disagreeable. Surrender to a pleasure, taking it to be one's happiness, is one of the surest ways of revealing or discovering what sort of a man one is. On the other hand, the pain which a miserly man feels in his first acts of generosity may be welcomed by him as, under the circumstances, an element in his good, since it is a sign of and factor in the improvement of character.

3. *The Unification of Character.*—Happiness as a sum of pleasures does not afford a basis for unifying or organizing the various tendencies and capacities of the self. It makes possible at best only a mechanical compromise or external adjustment. Take, for example, the satisfaction attendant upon acting from a benevolent or a malicious impulse. There can be no question that some pleasure is found in giving way to either impulse when it is strongly felt. Now if we regard the pleasure as a fixed state in itself, and good or happiness as a sum of such states, the only moral superiority that can attach to acting benevolently is that,

upon the whole, *more* units of pleasure come from it than from giving way to the opposite spring of action. It is simply a question of greater or less quantity in the long run. Each trait of character, each act, remains morally independent, cut off from others. Its only relation to others is that which arises when its results in the way of units of agreeable or painful feeling are compared, as to bulk, with analogous consequences flowing from some other trait, or act. But if the fundamental thing in happiness is the relation of the desire and intention of the agent to its own successful outlet, there is an inherent connection between our different tendencies. The satisfaction of one tendency strengthens itself, and strengthens allied tendencies, while it weakens others. A man who gives way easily to anger (and finds gratification in it) against the acts of those whom he regards as enemies, nourishes unawares a tendency to irritability in all directions and thus modifies the sources and nature of all satisfaction. The man who cherishes the satisfaction he derives from a landscape may increase his susceptibility to enjoyment from poetry and pictures.

The Final Question. —The final question of happiness, the question which marks off true and right happiness from false and wrong gratification, comes to this: Can there be found ends of action, desirable in themselves, which reenforce and expand not only the motives from which they directly spring, but also the other tendencies and attitudes which are sources of happiness? Can there be found powers whose exercise confirms ends which are stable and weakens and removes objects which occasion only restless, peevish, or transitory satisfaction, and ultimately thwart and stunt the growth of happiness? Harmony, reenforcement, expansion are the signs of a true or moral satisfaction. What is the good which while good in direct enjoyment also brings with it fuller and more continuous life?

Literature

For pleasure as the object of desire and the psychology of hedonism, see Bain, *Emotions and Will*, Part II, ch. viii; Rickaby, *Moral Philosophy*, pp. 54–61, and *Aquinas Ethicus*, Vol. I, pp.

104–21; Sidgwick, *Methods of Ethics* (1901), pp. 34–47, and the whole of Book II, and Book III, chs. xiii and xiv; Mackenzie, *Manual of Ethics*, Book II, ch. iv; Muirhead, *Elements of Ethics*, Book III, ch. i; Gizyeki, *A Student's Manual of Ethical Philosophy*; Green, *Prolegomena to Ethics*, pp. 163–77, 226–40, 374–88; James, *Principles of Psychology*, Vol. II, pp. 549–59; Martineau, *Types of Ethical Theory*, Vol. II, Part II, Book II.

For the history of hedonism, see Wallace, *Epicureanism*; Pater, *Marius the Epicurean*; Sidgwick, *History of Ethics*, ch. ii, *passim* and ch. iv, §§ 14–17; Hume, *Treatise of Human Nature*, Book III, and the references to Bentham and Mill in the text; Watson, *Hedonistic Theories from Aristippus to Spencer*.

For the utilitarian standard, see Lecky, *History of European Morals*, Vol. I, ch. i; Stephen, *Science of Ethics*, chs. iv and v; Spencer, *Principles of Ethics*, Part I; Höffding, *Ethik*, ch. vii, and *Monist*, Vol. I, p. 529; Paulsen, *System of Ethics*, pp. 222–86, and 404–14; Grote, *Examination of the Utilitarian Philosophy*; Wilson and Fowler, *Principles of Morals*, Vol. I, pp. 98–112; Vol. II, pp. 262–73; Green, *Prolegomena*, pp. 240–55, 399–415; Martineau, *Types*, pp. 308–34; Alexander, *Moral Order and Progress* (1891), pp. 204–11; Seth, *Ethical Principles*, pp. 94–111; Sidgwick, *Lectures on the Ethics of T. H. Green, Mr. Herbert Spencer, and J. Martineau*, Lectures I–IV of the Criticism of Spencer. Compare the references *sub voce* Happiness, 899–901, in Rand's *Bibliography*, Vol. III of Baldwin's *Dictionary of Philosophy and Psychology*.

15. HAPPINESS AND SOCIAL ENDS[1]

In form, the true good is thus an inclusive or expanding end. In substance, the only end which fulfills these conditions is the social good. The utilitarian standard is social consequences. To repeat our earlier quotation from Bentham (above, p. 242): "The greatest happiness of all those whose interest is in question is the right and proper, and the only right and proper and *universally desirable* end of human action." Mill says, "To do as you would be done by, and to love your neighbor as yourself, constitute the ideal perfection of utilitarian morality." And again: "The happiness which is the Utilitarian standard of what is right in conduct is not the agent's own happiness, but that of all concerned; as between his own happiness and that of others, Utilitarianism requires him to be as strictly impartial as a disinterested and benevolent spectator." So Sidgwick (*Methods of Ethics* [1877], p. 379):

> By Utilitarianism is here meant the ethical theory, first distinctly formulated by Bentham, that the conduct which under any given circumstances is externally or objectively right is that which produces the greatest amount of happiness *on the whole*; that is taking into account all whose happiness is affected by the conduct. It would tend to clearness if we might call this principle, and the method based upon it, by some such name as Universalistic hedonism.

And finally, Bain (*Emotions and Will*, p. 303): "Utility is opposed to the selfish principle, for, as propounded, it always implies the good of society generally and the subordination of individual interests to the general good."

Social Purpose of Utilitarianism.—Its aim, then, was the "greatest possible happiness of the greatest possible number," a democratic, fraternal aim. In the computation of the

1. The discussion of altruism and egoism in ch. 18 on the Self, considers some aspects of this question from another point of view.

elements of this aim, it insisted upon the principle of social and moral equality: "every one to count for one, and only for one." The standard was the well-being of the community conceived as a community of individuals, all of whom had equal rights and none of whom had special privileges or exclusive avenues of access to happiness. In a period in which the democratic spirit in England was asserting itself against vested interests and class-distinctions, against legalized inequalities of all sorts, the utilitarian philosophy became the natural and perhaps indispensable adjunct of the liberal and reforming spirit in law, education, and politics. Every custom, every institution, was cross-questioned; it was not allowed to plead precedent and prior existence as a basis for continued existence. It had to prove that it conduced to the happiness of the community as a whole, or be legislated out of existence or into reform. Bentham's fundamental objection to other types of moral theories than his own was not so much philosophic or theoretic as it was practical. He felt that every intuitional theory tended to dignify prejudice, convention, and fixed customs, and so to consecrate vested interests and inequitable institutions.

Recognition by an Opponent. — The following remarks by T. H. Green are the more noteworthy because coming from a consistent opponent of the theory:

> The chief theory of conduct which in Modern Europe has afforded the conscientious citizen a vantage-ground for judging of the competing claims on his obedience, and enabled him to substitute a critical and intelligent for a blind and unquestioning conformity, has no doubt been the Utilitarian. . . . Whatever the errors arising from its Hedonistic psychology, no other theory has been available for the social or political reformer, combining so much truth with such ready applicability. No other has offered so commanding a point of view from which to criticise the precepts and institutions presented as authoritative.[2]

And again, speaking of the possibility of practical service from theory, he says:

The form of philosophy which in the modern world has most conspicuously rendered this service has been the Utilitarian, because it has most definitely announced the interest of

2. Green, *Prolegomena to Ethics*, p. 361.

humanity, without distinction of persons or classes, as the end by reference to which all claims upon obedience are ultimately to be measured. . . . Impartiality of reference to human well-being has been the great lesson which the Utilitarian has had to teach.[3]

Irreconcilable Conflict of Motive and End. — But unfortunately the assertion that the happiness of all concerned is the "universally *desirable* end," is mixed up by early utilitarianism with an hedonistic psychology, according to which the *desired* object is private and personal pleasure. What is *desirable* is thus so different from what is *desired* as to create an uncrossable chasm between the true end of action — the happiness of all, — and the moving spring of desire and action — private pleasure. That there is a difference between what is *naturally* desired (meaning by "naturally" what first arouses interest and excites endeavor) and what is morally desirable (understanding by this the consequences which present themselves in adequate deliberation), is certain enough. But the desirable must be *capable of becoming* desired, or else there is such a contradiction that morality is impossible. If, now, the object of desire is always private pleasure, how can the recognition of the consequences upon the happiness or misery of others ever become an effective competitor with considerations of personal well-being, when the two conflict?[4]

Lack of Harmony among Pleasurable Ends. — If it so happens that the activities which secure the personal pleasure also manage to affect others favorably, so much the better; but since, by the theory, the individual *must* be moved exclusively by desire for his own pleasure, woe betide others if their happiness happens to stand in the way.[5] It could only

3. Green, *Prolegomena to Ethics*, pp. 365–66. Green then goes on to argue that this service has been in spite of its hedonistic factor, and that if the theory were generally applied with all the hedonistic implications to personal behavior in private life, it would put impediments in the way of moral progress.

4. It will be noted that we have here the same double rôle of pleasure that met us at the outset (see *ante*, p. 244): one sort of happiness is the moving spring of action, because object of desire; another and incompatible sort is the standard, and hence proper or right end.

5. It is this hedonistic element of the object of desire and moving spring which calls forth such denunciations as Carlyle's; on the

be by accident that activities of a large number of individuals all seeking their own private pleasures should coincide in effecting the desirable end of the common happiness. The outcome would, more likely, be a competitive "war of all against all." It is of such a situation that Kant says: "There results a harmony like that which a certain satirical poem depicts as existing between a married couple bent on going to ruin, 'O, marvellous harmony! what he wishes, she wishes too'; or like what is said of the pledge of Francis I. to the emperor Charles V., 'What my brother wants, that I want too' (namely Milan)."[6] The existence already noted of an unperceived and unreconcilable division between happiness *in the form of future consequences*, and pleasure *as object of desire and present moving spring*, thus becomes of crucial and, for hedonistic utilitarianism, of catastrophic importance. We shall first discuss the efforts of utilitarianism to deal with the problem.

Mill's Formal Method. — We mention first a purely logical or formal suggestion of Mill's, not because it is of very much significance one way or the other, but because it helps to bring out the problem.

No reason can be given why the general happiness is desirable, except that each person, so far as he believes it to be obtainable, desires his own happiness. This, however, being a fact, we have not only all the proof which the case admits of, but all which it is possible to require, that happiness is a good; that each person's happiness is a good to that person; and the general happiness, therefore, a good to the aggregate of all persons.[7]

It clearly does not follow that because the good of A and B and C, etc., is *collectively*, or aggregately, a good to A and B and C, etc., that therefore the good of A and B and C, etc., or of anybody beyond A himself, is regarded as a good by A— especially when the original premise is that A seeks his own

other hand, it is the assertion of the common happiness as the standard which calls out the indignant denial of the utilitarians; which, for example, leads Spencer to retort upon Carlyle's epithet of "pig-philosophy" with a counter charge that Carlyle's epithet is a survival of "devil-worship," since it assumes pain to be a blessing (*Principles of Ethics*, Vol. I, pp. 40–41).

6. Kant, *Theory of Ethics*, p. 116.
7. Mill, *Utilitarianism*, third paragraph of ch. iv.

good. Because all men want to be happy themselves, it hardly follows that each wants all to be so. It does follow, perhaps, that that would be the *reasonable* thing to want. If each man desires happiness for himself, to an outside spectator looking at the matter in the cold light of intelligence, there might be no reason why the happiness of one should be any more precious or desirable than that of another. From a mathematical standpoint, the mere fact that the individual knows he wants happiness, and knows that others are like himself, that they too are individuals who want happiness, might commit each individual, theoretically, to the necessity of regarding the happiness of every other as equally sacred with his own. But the difficulty is that there is no chance, upon the hedonistic psychology of desire, for this rational conviction to get in its work, even if it be intellectually entertained. The intellectual perception and the mechanism of human motivation remain opposed. Mill's statement, in other words, puts the problem which hedonistic utilitarianism has to solve.

Materially, as distinct from this formal statement, utilitarianism has two instrumentalities upon which it relies: one, internal, found in the nature of the individual; the other, external, or in social arrangements.

I. Bentham's View of Sympathetic Pleasures.—In the long list of pleasures moving men to action which Bentham drew up, he included what he called the social and the semisocial. The social are the pleasures of benevolence; the semisocial, the pleasures of amity (peace with one's fellows) and of reputation. "The pleasures of benevolence are the pleasures resulting from the view of any pleasures supposed to be possessed by the beings who may be the objects of benevolence" (*Principles of Morals and Legislation*). And if it be asked what motives lying within a man's self he has to consult the happiness of others,

In answer to this, it cannot but be admitted that the only interests which a man at all times and upon all occasions is sure to find *adequate* motives for consulting are his own. Notwithstanding this there are no occasions on which a man has not some motives for consulting the happiness of other men. In the first place, he has, on all occasions, the purely social motive of sympathy and benevolence; in the next place, he has, on most occasions, the semi-social motives of amity and love of reputation (*Principles,* ch. xvii, § 1).

So important finally are the sympathetic motives that he says "The Dictates of Utility are neither more nor less than the dictates of the most extensive and enlightened (that is, well-advised)[8] benevolence" (*Principles*, ch. x, § 4). In short, we are so constituted that the happiness of others gives us happiness, their misery creates distress in us. We are also so constituted that, even aside from direct penalties imposed upon us by others, we are made to suffer more or less by the knowledge that they have a low opinion of us, or that we are not "popular" with them. The more enlightened our activity, the more we shall see how by sympathy our pleasures are directly bound up with others, so that we shall get more pleasure by encouraging that of others. The same course will also indirectly increase our own, because others will be likely to esteem and honor us just in the degree in which our acts conduce to their pleasure. A wise or enlightened desire for our own pleasure will thus lead us to regard the pleasures of others in our activities.

Limitations of Doctrine. — To state the doctrine is almost to criticize it. It comes practically to saying that a sensible and prudent self-love will make us pay due heed to the effect of our activities upon the welfare of others. We are to be benevolent, but the reason is that we get more pleasure, or get pleasure more surely and easily, that way than in any other. We are to be kind, because upon the whole the net return of pleasure is greater that way. This does not mean that Bentham denied the existence of "disinterested motives" in man's make-up; or that he held that all sympathy is coldly calculating. On the contrary, he held that sympathetic reactions to the well-being and suffering of others are involved in our make-up. But as it relates to *motives* for action he holds that the sympathetic affections influence us only under the form of desire for our own pleasure: they make us rejoice in the rejoicing of others, and move us to act that others may rejoice so that we may thereby rejoice the more.

8. By this phrase Bentham refers to the necessity of controlling this spring to activity just as any other is regulated, by reference to its consequences.

They do not move us to act as direct interests in the welfare of others for their own sake.[9] We shall find that just as Mill transformed the utilitarian theory of motives by substituting quality of happiness for quantity of pleasures, so he also transformed the earlier Benthamite conception of both the internal and the external methods for relating the happiness of the individual and the welfare of society.

II. Mill's Criticism.—Mill charges Bentham with overlooking the motive in man which makes him love excellence for its own sake. "Even under the head of sympathy," he says:

his recognition does not extend to the more complex forms of the feeling—the love of *loving*, the need of a sympathising support, or of an object of admiration and reverence.[10]

Self-culture, the training by the human being himself of his affections and will . . . is a blank in Bentham's system. The other and co-equal part, the regulation of his outward actions, must be altogether halting and imperfect without the first; for how can we judge in what manner many an action will affect the worldly interests of ourselves or others unless we take in, as part of the question, its influence on the regulation of our or their affections and desires?[11]

In other words, Mill saw that the weakness of Bentham's theory lay in his supposition that the factors of character, the powers and desires which make up disposition, are of value only as moving us to seek pleasure; to Mill they have a worth of their own or are *direct* sources and ingredients of happiness. So Mill says: "I regard any considerable increase of human happiness, through mere changes in outward circumstances, unaccompanied by changes in the state of desires, as hopeless."[12] And in his *Autobiography*, speaking of his first reaction against Benthamism, he says:

I, for the first time, gave its proper place, among the prime necessities of human well-being, to the internal culture of the individual. I ceased to attach almost exclusive importance to the

9. Bentham himself was not a psychologist, and he does not state the doctrine in this extreme form. But those of the Benthamites who were psychologists, being hedonistic in their psychology, gave the doctrine this form.
10. Mill, *Early Essays*, p. 354. (Reprint by Gibbs, London, 1897.)
11. Mill, *Early Essays*, p. 357.
12. Mill, *Early Essays*, p. 404.

ordering of outward circumstances. . . . The cultivation of the feelings became one of the cardinal points in my ethical and philosophical creed.[13]

The Social Affections as Direct Interest in Others.—The importance of this changed view lies in the fact that it compels us to regard certain desires, affections, and motives as inherently worthy, because intrinsic constituent factors of happiness. Thus it enables us to *identify* our happiness with the happiness of others, to find our good in their good, not just to seek their happiness as, upon the whole, the most effective way of securing our own. Our social affections are direct interests in the well-being of others; their cultivation and expression is at one and the same time a source of good to ourselves, and, intelligently guided, to others. Taken in this light, it is sympathetic emotion and imagination which make the standard of general happiness not merely the "desirable end," but the desired end, the effectively working object of endeavor.

Intrinsic Motivation of Regard for Others.—If it is asked *why* the individual should thus regard the well-being of others as an inherent object of desire, there is, according to Mill, but one answer: We cannot think of ourselves save as to some extent *social* beings. Hence we cannot separate the idea of ourselves and of our own good from our idea of others and of their good. The natural sentiment which is the basis of the utilitarian morality, which gives the idea of the social good weight with us, is the

desire to be in unity with our fellow-creatures. . . . The social state is at once so natural, so necessary, and so habitual to man, that except in some unusual circumstances or by an effort of voluntary abstraction, *he never conceives himself otherwise than as a member of a body.* . . . Any condition, therefore, which is essential to a state of society becomes more and more an inseparable part of every person's conception of the state of things he is born into and which is the destiny of a human being.

This strengthening of social ties leads the individual "to identify his *feelings* more and more with the good" of others.

He comes, as though instinctively, to be conscious of himself as a being, who, *of course*, pays regard to others. The good

13. Mill, *Autobiography*, London, 1873, pp. 143–44.

of others becomes to him a thing naturally and necessarily to be attended to, like any of the physical conditions of our existence.

This social feeling, finally, however weak, does not present itself

as a superstition of education, or a law despotically imposed from without, but as an attribute which it would not be well to be without. . . . Few but those whose mind is a moral blank could *bear* to lay out their course of life on the line of paying no regard to others except so far as their own private interest compels.[14]

The transformation is tremendous. It is no longer a question of acting for the general interest because that brings most pleasure or brings it more surely and easily. It is a question of finding one's good in the good of others.

III. The Benthamite External Ties of Private and General Interests.—Aside from sympathy and love of peaceful relations and good repute, Bentham relied upon law, changes in political arrangements, and the play of economic interests which make it worth while for the individual to seek his own pleasure in ways that would also conduce to the pleasure of others. Penal law can at least make it painful for the individual to try to get his own good in ways which bring suffering to others. Civil legislation can at least abolish those vested interests and class privileges which inevitably favor one at the expense of others, and which make it customary and natural to seek and get happiness in ways which disregard the happiness of others. In the industrial life each individual seeks his own advantage under such conditions that he can achieve his end only by rendering service to others, that is, through exchange of commodities or services. The proper end of legislation is then to make political and economic conditions such that the individual while seeking his own good will at least not inflict suffering upon others, and positively, so far as possible, will promote their good.[15]

IV. Mill's Criticism.—Mill's criticism does not turn upon the importance of legislation and of social economic arrangements in promoting the identity of individual and general

14. Mill, *Utilitarianism*, ch. iii, *passim*.
15. Some phases of this view as respects legislation, etc., are touched upon later in ch. 18.

good. On the contrary, after identifying (in a passage already quoted, *ante,* p. 261) the ideal of utilitarian morality with love of neighbor, he goes on:

As the means of making the nearest approach to this ideal, utility would enjoin, first, that laws and social arrangements should place the happiness of every individual as nearly as possible in harmony with the interest of the whole; and, secondly, that education and opinion, which have so vast a power over human character, should so use that power as to establish in the mind of every individual an indissoluble association between his own happiness and the good of the whole.

The criticism turns upon the fact that *unless* the intrinsic social idea, already discussed, be emphasized, any association of private and general happiness which law and social arrangements can effect will be external, more or less artificial and arbitrary, and hence dissoluble either by intellectual analysis, or by the intense prepotency of egoistic desire.

Mill's Transformation.—If, however, this idea of inherent social ties and of oneself as a social being is presupposed, the various external agencies have something internal to work upon; and their effect is internal, not external. Their effect is not to establish a mere *coincidence* (as with Bentham) between pleasure to oneself and pleasure to others, but to protect, strengthen, and foster the sense, otherwise intermittent and feeble, of the social aspects and relations of one's own being. It is for this reason that Mill lays more stress on *education* than on mere external institutional changes, and, indeed, conceives of the ultimate moral value of the institutional arrangements as itself educative. Their value to him is not that they are contrivances or pieces of machinery for making the behavior of one conduce more or less automatically to the happiness of others, but that they train and exercise the individual in the recognition of the social elements of his own character.

Summary of Previous Discussion.—We have carried on our discussion of the relation between the common good as the standard for measuring rightness, and pleasure as the end and spring of the individual's activity, in terms of Mill's development of Bentham's utilitarianism. But of course our results are general, and they may be detached not only from this particular discussion, but from the truth or falsity of utilitarianism as a technical theory. Put positively, our results are these: (1) Moral quality is an attribute of character, of dispositions and attitudes which express themselves in desires and efforts. (2) Those attitudes and dispositions are morally good which aim at the production, the maintenance, and development of ends in which the agent and others affected alike find satisfaction. There is no difference (such as early utilitarianism made) between good as standard and as aim, because *only a voluntary preference for and interest in a social good is capable, otherwise than by coincidence or accident, of producing acts which have common good as their result.* Acts which are not motivated by it as aim cannot be trusted to secure it as result; *acts which are motived by it as a living and habitual interest are the guarantee, so far as conditions allow, of its realization.* Those who care for the general good for its own sake are those who are surest of promoting it.

The Good Moral Character.—The genuinely moral person is one, then, in whom the habit of regarding all capacities and habits of self from the social standpoint is formed and active. Such an one forms his plans, regulates his desires, and hence performs his acts with reference to the effect they have upon the social groups of which he is a part. He is one whose dominant attitudes and interests are bound up with associated activities. Accordingly he will find his happiness or satisfaction in the promotion of these activities irrespective of the particular pains and pleasures that accrue.

Social Interests and Sympathy.—A genuine social interest is then something much broader and deeper than an instinctive sympathetic reaction. Sympathy is a genuine natural instinct, varying in intensity in different individuals. It is a precious instrumentality for the development of social insight and socialized affection; but in and of itself it is upon the same plane as any natural endowment. It may lead to sentimentality or to selfishness; the individual may shrink from scenes of misery just because of the pain they cause him, or may seek jovial companions because of the sympathetic pleasures he gets. Or he may be moved by sympathy to labor for the good of others, but, because of lack of deliberation and thoughtfulness, be quite ignorant of what their good really is, and do a great deal of harm. One may wish to do unto others as he would they should do unto him, but may err egregiously because his conception of what is desirable for himself is radically false; or because he assumes arbitrarily that whatever he likes is good for others, and may thus tyrannically impose his own standards upon them. Again instinctive sympathy is partial; it may attach itself vehemently to those of blood kin or to immediate associates in such a way as to favor them at the expense of others, and lead to positive injustice toward those beyond the charmed circle.[16]

Transformation of Instinctive Sympathies.—It still remains true that the instinctive affectionate reactions in their various forms (parental, filial, sexual, compassionate, sympathetic) are the sole portions of the psychological structure or mechanism of a man which can be relied upon to work the identification of other's ends with one's own interests. What is required is a *blending*, a *fusing* of the sympathetic tendencies with all the other impulsive and habitual traits of the self. When interest in power is permeated with an affectionate impulse, it is protected from being a tendency to dominate and tyrannize; it becomes an interest in *effectiveness of regard for common ends*. When an interest in artistic or scientific objects is similarly fused, it loses the indifferent and coldly impersonal character which marks the specialist as such, and becomes an interest in the adequate aesthetic and intellectual development of the conditions of a common life. Sympathy does not merely *associate* one of these tendencies *with* another; still less does it make one a means to the other's end. It so intimately permeates them as to transform them both into a single new and moral interest. This same fusion protects sympathy from sentimentality and narrowness. Blended with interest in power, in science, in art, it

16. Mill in his article on Bentham says of him: "Personal affection, he well knew, is as liable to operate to the injury of third parties, and requires as much to be kept in check, as any other feeling whatever: and general philanthropy . . . he estimated at its true value when divorced from the feeling of duty, as the very weakest and most unsteady of all feelings" (Essay on Bentham, p. 362).

is liberalized in quality and broadened in range. In short, the fusion of affectionate reactions with the other dispositions of the self *illuminates, gives perspective and body to the former,* while it *gives social quality and direction to the latter.* The result of this reciprocal absorption is the disappearance of the natural tendencies in their original form *and the generation of moral,* i.e., *socialized interests.* It is sympathy transformed into a habitual standpoint which satisfies the demand for a standpoint which will render the person interested in foresight of all obscure consequences (*ante,* p. 240).

1. *Social Interest and the Happiness of the Agent.*— We now see what is meant by a distinctively *moral* happiness, and how this happiness is supreme in quality as compared with other satisfactions, irrespective of superior intensity and duration on the part of the latter. It is impossible to draw any fixed line between the *content* of the moral good and of natural satisfaction. The end, the right and only right end, of man, lies in the fullest and freest realization of powers in their appropriate objects. The good consists of friendship, family and political relations, economic utilization of mechanical resources, science, art, in all their complex and variegated forms and elements. There is no separate and rival moral good; no separate empty and rival "good will."

Nature of Moral Interest and Motivation.—Yet *the interest* in the social or the common and progressive realization of these interests may properly be called a distinctive moral interest. The degree of actual objective realization or achievement of these ends, depends upon circumstances and accidents over which the agent has little or no control. The more happily situated individual who succeeds in realizing these ends more largely we may call more fortunate; we cannot call him morally better. The interest in all other interests, the voluntary desire to discover and promote them within the range of one's own capacities, one's own material resources, and the limits of one's own surroundings, is, however, under one's control: *it is one's moral self. The nature and exercise of this interest constitutes then the distinctively moral quality in all good purposes.* They are morally good not so far as objectively accomplished and possessed, but so far as cherished in the dominant affections of the person.

The Moral Interest as Final Happiness.—Consequently the true or final happiness of an individual, the happiness which is not at the mercy of circumstance and change of circumstance, lies not in objective achievement of results, but in the supremacy within character of an alert, sincere, and persistent interest in those habits and institutions which forward common ends among men. Mill insisted that quality of happiness was morally important, not quantity. Well, that quality which is most important is the peace and joy of mind that accompanies the abiding and equable maintenance of socialized interests as central springs of action. To one in whom these interests live (and they live to some extent in every individual not completely pathological) their exercise brings happiness because it fulfills his life. To those in whom it is the supreme interest it brings supreme or final happiness. It is not preferred because it is the greater happiness, but in being preferred as expressing the only kind of self which the agent fundamentally wishes himself to be, it constitutes a kind of happiness with which others cannot be compared. It is unique, final, invaluable.[17]

Identity of the Individual and General Happiness.—No algebraic summing up of sympathetic pleasures, utilities of friendship, advantages of popularity and esteem, profits of economic exchange among equals, over against pains from legal penalties and disapproving public opinion, and lack of sympathetic support by others, can ever make it even approximately certain that an individual's own interest, in terms of quantity of pleasures and pains, is to regard the interest of others.[18] Such a demonstration, moreover, if possible, would not support but would weaken the moral life. It

17. "It is only a poor sort of happiness that could ever come by caring very much about our own narrow pleasures. We can only have the highest happiness, such as goes along with being a great man, by having wide thought and much feeling for the rest of the world as well as ourselves; and this sort of happiness often brings so much pain with it, that we can only tell it from pain by its being what we would choose before every thing else, because our souls see it is good." —George Eliot in *Romola*.

18. The recognition of this by many utilitarian hedonists has caused them to have recourse to the supernaturally inflicted penalties and conferred delights of a future life to make sure of balancing up the account of virtue as self-sacrificing action with happiness, its proper end.

would reduce the manifestation of character to selecting greater rather than less amounts of homogeneous ends. It would degrade reflection and consideration to ingenuity in detecting where larger quantities of pleasures lie, and to skill in performing sums of addition and subtraction. Even if such a scheme could be demonstrated, every one except the most languid and phlegmatic of pleasure-seekers would reject a life built upon it. Not only the "good," but the more vigorous and hearty of the "bad," would scorn a life in which character, selfhood, had no significance, and where the experimental discovery and testing of destiny had no place. The identity of individual and general happiness is a *moral* matter; it depends, that is, upon the reflective and intentional development of that type of character which identifies itself with common ends, and which is happy in these ends just because it has made them its own.

2. *Social Ends and the Happiness of Others.*—The same principle holds of the happiness of others. Happiness means the expression of the active tendencies of a self in their appropriate objects. Moral happiness means the satisfaction which comes when the dominant active tendencies are made interests in the maintenance and propagation of the things that make life worth living. Others, also, can be happy and should be happy only upon the same terms. Regard for the happiness of others means *regard for those conditions and objects which permit others freely to exercise their own powers from their own initiative, reflection, and choice.* Regard for their final happiness (i.e., for a happiness whose *quality* is such that it cannot be *externally* added to or subtracted from) demands that these others shall find the controlling objects of preference, resolution, and endeavor in the things that are worth while.

3. *Happiness and Common Ends.*—For all alike, in short, the chief thing is the discovery and promotion of those activities and active relationships in which the capacities of all concerned are effectively evoked, exercised, and put to the test. It is difficult for a man to attain a point of view from which steadily to apprehend how his own activities affect and modify those of others. It is hard, that is, to learn to accommodate one's ends to those of others; to adjust, to give

way here, and fit in there with respect to our aims. But difficult as this is, it is easy compared with the difficulty of acting
in such a way for ends which are helpful to others as will call
out and make effective their activities.

Moral Democracy.—If the vice of the criminal, and of
the coarsely selfish man is to disturb the aims and the good of
others; if the vice of the ordinary egoist, and of every man,
upon his egoistic side, is to neglect the interests of others; the
vice of the social leader, of the reformer, of the philanthropist
and the specialist in every worthy cause of science, or art,
or politics, is to seek ends which promote the social welfare
in ways which fail to engage the active interest and cooperation of others.[19] The conception of conferring the good upon
others, or at least of attaining it for them, which is our inheritance from the aristocratic civilization of the past, is so
deeply embodied in religious, political, and charitable institutions and in moral teachings, that it dies hard. Many a
man, feeling himself justified by the social character of his
ultimate aim (it may be economic, or educational, or political), is genuinely confused or exasperated by the increasing
antagonism and resentment which he evokes, because he has
not enlisted in his pursuit of the "common" end the freely
cooperative activities of others. This cooperation must be the
root principle of the morals of democracy. It must be confessed, however, that it has as yet made little progress.

Our traditional conceptions of the morally great man,
the moral hero and leader, the exceptionally good social and
political character, all work against the recognition of this
principle either in practice or theory. They foster the notion
that it is somebody's particular business to reach by his more
or less isolated efforts (with "following," or obedience, or unreflective subordination on the part of others) a needed
social good. Some genius is to lead the way; others are to
adopt and imitate. Moreover, the method of awakening and
enlisting the activities of all concerned in pursuit of the
end seems slow; it seems to postpone accomplishment indefinitely. But in truth a common end which is not made

19. The recognition of this type of spiritual selfishness is modern.
It is the pivot upon which the later (especially) of Ibsen's
tragedies turn.

such by common, free voluntary cooperation in process of achievement is common in name only. It has no support and guarantee in the activities which it is supposed to benefit, because it is not the fruit of those activities. Hence, it does not stay put. It has to be continually buttressed by appeal to external, not voluntary, considerations; bribes of pleasure, threats of harm, use of force. It has to be undone and done over. There is no way to escape or evade this law of happiness, that it resides in the exercise of the active capacities of a voluntary agent; and hence no way to escape or evade the law of a common happiness, that it must reside in the congruous exercise of the voluntary activities of all concerned. The inherent irony and tragedy of much that passes for a high kind of socialized activity is precisely that it seeks a common good by methods which forbid its being either common or a good.

Literature

See references upon utilitarianism at end of ch. 14. For happiness, see Aristotle, *Ethics*, Book I, and Book X, chs. vi–ix; Dickinson, *The Meaning of Good*; Paulsen, *System of Ethics*, pp. 268–86; Rickaby, *Aquinas Ethicus*, Vol. I, pp. 6–39; Mezes, *Ethics*, ch. xv; Santayana, *The Life of Reason*; Rashdall, *The Theory of Good and Evil*.

The following histories of utilitarianism bring out the social side of the utilitarian theory: Albee, *History of Utilitarianism*; Stephen, *The English Utilitarians*; Halévy, *La Formation du Radicalisme Philosophique*, especially Vols. I and II.

16. THE PLACE OF REASON
IN THE MORAL LIFE: MORAL KNOWLEDGE

§ 1. Problem of Reason and Desire

Intelligence and Reason in a Moral Act.—A voluntary act is one which involves intention, purpose, and thus some degree of deliberateness. It is this trait which marks off the voluntary act from a purely unconscious one (like that of a machine) and from one which yields to the superior urgency of present feeling, one which is pushed on from behind, as an instinctive or impulsive act, instead of being called out by some possibility ahead. This factor of forethought and of preference after comparison for some one of the ends considered, is the factor of intelligence involved in every voluntary act. To be intelligent in action is, however, a far-reaching affair. To know what one is really about is a large and difficult order to fill; so large and difficult that it is the heart of morality.[1] The relevant bearings of any act are subtler and larger than those which can be foreseen and than those which will be *unless* special care is taken. The tendencies which strongly move one to a certain act are often exactly those which tend to prevent one's seeing the effect of the act upon his own habits and upon the well-being of others. The internal forces and the external circumstance which evoke the idea of an end and of the means of attaining it are frequently also those which deflect intelligence to a narrow and partial view. The demand for a standard by which to regulate judgment of ends is thus the demand not only for intelligence, but for a certain kind of intelligence.

In short, a truly moral (or right) act is one which is intelligent in an emphatic and peculiar sense; it is a *reason-*

1. "Any one can be angry: that is quite easy. Any one can give money away or spend it. But to do these things to the right person, to the right amount, at the right time, with the right aim and in the right manner—this is not what any one can easily do."—Aristotle, *Ethics*, Book II, ix, 2.

able act. It is not merely one which is thought of, and thought of as good, at the moment of action, but one which will continue to be thought of as "good" in the most alert and persistent reflection.[2] For by "reasonable" action we mean such action as recognizes and observes all the necessary conditions; action in which impulse, instinct, inclination, habit, opinion, prejudice (as the case may be) are moderated, guided, and determined by considerations which lie outside of and beyond them. Not merely to form ends and select means, but to judge the *worth* of these means and ends by a standard, is then the distinctive province of reason in morals. Its outcome is *moral knowledge*; that is judgments of right and wrong, both in general, and in the particular and perplexing cases as they arise. This is the topic of the present chapter.

Typical Problems.—The problem of moral knowledge is in its general form: Is there a distinct and separate faculty of moral reason and knowledge, or is there but one power of judgment which varies with its object? The former view is the intuitional (from Latin, *intueor*: to look at); it is associated with theories, which, like the Kantian, emphasize attitudes, not results and intentions; while the view which holds that there is but one form of thought which, in morals, concerns itself with results, and with their association with the present aim, is the empirical. There are two especial difficulties which lead to the upholding of the intuitional point of view, difficulties which any theory of moral knowledge has to meet. They are (I) The Relation of Desire and Reason, and (II) The Knowledge of Private and General Good.

1. Desire and Reason.—Ordinary knowledge in practical matters follows the line set by desire. Hunger makes us think of food and of how to get it; sociable desire, of friends, and how to secure their companionship, and so on. Now a surging mass of desires, vehement and bulky, may concentrate itself upon the idea of any end; and as soon as it does so, it tends to shut out wider considerations. As we have just seen, it is the object of reason to give us a calm, objective, broad, and general survey of the field. Desires work against

2. Compare the sentence quoted on p. 246 from Hazlitt.

this, and unless (so runs the argument) there is a faculty which works wholly independent of desires, as our ordinary practical knowledge does not, it is absurd to suppose there can be a rational principle which will correct and curb desire.

2. *Private and General Good.* — Since the wide and permanent good is social, it is urged that unless we have an independent faculty of moral knowledge, our judgment will be subservient to the ends of private desire, and hence will not place itself at the public point of view. Or, if it does so, it will be simply as a matter of expediency to calculate better the means for getting our own pleasure. In general, it is urged that only a faculty of knowledge completely independent of personal wishes, habits, purposes can secure judgments possessing inherent dignity and authoritativeness; since these require an elevated, impartial, universal, and necessary point of view. We shall in the sequel attempt to show that this view of knowledge results from the false conception of desire as having pleasure for its object, and from a false conception of the relation of intent and motive. When these errors are corrected, there is no ground to assume any special faculty of moral intelligence, save as the one capacity of thought is specialized into a particular mental habit by being constantly occupied in judging values. We shall try to show that the broad and public point of view is secured by fusion of impulses with sympathetic affections. We shall begin with stating and criticizing the views of Kant, who upholds the doctrine of a separate independent Moral Reason in its most extreme form.

§ 2. *Kant's Theory of Practical Reason*

Kant is at one with the hedonist as regards the natural object of desire; it is pleasure. All purposes and ends that spring from inclination and natural tendency come under one head: self-love. Hence, the ordinary use of intelligence is confined to the matter of passing upon what constitutes the individual's private happiness and how he shall secure it. There are then fundamental contrasts between ordinary practical activity and genuinely moral activity, contrasts which reflect themselves in the theory of the nature and function of moral knowledge. (1) The moral end is *unqualified*, absolute, categorical. It is not something which we can pick or leave at our option. Morality is the region of final ends, ends not to be disputed or questioned; and reason must set forth such final ends. Since, however, happiness is not a morally necessary end, intelligence in its behalf can only give hypothetical counsel and advice: *if* you would be happy, or happy in this, or that way, then take such and such measures. Reason which promulgates ends must be of a different sort from the intelligence which simply searches for means.

(2) Morality is not qualified, but *certain* in its requirements. The most inexperienced, the humblest, the one most restricted in his circumstances and opportunities, must know what is morally required as surely as the wisest and most educated. Hence moral reason must utter its precepts clearly and unambiguously. But no one can be *sure* what happiness is, or whether a given act will bring joy or sorrow. "The problem of determining certainly what action would promote the happiness of a rational being is insoluble" (*Theory of Ethics*, p. 36). The demand for *certainty* of precepts in moral matters also requires a special faculty.

(3) Morality, which is inexorable and certain in its demands, is also *universal* in its requirements. Its laws are the same yesterday, to-day, and forever, the same for one as for another. Now happiness notoriously varies with the condition and circumstances of a person, as well as with the conditions of different peoples and epochs. Intelligence with reference to happiness can only give counsel, not even rules, so variable is happiness. It can only advise that upon the average, under certain conditions, a given course of action has usually promoted happiness. When we add that the commands of morality are also universal with respect to the different inclinations of different individuals, we are made emphatically aware of the necessity of a rational standpoint, which in its impartiality totally transcends the ends and plans that grow out of the ordinary experience of an individual.

An A Priori *Reason Kant's Solution.*—The net outcome is that only a reason which is separate and independent of all experience is capable of meeting the requirements of morality. What smacks in its origin and aim of experience is tainted with self-love; is partial, temporary, uncertain, and relative or dependent. The moral law is unqualified, necessary, and universal. Hence we have to recognize in man as a moral being a faculty of reason which expresses itself in the law of conduct *a priori* to all experience of desire, pleasure, and pain. Besides his sensuous nature (with respect to which knowledge is bound up with appetite) man has a purely rational nature, which manifests itself in the consciousness of the absolute authority of universal law.[3]

Formal Character of Such Reason. —This extreme separation of reason from experience brings with it, however, a serious problem. We shall first state this problem; and then show that its artificial and insoluble character serves as a refutation of Kant's theory of a transcendental, or wholly non-natural and non-empirical, mode of knowledge. Reason which is wholly independent of experience of desires and their results is, as Kant expressly declares, purely *formal* (*Theory of Ethics*, p. 33; p. 114). That is to say, it is *empty*; it does not point out or indicate anything particular to be done. It cannot say be industrious, or prudent, generous; give, or refrain from giving, so much money to this particular man at this particular time under just these circumstances. All it says is that morality is rational and requires man to follow the law of reason. But the law of reason is just that a man should follow the law of reason. And to the inevitable inquiry "What then is the law of reason?" the answer still is: To follow the law of reason. How do we break out of this empty circle into specific knowledge of the specific right things to be done? Kant has an answer, which we shall now consider.

Kant's Method. —He proceeds as follows: The law is indeed purely formal or empty (since, once more, all specific ends are "empirical" and changeable), but it is so because it is universal. Now nothing which is universal can contradict itself. All we need to do is to take any proposed principle of any act and ask ourselves whether it can be uni-

3. This means Duty. This phase will be discussed in the next chapter.

versalized without self-inconsistency. If it cannot be, the act is wrong. If it can be, the act is right. For example:

May I, when in distress, make a promise with the intention not to keep it? . . . The shortest way, and an unerring one to discover the answer to the question whether a lying promise is consistent with duty, is to ask myself, Should I be content that my maxim (to extricate myself from trouble by a false promise) should hold good as a universal law, for myself as well as for others? and should I be able to say to myself, every one may make a deceitful promise when he finds himself in a difficulty from which he cannot otherwise extricate himself? Then I personally become aware that while I can will the lie, I can by no means will that lying should be a universal law. For with such a law there would be no such thing as a promise. No one should have any faith in the proffered intention, or, if they do so over-hastily, would pay one back in one's own coin at the first opportunity (*Theory of Ethics*, p. 19).

The principle if made universal simply contradicts itself, and thus reveals that it is no principle at all, not rational. Summing this up in a formula, we get as our standard of right action the principle: "Act as if the maxim of thy action were to become by thy will a universal law of nature" (*Theory of Ethics*, p. 39).

The procedure thus indicated seems simple. As long as an individual considers the purpose or motive of his action as if it were merely a matter of that one deed, as if it were an isolated thing, there is no rationality, no consciousness of moral law or principle. But let the individual imagine himself gifted with such power that, if he acts, the motive of his act will become a fixed, a regular law in the constitution of things. Would he, as a rational being, be willing to bring about such a universalization,—can he, with equanimity as a reasonable being, contemplate such an outcome? If he can, the act is right; if not (as in the case of making a lying promise), wrong.

No sensible person would question the instructiveness of this scheme in the concrete. It indicates that the value of reason—of abstraction and generalization—in conduct is to help us escape from the partiality that flows from desire and emotion in their first and superficial manifestations, and to attain a more unified and permanent end. As a method (though not the only one) of realizing the *full meaning* of a proposed course of action, nothing could be better than asking ourselves how we should like to be committed forever to its principle; how we should like to have others committed to it and to treat us according to it? Such a method is well calculated to make us face our proposed end in its impartial consequences; to teach the danger of cherishing merely those results which are most congenial to our passing whim and our narrow conception of personal profit. In short, by generalizing a purpose we make its *general* character evident.

But this method does not proceed (as Kant would have it) from a mere consideration of moral law *apart from a concrete end, but from an end in so far as it persistently approves itself to reflection after an adequate survey of it in all its bearings*. It is the possibility of *generalizing the concrete end* that Kant falls back upon.

Other illustrations which Kant offers enforce the same lesson. He suggests the following:

(1) A man in despair from misfortune considers suicide. "Now he inquires whether the maxim of his action could become a universal law of nature. We see at once that a system of nature by which it should be a law to destroy life by means of the very feeling—self-love—whose nature it is to impel to the maintenance of life, would contradict itself and therefore could not exist."

(2) A man who has a certain talent is tempted from sluggishness and love of amusement not to cultivate it. But if he applies the principle he sees that, while a system of nature might subsist if his motive became a law (so that all people devoted their lives to idleness and amusement), yet he cannot *will* that such a system should receive absolute realization. As a rational being he necessarily also wills that faculties be developed since they serve for all sorts of possible purposes.

(3) A prosperous man, who sees some one else to be wretched, is tempted to pay no attention to it, alleging that it is no concern of his. Now, if this attitude were made a universal law of nature, the human race might subsist and even get on after a fashion; but it is impossible to will that such a principle should have the validity of a law of nature. Such a will would contradict itself, for many cases would occur in which the one willing would need the love and sympathy of others; he could not then without contradicting himself wish that selfish disregard should become a regular, a fixed uniformity.

The Social End is the Rational End.—These illustrations make it clear that the "contradiction" Kant really depends upon to reveal the wrongness of acts, is the introduction of friction and disorder among the various concrete ends of the individual. He insists especially that the social relations of an act bring out its general purport. A right end is one which can be projected harmoniously into the widest and broadest survey of life which the individual can make. A "system of nature" or of conduct in which love of life should lead to its own destruction certainly contradicts itself. A course of action which should include all the tendencies that make for amusement and sluggishness would be inconsistent with a scheme of life which would take account of other tendencies —such as interest in science, in music, in friendship, in business achievement, which are just as real constituents of the individual, although perhaps not so strongly felt at the moment. A totally callous and cruel mode of procedure certainly "contradicts" a course of life in which every individual is so placed as to be dependent upon the sympathy and upon the help of others. It is the province of reason to call up a sufficiently wide view of the consequences of an intention as to enable us to realize such inconsistencies and contradictions if they exist; to put before us, not through any logical manipulation of the principle of contradiction, but through memory and imagination a particular act, proposal, or suggestion as a portion of a connected whole of life; to make real to us that no man, no act, and no satisfaction of any man, falls or stands to itself, but that it affects and is affected by others. Our conclusion is: the right as the *rational* good means that which is harmonious with all the capacities and desires of the self, that which expands them into a cooperative whole.

Kant's Introduction of Social Factors.—The further development which Kant gives the formula already quoted (p. 283) goes far to remove the appearance of opposition between the utilitarian social standard and his own abstract rationalism. Kant points out that according to his view the moral or rational will is its own end. Hence every rational person is always an end, never a means:—this, indeed, is what we mean by a person. But every normal human being is a rational person. Consequently another formula for his maxim is: "So act as to treat humanity, whether in thine own person or in that of any other, as an end, never as a means merely." The man who contemplates suicide "uses a person merely as a means to maintaining a tolerable condition of life." He who would make a lying promise to another makes that other one merely a means to his profit, etc. Moreover, since all persons are equally ends in themselves and are to be equally regarded in behavior, we may say the standard of right is the notion of a "Kingdom of Ends"—the idea of "the union of different rational beings in a system by common laws."[4]

These propositions are rather formal, but the moment we put definite meaning into them, they suggest that the good for any man is that in which the welfare of others counts as much as his own. The right is that action which, so far as in it lies, combines into a whole of common interests and purposes the otherwise conflicting aims and interests of different persons. So interpreted, the Kantian formula differs in words, rather than in idea, from Bentham's happiness of all concerned "each counting for one and only one"; from Mill's statement that the "deeply rooted conception which every individual even now has of himself as a social being tends to make him feel it as one of his natural wants, that there should be harmony between his feelings and aims and those of his fellow-creatures." In all of these formulae we find re-statements of our conception that the good is the activities in which all men participate so that the powers of each are called out, put to use, and re-enforced.

Consequent Transformation of Theory of Reason.—Now if the common good, in the form of a society of individuals, as a kingdom of ends, is the object with reference to which the ends of desire have to be rationalized, Kant's theory of an *a priori* and empty Reason is completely made over. In strict logic Kant contradicts himself when he says that we are to generalize the end of desire, so as to see whether it could become a universal law. For according to him no end of desire (since it is private and a form of self-love) *can*

4. Kant, *Theory of Ethics*, trans. by Abbott, pp. 47–51.

possibly be generalized. He is setting up as a method of enlightenment precisely the very impossibility (impossible, that is, on his own theory that private happiness is the end of desire) which made him first resort to his *a priori* and transcendental reason. No more complete contradiction can be imagined.

On the other hand, if we neglect the concrete, empirical conditions and consequences of the object of desire, there is no motive whatsoever that may not be generalized. There is no *formal* contradiction in acting always on a motive of theft, unchastity, or insolence. All that Kant's method can require, in strict logic, is that the individual always, under similar circumstances, act from the same motive. Be willing to be always dishonest, or impure, or proud in your intent; achieve consistency in the badness of your motives, and you will be good! Doubtless no one, not even the worst man, would be willing to be universally consistent in his badness. But this is not in the least a matter of a purely formal, logical inconsistency of the motive with itself;[5] it is due rather to that *conflict among diverse desires, and different objects for which one strives, which makes him aware that at some time he should want to act kindly and fairly.*

Organization of Desires from the Social Standpoint.— What Kant is really insisting upon at bottom is, then, the demand for such a revision of desire as it casually and unreflectively presents itself as would make the desire a consistent expression of the whole body of the purposes of the self. What he demands is that a desire shall not be accepted as an adequate motive till it has been organized into desire for an end which will be compatible with the whole system of ends involved in the capacities and tendencies of the agent. This is true rationalization. And he further warns us that only when a particular desire has in view a good which is social will it meet this requirement. This brings us to our next problem. Just what is the process by which we judge of the worth of particular proposals, plans, courses of actions, desires? Granted that a generalized good, a socialized happi-

5. In last analysis Kant is trying to derive moral enlightenment from the most abstract principle of formal logic, the principle of Identity, that A is A!

ness, is the point of view at which we must place ourselves
to secure the reasonable point of view, how does this point
of view become an operative method?

§ 3. *Moral Sense Intuitionalism*

So far, our conclusions are (1) that the province of
reason is to enable us to generalize our concrete ends; to
form such ends as are consistent with one another, and reenforce one another, introducing continuity and force, where
otherwise there would be division and weakness; and (2)
that only social ends are ultimately reasonable, since they
alone permit us to organize our acts into consistent wholes.
We have now, however, to consider how this conception takes
effect in detail; how it is employed to determine the right or
the reasonable in a given situation. We shall approach this
problem by considering a form of intuitionalism historically
prior to that of Kant. This emphasizes the direct character of
moral knowledge in particular cases, and assimilates moral
knowledge to the analogy of sense perception, which also
deals directly with specific objects; it insists, however, that
a different kind of faculty of knowledge operates in the
knowledge of acts from that which operates in the knowledge of things. Our underlying aim here is to bring out the
relation of immediate appreciation to deliberate reflection,
with a view to showing that the reasonable standpoint, that
of the common good, becomes effective through the socialized
attitudes and emotions of a person's own character.

Moral Sense.—This theory holds that rightness is an
intrinsic, absolute quality of special acts, and as such is
immediately known or recognized for what it is. Just as a
white color is known as white, a high tone as high, a hard
body as existent, etc., so an act which is right is known as
right. In each case, the quality and the fact are so intimately
and inherently bound together that it is absurd to think of
one and not know the other. As a theory of moral judgment,
intuitionalism is thus opposed to utilitarianism, which holds
that rightness is not an inherent quality but one relative to
and borrowed from external and more or less remote conse-

quences. While some forms of intuitionalism hold that this moral quality belongs to general rules or to classes of ends, the form we are now to consider holds that the moral quality of an individual act cannot be borrowed even from a moral law, but shines forth as an absolute and indestructible part of the motive of the act itself. Because the theory in question sticks to the direct perception of the immediately present quality of acts, it is usually called, in analogy with the direct perception of eye or ear, the moral sense theory.

Objections to Theory.—The objections to this theory in the extreme form just stated may be brought under two heads: (1) There is no evidence to prove that all acts are directly characterized by the possession of absolute and self-evident rightness and wrongness; there is much evidence to show that this quality when presented by acts can, as a rule, be traced to earlier instruction, to the pressure of correction and punishment, and to association with other experiences. (2) While in this way many acts, perhaps almost all, of the average mature person of a good moral environment, have acquired a direct moral coloring, making unnecessary elaborate calculation or reference to general principles, yet there is nothing infallible in such intuitively presented properties. An act may present itself as thoroughly right and yet may be, in reality, wrong. The function of conscious deliberation and reasoning is precisely to detect the existence of and to correct such intuitive cases.[6]

I. Direct Perception as Effect of Habits.—It must be admitted, as a result of any unprejudiced examination, that a large part of the acts, motives, and plans of the adult who has had favorable moral surroundings seem to possess directly, and in their own intrinsic make-up, rightness or wrongness or moral indifference. To think of lying or stealing is one with thinking of it as wrong; to recall or suggest an act of kindness is the same as thinking of it as right; to think of going after mail is to think of an act free from either rightness or wrongness. With the average person it is probably rare for much time to be spent in figuring out whether

6. A student in an ethics class once made this remark: "Conscience is infallible, but we should not always follow it. Sometimes we should use our reason."

an act is right or wrong, after the idea of that act has once definitely presented itself. So far as the facts of moral experience in such cases are concerned, the "moral sense" theory appears to give a correct description.

(1) But the conclusion that, therefore, moral goodness or badness is and always has been an inherent, absolute property of the act itself, overlooks well-known psychological principles. In all perception, in all recognition, there is a funding or capitalizing of the results of past experience by which the results are rendered available in new experiences. Even a young child recognizes a table, a chair, a glass of milk, a dog, as soon as he sees it; there is no analysis, no conscious interpretation. Distance, direction, size, under normal circumstances, are perceived with the same assurance and ease. But there was a time when all these things were learning; when conscious experimentation involving interpretation took place. Such perceptions, moreover, take place under the guidance of others; pains are taken indelibly to stamp moral impressions by associating them with intense, vivid, and mysterious or awful emotional accompaniments.[7]

Anthropological and historical accounts of different races and peoples tell the same story. Acts once entirely innocent of moral distinctions have acquired, under differing circumstances and sometimes for trivial and absurd reasons, different moral values: —one and the same sort of act being stamped here as absolute guilt, there as an act of superior and heroic virtue. Now it would be fallacious to argue (as some do) that because distinctions of moral quality have been acquired and are not innate, they are therefore unreal when they are acquired. Yet the fact of gradual development proves that no fixed line exists where it can be said the case is closed; that just this is henceforth forever right or wrong; that there shall be no further observation of consequences, no further correction and revision of present "intuitions."

(2) Our immediate moral recognitions take place, moreover, only under usual circumstances. There is after all no such thing as complete moral maturity; all persons are still more or less children—in process of learning moral distinc-

7. Compare Locke, *Essay on Human Understanding*, Book I, ch. iii.

tions. The more intense their moral interests, the more child-like, the more open, flexible, and growing are their minds. It is only the callous and indifferent, or at least the conventional, who find all acts and projects so definitely right and wrong as to render reflection unnecessary. "New occasions teach new duties," but they teach them only to those who recognize that they are not already in possession of adequate moral judgments. Any other view destroys the whole meaning of reflective morality and marks a relapse to the plane of sheer custom. Extreme intuitionalism and extreme moral conservatism; dislike to calculation and reflection, for fear of innovations with attendant trouble and discomfort, are usually found to go together.

II. *Direct Perception No Guarantee of Validity.*—This suggests our second objection. The existence of immediate moral quality, the direct and seemingly final possession of rightness, as matter of fact, is not adequate proof of validity. At best, it furnishes a presumption of correctness, in the absence of grounds for questioning it, in fairly familiar situations. (a) There is nothing more direct, more seemingly self-evident, than inveterate prejudice. When class or vested interest is enlisted in the maintenance of the custom or institution which is expressed in a prejudice, the most vicious moral judgments assume the guise of self-conscious sanctity. (b) A judgment which is correct under usual circumstances may become quite unfit, and therefore wrong, if persisted in under new conditions. Life, individual and social, is in constant process of change; and there is always danger of error in clinging to judgments adjusted to older circumstances. "The good is the enemy of the better." It is not merely false ideas of the values of life that have to be re-formed, but ideas once true. When economic, political, and scientific conditions are modifying themselves as rapidly and extensively as they are in our day, it is reconstruction of moral judgment that needs emphasis, rather than the existence of a lot of ready-made "intuitions." When readjustment is required, deliberate inquiry is the only alternative to inconsiderate, undirected, and hence probably violent changes:— changes involving undue relaxation of moral ties on one side and arbitrary reactions on the other.

Deliberation and Intuition.—It is indeed absurd to set immediate recognition of quality and indirect calculation of more or less remote consequences, intuition and thought, over against each other as if they were rivals. For they are mutually supplementary. As we saw in a previous chapter, the foresight of future results calls out an *immediate reaction* of satisfaction and dissatisfaction, of happiness or dislike. (See pp. 248–49.) It is just as false to say that we calculate only future pains and pleasures (instead of changes in the world of things and persons) as it is to say that anticipations of the changes to be wrought in the world by our act are not accompanied by an immediate emotional appreciation of their value. The notion that deliberation upon the various alternatives open to us is simply a cold-blooded setting down of various items to our advantage, and various other items to our disadvantage (as Robinson Crusoe wrote down in bookkeeping fashion his miseries and blessings), and then striking an algebraic balance, implies something that never did and never could happen. Deliberation is a process of active, suppressed, rehearsal; of imaginative dramatic performance of various deeds carrying to their appropriate issues the various tendencies which we feel stirring within us. When we see in imagination this or that change brought about, there is a direct sense of the amount and kind of worth which attaches to it, as real and as direct, if not as strong, as if the act were really performed and its consequence really brought home to us.

Deliberation as Dramatic Rehearsal.—We, indeed, estimate the import or significance of any present desire or impulse by forecasting what it would come or amount to if carried out; literally its consequences define its *consequence*, its meaning and importance. But if these consequences were conceived *merely as remote*, if their picturing did not at once arouse a present sense of peace, of fulfillment, or of dissatisfaction, of incompletion and irritation, the process of thinking out consequences would remain purely intellectual. It would be as barren of influence upon behavior as the mathematical speculations of a disembodied angel. Any actual experience of reflection upon conduct will show that every foreseen result at once stirs our present affections, our likes and dislikes, our desires and aversions. There is developed a running commentary which stamps values at once as good or evil. It is this direct sense of value, not the consciousness of general rules or ultimate goals, which finally determines the worth of the act to the agent. Here is the inexpugnable element of truth in the intuitional theory. Its error lies in conceiving this immediate response of appreciation as if it excluded reflection instead of following directly upon its heels. Deliberation is actually an imaginative rehearsal of various courses of conduct. We give way, *in our mind*, to some impulse; we try, *in our mind*, some plan. Following its career through various steps, we find ourselves in imagination in the presence of the consequences that would follow; and as we then like and approve, or dislike and disapprove, these consequences, we find the original impulse or plan good or bad. Deliberation is dramatic and active, not mathematical and impersonal; and hence it has the intuitive, the direct factor in it. The advantage of a mental trial, prior to the overt trial (for the act after all is itself also a trial, a proving of the idea that lies back of it), is that it is retrievable, whereas overt consequences remain. They cannot be recalled. Moreover, many trials may mentally be made in a short time. The imagining of various plans carried out furnishes an opportunity for many impulses which at first are not in evidence at all, to get under way. Many and varied direct sensings, appreciations, take place. When many tendencies are brought into play, there is clearly much greater probability that the capacity of self which is really needed and appropriate will be brought into action, and thus a truly reasonable happiness result. The tendency of deliberation to "polarize" the various lines of activity into opposed alternatives, into incompatible "either this or that," is a way of forcing into clear recognition the importance of the issue.

The Good Man's Judgments as Standard.—This explains the idea of Aristotle that only the good man is a good judge of what is really good. Such an one will take satisfaction in the thought of noble ends and will recoil at the idea of base results. Because of his formed capacities, his organized habits and tendencies, he will respond to a suggested end with an emotion which confers its appropriate kind and shade of value. The brave man is sensitive to all acts and plans so far as they involve energy and endurance in overcoming painful obstacles; the kindly man responds at once to the elements that affect the well-being of others. The moral sense or direct appreciations of the good man may thus be said to furnish the standard of right and wrong. There are few persons who, when in doubt regarding a difficult matter of conduct, do not think of some other person in whose goodness they believe, and endeavor to direct and clinch their own judgment by imagining how such an one would react in a similar situation—what he would find congenial and what disagreeable. Or else they imagine what that other person would think of them if he knew of their doing such and such an act. And while this method cannot supply the standard of their own judgment, cannot determine the right or wrong for their own situations, it helps emancipate judgment from selfish partialities, and it facilitates a freer and more flexible play of imagination in construing and appreciating the situation.

§ 4. The Place of General Rules

Between such a highly generalized and formal principle as that of Kant, and the judgment of particular cases, we have intermediate generalizations; rules which are broad as compared with individual deeds, but narrow as compared with some one final principle. What are their rational origin, place, and function? We have here again both the empirical and the intuitional theories of knowledge, having to deal with the same fundamental difficulty: What is the relation of the special rule to the general principle on one side and to the special case on the other? The more general, the more abstractly rational the rule, the vaguer and less applicable it is. The more definite and fixed it is, the greater the danger that it will be a Procrustean bed, mutilating the rich fullness of the individual act, or destroying its grace and freedom by making it conform servilely to a hard and fast rule. Our analysis will accordingly be devoted to bringing to light the conditions under which a rule may be rational and yet be of specific help.

I. Intuitionalism and Casuistry.—Utilitarianism at least holds that rules are derived from actual cases of conduct; hence there must be points of likeness between the cases to be judged and the rules for judging them. But rules which do not originate from a consideration of special cases, which simply descend out of the blue sky, have only the most mechanical and external relation to the individual acts to be judged. Suppose one is convinced that the rule of honesty was made known just in and of itself by a special faculty, and had absolutely nothing to do with the recollection of past cases or the forecast of possible future circumstances. How would such a rule apply itself to any particular case which needed to be judged? What bell would ring, what signal would be given, to indicate that just *this* case is the appropriate case for the application of the rule of honest dealing? And if by some miracle this question were answered so one knows that here is a case for the rule of honesty, how would we know just what course in detail the rule calls for? For the rule, to be applicable to all cases, must omit the conditions which differentiate one case from another; it must contain only the very few similar elements which are to be found in all honest deeds. Reduced to this skeleton, not much would be left save the bare injunction to be honest whatever happens, leaving it to chance, the ordinary judgment of the individual, or to external authority to find out just *what* honesty specifically means in the given case.

This difficulty is so serious that all systems which have committed themselves to belief in a number of hard and fast rules having their origin in conscience, or in the word of God impressed upon the human soul or externally revealed, always have had to resort to a more and more complicated procedure to cover, if possible, all the cases. The moral life is finally reduced by them to an elaborate formalism and legalism.

Illustration in Casuistry.—Suppose, for example, we take the Ten Commandments as a starting-point. They are only ten, and naturally confine themselves to general ideas, and ideas stated mainly in negative form. Moreover, the same act may be brought under more than one rule. In order to resolve the practical perplexities and uncertainties which inevitably arise under such circumstances, *Casuistry* is built up (from the Latin *casus*, case). The attempt is made to foresee all the different cases of action which may conceivably occur, and provide in advance the exact rule for each case. For example, with reference to the rule "do not kill," a list will be made of all the different situations in which killing might occur: — accident, war, fulfillment of command of political superior (as by a hangman), self-defense (defense of one's own life, of others, of property), deliberate or premeditated killing with its different motives (jealousy, avarice, revenge, etc.), killing with slight premeditation, from sudden impulse, from different sorts and degrees of provocation. To each one of these possible cases is assigned its exact moral quality, its exact degree of turpitude and innocency. Nor can this process end with overt acts; all the inner springs of action which affect regard for life must be similarly classified: envy, animosity, sudden rage, sullenness, cherishing of sense of injury, love of tyrannical power, hardness or hostility, callousness — all these must be specified into their different kinds and the exact moral worth of each determined. What is done for this one kind of case must be done for every part and phase of the entire moral life until it is all inventoried, catalogued, and distributed into pigeonholes definitely labeled.

    Dangers of Casuistry.—Now dangers and evils attend this way of conceiving the moral life. (a) *It tends to magnify the letter of morality at the expense of its spirit.* It fixes attention not upon the positive good in an act, not upon the underlying agent's disposition which forms its spirit, nor upon the unique occasion and context which form its atmosphere, but upon its literal conformity with Rule A, Class I, Species 1, sub-head (1), etc. The effect of this is inevitably to narrow the scope and lessen the depth of conduct. (i.) It tempts some to hunt for that classification of their act which will make it the most convenient or profitable for themselves. In popular speech, "casuistical" has come to mean a way of judging acts which splits hairs in the effort to find a way of acting that conduces to personal interest and profit, and which yet may be justified by some moral principle. (ii.) With others, this regard for the letter makes conduct formal and pedantic. It gives rise to a rigid and hard type of character illustrated among the Pharisees of olden and the Puritans of modern time—the moral schemes of both classes being strongly impregnated with the notion of fixed moral rules.

(b) *This ethical system also tends in practice to a legal view of conduct.*—Historically it always has sprung from carrying over legal ideas into morality. In the legal view, liability to blame and to punishment inflicted from without by some superior authority, is necessarily prominent. Conduct is regulated through specific injunctions and prohibitions: Do this, Do not do that. Exactly the sort of analysis of which we have spoken above (p. 296) in the case of killing is necessary, so that there may be definite and regular methods of measuring guilt and assigning blame. Now the ideas of liability and punishment and reward are, as we shall see in our further discussion (chs. 17 and 21), important factors in the conduct of life, but any scheme of morals is defective which puts the question of avoiding punishment in the foreground of attention, and which tends to create a Pharisaical complacency in the mere fact of having conformed to command or rule.

(c) *Probably the worst evil of this moral system is that it tends to deprive moral life of freedom and spontaneity* and to reduce it (especially for the conscientious who take it seriously) to a more or less anxious and servile conformity to externally imposed rules. Obedience as loyalty to principle is a good, but this scheme practically makes it the only good and conceives it not as loyalty to ideals, but as conformity to commands. Moral rules exist just as independent deliverances on their own account, and the right thing is merely to follow them. This puts the centre of moral gravity outside the concrete processes of living. All systems which emphasize the letter more than the spirit, legal consequences more than vital motives, put the individual under the weight of external authority. They lead to the kind of conduct described by St. Paul as under the law, not in the spirit, with its constant attendant weight of anxiety, uncertain struggle, and impending doom.

All Fixed Rules Have Same Tendencies.—Many who strenuously object to all of these schemes of conduct, to everything which hardens it into forms by emphasizing external commands, authority and punishments and rewards, fail to see that such evils are logically connected with any acceptance of the finality of fixed rules. They hold certain bodies of people, religious officers, political or legal authorities, responsible for what they object to in the scheme; while they still cling to the idea that morality is an effort to apply to particular deeds and projects a certain number of absolute unchanging moral rules. They fail to see that, if this were its nature, those who attempt to provide the machinery which would render it practically workable deserve praise rather than blame. In fact, the notion of absolute rules or precepts cannot be made workable except through certain superior authorities who declare and enforce them. Said Locke: "It is no small power it gives one man over another to be the dictator of principles and teacher of unquestionable truths."

II. Utilitarian View of General Rules.—The utilitarians escape the difficulties inherent in the application to particular cases of a rule which has nothing to do with particular cases. Their principles for judging right and wrong in particular cases are themselves generalizations from particular observations of the effect of certain acts upon happiness and misery. But if we take happiness in the technical sense of Bentham (as meaning, that is, an aggregate of isolated pleasures) it is impossible for general rules to exist—there is nothing to generalize. If, however, we take happiness in its common-sense form, as welfare, a state of successful achievement, satisfactory realization of purpose, there can be no doubt of the existence of maxims and formulae in which mankind has registered its experience. The following quotations from Mill bring out the essential points:

> We think utility or happiness much too complex and indefinite an end to be sought except through the medium of various secondary ends concerning which there may be, and often is, agreement among persons who differ in their ultimate standard; and about which there does in fact prevail a much

greater unanimity among thinking persons, than might be supposed from their diametrical divergence on the great questions
of moral metaphysics (Essay on Bentham).

These secondary ends or principles are such matters as regard for health, honesty, chastity, kindness, and the like.
Concerning them he says in his *Utilitarianism* (ch. ii):

Mankind must by this time have acquired positive beliefs as to
the effects of some actions on their happiness; and the beliefs
which have thus come down are rules of morality for the multitude and for the philosopher until he has succeeded in finding
better. . . . To consider the rules of morality as improvable is
one thing; to pass over the intermediate generalizations entirely
and endeavor to test each individual action directly by the first
principle, is another. . . . Nobody argues that the act of navigation is not founded on astronomy, because sailors cannot wait
to calculate the "Nautical Almanac." Being rational creatures,
they go to sea with it already calculated; and all rational creatures go out upon the sea of life with their minds made up on
the common questions of right and wrong, as well as on many
of the far more difficult questions of wise and foolish.

Empirical Rules Run into Fixed Customs.—It cannot be
denied that Mill here states considerations which are of great
value in aiding present judgments on right and wrong. The
student of history will have little doubt that the rules of
conduct which the intuitionalist takes as ultimate deliverances of a moral faculty are in truth generalizations of the
sort indicated by Mill. But the truth brought out by Mill does
not cover the ground which needs to be covered. Such rules
at best cover customary elements; they are based upon past
habits of life, past natural economic and political environments. And, as the student of customs knows, greater store
is often set upon trivial, foolish, and even harmful things
than upon serious ones—upon fashions of hair-dressing, ablutions, worship of idols. Coming nearer our own conditions,
past customs certainly tolerate and sanction many practices,
such as war, cruel business competition, economic exploitation of the weak, and absence of cooperative intelligent foresight, which the more sensitive consciences of the day will
not approve.

Hence are Unsatisfactory.—Yet such things have been
so identified with happiness that to forego them means

misery, to alter them painful disturbance. To take the rules of the past with any literalness as criteria of judgment in the present, would be to return to the unprogressive morality of the régime of custom—to surrender the advance marked by reflective morality. Since Bentham and Mill were both utilitarians, it is worth noting that Bentham insisted upon the utilitarian standard just because he was so convinced of the unsatisfactory character of the kind of rules upon which Mill is dwelling. The "Nautical Almanac" has been *scientifically* calculated; it is adapted rationally to its end; but the rules which sum up custom are a confused mixture of class interest, irrational sentiment, authoritative pronunciamento, and genuine consideration of welfare.

Empirical Rules Also Differ Widely.—The fact is, moreover, that it is only when the "intermediate generalizations" are taken vaguely and abstractly that there is as much agreement as Mill claims. All educated and virtuous persons in the same country practically agree upon the rules of justice, benevolence, and regard for life, so long as they are taken in such a vague way that they mean anything in general and nothing in particular. Every one is in favor of justice in the abstract; but existing political and economic discussions regarding tariff, sumptuary laws, monetary standards, trades unions, trusts, the relation of capital and labor, the regulation or ownership of public utilities, the nationalization of land and industry, show that large bodies of intelligent and equally well-disposed people are quite capable of finding that the principle of justice requires exactly opposite things.

Custom still forms the background of all moral life, nor can we imagine a state of affairs in which it should not. Customs are not external to individuals' courses of action; they are embodied in the habits and purposes of individuals; in the words of Grote (quoted above, p. 161), they "reign under the appearance of habitual, *self-suggested* tendencies." Laws, formulated and unformulated, social conventions, rules of manners, the general expectations of public opinion, are all of them sources of instruction regarding conduct. Without them the individual would be practically helpless in determining the right courses of action in the various situations in which he finds himself. Through them he has provided himself in advance with a list of questions, an organized series of points-of-view, by which to approach and estimate each state of affairs requiring action. Most of the moral judgments of every individual are framed in this way.

For Customs Conflict.—If social customs, or individual habits, never conflicted with one another, this sort of guidance would suffice for the determination of right and wrong. But reflection is necessitated because opposite habits set up incompatible ends, forms of happiness between which choice has to be made. Hence the need of *principles in judging.* Principles of judgment cannot simply reinstate past rules of behavior, for the simple reason that as long as these rules suffice there is no reflection and no demand for principles. Good and evil, right and wrong, are embodied in the injunctions and prohibitions of customs and institutions and are not thought about.

Moral Import of Principles is Intellectual, Not Imperative.—This brings us to the essential point in the consideration of the value of general principles. *Rules are practical; they are habitual ways of doing things. But principles are intellectual; they are useful methods of judging things.* The fundamental error of the intuitionalist and of the utilitarian (represented in the quotation from Mill) is that they are on the lookout for rules which will of themslves tell agents just what course of action to pursue; *whereas the object of moral principles is to supply standpoints and methods which will enable the individual to make for himself an analysis of the elements of good and evil in the particular situation in which he finds himself.* No genuine moral principle prescribes a specific course of action; rules,[8] like cooking recipes, may tell just what to do and how to do it. A moral principle, such as that of chastity, of justice, of the golden rule, gives the agent a basis for looking at and examining a particular question that comes up. It holds before him certain possible aspects of the act; it warns him against taking a short or partial view of the act. It economizes his thinking by supplying him with the main heads by reference to which to con-

---

8. Of course, the word "rule" is often used to designate a principle—as in the case of the phrase "golden-rule." We are speaking not of the words, but of their underlying ideas.

sider the bearings of his desires and purposes; it guides him
in his thinking by suggesting to him the important considerations for which he should be on the lookout.

Golden Rule as a Tool of Analysis.—A moral principle,
then, is not a command to act or forbear acting in a given
way: *it is a tool for analyzing a special situation,* the right
or wrong being determined by the situation in its entirety,
and not by the rule as such. We sometimes hear it stated,
for example, that the universal adoption of the Golden Rule
would at once settle all industrial disputes and difficulties.
But supposing that the principle were accepted in good faith
by everybody; it would not at once tell everybody just what
to do in all the complexities of his relations to others. When
individuals are still uncertain of what their real good may
be, it does not finally decide matters to tell them to regard
the good of others as they would their own. Nor does it mean
that whatever in detail we want for ourselves we should
strive to give to others. Because I am fond of classical music
it does not follow that I should thrust as much of it as possible upon my neighbors. But the "Golden Rule" does furnish
us a *point of view from which to consider acts*; it suggests
the necessity of considering how our acts affect the interests
of others as well as our own; it tends to prevent partiality of
regard; it warns against setting an undue estimate upon a
particular consequence of pain or pleasure, simply because
it happens to affect us. In short, the Golden Rule does not
issue special orders or commands; but it does simplify judgment of the situations requiring intelligent deliberation.

*Sympathy as Actuating Principle of a Reasonable Judg-
ment.*—We have had repeated occasion (as in the discussion
of intent and motive, of intuition and deliberate calculation)
to see how artificial is the separation of emotion and thought
from one another. As the only effective thought is one fused
by emotion into a dominant interest, so the only truly general, the reasonable as distinct from the merely shrewd or
clever thought, is the *generous* thought. Sympathy widens
our interest in consequences and leads us to take into account such results as affect the welfare of others; it aids us
to count and weigh these consequences as counting for as
much as those which touch our own honor, purse, or power.

To put ourselves in the place of another, to see from the standpoint of his purposes and values, to humble our estimate of our own claims and pretensions to the level they would assume in the eyes of a sympathetic and impartial observer, is the surest way to attain universality and objectivity of moral knowledge. Sympathy, in short, is the general principle of moral knowledge, not because its commands take precedence of others (which they do not necessarily), but because it furnishes the most reliable and efficacious *intellectual* standpoint. It supplies the tool, *par excellence*, for analyzing and resolving complex cases. As was said in our last chapter, it is the *fusion* of the sympathetic impulses with others that is needed; what we now add is that in this fusion, sympathy supplies the *pou sto* for an effective, broad, and objective survey of desires, projects, resolves, and deeds. It translates the formal and empty reason of Kant out of its abstract and theoretic character, just as it carries the cold calculations of utilitarianism into recognition of the common good.

Literature

For criticisms of Kant's view of reason, see Caird, *Philosophy of Kant*, Vol. II, Book II, ch. ii; Paulsen, *System of Ethics*, pp. 194–203 and 355–63; Fite, *Introductory Study*, pp. 173–88; Muirhead, *Elements of Ethics*, pp. 112–24.

For intuitionalism, see Calderwood, *Handbook of Moral Philosophy*; Maurice, *Conscience*; Whewell, *The Elements of Morality*; Martineau, *Types of Ethical Theory*, Vol. II, pp. 96–115; Mezes, *Ethics*, ch. iii; Sidgwick, *Methods of Ethics* (1901), Book I, chs. viii–ix, and Book III entire, but especially ch. i; *History of Ethics*, 170–204, and 224–36, and *Lectures on the Ethics of Green, Spencer, and Martineau*, 361–74.

For the moral sense theory, see Sidgwick, *History of Ethics*, p. 189; Shaftesbury, *Characteristics*; Hutcheson, *System of Moral Philosophy*.

For casuistry, see references in Rand's *Bibliography*, Vol. III, Part II, p. 880.

For the variability of moral rules, see Locke, *Essay on Human Understanding*, Book I; Bain, *Moral Science*, Part I, ch. iii; Spencer, *Principles of Ethics*, Vol. I, Part II; Williams, *A Review of the Systems of Ethics Founded on the Theory of Evolution*, pp. 423–65; Bowne, *Principles of Ethics*, ch. v; Schurman, *The Ethical Import of Darwinism*; the writings of Westermarck and Hobhouse elsewhere referred to, and Darwin, *Descent of Man*, Part I, chs. iv–v.

For the nature of moral judgment and the function of reason in conduct, see Aristotle, Book III, chs. ii–iii, and Book VI; Ladd, *Philosophy of Conduct*, ch. vii; Sharp, Essay on Analysis of the Moral Judgment, in *Studies in Philosophy and Psychology* (Garman Commemorative Volume); Santayana, *Life of Reason*, Vol. I, chs. x–xii; Bryant, *Studies in Character*, Part II, chs. iv–v.

For the social character of conscience, see Cooley, *Human Nature and the Social Order*, ch. x.

For sympathy and conscience, see Adam Smith, *Theory of Moral Sentiments*, especially Part III, chs. i and iv, and Part IV, chs. i–ii; Stephen, *Science of Ethics*, pp. 228–38.

Conflict of Ends as Attractive and as Reasonable.—The
previous discussion has brought out the contrast between a
Good or Satisfaction which is such *directly*, immediately, by
appealing attractively to desire; and one which is such indirectly, through considerations which reflection brings up.
As we have seen, the latter must, if entertained at all, arouse
some direct emotional response, must be felt to be in some
way satisfactory. But the *way* may be quite unlike that of
the end which attracts and holds a man irrespective of the
principle brought to light by reflection. The one may be intense, vivid, absorbing, passing at once into overt action,
unless checked by a contrary reason. The good whose claim
to be good depends mainly on projection of remote considerations, may be theoretically recognized and yet the direct appeal to the particular agent at the particular time be feeble
and pallid. The "law of the mind" may assert itself less ur-
gently than the "law of the members" which wars against it.

Two Senses of Term Duty.—This contrast gives rise to
the fact of Duty. On one side is the rightful supremacy of
the reasonable but remote good; on the other side is the
aversion of those springs to action which are immediately
most urgent. Between them exists the necessity of securing
for the reasonable good efficacy in operation; or the necessity of redirecting the play of naturally dominant desires.
Duty is also used, to be sure, in a looser and more external
sense. To identify the dutiful with the right apart from conflict, to say that a man did his duty, may mean that he did
right, irrespective of the prior state of his inclinations. It
frequently happens that the wider and larger good which is
developed through reflective memory and foresight is welcomed, is directly appreciated as good, since it is thoroughly
attractive. Without stress and strain, without struggle, it
just displaces the object which unreflective impulse had sug-

gested. It is the fit and proper, the only sensible and wise thing, under the circumstances. The man does his duty, but is glad to do it, and would be troubled by the thought of another line of action. So far as calling the act "duty" brings in any new meaning, it means that the right act is one which is found to meet the demands, the necessities, of the situation in which it takes place. The Romans thus spoke of duties as *offices*, the performance of those functions which are appropriate to the status which every person occupies because of his social relations.

Conscious Conflict.—But there are other cases in which the *right* end is distinctly apprehended by the person as standing in opposition to his natural inclinations, as a principle or law which *ought* to be followed, but which *can* be followed only by constraining the inclinations, by snubbing and coercing them. This state of affairs is well represented by the following quotation from Matthew Arnold, if we take it as merely describing the facts, not as implying a theory as to their explanation:

All experience with conduct brings us at last to the fact of two selves, or instincts, or forces—name them, however we may and however we may suppose them to have arisen—contending for the mastery over men: one, a movement of first impulse and more involuntary, leading us to gratify any inclination that may solicit us and called generally a movement of man's ordinary or passing self, of sense, appetite, desire; the other a movement of reflexion and more voluntary, leading us to submit inclination to some rule, and called generally a movement of man's higher or enduring self, of reason, spirit, will.[1]

We shall (I) present what we consider the true account of this situation of conflict in which the sense of duty is found; (II) turn to explanations which are one-sided, taking up (1) the intuitive, (2) the utilitarian theory; and finally (III) return with the results of this criticism to a restatement of our own theory.

§1. The Subjection of Desire to Law

Ordinary language sets before us some main facts: duty suggests what is due, a debt to be paid; ought is connected

1. Arnold, *Last Essays on Church and Religion*, "Preface."

with owe; obligation implies being bound to something— as we speak of "bounden duty." We speak naturally of "meeting obligations"; of duties being "imposed," "laid upon" one. The person who is habitually careless about his duties is "unruly" or "lawless"; one who evades or refuses them is "unprincipled." These ideas suggest there is something required, exacted, having the sanction of law, or a regular and regulative principle; and imply natural aversion to the requirements exacted, a preference for something else. Hence duty as a conscious factor means constraint of inclination; an unwillingness or reluctance which *should* be overcome but which it is difficult to surmount, requiring an effort which only adequate recognition of the rightful supremacy of the dutiful end will enable one to put forth. Thus we speak of interest conflicting with principle, and desire with duty. While they are inevitably bound together, it will be convenient to discuss separately (1) Inclination and impulse as averse to duty, and (2) Duty as having authority, as expressing law.

I. *Inclination Averse to Duty.*—Directly and indirectly, all desires root in certain fundamental organic wants and appetites. Conduct, behavior, implies a living organism. If this organism were not equipped with an intense instinctive tendency to keep itself going, to sustain itself, it would soon cease to be amid the menaces, difficulties, rebuffs, and failures of life. Life means appetites, like hunger, thirst, sex; instincts like anger, fear, and hope, which are almost imperious in their struggles for satisfaction. They do not arise from reflection, but antedate it; their existence does not depend upon consideration of consequences, but their existence it is which tends to call out reflection. Their very presence in a healthy organism means a certain reservoir of energy which overflows almost spontaneously. They are impulsive. Such tendencies, then, constitute an essential and fundamental part of the capacities of a person; their realization is involved in one's happiness. In all this there is nothing abnormal nor immoral. But a human being is something more than a mere demand for the satisfaction of instincts of food, sex, and protection. If we admit (as the theory of organic evolution requires) that all other desires and purposes are *ultimately* derived from these tendencies of the organism,

still it is true that the refined and highly developed forms
exist side by side with crude, organic forms, and that the
simultaneous satisfaction of the two types, just as they stand,
is impossible.

Organic and Reflectively Formed Tendencies Conflict.—
Even if it be true, as it may well be, that the desires and
purposes connected with property were developed out of
instincts having to do with food for self and offspring, it
is still true that the developed desires do not wholly displace
those out of which they developed. The presence of the purposes elaborated by thought side by side with the more organic demands causes strife and the need of resolution. The
accumulation of property may involve subordinating the
immediate urgency of hunger; property as an institution implies that one is not free to satisfy his appetite just as he
pleases, but may have to postpone or forego satisfaction, because the food supply belongs to another; or that he can
satisfy hunger only through some labor which in itself is
disagreeable to him. Similarly the family springs originally
out of the instinct of reproduction. But the purposes and
plans which go with family life are totally inconsistent with
the mere gratification of sexual desire in its casual and
spontaneous appearance. The refined, highly developed, and
complex purposes exact a checking, a regulation and subordination of inclinations as they first spring up—a control
to which the inclinations are not of themselves prone and
against which they may rebelliously assert themselves.

*Duty May Reside on the More Impulsive Side.—*It would
be a great mistake, however, to limit the need of subordination simply to the unruly agencies of appetite. Habits which
have been consciously or reflectively formed, even when in
their original formation these habits had the sanction and
approval of reason, require control. The habits of a professional man, of an investigator, or a lawyer, for example,
have been formed through careful and persistent reflection
directed upon ends adjudged right. Virtues of painstaking
industry, of perseverance, have been formed; untimely and
unseemly desires have been checked. But as an outcome
these habits, and the desires and purposes that express them,
have perhaps become all-engrossing. Occupation is preoccu-

pation. It encroaches upon the attention needed for other concerns. The skill gained tends to shut the individual up to narrow matters and to shut out other "universes" of good which should be desired. Domestic and civic responsibilities are perhaps felt to be insignificant details or irritating burdens unworthy of attention. Thus a reflective habit, legitimate in itself, right in its right place, may give rise to desires and ends which involve a corrosive selfishness.

Moreover, that the insubordination does not reside in appetites or impulses, just as appetites and impulses, is seen in the fact that duty may lie on the side of a purpose connected with them, and be asserted against the force of a habit formed under the supervision of thought. The student or artist may find his pursuit makes him averse to satisfying the needful claims of hunger and healthy exercise. The prudent business man may find himself undutifully cold to the prompting of an impulse of pity; the student of books or special intellectual or artistic ends may find duty on the side of some direct human impulse.

Statement of Problem.—Such considerations show that we cannot attribute the conflict of duty and inclination simply to the existence of appetites and unreflective impulses, as if these were in and of themselves opposed to regulation by any principle. We must seek for an explanation which will apply equally to appetites and to habits of thought. What is there common to the situations of him who feels it his duty to check the satisfaction of strong hunger until others have been properly served, and of the scientific investigator who finds it his duty to check the exercise of his habit of thinking in order that he may satisfy the demands of his body?

Statement of Explanation.—Any habit, like any appetite or instinct, represents something formed, set; whether this has occurred in the history of the race or of the individual makes little difference to its established urgency. Habit is second, if not first, nature. (1) Habit represents *facilities*; what is set, organized, is relatively easy. It *marks the line of least resistance*. A habit of reflection, so far as it is a specialized habit, is as easy and natural to follow as an organic appetite. (2) Moreover, the exercise of any easy, frictionless habit is pleasurable. It is a commonplace that use and wont deprive situations of originally disagreeable features. (3) Finally, a formed habit is an active *tendency*. It only needs an appropriate stimulus to set it going; frequently the mere absence of any strong obstacle serves to release its pent-up energy. It is a propensity to act in a certain way whenever opportunity presents. Failure to function is uncomfortable and arouses feelings of irritation or lack.

Reluctance to the right end, an aversion requiring to be overcome, if at all, by recognition of the superior value of the right end, is then to be accounted for *on the ground of the inertia or momentum of any organized, established tendency*. This momentum gives the common ground to instinctive impulses and deliberately formed habits. The momentum represents the *old*, an adaptation to familiar, customary conditions. So far as similar conditions recur, the formed power functions economically and effectively, supplying ease, promptness, certainty, and agreeableness to the execution of an act.

But if new, changed conditions require a serious readjustment of the old habit or appetite, the natural tendency will be to resist this demand. Thus we have precisely the traits of reluctance and constraint which mark the consciousness of duty. A self without habits, one loose and fluid, in which change in one direction is just as easy as in another, would not have the sense of duty. A self with no new possibilities, rigidly set in conditions and perfectly accommodated to them, would not have it. But definite, persistent, urgent tendencies to act in a given way, occurring at the same time with other incompatible tendencies which represent the self more adequately and yet are not organized into habits, afford the conditions of the sense of restraint. If for any reason the unorganized tendency is judged to be the truer expression of self, we have also the sense of lawful constraint. *The constraint of appetite and desire is a phenomenon of practical readjustment, within the structure of character, due to conflict of tendencies so irreconcilable in their existing forms as to demand radical redirection.*

When an appetite is in accord with those habits of an individual which enable him to perform his social functions, or which naturally accrue from his social relations, it is legitimate and good; when it conflicts, it is illicit, it is lust; we call it by hard names and we demand that it be curbed; we regard its force as a menace to the integrity of the agent and a threat to social order. When the reflective habits of an individual come into conflict with natural appetites and impulses, the manifestation of which would enlarge or make more certain the powers of the individual in his full relations to others, it is the reflective habits which have to be held in and redirected at the cost of whatever disagreeableness.

II. *The Authority of Duty.*—A duty, in Kant's words, is a *categorical* imperative—it claims the absolute right of way as against immediate inclination. That which, on one side, is the constraint of natural desire, is, on the other, the authoritative claim of the right end to regulate. Over against the course of action most immediately urgent, most easy and comfortable, so congenial as at once to motivate action unless checked, stands another course, representing a wider and more far-reaching point of view, and hence furnishing the rational end of the situation. However lacking in intensity, however austere this end, it stands for the whole self, and is therefore felt to be rightly supreme over any partial tendency. But since it looks to realization in an uncertain future, rather than permission just to let go what is most urgent at the moment, it requires effort, hard work, work of attention more or less repulsive and uncongenial. Hence that sense of stress and strain, of being pulled one way by inclination and another by the claims of right, so characteristic of an experience of obligation.

Social Character of Duties.—But this statement describes the experience only on its formal side. In the concrete, that end which possesses claim to regulate desire is the one which grows out of the social position or function of the agent, out of *a course of action to which he is committed by a regular, socially established connection between himself and others*. The man who has assumed the position of a husband and a parent has by that very fact entered upon a *line* of action, something continuous, running far into the future; something so fundamental that it modifies and pervades his other activities, requiring them to be coordinated or rearranged from its point of view. The same thing holds, of course, of the calling of a doctor, a lawyer, a merchant, a banker, a judge, or other officer of the State. Each social calling implies a continuous, regular mode of action, binding together into a whole a multitude of acts occurring at different times, and giving rise to definite expectations and demands on the part of others. Every relationship in life, is, as it were, *a tacit or expressed contract with others*, committing one, by the simple fact that he occupies that relationship, to a corresponding mode of action. Every one, willynilly, occupies a social position; if not a parent, he is a child; if not an officer, then a citizen of the State; if not pursuing an occupation, he is in preparation for an occupation, or else is living upon the results of the labors of others.

Connection with Selfhood.—Every one, in short, is in *general relations to others,*—relationships which enter so internally and so intimately into the very make-up of his being that he is not morally free to pick and choose, saying, this good is really my affair, that other one not. The mode of action which is required by the fact that the person is a member of a complex social network is a more final expression of his own nature than is the temporarily intense instinctive appetite, or the habit which has become "second nature." It is not for the individual to say, the latter is attractive and therefore really mine, while the former is repellant and therefore an alien intruder, to be surrendered to only if it cannot be evaded. From this point of view, the conflict of desire and duty, of interest and principle, expresses itself as a conflict between tendencies which have got organized into one's *fixed character* and which therefore appeal to him just as he is; and those tendencies which relate to the development of a larger self, a self which should take fuller account of social relations. The Kantian theory emphasizes the fact brought out above: *viz.*, that duty represents the authority of an act expressing the reasonable and "universal" self over a casual and partial self; while the utilitarian theory emphasizes the part played by social institutions and demands in creating and enforcing both special duties and the sense of duty in general.

§ 2. *Kantian Theory*

"Accord with" Duty versus "from" Duty.—Kant points out that acts may be "in accordance with duty" and yet not be done "from duty." "It is always, for example, a matter of duty that a dealer should not overcharge an inexperienced purchaser, and wherever there is much commerce the prudent tradesman does not overcharge. . . . Men are thus honestly served; but this is not enough to prove that the tradesman so acted from duty and from principles of honesty; his own advantage required it" (*Theory of Ethics*, Abbott's translation, p. 13). In such a case the act externally viewed is in *accordance* with duty; morally viewed, it proceeds from selfish calculation of personal profit, not from duty. This is true in general of all acts which, though outwardly right, spring from considerations of expediency, and are based on the consideration that "honesty (or whatever) is the best policy." Persons are naturally inclined to take care of their health, their property, their children, or whatever belongs to them. Such acts, no matter how much they accord with duty, are not done *from duty*, but from inclination. If a man is suffering, unfortunate, desirous of death, and yet cherishes his life with no love for it, but from the duty to do so, his motive has truly moral value. So if a mother cares for her child, *because* she recognizes that it is her duty, the act is truly moral.

From Duty alone Moral.—According to Kant, then, acts alone have moral import that are consciously performed "from duty," that is, with recognition of its authority as their animating spring. *"The idea of good and evil (in their moral sense) must not be determined before the moral law, but only after it and by means of it"* (*Theory of Ethics*, p. 154). All our desires and inclinations seek naturally for an *end* which is good—for happiness, success, achievement. No one of them nor all of them put together, then, can possibly supply the motive of acting *from* duty. Hence duty and its authority must spring from another source, from reason itself, which supplies the consciousness of a law which *ought* to be the motive of every act, whether it is or not. The utilitarians completely reverse the truth of morals when they say that the idea of the good end comes first and the "right" is that which realizes the good end.

Dual Constitution of Man.—We are all familiar with the notion that man has a dual constitution; that he is a creature both of sense and spirit; that he has a carnal and an ideal nature; a lower and a higher self, a self of appetite and of reason. Now Kant's theory of duty is a peculiar version of this common notion. Man's special ends and purposes all spring from desires and inclinations. These are all for personal happiness and hence without moral worth. They form man's sensuous, appetitive nature, which if not "base" in itself easily becomes so, because it struggles with principle for the office of supplying motives for action. The principle of a law absolutely binding, requires the complete expulsion of the claim of desires to *motivate* action (see *Theory of Ethics*, pp. 70–79; 132–36; 159–63). If a man were an animal, he would have only appetite to follow; if he were a god or angel, he would have only reason. Being man, being a peculiar compound of sense and reason, he has put upon him the problem of resisting the natural prompting of inclination and of accepting the duty of acting from reverence for duty.

Criticism of Kant's Theory.—There is an undoubted fact back of Kant's conception which gives it whatever plausibility it has—the fact that inclinations which are not necessarily evil tend to claim a controlling position, a claim which has to be resisted. The peculiarity of Kant's interpretation lies in its complete and final separation of the two aspects, "higher" and "lower," the appetitive and rational, of man's nature, and it is upon this separation, accordingly, that our discussion will be directed.

I. Duty and the Affections.—In the first place, Kant's absolute separation of sense or appetite from reason and duty, because of its necessary disparagement of the affections, leads to a formal and pedantic view of morality. It is one thing to say that desire as it *first* shows itself *sometimes* prompts to a morally inadequate end; it is quite another thing to say that *any* acceptance of an end of desire as a motive is morally wrong—that the act to be right must be first brought under a conscious acknowledgment of some law or principle. Only the exigencies of a ready-made theory would lead any one to think that habitual purposes that express the habitually dominant tendencies and powers of the agent, may not suffice to keep morally sound the main tenor of behavior; that it is impossible for regard for right ends to become organized into character and to be fused into working unity with natural impulses. Only a metaphysical theory regarding the separation of sense and reason in man leads to the denial of this fact.

Between the merchant who is honest in his weights and fixed in his prices merely because he calculates that such a course is to his own advantage, and the merchant (if such a person could exist) who should never sell a spool of thread or a paper of pins without having first reminded himself that his ultimate motive for so doing was respect for the law of duty, there is the ordinary merchant who is honest because he has the desires characteristic of an honest man. Schiller has made fun of the artificial stringency of Kant's theory in some verses which represent a disciple coming to Kant with his perplexity:

Willingly serve I my friends, but I do it, alas with affection.
Hence I am plagued with this doubt, virtue I have not attained!

to which he received the reply:

This is your only resource, you must stubbornly seek to abhor them;
Then you can do with disgust that which the law may enjoin.

These verses are a caricature of Kant's position; he does not require that affections should be crushed, but that they should be stamped with acknowledgment of law before being accepted as motives. But the verses bring out the absurd element in the notion that the affections and inclinations may not of themselves be morally adequate springs to action,—as if a man could not eat his dinner simply because he was hungry, or be amiable to a companion because he wanted to be, or relieve distress because his compassionate nature urged him to it.

It is worth while noting that some moralists have gone to the opposite extreme and have held that an act is not right unless it expresses the overflowing spontaneity of the affections; that a man's act is only imperfectly right when he performs it not from affection, but from coercion by duty. Thus Emerson speaks of men who "do by knowledge what the stones do by structure." And again, "We love characters in proportion as they are impulsive and spontaneous. When we see a soul whose acts are all regal, graceful, and pleasant as roses, we must thank God that such things can be and are, and not turn sourly on the angel and say, 'Crump is a better man with his grunting resistance to all his native devils.' " The facts seem to be that while, in a good man, natural impulses and formed habits are adequate motive powers under ordinary conditions, there are times when an end, somewhat weak in its motive force because it does not express an habitually dominant power of the self, needs to be reenforced by associations which have gathered at all periods of his past around the experience of good. There is a certain reservoir of emotional force which, while far from fluid, is capable of transfer and application, especially in a conscientious person. Kant criticizes the moral sense theory on the ground that "in order to imagine the vicious man tormented with a sense of his transgressions, it must first represent him as morally good in the main trend of his character" (*Theory of Ethics*, p. 128). Well, a man who is capable of making appeal to the sense of duty in general, is the one in whom love of good is already dominant.

II. *Tendency to Fanaticism and Idealization of Authority.*—Kant's theory of fixed and final separation between desire and reason leads us into a fatal dilemma; either a right end is impossible, or any end is right provided we fall back on a belief that it is our duty to perform it. Kant holds that every concrete end, every definite purpose which we entertain, comes from desire. Law utters no specific command except "do your duty"; it stamps an end of desire as right only when it is pursued, not because it is an end of desire, but "from duty." The actual end which is before us is, in any case, supplied through inclination and desire. Reason furnishes *principle* as a *motive*. We have here, in another form, the separation of end and motive which has already occupied us (p. 227). End and motive are so disconnected, so irrelevant to one another, that we have no alternative except either to condemn every end, because, being prompted by desire, it falls so far short of the majesty of duty; or else fanatically to persist in any course when once we have formally brought it under the notion of duty.

The latter alternative would be the one chosen by a truly Kantian agent because it is alone possible in practice. But the moral fanatic does about as much evil in the world as the man of no moral principle. Religious wars, persecutions, intolerance, harsh judgment of others, obstinate persistence in a course of action once entered upon in spite of the testimony of experience to the harm that results; blind devotion to narrow and one-sided aims; deliberate opposition to art, culture, social amenities, recreations, or whatever the "man of principle" happens to find obnoxious: pharisaical conviction of superiority, of being the peculiar, chosen instrument of the moral law; — these and the countless ills that follow in their wake, are inevitable effects of erecting the isolated conviction of duty into a sufficient motive of action. So far as these evils do not actually flow from an acceptance of the Kantian principle, it is because that has been promulgated and for the most part adopted, where reverence for authority and law is strong. In Germany the Kantian philosophy has, upon the whole, served as a help in criticizing law and procedure on the basis of their rationality, while it has also served as a convenient stamp of rational sanction upon a politically authoritative régime, already fairly reasonable, as such matters go, in the content of its legislation and administration.

III. *Meaning of Duty for Duty's Sake.*—It is a sound principle to do our duty *as* our duty, and not for the sake of something else. "Duty for duty's sake" means, in truth, *an act for the act's own sake*: the gift of cold water, the word of encouragement, the sweeping of the room, the learning of the lesson, the selling of the goods, the painting of the picture, because they are the things really called for at a given time, and hence their own excuses for being. *No moral act is a means to anything beyond itself,—not even to morality.* But, upon Kant's theory, duty for duty's sake means a special act not for its own sake, but for the sake of abstract principle. Just as the hedonists regard a special act as a mere means to happiness, so Kant makes the concrete act a mere means to virtue. As there is a "hedonistic paradox," namely that the way to get happiness is to forget it, to devote ourselves to things and persons about us; so there is a "moralistic" paradox, that the way to get goodness is to cease to think of it—as something separate—and to devote ourselves to the realization of the full value of the practical situations in which we find ourselves. Men can really think of their "duty" only when they are thinking of specific things to be done; to think of Duty at large or in the abstract is one of the best ways of avoiding doing it, or of doing it in a partial and perverted way.

Summary of Criticism of Kant.—To sum up, the theory which regards duty as having its source in a rational self which is independent of and above the self of inclination and affection (1) deprives the habitual desires and affections, which make the difference between one concrete character and another, of moral significance; (2) commits us to an unenlightened performance of what is called duty irrespective of its real goodness; and (3) makes moral principle a remote abstraction, instead of the vivifying soul of a concrete deed. Its strongest point, its insistence upon the *autonomous* character of duty, or that duty is organically connected with the self in some of its phases or functions, will appear more clearly as we contrast it with the utilitarian theory.

§ 3. *The Utilitarian Theory of Duty*

Problem of Duty on Hedonistic Basis.—The utilitarians' explanation of the constraint of desire by the authority of right is framed to meet the peculiar difficulty in which their hedonistic theory places them. If pleasure is the good, and if all desire is naturally for the good, why should desire have to be constrained? How can such a thing as "duty" exist at all? For to say that a man is obliged or bound to seek that which he just can't help seeking is absurd. There is, according to the utilitarian, a difference, however, between the pleasure which is the object of desire and that which is the standard of judgment. The former is the person's own pleasure; it is private. The happiness which measures the rightness of the act is that of all persons who are affected by it. In view of this divergence, there must, if right action is to occur, be agencies which operate upon the individual so as to make him find his personal pleasure in that which conduces to the general welfare. These influences are the expectations and demands of *others so far as they attach consequences in the way of punishment, of suffering, and of reward and pleasure, to the deeds of an individual.*

In this way the natural inclination of an individual towards a certain pleasure, or his natural revulsion from a certain pain, may be checked and transformed by recognition that if he seeks the pleasure, others will inflict more than an equivalent pain, or if he bears the pain, others will reward him with more than compensating pleasures. In such cases, we have the fact of duty or obligation. There is constraint of first inclination through recognition of superior power, this power being asserted in its expressly declared intention of rewarding and penalizing according as its prescriptions are or are not followed. These are the factors: (1) demands, expectations, rules externally imposed; (2) consequences in the way of proffered reward of pleasure, and penalty of pain; (3) resulting constraint of the natural manifestation of desires. In the main, the theory is based on the analogy of legal obligations.[2]

(*a*) *Bentham's Account.*—Bentham dislikes the very word duty; and speaks preferably of the "sanctions" of an act. The following quotation will serve to confirm the foregoing statements.

The happiness of the individuals of whom a community is composed is . . . the sole standard, in conformity to which each individual *ought* to be made to fashion his behaviour. But whether it be this, or any thing else that is to be done, there is nothing by which a man can ultimately be *made* to do it, but either pain or pleasure.

2. Historically it has often taken theological form. Thus Paley defined virtue as "doing good to mankind in obedience to the will of God, and for the sake of everlasting happiness." Of obligation he said, "A man is said to be obliged, 'when he is urged by a violent motive, resulting from the command of another.'"

A kind of pain or pleasure which tends to *make* an individual find his own good in the good of the community is a *sanction*. Of these Bentham mentions four kinds, of which the first alone is not due to the will of others, but is *physical*. Thus the individual may check his inclination to drink by a thought of the ills that flow from drunkenness. Metaphorically, then, he may be said to have a duty not to drink; strictly speaking, however, this is his own obvious interest. The sanctions proper are (a) political, consequences in the way of pleasure and pain (especially pain) attached to injunctions and prohibitions by a legal superior; (b) popular, the consequences following from the more indefinite influence of public opinion—such as being "sent to Coventry," being shunned, rendered unpopular, losing reputation, or honor, etc.; and (c) religious, penalties of hell and rewards of heaven attached to action by a divine being, or similar penances and rewards by the representatives on earth (church, priests, etc.) of this divine being.[3]

Value and Deficiencies of This View.—The strong point of this explanation of duty is obviously that it recognizes the large, the very large, rôle played by social institutions, regulations, and demands in bringing home to a person the fact that certain acts, whether he is naturally so inclined or not, should be performed. But its weak point is that it tends to identify duty with coercion; to change the "ought" if not into a physical "must," at least into the psychological "must" of fear of pain and hope of pleasure. Hope of reward and fear of penalty are real enough motives in human life; but acts performed mainly or solely on their account do not, in the unprejudiced judgment of mankind, rank very high morally. Habitually to appeal to such motives is rather to weaken than to strengthen the tendencies in the individual which make for right action. The difficulty lies clearly in the purely *external* character of the "sanctions," and this in turn is due

---

3. The earlier English utilitarians (though not called by that name), such as Tucker and Paley, assert that upon this earth there is no exact coincidence of the right and the pleasure-giving; that it is future rewards and punishments which make the equilibrium. Sidgwick, among recent writers, has also held that no complete identification of virtue and happiness can be found apart from religious considerations. (See *Methods of Ethics*, p. 505. For theological utilitarianism see Albee, *History*.)

to the fact that the obligations imposed by the demands and expectancies of others do not have any intrinsic connection with the character of the individual of whom they are exacted. They are wholly external burdens and impositions.

The individual, with his desires and his pleasures, being made up out of particular states of feeling, is complete in himself. Social relationships must then be alien and external; if they modify in any way the existing body of feelings they are artificial constraints. One individual merely *happens* to live side by side with other individuals, who are in themselves isolated, and are complete in their isolation. If their external acts conflict, it may be necessary to invade and change the body of feelings which make up the self from which the act flows. Hence duty.

The later development of utilitarianism tended to get away from this psychical and atomic individualism; and to conceive the good of an individual as including *within* himself relations to others. So far as this was done, the demands of others, public opinion, laws, etc., became factors *in the development of the individual, and in arousing him to an adequate sense of what his good is, and of interest in effecting it.* Later utilitarianism dwells less than Bentham upon external sanctions, and more upon an unconscious shaping of the individual's character and motives through imitation, education, and all the agencies which mold the individual's desires into natural agreement with the social type. While it is John Stuart Mill who insists most upon the internal and qualitative change of disposition that thus takes place,[4] it is Bain and Spencer who give the most detailed account of the methods by which it is brought about.

(*b*) *Bain's Account.*—His basis agrees with Bentham's: "The proper meaning, or import, of the terms (duty, obligation) refers to that class of action which is enforced by the sanction of punishment" (Bain, *Emotions and Will*, p. 286). But he sets less store by political legislation and the force of vague public opinion, and more by the gradual and subtle processes of family education. The lesson of obedience, that there are things to be done whether one wishes or no, is im-

4. See his *Utilitarianism*, ch. iii.

pressed upon the child almost unremittingly from the very first moment of life. There are three stages in the complete evolution of the sense of duty. The first, the lowest and that beyond which some persons never go, is that in which "susceptibility to pleasure and pain is made use of to bring about obedience, and a mental association is rapidly formed between the disobedience and apprehended pain, more or less magnified by fear." The fact that punishment may be kept up until the child desists from the act "leaves on his mind a certain dread and awful impression as connected with forbidden actions." Here we have in its germ conscience, acknowledgment of duty, in its most external form.

A child in a good home (and a citizen in a good state) soon adds other associations. The command is uttered, the penalty threatened, by those whom he admires, respects, and loves. This element brings in a new dread—the fear of giving pain to the beloved object. Such dread is more disinterested. It centres rather about the point of view from which the act is held wrong than about the thought of harm to self. As intelligence develops, the person apprehends the positive ends, the goods, which are protected by the command put on him; he sees the use and reason of the prohibition to which he is subject, and approving of what it safeguards, approves the restriction itself. "A new motive is added on and begirts the action with a threefold fear. . . . If the duty prescribed has been approved of by the mind as *protective of the general interests of persons engaging our sympathies*, the violation of this on our part affects us with all the pain that we feel from inflicting *an injury upon those interests*."

Transformation into an Internal Power.—When the child appreciates *the reasons for the command, "the character of conscience is entirely transformed."* The fear which began as fear of the penalty that a superior power may inflict, adds to itself the fear of displeasing a beloved person; and is finally transformed into the dread of injuring interests the worth of which the individual appreciates and in which he shares. The sense of duty now "stands upon an independent foundation." It is an internal "ideal resemblance of public authority," "an imitation (or facsimile) within ourselves of the government without us." "Regard is now had to the intent and meaning of the law and not to the mere fact of its being prescribed by some power." Thus there is developed a sense of obligation in general, which may be detached from the particular deeds which were originally imposed under the sanction of penalty, and transferred to new ends which have never even been socially imposed, which the individual has perhaps for the first time conceived within himself. "The feeling and habit of obligation" which was generated from social pressure remains, but as a distinct individually cherished thing (Bain, *Emotions and Will*, p. 319 n.). This view of the *final* sense of obligation thus approximates Kant's view of the autonomous character of duty.

(c) *Spencer's Account.*—Herbert Spencer (like Bentham) lays emphasis upon the restraining influence of various social influences, but lays stress, as Bentham does not, upon the *internal* changes effected by long-continued, unremitting pressure exercised through the entire period of human evolution. Taken in itself, the consciousness of duty —the distinctively moral consciousness—is the control of proximate ends by remote ones, of simple by complex aims, of the sensory or presentative by the ideal or representative. An undeveloped individual or race lives and acts in the present; the mature is controlled by foresight of an indefinitely distant future. The thief who steals is actuated by a simple feeling, the mere impulse of acquisition; the business man conducts his acquisition in view of highly complex considerations of property and ownership. A low-grade intelligence acts only upon sensory stimulus, immediately present; a developed mind is moved by elaborate intellectual constructions, by imaginations and ideas which far outrun the observed or observable scene. Each step of the development of intelligence, of culture, whether in the individual or the race, is dependent upon ability to *subordinate* the immediate simple, physically present tendency and aim to the remote, compound, and only ideally present intention (Spencer, *Principles of Ethics*, Vol. I, Part I, ch. vii).

Subordination of Near to Remote Good Dependent on Social Influences.—"The conscious relinquishment of immediate and special good to gain distant and general good . . . is a cardinal trait of the self-restraint called moral." But this develops out of forms of restraint which are not moral; where the "relinquishment" and subordination of the present and temporary good is not consciously willed by the individual in view of a conscious appreciation of a distant and inclusive good; but where action in view of the latter is forced upon the individual by outside authority, operating by menace, and having the sanction of fear. These outside controls are three in number: political or legal; supernatural, priestly, or religious; and popular. All these external controls, working through dread of pain and promise of reward, bring about, however, in the individual a habit of looking to the remote, rather than to the proximate, end. At first the thought of these extrinsic consequences, those which do not flow from the act but from the reaction of others to it, is mixed up with the thought of its own proper consequences. But this association causes attention at least to be fixed upon intrinsic consequences that, because of their remoteness and complexity, might otherwise escape attention. Gradually the thought of them grows in clearness and efficacy and dissociates itself as a motive from the externally imposed consequences, and there is a control which alone is truly moral.

The Internal Sanction. —

The truly moral deterrent from murder, is not constituted by a representation of hanging as a consequence, or by a representation of tortures in hell as a consequence, or by a representation of the horror and hatred excited in fellow men; but by a representation of the *necessary natural results*—the infliction of death-agony on the victim, the destruction of all his possibilities of happiness, the entailed sufferings to his belongings (Spencer, *Principles of Ethics*, Vol. I, p. 120).

The external constraints thus serve as a schoolmaster to bring the race and the individual to internal restraint. Gradually the abstract sense of coerciveness, authoritativeness, the need of controlling the present by the future good is disentangled, and there arises the sense of duty in general. But even this "is transitory and will diminish as fast as moralization increases" (Spencer, *Principles of Ethics*, Vol. I, p. 127). Persistence in performance of a duty makes it a pleasure; an habitually exercised obligation is naturally agreeable.

In the present state of evolutionary development, obligation, or the demands made by the external environment, and spontaneous inclination, or the demand of the organism, cannot coincide. But at the goal of evolution, the organism and environment will be in perfect adjustment. Actions congenial to the former and appropriate to the latter will completely coincide. "In their proper times and places, and proportions, the moral sentiments will guide men just as spontaneously and adequately as now do the sensations" (Spencer, *Principles of Ethics*, Vol. I, p. 129).

Criticism of Utilitarianism.—The utilitarian account of the development of the consciousness of duty or its emphasis upon concrete facts of social arrangements and education affords a much-needed supplement to the empty and abstract formalism of Kant. (i.) The individual is certainly brought to his actual recognition of specific duties and to his consciousness of obligation or moral law in general through social influences. Bain insists more upon the family training and discipline of its immature members; Bentham and Spencer more upon the general institutional conditions, or the organization of government, law, judicial procedure, crystallized custom, and public opinion. In reality, these two conditions imply and reenforce each other. It is through the school of the family, for the most part, that the meaning of the requirements of the larger and more permanent institutions are brought home to the individual; while, on the other hand, the family derives the aims and values which it enforces upon the attention of its individual members mainly from the larger society in which it finds its own setting. (ii.) The later utilitarianism, in its insistence upon an "internal sanction," upon the ideal personal, or free facsimile of public authority, upon regard for "intrinsic consequences," corrects the weak point in Bentham (who relies so unduly upon mere threat of punishment and mere fear of pain) and approximates in practical effect, though not in theory, Kant's doctrine of the connection of duty with the rational or "larger" self which is social, even if individual. Even in its revised version utilitarianism did not wholly escape from the rigid unreal separation between the selfhood of the agent and his social surroundings forced upon it by its hedonistic psychology.

Fictitious Theory of Nature of Self.—The supposition that the individual starts with mere love of private pleasure,

and that, if he ever gets beyond to consideration of the good
of others, it is because others have forced their good upon
him by interfering with his private pleasures, is pure fiction.
The requirements, encouragements, and approbations of others react not primarily upon the pleasures and calculations
of the individual, but upon his *activities*, upon his inclinations, desires, habits. There is a common defect in the utilitarian and Kantian psychology. Both neglect the importance
of the active, the organically spontaneous and direct tendencies which enter into the individual. Both assume unreal
"*states* of consciousness," passive sensations, and feelings.
Active tendencies may be internally modified and redirected
by the very conditions and consequences of their own exercise. Family discipline, jural influences, public opinion, may
do little, or they may do much. But their educative influence
is as far from the mere association of feelings of pleasure
and pain as it is from Kant's purely abstract law. *Social influences enable an individual to realize the weight and import of the socially available and helpful manifestations of
the tendencies of his own nature and to discriminate them
from those which are socially harmful or useless*. When the
two conflict, the perception of the former is the recognition of
duties as distinct from *mere* inclinations.

§ *4. Final Statement*

Duty and a Growing Character.—Duty is what is owed
by a partial isolated self embodied in established, facile, and
urgent tendencies, to that ideal self which is presented in
aspirations which, since they are not yet formed into habits,
have no organized hold upon the self and which can get organized into habitual tendencies and interests only by a
more or less painful and difficult reconstruction of the habitual self. For Kant's fixed and absolute separation between
the self of inclination and the self of reason, we substitute
the relative and shifting distinction between those factors
of self which have become so definitely organized into set
habits that they take care of themselves, and those other factors which are more precarious, less crystallized, and which

depend therefore upon conscious acknowledgment and intentionally directed affection. The consciousness of duty grows out of the complex character of the self; the fact that at any given time, it has tendencies relatively set, engrained, and embodied in fixed habits, while it also has tendencies in process of making, looking to the future, taking account of unachieved possibilities. The former give the solid relatively formed elements of character; the latter, its ideal or unrealized possibilities. Each must play into the other; each must help the other out.

The conflict of duty and desire is thus an accompaniment of a *growing* self. Spencer's complete disappearance of obligation would mean an exhausted and fossilized self; wherever there is progress, tension arises between what is already accomplished and what is possible. In a being whose "reach should exceed his grasp," a conflict within the self making for the readjustment of the direction of powers must always be found. The value of continually *having to meet the expectations and requirements of others is in keeping the agent from resting on his oars, from falling back on habits already formed as if they were final.* The phenomena of duty in all their forms are thus phenomena attendant upon the expansion of ends and the reconstruction of character. So far, accordingly, as the recognition of duty is capable of operating as a distinct reenforcing motive, it operates most effectively, not as an interest in duty, or law in the abstract, but as an interest in progress in the face of the obstacles found within character itself.

Literature

The most important references on the subject of duty are given in the text. To these may be added: Ladd, *Philosophy of Conduct*, chs. v and xv; Mackenzie, *Manual*, Part I, ch. iv; Green, *Prolegomena*, pp. 315–20, 353–54 and 381–88; Sharp, *International Journal of Ethics*, Vol. II, pp. 500–513; Muirhead, *Elements of Ethics*, Book II, ch. ii; McGilvary, *Philosophical Review*, Vol. XI, pp. 333–52; Stephen, *Science of Ethics*, pp. 161–71; Sturt, *International Journal of Ethics*, Vol. VII, 334–45; Schurman, *Philosophical Review*, Vol. III, pp. 641–54; Guyau, *Sketch of Morality Independent of Obligation or Sanction.*

18. THE PLACE OF THE SELF IN THE MORAL LIFE

We have reached the conclusion that disposition as manifest in endeavor is the seat of moral worth, and that this worth itself consists in a readiness to regard the general happiness even against contrary promptings of personal comfort and gain. This brings us to the problems connected with the nature and functions of the self. We shall, in our search for the moral self, pass in review the conceptions which find morality in (1) Self-Denial or Self-Sacrifice, (2) Self-Assertion, (3) Combination of Regard for Self and for Others, (4) Self-Realization.

§ 1. The Doctrine of Self-Denial

Widespread Currency of the Doctrine. — The notion that real goodness, or virtue, consists essentially in abnegation of the self, in denying and, so far as may be, eliminating everything that is of the nature of the self, is one of the oldest and most frequently recurring notions of moral endeavor and religion, as well as of moral theory. It describes Buddhism and, in large measure, the monastic ideal of Christianity, while, in Protestantism, Puritanism is permeated with its spirit. It characterized Cynicism and Stoicism. Kant goes as far as to say that every rational being must wish to be wholly free from inclinations. Popular morality, while not going so far as to hold that all moral goodness is self-denial, yet more or less definitely assumes that self-denial on its own account, irrespective of what comes out of it, is morally praiseworthy. A notion so deeply rooted and widely flourishing must have strong motives in its favor, all the more so because its practical vogue is always stronger than any reasons which are theoretically set forth.

Origin of the Doctrine. — The notion arises from the tendency to identify the self with one of its own factors. It is one and the same self which conceives and is interested in some generous and ideal good that is also tempted by some near, narrow, and exclusive good. The force of the latter resides in the *habitual* self, in purposes which have got themselves inwrought into the texture of ordinary character. Hence there is a disposition to overlook the complexity of selfhood, and to identify it with those factors in the self which resist ideal aspiration, and which are recalcitrant to the thought of duty; to identify the self with impulses that are inclined to what is frivolous, sensuous and sensual, pleasure-seeking. All vice being, then, egoism, selfishness, self-seeking, the remedy is to check it at its roots; to keep the self down in its proper place, denying it, chastening it, mortifying it, refusing to listen to its promptings. Ignoring the variety and subtlety of the factors that make up the self, all the different elements of right and of wrong are gathered together and set over against each other. All the good is placed once for all in some outside source, some higher law or ideal; and the source of all evil is placed within the corrupted and vile self. When one has become conscious of the serious nature of the moral struggle; has found that vice is easy, and to err "natural," needing only to give way to some habitual impulse or desire; that virtue is arduous, requiring resistance and strenuous effort, one is apt to overlook the habitual tendencies which are the ministers of the higher goods. One forgets that unless ideal ends were also rooted in some natural tendencies of the self, they could neither occur to the self nor appeal to the self. Hence everything is swept into the idea that the self is inherently so evil that it must be denied, snubbed, sacrificed, mortified.

In general, to point out the truth which this theory perverts, to emphasize the demand for constant reconstruction and rearrangement of the habitual powers of the self—is sufficient criticism of it. But in detail the theory exercises such pervasive influence that it is worth while to mention specifically some of the evils that accrue from it.

1. It so Maims and Distorts Human Nature as to Narrow the Conception of the Good.—In its legitimate antagonism to pleasure-seeking, it becomes a foe to happiness, and an implacable enemy of all its elements. Art is suspected, for beauty appeals to the lust of the eye. Family life roots in sexual impulses, and property in love of power, gratification, and luxury. Science springs from the pride of the intellect; the State from the pride of will. *Asceticism* is the logical result; a purely negative conception of virtue. But it surely does dishonor, not honor, to the moral life to conceive it as mere negative subjection of the flesh, mere holding under control the lust of desire and the temptations of appetite. All positive content, all liberal achievement, is cut out and morality is reduced to a mere struggle *against* solicitations to sin. While asceticism is in no danger of becoming a popular doctrine, there is a common tendency to conceive self-control in this negative fashion; to fail to see that the important thing is some positive good *for* which a desire is controlled. In general we overemphasize that side of morality which consists in abstinence and *not* doing wrong.

2. *To Make so Much of Conflict with the "Flesh," is to Honor the Latter too Much.*—It is to fix too much attention on it. It is an open lesson of psychology that to oppose doing an act by mere injunction *not* to do it, is to increase the power of the thing not to be done, and to weaken the spring and effectiveness of the other motives, which, if positively attended to, might keep the obnoxious motive from gaining supremacy. The "expulsive power" of a generous affection is more to be relied upon than effort to suppress, which keeps alive the very thing to be suppressed. The history of monks and Puritan saints alike is full of testimony to the fact that withdrawal from positive generous and wholesome aims reenforces the vitality of the lower appetites and stimulates the imagination to play about them. Flagellation and fasting work as long as the body is exhausted; but the brave organism reasserts itself, and its capacities for science, art, the life of the family and the State not having been cultivated, sheer ineradicable physical instinct is most likely to come to the front.

3. *We Judge Others by Ourselves Because We Have No Other Way to Judge.*—It is impossible for a man who conceives his own good to be in "going without," in just restricting himself, to have any large or adequate idea of the good of others. Unconsciously and inevitably a hardening and narrowing of the conditions of the lives of others accom-

panies the reign of the Puritanic ideal. The man who takes
a high view of the capacities of human nature in itself, who
reverences its possibilities and is jealous for their high maintenance in himself, is the one most likely to have keen and
sensitive appreciation of the needs of others. There is, moreover, no selfishness, no neglect of others more thoroughgoing, more effectively cruel than that which comes from pre-
occupation with the attainment of personal goodness, and
this interest is an almost inevitable effect of devotion to the
negative ideal of self-denial.

4. *The Principle Radically Violates Human Nature.*—
This indeed is its claim—that human nature, just as human
nature, requires to have violence done it. But the capacities
which constitute the self demand fulfillment. The place, the
time, the manner, the degree, and the proportion of their
fulfillment, require infinite care and pains, and to secure
this attention is the business of morals. Morals is a matter
of direction, not of suppression. The urgency of desires and
capacities for expression cannot be got rid of; nature cannot
be expelled. If the need of happiness, of satisfaction of
capacity, is checked in one direction, it will manifest itself
in another. If the direction which is checked is an unconscious and wholesome one, that which is taken will be likely
to be morbid and perverse. The one who is conscious of continually denying himself cannot rid himself of the idea that
it ought to be "made up" to him; that a compensating happiness is due him for what he has sacrificed, somewhat increased, if anything, on account of the unnatural virtue he
has displayed.[1] To be self-sacrificing is to "lay up" merit, and
this achievement must surely be rewarded with happiness—
if not now, then later. Those who habitually live on the basis
of conscious self-denial are likely to be exorbitant in the demands which they make on some one near them, some member of their family or some friend; likely to blame others if
their own "virtue" does not secure for itself an exacting
attention which reduces others to the plane of servility. Often
the doctrine of self-sacrifice leads to an inverted hedonism:

1. Compare the opening words of Emerson's *Essay on Compensation.*

we are to be good—that is, to forego pleasure—now, that we may have a greater measure of enjoyment in some future paradise of bliss. Or, the individual who has taken vows of renunciation is entitled by that very fact to represent spiritual authority on earth and to lord it over others.

§ 2. Self-Assertion

The idea that morality consists in an unbridled assertion of self, in its forceful aggressive manifestation, rarely receives consistent theoretical formulation—possibly because most men are so ready to act upon it practically that explicit acknowledgment would be a hindrance rather than a help to the idea. But it is a doctrine which tends to be invoked more or less explicitly as a reaction from the impotency of the self-denial dogma. In reference to some superior individual or class, some leader or group of aristocratically ordained leaders, it is always a more or less conscious principle. Concerning these it is held that ordinary morality holds eventually only for the "common herd," the activities of the leader being amenable to a higher law than that of common morality.[2] Moreover, since the self-sacrifice morality is almost never carried out consistently—that is, to the point of monastic asceticism,—much popular morality is an unbalanced combination of self-sacrifice in some regards and ruthless self-assertion in others. It is not "practicable" to carry out the principle of self-denial everywhere; it is reserved for the family life, for special religious duties; in business (which is business, not morals), the proper thing is aggressive and unremitting self-assertion. In business, the end is success, to "make good"; weakness is failure, and failure is disgrace, dishonor. Thus in practice the two conceptions of self-denial in one region and self-assertion in another mutually support each other. They give occasion for the more or less unformulated, yet prevalent, idea that moral considerations (those of self-denial) apply to a limited phase of life, but have noth-

2. The principle of a "higher law" for the few who are leaders was first explicitly asserted in modern thought by Machiavelli.

ing to do with other regions in which accordingly the principle of "efficiency" (that is, personal success, wealth, power obtained in competitive victory) holds supreme sway.

Recently, however, there has sprung up a so-called "naturalistic" school of ethics which has formulated explicitly the principle of self-assertion, and which claims to find scientific sanction for it in the evolutionary doctrine of Darwin. Evolution, it says, is the great thing, and evolution means the *survival of the fit in the struggle for existence.* Nature's method of progess is precisely, so it is said, ruthless self-assertion — to the strong the victory, to the victorious the spoils, and to the defeated, woe. Nature affords a scene of egoistic endeavor or pressure, suffer who may, of struggle to get ahead, that is, ahead of others, even by thrusting them down and out. But the justification of this scene of rapine and slaughter is that out of it comes progress, advance, everything that we regard as noble and fair. Excellence is the sign of excelling; the goal means outrunning others. The morals of humility, of obedience to law, of pity, sympathy, are merely a self-protective device on the part of the weak who try to safeguard their weakness by setting fast limitations to the activities of the truly strong (compare what was said of the not dissimilar doctrine among the Greeks, pp. 114–16). But the truly moral man, in whom the principle of progress is embodied, will break regardlessly through these meshes and traps. He will carry his own plans through to victorious achievement. He is the super-man. The mass of men are simply food for his schemes, valuable as furnishing needed material and tools.[3]

Practical Vogue of the Underlying Idea.—Such a theory, in and of itself, is a literary diversion for those who, not being competent in the fields of outer achievement, amuse

3. Some phases of the writings of Nietzsche supply relevant material for this sketch. (See especially his *Will for Power, Beyond Good and Evil*, and such statements as: "The loss of force which suffering has already brought upon life is still further increased and multiplied by sympathy. Suffering itself becomes contagious through sympathy" (overlooking the reaction of sympathy to abolish the source of suffering and thus increase force). "Sympathy thwarts, on the whole, in general, the law of development, which is the law of selection."—*Works*, Vol. XI, p. 242.

themselves by idealizing it in writing. Like most literary ver-
sions of science, it rests upon a pseudo-science, a parody of
the real facts. But at a time when economic conditions are
putting an extraordinary emphasis upon outward achievement, upon success in manipulating natural and social
resources, upon "efficiency" in exploiting both inanimate energies and the minds and bodies of other persons, the underlying principle of this theory has a sanction and vogue which
is out of all proportion to the number of those who consciously entertain it as a theory. For a healthy mind, the
frank statement and facing of the theory is its best criticism.
Its bald brutalism flourishes freely only when covered and
disguised. But in view of the forces at present, and especially
in America, making for a more or less unconscious acceptance of its principle in practice, it may be advisable to say
something (1) regarding its alleged scientific foundation,
and (2) the inadequacy of its conception of efficiency.

 *1. The Theory Exaggerates the Rôle of Antagonistic
Competitive Struggle in the Darwinian Theory.*—(a) The
initial step in any "progress" is *variation*; this is not so much
struggle *against* other organisms, as it is *invention* or discovery of some *new* way of acting, involving better adaptation of hitherto merely latent natural resources, use of some
possible food or shelter not previously utilized. The struggle
against other organisms at work preserves from elimination
a species already fixed—quite a different thing from the
variation which occasions the introduction of a higher or
more complex species. (b) Moreover, so far as the Darwinian
theory is concerned, the "struggle for existence" may take
any conceivable form; rivalry in generosity, in mutual aid
and support, may be the kind of competition best fitted to
enable a species to survive. It not only may be so, but it is
so within certain limits. The rage for survival, for power,
must not be asserted indiscriminately; the mate of the other
sex, the young, to some extent other individuals of the same
kin, are spared, or, in many cases, protected and nourished.[4]
(c) The higher the form of life, the *more* effective the two

 4. This phase of the matter has been brought out (possibly with
some counter-exaggeration) by Kropotkin in his *Mutual Aid.*

methods just suggested: namely, the method of intelligence in discovering and utilizing new methods, tools, and resources as substituted for the direct method of brute conflict; and the method of mutual protection and care substituted for mutual attack and combat. It is among the lower forms of life, not as the theory would require among the higher types, that conditions approximate its picture of the gladiatorial show. The higher species among the vertebrates, as among insects (like ants and bees), are the "sociable" kinds. It is sometimes argued that Darwinism carried into morals would abolish charity: all care of the hopelessly invalid, of the economically dependent, and in general of all the weak and helpless except healthy infants. It is argued that our current standards are sentimental and artificial, aiming to make survive those who are unfit, and thus tending to destroy the conditions that make for advance, and to introduce such as make towards degeneration. But this argument (1) wholly ignores the reflex effect of interest in those who are ill and defective in strengthening social solidarity—in promoting those ties and reciprocal interests which are as much the prerequisites of strong individual characters as they are of a strong social group. And (2) it fails to take into account the stimulus to foresight, to scientific discovery, and practical invention, which has proceeded from interest in the helpless, the weak, the sick, the disabled, blind, deaf, and insane. Taking the most coldly scientific view, the gains in these two respects have, through the growth of social pity, of care for the unfortunate, been purchased more cheaply than we can imagine their being bought in any other way. In other words, the chief objection to this "naturalistic" ethics is that it overlooks the fact that, even from the Darwinian point of view, the human *animal* is a *human* animal. It forgets that the sympathetic and social instincts, those which cause the individual to take the interests of others for his own and thereby to restrain his sheer brute self-assertiveness, are the highest achievements, the high-water mark of evolution. The theory urges a systematic relapse to lower and foregone stages of biological development.

2. *Its Conception of "Power," "Efficiency," "Achievement" is Perverse.*—Compared with the gospel of abstinence,

of inefficiency, preached by the self-denial school, there is an element of healthy reaction in any ethical system which stresses positive power, positive success, positive attainment. Goodness has been too much identified with practical feebleness and ineptitude; strength and solidity of accomplishment, with unscrupulousness. But power for the sake of power is as unreal an abstraction as self-denial for the sake of sacrifice, or self-restraint for the sake of the mere restraint. Erected into a central principle, it takes means for end—the fallacy of all materialism. It makes little of many of the most important and excellent *inherent ingredients* of happiness in its eagerness to master *external conditions* of happiness. Sensitive discrimination of complex and refined distinctions of worth, such as good taste, the resources of poetry and history, frank and varied social converse among intellectual equals, the humor of sympathetic contemplation of the spectacle of life, the capacity to extract happiness from solitude and society, from nature and from art:—all of these, as well as the more obvious virtues of sympathy and benevolence, are swept aside for one coarse undiscriminating ideal of external activity, measured by sheer quantity of external changes made and external results accumulated. Of such an ideal we may say, as Mill said, that the judge of good, of happiness, is the one who has experienced its various forms; and that as "no intelligent person would consent to be a fool" on account of the pleasures of the fool, so no man of cultivated spirit would consent to be a lover of "efficiency" and "power" for the sake of brute command of the external commodities of nature and man.

Present Currency of This Ideal.—In spite of the extraordinary currency of this ideal at present, there is little fear that it will be permanently established. Human nature is too rich and varied in its capacities and demands; the world of nature and society is too fruitful in sources of stimulus and interest for man to remain indefinitely content with the idea of power for power's sake, command of means for the mere sake of the means. Humanity has long lived a precarious and a stunted life because of its partial and easily shaken hold on natural resources. Starved by centuries of abstinence enforced through lack of control of the forces and methods of nature, taught the gospel of the merit of abstention, it is not surprising that it should be intoxicated when scientific discovery bears its fruit of power in utilization of natural forces, or that, temporarily unbalanced, it should take the external conditions of happiness for happiness itself. But when the values of material acquisition and achievement become familiar they will lose the contrast value they now possess; and human endeavor will concern itself mainly with the problem of rendering its conquests in power and efficiency tributary to the life of intelligence and art and of social communication.[5] Such a moral idealism will rest upon a more secure and extensive natural foundation than that of the past, and will be more equitable in application and saner in content than that with which aristocracies have made us familiar. It will be a democratic ideal, a good for all, not for a noble class; and it will include, not exclude, those physical and physiological factors which aristocratic idealisms have excluded as common and unclean.

§ 3. Self-Love and Benevolence; or, Egoism and Altruism

For the last three centuries, the most discussed point in English ethical literature (save perhaps whether moral knowledge is intuitive or derived from experience) has been the relation of regard for one's own self and for other selves as motives of action—"the crux of all ethical speculation," Spencer terms it. All views have been represented: (a) that man naturally acts from purely selfish motives and that

5. Spencer puts the matter truly, if ponderously, in the following: "The citizens of a large nation industrially organized, have reached their possible ideal of happiness when the producing, distributing and other activities, are such in their kinds and amounts, that each individual finds in them a place for all his energies and aptitudes, while he obtains the means of satisfying all his desires. Once more we may recognize as not only possible, but probable, the eventual existence of a community, also industrial, the members of which, having natures similarly responding to these requirements, are also characterized by dominant aesthetic faculties, and achieve complete happiness only when a large part of life is filled with aesthetic activities" (*Principles of Ethics*, Vol. I, p. 169).

morality consists in an enforced subjection of self-love to the laws of a common social order. (b) That man is naturally selfish, while morality is an "enlightened selfishness," or a regard for self based upon recognition of the extent to which its happiness requires consideration of others. (c) That the tendencies of the agent are naturally selfish, but that morality is the subjection of these tendencies to the law of duty. (d) That man's interests are naturally partly egoistic and partly sympathetic, while morality is a compromise or adjustment of these tendencies. (e) That man's interests are naturally both, and morality a subjection of both to conscience as umpire. (f) That they are both, while morality is a subjection of egoistic to benevolent sentiments. (g) That the individual's interests are naturally in objective ends which primarily are neither egoistic nor altruistic; and these ends become either selfish or benevolent at special crises, at which times morality consists in referring them, equally and impartially for judgment, to a situation in which the interests of the self and of others concerned are involved: *to a common good.*

Three Underlying Psychological Principles.—We shall make no attempt to discuss these various views in detail; but will bring into relief some of the factors in the discussion which substantiate the view (g) stated last. It will be noted that the theories rank themselves under three heads with reference to the constitution of man's tendencies: holding they (1) naturally have in view personal ends exclusively or all fall under the principle of self-love or self-regard; that (2) some of them contemplate one's own happiness and some of them that of others; that (3) primarily they are not *consciously* concerned with either one's own happiness or that of others. Memory and reflection may show (just as it shows other things) that their consequences affect both the self and others, when the recognition of this fact becomes an additional element, either for good or for evil, in the motivation of the act. We shall consider, first, the various senses in which action occurs, or is said to occur, in behalf of the person's own self; and then take up, in similar fashion, its reference to the interests of others.

I. Action in Behalf of Self.—1. *Motives as Selfish:* The Natural Selfishness of Man is maintained from such different standpoints and with such different objects in view that it is difficult to state the doctrine in any one generalized form. By some theologians, it has been associated with an innate corruption or depravity of human nature and been made the basis of a demand for supernatural assistance to lead a truly just and benevolent life. By Hobbes (1588–1679) it was associated with the anti-social nature of individuals and made the basis for a plea for a strong and centralized political authority[6] to control the natural "war of all against all" which flows inevitably from the psychological egoism. By Kant, it was connected with the purely sense origin of desires, and made the basis for a demand for the complete subordination of desire to duty as a motive for action. Morals, like politics, make strange bedfellows! The common factor in these diverse notions, however, is that every act of a self must, when left to its *natural* or psychological course, have the interest of the self in view; otherwise there would be no motive for the deed and it would not be done. This theoretical and *a priori* view is further supported by pointing out, sometimes in reprobation of man's sinful nature, sometimes in a more or less cynical vein, the lurking presence of some subtle regard for self in acts that apparently are most generous and "disinterested."[7]

Ambiguity of the Psychological Basis.—The notion that all action is "for the self" is infected with the same ambiguity as the (analogous) doctrine that all desire is for happiness. Like that doctrine, in one sense it is a truism, in another a falsity—this latter being the sense in which its upholders maintain it. Psychologically, any object that moves us, any object in which we imagine our impulses to rest satisfied or to find fulfillment, *becomes,* in virtue of that fact, a factor in the self. If I am enough interested in collecting postage stamps, a collection of postage stamps becomes a part of my "ego," which is incomplete and restless till filled out in that way. If my habits are such that I am not content when I know my neighbor is suffering from a lack of food until I have relieved him, then relief of his suffering be-

6. Machiavelli, transferring from theology to statecraft the notion of the corruption and selfishness of all men, was the first modern to preach this doctrine.
7. See, for example, Hobbes, *Leviathan*; Mandeville, *Fable of the Bees*; and Rochefoucauld, *Maxims*.

comes a part of my selfhood. If my desires are such that I have no rest of mind until I have beaten my competitor in business, or have demonstrated my superiority in social gifts by putting my fellow at some embarrassing disadvantage, then that sort of thing constitutes my self. Our instincts, impulses, and habits all demand appropriate objects in order to secure exercise and expression; and these ends in their office of furnishing outlet and satisfaction to our powers form a cherished part of the "me." In this sense it is true, and a truism, that all action involves the interest of self.

True and False Interpretation.—But this doctrine is the exact opposite of that intended by those who claim that all action is from self-love. The true doctrine says, *the self is constituted and developed through instincts and interests which are directed upon their own objects with no conscious regard necessarily for anything except those objects themselves.* The false doctrine implies that the self *exists by itself apart from these objective ends, and that they are merely means for securing it a certain profit or pleasure.*

Suppose, for example, it is a case of being so disturbed in mind by the thought of another in pain that one is moved to do something to relieve him. This means that certain native instincts or certain acquired habits demand relief of others as part of themselves. The well-being of the other is an interest of the self: is a part of the self. This is precisely what is meant ordinarily by unselfishness: not lack or absence of a self, but *such* a self as identifies itself in action with others' interests and hence is satisfied only when they are satisfied. To find pain in the thought of others pained and to take pleasure in the thought of their relief, is to have and to be moved by personal motives, by states which are "selfish" in the sense of making up the self; but which are the exact opposite of selfish in the sense of being the thought of some private advantage to self.[8] Putting it roundly, then, the

8. Compare what was said above, p. 249, on the confusion of pleasure as end, and as motive. Compare also the following from Leslie Stephen, *Science of Ethics*, p. 241. It is often "insinuated that I dislike your pain because it is painful to me in some special relation. I do not dislike it *as* your pain, but in virtue of some particular consequence, such, for example, as its making you less able to render me a service. In that case I do not really

fallacy of the selfish motive theory is that it fails to see that *instincts and habits directed upon objects are primary*, and that they come before any conscious thought of self as end, since they are necessary to the constitution of that thought.

The following quotation from James[9] states the true doctrine:

When I am led by self-love to keep my seat whilst ladies stand, or to grab something first and cut out my neighbor, what I really love is the comfortable seat; it is the thing itself which I grab. I love *them* primarily, as the mother loves her babe, or a generous man an heroic deed. Wherever, as here, self-seeking is the outcome of simple instinctive propensity, it is but a name for certain reflex acts. Something rivets my attention fatally and fatally provokes the "selfish" response. . . . It is true I am no automaton, but a thinker. But my thoughts, like my acts, are here concerned only with the outward things. . . . In fact the more utterly selfish I am in this primitive way, the more blindly absorbed my thought will be in the objects and impulses of my lust and the more devoid of any inward looking glance.

2. *Results as Selfish: Ambiguity in the Notion.*—We must then give up the notion that motives are inherently self-seeking, in the sense that there is in voluntary acts a thought of the self as the end for the sake of which the act is performed. The self-seeking doctrine may, however, be restated in these terms: Although there is no thought of self or its advantage consciously entertained, yet our original instincts are such that their objects do as *matter of result* conduce primarily to the well-being and advantage of the self. In this sense, anger, fear, hunger, and thirst, etc., are said to be egoistic or self-seeking—not that their *conscious* object is the self, but that their inevitable effect is to preserve and protect the self. The fact that an instinct secures self-preservation or self-development does not, however, make it "egoistic" or "selfish" in the moral sense; nor does it throw any light upon the moral status of the instinct. *Everything depends upon the sort of self which is maintained.*

---

object to your pain as your pain at all, but only to some removable and accidental consequences." The entire discussion of sympathy (pp. 230–45), which is admirable, should be consulted.

9. James, *Psychology*, Vol. I, p. 320. The whole discussion, pp. 317–29, is very important.

There is, indeed, some presumption (see *ante,* p. 268) that
the act sustains a *social* self, that is, a self whose maintenance is of social value. If the individual organism did not
struggle for food; strive aggressively against obstacles and
interferences; evade or shelter itself against menacing superior force, what would become of children, fathers and
mothers, lawyers, doctors and clergymen, citizens and patriots—in short, of society? If we avoid setting up a purely
abstract self, if we keep in mind that every actual self is a
self which *includes* social relations and offices, both actual
and potential, we shall have no difficulty in seeing that self-
preservative instincts *may* be, and taken by and large, *must*
be, socially conservative. Moreover, while it is not true that
if "a man does not look after his own interests no one else
will" (if that means that his interests are no one else's affair
in any way), it is true that no one has a right to neglect his
own interests in the hope that some one else will care for
them. "His own interests," properly speaking, are precisely
the ends which concern him more directly than they concern any one else. Each man is, so to say, nearer himself
than is any one else, and, therefore, has certain duties to
and about himself which cannot be performed by any other
one. Others may present food or the conditions of education,
but the individual alone can digest the food or educate himself. It is profitable for society, not merely for an individual,
that each of us should instinctively have his powers most
actively and intensely called out by the things that distinctively affect him and his own welfare. Any other arrangement would mean waste of social energy, inefficiency in securing social results.

The quotation from James also makes it clear, however, that under certain circumstances the mere absorption
in a thing, even without conscious thought of self, is morally
offensive. The "pig" in manners is not necessarily thinking
of himself; all that is required to make him a pig is that he
should have too narrow and exclusive an object of regard.
The man sees simply the seat, not the seat *and* the lady.
The boor in manners is unconscious of many of the objects
in the situation which *should* operate as stimuli. One impulse
or habit is operating at the expense of others; the self in play

is too petty or narrow. Viewed from the standpoint of results, the fact which constitutes selfishness in the moral sense is not that certain impulses and habits secure the well-being of the self, *but that the well-being secured is a narrow and exclusive one.* The forms of coarse egoism which offend us most in ordinary life are not usually due to a deliberate or self-conscious seeking of advantage for self, but to such pre-occupation with certain ends as blinds the agent to the thought of the interests of others. Many whose behavior seems to others most selfish would deny indignantly (and, from the standpoint of their *definite* consciousness, honestly) any self-seeking motives: they would point to certain objective results, which in the abstract are desirable, as the true ends of their activities. But none the less, they *are* selfish, because the limitations of their interests make them overlook the consequences which affect the freedom and happiness of others.

3. *There are also Cases in Which the Thought of the Resulting Consequence to the Self Consciously Enters in and Modifies the Motive of the Act.*—With increasing memory and foresight, one can no more ignore the lesson of the past as to the consequences of an act upon himself than he can ignore other consequences. A man who has learned that a certain act has painful consequences to himself, whether to his body, his reputation, his comfort, or his character, is quite likely to have the thought of himself present itself as part of the foreseen consequences when the question of a similar act recurs. In and of itself, once more, this fact throws no light upon the moral status of the act. Everything depends upon what sort of a self moves and how it moves. A man who hesitated to rush into a burning building to rescue a suit of clothes because he thought of the danger to himself, would be sensible; a man who rushed out of the building just because he thought of saving himself when there were others he might have assisted, would be contemptible.

The one who began taking exercise because he thought of his own health, would be commended; but a man who thought so continually of his own health as to shut out other objects, would become an object of ridicule or worse. *There*

is a moral presumption that a man should make considera-
tion of himself a part of his aim and intent. A certain care of
health, of body, of property, of mental faculty, because they
are one's own is not only permissible, but obligatory. This is
what the older moral writers spoke of as "prudence," or as
"reasonable self-love."

(i.) It is a stock argument of the universal selfishness
theory to point out that a man's acknowledgment of some
public need or benefit is quite likely to coincide with his
recognition of some private advantage. A statesman's recognition of some measure of public policy happens to coincide
with perceiving that by pressing it he can bring himself into
prominence or gain office. A man is more likely to see the
need of improved conditions of sanitation or transportation
in a given locality if he has property there. A man's indignation at some prevalent public ill may sleep till he has had a
private taste of it. We may admit that these instances describe a usual, though not universal, state of affairs. But
does it follow that such men are moved *merely* by the
thought of gain to themselves? Possibly this sometimes happens; then the act is selfish in the obnoxious sense. The
man has isolated his thought of himself as an end and made
the thought of the improvement or reform merely an external means. The latter is not truly his *end* at all; he has not
identified it with himself. In other cases, while the individual
would not have recognized the end if the thought of himself
had not been implicated, yet *after* he has recognized it, the
two—the thought of himself and of the public advantage—
may blend. His thought of himself may lend warmth and
intimacy to an object which otherwise would have been cold,
while, at the same time, the self is broadened and deepened
by taking in the new object of regard.

(ii.) Take the case of amusement or recreation. To an
adult usually engaged in strenuous pursuits, the thought of
a pleasure for the mere sake of pleasure, of enjoyment, of
having a "good time," may appeal as an end. And if the
pleasure is itself "innocent," only the requirements of a
preconceived theory (like the Kantian) would question its
legitimacy. Even its moral necessity is clear when relaxation
is conducive to cheerfulness and efficiency in more serious

pursuits. But if a man discriminates mentally between himself and the play or exercise in which he finds enjoyment and relief, thinking of himself as a distinct end to which the latter is merely means, he is not likely to get the recreation. It is by forgetting the self, that is by taking the light and easy activity *as* the self of the situation, that the benefit comes. To be a "lover of pleasure" in the bad sense is precisely to seek amusements as excitements for a self which somehow remains outside them as their fixed and ulterior end.

(iii.) Exactly the same analysis applies to the idea of the moral culture of the self, of its moral perfecting. Every serious-minded person has, from time to time, to take stock of his status and progress in moral matters—to take thought of the moral self just as at other times he takes thought of the health of the bodily self. But woe betides that man who, having entered upon a course of reflection which leads to a clearer conception of his own moral capacities and weaknesses, maintains that thought as a distinct mental end, and thereby makes his subsequent acts simply means to improving or perfecting his moral nature. Such a course defeats itself. At the least, it leads to priggishness, and its tendency is towards one of the worst forms of selfishness: a habit of thinking and feeling that persons, that concrete situations and relations, exist simply to render contributions to one's own precious moral character. The worst of such selfishness is that having protected itself with the mantle of interest in moral goodness, it is proof against that attrition of experience which may always recall a man to himself in the case of grosser and more unconscious absorption. A sentimentally refined egoism is always more hopeless than a brutal and naïve one—though a brutal one not infrequently protects itself by adoption and proclamation of the language of the former.

II. Benevolence or Regard for Others.—*Ambiguity in Conception*: There is the same ambiguity in the idea of sympathetic or altruistic springs to action that there is in that of egoistic and self-regarding. Does the phrase refer to their conscious and express intent? or to their objective results when put into operation, irrespective of explicit desire and aim? And, if the latter, are we to believe contribution to the welfare of others to be the sole and exclusive character of some springs of action, or simply that, under certain circumstances, the *emphasis* falls more upon the good resulting to others than upon other consequences? The discussion will show that the same general principles hold for "benevolent" as for self-regarding impulses: namely (1) that there are none which from the start are consciously such; (2) that while reflection may bring to light their bearing upon the welfare of others so that it becomes an element in the conscious desire, this is a matter of relative preponderance, not of absolute nature; and (3) that just as conscious regard for self is not necessarily bad or "selfish," so conscious regard for others is not necessarily good: the criterion is the whole situation in which the desire takes effect.

1. *The Existence of Other-Regarding Springs to Action.*—Only the preconceptions of hedonistic psychology would ever lead one to deny the existence of reactions and impulses called out by the sight of others' misery and joy and which tend to increase the latter and to relieve the former. Recent psychologists (writing, of course, quite independently of ethical controversies) offer lists of native instinctive tendencies such as the following: Anger, jealousy, rivalry, secretiveness, acquisitiveness, fear, shyness, sympathy, affection, pity, sexual love, curiosity, imitation, play, constructiveness.[10] In this inventory, the first seven may be said to be aroused specially by situations having to do with the preservation of the self; the next four are responses to stimuli proceeding especially from others and tending to consequences favorable to them, while the last four are mainly impersonal. But the division into self-regarding and other-regarding is not exclusive and absolute. Anger *may* be wholly other-regarding, as in the case of hearty indignation at wrongs suffered by others; rivalry may be generous emulation or be directed toward surpassing one's own past record. Love between the sexes, which should be the source of steady, far-reaching interest in others, and which at times expresses itself in supreme abnegation of devotion, easily becomes the cause of brutal and persistent egoism. In short,

10. See, for example, James, *Psychology*, Vol. II, ch. xxiv.

the division into egoistic and altruistic holds only "other things being equal."

Confining ourselves for the moment to the native psychological equipment, we may say that man is endowed with instinctive promptings which naturally (that is, without the intervention of deliberation or calculation) tend to preserve the self (by aggressive attack as in anger, or in protective retreat as in fear); and to develop his powers (as in acquisitiveness, constructiveness, and play); and which equally, without consideration of resulting ulterior benefit either to self or to others, tend to bind the self closer to others and to advance the interests of others—as pity, affectionateness, or again, constructiveness and play. Any given individual is *naturally* an erratic mixture of fierce insistence upon his own welfare and of profound susceptibility to the happiness of others—different individuals varying much in the respective intensities and proportions of the two tendencies.

2. *The Moral Status of Altruistic Tendencies.*—We have expressly devoted considerable space (ch. 13) to showing that there are no motives which in and of themselves are right; that any tendency, whether original instinct or acquired habit, requires sanction from the special consequences which, in the special situation, are likely to flow from it. The mere fact that pity in general tends to conserve the welfare of others does not guarantee the rightness of giving way to an impulse of pity, just as it happens to spring up. This might mean sentimentalism for the agent, and weakening of the springs of patience, courage, self-help, and self-respect in others. The persistence with which the doctrine of the evils of indiscriminate charity has to be taught is sufficient evidence that the so-called other-regarding impulses require the same control by reason as do the "egoistic" ones. They have no inherent sacredness which exempts them from the application of the standard of the common and reasonable happiness.

Evils of Unregulated Altruism.—So much follows from the general principles already discussed. But there are special dangers and evils attendant upon an exaggeration of the altruistic idea. (i.) *It tends to render others dependent*, and thus contradicts its own professed aim: the helping of others.

Almost every one knows some child who is so continuously "helped" by others, that he loses his initiative and resourcefulness. Many an invalid is confirmed in a state of helplessness by the devoted attention of others. In large social matters there is always danger of the substitution of an ideal of conscious "benevolence" for justice: it is in aristocratic and feudal periods that the idea flourishes that "charity" (conceived as conferring benefits *upon* others, doing things *for* them) is inherently and absolutely a good. The idea assumes the continued and necessary existence of a dependent "lower" class to be the recipients of the kindness of their superiors; a class which serves as passive material for the cultivation in others of the virtue of charity, the higher class "acquiring merit" at expense of the lower, while the lower has gratitude and respect for authority as its chief virtues.

(ii.) *The erection of the "benevolent" impulse into a virtue in and of itself tends to build up egoism in others.* The child who finds himself unremittingly the object of attention from others is likely to develop an exaggerated sense of the relative importance of his own *ego*. The chronic invalid, conspicuously the recipient of the conscious altruism of others, is happy in nature who avoids the slow growth of an insidious egoism. Men who are the constant subjects of abnegation on the part of their wives and female relatives rarely fail to develop a self-absorbed complacency and unconscious conceit.

(iii.) Undue emphasis upon altruism as a motive is quite likely to react to form a *peculiarly subtle egoism in the person who cultivates it*. Others cease to be *natural* objects of interest and regard, and are converted into excuses for the manifestation and nurture of one's own generous goodness. Underlying complacency with respect to social ills grows up because they afford an opportunity for developing and displaying this finest of virtues. In our interest in the maintenance of our own benign altruism we cease to be properly disturbed by conditions which are intrinsically unjust and hateful.[11] (iv.) As present circumstances amply

11. Measures of public or state activity in the extension, for example, of education (furnishing free text-books, adequate medi-

demonstrate, there is the danger that the erection of benevolence into a conscious principle in some things will serve to supply rich persons with a cloak for selfishness in other directions. Philanthropy is made an offset and compensation for brutal exploitation. A man who pushes to the breaking-point of legality aggressively selfish efforts to get ahead of others in business, squares it in his own self-respect and in the esteem of those classes of the community who entertain like conceptions, by gifts of hospitals, colleges, missions, and libraries.

Genuine and False Altruism.—These considerations may be met by the obvious retort that it is not true altruism, genuine benevolence, sincere charity, which we are concerned with in such cases. This is a true remark. We are not of course criticizing true but spurious interest in others. But why is it counterfeit? What is the nature of the genuine article? The danger is not in benevolence or altruism, but in that conception of them which makes them equivalent to regard for others *as others*, irrespective of a social situation to which all alike belong. There is nothing in the selfhood of others, because they are others, which gives it any supremacy over selfhood in oneself. Just as it is exclusiveness of objective ends, the ignoring of relations, which is objectionable in selfishness, so it is taking the part for the whole which is obnoxious in so-called altruism. To include in our view of consequences the needs and possibilities of others on the same basis as our own, is to take the only course which will give an adequate view of the situation. There is no situation into which these factors do not enter. To have a generous view of others is to have a larger world in which to act. To remember that they, like ourselves, are persons, are individuals who are centres of joy and suffering, of lack and of potentiality, is alone to have a just view of the conditions and issues of behavior. Quickened sympathy means liberality of intelligence and enlightened understanding.

The Social Sense versus Altruism.—There is a great difference in principle between modern philanthropy and the

---

cal inspection, and remedy of defects), are opposed by "good people" because there are "charitable" agencies for doing these things.

"charity" which assumes a superior and an inferior class. The latter principle tries to acquire merit by employing one's superior resources to lessen, or to mitigate, the misery of those who are fixed in a dependent status. Its principle, so far as others are concerned, is negative and palliative merely. The motive of what is vital in modern philanthropy is constructive and expansive because it looks to the well-being of society as a whole, not to soothing or rendering more tolerable the conditions of a class. It realizes the interdependence of interests: that complex and variegated interaction of conditions which makes it impossible for any one individual or "class" really to secure, to assure, its own good as a separate thing. Its aim is general social advance, constructive social reform, not merely doing something kind for individuals who are rendered helpless from sickness or poverty. Its aim is the equity of justice, not the inequality of conferring benefits. That the sight of the misery that comes from sickness, from insanity, from defective organic structure (as among the blind and deaf), from poverty that destroys hope and dulls initiative, from bad nutrition, should stimulate this general quickening of the social sense is natural. But just as the activities of the parent with reference to the welfare of a helpless infant are wisely directed in the degree in which attention is mainly fixed not upon weakness, but upon positive opportunities for growth, so the efforts of those whose activities, by the nature of circumstances, have to be especially remedial and palliative are most effective when centered on the social rights and possibilities of the unfortunate individuals, instead of treating them as separate individuals to whom, in their separateness, "good is to be done."

The best kind of help to others, whenever possible, is indirect, and consists in such modifications of the conditions of life, of the general level of subsistence, as enables them independently to help themselves.[12] Whenever conditions require purely direct and personal aid, it is best given when it proceeds from a natural social relationship, and not from

12. Compare Spencer's criticisms of Bentham's view of happiness as a social standard in contrast with his own ideal of freedom. See *Ethics*, Vol. I, pp. 162–68.

a motive of "benevolence" as a separate force.[13] The gift that pauperizes when proceeding from a philanthropist in his special capacity, is a beneficent acknowledgment of the relationships of the case when it comes from a neighbor or from one who has other interests in common with the one assisted.

The Private and the Social Self.—The contrast between the narrow or restrictive and the general or expansive good explains why evil presents itself as a selfish end in contrast with an authoritative, but faint, good of others. This is not, as we have seen, because regard for the good of self is inherently bad and regard for that of others intrinsically right; but because we are apt to identify the self with the habitual, with that to which we are best adjusted and which represents the customary occupation. Any moral crisis is thus fairly pictured as a struggle to overcome selfishness. The tendency under such circumstances is to contract, to secrete, to hang on to what is already achieved and possessed. The habitual self needs to go out of the narrowness of its accustomed grooves into the spacious air of more generous behavior.

§ 4. The Good as Self-Realization

We now come to the theory which attempts to do justice to the one-sided truths we have been engaged with, *viz.*, the idea that the moral end is *self-realization*. Like self-assertion in some respects, it differs in conceiving the self to be realized as universal and ultimate, involving the fulfillment of *all* capacities and the observance of *all* relations. Such a comprehensive self-realization includes also, it is urged, the truth of altruism, since the "universal self" is realized only when the relations that bind one to others are fulfilled. It avoids also the inconsistencies and defects of the notion of self-sacrifice for its own sake, while emphasizing that the present incomplete self must be denied for the sake of attainment of a more complete and final self. A discussion of this theory accordingly furnishes the means of gathering together and

13. See Addams, *Democracy and Social Ethics*, ch. ii.

summarizing various points regarding the rôle of the self in the moral life.

Ambiguity in the Conception.—Is self-realization the end? As we have had such frequent occasion to observe, "end" means either the consequences actually effected, the closing and completing phase of an act, or the aim held deliberately in view. Now realization of self is an end (though not the only end) in the former sense. Every moral act in its outcome marks a development or fulfillment of selfhood. But the very nature of right action forbids that the self should be the end in the sense of being the conscious aim of moral activity. For there is no way of discovering the nature of the self except in terms of objective ends which fulfill its capacities, and there is no *way* of realizing the self except as it is forgotten in devotion to these objective ends.

1. Self-Realization as Consequence of Moral Action.— Every good act realizes the selfhood of the agent who performs it; every bad act tends to the lowering or destruction of selfhood. This truth is expressed in Kant's maxim that every personality should be regarded as always an end, never as a means, with its implication that a wrong intent always reduces selfhood to the status of a mere tool or device for securing some end beyond itself—the self-indulgent man treating his personal powers as mere means to securing ease, comfort, or pleasure. It is expressed by ordinary moral judgment in its view that all immoral action is a sort of prostitution, a lowering of the dignity of the self to base ends. The destructive tendency of evil deeds is witnessed also by our common language in its conception of wrong as dissipation, dissoluteness, duplicity. The bad character is one which is shaky, empty, "naughty," unstable, gone to pieces, just as the good man is straight, solid, four-square, sound, substantial. This conviction that at bottom and in the end, in spite of all temporary appearance to the contrary, the right act effects a realization of the self, is also evidenced in the common belief that virtue brings its own bliss. No matter how much suffering from physical loss or from material and mental inconvenience or loss of social repute virtue may bring with it, the *quality of happiness* that accompanies devotion to the right end is so unique, so *invaluable*, that pains and discomforts do not weigh in the balance. It is indeed possible to state this truth in such an exaggerated perspective that it becomes false; but taken just for what it is, it acknowledges that whatever harm or loss a right act may bring to the self in some of its aspects, —even extending to destruction of the bodily self, —the inmost moral self finds fulfillment and consequent happiness in the good.

2. *Self-Realization as Aim of Moral Action.*—This realization of selfhood in the right course of action is, however, not *the* end of a moral act—that is, it is not the only end. The moral act is one which sustains a whole complex system of social values; one which keeps vital and progressive the industrial order, science, art, and the State. The patriot who dies for his country may find in that devotion his own supreme realization, but none the less the aim of his act is precisely that for which he performs it: the conservation of his nation. He dies *for* his country, not *for* himself. He is what he would be in dying for his country, not in dying for himself. To say that his conscious aim is self-realization is to put the cart before the horse. That his willingness to die for his country proves that his country's good is taken by him to constitute himself and his own good is true; but his aim is his country's good *as constituting* his self-realization, not the self-realization. It is impossible that genuine artistic creation or execution should not be accompanied with the joy of an expanding selfhood, but the artist who thinks *of* himself and allows a view of himself to intervene between his performance and its result, has the embarrassment and awkwardness of "self-consciousness," which affects for the worse his artistic product. And it makes little difference whether it is the thought of himself as materially profiting, or as famous, or as technical performer, or as benefiting the public, or as securing his own complete artistic culture, that comes in between. In any case, there is loss to the work, and loss in the very thing taken as end, namely, development of his own powers. The problem of morality, upon the intellectual side, is the discovery of, the finding of, the self, in the objective end to be striven for; and then upon the overt practical side, it is the losing of the self in the endeavor for the objective realization. This is the lasting truth in the con-

ception of self-abnegation, self-forgetfulness, disinterested interest.

The Thought of Self-Realization. — Since, however, the realization of selfhood, the strengthening and perfecting of capacity, is as matter of fact one phase of the objective end, it may, *at times*, be definitely present in thought as part of the foreseen consequences; and even, *at times*, may be the most prominent feature of the conceived results. The artist, for example a musician or painter, may practice for the sake of acquiring skill, that is, of developing capacity. In this case, the usual relationship of objective work and personal power is reversed; the product or performance being subordinated to the perfecting of power, instead of power being realized in the use it is put to. But the development of power is not conceived as a final end, but as *desirable because of an eventual more liberal and effective use*. It is matter of temporary emphasis. Something of like nature occurs in the moral life — not that one definitely rehearses or practices moral deeds for the sake of acquiring more skill and power. At times the effect upon the self of a deed becomes the conspicuously controlling element in the forecast of consequences. (See p. 343.) For example, a person may realize that a certain act is trivial in its effects upon others and in the changes it impresses upon the world; and yet he may hesitate to perform it because he realizes it would intensify some tendency of his own in such a way as, in the delicate economy of character, to disturb the proper balance of the springs to action. Or, on the other hand, the agent may apprehend that some consequences that are legitimate and important in themselves involve, in their attainment, an improper sacrifice of personal capacity. In such cases, the consideration of the effect upon self-realization is not only permissible, but imperative as *a part or phase of the total end*.

The Problem of Equating Personal and General Happiness. — Much moral speculation has been devoted to the problem of equating personal happiness and regard for the general good. Right moral action, it is assumed, consists especially of justice and benevolence, — attitudes which aim at the good of others. But, it is also assumed, a just and righteous order of the universe requires that the man who seeks the happiness of others should also himself be a happy man. Much ingenuity has been directed to explaining away and accounting for the seeming discrepancies: the cases where men not conspicuous for regard for others or for maintaining a serious and noble view of life seem to maintain a banking-credit on the side of happiness; while men devoted to others, men conspicuous for range of sympathetic affections, seem to have a debit balance. The problem is the more serious because the respective good and ill fortunes do not seem to be entirely accidental and external, but to come as results from the moral factors in behavior. It would not be difficult to build up an argument to show that while extreme viciousness or isolated egoism is unfavorable to happiness, so also are keenness and breadth of affections. The argument would claim that the most comfortable course of life is one in which the man cultivates enough intimacies with enough persons to secure for himself their support and aid, but avoids engaging his sympathies too closely in their affairs and entangling himself in any associations which would require self-sacrifice or exposure to the sufferings of others: a course of life in which the individual shuns those excesses of vice which injure health, wealth, and lessen the decent esteem of others, but also shuns enterprises of precarious virtue and devotion to high and difficult ends.

Real and Artificial Aspects of the Problem.—The problem thus put seems insoluble, or soluble only upon the supposition of some prolongation of life under conditions very different from those of the present, in which the present lack of balance between happiness and goodness will be redressed. *But the problem is insoluble because it is artificial.*[14]

14. Compare the following extreme words of Sumner (*Folkways*, p. 9): "The great question of world philosophy always has been, What is the real relation between happiness and goodness? It is only within a few generations that men have found courage to say there is none." But when Sumner, in the next sentence, says, "The whole strength of the notion that they are correlated is in the opposite experience which proves that no evil thing brings happiness," one may well ask what more relation any reasonable man would want. For it indicates that "goodness" consists in active interest in those things which really bring happiness; and while it by no means follows that this interest will *bring* even a preponderance of pleasure over pain to the person, it is always

It assumes a ready-made self and hence a ready-made type of satisfaction or happiness. It is not the business of moral theory to demonstrate the existence of mathematical equations, in this life or another one, between goodness and virtue. It is the business of men to develop such capacities and desires, such selves as render them capable of finding their own satisfaction, their invaluable value, in fulfilling the demands which grow out of their associated life. Such happiness may be short in duration and slight in bulk: but that it outweighs in quality all accompanying discomforts as well as all enjoyments which may have been missed by not doing something else, is attested by the simple fact that men do consciously choose it. Such a person has found *himself*, and has solved the problem in the only place and in the only way in which it can be solved: *in action*. To demand in advance of voluntary desire and deliberate choice that it be demonstrated that an individual shall get happiness in the measure of the rightness of his act, is to demand the obliteration of the essential factor in morality: the constant discovery, formation, and reformation of the self in the ends which an individual is called upon to sustain and develop in virtue of his membership in a social whole. The solution of the problem through the individual's voluntary identification of himself with social relations and aims is neither rare nor utopian. It is achieved not only by conspicuous social figures, but by multitudes of "obscure" figures who are faithful to the callings of their social relationships and offices. That the conditions of life for all should be enlarged, that wider opportunities and richer fields of activity should be opened, in order that happiness may be of a more noble and variegated sort, that those inequalities of status which lead men to find their advantage in disregard of others should be destroyed— these things are indeed necessary. But under the most ideal conditions which can be imagined, if there remain any moral element whatsoever, it will be only through personal deliberation and personal preference as to objective and social ends that the individual will discover and constitute himself,

---

open to him to *find* and *take* his dominant happiness in making this interest dominant in his life.

and hence discover the sort of happiness required as his good.

Our final word about the place of the self in the moral life is, then, that the problem of morality is the formation, out of the body of original instinctive impulses which compose the natural self, of a voluntary self in which socialized desires and affections are dominant, and in which the last and controlling principle of deliberation is the love of the objects which will make this transformation possible. If we identify, as we must do, the interests of such a character with the virtues, we may say with Spinoza that happiness is not the reward of virtue, but is virtue itself. What, then, are the virtues?

Literature

For asceticism, see Lecky, *History of European Morals.*

For self-denial, Mackenzie, *International Journal of Ethics,* Vol. V, pp. 273–95.

For egoism and altruism: Comte, *System of Positive Polity,* Vol. I, "Introductory Principles," ch. iii, and Vol. II, ch. ii; Spencer, *Principles of Ethics,* Vol. I, Part I, chs. xi–xiv; Stephen, *Science of Ethics,* ch. vi; Paulsen, *System of Ethics,* pp. 379–99; Sorley, *Recent Tendencies in Ethics;* Sidgwick, *Methods of Ethics* (1901), pp. 494–507.

For the doctrine of self-interest, see Mandeville, *Fable of the Bees;* Sidgwick, *Methods of Ethics* (1901), Book I, ch. vii, and Book II, ch. v; Stephen, *Science of Ethics,* ch. x; Martineau, *Types of Ethical Theory,* Part II, Book II, Branch I, ch. i; Fite, *Introductory Study,* ch. ii.

For historic development of sympathy, see Sutherland, *Origin and Growth of the Moral Instinct.*

For the doctrine of self-realization, see Aristotle, *Ethics;* Green, *Prolegomena to Ethics;* Seth, *Ethical Principles,* Part I, ch. iii; Bradley, *Ethical Studies,* Essay II; Fite, *Introductory Study,* ch. xi; Paulsen, *System of Ethics,* Book II, ch. i; Taylor, *International Journal of Ethics,* Vol. VI, pp. 356–71; Palmer, *The Field of Ethics,* and *The Nature of Goodness;* Calderwood, *Philosophical Review,* Vol. V, pp. 337–51; Dewey, *Philosophical Review,* Vol. II, pp. 652–64; Bryant, *Studies in Character,* pp. 97–117.

For the ethics of success, besides the writings of Nietzsche, see Plato, *Gorgias* and *Republic,* Book I, and Sumner, *Folkways,* ch. xx.

For the social self: Cooley, *Human Nature and the Social Order*, chs. v and vi; for the antagonistic self, chs. vii–ix.

For a general discussion of the Moral Self, see Bosanquet, *Psychology of the Moral Self*; Ladd, *Philosophy of Conduct*, ch. ix (see also ch. xviii on the Good Man).

Introductory

Definition of Virtue.—It is upon the self, upon the agent, that ultimately falls the burden of maintaining and of extending the values which make life reasonable and good. The worth of science, of art, of industry, of relationship of man and wife, parent and child, teacher and pupil, friend and friend, citizen and State, exists only as there are characters consistently interested in such goods. Hence any trait of character which makes for these goods is esteemed; it is given positive value; while any disposition of selfhood found to have a contrary tendency is condemned—has negative value. The habits of character whose effect is to sustain and spread the rational or common good are virtues; the traits of character which have the opposite effect are vices.

Virtue and Approbation; Vice and Condemnation.—The approbation and disapprobation visited upon conduct are never purely intellectual. They are also emotional and practical. We are stirred to hostility at whatever disturbs the order of society; we are moved to admiring sympathy of whatever makes for its welfare. And these emotions express themselves in appropriate conduct. To disapprove and dislike is to reprove, blame, and punish. To approve is to encourage, to aid, and support. Hence the judgments express the character of the one who utters them—they are traits of his conduct and character; and they react into the character of the agent upon whom they are directed. They are part of the process of forming character. The commendation is of the nature of a reward calculated to confirm the person in the right course of action. The reprobation is of the nature of punishment, fitted to dissuade the agent from the wrong course. This encouragement and blame are not necessarily of an external sort; the reward and the punishment may not be in material things. It is not from ulterior design that society esteems and respects those attributes of an agent which tend to its own peace and welfare; it is from natural, instinctive response to acknowledge whatever makes for its good. None the less, the social esteem, the honor which attend certain acts inevitably educate the individual who performs these acts, and they strengthen, emotionally and practically, his interest in the right. Similarly, there is an instinctive reaction of society against an infringement of its customs and ideals; it naturally "makes it hot" for any one who disturbs its values. And this disagreeable attention instructs the individual as to the consequences of his act, and works to hinder the formation of dispositions of the socially disliked kind.

Natural Ability and Virtue.—There is a tendency to use the term virtue in an abstract "moralistic" sense—a way which makes it almost Pharisaic in character. Hard and fast lines are drawn between certain traits of character labeled "virtues" and others called talents, natural abilities, or gifts of nature. Apart from deliberate or reflective nurture, modesty or generosity is no less and no more a purely natural ability than is good-humor, a turn for mechanics, or presence of mind. Every natural capacity, every talent or ability, whether of inquiring mind, of gentle affection or of executive skill, becomes a virtue when it is turned to account in supporting or extending the fabric of social values; and it turns, if not to vice at least to delinquency, when not thus utilized. The important habits conventionally reckoned virtues are barren unless they are the cumulative assemblage of a multitude of anonymous interests and capacities. Such natural aptitudes vary widely in different individuals. Their endowments and circumstances occasion and exact different virtues, and yet one person is not more or less virtuous than another because his virtues take a different form.

Changes in Virtues.—It follows also that the meaning, or content, of virtues changes from time to time. Their abstract form, the man's attitude towards the good, remains the same. But when institutions and customs change and natural abilities are differently stimulated and evoked, ends vary, and habits of character are differently esteemed both by the individual agent and by others who judge. No social group could be maintained without patriotism and chastity, but the actual meaning of chastity and patriotism is widely different in contemporary society from what it was in savage tribes or from what we may expect it to be five hundred years from now. Courage in one society may consist almost wholly in willingness to face physical danger and death in voluntary devotion to one's community; in another, it may be willingness to support an unpopular cause in the face of ridicule.

Conventional and Genuine Virtue.—When we take these social changes on a broad scale, in the gross, the point just made is probably clear without emphasis. But we are apt to forget that minor changes are going on all the while. The community's formulated code of esteem and regard and praise at any given time is likely to lag somewhat behind its practical level of achievement and possibility. It is more or less traditional, describing what used to be, rather than what are, virtues. The "respectable" comes to mean tolerable, passable, conventional. Accordingly the prevailing scheme of assigning merit and blame, while on the whole a mainstay of moral guidance and instruction, is also a menace to moral growth. Hence men must look behind the current valuation to the real value. Otherwise, mere conformity to custom is conceived to be virtue;[1] and the individual who deviates from custom in the interest of wider and deeper good is censured.

Moral Responsibility for Praise and Blame.—The practical assigning of value, of blame and praise, is a measure and exponent of the character of the one from whom it issues. In judging others, in commending and condemning, we judge ourselves. What we find to be praiseworthy and blameworthy is a revelation of our own affections. Very literally the measure we mete to others is meted to us. To be free in our attributions of blame is to be censorious and uncharitable; to be unresentful to evil is to be indifferent, or interested perhaps chiefly in one's own popularity, so that one avoids giving offense to others. To engage profusely in blame and approbation in speech without acts which back up or attack the ends verbally honored or condemned, is to have a perfunctory morality. To cultivate complacency and remorse

1. This is, of course, the point made in ch. 4 on "Customs or Mores," save that there the emphasis was upon the epoch of customary as distinct from the reflective morals, while here it is upon the customary factor in the present.

apart from effort to improve is to indulge in sentimentality. In short, to approve or to condemn is itself a moral act for which we are as much responsible as we are for any other deed.

Impossibility of Cataloguing Virtues.—These last three considerations: (1) the intimate connection of virtues with all sorts of individual capacities and endowments, (2) the change in types of habit required with change of social customs and institutions, (3) the dependence of judgment of vice and virtue upon the character of the one judging,[2] make undesirable and impossible a catalogued list of virtues with an exact definition of each. Virtues are numberless. Every situation, not of a routine order, brings in some special shading, some unique adaptation, of disposition.

Twofold Classification.—We may, however, classify the chief institutions of social life—language, scientific investigation, artistic production, industrial efficiency, family, local community, nation, humanity—and specify the types of mental disposition and interest which are fitted to maintain them flourishingly; or, starting from typical impulsive and instinctive tendencies, we may consider the form they assume when they become intelligently exercised habits. A virtue may be defined, accordingly, either as *the settled intelligent identification of an agent's capacity with some aspect of the reasonable or common happiness*; or, as *a social custom or tendency organized into a personal habit of valuation*. From the latter standpoint, truthfulness is the social institution of language maintained at its best pitch of efficiency through the habitual purposes of individuals; from the former, it is an instinctive capacity and tendency to communicate emotions and ideas directed so as to maintain social peace and prosperity. In like fashion, one might catalogue all forms of social custom and institution on one hand; and all the species and varieties of individual equipment on the other, and enumerate a virtue for each. But the performance is so formal as not to amount to much.

2. This fact might be employed to reenforce our prior conclusion that moral rules, classifications, etc., are not of final importance but are of value in clarifying and judging individual acts and situations. Not the rule, but the use which the person makes of the rule in approving and disapproving himself and others, is the significant thing.

Aspects of Virtue.—Any virtuous disposition of character exhibits, however, certain main traits, a consideration of which will serve to review and summarize our analysis of the moral life.

I. The Interest Must be Entire or Whole-hearted.—The whole self, without division or reservation, must go out into the proposed object and find therein its own satisfaction. Virtue is integrity; vice duplicity. Goodness is straight, right; badness is crooked, indirect. Interest that is incomplete is not interest, but (so far as incomplete) indifference and disregard. This totality of interest we call affection, love; and love is the fulfilling of the law. A grudging virtue is next to no virtue at all; thorough heartiness in even a bad cause stirs admiration, and lukewarmness in every direction is always despised as meaning lack of character. Surrender, abandonment, is of the essence of identification of self with an object.

II. The Interest Must be Energetic and Hence Persistent. —One swallow does not make a summer nor a sporadic right act a virtuous habit. Fair-weather character has a proverbially bad name. Endurance through discouragement, through good repute and ill, weal and woe, tests the vigor of interest in the good, and both builds up and expresses a formed character.

III. The Interest Must be Pure or Sincere.—Honesty is, doubtless, the best policy, and it is better a man should be honest from policy than not honest at all. If genuinely honest from considerations of prudence, he is on the road to learn better reasons for honesty. None the less, we are suspicious of a man if we believe that motives of personal profit are the only stay of his honesty. For circumstances might arise in which, in the exceptional case, it would be clear that personal advantage lay in dishonesty. The motive for honesty would hold in most cases, in ordinary and routine circumstances and in the glare of publicity, but not in the dark of secrecy, or in the turmoil of disturbed circumstance. The eye single to the good, the "disinterested interest" of moralists, is required. The motive that has to be coaxed or coerced to its work by some promise or threat is imperfect.

Cardinal or Indispensable Aspects of Virtue.—Bearing in mind that we are not attempting to classify various acts or habits, but only to state traits essential to all morality, we have the "cardinal virtues" of moral theory. As whole-hearted, as complete interest, any habit or attitude of character involves justice and love; as persistently active, it is courage, fortitude, or vigor; as unmixed and single, it is temperance—in its classic sense. And since no habitual interest can be integral, enduring, or sincere, save as it is reasonable, save, that is, as it is rooted in the deliberate habit of viewing the part in the light of the whole, the present in the light of the past and future, interest in the good is also wisdom or conscientiousness:—interest in the discovery of the true good of the situation. Without this interest, all our interest is likely to be perverted and misleading—requiring to be repented of.

Wisdom, or (in modern phrase) conscientiousness, is the nurse of all the virtues. Our most devoted courage is in the will to know the good and the fair by unflinching attention to the painful and disagreeable. Our severest discipline in self-control is that which checks the exorbitant pretensions of an appetite by insisting upon knowing it in its true proportions. The most exacting justice is that of an intelligence which gives due weight to each desire and demand in deliberation before it is allowed to pass into overt action. That affection and wisdom lie close to each other is evidenced by our language; thoughtfulness, regard, consideration for others, recognition of others, attention to others.

§ 1. Temperance

The English word "temperance" (particularly in its local association with agitation regarding use of intoxicating liquors) is a poor substitute for the Greek *sophrosyne* which, through the Latin *temperantia*, it represents. The Athenian Greek was impressed with the fact that just as there are lawless, despotically ruled, and self-governed communities, so there are lawless, and servile, and self-ruled individuals. Whenever there is a self-governed soul, there is a happy blending of the authority of reason with the force of appetite. The individual's diverse nature is tempered into a living harmony of desire and intelligence. Reason governs not as a tyrant from without, but as a guide to which the impulses and emotions are gladly responsive. Such a well-attuned nature, as far from asceticism on one side as from random indulgence on the other, represented the ideal of what was fair and graceful in character, an ideal embodied in the notion of *sophrosyne*. This was a *whole-mindedness* which resulted from the happy furtherance of all the elements of human nature under the self-accepted direction of intelligence. It implied an *aesthetic* view of character; of harmony in structure and rhythm in action. It was the virtue of judgment exercised in the estimate of pleasures: —since it is the agreeable, the pleasant, which gives an end excessive hold upon us.

Roman Temperantia.—The Roman conceived this virtue under the term *temperantia*, which conveys the same idea, but accommodated to the Roman genius. It is connected with the word *tempus*, time, which is connected also with a root meaning divide, distribute; it suggests a consecutive orderliness of behavior, a freedom from excessive and reckless action, first this way, and then that. It means seemliness, decorum, decency. It was "moderation," not as quantity of indulgence, but as a moderating of each act in a series by the thought of other and succeeding acts—keeping each in sequence with others in a whole. The idea of time involves time to think; the sobering second thought expressed in seriousness and gravity. The negative side, the side of restraint, of inhibition, is strong, and functions for the consistent calm and gravity of life.

Christian Purity.—Through the Christian influence, the connotation which is marked in the notion of control of sexual appetite, became most obvious—*purity*. Passion is not so much something which disturbs the harmony of man's nature, or which interrupts its orderliness, as it is something which defiles the purity of spiritual nature. It is the grossness, the contamination of appetite which is insisted upon, and temperance is the maintenance of the soul spotless and unsullied.

Negative Phase: Self-control.—A negative aspect of self-control, restraint, inhibition is everywhere involved.[3] It is not, however, desire, or appetite, or passion, or impulse, which

3. Less is said on this point because this phase of the matter has been covered in the discussion of self-denial in the previous chapter. See pp. 328–32.

has to be checked (much less eliminated); it is rather that tendency of desire and passion so to engross attention as to destroy our sense of the other ends which have a claim upon us. This moderation of pretension is indispensable for every desire. In one direction, it is modesty, humility; the restraint of the tendency of self-conceit to distort the relative importance of the agent's and others' concerns; in another direction, it is chastity; in another, "temperance" in the narrower sense of that word—keeping the indulgence of hunger and thirst from passing reasonable bounds; in another, it is calmness, self-possession—moderation of the transporting power of excitement; in yet another, it is discretion, imposing limits upon the use of the hand, eye, or tongue. In matters of wealth, it is decent regulation of display and ostentation. In general, it is prudence, control of the present impulse and desire by a view of the "long run," of proximate by remote consequences.[4]

Positive Phase: Reverence.—The tendency of dominant passion is to rush us along, to prevent our thinking. The one thing that desire emphasizes is, for the time being, the most important thing in the universe. This is necessary to heartiness and effectiveness of interest and behavior. But it is important that the thing which thus absorbs desire should be an end capable of justifying its power to absorb. This is possible only if it expresses the entire self. Otherwise capacities and desires which will occur later will be inconsistent and antagonistic, and conduct will be unregulated and unstable. The underlying idea in "temperance" is then a care of details for the sake of the whole course of behavior of which they are parts; heedfulness, painstaking devotion. Laxness in conduct means carelessness; lack of regard for the whole life permits temporary inclinations to get a sway that the outcome will not justify. In its more striking forms, we call this care and respect *reverence*; recognition of the unique, invaluable worth embodied in any situation or act of life, a recognition which checks that flippancy of surrender to momentary excitement coming from a superficial view of be-

4. Strict hedonism would tend to reduce all virtue to prudence—the calculation of subtler and remoter consequences and the control of present behavior by its outcome.

havior. A sense of momentous issues at stake means a sobering and deepening of the mental attitude. The consciousness that every deed of life has an import clear beyond its immediate, or first significance, attaches dignity to every act. To live in the sense of the larger values attaching to our passing desires and deeds is to be possessed by the virtue of temperance.

Control of Excitement.—What hinders such living is, as we have seen, the exaggerated intensity, the lack of proportion and perspective, with which any appetite or desire is likely to present itself. It is this which moralists of all ages have attacked under the name of pleasure—the alluring and distracting power of the momentarily agreeable. Seeing in this the enemy which prevents the rational survey of the whole field and the calm, steady insight into the true good, it is hardly surprising that moralists have attacked "pleasure" as the source of every temptation to stray from the straight path of reason. But it is not pleasure, it is one form of pleasure, the *pleasure of excitement*, which is the obstacle and danger.[5] Every impulse and desire marks a certain disturbance in the order of life, an exaltation above the existing level, a pressure beyond its existing limit. To give way to desire, to let it grow, to taste to the full its increasing and intensifying excitement, is the temptation. The bodily appetites of hunger and thirst and sex, with which we associate the grossest forms of indulgence and laxity, exemplify the principle of expanding waves of organic stimulation. But so also do many of the subtler forms of unrestraint or intemperate action. The one with a clever and lively tongue is tempted to let it run away with him; the vain man feeds upon the excitement of a personality heightened by display and the notice of others; the angry man, even though he knows he will later regret his surrender, gives away to the sense of

5. Says Hazlitt, "The charm of criminal life, like that of savage life, consists in liberty, in hardship, in danger, and in the contempt of death: in one word, in *extraordinary excitement*" (Essay on Bentham). But this is equally true in principle (though not in degree) of every temptation to turn from the straight and narrow path. Virtue seems dull and sober, uninteresting, in comparison with the increasing excitation of some desire. There are as many forms of excitement as there are individual men.

expanding power coincident with his discharge of rage. The shiftless person finds it easier to take chances and let consequences take care of themselves, while he enjoys local and casual stimulations. Trivialities and superficialities entangle us in a flippant life, because each one as it comes promises to be "thrilling," while the very fear that this promise will not be kept hurries us on to new experiences. To think of alternatives and consequences is not "thrilling," but serious.

Necessity of Superior Interest.—Now calculation of the utilitarian type is not adequate to deal with this temptation. Those who are prone to reflection upon results are just those who are least likely to be carried away by excitement—unless, as is the case with some specialists, thinking is itself the mode of indulgence in excitement.[6] With those who are carried away habitually by some mode of excitement, the disease and the incapacity to take the proffered remedy of reflection are the same thing. Only some *other* passion will accomplish the desired control. With the Greeks, it was aesthetic passion, love of the grace and beauty, the rhythm and harmony, of a self-controlled life. With the Romans, it was the passion for dignity, power, honor of personality, evidenced in rule of appetite. Both of these motives remain among the strong allies of ordered conduct. But the passion for purity, the sense of something degrading and foul in surrender to the base, an interest in something spotless, free from adulteration, are, in some form or other, the chief resource in overcoming the tendency of excitement to usurp the governance of the self.[7]

§ 2. *Courage*[8] *or Persistent Vigor*

While love of excitement allures man from the path of reason, fear of pain, dislike to hardship, and laborious effort,

6. There is something of the nature of gambling, of taking chances on future results for the sake of present stimulation, in all unrestraint or intemperate action. And the reflection of the specialist—that is, the one whose reflection is not subjected to responsible tests in social behavior—is a more or less exciting adventure—a "speculation."
7. In the last words of Spinoza's *Ethics*, "No one delights in the good because he curbs his appetites, but because we delight in the good we are able to curb our lusts."
8. What has been said about Self-assertion, in the last chapter, anticipates in some measure what holds of this virtue.

hold him back from entering it. Dislike of the disagreeable inhibits or contracts the putting forth of energy, just as liking for agreeable stimulation discharges and exhausts it. Intensity of active interest in the good alone subdues that instinctive shrinking from the unpleasant and hard which slackens energy or turns it aside. Such energy of devotion is courage. Its etymological connection with the Latin word for *heart*, suggests a certain abundant spontaneity, a certain overflow of positive energy; the word was applied to this aspect of virtue when the heart was regarded as literally (not metaphorically) the seat of vital impulse and abundant forcefulness.

Courage and the Common Good.—One of the problems of early Greek thought was that of discriminating courage as virtuous from a sort of animal keenness and alacrity, easily running into recklessness and bravado. It was uniformly differentiated from mere overflow of physical energy by the fact that it was exhibited in support of some common or social good. It bore witness to its voluntary character by abiding in the face of threatened evil. Its simplest form was patriotism—willingness to brave the danger of death in facing the country's enemy from love of country. And this basic largeness of spirit in which the individual sinks considerations of personal loss and harm in allegiance to an objective good remains a cardinal aspect of all right disposition.

Courage is Preeminently the Executive Side of Every Virtue.—The good will, as we saw, means endeavor, effort, towards certain ends; unless the end stirs to strenuous exertion, it is a sentimental, not a moral or practical end. And endeavor implies obstacles to overcome, resistance to what diverts, painful labor. It is the degree of threatened harm— in spite of which one does not swerve—which measures this depth and sincerity of interest in the good.

Aspects of Interest in Execution.—Certain formal traits of courage follow at once from this general definition. In its onset, willingness in behalf of the common good to endure attendant private evils is alacrity, promptness. In its abiding and unswerving devotion, it is constancy, loyalty, and faithfulness. In its continual resistance to evil, it is fortitude, patience, perseverance, willingness to abide for justification an ultimate issue. The *totality* of commitment of self to the good is decision and firmness. Conviction and resolution accompany all true moral endeavor. These various dimensions (intensity, duration, extent, and fullness) are, however, only differing expressions of one and the same attitude of vigorous, energetic identification of agency with the object.

Goodness and Effectiveness.—It is the failure to give due weight to this factor of morality (the "works" of theological discussion) which is responsible for the not uncommon idea that moral goodness means loss of practical efficacy. When inner disposition is severed from outer action, wishing divorced from executive willing, morality is reduced to mere harmlessness; outwardly speaking, the best that can then be said of virtue is that it is innocent and innocuous. Unscrupulousness is identified with energy of execution; and a minute and paralyzing scrupulosity with goodness. It is in reaction from such futile morality that the gospel of force and of shrewdness of selecting and adapting means to the desired end, is preached and gains hearers—as in the Italy of the Renaissance[9] in reaction against mediaeval piety, and again in our own day (see *ante*, p. 336).

Moral Courage and Optimism.—A characteristic modern development of courageousness is implied in the phrase "moral courage,"—as if all genuine courage were not moral. It means devotion to the good in the face of the customs of one's friends and associates, rather than against the attacks of one's enemies. It is willingness to brave for sake of a new idea of the good the unpopularity that attends breach of custom and convention. It is this type of heroism, manifested in integrity of memory and foresight, which wins the characteristic admiration of to-day, rather than the outward heroism of bearing wounds and undergoing physical dangers. It is *attention* upon which the stress falls.[10] This supplies, perhaps, the best vantage point from which to survey optimism and pessimism in their direct moral bearings. The individual whose pursuit of the good is colored by honest recognition of existing and threatening evils is almost always charged with being a pessimist; with cynical delight in dwelling upon what

9. See Sumner, *Folkways*, ch. xx.
10. Upon this point see James, *Psychology*, Vol. II, pp. 561–67, and Royce, *World and Individual*, Second Series, pp. 354–60.

is morbid, base, or sordid; and he is urged to be an "optimist," meaning in effect to conceal from himself and others evils that obtain. Optimism, thus conceived, is a combination of building rosy-colored castles in the air and hiding, ostrich-like, from actual facts. As a general thing, it will be those who have some interest at stake in evils remaining unperceived, and hence unremedied, who most clamor in the cause of such "optimism." Hope and aspiration, belief in the supremacy of good in spite of all evil, belief in the realizability of good in spite of all obstacles, are necessary inspirations in the life of virtue. The good can never be demonstrated to the senses, nor be proved by calculations of personal profit. It involves a radical venture of the will in the interest of what is unseen and prudentially incalculable. But such optimism of *will*, such determination of the man that, so far as his choice is concerned, only the good shall be recognized as real, is very different from a sentimental refusal to look at the realities of the situation just as they are. In fact a certain intellectual pessimism, in the sense of a steadfast willingness to uncover sore points, to acknowledge and search for abuses, to note how presumed good often serves as a cloak for actual bad, is a necessary part of the moral optimism which actively devotes itself to making the right prevail. Any other view reduces the aspiration and hope, which are the essence of moral courage, to a cheerful animal buoyancy; and, in its failure to see the evil done to others in its thoughtless pursuit of what it calls good, is nextdoor to brutality, to a brutality bathed in the atmosphere of sentimentality and flourishing the catchwords of idealism.

§ 3. *Justice*

In Ethical Literature Justice Has Borne at Least Three Different Senses. — (1) In its widest sense, it means righteousness, uprightness, rectitude. It sums up morality. It is not *a* virtue, but it is virtue. The just act is the *due* act; justice is fulfillment of obligation. (2) This passes over into fairness, equity, impartiality, honesty in all one's dealing with others. (3) The narrowest meaning is that of *vindication* of right through the administration of law.[11] Since Aristotle's time (and following his treatment) this has been divided into (i.) the *distributive*, having to do with the assignment of honor, wealth, etc., in proportion to desert, and (ii.) the *corrective*, vindicating the law against the transgressor by effecting a requital, redress, which restores the supremacy of law.

A Thread of Common Significance Runs through These Various Meanings.—The rational good means a comprehensive or complete end, in which are harmoniously included a variety of special aims and values. The just man is the man who takes in the whole of a situation and reacts to it in its wholeness, not being misled by undue respect to some particular factor. Since the general or inclusive good is a common or social good, reconciling and combining the ends of a multitude of private or particular persons, justice is the preeminently social virtue: that which maintains the due order of individuals in the interest of the comprehensive or social unity.

Justice, as equity, fairness, impartiality, honesty, carries the recognition of the whole over into the question of right distribution and apportionment among its parts. The equitable judge or administrator is the one who makes no unjustifiable distinctions among those dealt with. A fair price is one which recognizes the rights of both buyer and seller. An honest man is the one who, with respect to whatever he has to distribute to others and to receive from them, is desirous of giving and taking just what belongs to each party concerned. The fair-minded man is not bribed by pleasure into giving undue importance to some element of good nor coerced by fear of pain into ignoring some other. He *distributes* his attention, regard, and attachment according to the reasonable or objective claims of each factor.

Justice and Sympathy or Love.—The most significant questions regarding justice are as to its connection with love and with condemnation and punishment. It is a common notion that justice is harsh or hard in its workings and that it requires to be supplemented, if not replaced, by mercy. Taken literally this would mean that justice is not just in

11. This receives more attention in ch. 21 of Part III.

its workings. The truth contained is that what is frequently regarded as justice is not justice, but an imperfect substitute for it. When a legal type of morality is current, justice is regarded as the working of some fixed and abstract law; it is the law as law which is to be reverenced; it is law as law whose majesty is to be vindicated. It is forgotten that the nobility and dignity of law are due to the place of law in securing the order involved in the realization of human happiness. Then the law instead of being a servant of the good is put arbitrarily above it, as if man was made for law, not law for man. The result is inevitably harshness; indispensable factors of happiness are ruthlessly slighted, or ruled out; the loveliness and grace of behavior responding freely and flexibly to the requirements of unique situations are stiffened into uniformity. The formula *summum jus summa injuria* expresses the outcome when abstract law is insisted upon without reference to the needs of concrete cases. Under such conditions, there arises a demand for tempering the sternness of justice with mercy, and supplementing the severity of law with grace. This demand means that the neglected human values shall be restored into the idea of what is just.

"Social Justice."—Our own time has seen a generous quickening of the idea of social justice due to the growth of love, or philanthropy, as a working social motive. In the older scheme of morals, justice was supposed to meet all the necessary requirements of virtue; charity was doing good in ways not obligatory or strictly exacted. Hence it was a source of peculiar merit in the doer, a means of storing up a surplus of virtue to offset vice. But a more generous sense of inherent social relationships binding the aims of all into one comprehensive good, which is the result of increase of human intercourse, democratic institutions, and biological science, has made men recognize that the greater part of the sufferings and miseries which afford on the part of a few the opportunity for charity (and hence superior merit), are really social inequities, due to causes which may be remedied. That justice requires radical improvement of these conditions displaces the notion that their effects may be here and there palliated by the voluntary merit of morally superior individuals. The change illustrates, on a wide scale, the transforma-

tion of the conception of justice so that it joins hands with love and sympathy. That human nature should have justice done it under all circumstances is an infinitely complicated and difficult requirement, and only a vision of the capacities and accomplishments of human beings rooted in affection and sympathy can perceive and execute justly.

Transformation of Punitive Justice.—The conception of punitive or corrective justice is undergoing the same transformation. Aristotle stated the rule of equity in the case of wrongdoing as an arithmetical requital: the individual was to suffer according to his deed. Later, through conjunction with the idea of a divine judge inflicting retribution upon the sinner, this notion passed into the belief that punishment is a form of justice restoring the balance of disturbed law by inflicting suffering upon the one who has done wrong. The end and aim of punishment was retribution, bringing back to the agent the evil consequences of his own deed. That punishment *is* suffering, that it inevitably involves pain to the guilty one, there can be no question; this, whether the punishment is externally inflicted or is in the pangs of conscience, and whether administered by parent, teacher, or civil authority. But that suffering is for the sake of suffering, or that suffering can in any way restore or affect the violated majesty of law, is a different matter.

What erring human nature deserves or merits, it is just it should have. But in the end, a moral agent deserves to *be* a moral agent; and hence deserves that punishments inflicted should be *corrective*, not merely retributive. Every wrongdoer should have his due. But what is his due? Can we measure it by his past alone; or is it due every one to regard him as a man with a future as well? as having possibilities for good as well as achievements in bad? Those who are responsible for the infliction of punishment have, as well as those punished, to meet the requirements of justice; and failure to employ the means and instrumentalities of punishment in a way to lead, so far as possible, the wrongdoer to reconsideration of conduct and re-formation of disposition, cannot shelter itself under the plea that it vindicates law. Such failure comes rather from thoughtless custom; from a lazy unwillingness to find better means; from an admixture of pride with lack of sympathy for others; from a desire to maintain things as they are rather than go to the causes which generate criminals.

§ 4. *Wisdom or Conscientiousness*

As we have repeatedly noted, the heart of a voluntary act is its intelligent or deliberate character. The individual's *intelligent* concern for the good is implied in his sincerity, his faithfulness, and his integrity. Of all the habits which constitute the character of an individual, the habit of *judging* moral situations is the most important, for this is the key to the *direction* and to the *remaking* of all other habits. When an act is overt, it is irretrievably launched. The agent has no more control. The moral life has its centre in the periods of suspended and postponed action, when the energy of the individual is spent in recollection and foresight, in severe inquiry and serious consideration of alternative aims. Only through reflection can habits, however good in their origin and past exercise, be readapted to the needs of the present; only through reflection can impulses, not yet having found direction, be guided into the haven of a reasonable happiness.

Greek Emphasis upon Insight or Wisdom.—It is not surprising that the Greeks, the first seriously to inquire into the nature of behavior and its end or good, should have eulogized *wisdom*, *insight*, as the supreme virtue and the source of all the virtues. Now, indeed, it seems paradoxical to say with Socrates that ignorance is the only vice; that man is bad not voluntarily, from deliberate choice, but only from ignorance. But this is largely because we discriminate between different kinds of knowledge as the Greeks did not, and as they had no occasion for doing. We have a second-hand knowledge, a knowledge from books, newspapers, etc., which was practically non-existent even in the best days of Athens. Knowledge meant to them something more personal; something like what we call a "realizing sense"; an intimate and well-founded conviction. To us knowledge suggests information about what others have found out, and hence is more remote in its meaning. Greek knowledge was mostly directly connected with the affairs of their common associated life. The very words for knowledge and art, understanding and skill, were hardly separated. Knowledge was knowledge about the city, its traditions, literature, history, customs, purposes, etc. Their astronomy was connected with their civic religion; their geography with their own topography; their mathematics with their civil and military pursuits. Now we have immense bodies of impersonal knowledge, remote from direct bearing upon affairs. Knowledge has accordingly subdivided itself into theoretical or scientific and practical or moral. We use the term knowledge usually only for the first kind; hence the Socratic position seems gratuitously paradoxical. But under the titles of *conscience* and *conscientiousness* we preserve the meaning which was attached to the term knowledge. It is not paradoxical to say that unconscientiousness is the fundamental vice, and genuine conscientiousness is guarantee of all virtue.

Conscientiousness.—In this change from Greek wisdom to modern conscientiousness there have been some loss and some gain. The loss lies in a certain hardening of the idea of insight and deliberation, due to the 'isolation of the moral good from the other goods of life. The good man and the bad man have been endowed with the same faculty; and this faculty has been treated as automatically delivering correct conclusions. On the other hand, modern conscientiousness contains less of the idea of intellectual accomplishment, and more of the idea of interest in finding out the good in conduct. "Wisdom" tended to emphasize achieved insight; knowledge which was proved, guaranteed, and unchangeable. "Conscientiousness" tends rather to fix attention upon that voluntary attitude which is interested in *discovery.*

This implies a pretty radical change in wisdom as virtue. In the older sense it is an attainment; something possessed. In the modern, it resides in the active desire and effort, in pursuit rather than in possession. The *attainment* of knowledge varies with original intellectual endowment; with opportunity for leisurely reflection; with all sorts of external conditions. Possession is a *class* idea and tends to mark off a moral aristocracy from a common herd. Since the activities of the latter must be directed, on this assumption, by attained knowledge, its practical outcome is the necessity of the regulation of their conduct by the wisdom possessed by the superior class. When, however, the morally important thing is the desire and effort to discover the good, every one is on the same plane, in spite of differences in intellectual endowment and in learning.

Moral knowing, as a fundamental or cardinal aspect of virtue, is then the completeness of the interest in good exhibited in effort to discover the good. Since knowing involves two factors, a direct and an indirect, conscientiousness involves both *sensitiveness* and *reflectiveness*.[12]

(*1*) *Moral Sensitiveness.*—The individual who is not directly aware of the presence of values needing to be perpetuated or achieved, in the things and persons about him, is hard and callous or tough. A "tender" conscience is one which is immediately responsive to the presentation of good and evil. The modern counterpart to the Socratic doctrine that ignorance is the root of vice, is that being morally "cold" or "dead," being indifferent to moral distinctions, is the most hopeless of all conditions. One who cares, even if he cares in the wrong way, has at least a spring that may be touched; the one who is just irresponsive offers no leverage for correction or improvement.

(*2*) *Thoughtfulness.*—While the possession of such an immediate, unreflective responsiveness to elements of good and bad must be the mainstay of moral wisdom, the character which lies back of these intuitive apprehensions must be thoughtful and serious-minded. There is no individual who, however morally sensitive, can dispense with cool, calm reflection, or whose intuitive judgments, if reliable, are not largely the funded outcome of prior thinking. Every voluntary act is intelligent: i.e., includes an idea of the end to be reached or the consequences to accrue. Such ends are ideal in the sense that they are present to thought, not to sense. But special ends, because they are limited, are not what we mean by ideals. They are specific. With the growth of the habit of reflection, agents become conscious that the values of their particular ends are not circumscribed, but extend far beyond the special case in question; so far indeed that their range of influence cannot be foreseen or defined. A kindly act

12. Compare what was said concerning the intuitive and the discursive factors in moral knowledge in ch. 16.

may not only have the particular consequence of relieving present suffering, but may make a difference in the entire life of its recipient, or may set in radically different directions the interest and attention of the one who performs it. These larger and remoter values in any moral act transcend the end which was consciously present to its doer. The person has always to aim at something definite, but as he becomes aware of this penumbra or atmosphere of far-reaching ulterior values the meaning of his special act is thereby deepened and widened. An act is outwardly temporary and circumstantial, but its meaning is permanent and expansive. The act passes away; but its significance abides in the increment of meaning given to further growth. To live in the recognition of this deeper meaning of acts is to live in the ideal, in the only sense in which it is profitable for man to dwell in the ideal.

Our "ideals," our types of excellence, are the various ways in which we figure to ourselves the outreaching and ever-expanding values of our concrete acts. Every achievement of good deepens and quickens our sense of the inexhaustible value contained in every right act. With achievement, our conception of the possible goods of life increases, and we find ourselves called to live upon a still deeper and more thoughtful plane. An ideal is not some remote allexhaustive goal, a fixed *summum bonum* with respect to which other things are only means. It is not something to be placed in contrast to the direct, local, and tangible quality of our actual situations, so that by contrast these latter are lightly esteemed as insignificant. On the contrary, an ideal is the conviction that each of these special situations carries with it a final value, a meaning which in itself is unique and inexhaustible. To set up "ideals" of perfection which are other than the serious recognition of the possibilities of development resident in each concrete situation, is in the end to pay ourselves with sentimentalities, if not with words, and meanwhile it is to direct thought and energy away from the situations which need and which welcome the perfecting care of attention and affection.

Thoughtfulness and Progress. — This sense of wider values than those definitely apprehended or definitely attained is a constant warning to the individual not to be content with an accomplishment. Conscientiousness takes more and more the form of interest in improvement, in progress. Conscientiousness as sensitiveness may rest upon the plane of already secured satisfactions, upon discriminating with accuracy their quality and degree. As thoughtfulness, it will always be on the lookout for the better. The good man not only measures his acts by a standard, but he is concerned to revise his standard. His sense of the ideal, of the undefinable because ever-expanding value of special deeds, forbids his resting satisfied with any formulated standard, for the very formulation gives the standard a technical quality, while the good can be maintained only in enlarging excellence. The highest form of conscientiousness is interest in constant progress.

Love and Courage Required for Thoughtfulness.—We may close this chapter by repeating what we have already noted, that genuine moral knowledge involves the affections and the resolute will as well as the intelligence. We cannot know the varied elements of value in the lives of others and in the possibilities of our own, save as our affections are strong. Every narrowing of love, every encroachment of egoism, means just so much blindness to the good. The man who pleads "good motives" as excuse for acts which injure others is always one whose absorption in himself has wrought harm to his powers of perception. Every widening of contact with others, every deepening of the level of sympathetic acquaintance, magnifies in so much vision of the good. Finally, the chief ally of moral thoughtfulness is the resolute courage of willingness to face the evil for the sake of the good. Shrinking from apprehension of the evil to others consequent upon our behavior, because such realization would demand painful effort to change our own plans and habits, maintains habitual dimness and narrowness of moral vision.

Literature

Upon the principle of virtue in general, see Plato, *Republic*, 427–43; Aristotle, *Ethics*, Books II and IV; Kant, *Theory of Ethics* (Abbott's trans.), pp. 164–82, 305, 316–22; Green,

Prolegomena, pp. 256–314 (and for conscientiousness, 323–37); Paulsen, *System of Ethics,* pp. 475–82; Alexander, *Moral Order and Progress* (1891), pp. 242–53; Ladd, *Philosophy of Conduct,* chs. x and xiv; Stephen, *Science of Ethics,* ch. v; Spencer, *Principles of Ethics,* Vol. II, pp. 3–34 and 263–76; Sidgwick, *Methods of Ethics* (1901), pp. 2–5 and 9–10; Rickaby, *Aquinas Ethicus,* Vol. I, pp. 155–95; Mezes, *Ethics,* chs. ix and xvi.

For natural ability and virtue: Hume, *Treatise,* Part II, Book III, and "Inquiry," Appendix IV; Bonar, *Intellectual Virtues.*

For discussions of special virtues: Aristotle, *Ethics,* Book III, and Book VII, chs. i–x; for justice: Aristotle, *Ethics,* Book V; Rickaby, *Moral Philosophy,* pp. 102–8, and *Aquinas Ethicus* (see Index); Paulsen, *System of Ethics,* pp. 599–637; Mezes, *Ethics,* ch. xiii; Mill, *Utilitarianism,* ch. v; Sidgwick, *Methods of Ethics* (1901), Book III, ch. v, and see Index; also criticism of Spencer in his *Lectures on the Ethics of Green, Spencer, and Martineau,* pp. 272–302; Spencer, *Principles of Ethics,* Vol. II; Stephen, *Science of Ethics,* ch. v.

For benevolence, see Aristotle, *Ethics,* Books VIII–IX (on friendship); Rickaby, *Moral Philosophy,* pp. 237–44, and *Aquinas Ethicus* (see charity and almsgiving in Index); Paulsen, *System,* chs. viii and x of Book III; Mezes, *Ethics,* ch. xii; Sidgwick, *Methods of Ethics* (1901), Book III, ch. iv; Spencer, *Principles of Ethics,* Vol. II; see also the references under sympathy and altruism at end of ch. xviii. Courage and temperance are discussed in chs. x and xi of Mezes; in pp. 484–504 of Paulsen; pp. 327–36 of Sidgwick, *Methods of Ethics* (1901); ch. xi of Ladd's *Philosophy of Conduct.*

Part III   The World of Action

General Literature for Part III

Addams, *Democracy and Social Ethics*, 1902, *Newer Ideals of Peace*, 1907; Santayana, *The Life of Reason*, Vol. II, 1905; Bergemann, *Ethik als Kulturphilosophie*, 1904, especially pp. 154–304; Wundt, *Ethics*, Vol. III, *The Principles of Morality and the Departments of the Moral Life* (trans. 1901); Spencer, *Principles of Ethics*, 1893, Vol. II, *Principles of Sociology*, 1882, Vol. I, Part II; Leslie, *Essays in Political and Moral Philosophy*, 1879; 2d ed., 1888; Bosanquet, *Philosophical Theory of the State*, 1899; Willoughby, *Social Justice*, 1900; Cooley, *Human Nature and the Social Order*, 1902; Paulsen, *System der Ethik*, 5th ed., 1900, Book IV; Runze, *Praktische Ethik*, 1891; Janet, *Histoire de la Science Politique dans ses Rapports avec la Morale*, 3d ed., 1887; Plato, *The Republic*; Aristotle, *Ethics*, Book V, and *Politics* (trans. by Welldon, 1883); Hegel, *Philosophy of Right* (pub. 1821, trans. by Dyde, 1896); Mackenzie, *An Introduction to Social Philosophy*, 1890; Dunning, *History of Political Theories* (1902, 1905); Stein, *Die Sociale Frage im Licht der Philosophie*, 1897.

20. SOCIAL ORGANIZATION AND THE INDIVIDUAL

Object of Part and Chapter.—The history of morals manifests a twofold movement. It reveals, on one side, constantly increasing stress on *individual* intelligence and affection. The transformation of customary into reflective morals is the change from "Do those things which our kin, class, or city do" to "Be a person with certain habits of desire and deliberation." The moral history of the race also reveals constantly growing emphasis upon the *social* nature of the objects and ends to which personal preferences are to be devoted. While the agent has been learning that it is his personal attitude which counts in his deeds, he has also learnt that there is no attitude which is exclusively private in scope, none which does not need to be socially valued or judged. Theoretic analysis enforces the same lesson as history. It tells us that moral quality *resides in* the habitual dispositions of an agent; and that it *consists of* the tendency of these dispositions to secure (or hinder) values which are sociably shared or sharable.

In Part One we sketched the historical course of this development; in Part Two we traced its theoretic analysis. In the present and concluding Part, our purpose is to consider the distinctively social aspects of morality. We shall consider how social institutions and tendencies supply value to the activities of individuals, impose the conditions of the formation and exercise of their desires and aims; and, especially, how they create the peculiarly urgent problems of contemporary moral life. The present chapter will take up the general question, that of the relation of social organization to individual life.

§ 1. Growth of Individuality
Through Social Organizations

From one point of view, historic development represents the increasing liberation of individual powers from rigid social control. Sir John Lubbock remarks: "No savage is free. All over the world his daily life is regulated by a complicated and apparently most inconvenient set of customs (as forcible as laws), of quaint prohibitions and privileges." Looked at from another point of view, emancipation from one sort of social organization means initiation into some other social order; the individual is liberated from a small and fixed (customary) social group, to become a member of a larger and progressive society. The history of setting free individual power in desire, thought, and initiative is, upon the whole, the history of the formation of more complex and extensive social organizations. Movements that look like the disintegration of the order of society, when viewed with reference to what has preceded them, are factors in the construction of a new social order, which allows freer play to individuals, and yet increases the number of social groupings and the depth of social combinations.

This fact of historical development is well summed up in the following words of Hobhouse, set forth as a summary of a comprehensive survey of the historic development of law and justice, of the family including the status of women and children, of the relations between communities, and between classes, the rich and the poor. He says:

Amid all the variety of social institutions and the ebb and flow of historical change, it is possible in the end to detect a double movement, marking the transition from the lower to the higher levels of civilized law and custom. On the one hand, the social order is strengthened and extended. . . . On this side the individual human being becomes more and more subject to social constraint, and, as we have frequently seen, the changes making for the tightening of the social fabric may diminish the rights which the individual or large classes of individuals can claim. . . . In this relation liberty and order become opposed. But the opposition is not essential. From the first the individual relies on social forces to maintain him in his rights, and in the higher form of social organization we have seen order and liberty drawing together again. . . . The best ordered community is that which gives most scope to its component members to make the best of themselves, while the "best" in human nature is that which contributes to the harmony and onward movement of society. . . . The responsible human being, man or woman, is the centre of modern ethics as of modern law, free so far as custom and law are concerned to make his own life. . . . The social nature of man is not diminished either on the side of its needs or its duties by the fuller recognition of personal rights. The difference is that, so far as rights and duties are conceived as attaching to human beings as such, they become universalized, *and are therefore the care of society as a whole rather than of any partial group organization.*[1]

With this statement may be compared the words of Green and Alexander. According to Green, moral progress consists in the *extension* of the area or range of persons whose common good is concerned, and in the deepening or *intensification* in the individual of his social interest: "the settled disposition on each man's part to make the most and best of humanity in his own person and in the person of others."[2] Alexander's formulae for moral growth are the "laws of differentiation and of comprehension." The first means diversification, specialization, differentiating the powers of an individual with increased refinement of each. The law of comprehension means the steady enlargement of the size and scope of the social group (as from clan to modern national state) with its increased complexity of ways in which men are brought into contact with one another.[3]

Social Life Liberates and Directs Individual Energies. — Breadth in extent of community life goes hand in hand with multiplication of the stimuli which call out an individual's powers. Diversification of social activities increases opportunities for his initiative and endeavor. Narrow and meagre social life means limitation of the scope of activities in which its members may engage. It means little occasion for the exercise of deliberation and choice, without which character is both immature and fossilized; it means, in short, restricted personality. But a rich and varied society, one which liberates powers otherwise torpid and latent, also exacts that they

1. Hobhouse, *Morals in Evolution*, Vol. I, pp. 367–68, italics not in original.
2. Green, *Prolegomena to Ethics*, p. 262; see chs. iii and iv of Book III.
3. Alexander, *Moral Order and Progress* (1891), pp. 384–98.

be employed in ways consistent with its own interests. A society which is extensive and complex would dissolve in anarchy and confusion were not the activities of its various members upon the whole mutually congruent. The world of action is a world of which the individual is one limit, and humanity the other; between them lie all sorts of associative arrangements of lesser and larger scope, families, friendships, schools, clubs, organizations for making or distributing goods, for gathering and supplying commodities; activities politically organized by parishes, wards, villages, cities, counties, states, nations. Every maladjustment in relations among these institutions and associated activities means loss and friction in the relations between individuals; and thereby introduces defect, division, and restriction into the various powers which constitute an individual. All harmonious cooperation among them means a fuller life and greater freedom of thought and action for the individual person.

Order and Laws. — The world of action as a scene of organized activities going on in regular ways[4] thus presents a public or common order and authority, with its established modes of operation, its laws. Organized institutions, from the more permanent to the more casual, with their orderly rules of conduct, are not, of course, prior to individual activity; for their elements are individual activities related in certain ways. But with respect to *any one* individual in his separate or distributive capacity, there is a genuine and important sense in which the institution comes first. A child is born into an already existing family with habits and beliefs already formed, not indeed rigid beyond readaptation, but with their own order (arrangements). He goes to schools which have their established methods and aims; he gradually assumes membership in business, civic, and political organizations, with their own settled ways and purposes. Only in participating in already fashioned systems of conduct does he apprehend his own powers, appreciate their worth and realize their possibilities, and achieve for himself a controlled and orderly body of physical and mental habits. He finds the

4. This does not of course exclude change and reform. It means that, so far as a society is organized, these changes themselves occur in regular and authorized ways.

value and the principles of his life, his satisfaction and his norms of authority, in being a member of associated groups of persons and in playing his part in their maintenance and expansion.

The Social and the Moral.—In customary society, it does not occur to any one that there is a difference between what he ought to do, i.e., the moral, and what those about him customarily do, i.e., the social. The socially established *is* the moral. Reflective morality brings with it, as we have seen, a distinction. A thoughtfully minded person reacts against certain institutions and habits which obtain in his social environment; he regards certain ideas, which he frames himself and which are not embodied in social habits, as more moral than anything existing about him. Such reactions against custom and such projections of new ideas are necessary if there is to be progress in society. But unfortunately it has often been forgotten that this distinctly *personal* morality, which takes its stand against some established usage, and which, therefore, for the time being has its abode only in the initiative and effort of an individual, is simply the means of *social* reconstruction. It is treated as if it were an end in itself, and as if it were something higher than any morality which is or can be socially embodied.

At some periods, this view has led to a monastic retreat from all social affairs for the sake of cultivating personal goodness. At other times, it has led to the political indifference of the Cynic and Stoic. For ages, it led to a morality of "other worldliness"; to the belief that true goodness can be attained only in another kind of life and world—a belief which carried with it relative contempt and neglect of concrete social conditions in this life. Social affairs at best were only "secular" and temporal, and, in contrast with the eternal and spiritual salvation of the individual's own soul, of little account. After the Renaissance and the Protestant Revolt, this kind of moral individualism persisted in different forms. Among the hedonists, it took the form of assuming that while social arrangements are of very great importance, their importance lies in the fact that they hinder or help individuals in the attainment of their own private pleasures. The transcendentalists (such as Kant) asserted that, since morality is wholly a matter of the inner motive, of the personal attitude towards the moral law, social conditions are wholly external. Good or evil lies wholly inside the individual's own will. Social institutions may help or hinder the outward *execution* of moral purpose; they may be favorable or hostile to the successful outward display of virtue. But they have nothing to do with originating or developing the moral purpose, the Good Will, and hence, in themselves, are lacking in moral significance. Thus Kant made a sharp and fast distinction between *morality*, appertaining solely to the individual's own inner consciousness, and *legality*, appertaining to the social and political conditions of outward behavior. Social institutions and laws may indeed regulate men's outer acts. So far as men externally conform, their conduct is legal. But laws cannot regulate or touch men's motives, which alone determine the morality of their behavior.

We shall not repeat here our prior criticisms of hedonism and utilitarianism in order to point out the falsity of this division of moral action into unrelated inner (or private) and outer (or social) factors. We may recall to memory, however, that Kant himself virtually passed beyond his own theory of moral individualism in insisting upon the promotion of a "Kingdom of Ends," in which every person is to be treated as an end in himself. We may recall that the later utilitarians (such as Mill, Leslie Stephen, Bain, and Spencer) insisted upon the *educative* value of social institutions, upon their importance in forming certain interests and habits in the individual. Thus social arrangements were taken out of the category of mere means to private good, and made the necessary factors and conditions of the development of an individuality which should have a reasonable and just conception of its own nature and of its own good. We may also enumerate some of the more fundamental ways in which social institutions determine individual morality.

1. Apart from the social medium, the individual would never "know himself"; he would never become acquainted with his own needs and capacities. He would live the life of a brute animal, satisfying as best he could his most urgent appetites of hunger, thirst, and sex, but being, as regards even that, handicappd in comparison with other animals.

And, as we have already seen, the wider and the richer the social relationships into which an individual enters, the more fully are his powers evoked, and the more fully is he brought to recognize the possibilities latent in them. It is from seeing noble architecture and hearing harmonious music that the individual learns to know to what his own constructive and rhythmic tendencies, otherwise blind and inchoate, may come. It is from achievement in industrial, national, and family life that he is initiated into perception of his own energy, loyalty, and affection.

2. Social conditions not only evoke what is latent, and bring to conscious recognition what is blind, but they select, encourage, and confirm certain tendencies at the expense of others. They enable the individual to discriminate the better and the worse among his tendencies and achievements. There is no limit in the power of society to awaken and strengthen this habit of discrimination, of choice after comparison, in its individual members. A small social group with fixed habits, a clan, a gang, a narrow sect, a dogmatic party, will restrict the formation of critical powers—i.e., of conscientiousness or moral thoughtfulness. But an individual who *really* becomes a member of modern society, with its multiple occupations, its easy intercourse, its free mobility, its rich resources of art and science, will have only too many opportunities for reflective judgment and personal valuation and preference. *The very habits of individual moral initiative, of personal criticism of the existent order, and of private projection of a better order, to which moral individualists point as proofs of the purely "inner" nature of morality, are themselves effects of a variable and complex social order.*

The Moral Value of the State.—If then we take modern social life in its broadest extent, as including not only what has become institutionalized and more or less fossilized, but also what is still growing (forming and re-forming), we may justly say that it is as true of progressive as of stationary society, that the moral and the social are one. The virtues of the individual in a progressive society are more reflective, more critical, involve more exercise of comparison and selection, than in customary society. But they are just as socially conditioned in their origin and as socially directed in their manifestation.

In rudimentary societies, customs furnish the highest ends of achievement; they supply the principles of social organization and combination; and they form binding laws whose breach is punished. The moral, political, and legal are not differentiated. But village communities and city-states, to say nothing of kingdoms and empires and modern national States, have developed special organs and special regulations for maintaining social unity and public order. Small groups are usually firmly welded together and are exclusive. They have a narrow but intense social code: —like a patriarchal family, a gang, a social set, they are clannish. But when a large number of such groups come together within a more inclusive social unity, some institution grows up to represent the interests and activities of the whole as against the narrow and centrifugal tendencies of the constituent factors. A society is then *politically* organized; and a true public order with its comprehensive laws is brought into existence. The moral importance of the development of this public point of view, with its extensive common purposes and with a general will for maintaining them, can hardly be overestimated. Without such organization, society and hence morality would remain sectional, jealous, suspicious, unfraternal. Sentiments of intense cohesion within would have been conjoined with equally strong sentiments of indifference, intolerance, and hostility to those without. In the wake of the formation of States have followed more widely cooperative activities, more comprehensive and hence more reasonable principles of judgment and outlook. The individual has been emancipated from his relative submergence in the local and fixed group, and set upon his own feet, with varied fields of activity open to him in which to try his powers, and furnished with principles of judging conduct and projecting ideals which in theory, at least, are as broad as the possibilities of humanity itself.

§ 2. *Responsibility and Freedom*

The more comprehensive and diversified the social order, the greater the responsibility and the freedom of the individual. His freedom is the greater, because the more numerous are the effective stimuli to action, and the more varied and the more certain the ways in which he may fulfill his powers. His responsibility is greater because there are more demands for considering the consequences of his acts; and more agencies for bringing home to him the recognition of consequences which affect not merely more persons individually, but which also influence the more remote and hidden social ties.

Liability.—Freedom and responsibility have a relatively superficial and negative meaning and a relatively positive central meaning. In its external aspect, responsibility is *liability.* An agent is free to act; yes, but—. He must stand the consequences, the disagreeable as well as the pleasant, the social as well as the physical. He may do a given act, but if so, let him look out. His act is a matter that concerns others as well as himself, and they will prove their concern by calling him to account; and if he cannot give a satisfactory and credible account of his intention, subject him to correction. Each community and organization informs its members what it regards as obnoxious, and serves notice upon them that they have to answer if they offend. The individual then is (1) likely or liable to have to explain and justify his behavior, and is (2) liable or open to suffering consequent upon inability to make his explanation acceptable.

Positive Responsibility.—In this way the individual is made aware of the stake the community has in his behavior; and is afforded an opportunity to take that interest into account in directing his desires and making his plans. If he does so, he is a responsible person. The agent who does not take to heart the concern which others show that they have in his conduct, will note his liability only as an evil to which he is exposed, and will take it into consideration only to see how to escape or evade it. But one whose point of view is sympathetic and reasonable will recognize the justice of the community interest in his performances; and will recognize the value to him of the instruction contained in its assertions of its interest. Such an one responds, answers, to the social demands made; he is not merely called to answer. He holds himself responsible for the consequences of his acts; he does not wait to be held liable by others. When society looks for responsible workmen, teachers, doctors, it does not mean merely those whom it may call to account; it can do that in any case. It wants men and women who habitually form their purposes after consideration of the social consequences of their execution. Dislike of disapprobation, fear of penalty, play a part in generating this responsive habit; but fear, operating directly, occasions only cunning or servility. Fused, through reflection, with other motives which prompt to action, it helps bring about that apprehensiveness, or susceptibility to the rights of others, which is the essence of responsibility, which in turn is the sole *ultimate* guarantee of social order.

The Two Senses of Freedom.—In its external aspect, freedom is negative and formal. It signifies freedom *from* subjection to the will and control of others; exemption from bondage; release from servitude; capacity to act without being exposed to direct obstructions or interferences from others. It means a clear road, cleared of impediments, for action. It contrasts with the limitations of prisoner, slave, and serf, who have to carry out the will of others.

Effective Freedom.—Exemption from restraint and from interference with overt action is only a condition, though an absolutely indispensable one, of effective freedom. The latter requires (1) positive control of the resources necessary to carry purposes into effect, possession of the means to satisfy desires; and (2) mental equipment with the trained powers of initiative and reflection requisite for free preference and for circumspect and far-seeing desires. The freedom of an agent who is merely released from direct external obstructions is formal and empty. If he is without resources of personal skill, without control of the tools of achievement, he must inevitably lend himself to carrying out the directions and ideas of others. If he has not powers of deliberation and invention, he must pick up his ideas casually and superficially from the suggestions of his environment and appropriate the notions which the interests of some class insinuate into his mind. If he have not powers of intelligent self-control, he will be in bondage to appetite, enslaved to routine, imprisoned within the monotonous round of an imagery flowing from illiberal interests, broken only by wild forays into the illicit.

Legal and Moral.—Positive responsibility and freedom may be regarded as moral, while liability and exemption are legal and political. A particular individual at a given time is possessed of certain secured resources in execution and certain formed habits of desire and reflection. In so far, he is positively free. Legally, his sphere of activity may be very much wider. The laws, the prevailing body of rules which define existing institutions, would protect him in exercising claims and powers far beyond those which he can actually put forth. He is exempt from interference in travel, in reading, in hearing music, in pursuing scientific research. But if he has neither material means nor mental cultivation to enjoy these legal possibilities, mere exemption means little or nothing. It does, however, create a moral demand that the practical limitations which hem him in should be removed; that practical conditions should be afforded which will enable him effectively to take advantage of the opportunities formally open. Similarly, at any given time, the liabilities to which an individual is actually held come far short of the accountability to which the more conscientious members of society hold themselves. The morale of the individual is in advance of the formulated morality, or legality, of the community.

Relation of Legal to Moral.—It is, however, absurd to separate the legal and the ideal aspects of freedom from one another. It is only as men are held liable that they become responsible; even the conscientious man, however much in some respects his demands upon himself exceed those which would be enforced against him by others, still needs in other respects to have his unconscious partiality and presumption steadied by the requirements of others. He needs to have his judgment balanced against crankiness, narrowness, or fanaticism, by reference to the sanity of the common standard of his times. It is only as men are exempt from external obstruction that they become aware of possibilities, and are awakened to demand and strive to obtain more positive freedom. Or, again, it is the possession by the more favored individuals in society of an effectual freedom to do and to enjoy things with respect to which the masses have only a formal and legal freedom, that arouses a sense of inequity, and that stirs the social judgment and will to such reforms of law, of administration and economic conditions as will transform the empty freedom of the less favored individuals into constructive realities.

§ 3. Rights and Obligations

The Individual and Social in Rights and Obligations.— That which, taken at large or in a lump, is called freedom breaks up in detail into a number of specific, concrete abilities to act in particular ways. These are termed *rights*. Any right includes within itself in intimate unity the individual and social aspects of activity upon which we have been insisting. As a capacity for exercise of power, it resides in and proceeds from some special agent, some individual. As exemption from restraint, a secured release from obstruction, it indicates at least the permission and sufferance of society, a tacit social assent and confirmation; while any more positive and energetic effort on the part of the community to guarantee and safeguard it, indicates an active acknowledgment on the part of society that the free exercise by individuals of the power in question is positively in its own interest. Thus a right, individual in residence, is social in origin and intent. The social factor in rights is made explicit in the demand that the power in question be exercised in certain ways. A right is never a claim to a wholesale, indefinite activity, but to a *defined* activity; *to one carried on*, that is, *under certain conditions*. This limitation constitutes the *obligatory* phases of every right. The individual is free; yes, that is his right. But he is free to act only according to certain regular and established conditions. That is the obligation imposed upon him. He has a right to use public roads, but he is obliged to turn in a certain way. He has a right to use his property, but he is obliged to pay taxes, to pay debts, not to harm others in its use, and so on.

*Correspondence of Rights and Obligations.—*Rights and obligations are thus strictly correlative. This is true both in their external employment and in their intrinsic natures. Externally the individual is under obligation to use his right in a way which does not interfere with the rights of others. He is free to drive on the public highways, but not to exceed a certain speed, and on condition that he turns to right or left as the public order requires. He is entitled to the land which he has bought, but this possession is subject to conditions of public registration and taxation. He may use his property, but not so that it menaces others or becomes a nuisance. Absolute rights, if we mean by absolute those not relative to any social order and hence exempt from any social restriction, there are none. But rights correspond even more intrinsically to obligations. The right is itself a social outcome: it is the individual's in so far as he is himself a social member not merely physically, but in his habits of thought and feeling. He is under obligation to use his rights in social ways. The more we emphasize the free right of an individual to his property, the more we emphasize what society has done for him: the avenues it has opened to him for acquiring; the safeguards it has put about him for keeping; the wealth achieved by others which he may acquire by exchanges themselves socially buttressed. So far as an individual's own merits are concerned these opportunities and protections are "unearned increments," no matter what credit he may deserve for initiative and industry and foresight in using them. The only fundamental anarchy is that which regards rights as private monopolies, ignoring their social origin and intent.

Classes of Rights and Obligations.—We may discuss freedom and responsibility with respect to the social organization which secures and enforces them; or from the standpoint of the individual who exercises and acknowledges them. From the latter standpoint, rights are conveniently treated as physical and mental: not that the physical and mental can be separated, but that emphasis may fall primarily on control of the conditions required to execute ideas and intentions, or upon the control of the conditions involved in their personal formation and choice. From the standpoint of the public order, rights and duties are civil and political. We shall consider them in the next chapter in connection with the organization of society in the State. Here we consider rights as inhering in an individual in virtue of his membership in society.

I. Physical Rights.—These are the rights to the free unharmed possession of the body (the rights to life and limb), exemption from homicidal attack, from assault and battery, and from conditions that threaten health in more obscure ways; and positively, the right to free movement of the body, to use its members for any legitimate purpose, and the right to unhindered locomotion. Without the exemption, there is no security in life, no assurance; only a life of constant fear and uncertainty, of loss of limb, of injury from others, and of death. Without some positive assurance, there is no chance of carrying ideas into effect. Even if sound and healthy and extremely protected, a man lives a slave or prisoner. Right to the control and use of physical conditions of life takes effect then in property rights, command of the natural tools and materials which are requisite to the maintenance of the body in a due state of health and to an effective and competent use of the person's powers. These physical rights to life, limb, and property are so basic to all achievement and capability that they have frequently been termed "natural rights." They are so fundamental to the existence of personality that their insecurity or infringement is a direct menace to the social welfare. The struggle for human liberty and human responsibility has accordingly been more acute at this than at any other point. Roughly speaking, the history of personal liberty is the history of the efforts which have safeguarded the security of life and property and which have emancipated bodily movement from subjection to the will of others.

Unsolved Problems: War and Punishment.—While history marks great advance, especially in the last four or five centuries, as to the negative aspect of freedom or release from direct and overt tyranny, much remains undone on the positive side. It is at this point of free physical control that all conflicts of rights concentrate themselves. While the limitation by war of the right to life may be cited as evidence for the fact that even this right is not absolute but is socially conditioned, yet that kind of correspondence between individual activity and social well-being which exacts exposure to destruction as its measure, is too suggestive of the tribal morality in which the savage shows his social nature by participation in a blood feud, to be satisfactory. Social organization is clearly defective when its constituent portions are so set at odds with one another as to demand from individuals their death as their best service to the community. While one may cite capital punishment to enforce, as if in large type, the fact that the individual holds even his right to life subject to the social welfare, the moral works the other way to underline the failure of society to socialize its members, and its tendency to put undesirable results out of sight and mind rather than to face responsibility for causes. The same limitation is seen in methods of imprisonment, which, while supposed to be protective rather than vindictive, recognize only in a few and sporadic cases that the sole sure protection of society is through education and correction of individual character, not by mere physical isolation under harsh conditions.

Security of Life.—In civilized countries the blood feud, infanticide, putting to death the economically useless and the aged, have been abolished. Legalized slavery, serfdom, the subjection of the rights of wife and child to the will of husband and father, have been done away with. But many modern industries are conducted with more reference to financial gain than to life, and the annual roll of killed, injured, and diseased in factory and railway practically equals the list of dead and wounded in a modern war.[5] Most of these accidents are preventable. The willingness of parents on one side and of employers on the other, conjoined with the indifference of the general public, makes child-labor an effective substitute for exposure of children and other methods of infanticide practiced by savage tribes. Agitation for old-age pensions shows that faithful service to society for a lifetime is still inadequate to secure a prosperous old age.

Charity and Poverty.—Society provides assistance and remedial measures, poorhouses, asylums, hospitals. The exceedingly poor are a public charge, supported by taxes as well as by alms. Individuals are not supposed to die from starvation nor to suffer without any relief or assistance from

5. It is stated, upon good authority, that a street railway system in a large American city declined to adopt an improved fender, which made it practically impossible to kill persons, because the annual cost would be $5,000 more than the existing expense for damages. This same system declined to adopt improved brakes which would reduce accidents to life and limb; and it was discovered that one of its directors was largely interested in the manufacture of the old brakes.

physical defects and disease. So far, there is growth in positive provision for the right to live. But the very necessity for
such extensive remedial measures shows serious defects farther back. It raises the question of social responsibility for
the causes of such wholesale poverty and widespread misery.
Taken in conjunction with the idleness and display of the
congested rich, it raises the question how far we are advanced beyond barbarism in making organic provision for an
effective, as distinct from formal, right to life and movement.
It is hard to say whether the heavier indictment lies in the
fact that so many shirk their share of the necessary social
labor and toil, or in the fact that so many who are willing
to work are unable to do so, without meeting recurrent crises
of unemployment, and except under conditions of hours,
hygiene, compensation, and home conditions which reduce to
a low level the positive rights of life. The social order protects the property of those who have it; but, although historic
conditions have put the control of the machinery of production in the hands of a comparatively few persons, society
takes little heed to see that great masses of men get even that
little property which is requisite to secure assured, permanent, and properly stimulating conditions of life. Until there
is secured to and imposed upon all members of society the
right and the duty of work in socially serviceable occupations, with due return in social goods, rights to life and free
movement will hardly advance much beyond their present
largely nominal state.

II. *Rights to Mental Activity.*—These rights of course
are closely bound up with rights to physical well-being and
activity. The latter would have no meaning were it not that
they subserve purposes and affections; while the life of mind
is torpid or remote, dull or abstract, save as it gets impact in
physical conditions and directs them. Those who hold that
the limitations of physical conditions have no *moral* signification, and that their improvement brings at most an increase of more or less materialistic comfort, not a moral
advance, fail to note that the development of concrete purposes and desires is dependent upon so-called outward conditions. These conditions affect the execution of purposes
and wants; and this influence reacts to determine the further

arrest or growth of needs and resolutions. The sharp and unjustifiable antithesis of spiritual and material in the current
conception of moral action leads many well-intentioned people to be callous and indifferent to the moral issues involved in physical and economic progress. Long hours of
excessive physical labor, joined with unwholesome conditions
of residence and work, restrict the growth of mental activity,
while idleness and excess of physical possession and control
pervert mind, as surely as these causes modify the outer and
overt acts.

Freedom of Thought and Affection.—The fundamental
forms of the right to mental life are liberty of judgment and
sympathy. The struggle for spiritual liberty has been as prolonged and arduous as that for physical freedom. Distrust of
intelligence and of love as factors in concrete individuals has
been strong even in those who have proclaimed most vigor-
ously their devotion to them as abstract principles. Disbelief
in the integrity of mind, assertion that the divine principles
of thought and love are perverted and corrupt in the individual, have kept spiritual authority and prestige in the
hands of the few, just as other causes have made material
possessions the monopoly of a small class. The resulting
restriction of knowledge and of the tools of inquiry have
kept the masses where their blindness and dullness might be
employed as further evidence of their natural unfitness for
personal illumination by the light of truth and for free direction of the energy of moral warmth.[6] Gradually, however,
free speech, freedom of communication and intercourse, of
public assemblies, liberty of the press and circulation of
ideas, freedom of religious and intellectual conviction (commonly called freedom of conscience), of worship, and to
some extent the right to education, to spiritual nurture, have
been achieved. In the degree the individual has won these
liberties, the social order has obtained its chief safeguard
against explosive change and intermittent blind action and
reaction, and has got hold of the method of graduated and
steady reconstruction. Looked at as a mere expedient, liberty

6. Said Emerson: "If a man is sick, is unable, is mean-spirited and
   odious, it is because there is so much of his nature which is
   unlawfully withholden from him."

of thought and expression is the most successful device ever hit upon for reconciling tranquillity with progress, so that peace is not sacrificed to reform nor improvement to stagnant conservatism.[7]

Right and Duty of Education.—It is through education in its broadest sense that the right of thought and sympathy become effective. The final value of all institutions is their educational influence; they are measured morally by the occasions they afford and the guidance they supply for the exercise of foresight, judgment, seriousness of consideration, and depth of regard. The family, the school, the church, art, especially (to-day) literature, nurture the affections and imagination, while schools impart information and inculcate skill in various forms of intellectual technique. In the last one hundred years, the right of each individual to spiritual self-development and self-possession, and the interest of society as a whole in seeing that each of its members has an opportunity for education, have been recognized in publicly maintained schools with their ladder from kindergarten through the college to the engineering and professional school. Men and women have had put at their disposal the materials and tools of judgment; have had opened to them the wide avenues of science, history, and art that lead into the larger world's culture. To some extent negative exemption from arbitrary restriction upon belief and thought has been developed into positive capacities of intelligence and sentiment.

Restrictions from Inadequate Economic Conditions.— Freedom of thought in a developed constructive form is, however, next to impossible for the masses of men so long as their economic conditions are precarious, and their main problem is to keep the wolf from their doors. Lack of time, hardening of susceptibility, blind preoccupation with the machinery of highly specialized industries, the combined

---

7. Recent suppression by the police in the larger American cities of public meetings called to discuss unemployment or other matters deemed by some dangerous to vested interests, shows that the value of free speech as a "safety-valve" has not even yet been thoroughly learned. It also shows how the victories of freedom in the past have to be fought and won over again under new conditions, if they are to be kept alive.

apathy and worry consequent upon a life maintained just above the level of subsistence, are unfavorable to intellectual and emotional culture. Intellectual cowardice, due to apathy, laziness, and vague apprehension, takes the place of despotism as a limitation upon freedom of thought and speech. Uncertainty as to security of position, the welfare of a dependent family, close men's mouths from expressing their honest convictions, and blind their minds to clear perception of evil conditions. The instrumentalities of culture— churches, newspapers, universities, theatres—themselves have economic necessities which tend to make them dependent upon those who can best supply their needs. The congestion of poverty on one side and of "culture" on the other is so great that, in the words of a distinguished economist, we are still questioning "whether it is really impossible that all should start in the world with a fair chance of leading a cultured life free from the pains of poverty and the stagnating influences of a life of excessive mechanical toil."[8] We provide free schools and pass compulsory education acts, but actively and passively we encourage conditions which limit the mass of children to the bare rudiments of spiritual nurture.

Restriction of Educational Influences.—Spiritual resources are practically as much the possession of a special class, in spite of educational advance, as are material resources. This fact reacts upon the chief educative agencies— science, art, and religion. Knowledge in its ideas, language, and appeals is forced into corners; it is overspecialized, technical, and esoteric because of its isolation. Its lack of intimate connection with social practice leads to an intense and elaborate over-training which increases its own remoteness. Only when science and philosophy are one with literature, the art of successful communication and vivid intercourse, are they liberal in effect; and this implies a society which is already intellectually and emotionally nurtured and alive. Art itself, the embodiment of ideas in forms which are socially contagious, becomes what it is so largely, a development of technical skill, and a badge of class differences.

8. Marshall, *Principles of Economics.*

Religious emotion, the quickening of ideas and affections by recognition of their inexhaustible signification, is segregated into special cults, particular days, and peculiar exercises, and the common life is left relatively hard and barren.

In short, the limitations upon freedom both of the physical conditions and the mental values of life are at bottom expressions of one and the same divorce of theory and practice,—which makes theory remote, sterile, and technical, while practice remains narrow, harsh, and also illiberal. Yet there is more cause for hope in that so much has been accomplished, than for despondency because mental power and service are still so limited and undeveloped. The intermixture and interaction of classes and nations are very recent. Hence the opportunities for an effective circulation of sympathetic ideas and of reasonable emotions have only newly come into existence. Education as a public interest and care, applicable to all individuals, is hardly more than a century old; while a conception of the richness and complexity of the ways in which it should touch any one individual is hardly half a century old. As society takes its educative functions more seriously and comprehensively into account, there is every promise of more rapid progress in the future than in the past. For education is most effective when dealing with the immature, those who have not yet acquired the hard and fixed directing forms of adult life; while, in order to be effectively employed, it must select and propagate that which is common and hence typical in the social values that form its resources, leaving the eccentric, the partial, and exclusive gradually to dwindle. Upon some generous souls of the eighteenth century there dawned the idea that the cause of the indefinite improvement of humanity and the cause of the little child are inseparably bound together.

Literature

Kant, *Philosophy of Law*, 1796 (trans. by Hastie, 1887); Fichte, *The Science of Rights*, 1796 (trans. by Kroeger, 1869); Rousseau, *Social Contract*, 1762 (trans. by Tozer, 1895); Bonar,

Philosophy and Political Economy, 1893; Stephen, *Science of Ethics*, ch. iii (on Social Motives); Caird, *Social Philosophy of Comte*, 1885; Sidgwick, *Practical Ethics*, 1898, Essay on Public Morality; Sidgwick, *Elements of Politics*, 1891, ch. iv on Individualism, vi on Contract, x on Socialistic Interferences, xiii on Law and Morality; Maine, *Ancient Law*, 1861, Pollock's ed., 1906, chs. iii and iv on law of nature and equity; Leslie, *Essays in Political and Moral Philosophy*, 1879; 2d ed., 1888; Rickaby, *Political and Moral Essays*, 1902; Hobhouse, *Morals in Evolution*, Vol. II, ch. vii (on the general relation of the social and the moral). On the development of rights to life, limb, and freedom of movement, see Westermarck, chs. xiv–xxii, and Sumner, *Folkways*, chs. vi, vii, and viii; Hobhouse, Vol. I, ch. vii (on slavery); Spencer, *Ethics*, Vol. II, Part IV. For charity, see Loch on Charity and Charities, *Encyclopædia Britannica*; Uhlhorn, *Christian Charity in the Ancient Church*; Lallemand, *Histoire de la Charité*; Nicholl, *History of the English Poor Law*, 2 vols., 1898–99.

We have been considering responsible freedom as it centres in and affects individuals in their distinctive capacities. It implies a public order which guarantees, defines, and enforces rights and obligations. This public order has a two-fold relation to rights and duties: (1) As the social counterpart of their exercise by individuals, it constitutes *Civil Society*. It represents those forms of associated life which are orderly and authorized, because constituted by individuals in the exercise of their rights, together with those special forms which protect and insure them. Families, clubs, guilds, unions, corporations come under the first head; courts and civil administrative bodies, like public railway and insurance commissions, etc., come under the second. (2) The public order also fixes the fundamental terms and conditions on which at any given time rights are exercised and remedies secured; it is organized for the purpose of defining the basic methods of exercising the activities of its constituent elements, individual and corporate. In this aspect it is the *State*.

§ 1. *Civil Rights and Obligations*

Every act brings the agent who performs it into association with others, whether he so intends or not. His act takes effect in an organized world of action; in social arrangement and institutions. So far as such combinations of individuals are recurrent or stable, their nature and operations are definitely formulated and definitely enforceable. Partnerships, clubs, corporations, guilds, families are such stable unions, with their definite spheres of action. Buying and selling, teaching and learning, producing and consuming, are recurrent activities whose legitimate methods get prescribed. These specific provinces and methods of action are defined in Civil Rights. They express the guaranteed and regular ways in which an individual, through action, voluntarily enters into association or combination with others for the sake of a common end. They differ from political rights and obligations in that the latter concern modes of social organization which are so fundamental that they are not left to the voluntary choice and purpose of an individual. As a social being, he must have political relationships, must be subject to law, pay taxes, etc.

Modes of association are so numerous and variable that we can only select those aspects of civil rights which are morally most significant. We shall discriminate them according as they have to do (1) with the more temporary and casual combinations of individuals, for limited and explicit purposes; and (2) with more permanent, inclusive, and hence less definable ends; and (3) with the special institutions which exist for guaranteeing individuals the enjoyment of their rights and providing remedies if these are infringed upon.

1. Contract Rights.—Rights of the first type are rights resulting from express or implied agreements of certain agents to do or refrain from doing specific acts, involving exchange of services or goods to the mutual benefit of both parties in the transaction. Every bargain entered into, every loaf of bread one buys or paper of pins one sells, involves an implied and explicit contract. A genuinely free agreement or contract means (i.) that each party to the transaction secures the benefit he wants; (ii.) that the two parties are brought into cooperative or mutually helpful relations; and that (iii.) the vast, vague, complex business of conducting social life is broken up into a multitude of specific acts to be performed and of specific goods to be delivered, at definite times and definite places. Hence it is hardly surprising that one school of social moralists has found in the conception of free contract its social ideal. Every individual concerned assumes obligations which it is to his interest to perform so that the performance is voluntary, not coerced; while, at the same time, some other person is engaged to serve him in some way. The limitations of the contract idea will concern us later.

2. *The Permanent Voluntary Associations.*—Partnerships, limited liability corporations, guilds, trades unions, churches, schools, clubs, are more permanent and comprehensive associations, involving more far-reaching rights and obligations. Societies organized for conversation and sociability or conviviality, "corporations not for profit," but for mutual enjoyment or for benevolent ends, come under the same head. Most significant are the associations which, while entered only voluntarily and having therefore a basis in contract, are for generic ends. Thus they are permanent, and cover much more than can be written in the contract. Marriage, in modern society, is entered into by contract; but married life is not narrowed to the exchange of specific services at specific times. It is a union for mutual economic and spiritual goods which are coextensive with all the interests of the parties. In its connection with the generation and rearing of children, it is a fundamental means of guarding all social interests and of directing their progress. Schools, colleges, churches, federations of labor, organizations of employers, and of both together, represent other forms of permanent voluntary organizations which may have the most far-reaching influence both upon those directly concerned and upon society at large.

3. *Right to Use of Courts.*—All civil rights get their final application and test in the right to have conflicting rights defined and infringed rights remedied by appeal to a public authority having general and final jurisdiction. "The right to sue and be sued" may seem too legal and external a matter to be worthy of much note in an ethical treatise; but it represents the culmination of an age-long experimentation with the problem of reconciling individual freedom and public order. No civil right is effective unless it carries with it a statement of a method of enforcement and, if necessary, of redress and remedy. Otherwise it is a mere name. Moreover, conflicts of civil rights are bound to occur even when there is good faith on the part of all concerned, just because new situations arise. Unless there is a way of defining the respective rights of each party in the new situation, each will arbitrarily and yet in good faith insist upon asserting his rights on the old basis: private war results. A new order

is not achieved and the one already attained is threatened or disrupted. The value of rights to the use of courts resides, then, to a comparatively small degree, in the specific cases of deliberate wrong which are settled. What is more important is that men get instruction as to the proper scope and limits of their activities, through the provision of an effective mechanism for amicable settlement of disputes in those cases in which rights are vague and ambiguous because the situations are novel.

Classes of Wrongs and Remedies. —Infringements upon rights, such as murder, theft, arson, forgery, imply a character which is distinctly anti-social in its bent. The wrong, although done to one, is an expression of a disposition which is dangerous to all. Such a wrong is a crime; it is a matter for the direct jurisdiction of public authority. It is the business of all to cooperate in giving evidence, and it may render one a criminal accomplice to conceal or suppress evidence, just as it is "compounding a felony" for the wronged individual to settle the wrong done him by arranging privately for compensation. The penalty in such cases is generally personal; imprisonment or at least a heavy fine. The violation may, however, be of the nature of a wrong or "tort," rather than of a crime; it may indicate a disposition indifferent to social interests or neglectful of them rather than one actively hostile to them. Such acts as libels, trespasses upon the land of another, are illustrations. In such cases, the machinery of justice is put in motion by the injured individual, not by the commonwealth. This does not mean that society as a whole has no interest in the matter; but that under certain circumstances encouraging individuals to look out for their own rights and wrongs is socially more important than getting certain wrongs remedied irrespective of whether men stand up for their own rights or not. Then again, there are civil disputes which indicate neither a criminal nor a harmful disposition, but rather uncertainty as to what the law really is, leading to disputes about rights—interpretations of a contract, express or implied. Here the interest of society is to provide a method of settlement which will hinder the growth of ill will and private retaliation; and which also will provide precedents and principles that will lessen uncertainty and conflict in like cases in the future.

Peace and tranquillity are not merely the absence of open friction and disorder. They mean specific, easily-known, and generally recognized principles which determine the province and limits of the legitimate activity of every person. Publicity, standards, rules of procedure, remedies acknowledged in common, are their essence. *Res publica*, the common concern, remains vague and latent till defined by impartial, disinterested social organs. Then it is expressed in regular and guaranteed modes of activity. In the pregnant phrase of Aristotle, the administration of justice is also its determination: that is, its discovery and promulgation.

§ 2. *Development of Civil Rights*

Contrast of Primitive with Present Justice. —The significance of the accomplishments and the defects of the present administration of law may be brought out by a sketch of its contrast with primitive methods. In savage and barbarian society, on account of the solidarity of the kin-group, any member of the group is likely to be attacked for the offense of any other (see p. 33). He may not have participated in the act, or have had complicity in planning it. His guilt is that the same blood runs in his veins.[1] The punitive attack, moreover, is made directly and promiscuously by the injured man and by his blood-relatives; it is made in the heat of passion or in the vengeance of stealth as custom may decree. Says Hearn, the state "did not interfere in the private quarrels of its citizens. Every man took care of his own property and his own household, and every hand guarded its own head. If any injury were done to any person, he retaliated, or made reprisals, or otherwise sought redress, as custom prescribed."[2] The reprisal may itself have

1. A traveler tells of overhearing children in Australia, when one of their kin had injured some one in another clan, discuss whether or no they came within the degree of nearness of relationship which made them liable to suffer.
2. Hearn, *The Aryan Household*, p. 431. Hearn is speaking, moreover, of a later and more advanced condition of society, one lying well within "civilization."

called for another, and the blood-feud was on. In any case, the state of affairs was one literally, not metaphorically, described as "private war."

Changes Now Effected.—This state of affairs has been superseded by one in which a third, a public and impartial authority (1) takes cognizance of offenses against another individual as offenses against the commonwealth; (2) apprehends the supposed offender; (3) determines and applies an objective standard of judgment, the same for all, the law; (4) tries the supposed offender according to rules of procedure, including rules of evidence or proof, which are also publicly promulgated; and (5) takes upon itself the punishment of the offender, if found guilty. The history of this change, important and interesting as it is, does not belong here. We are concerned here only with the relation of public authority, public law, and public activity to the development of the freedom of the individual on one side and of his responsibility on the other.[3] We shall point out in a number of particulars that the evolution of freedom and responsibility in individuals has coincided with the evolution of a public and impartial authority.

1. Good and Evil as Quasi-Physical.—There are two alternatives in the judgment of good and evil. (1) They may be regarded as having *moral* significance, that is, as having a voluntary basis and origin. (2) Or they may be considered as substantial properties of things, as a sort of essence diffused through them, or as a kind of force resident in them, in virtue of which persons and things are noxious or helpful, malevolent or kindly. Savage tribes, for instance, cannot conceive either sickness or death as natural evils; they are attributed to the malicious magic of an enemy. Similarly the evil which follows from the acts of a man is treated as

---

3. Those interested in this important history, as every student of morals may well be, will find easily accessible material in the following references: Hobhouse, *Morals in Evolution*, ch. iii of Vol. I; Hearn, *The Aryan Household*, ch. xix; Westermarck, *Origin and Development*, Vol. I, pp. 120–85, and parts of ch. xx; Sutherland, *Origin and Growth*, chs. xx and xxi; Pollock and Maitland, *History of English Law*, Vol. II, pp. 447–60 and ch. ix; Pollock, *Oxford Lectures* ("The King's Peace"); Cherry, *Criminal Law in Ancient Communities*; Maine, *Ancient Law*. References to anthropological literature, dealing with savage and barbarian customs, will be found especially in Westermarck and Hobhouse.

a sign of some metaphysical tendency inherent in him. Some
men bring bad luck upon everything and everybody they
have anything to do with. A curse is on their doings. No distinction is made between such evils and those which flow
from intention and character. The notion of the moral or
voluntary nature of good and evil hardly obtains. The quasi-
physical view, bordering upon the magical, prevails. The
result is that evil is thought of as a contagious matter, trans-
mitted from generation to generation, from class or person
to class or person; and as something to be got rid of, if at all,
by devices which are equally physical. Natural evils, plagues,
defeats, earthquakes, etc., *are treated as quasi-moral, while
moral evils are treated as more than half physical.* Sins are
infectious diseases, and natural diseases are malicious interferences of a human or divine enemy. Morals are material-
ized, and nature is moralized or demoralized.[4]

Now it is hardly necessary to point out the effect of such
conceptions in restricting the freedom and responsibility of
the individual person. Man is hemmed in as to thought and
action on all sides by all kinds of mysterious forces working
in unforeseeable ways. This is true enough in his best estate.
When to this limitation is added a direction of energy into
magical channels, away from those controllable sources of
evil which reside in human disposition, the amount of effective freedom possible is slight. This same misplacing of
liability holds men accountable for acts they have not committed, because some magic tendency for evil is imputed to
them. Famine, pestilence, defeat in war are evils to be
remedied by sacrifice of goods or persons or by ritualistic
ceremonies; while the remediable causes of harm in human
ignorance and negligence go without attention.

2. *Accident and Intention.*—Under such circumstances,
little distinction can be made between the good and evil

4. For facts regarding the importance and nature of these conceptions, see Westermarck, *Origin and Development,* Vol. I, pp.
   52–72; Robertson Smith, *The Religion of the Semites,* pp. 427–
   35 and 139–49; Jevons, *Introduction to the History of Religion;*
   Hobhouse, *Morals in Evolution,* Vol. II, chs. i and ii; and in
   general facts bearing on the relations between taboos, holiness,
   and uncleanness; ablutions, purifications by fire, transference by
   scapegoats; also the evil power of curses, and the early conceptions of doom and fate. For a suggestive interpretation of the
   underlying facts, see Santayana, *The Life of Reason,* Vol. III,
   chs. iii and iv.

which an individual *meant* to do and that which he *happened* to do. The working presumption of society, up to a comparatively late stage of its history, was that every harmful consequence is an evidence of evil disposition in those who were in any way concerned. This limitation of freedom was accompanied by a counterpart limitation of responsibility. Where no harm actually resulted, there was thought to be no harmful intent. Animals and even inanimate objects which do injury are baleful things and come under disapprobation and penalty. Even in civilized Athens there was a survival of the practice of holding inanimate things liable. If a tree fell on a man and killed him, the tree was to be brought to trial, and after condemnation cast beyond the civic borders, i.e., outlawed.[5] Anyhow, the owner of an offending article was almost always penalized. Westermarck,[6] with reference to the guilt of animals, cites an instance, dated in 1457, "when a sow and her six young ones were tried on a charge of their having murdered and partly eaten a child; the sow, being found guilty, was condemned to death, the young pigs were acquitted on account of their youth and the bad example of their mother." When sticks, stones, and animals are held accountable for evil results, there is little chance of discriminating intent and accident or misadventure in the case of personal agents. "The devil himself knoweth not the intent, the 'thought' of man" was the mediaeval maxim; all that can be certain is that harm has come and the one who caused it must suffer; or else no overt harm has come and no one is to blame.[7] Harm has been done and any one concerned, even remotely, in the injurious situation, is *ex officio* guilty; it will not do to take chances. The remoteness of an implication which may involve liability is seen in the condition of English law in the thirteenth century: "At your request I accompany you when you are about

5. See Plato, *Laws*, IX, §§ 873–74. Compare Holmes, *Common Law*. In mediaeval and early modern Europe, offending objects were "deodand," that is, devoted to God. They were to be appropriated by the proper civil or ecclesiastical authority, and used for charity. In theory, this lasted in England up to 1846. See Tylor, *Primitive Culture*, Vol. I, pp. 286–87; and Pollock and Maitland, *History of English Law*, Vol. II, pp. 471–72.
6. Westermarck, *Origin and Development*, Vol. I, p. 257.
7. The very words "cause" and "to blame" are closely connected in their origin. Cf. the Greek αἰτία.

your own affairs: my enemies fall upon and kill me: you must pay for my death. You take me to see a wild-beast-show, or that interesting spectacle a madman: beast or madman kills me; you must pay. You hang up your sword; some one else knocks it down so that it cuts me; you must pay."[8] Only gradually did intent clearly evolve as the central element in an act, and thus lead to the idea of a voluntary or free act.

That the limitation upon the side of responsibility was equally great is obvious. If a man is held liable for what he did not and could not foresee or desire, there is no ground for his *holding himself* responsible for anticipating the consequences of his acts, and forming his plans according as he foresees. This comes out clearly in the obverse of what has just been said. If no harm results from a willful attempt to do evil, the individual is not blamed. He goes scot free. "An attempt to commit a crime is no crime."[9]

3. *Character and Circumstances.*—Even in law, to say nothing of personal moral judgments, we now almost as a matter of course take into account, in judging an agent's intent, both circumstances, and character as inferred from past behavior. We extend our view of consequences, taking into account in judging the moral quality of a particular deed, consequences its doer is *habitually* found to effect. We blame the individual less for a deed if we find it contrary to his habitual course. We blame him more, if we find he has a character given to that sort of thing. We take into account, in short, the permanent attitude and disposition of the agent. We also discriminate the conditions and consequences of a deed much more carefully. Self-defense, protection of others or of property, come in as "extenuating circumstances"; the degree of provocation, the presence of immediate impulsive fear or anger, as distinct from a definitely formed, long-cherished idea, are considered. The questions of first or of repeated offense, of prior criminality or good behavior, enter

8. Pollock and Maitland, *History of English Law*, Vol. II, p. 469; Vol. I, p. 30. For the history of the idea of accident in English law with reference to homicide, see also Vol. II, pp. 477–83. Also Stephen, *History of the Criminal Law of England*, Vol. III, pp. 316–76.
9. Pollock and Maitland, *History of English Law*, Vol. II, p. 473; see Westermarck, *Origin and Development*, Vol. I, pp. 240–47.

in. Questions of heredity, of early environment, of early education and opportunity are being brought to-day into account.

We are still very backward in this respect, both in personal and in public morals; in private judgment and in legal procedure and penalty. Only recently have we, for example, begun to treat juvenile delinquents in special ways; and the effort to carry appropriate methods further meets with strong opposition and the even stronger inertia of indifference. It is regarded by many good people as lowering the bars of responsibility to consider early training and opportunity, just as in its day it was so regarded to plead absence of intent in cases where evil had actually resulted. It is not "safe" to let any one off from the rigor of the law. The serious barrier, now as earlier, is upon the scientific or intellectual side. There was a time when it did not seem feasible to pass upon intent; it was hidden, known only to God. But we have now devised ways, adequate in principle, though faulty in detail, to judge immediate intent; similarly, with the growth of anthropology, psychology, statistics, and the resources of publicity in social science, we shall in time find it possible to consider the effects of heredity, early environment, and training upon character and so upon intent. We shall then regard present methods of judging intent to be almost as barbarous as we now consider the earlier disregard of accident and provocation. Above all we shall learn that increased, not relaxed responsibility, comes with every increase of discrimination of causes lying in character and conditions.[10]

4. *Intellectual Incapacity and Thoughtlessness.*—With increasing recognition of character as the crucial element in voluntary action, we now take into account such matters as age, idiocy, and insanity as factors of judgment. But this also has been a slow growth. If we take the one question of insanity, for example, in 1724 exculpation for harm result-

10. The slowness and indirectness of change throw light upon the supposed distinction of justice and mercy (see *ante*, p. 372). When the practical injustice of regarding accidental homicide or killing in self-defense as murder began to be felt, the theory was still that the man in justice was guilty, but that he was to be recommended to the crown for mercy or pardon. This was a mean term in the evolution of our present notion of justice.

ing from a madman's acts required that the person excused "be a man that is totally deprived of his understanding and memory, and doth not know what he is doing, no more than an infant, than a brute, or a wild beast." At the beginning of the nineteenth century, the excuse was no longer that of being such a raving lunatic as is here implied; but of knowing right and wrong from each other *in the abstract.* By a celebrated case in 1843, the rule was changed, in English law, to knowledge of the difference between right and wrong in the particular case. Further advance waits upon progress of science which will make it more possible to judge the specific mental condition of the person acting; and thus do away with the abuses of the present system which tend, on the one hand, to encourage the pleading of insanity where none may exist; and, on the other hand (by a rigid application of a technical rule), to condemn persons really irresponsible.[11] Popular judgment still inclines to impute clear and definite intention on the basis of results and to ignore conditions of intellectual confusion and bewilderment, and justifies itself in its course on the ground that such is the only "safe" course.[12]

Responsibility for Thoughtlessness.—But the release from responsibility for deeds in which the doer is intellectually incapacitated, is met on the other side by holding individuals of normal mental constitution responsible for some consequences which were not thought of at all. We even hold men accountable for *not* thinking to do certain acts. The former are acts of heedlessness or carelessness, as when a mason on top of a building throws rubbish on to a street below which injures some one, without any thought on his part of this result, much less any deliberate desire to effect it. The latter are acts of negligence, as when, say, an engineer fails to note a certain signal. In such cases even when no harm results, we now hold the agent morally

11. For some of the main historic facts on intellectual disability, see Westermarck, *Origin and Development*, Vol. I, pp. 264–77.
12. Popular judgment, we may say, tends to be as grossly utilitarian in its practice as it is grossly intuitional in its theoretical standpoint. In assuming the possibility of an almost infallible, offhand, pat perception of right and wrong, it commits itself practically to judging in an offhand, analyzed way, on the basis of the evils which overtly result.

culpable. Similarly we blame children for *not* thinking of the consequences of their acts; we blame them for *not* thinking to do certain things at a certain time—to come home when told, and so on. This is not merely a matter of judgment by others. The more conscientious a person is, the more occasions he finds to judge *himself* with respect to results which *happened because he did not think or deliberate or foresee at all*—provided he has reason to believe he would have thought of the harmful results if he had been of a different character. Because we were absorbed in something else we did not think, and while, in the abstract, this something else may have been all right, in the concrete it may be proof of an unworthy character. The very fact that we permitted ourselves to become so absorbed that the thought of an engagement, or of an opportunity to help some friend whom we knew to be in need, did not occur to us, is evidence of a selfish, i.e., inconsiderate, character.

The case seems paradoxical and is crucial. Others hold us responsible because we *were* irresponsible in action and *in order* that we may *become* responsible. We blame ourselves precisely because we discover that an unconscious preference for a private or exclusive good led us to be careless of the good of others. The effect (if the regret is genuine, not simulated) is to develop a habit of greater thoughtfulness in the future. Less and less do men accept for others or for themselves ignorance as an excuse for bad consequences, when the ignorance itself flows from character. Our chief moral business is to become acquainted with consequences. Our moral character surely does not depend in this case, then, upon the fact that we had alternatives clearly in mind and chose the worse; the difficulty is that we had only one alternative in mind and did not *consciously* choose at all. Our freedom lies in the *capacity* to alter our mode of action, through having our ignorance enlightened by being held for the neglected consequences when brought to accountability by others, or by holding ourselves accountable in subsequent reflection. Cases of careless acts and of acts omitted through negligence are thus crucial for any theory of freedom and responsibility. Either we are all wrong in blaming ourselves or others in such cases, because there is no free or voluntary element in them; or else there is responsibility when deliberate comparison of alternatives and conscious preference are absent. There is responsibility for the absence of deliberation. Nature does not forbear to attach consequences to acts because of the ignorance of the one who does the deed. The evil results that follow in the wake of a thoughtless act are precisely the reminders that make one take thought the next time. Similarly, to be held liable by others or to take ourselves to task for forgetfulness, inconsiderateness, and negligence, is the way in which to build up conscientious foresight and deliberate choice. The increased complexity and danger of modern industrial activity, the menace of electric power, of high explosives, of railway trains and trolley cars, of powerful machines, have done much to quicken recognition that negligence may be criminal, and to reawaken the conviction of Greek thought that thoughtless ignorance, where knowledge is possible, is the worst of evils. The increased interdependence of men, through travel and transportation, collective methods of production, and crowding of population in cities, has widened the area of the harm likely to result from inconsiderate action, and has strengthened the belief that adequate thoughtfulness is possible only where there is sympathetic interest in others.

5. *The Conflict of Form and Substance.*—The technical forms of procedure concerned in establishing and remedying rights were, for long ages, more important than the substantial ends by which alone the forms may be justified. Any effort for a remedy was nullified if the minutiae of complicated formulae (largely magical or ritualistic in their origin) were deviated from. Almost any obligation might be escaped by some quirk or turn in some slight phrase or motion, without which no agreement was binding, so sacramental was the importance of the very words. In early days the rigidity of these semi-ritualistic performances doubtless served to check arbitrary and reckless acts, and to impress the sense of the value of a standard.[13] But they survived as "rudimentary

___

13. See Pollock and Maitland, *History of English Law*, Vol. II, p. 561, who quote from Ihering: "Formulation is the sworn enemy of arbitrariness, the twin-sister of liberty"; and who add: "As

organs" long after they had done their work in this respect; and after they had been eliminated from legal procedure they survived as habits of judging conduct.

Survivals of Spirit of Individualistic Litigation.—The fact that the procedure of justice originated as methods of supplying impartial umpires for conflicts waged between individuals, has had serious consequences. It has had indeed the desirable consequence of quickening men to the perception of their rights and to their obligation as social members to maintain them intact. But it has also had the undesirable result of limiting the function of the public interest to the somewhat negative one of securing fair play between contentious individuals. The battle is not now fought out with fists or spears or oaths or ordeals: but it is largely a battle of wits and of technical resources between the opposite parties and their lawyers, with the State acting the part of a benevolently neutral umpire. The ignorant, the poor, the foreign, and the *merely* honest are almost inevitably at a discount in this battle.[14] And, in any case, the technical aspect of justice, that is, the question of proper forms gets out of true perspective. The "legally-minded" man is likely to be one with whom technical precedents and rules are more important than the goods to be achieved and the evils to be avoided. With increase of publicity and scientific methods of determining and interpreting facts, and with a public and professional criticism which is impartial and wise, we may anticipate that the supremacy of the general good will be increasingly recognized in cases of litigation, and that the courts, as organs of public justice, will take a more active and substantial part in the management of all legal controversies.[15]

Legal and Moral.—But, at the best, definitions of rights and of remedial procedures only (1) lay down general, not

---

time goes on there is always a larger room for discretion in the law of procedure: but discretionary powers can only be safely entrusted to judges whose impartiality is above suspicion and whose every act is exposed to public and professional criticism."

14. A lawyer, asked if the poor were not at a disadvantage in the legal maintenance of their rights, replied: *"Not any more than they are in the other relations of life."*

15. The devices of "equity" as distinct from strict legality are of course in part intended to secure this result.

individual conditions, and (2), so far as they are strict, register precedent and custom rather than anticipate the novel and variable. They can state what shall not be done. Except in special cases, they cannot state what shall be done, much less the spirit and disposition in which it shall be done. In their formulations, they present a sort of minimum limit of morality not to be overstepped by those inclined to ill. They throw little light on the positive capacities and responsibilities of those who are socially minded. They have a moral purpose: they free energy from the friction attendant upon vague, obscure, and uncertain situations, by enlightening men as to what they may do and how they may do it. But the exaggeration of form at the expense of the substantial end and good, leads to misplaced emphasis and false perspective. The rules are treated as ends; they are employed not to get insight into consequences, but as justifying, apart from consequences, certain acts. The would-be conscientious agent is led into considering goodness as a matter of obeying rules, not of fulfilling ends. The average individual conceives he has satisfied the requirements of morality when he has conformed to the average level of legal definition and prescription. Egoistic, self-seeking men regard their actions as sanctioned if they have *not* broken the laws; and decide this question by success in evading penalties. The intelligence that should go to employing the spirit of laws to enlighten behavior is spent in ingenious inventions for observing their letter. The "respectable" citizen of this type is one of the unsocialized forces that social reformers find among their most serious obstacles.

This identification of morality with the legal and jural leads to a reaction which is equally injurious: the complete separation of the legal and the moral, the former conceived as merely "outer," concerned entirely with acts, not at all with motive and character. The effect of this divorce is perhaps more serious upon the moral than upon the legal. The separation makes morals sentimental and whimsical, or else transcendental and esoteric. It leads to neglect of the social and institutional realities which form a world of action as surely as natural objects and energies form a physical world, and ends in the popular conception of morals as just a matter of "goodness" (the goody-goodiness) of individuals. One of the most fundamental of moral duties is that of making the legal order a more adequate expression of the common good.

Special Problems. — Civil Society thus imposes upon its members not only specific obligations, but it also imposes upon all who enjoy its benefits the supreme obligation of seeing that the civic order is itself intelligently just in its methods of procedure. The peculiar moral problems which men have to face as members of civil society change, of course, from time to time with change of conditions; among the more urgent of present problems, we may mention:

1. Reform of Criminal Procedure. — The negative side of morality is never so important as the positive, because the pathological cannot be as important as the physiological of which it is a disturbance and perversion. But no fair survey of our methods, either of locating criminality or of punishing it, can fail to note that they contain far too many survivals of barbarism. Compared with primitive times we have indeed won a precious conquest. Even as late as 1813, a proposal to change the penalty for stealing five shillings from death to transportation to a remote colony, was defeated in England.[16] But we are likely in flattering ourselves upon the progress made to overlook that which it remains to make. Our trials are technical rather than human: they assume that just about so much persistent criminality must persist in any case. They endeavor, in rather routine and perfunctory ways, to label this and that person as criminal in such and such degrees, or, by technical devices and resources, to acquit. In many American states, distrust of government, inherited from days of tyrannical monarchy or oligarchy, protects the accused in all sorts of ways. For fear the government will unjustly infringe upon the liberty of the individual, the latter is not only — as is just — regarded as innocent till proved guilty; but is provided with every possible technical advantage in rules of evidence, postponements and appeals, advantages backed up, in many cities, by association with political bosses which gives him a corrupt "pull."

On the other hand, there is as yet no general recognition

16. Robinson and Beard, *Development of Modern Europe*, Vol. II, p. 207.

of the possibility of an unbiased scientific investigation into all the antecedents (hereditary and environmental) of evildoers; an investigation which would connect the wrong done with the *character of the individual* committing it, and not merely with one of a number of technical degrees of crime, laid down in the statute books in the abstract, without reference to particular characters and circumstances. Thus while the evildoer has in one direction altogether too much of a chance to evade justice, he has in another direction a chance at only technical, rather than at moral, justice—justice as an individual human being. It is not possible to discuss here various methods which have been proposed for remedying these defects. But it is clearly the business of the more thoughtful members of society to consider the evils seriously and to interest themselves actively in their reform. We need, above all, a change in two respects: (a) recognition of the possibilities of new methods of judgment which the sciences of physiology, psychology, and sociology have brought about; and (b) surrender of that feudal conception according to which men are divided, as it were essentially, into two classes: one the criminal and the other the meritorious. We need to consider the ways in which the pressure and the opportunities of environment and education, of poverty and comfortable living, of extraneous suggestion and stimulation, make the differences between one man and another; and to recognize how fundamentally one human nature is at bottom. Juvenile courts, probation officers, detention officers, mark the beginnings of what is possible, but only the beginnings. For the most part crime is still treated sordidly and by routine, except when, being sensational, it is the occasion for a great battle of wits between keen prosecuting attorney and clever "criminal lawyer," with the world through the newspapers watching the display.

2. *Reform of Punishment.*—Emerson's bitter words are still too applicable. "Our distrust is very expensive. The money we spend for courts and prisons is very ill laid out. We make, by distrust, the thief and burglar and incendiary, and by our court and jail we keep him so."[17] Reformatories,

17. Emerson, "Man the Reformer."

whose purpose is change of disposition, not mere penaliza-
tion, have been founded; but there are still many more prisons than reformatories. And, if it be argued that most criminals are so hardened in evil-doing that reformatories are of
no use, the answer is twofold. We do not know, because we
have never systematically and intelligently tried to find out;
and, even if it were so, nothing is more illogical than to turn
the unreformed criminal, at the end of a certain number of
months or years, loose to prey again upon society. Either reform or else permanent segregation is the logical alternative.
Indeterminate sentences, release on probation, discrimination of classes of offenders, separation of the first and more
or less accidental and immature offender from the old and
experienced hand, special matrons for women offenders, introduction of education and industrial training into pen-
itentiaries, the finding of employment for those released—
all mark improvements. They are, however, as yet inchoate.
Intelligent members of society need to recognize their own
responsibility for the promotion of such reforms and for the
discovery of new ones.

   3. *Increase of Administrative Efficiency.*—In the last one
hundred years, society has rapidly grown in internal complexity. Commercial changes have brought about an intense
concentration of population in cities; have promoted migra-
tory travel and intercourse, with destruction of local ties;
have developed world markets and collective but impersonal
(corporate) production and distribution. Many new problems have been created, while at the same time many of the
old agencies for maintaining order have been weakened or
destroyed, especially such as were adapted to small groups
with fixed habits. A great strain has thus been put upon the
instrumentalities of justice. Pioneer conditions retarded in
America the development of the problems incident upon industrial reconstruction. The possibility of moving on, of
taking up new land, finding unutilized resources of forest
and mine, the development of new professions, the growth of
population with new needs to be met, stimulated and rewarded individual enterprise. Under such circumstances
there could be no general demand for public agencies of inspection, supervision, and publicity. But the pioneer days of

America are practically ended. American cities and states find themselves confronted with the same problems of public health, poverty and unemployment, congested population, traffic and transportation, charitable relief, tramps and vagabondage, and so forth, that have troubled older countries.

We face these problems, moreover, with traditions which are averse to "bureaucratic" administration and public "interference." Public regulation is regarded as a "paternalistic" survival, quite unsuited to a free and independent people. It would be foolish, indeed, to overlook or deny the great gains that have come from our American individualistic convictions: the quickening of private generosity, the growth of a generalized sense of *noblesse oblige*—of what every successful individual owes to his community; of personal initiative, self-reliance, and versatile "faculty"; of interest in all the voluntary agencies which by education and otherwise develop the individuality of every one; and of a demand for equality of opportunity, a fair chance, and a square deal for all. But it is certain that the country has reached a state of development, in which these individual achievements and possibilities require new civic and political agencies if they are to be maintained as realities. Individualism means inequity, harshness, and retrogression to barbarism (no matter under what veneer of display and luxury), unless it is a *generalized* individualism: an individualism which takes into account the real good and effective—not merely formal—freedom of *every* social member.

Hence the demand for civic organs—city, state, and federal,—of expert inquiry, inspection, and supervision with respect to a large number of interests which are too widespread and too intricate to be well cared for by private or voluntary initiative. The well-to-do in great cities may segregate themselves in the more healthful quarters; they may rely upon their automobiles for local transportation; they may secure pure milk and unadulterated foods from personal resources; they may, by their combined "pull," secure good schools, policing, lighting, and well-paved streets for their own localities. But the great masses are dependent upon public agencies for proper air, light, sanitary conditions of work and residence, cheap and effective transportation, pure food, decent educative and recreative facilities in schools, libraries, museums, parks.

The problems which fall to the lot of the proper organs of administrative inspection and supervision are essentially *scientific* problems, questions for expert intelligence conjoined with wide sympathy. In the true sense of the word political, they are political questions: that is, they relate to the welfare of society as an organized community of attainment and endeavor. In the cant sense of the term political, the sense of conventional party-issues and party-lines, they have no more to do with politics than have the multiplication table and the laws of hygiene. Yet they are at present almost hopelessly entangled with irrelevant "political" issues, and are almost hopelessly under the heel of party-politicians whose least knowledge is of the scientific questions involved, just as their least interest is for the human issues at stake. So far "civil service reform" has been mainly negative: a purging away of some of the grosser causes which have influenced appointments to office. But now there is needed a constructive reform of civil administration which will develop the agencies of inquiry, oversight, and publicity required by modern conditions; and which will necessitate the selection of public servants of scientifically equipped powers.

§ 3. *Political Rights and Obligations*

No hard and fast line can be drawn between civil society and the State. By the State, however, we denote those conditions of social organization and regulation which are most fundamental and most general: —conditions which are summed up in and expressed through the general will as manifested in legislation and its execution. As a civil right is technically focused in the right to use the courts, "to sue and be sued," that is in the right to have other claims adjudicated and enforced by a public, impartial authority, so a political right is technically summed up in the power to vote—either to vote directly upon laws or to vote for those who make and carry out laws. To have the right in a legislative assembly to speak for or against a certain measure; to be able to say "yea" or "nay" upon a roll-call; to be able to put into a ballot-box a piece of paper with a number of names written thereon, are not acts which of themselves possess the inherent value of many of the most ordinary transactions of daily life. But the representative and potential significance of political rights exceeds that of any other class of rights. Suffrage stands for direct and active participation in the regulation of the terms upon which associated life shall be sustained, and the pursuit of the good carried on. Political freedom and responsibility *express an individual's power and obligation to make effective all his other capacities by fixing the social conditions of their exercise.*

Growth of Democracy.—The evolution of democratically regulated States, as distinct from those ordered in the interests of a small group, or of a special class, is the social counterpart of the development of a comprehensive and common good. Externally viewed, democracy is a piece of machinery, to be maintained or thrown away, like any other piece of machinery, on the basis of its economy and efficiency of working. Morally, it is the effective embodiment of the moral ideal of a good which consists in the development of all the social capacities of every individual member of society.

Present Problems: 1. Distrust of Government.—Present moral problems connected with political affairs have to do with safeguarding the democratic ideal against the influences which are always at work to undermine it, and with building up for it a more complete and extensive embodiment. The historic antecedent of our own governmental system was the exercise of a monopoly by a privileged class.[18] It became a democratic institution partly because the King, in order to secure the monopoly, had to concede and guarantee to the masses of the people certain rights as against the oligarchical interests which might rival his powers; and partly because the centralization of power, with the arbitrary despotism it

18. The term "the King's Peace," as the equivalent in England for the peace and order of the commonwealth, goes back to a time when literally it meant a private possession. Pollock says that the desire to collect larger revenues was the chief motive for pushing the royal jurisdiction against lesser local authorities. Essay on the King's Peace in *Oxford Lectures.*

created, called out protests which finally achieved the main popular liberties: safety of life and property from arbitrary forfeiture, arrest, or seizure by the sovereign; the rights of free assembly, petition, a free press, and of representation in the law-making body.

Upon its face, the struggle for individual liberty was a struggle against the overbearing menace of despotic rulers. This fact has survived in an attitude towards government which cripples its usefulness as an agency of the general will. Government, even in the most democratic countries, is still thought of as an external "ruler," operating from above, rather than as an organ by which people associated in pursuit of common ends can most effectively cooperate for the realization of their own aims. Distrust of government was one of the chief traits of the situation in which the American nation was born. It is embodied not only in popular tradition, and party creeds, but in our organic laws, which contain many provisions expressly calculated to prevent the corporate social body from effecting its ends freely and easily through governmental agencies.[19]

There can be no doubt that the movement to restrict the functions of government, the *laissez-faire* movement, was in its time an important step in human freedom, because so much of governmental action was despotic in intention and stupid in execution. But it is also a mistake to continue to think of a government which is only the people associated for the assuring of their own ends as if it were the same sort of thing as a government which represented the will of an irresponsible class. The advance of means of publicity, and of natural and social science, provides not only protection against ignorant and unwise public action, but also con-

19. Says President Hadley: "The fundamental division of powers in the Constitution of the United States is between voters on the one hand, and property owners on the other. The forces of democracy on one side, divided between the executive and the legislature, are set over against the forces of property on the other side, with the judiciary as arbiter between them. . . . The voter could elect what officers he pleased, so long as these officers did not try to do certain duties confided by the Constitution to the property holders. Democracy was complete as far as it went, but constitutionally it was bound to stop short of *social* democracy."

structive instrumentalities of intelligent administrative activities. One of the chief moral problems of the present day is, then, that of making governmental machinery such a prompt and flexible organ for expressing the *common* interest and purpose as will do away with that distrust of government which properly must endure so long as "government" is something imposed from above and exercised from without.

2. *Indifference to Public Concerns.*—The multiplication of private interests is a measure of social progress: it marks the multiplication of the sources and ingredients of happiness. But it also invites neglect of the fundamental general concerns which, seeming very remote, get pushed out of sight by the pressure of the nearer and more vivid personal interests. The great majority of men have their thoughts and feelings well occupied with their family and business affairs; with their clubs for recreation, their church associations, and so on. "Politics" becomes the trade of a class which is especially expert in the manipulation of their fellows and skilled in the "acceleration" of public opinion. "Politics" then gets a bad name, and the aloofness from public matters of those best fitted, theoretically, to participate in them is further promoted. The saying of Plato, twenty-five hundred years ago, that the penalty good men pay for not being interested in government is that they are then ruled by men worse than themselves, is verified in most of our American cities.

3. *Corruption.*—This indifference of the many, which throws the management of political affairs into the hands of a few, leads inevitably to corruption. At the best, government is administered by human beings possessed of ordinary human frailties and partialities; and, at the best, therefore, its ideal function of serving impartially the common good must be compromised in its execution. But the control of the inner machinery of governmental power by a few who can work in irresponsible secrecy because of the indifference and even contempt of the many, incites to deliberate perversion of public functions into private advantages. As embezzlement is appropriation of trust funds to private ends, so corruption, "graft," is prostitution of public resources, whether of power

or of money, to personal or class interests. That a "public office is a public trust" is at once an axiom of political ethics and a principle most difficult to realize.

In our own day, a special field has been opened within which corruption may flourish, in the development of public utility companies. Railways, city transportation systems, telegraph and telephone systems, the distribution of water and light, require public franchises, for they either employ public highways or they call upon the State to exercise its power of eminent domain. These enterprises can be carried on efficiently and economically only as they are either monopolies, or quasi-monopolies. All modern life, however, is completely bound up with and dependent upon facilities of communication, intercourse, and distribution. Power to control the various public-service corporations carries with it, therefore, power to control and to tax all industries, power to build up and cast down communities, companies, and individuals, to an extent which might well have been envied by royal houses of the past. It becomes then a very special object for great corporations to control the agencies of legislation and administration; and it becomes a very special object for party leaders and bosses to get control of party machinery in order to act as brokers in franchises and in special favors —sometimes directly for money, sometimes for the perpetuation and extension of their own power and influence, sometimes for the success, through influential support and contribution to party funds, of the national party with which they are identified.

4. Reforms in Party Machinery.—The last decade or so of our history has been rife with schemes to improve political conditions. It has become clear, among other things, that our national growth has carried with it the development of secondary political agencies, not contemplated by the framers of our constitutions, agencies which have become primary in practical matters. These agencies are the "machines" of political parties, with their hierarchical gradation of bosses from national to ward rulers, bosses who are in close touch with great business interests at one extreme, and with those who pander to the vices of the community (gambling, drink, and prostitution) at the other; parties with their committees, conventions, primaries, caucuses, party-funds, societies, meetings, and all sorts of devices for holding together and exciting masses of men to more or less blind acquiescence.

It is not necessary to point out the advantages which parties have subserved in concentrating and defining public opinion and responsibility in large issues; nor to dwell upon their value in counteracting tendencies which break up and divide men into a multitude of small groups having little in common with one another. But behind these advantages a vast number of abuses have sheltered themselves. Recent legislation and recent discussion have shown a marked tendency formally to recognize the part actually played by party machinery in the conduct of the State, and to take measures to make this factor more responsible in its exercise. Since these measures directly affect the conditions under which the government as the organ of the general will does its work of securing the fundamental conditions of equal opportunity for all, they have a direct moral import. Such questions as the Australian ballot, the recognition of party emblems and party groupings of names; laws for direct primary nominations; the registering of voters for primary as well as for final elections; legal control of party committees and party conventions; publicity of accounts as to the reception and use of party funds; forbidding of contributions by corporations, are thus as distinctly moral questions as are bribery and ballot-box stuffing.

5. *Reforms in Governmental Machinery.*—Questions that concern the respective advantages of written versus unwritten constitutions are in their present state problems of technical political science rather than of morals. But there are problems, growing out of the fact that for the most part American constitutions were written and adopted under conditions radically unlike those of the present, which have a direct ethical import. As already noted, our constitutions are full of evidences of distrust of popular cooperative action. They did not and could not foresee the direction of industrial development, the increased complexity of social life, nor the expansion of national territory. Many measures which have proved indispensable have had therefore to be as it were smuggled in; they have been justified by "legal fictions" and

by interpretations which have stretched the original text to uses undreamed of. At the same time, the courts, which are the most technical and legal of our political organs, are supreme masters over the legislative branch, the most popular and general. The distribution of functions between the states and the nation is curiously ill-adapted to present conditions (as the discussions regarding railway regulation indicate); and the distribution of powers between the state and its municipalities is hardly less so, resting in theory upon the idea of local self-government, and in practice doing almost everything possible to discourage responsible initiative for the conduct of their own affairs on the part of municipalities.

These conditions have naturally brought forth a large crop of suggestions for reforms. It is not intended to discuss them here, but the more important of them, so far as involving moral questions, may be briefly noted. The proposals termed the initiative and the referendum and the "recall" (this last intended to enable the people to withdraw from office any one with whose conduct of affairs they are dissatisfied) are clearly intended to make the ideal of democratic control more effective in practice. Proposals for limited or complete woman's suffrage call attention to the fact that one-half of the citizenship does the political thinking for the other half, and emphasize the difficulty under such conditions of getting a comprehensive social standpoint (which, as we have already seen, is the sympathetic and reasonable standpoint) from which to judge social issues. Many sporadic propositions from this and that quarter indicate a desire to revise constitutions so as to temper their cast-iron quality and increase their flexible adaptation to the present popular will, and so as to emancipate local communities from subjection to State legislatures in such a way as to give them greater autonomy and hence greater responsibility, in the management of their own corporate affairs. It is not the arguments *pro* and *con* that we are here concerned with; but we are interested to point out that moral issues are involved in the settlement of these questions. It may, moreover, be noted that dividing lines in the discussion are generally drawn, consciously or unconsciously, on the basis of the degree of faith which exists in the democratic principle and ideal, as against the class idea in some of its many forms.

6. *Constructive Social Legislation.* — The rapid change of economic methods, the accumulation and concentration of wealth, the aggregation of capital and labor into distinct bodies of corporations and trusts, on one side, and federated labor unions, on the other; the development of collective agencies of production and distribution, have brought to the focus of public attention a large number of proposals for new legislation, almost all of which have a direct moral import. These matters are discussed at length in subsequent chapters (chs. 22–25); and so are passed over here with the reminder that, while on one side they are questions of the ethics of industry, they are also questions of the right and wrong use of political power and authority. We may also note that the theoretical principle at issue, the extension versus the restriction of governmental agencies, so far as it is not simply a question of what is expedient under the given circumstances, is essentially a question of a *generalized* versus a *partial* individualism. The democratic movement of emancipation of personal capacities, of securing to each individual an *effective* right to count in the order and movement of society as a whole (that is, in the common good), has gone far enough to secure to many, more favored than others, peculiar powers and possessions. It is part of the irony of the situation that such now oppose efforts to secure equality of opportunity to *all* on the ground that these efforts would effect an invasion of individual liberties and rights: i.e., of privileges based on inequality. It requires perhaps a peculiarly sympathetic imagination to see that the question really involved is not one of magnifying the powers of the State against individuals, but is one of making individual liberty a more extensive and equitable matter.

7. *The International Problem.* — The development of national States marks a tremendous step forward in the realization of the principle of a truly inclusive common good. But it cannot be the final step. Just as clans, sects, gangs, etc., are intensely sympathetic within and intensely exclusive and jealous without, so States are still arrayed against States, with patriotism, loyalty, as an internal virtue, and the distrust and hatred of divisive hostility as the counterpart vice.

The idea of humanity in the abstract has been attained as a moral ideal. But the political organization of this conception, its embodiment in law and administrative agencies, has not been achieved. International law, arbitration treaties, and even a court like the Hague tribunal, whose power is sentimental rather than political, mark steps forward. Nothing could be more absurd, from the historic point of view, than to regard the conception of an international State of federated humanity, with its own laws and its own courts and its own rules for adjudicating disputes, as a mere dream, an illusion of sentimental hope. It is a very slight step to take forward compared with that which has substituted the authority of national States for the conflict of isolated clans and local communities; or with that which has substituted a publicly administered justice for the régime of private war and retaliation. The argument for the necessity (short of the attainment of a federated international State with universal authority and policing of the seas) of preparing in peace by enlarged armies and navies for the possibility of war, must be offset at least by recognition that the possession of irresponsible power is always a direct temptation to its irresponsible use. The argument that war is necessary to prevent moral degeneration of individuals may, under present conditions, where every day brings its fresh challenge to civic initiative, courage, and vigor, be dismissed as unmitigated nonsense.

§ 4. *The Moral Criterion of Political Activity*

The moral criterion by which to try social institutions and political measures may be summed up as follows: The test is whether a given custom or law sets free individual capacities in such a way as to make them available for the development of the general happiness or the common good. This formula states the test with the emphasis falling upon the side of the individual. It may be stated from the side of associated life as follows: The test is whether the general, the public, organization and order are promoted in such a way as to equalize opportunity for all.

Comparison with the Individualistic Formula.—The

formula of the individualistic school (in the narrow sense of that term—the *laissez-faire* school) reads: The moral end of political institutions and measures is the maximum possible freedom of the individual consistent with his not interfering with like freedom on the part of other individuals. It is quite possible to interpret this formula in such a way as to make it equivalent to that just given. But it is not employed in that sense by those who advance it. An illustration will bring out the difference. Imagine one hundred workingmen banded together in a desire to improve their standard of living by securing higher wages, shorter hours, and more sanitary conditions of work. Imagine one hundred other men who, because they have no families to support, no children to educate, or because they do not care about their standard of life, are desirous of replacing the first hundred at lower wages, and upon conditions generally more favorable to the employer of labor. It is quite clear that in offering themselves and crowding out the others, they are not interfering with the *like* freedom on the part of others. The men already engaged are "free" to work for lower wages and longer time, if they want to. But it is equally certain that they are interfering with the *real* freedom of the others: that is, with the effective expression of their *whole* body of activities.

The formula of *"like* freedom" artificially isolates some one power, takes that in the abstract, and then inquires whether *it* is interfered with. The one truly moral question is what relation this particular power, say the power to do a certain work for a certain reward, sustains to all the other desires, purposes, and interests of the individual. How are *they* affected by the way in which some one activity is exercised? It is in them that the concrete freedom of the man resides. We do not know whether the freedom of a man is interfered with or is assisted until we have taken into account his whole system of capacities and activities. The maximum freedom of one individual consistent with equal *concrete* or *total* freedom of others, would indeed represent a high moral ideal. But the individualistic formula is condemned by the fact that it has in mind only an abstract, mechanical, external, and hence formal freedom.

Comparison with the Collectivistic Formula.—There is a rival formula which may be summed up as the subordination of private or individual good to the public or general good: the subordination of the good of the part to the good of the whole. This notion also *may* be interpreted in a way which renders it identical with our own criterion. But it is usually not so intended. It tends to emphasize quantitative and mechanical considerations. The individualistic formula tends in practice to emphasize the freedom of the man who has power at the expense of his neighbor weaker in health, in intellectual ability, in worldly goods, and in social influence. The collectivistic formula tends to set up a static social whole and to prevent the variations of individual initiative which are necessary to progress. An individual variation may involve opposition, not conformity or subordination, to the existing social good taken statically; and yet may be the sole means by which the existing State is to progress. Minorities are not always right; but every advance in right begins in a minority of one, when some individual conceives a project which is at variance with the social good as it *has* been established.

A true public or social good will accordingly not subordinate individual variations, but will encourage individual experimentation in new ideas and new projects, endeavoring only to see that they are put into execution under conditions which make for securing responsibility for their consequences. A just social order promotes in all its members habits of criticizing its attained goods and habits of projecting schemes of new goods. It does not aim at intellectual and moral subordination. Every form of social life contains survivals of the past which need to be reorganized. The struggle of some individuals *against* the existing subordination of their good to the good of the whole is the method of the reorganization of the whole in the direction of a more generally distributed good. Not order, but orderly progress, represents the social ideal.

Literature

Green, *Principles of Political Obligation*, 1895; Ritchie, *Principles of State Interference*, 1891, *Natural Rights*, 1895; Lioy, *Philosophy of Right*, 2 vols., 1891; Willoughby, *An Examination of the Nature of the State*, 1896; Wilson, *The State*, 1889; Donisthorpe, *Individualism*, 1889; Giddings, *Democracy and Empire*, 1900; Mulford, *The Nation*, 1872; Spencer, *Principles of Sociology*, Vol. II, Part V, 1882, on Political Institutions; Bentham, "Fragment on Government," 1776; Mill, *Considerations on Representative Government*, 1861, *On Liberty*, 1859, and *The Subjection of Women*, 1869; Austin, *Jurisprudence*, 2 vols., 4th ed., 1873; Hadley, *The Relations Between Freedom and Responsibility in the Evolution of Democratic Government*, 1903; Pollock, *Expansion of the Common Law*, 1904; Hall, *Crime in Its Relations to Social Progress*, 1901; Addams, *Philanthropy and Social Progress: Seven Essays*, 1893; Stephen (J. F.), *Liberty, Equality, Fraternity*, 1873 (a criticism of Mill's *Liberty*); Tufts, "Some Contributions of Psychology to the Conception of Justice," *Philosophical Review*, Vol. XV, pp. 361–79.

22. THE ETHICS OF THE ECONOMIC LIFE

In considering the ethics of the economic life and of property, so far as this latter topic has not received treatment elsewhere, we give (1) a general analysis of the ethical questions involved, (2) a more specific account of the problems raised by the present tendencies of industry, business, and property; we follow these analyses with (3) a statement of principles, and (4) a discussion of unsettled problems.

§ 1. General Analysis

Both the economic process and property have three distinct ethical aspects corresponding respectively to the ethical standpoint of happiness, character, and social justice. (1) The economic process supplies men with goods for their bodily wants and with many of the necessary means for satisfying intellectual, aesthetic, and social needs; property represents permanence and security in these same values. (2) Through the difficulties it presents, the work it involves, and the incitements it offers, the economic process has a powerful influence in evoking skill, foresight, and scientific control of nature, in forming character, and stimulating ambition to excel. Property means power, control, and the conditions for larger freedom. (3) The economic process has an important social function. Through division of labor, cooperation, and exchange of goods and services, it affords one of the fundamental expressions of the organic nature of society in which members are reciprocally ends to each other. Property, likewise, is not only a possessing, but a "right," and thus, like all rights, involves the questions why and how far society should support the individual in his interests and claims. Let us examine each of these aspects further.

1. *The Economic in Relation to Happiness.*—Subject to the important qualifications to be made below under this and

the succeeding sections, we note first that the supply of needs and wants by industry and commerce is ethically a good. A constant increase in production and consumption is at least a possible factor in a fuller life. Wealth is a possible condition of weal, even if it is not to be gratuitously identified with it. Rome is frequently cited as an example of the evil effects of material wealth. But it was not wealth *per se,* but wealth (a) gained by conquest, and exploitation, rather than by industry; (b) controlled by a minority; and (c) used in largesses or in crude spectacles—rather than democratically distributed and used to minister to higher wants. The present average income in the United States is about two hundred dollars a year per capita, too small a sum to permit comfortable living, sufficient education for children, and the satisfaction which even a very moderate taste may seek. From this point of view we may then ask of any industrial process or business method whether it is an economical and efficient method of production, and whether it naturally tends to stimulate increased production. To do this is—so far as it goes—ethically as well as economically desirable.

If wealth is a good, it might seem that property must be judged by the same standard, since it represents security in the satisfactions which wealth affords. But there is an important distinction. Wealth means enjoyment of goods and satisfaction of wants. Property means the title to the exclusive use or possession of goods. Hence the increase of property may involve increasing exclusion of part of the community from wealth, although the owners of the property may be increasing their own enjoyments. For, as pointed out very forcibly by Hadley in the first chapter of his *Economics,* the public wealth of a community is by no means equal to the sum of its private property. If all parks were divided up into private estates, all schoolhouses controlled by private owners, all water supplies and highways given into private control, the sum of private property might be very much increased; but the public wealth would be decreased. Property is one of the means of dealing with public wealth. It is important to bear in mind, however, that it is only one means. Wealth may be (1) privately owned and privately used; (2) privately owned and publicly or commonly used; (3) publicly owned, but privately used; (4) publicly owned and publicly or commonly used. Illustrations of these four methods are, for the first, among practically all peoples, clothing and tools; of the second, a private estate opened to public use—as a park; of the third, public lands or franchises leased to individuals; of the fourth, public highways, parks, navigable rivers, public libraries. Whether property in any given case is a means to happiness will depend, then, largely upon whether it operates chiefly to increase wealth or to diminish it. The view has not been infrequent that the wealth of the community is the sum of its private property. From this it is but a step to believe "that the acquisition of property is the production of wealth, and that he best serves the common good who, other things equal, diverts the larger share of the aggregate wealth to his own possession."[1] The ethical questions as to the relation of property to happiness involve accordingly the problem of justice and can be more conveniently considered under that head.

2. *Relation to Character.*—Even in its aspect of satisfying human wants, quantity of production is not the only consideration. As was pointed out in the chapters on Happiness, the satisfaction of any and every want is not necessarily a moral good. It depends upon the nature of the wants; and as the nature of the wants reflects the nature of the man who wants, the moral value of the economic process and of the wealth it provides must depend upon the relation of goods to persons. As economists we estimate values in terms of external goods or commodities; as ethical students we estimate values in terms of a certain quality of life. We must ask first how the satisfaction of wants affects the consumers.

Moral Cost of Production.—Consider next the producers. It is desirable to have cheap goods, but the price of goods or service is not measurable solely in terms of other commodities or service; the price of an article is also, as Thoreau has said, what it costs in terms of human life. There is cheap production which by this standard is dear. The introduction of machinery for spinning and weaving cotton cheapened

1. Veblen, *Theory of Business Enterprise*, p. 291.

cotton cloth, but the child labor which was supposedly necessary as a factor in cheap production, involving disease, physical stunting, ignorance, and frequently premature exhaustion
or death, made the product too expensive to be tolerated. At
least, it was at last recognized as too expensive in England;
apparently the calculation has to be made over again in
every community where a new system of child labor is introduced. What is true of child labor is true of many other
forms of modern industry—the price in human life makes the
product dear. The minute subdivision of certain parts of industry with the consequent monotony and mechanical quality of the labor, the accidents and diseases due to certain
occupations, the devices to cheapen goods by ingredients
which injure the health of the consumer, the employment of
women under unsanitary conditions and for excessive hours
with consequent risk to the health of themselves and their
offspring—all these are part of the moral price of the present
processes of industry and commerce.

Moreover, the relation of production to physical welfare
is only one aspect of its effects upon life and character. We
may properly ask of any process or system whether it quickens intelligence or deadens it, whether it necessitates the
degradation of work to drudgery, and whether it promotes
freedom or hampers it. To answer this last question we shall
have to distinguish formal from real freedom. It might be
that a system favorable to the utmost formal freedom—
freedom of contract—would result in the most entire absence of that real freedom which implies real alternatives.
If the only alternative is, this or starve, the real freedom is
limited.

Property and Character.—Viewed on its positive side,
property means an expansion of power and freedom. To seize,
master, and possess is an instinct inbred by the biological
process. It is necessary for life; it is a form of the *Wille zum
Leben* or *Wille zur Macht* which need not be despised. But in
organized society possession is no longer mere animal instinct; through expression in a social medium and by a social
person it becomes a *right* of property. This is a far higher
capacity; like all rights it involves the assertion of personality
and of a rational claim upon fellow members of society for

their recognition and backing. Fichte's doctrine, that property is essential to the effective exercise of freedom, is a strong statement of its moral importance to the individual.

Over against these positive values of property are certain evils which moralists have always recognized, evils both to the property owner and to society. Avarice, covetousness, hardness toward others, seem to be the natural effects of the enormous possibilities of power offered by property, joined with its exclusive character. The prophets of Israel denounced the rich, and Jesus's image of the difficulty found by the rich man in entering the kingdom of God—a moral society—has met general acceptance. Plato's portrayal of the State in which the wealthy rule sketches the perversion and disobedience of laws, the jealousies and class hatred, the evasion of taxes for public defense, and gives the moral outcome: —

And henceforth they press forward on the path of money-getting, losing their esteem for virtue as the esteem for wealth grows upon them. For can you deny that there is such a gulf between wealth and virtue, that when weighed as it were in the two scales of a balance one of the two always falls, as the other rises?[2]

Even apart from questions of just distribution, the moral question arises as to whether an unlimited power should be given to individuals in this form, and whether there should be unlimited right of inheritance. But all these tend to pass over at once into questions of justice.

3. *Social Aspects.*—The various relations of man to man, political, friendly, kindred, are developed forms of the interdependence implicit in the early group life. A group of units, each independent of the others, would represent mass only, but such a group as is made up of men, women, and children, sustaining all the relations found in present human life, represents something vastly more than a mass of individuals. Every life draws from the rest. Man without friendship, love, pity, sympathy, communication, cooperation, justice, rights, or duties, would be deprived of nearly all that gives life its value.

2. Plato, *Republic*, § 550. Davies and Vaughan.

The necessary help from others is obtained in various ways. Parental, filial, and other kinship ties, friendship and pity, give rise to certain services, but they are necessarily limited in their sphere and exact in return a special attitude that would be intolerable if made universal. The modern man does not want to be cousin to every one, to give every one his personal friendship, to be in a perpetual attitude of receiving favors, or of asking and not receiving. Formerly the way of getting service from men outside these means was by slavery. The economic relation provides for the mutual exchange of goods and services on a basis of self-respect and equality. Through its system of contracts it provides for future as well as present service. It enables each to obtain the services of all the rest, and in turn to contribute without incurring any other claims or relations. Nor does it at all diminish the moral value of these mutual exchanges of goods and services that they may be paid for. It used to be the theory that in every bargain one party gained and the other lost. It is now recognized that a normal transaction benefits both parties. The "cash payment basis," which was at first denounced as substituting a mechanical nexus for the old personal tie, is in reality a means for establishing a greater independence instead of the older personal relation of "master" and "servant." It enabled a man, as Toynbee puts it, to sell his labor like any other commodity without selling himself.

But while the economic process has these moral possibilities, the morality of any given system or practice will depend on how far these are actually realized.

First of all, we may fairly ask of a process, Does it give to each member the kind of service needed by him? In economic terms, Does it produce the kinds of goods which society needs and desires? A method which provides for this successfully will in so far be providing against scarcity of some goods and oversupply of others, and thus against one of the sources of crises, irregularity of work and wages, and ultimately against suffering and want.

Secondly, if the process is an expression of the mutual dependence and service of members who as persons all have, as Kant puts it, intrinsic worth, and who in our political society are recognized as equal, we may fairly ask how it distributes the results of services rendered. Does the process tend to a broad and general distribution of goods in return for services rendered, or to make "the rich richer and the poor poorer?" Or, from another point of view, we might ask, Does the process tend to reward members on a moral or equitable basis, or upon a basis which is non-moral if not immoral or unjust.

Thirdly, the problem of *conflicting services* presents itself under several forms. There is, first, the ever-present conflict between producer and consumer. Higher wages and shorter hours are good for the carpenter or the weaver, until he pays his rent or buys clothes, when he is interested in cheaper goods. What principle can be employed to adjust such a question? Again, service to the consumer may lead a producer to a price-list implying a minimum of profits. One producer can afford this because of his larger business, but it will drive his competitor from the field. Shall he agree to a higher price at which all can do business, or insist on the lower which benefits the consumer and also himself? The labor union is a constant embodiment of the problem of conflicting services. How far shall it serve a limited group, the union, at the expense of other workers in the same trade—non-unionists? Does it make a difference whether the union is open to all, or whether the dues are fixed so high as to limit the membership? Shall the apprentices be limited to keep up the wage by limiting the supply? If so, is this fair to the boys or unskilled laborers who would like to enter? And granting that it is a hardship to these, is it harder or is it kinder to them than it would be to leave the issue to the natural weeding-out or starving-out procedure of natural selection in case too many enter the trade? Shall the hours be reduced and wages raised as high as possible, or is there a "fair" standard—fair to both consumer and laborer? How far may the union combine with the capitalist to raise prices to the consumer?

Private Property and Social Welfare.—The social value of property is obviously indirect, just as in law, private rights are regarded as indirectly based on social welfare. It is society's aim to promote the worth of its members and to favor the development of their personal dignity and freedom.

Property may, therefore, claim social value in so far as it serves these ends, unless it interferes with other social values. The effect of private property has seemed to some disastrous to community of interest and feeling. Plato, for example, in his ideal state would permit his guardians no private property. There would, then, be no quarrels over "meum" and "tuum," no suits or divisions, no petty meanness or anxieties, no plundering of fellow-citizens, no flattery of rich by poor. The mediaeval church carried out his theory. Even modern society preserves a certain trace of its spirit. For the classes that Plato called guardians—soldiers, judges, clergy, teachers—have virtually no property, although they are given support by society. It would probably be generally agreed that it is better for the public that these classes should not have large possessions. But it is obvious that private property is not the sole cause of division between individuals and classes. Where there is a deep-going unity of purpose and feeling, as in the early Christian community, or in various other companies that have attempted to practice communism, common ownership of wealth may be morally valuable as well as practically possible. But without such unity, mere abolition of property is likely to mean more bitter divisions, because there is no available method for giving to each the independence which is necessary to avoid friction and promote happiness.

Granting, however, the general position that some parts of wealth should be privately owned, we must recognize that a great number of moral problems remain as to the precise conditions under which society will find it wise to entrust the control of wealth to private ownership. For it must be clearly kept in mind that there is no absolute right of private property. Every right, legal or moral, derives from the social whole, which in turn, if it is a moral whole, must respect the individuality of each of its members. On this basis moral problems, such as the following, must be considered. What kind of public wealth should be given into absolute control of private individuals or impersonal corporations? Does the institution in its present form promote the good of those who have no property as well as of those who have it, or only of those who own? Would the welfare of society as a whole be promoted by giving a larger portion of public wealth into private control, or by retaining a larger proportion than at present under public ownership? Should there be any limit to the amount of land or other property which an individual or corporation may own? Are there any cases in which private ownership operates rather to exclude the mass of society from the benefits of civilization than to give them a share of those benefits? Should a man be allowed to transmit all his property to his heirs, or should it be in part reserved by society?

The preceding analysis has aimed to state some of the problems which belong necessarily to the economic life. At the present time, however, the moral issues assume a new and puzzling aspect because of the changes in economic conditions. It will be necessary to consider briefly these changed conditions.

§ 2. *The Problems Set by the New Economic Order*

The Collective and Impersonal Organizations.—Two changes have come over a large part of the economic and industrial field. The first is the change from an individual to a collective basis. The second, which is in part a consequence of the first, is a change from personal to impersonal or corporate relations. Corporations are of course composed of persons, but when organized for economic purposes they tend to become simply economic purpose incorporate, abstracted from all other human qualities. Although legally they may be subjects of rights and duties, they have but one motive, and are thus so abstract as to be morally impersonal. They tend to become machines for carrying on business, and, as such, may be as powerful—and as incapable of moral considerations—as other machines.

Ethical Readjustment.—Both these changes require readjustment of our ethical conceptions. Our conceptions of honesty and justice, of rights and duties, got their present shaping largely in an industrial and business order when mine and thine could be easily distinguished; when it was easy to tell how much a man produced; when the producer sold to his neighbors, and an employer had also the relations of neighbor to his workmen; when responsibility could be personally located, and conversely a man could control the business he owned or make individual contracts; when each man had his own means of lighting, heating, water supply, and frequently of transportation, giving no opportunity or necessity for public service corporations. Such conceptions are inadequate for the present order. The old honesty could assume that goods belonged to their makers, and then consider exchanges and contracts. The new honesty will first have to face a prior question, *Who owns what is collectively produced,* and are the present "rules of the game" distributing the returns honestly and fairly? The old justice in the economic field consisted chiefly in securing to each individual his rights in property or contracts. The new justice must consider how it can secure for each individual a standard of living, and such a share in the values of civilization as shall make possible a full moral life. The old virtue allowed a man to act more as an individual; the new virtue requires him to act in concerted effort if he is to achieve results. Individualist theories cannot interpret collectivist facts.

The changes in the economic and industrial processes by which not only the associated powers of present human knowledge, skill, and endurance, but also the combined results of past and future skill and industry are massed and wielded, depend on several concurrent factors. We shall notice the social agency, the technique of industry, the technique of business, the means of fixing value, and the nature of property.

§ 3. *The Agencies for Carrying on Commerce and Industry*

Early Agencies.—The early agencies for carrying on trade and industry were not organized purely for economic purposes. The kindred or family group engaged in certain industries, but this was only part of its purpose. So in the various territorial groups. The Athenian city-state owned the mines; the German village had its forest, meadow, and water as a common possession; and the "common" survived long in English and American custom, though the cattle pastured on it might be individually owned. In the United States certain land was reserved for school purposes, and if retained would now in some cases be yielding an almost incredible amount for public use; but it has usually been sold to private individuals. The national government still retains certain land for forest reserve, but until the recent movement toward municipal ownership, the civic community had almost ceased to be an economic factor in England and America, except in the field of roads, canals, and the postoffice. In both family and territorial or community control of industry, we have the economic function exercised as only one among several others. The economic helped to strengthen the other bonds of unity. On the other hand, the economic motive could not disentangle itself and stand out in all its naked force. Within either family or civic group the effects of the acquisitive instincts were limited by the fact that individuals in their industrial relations were also kin or neighbors.

The Business Enterprise.—In the business enterprise— partnership, company, corporation, "trust,"—on the other hand, men are organized solely for economic purposes. No other interests or ends are regarded. Corporations organized for this purpose "have no souls," because they consist of merely the abstract economic interests. While in domestic and territorial agencies the acquisitive forces were to some degree beneficially controlled, they were also injuriously hampered. With the rise of business enterprise as a distinct sphere of human action, the way was opened for a new force to manifest itself. This brought with it both advantages and disadvantages for the moral and social life as a whole. On the one hand, it increased tremendously the possibilities of economic and industrial efficiency. The size of the enterprise could be as large or as small as was needed for the most efficient production, and was not, as in family or community agency, sometimes too small and sometimes too large. The enterprise could group men according to their capacity for a particular task, and not, as in the other forms, be compelled to take a group already constituted by other than economic or industrial causes. Further, it could without difficulty dis-

pense with the aged or those otherwise unsuited to its purposes. When, moreover, as is coming to be increasingly the
case, great corporations, each controlling scores or even
hundreds of millions of capital, are linked together in common control, we have a tremendous force which may be
wielded as a unit. It is easy to assume—indeed it is difficult
for managers not to assume—that the interests of such colos-
sal organizations are of supreme importance, and that diplo-
macy, tariffs, legislation, and courts should be subordinate.
The moral dangers attaching to such corporations formed
solely for economic purposes are obvious, and have found
frequent illustration in their actual workings. Knowing few
or none of the restraints which control an individual, the
corporation has treated competitors, employees, and the public in a purely economic fashion. This insures certain limited
species of honesty, but does not include motives of private
sympathy or public duty.

The Labor Union.—Correlative to these corporate combinations of capital are Labor Unions of various types. They
are usually when first organized more complex in motive,
including social and educational ends, and are more emotional, or even passionate in conduct. With age they tend to
become more purely economic. In the United States they have
sought to secure better wages, to provide benefits or insurance
in case of sickness and death, and to gain better conditions
in respect of hours, of child-labor, and of protection against
dangerous machinery, explosions, and occupational diseases.
In Great Britain they have also been successful in applying
the cooperative plan to the purchase of goods for consumption. The organizations have been most successful among the
skilled trades. For so far as the aim is collective bargaining,
it is evident that the union will be effective in proportion as
it controls the whole supply of labor in the given trade. In
the unskilled forms of labor, especially with a constant flow
of immigration, it is difficult, if not impossible, to maintain
organizations comparable with the organizations of capital.
Hence in conflicts it is natural to expect the moral situations
which frequently occur when grossly unequal combatants
are opposed. The stronger has contempt for the weaker and
refuses to "recognize" his existence. The weaker, rendered

desperate by the hopelessness of his case when he contends under rules and with weapons prescribed by the stronger, refuses to abide by the rules and resorts to violence—only to find that by this he has set himself in opposition to all the forces of organized society.

Group Morality Again.—The striking feature of the new conditions is that it means a *reversion to group morality.* That is, it has meant this so far. Society is struggling to re-assert a general moral standard, but it has not yet found a standard, and has wavered between a rigid insistence upon outgrown laws on the one hand, and a more or less emotional and unreasoned sympathy with new demands, upon the other.[3] Group morality meant impersonal, collective life. It meant loyalty to one's own group, little regard for others, lack of responsibility, and lack of a completely social standard. There is, of course, one important difference. The present collective, impersonal agencies are not so naïve as the old kinship group. They can be used as effective agencies to secure definite ends, while the manipulators secure all the advantages of the old solidarity and irresponsibility.

Members and Management.—The corporation in its idea is democratic. For it provides for the union of a number of owners, some of them it may be small owners, under an elected management. It would seem to be an admirable device for maintaining concentration of power with distribution of ownership. But the very size of modern enterprises and unions prevents direct control by stockholders or members. They may dislike a given policy, but they are individually helpless. If they attempt to control, it is almost impossible, except in an extraordinary crisis, to unite a majority for common action.[4] The directors can carry on a policy and at the same time claim to be only agents of the stockholders, and therefore not ultimately responsible. What influence can the small shareholders in a railway company, or a great industrial corporation, or labor union, have? They unite with

---

3. E.g., in a strike there is sometimes a toleration by public senti-ment of a certain amount of violence where it is believed that there is no legal remedy for unfair conditions.
4. Recent elections in the great insurance companies have shown this.

ease upon one point only: they want dividends or results. When an illegal policy is to be pursued, or a legislature or jury is to be bribed, or a non-union man is to be "dealt with," the head officials likewise seek only "results." They turn over the responsibility to the operating or "legal" department, or to the "educational committee," and know nothing further. These departments are "agents" for the stockholders or union, and therefore, feel quite at ease. The stockholders are sure they never authorized anything wrong. Some corporations are managed for the interest of a large number of owners; some, on the other hand, by ingenious contracts with side corporations formed from an inner circle, are managed for the benefit of this inner circle. The tendency, moreover, in the great corporations is toward a situation in which boards of directors of the great railroad, banking, insurance, and industrial concerns are made up of the same limited group of men. This aggregate property may then be wielded as absolutely as though owned by these individuals. If it is used to carry a political election the directors, according to New York courts, are not culpable.

Employer and Employed.—The same impersonal relation often prevails between employer and employed. The ultimate employer is the stockholder, but he delegates power to the director, and he to the president, and he to the foreman. Each is expected to get results. The employed may complain about conditions to the president, and be told that he cannot interfere with the foreman, and to the foreman and be told that such is the policy of the company. The union may serve as a similar buffer. Often any individual of the series would act humanely or generously, if he were acting for himself. He cannot be humane or generous with the property of others, and hence there is no humanity or generosity in the whole system. This system seems to have reached its extreme in the creation of corporations for the express purpose of relieving employers of any personal responsibility. Companies organized to insure employers against claims made by employees on account of injuries may be regarded as a device for distributing the burden. But as the company is organized, not primarily to pay damages, as are life insurance companies, but to avoid such payment, it has a powerful motive in contesting every claim, however just, and in making it so expensive to prosecute a claim that the victims may prefer not to make the attempt. The "law's delay" can nearly always be counted upon as a powerful defense when a poor man is plaintiff and a rich corporation is defendant.

Relations to the Public.—The relations of corporations to the public, and of the public to corporations, are similarly impersonal and non-moral. A convenient way of approach to this situation is offered by the ethical, or rather non-ethical, status of the various mechanical devices which have come into use in recent years for performing many economic services. The weighing machines, candy machines, telephones, are supposed to give a certain service for a penny or a nickel. But if the machine is out of order, the victim has no recourse. His own attitude is correspondingly mechanical. He regards himself as dealing, not with a person, but with a thing. If he can exploit it or "beat" it, so much the better. Now a corporation, in the attitude which it takes and evokes, is about half-way between the pure mechanism of a machine and the completely personal attitude of a moral individual. A man is overcharged, or has some other difficulty with an official of a railroad company. It is as hopeless to look for immediate relief as it is in the case of a slot machine. The conductor is just as much limited by his orders as the machine by its mechanism. The man may later correspond with some higher official, and if patience and life both persist long enough, he will probably recover. But to prevent fraud, the company is obliged to be more rigorous than a person would be who was dealing with the case in a personal fashion. Hence the individual with a just grievance is likely to entertain toward the corporation the feeling that he is dealing with a machine, not with an ethical being, even as the company's servants are not permitted to exercise any moral consideration in dealing with the public. They merely obey orders. Public sentiment, which would hold an individual teamster responsible for running over a child, or an individual stage owner responsible for reckless or careless conduct in carrying his passengers, feels only a blind rage in the case of a railroad accident. It cannot fix moral responsibility definitely upon either stockholder or management or employee, and conversely neither stockholder, nor manager, nor employee[5] feels the moral restraint which the individual would feel. He is not wholly responsible, and his share in the collective responsibility is so small as often to seem entirely negligible.

Relations to the Law.—The collective business enterprises, when incorporated, are regarded as "juristic persons," and so gain the support of law as well as become subject to its control. If the great corporation can thus gain the right of an individual, it can enter the field of free contract with great advantage. Labor unions have not incorporated, fearing, perhaps, to give the law control over their funds. They seek a higher standard of living, but private law does not recognize this as a right. It merely protects contracts, but leaves it to the individual to make the best contract he can. As most wage-earners have no contracts, but are liable to dismissal at any time, the unions have seen little to be gained by incorporation. They have thus missed contact with the institution in which society seeks to embody, however tardily, its moral ideas and have been, in a sense, outlaws. They were such at first by no fault of their own, for the law treated such combinations as conspiracies. And they are still at two decided disadvantages. First, the capitalistic or employing corporation acting as a single juristic person may refuse to buy the labor of a union; indeed, according to a recent decision, it cannot be forbidden to discharge its employees because of their membership in a union. As the corporation may employ scores of thousands, and be practically the only employer of a particular kind of labor, it can thus enforce a virtual boycott and prevent the union from selling its labor. It does not need to use a "blacklist" because the employers are all combined in one "person." On the other hand, the union is adjudged to act in restraint of interstate commerce if it boycotts the employing corporation. The union is here treated as a combination, not as a single person. The second point in which the employing body has greatly the legal advantage appears in the case of a strike. Men are allowed to quit work, but this is not an effective method of exerting

5. "J. O. Fagan," in the *Atlantic Monthly* (1908), has called attention to the influence of the union in shielding individuals from the penalties of carelessness.

pressure unless the employer is anxious to keep his plant in operation and can employ no one else. If he can take advantage of an open labor market and hire other workmen, the only resource of the strikers is to induce these to join their ranks. But they·have been enjoined by the courts, not only from intimidating, but even from persuading[6] employees to quit work. The method of procedure in enforcing the injunction, which enables the judge to fix the offense, eliminate trial by jury, determine the guilt, and impose any penalty he deems fit, has all the results of criminal process with none of its limitations, and forms a most effective agency against the unions. Where persuasion is enjoined it is difficult to see how a union can exert any effective pressure except in a highly skilled trade, where it can control all the labor supply. In the field of private rights and free contract, the labor unions are then at a disadvantage because they have no rights which are of any value for their purposes, except, under certain conditions, the right to refuse to work. And since this is, in most cases, a weapon that injures its wielder far more than his opponent, it is not effective.

Disappointed in the field of free contract, the labor unions seek to enlist public agency in behalf of better sanitary conditions and in prevention of child-labor, long hours for

6. Recent Illinois decisions (216 Ill., pp. 358 f., and especially 232 Ill., pp. 431–40) uphold sweeping injunctions against persuasion, no matter how peaceable. "Lawful competition, which may injure the business of a person, even though successfully directed to driving him out of business, is not actionable." But for a union to hire laborers away from an employer by money or transportation is not "lawful competition." The object is assumed by the court to be malicious, i.e., the injury of the employer. The court does not entertain the possibility that to obtain an eight-hour day is as lawful an aim for the labor union as to acquire property is for an employer. The decision shows clearly the difference in legal attitude toward pressure exerted by business corporations for the familiar end of acquisition, and that exerted by the union for the novel end of a standard of living. The court regards the injury to others as incidental in the former, but as primary and therefore as malicious in the latter. It may be that future generations will regard this judicial psychology somewhat as we regard some of the cases cited above, Chapter 21. Other courts have not always taken this view, and have permitted persuasion unless it is employed in such a manner or under such circumstances as to "operate on fears rather than upon their judgments or their sympathies" (17., *N. Y. Supp.*, 264). For other cases, *American and English Decisions in Equity*, 1905, pp. 565 f.; also Eddy on Combinations.

women, unfair contracts, and the like. Capitalistic corporations frequently resist this change of venue on the ground that it interferes with free contract or takes away property without "due process of law," and many laws have been set aside as unconstitutional on these grounds,[7] several of them no doubt because so drawn as to appear to be in the interest of a class, rather than in that of the public. The trend in the direction of asserting larger public control both under the police power and over corporations in whose service the pub-

7. The list appended was bulletined at the Chicago Industrial Exhibit of 1906, and reprinted by Taylor in *Charities and The Commons.*
"What 'Freedom of Contract' has Meant to Labor:
  1. Denial of eight-hour law for women in Illinois.
  2. Denial of eight-hour law for city labor or for mechanics and ordinary laborers.
  3. Denial of ten-hour law for bakers.
  4. Inability to prohibit tenement labor.
  5. Inability to prevent by law employer from requiring employee as condition of securing work, to assume all risk from injury while at work.
  6. Inability to prohibit employer selling goods to employees at greater profit than to non-employees.
  7. Inability to prohibit mine owners screening coal which is mined by weight before crediting same to employees as basis of wages.
  8. Inability to legislate against employer using coercion to prevent employee becoming a member of a labor union.
  9. Inability to restrict employer in making deductions from wages of employees.
 10. Inability to compel by law, weekly or bi-weekly payment of wages.
 11. Inability to compel by law payment of wages at regular intervals.
 12. Inability to provide by law that laborers on public works shall be paid prevailing rate of wages.
 13. Inability to compel by law payment of extra compensation for overtime.
 14. Inability to prevent by law employer from holding back part of wages.
 15. Inability to compel payment of wages in cash; so that employer may pay in truck or scrip not redeemable in lawful money.
 16. Inability to forbid alien labor on municipal contracts.
 17. Inability to secure by law union label on city printing."
Labor representatives speak of "the ironic manner in which the courts guarantee to workers: The right to be maimed and killed without liability to the employer; the right to be discharged for belonging to a union; the right to work as many hours as employers please and under any considerations which they may impose." The "irony" is, of course, not intended by the courts. It is the irony inherent in a situation when rules designed to secure justice become futile, if not a positive cause of injustice, because of changed conditions.

lic has a direct interest, will be noted later. Against other corporations the general public or the unsuccessful competitor has sought legal aid in legislation against "trusts," but this has mainly proved to be futile. It has merely induced a change in form of organization. Nor has it been easy as yet for the law to exercise any effective control over the business corporation on any of the three principles invoked—namely: to prevent monopoly, to secure the public interest in the case of public service corporations, and to assert police power. For penalties by fine frequently fail to reach the guilty persons, and it is difficult to fix any personal responsibility. Juries are unwilling to convict subordinate officials of acts which they believe to have been required by the policy of the higher officials, while, on the other hand, the higher officials are seldom directly cognizant of criminal acts. Gradually, however, we may believe that the law will find a way to make both capital and labor organizations respect the public welfare, and to give them support in their desirable ends. The cooperative principle cannot be outlawed; it must be more fully socialized.

§ 4. The Methods of Production, Exchange, and Valuation

The Machine.—The technique of production has shown a similar progress from individual to collective method. The earlier method was that of handicraft. The present method in most occupations, aside from agriculture, is that of the machine. But the great economic advantage of the machine is not only in the substitution of mechanical power for muscle; it is also in the substitution of collective for individual work. It is the machine which makes possible on a tremendously effective basis the division of labor and its social organization. The extraordinary increase in wealth during the past century depends upon these two factors. The machine itself moreover, in its enormous expansion, is not only a social tool, but a social product. The invention and discovery which gave rise to the new processes in industry of every sort were largely the outcome of scientific researches carried on at public expense to a great extent by men other than those who finally utilize their results. They become in turn the instruments for the production of wealth, which is thus doubly social in origin.

This machine process has an important bearing upon the factors of character mentioned in our analysis. It standardizes efficiency; it calls for extraordinary increase of speed; it requires great specialization of function and often calls for no knowledge of the whole process. On the other hand, it gives a certain sense of power to control and direct highly complicated machinery. In the more skilled trades there is more time and resource for intellectual, aesthetic, or social satisfactions. The association of workmen favors discussion of common interests, sympathy, and cooperation; this may evoke a readiness to sacrifice individual to group welfare, which is quite analogous to patriotic sentiment at its best, even if it is liable to such violent expressions as characterize patriotic sentiment at its worst. The association of workmen is one of the most significant features of modern industry.

Capital and Credit.—The technique of exchange of services and goods has undergone a transformation from an individual and limited to a collective and almost unlimited method. The earlier form of exchange and barter limited the conduct of business to a small area, and the simpler form of personal service involved either slavery or some personal control which was almost as direct. With the use of money it became possible to make available a far greater area for exchange and to accumulate capital which represented the past labors of vast numbers of individuals. With the further discovery of the possibilities of a credit system which business enterprise now employs, it is possible to utilize in any enterprise not merely the results of the labor of the past, but the anticipated income of the future. A corporation, as organized at present, issues obligations in the form of bonds and stock which represent no value as yet produced, but only the values of labor or privilege anticipated. The whole technique, therefore, of capital and credit means a collective business enterprise. It masses the work and the abilities of thousands and hundreds of thousands in the past and the future, and wields the product as an almost irresistible agency to achieve new enterprises or to drive from the field rival enterprises.

Basis of Valuation.—The whole basis for value and prices has also been changed. The old basis, employed for the most part through the Middle Ages in fixing the value of labor or goods, was the amount of labor and material which had been expended. The modern basis is that of supply and demand. This proceeds on the theory that it is human wants which after all give value to any product. I may have expended time and labor upon a book or carving, or in the cultivation of a new vegetable, or in the manufacture of an article for apparel, but if no one cares to read the book or look at the carving, if the vegetable is one that no one can eat, or the garment is one that no one will wear, it has no value. Starting then from this, we can see how the two elements in valuation—namely, demand and supply—are affected by social factors. The demand for an article depends upon the market: i.e., upon how many buyers there are, and what wants they have. Modern methods of communication and transportation have made the market for goods as large as the civilized world. Education is constantly awakening new wants. The facilities for communication, for travel, and for education are constantly leading one part of the world to imitate the standards or fashions set by other parts. We have, therefore, a social standard for valuation which is constantly extending in area and in intensity.

The other factor in valuation, namely, the supply, is likewise being affected in an increasing degree by social forces. With many, if not with most, of the commodities which are of greatest importance, it has been found that there is less profit in an unrestricted supply than in a supply regulated in the interest of the producers. The great coal mines, the iron industries, the manufacturers of clothing, find it more profitable to combine and produce a limited amount. The great corporations and trusts have usually signalized their acquisition of a monopoly or an approximate control of any great field of production by shutting down part of the factories formerly engaged. The supply of labor is likewise limited by the policies of labor unions in limiting the number of apprentices allowed, or by other means of keeping the union small. Tariffs, whether in the interest of capital or of labor, are a social control of the supply. Franchises, whether of steam railroads, street transportation, gas, electric lighting, or other public utilities so-called, are all of them in the nature of monopolies granted to a certain group of individuals. Their value is dependent upon the general need of these utilities, coupled with the public limitation of supply. In many cases the services are so indispensable to the community that the servant does not need to give special care or thought to the rendering of especially efficient service. The increase in population makes the franchises enormously profitable without any corresponding increase of risk or effort on the part of the utility company.

But the most striking illustration of the creation of values by society is seen in the case of land. That an acre of land in one part of the country is worth fifty dollars, and in another part two hundred thousand dollars,[8] is not due to any difference in the soil, nor for the most part to any labor or skill or other quality of the owner. It is due to the fact that in the one case there is no social demand, whereas, in the other, the land is in the heart of a city. In certain cases, no doubt, the owner of city real estate may help by his enterprise to build up the city, but even if so this is incidental. The absentee owner profits as much by the growth of the city as the foremost contributor to that growth. The owner need not even improve the property by a building. This enormous increase in land values has been called the "unearned increment." In America it is due very largely to features of natural location and transportation. It has seemed to some writers, such as Henry George, not only a conspicuous injustice, but the root of all economic evil. It is, no doubt, in many cases, a conspicuous form of "easy money," but the principle is not different from that which is involved in nearly all departments of modern industry. The wealth of modern society is really a gigantic pool. No individual knows how much he creates; it is a social product. To estimate what any one should receive by an attempted estimate of what he has individually contributed is absolutely impossible.

8. In Greater New York. An acre on Manhattan Island is of course worth much more. The Report of the New York Tax Department for 1907 is very suggestive.

§ 5. *The Factors Which Aid Ethical Reconstruction*

The two distinctive features of the modern economic situation, its collective character and its impersonal character, are themselves capable of supplying valuable aid toward understanding the ethical problems and in making the reconstruction required. For *the very magnitude of modern operations and properties serves to bring out more clearly the principles involved. The impersonal character allows economic forces pure and simple to be seen in their moral bearings.* Publicity becomes a necessity. Just as the factories are compelled to have better light, air, and sanitation than the sweat shops, so public attention is aroused and the conscience stimulated by practices of great corporations, although these practices may be in principle precisely the same as those of private persons which escape moral reprobation. In some cases, no doubt, the very magnitude of the operation does actually change the principle. A "lift" on the road from an oldtime stage-driver, or a "special bargain" at a country store was not likely to disturb the balance of competition as a system of free passes or secret rebates may in modern business. But in other cases what the modern organizations have done is simply to exhibit the workings of competition or other economic forces *on a larger scale*. An illustration of this is seen in the familiar fact that a law passed to correct some corporate practice is often found to apply to many practices not contemplated by the makers of the law.

The effect of getting a principle out into the open and at work on a large scale is to make public judgment clear and reprobation of bad practices more effective. The impersonal factor likewise contributes powerfully to make condemnation easy. Criticism is unhampered by the considerations which complicate the situation when the conduct of an individual is in question. The individual may be a good neighbor, or a good fellow, or have had bad luck. But no one hesitates to express his opinion of a corporation, and the average jury is not biased in its favor, whatever may be true of the bench. Even the plea that the corporation includes widows and orphans among its shareholders, which is occasionally put forth to avert interference with corporate practices, usually falls on unsympathetic ears. A higher standard

will be demanded for business conduct, a more rigid regard
for public service will be exacted, a more moderate return
for invested capital in public service, and a more liberal
treatment of employees will be insisted upon from corporations than from private individuals. Nor does the organization of labor escape the same law. When an agent of a union
has been detected in calling a strike for private gain, public
sentiment has been as severe in condemnation as in the case
of corporate officials who have profited at the expense of
stockholders.

Summary.—We may summarize some of the chief points
brought out by our analysis. Modern technique has increased
enormously the productivity of labor, but has increased its
dangers to health and life, and to some extent diminished its
educating and moralizing values. The impersonal agencies
give vast power, but make responsibility difficult to locate.
The collective agencies and the social contributions make the
economic process a great social pool. Men put in manual
labor, skill, capital. Some of it they have inherited from their
kin; some they have inherited from the inventors and scientists who have devised tools and processes; some they have
wrought themselves. This pooling of effort is possible because
of good government and institutions which were created by
statesmen, patriots, and reformers, and are maintained by
similar agencies. The pool is immensely productive. But no
one can say just how much his contribution earns. Shall
every one keep what he can get? Shall all share alike? Or
shall there be other rules for division—either made and enforced by society or made by the individual and enforced
by his own conscience? Are our present rules adequate to
such a situation as that of the present? These are some of
the difficult questions that modern conditions are pressing
upon the man who thinks.

Literature

Besides the classic treatises of Adam Smith, J. S. Mill, and
Karl Marx, which are important for the relation of the economic
to the whole social order during the past century, the following

recent works in the general field give especial prominence to the ethical problems involved: Marshall, *Principles of Economics,* 1898; Hadley, *Economics,* 1896; Clark, *Essentials of Economic Theory as Applied to Modern Problems of Industry and Public Policy,* 1907; George, *Progress and Poverty,* 1879; Schmoller, *Grundriss der allgemeinen Volkswirtschaftslehre,* 1900–04; Bonar, *Philosophy and Political Economy,* 1893; Hobson, *The Social Problem,* 1901; Brooks, *The Social Unrest,* 1903.

ON MODERN BUSINESS AND INDUSTRY: Veblen, *The Theory of Business Enterprise,* 1904; Cooke-Taylor, *The Modern Factory System,* 1891; Hobson, *Evolution of Modern Capitalism,* 1894; Toynbee, *The Industrial Revolution,* 1890; Adams and Sumner, *Labor Problems,* 1905; S. and B. Webb, *History of Trade Union-ism,* 1894, *Problems of Modern Industry,* 1898, and *Industrial Democracy,* 1902; Mitchell, *Organized Labor,* 1903; Ely, *The Labor Movement in America,* 1886; Hollander and Barnett, *Studies in American Trades Unionism,* 1906; Henderson, *Social Elements,* 1898, chs. vii–x.

Certain problems suggested by the foregoing analysis are unsettled, for the issues are so involved, and in some cases, both the facts and their interpretations are so much in controversy, that we cannot yet formulate sure moral judgments. On the other hand, certain principles emerge with a good degree of clearness. We state some of the more obvious.

1. Wealth and Property are Subordinate in Importance to Personality.—The life is more than meat. Most agree to this, stated abstractly, but many fail to make the application. They may sacrifice their own health, or human sympathy, or family life; or they may consent to this actively or passively as employers, or consumers, or citizens, in the case of others. A civilization which loses life in providing the means to live is not highly moral. A society which can afford luxuries for some cannot easily justify unhealthful conditions of production, or lack of general education. An individual who gratifies a single appetite at the expense of vitality and efficiency is immoral. A society which considers wealth or property as ultimate, whether under a conception of "natural rights" or otherwise, is setting the means above the end, and is therefore unmoral or immoral.

2. Wealth should Depend on Activity.—The highest aspect of life on its individual side is found in active and resolute achievement, in the embodying of purpose in action. Thought, discovery, creation, mark a higher value than the satisfaction of wants, or the amassing of goods. If the latter is to be a help it must stimulate activity, not deaden it. Inherited wealth without any accompanying incitement from education or class feeling or public opinion would be a questionable institution from this point of view. Veblen in his *Theory of the Leisure Class* points out various forms of degeneration that may attend upon leisure, when leisure means not merely release from mechanical labor in the interest of more intellectual activity, but a relinquishing of all serious labor. As the race has made its ascent in the presence of an environment which has constantly selected the more active persons, society in its institutions and consciously directed processes may well plan to keep this balance between activity and reward. Modern charity has adopted this principle. We fear to pauperize by giving aid to the poor unless we can provide some form of self-help. But in its treatment of the rich, society is not solicitous. Our provisions for inheritance of property undoubtedly pauperize a certain proportion of those who inherit. Whether this can be prevented without interfering with motives to activity on the part of those who acquire the property, or whether the rich thus pauperized are not as well worth saving to society as the poor, will undoubtedly become more pressing problems as the number of inheritors increases, and society recognizes that it may have a duty to its idle rich as well as to its idle poor.

3. *Public Service Should Go Along with Wealth.*—Note that we do not say, "wealth should be proportionate to public service." This would take us at once into the controversy between the individualist and the socialist which we shall consider later among the unsettled problems. The individualist, as represented, for example, by Herbert Spencer, would say that except for the young, the aged, or the sick, reward should be proportioned to merit. The socialist, on the other hand, is more inclined to say, "From each according to his ability, to each according to his needs." In either case, it is assumed that there should be public service. Leaving for later consideration the question whether we can fix any quantitative rule, let us notice at this time why some service is a fundamental moral principle.

Such service in the form of some economically useful contribution, whether to the production and distribution of goods, to the public order, to education, to the satisfaction of aesthetic and religious wants, might be demanded as a matter of common honesty. This would be to treat it as a just claim made by society upon each of its members. There is, of course, no legal claim. The law is far from adopting as a universal maxim, "If any man will not work, neither let him

eat." Vagrancy is not a term applied to all idlers. It is sufficient for the law if some of a man's ancestors obtained possession and title by service, or force, or gift. Modern law,
in its zeal to strengthen the institution of property, releases
all the owner's posterity forever from the necessity of any
useful service. The old theology used to carry the conception
of inherited or imputed sin and merit to extremes which
modern individualism rejects. But the law—at least in the
United States—permits a perpetual descent of inherited property; i.e., of inherited permission to receive from society
without rendering any personal return. Theologically and
morally, however, the man of to-day repudiates any conception which would reduce him to a shadow of another. He
wishes to stand on his own feet, to be rewarded or blamed
according to his own acts, not because of a deed of some one
else. To follow out this principle in the economic sphere
would require that every man who receives aught from others
should feel in duty bound to render some service. Merely "to
have been born" is hardly sufficient in a democratic society,
however munificent a contribution to the social weal the
French aristocrat may have felt this to be.

But it is only one aspect of the case to say that society
may claim service as a just due. There is another aspect—
what this service means to the person himself. It is his opportunity to fulfill his function in the social organism. Now
a person is as large as his purpose and will. The person,
therefore, who identifies his purposes with the welfare of
the public is thereby identifying himself with the whole social body. He is no longer himself alone; he is a social power.
Not only the leader of society, but every efficient servant
makes himself an organ through which society itself acts
and moves forward. This is perhaps most conspicuous in the
case of the great inventors or organizers of industry and society. By serving civilization they have become its bearers
and have thus shared its highest pulses. But it is true of every
laborer. As he is an active contributor he becomes creative,
not merely receptive.

4. *The Change from Individual to Collective Methods
of Industry and Business Demands a Change from Individual
to Collective Types of Morality.*—Moral action is either to accomplish some positive good or to hinder some wrong or evil.

But under present conditions the individual by himself is practically helpless and useless for either purpose. It was formerly possible for a man to set a high standard and live up to it, irrespective of the practice or cooperation of others. When a seller's market was limited to his acquaintance or a limited territory, it might well be that honesty or even fair dealing was the best policy. But with the changes that have come in business conditions the worse practices, like a baser coinage, tend to drive out the morally better. This may not apply so thoroughly to the relations between seller and buyer, but it applies to many aspects of trade. A merchant may desire to pay his women clerks wages on which they can support life without selling their souls. But if his rival across the street pays only half the wage necessary for subsistence, it is evident the former is in so far at a disadvantage. Extend the same policy. Let the former have his goods made under good conditions and the latter have no scruple against "sweating"; let the former pay taxes on an honest estimate and the latter "see" the assessor, or threaten to move out of town if he is assessed for more than a figure named by himself; let the former ask only for a fair chance, while the latter secures legislation that favors his own interests, or gets specifications for bids worded so that they will exclude his opponents, or in selling to public bodies "fixes" the councils or school committees, or obtains illegal favors in transportation. Let this continue, and how long will the former stay in the field? Even as regards quality of goods, where it would seem more plausible that honest dealing might succeed, experience has shown that this depends on whether the frauds can be easily detected. In the case of drugs and goods where the adulterations cannot be readily discovered, there is nothing to offset the more economical procedure of the fraudulent dealer. The fact that it is so difficult to procure pure drugs and pure food would seem to be most plausibly due to the fatal competition of the adulterated article.

Or, suppose a person has a little property invested in some one of the various corporations which offer the most convenient method for placing small sums as well as large. This railroad defies the government by owning coal mines as well as transporting the product; that public service corporation has obtained its franchise by bribery; this corpora-

tion is an employer of child labor; that finds it less expensive
to pay a few damage suits—those it cannot fight successfully
—than to adopt devices which will protect employees. Does
a man, or even an institution, act morally if he invests in
such corporations in which he finds himself helpless as an
individual stockholder? And if he sells his stock at the market
price to invest the money elsewhere, is it not still the price
of fraud or blood? If, finally, he buys insurance for his family's support, recent investigation has shown that he may
have been contributing unawares to bribery of legislatures,
and to the support of political theories to which he may be
morally opposed. The individual cannot be moral in independence. The modern business collectivism forces a collective morality. Just as the individual cannot resist the combination, so individual morality must give place to a more
robust or social type.

5. *To Meet the Change to Corporate Agency and Ownership, Ways Must be Found to Restore Personal Control and
Responsibility.*—Freedom and responsibility must go hand in
hand. The "moral liability limited" theory cannot be accepted
in the simple form in which it now obtains. If society holds
stockholders responsible, they will soon cease to elect managers merely on an economic basis and will demand morality.
If directors are held personally responsible for their "legal
department," or union officials for their committees, directors
and officials will find means to know what their subordinates
are doing. "Crime is always personal," and it is not usual
for subordinates to commit crimes for the corporation against
the explicit wishes of the higher officials. In certain lines the
parties concerned have voluntarily sought to restore a more
personal relation.[1] It has been found profitable to engage
foremen who can get on smoothly with workmen. It has
proved to be good economy to treat men, whether they sell
labor or buy it, with respect and fairness.

The managers of some of the great public service corporations have also recently shown a disposition to recognize
some public obligations, with the naïve admission that this
has been neglected. Labor unions are coming to see the need

1. Hayes Robbins in the *Atlantic Monthly* for June, 1907, "The
Personal Factor in the Labor Problem."

of conciliating public opinion if they are to gain their contests.

6. *To Meet the Impersonal Agencies Society Must Require Greater Publicity and Express Its Moral Standards More Fully in Law.*—Publicity is not a cure for bad practices, but it is a powerful deterrent agency so long as the offenders care for public opinion and not solely for the approval of their own class. Professor Ross[2] maintains that in the United States classes are still so loosely formed that general approval is desired by the leaders. Hence he urges that it is possible to enforce moral standards by the "grilling of sinners." But to make this "grilling" a moral process society needs much more accurate information and a more impartial basis for selecting its sinners than present agencies afford. The public press is itself in many respects one of the most conspicuous examples of the purely economic motive. The newspaper or magazine must interest readers and not displease advertisers. The news is selected, or colored, or worked up to suit particular classes. If a speaker says what the reporter does not regard as interesting he is likely to find himself reported as saying something more striking. Publicity bureaus are able to point with pride to the amount of matter, favorable to certain interests, which they place before the public as news. The particular interests singled out for "exposure" are likely to be determined more by the anticipated effects on circulation or advertising than by the merits of the case. It is scarcely more satisfactory to leave all the education of public opinion to commercial control than to leave all elementary education to private interests. Publicity—scientific investigation and public discussion—is indeed indispensable, and its greatest value is probably not in the exhilarating discharge of righteous indignation, but in the positive elevation of standards, by giving completer knowledge and showing the fruits of certain practices. A large proportion of the public will wish to do the right thing if they can see it clearly, and can have public support, so that right action will not mean suicide.

But the logical way to meet the impersonal character

2. Ross, *Sin and Society.*

of modern economic agencies is by the moral consciousness embodied in an impersonal agency, the law. The law is not to be regarded chiefly as an agency for punishing criminals. It, in the first place, defines a standard; and, in the next place, *it helps the morally disposed to maintain this standard by freeing him from unscrupulous competition.* It is a general principle that to resort to the law is an ethical gain only when the getting something done is more important than to get it done from the right motive. This evidently applies to acts of corporate bodies. We do not care for their motives. We are not concerned to save their souls. We are concerned only for results—just the place where we have seen that the personal responsibility breaks down. The value of good motives and moral purpose is in this case located in those who strive to secure and execute progressive legislation for the public good, and in the personal spirit with which this is accepted and carried out by officials.[3]

7. *Every Member of Society Should Share in Its Wealth and in the Values Made Possible by It.*—The quantitative basis of division and the method for giving each a share belong to the unsettled problems. But the worth and dignity of every human being of moral capacity is fundamental in nearly every moral system of modern times. It is implicit in the Christian doctrine of the worth of the soul, in the Kantian doctrine of personality, in the Benthamic dictum, "every man to count as one." It is imbedded in our democratic theory and institutions. With the leveling and equalizing of physical and mental power brought about by modern inventions and the spread of intelligence, no State is permanently safe except on a foundation of justice. And justice cannot be fundamentally in contradiction with the essence of democracy. This means that wealth must be produced, distributed, and owned justly: that is, so as to promote the individuality of every member of society, while at the same time he must always function as a member, not as an individual. In defining justice some will place freedom first; others, a standard of living. Some will seek fairness by distributing to each an actual share of the goods; others, by giving to each a fair

3. See Florence Kelley, *Some Ethical Gains Through Legislation.*

chance to get his share of goods. Others again have held that if no moral purpose is proposed and each seeks to get what he can for himself, the result will be a just distribution because of the beneficent effects of competition. Still others have considered that if the economic process has once been established on the basis of contracts rather than status or slavery, justice may be regarded as the maintenance of these contracts, whatever the effect in actual benefits. These views will be considered under the next topic as unsettled problems.

Literature

In addition to the works cited at the close of the last chapter, Giddings, "The Costs of Progress," in *Democracy and Empire*, 1901; Bosanquet (Mrs. B.), *The Standard of Life*, 1898; Bosanquet, B., *Aspects of the Social Problem*, 1895; Stephen, *Social Rights and Duties*, 1896; Tufts, "Some Contributions of Psychology to the Conception of Justice," *Philosophical Review*, XV, 1906, pp. 361–79; Woods, "Democracy, A New Unfolding of Human Power," in *Studies in Philosophy and Psychology* (Garman Commemorative Volume), 1906.

24. UNSETTLED PROBLEMS
IN THE ECONOMIC ORDER

Under this head we propose to consider one general and three special problems on which society is at present at work, framing new moral standards to meet new conditions. Many of the questions involved in the new order marshal themselves under a single antithesis. Will the moral values of wealth be most fully secured and justly distributed by leaving to individuals the greatest possible freedom and holding them morally responsible, or by social agency and control? The first theory is known as *individualism*. The most convenient term for the second position would be *socialism*.

Socialism, however, is, for many, an epithet rather than a scientific conception. It is supposed to mean necessarily the abolition of all private enterprise or private property. In its extreme form it might mean this, as individualism in its extreme form would mean anarchy. But as a practical ethical proposition we have before us neither the abolition of public agency and control—extreme individualism—nor the abolition of private agency and control. We have the problem of getting the proper amount of each in order that the highest morality may prevail. Each theory professes to desire the fullest development and freedom of the individual. The individualist seeks it through formal freedom and would limit public agency to a minimum. The socialist is willing to permit limitations on formal freedom in order to secure the "real" freedom which he regards as more important and substantial. Between the extremes, and borrowing from each, is a somewhat indefinite programme known as the demand for equal opportunity. Let us consider each in a brief statement and then in a more thorough analysis.

§ *1*. *General Statement of the Positions of Individualism and of Public Agency and Control*

1. Individualism. — Individualism[1] believes that each man can secure his own welfare better than any one else can secure it for him. It further holds that society is made up of individuals, and hence, if each is provided for, the welfare of the whole is secured. Such goods as are social can be secured by voluntary association. Believing that the course of civilization has been "from status to contract," it makes free contract its central principle. It should be the chief business of organized society to maintain and safeguard this freedom. It locates the important feature of freedom precisely in the act of assent, rather than in any consideration of whether the after consequences of the assent are good or bad; nor does it ask what motives (force and fraud aside) brought about the assent, or whether there was any other alternative. In other words, it regards formal freedom as fundamental. If not in itself all that can be desired, it is the first step, and the only one which law need recognize. The individual may be trusted to take other steps, if protected in this. The only restriction upon individual freedom should be that it must not interfere with the equal freedom of others. In the economic sphere this restriction would mean, "must not interfere by force." The theory does not regard economic pressure by competition as interference. Hence it favors free competition. Leaving out of account benevolence, it holds that in business each should be allowed, or even recommended, to seek his own advantage. But when the question as to the justice of the distribution reached by this method is raised, a division appears between the *democratic* individualists and the *"survival of the fittest"* individualists. The democratic individualists — Adam Smith, Bentham, Mill[2] — believed that individualism would promote the welfare of *all* members of society. The "survival of the fittest" school maintains that the welfare of the race or of civilization depends on the sifting and selecting process known as the "struggle for exist-

---

1. See above, pp. 384 f., 421–26, 432.
2. In his later years Mill had much more confidence in the value of social agency.

ence." If the "fittest" are thus selected and survive, it matters
not so much what is the lot of the rest. We must choose between progress through aristocratic selection and degeneration through democratic leveling.

2. *Theory of Public Agency and Control.*—Socialism
(using the word in a broad sense) holds that society should
secure to all its members the goods of life. It holds that an
unrestrained liberty of struggle for existence may secure the
survival of the strongest, but not necessarily of the morally
best. The individualist's theory emphasizes formal freedom.
"Seek first freedom and all other things will be added." The
socialist view emphasizes the content. It would have all members of society share in education, wealth, and all the goods
of life. In this it agrees with democratic individualism. But
it considers this impossible on the basis of individual effort.
To hold that society as a whole can do nothing for the individual either ignores social goods or supposes the social
will, so powerful for democracy in the political sphere, to be
helpless and futile in the economic world. To assume that
all the control of economic distribution—the great field of
justice—may be left to individual freedom and agency, is as
archaic as to leave the collection of taxes, the administration
of provinces, and the education of citizens to private enterprise. It regards the unregulated struggle for existence as
economically wasteful and morally vicious, both in its inequality of distribution and in the motives of egoism on
which it relies. Individualism, on the other hand, so far as
it is intelligent and does not lump socialism with anarchy
and all other criticisms on the established order, regards socialism as ignoring the supreme importance of active personal effort, and the value of freedom as the keynote to
progress.

3. *Equal Opportunity.*—An intermediate view has for
its maxim, "equal opportunity." It holds with individualism
that the active personality is to be stimulated and made a
prime end. But because it believes that not merely a few but
all persons should be treated as ends, it finds individualism
condemned. For it holds that an unregulated struggle for
existence does not secure the end individualism professes to
seek. When individuals start in the race handicapped by dif-

ferences in birth, education, family, business, friends, and inherited wealth, *there is no selection of ability*; there is *selection of the privileged.* Hence it would borrow so much from socialism as to give each individual a "fair start." This would include public schools, and an undefined amount of provision for sanitation, and for governmental regulation of the stronger.

It is manifest, however, that this theory of the "square deal" is a name for a general aim rather than for a definite programme. For a "square deal," or equality of opportunity, might be interpreted to call for a great variety of concrete schemes, ranging all the way from an elementary education up to public ownership of all the tools for production, and to abolition of the right to bequeath or inherit property. The peoples of America, Europe, and Australasia are at present working out policies which combine in various degrees the individualistic and the socialistic views. Most have public schools. Some have provision for old age and accident through either mutual or State systems of insurance and pensions. Let us analyze the moral aspects of the two opposing theories more thoroughly. It is obvious that the third view is only one of a number of mediating positions.

§ 2. *Individualism or Free Contract Analyzed: Its Values*

Efficiency in Production.—Individualism can make out a strong case in respect to several of the ethical qualities which are demanded: *viz.*, efficiency in production of goods, stimulation of active and forceful character, promotion of freedom and responsibility, encouragement to wide diversification of occupation and thus of services, and, finally, the supply to society of the kinds of goods which society wants. It would be absurd to credit the enormous increase in production of wealth during the past century to individualism alone, ignoring the contributions of science and education which have been mainly made under social auspices. It would be as absurd to credit all the gains of the century in civilization and freedom to individualism as it would be to charge all the wretchedness and iniquity of the century to this same policy. But, setting aside extravagant claims, it can scarcely be doubted that Adam Smith's contentions for greater individual freedom have been justified as regards the tests named. Granting that the great increase in amount and variety of production, and in means of communication and distribution, has been primarily due to two agencies, the machine and association, it remains true that individualism has permitted and favored association and has stimulated invention.

Initiative and Responsibility.—Moreover, the general policy of turning over to individuals the power and responsibility to regulate their own acts, is in accord with one great feature of moral development. The evolution of moral personality, as traced in our early chapters, shows the individual at first living as a member of a kinship group which determines his economic as well as his religious and social life, and permits him neither to strike out independently, nor, on the other hand, to suffer want so long as the group has supplies. Individual initiative and responsibility have steadily increased, and the economic development has undoubtedly strengthened the development of religious, political, and moral freedom. It is the combination of these which gives the person of to-day the worth and dignity belonging to autonomy, self-government, and democracy.

Regulation of Production.—Further, it may be said that supply and demand, individualism's method of regulating prices and the kinds of goods produced, not only accords with a principle of freedom, but also gets those goods made which society most needs or wants. If goods of a certain kind are scarce, the high price stimulates production. While it permits crises, panics, and hardship, it at least throws the burden of avoiding hardship upon the foresight of a great many: namely, all producers, rather than upon a few persons who might be designated for the purpose. In thus providing a method to find out what society wants and how much, it is performing a social service, and, as we have pointed out, it is none the less a service because the goods are to be paid for; it is all the more so because they can be paid for. So far, then, individualism has a strong case.

§ 3. *Criticisms upon Individualism*

There is undoubtedly great waste in some of its methods, e.g., its advertising and its competitions, but the most serious objections to individualism are not to be found here; they arise in connection with the other ethical criteria of economic morality. They fall chiefly under two heads. (1) Does individualism provide for real as well as formal freedom? (2) Does it distribute the benefits widely or to the few? Does it distribute them justly or unjustly?

It Does Not Secure Real Freedom.—The distinction between real and formal[3] freedom has been forced into prominence by several causes. The division of labor trains a man for a specific kind of work. If there is no opening in this he is unable to find work. The continual invention of improved machinery is constantly displacing particular sets of workers and rendering their special training worthless. A business panic causes immediate discharge of thousands of laborers. A "trust" closes several of its shops, and workmen who have purchased homes must lose their jobs or their investments, or perhaps both. The employer is no less limited in his conduct by the methods of competing firms; but it is the wage-workers who have felt this lack of real freedom most keenly. Theoretically, no one is forced to labor. Every one is free to choose whether he will work, and what work he will do. But in effect, freedom of choice depends for its value upon what the alternative is. If the choice is, do this or—starve—the freedom is not worth much. Formal freedom excludes constraint by the direct control or will of others. It excludes violence or fear of violence. But subjection to the stress or fear of want, or to the limits imposed by ignorance, is just as fatal to freedom. Hunger is as coercive as violence; ignorance fetters as hopelessly as force. Whether a man has any choice of occupation, employment, residence, or wage, depends on his physical strength, education, family ties, and accumulated resources, and on the pressure of present need. To speak of free contract where there is gross inequality between the parties, is to use a mere form of words. Free contract in

---

3. See above, p. 392 f.

this case means simply the right of the stronger to exploit the weaker.

Individualism and Justice.—Individualists, as stated, belong to two very different schools, which we may call the democratic and aristocratic, or perhaps more correctly, if we may coin a word, "oligocratic." Democratic individualism would have every man count as one. It would distribute benefits widely. It holds that since society is made up of individuals all social goods will be secured if each individual seeks and finds his own. Aristocratic individualism[4] has been reenforced by the Darwinian theory of the struggle for existence as a condition for "survival of the fittest," by race prejudice, and by imperialism. It holds that civilization is for the few "best," not necessarily for the many. Progress lies through the selection of the few efficient, masterful, aggressive individuals, races, or nations. Individualism is a policy which favors these few. It is Nature's method of dealing. It is of course regrettable that there should be weak, backward, ineffective individuals or races, but their exploitation serves the advance of the rest, and benevolence or charity may mitigate the most painful results.

The older economists of democratic individualism could properly claim two respects in which economic justice was furthered by economic processes under free management and exchange. The social body is in truth made up of members, and the old policy had been to tie up the members to make the body grow. It did promote justice to remove needless and excessive restrictions. In the second place, it is true, as the economists insisted, that in a free exchange each party profits if he gets what he wants. There is mutual benefit, and so far as this goes there is an element of justice. But while the benefit may be mutual, the *amount* of advantage each gets is not necessarily the same, and if the party who has greater shrewdness or resources takes advantage of a great need on the part of the other, the result may be a very unequal division. Exchanges of a birthright for a mess of pottage will be common. Very well, says the individualist, Esau will know better next time—or if he doesn't, he is an object

4. See above, p. 332 f.

for charity. But the trouble is that even if Esau does "know better" he is in even poorer condition next time to make a bargain if his birthright is gone; besides, if starvation or misery for himself or his family is his only alternative, what good will it do him to "know better"? Can the result, then, be just or fair? This depends on how we define "just" and "fair." If we take a purely formal view and make formal freedom of contract the only criterion, then any price is fair which both parties agree to. The law for the most part takes this view, assuming absence of force or fraud. But this leaves out of account everything except the bare formal act of assent. It is too abstract a conception of personality on which to base a definition of justice. To get the true organic relation of mutual service and benefit by a system of individualism we must have the two parties to the bargain equal. *But in a large part of the exchange of business and services the two parties are not equal.* One has greater shrewdness, better education, more knowledge of the market, more accumulated resources, and, therefore, less pressing need than the other. The moral consciousness will call prices or contracts unfair where the stronger takes advantage of the weaker's necessities, even if the law does not.

Competition.—The fact of competition is depended upon by the individualist to obviate the disadvantages of the weaker party. If A is ignorant of the market, B may impose upon him; but if C and D are competing with B for A's goods or services, A will soon find out what they are "worth." That is, he will get for them a social and not a purely individual valuation. There is doubtless such a gain to A. But in considering competition as removing the objections to the unfairness possible in bargaining, we must bear in mind two things. First, competition cuts both ways. It helps A when several compete for his goods or labor; but, on the other hand, it may ruin one of the competitors. If A is a laborer, it is a good thing if X, Y, and Z, employers, compete for his services. But if the boot is on the other foot, if B, C, and D also are laborers and compete with A for a place, we have the conditions which may lead to the sweat-shop. Whether there is any better way to avoid unequal distribution will be considered later. The second and seemingly fatal objection to competition as a means to justice, is that *free competition under an individualistic system tends to destroy itself*. For the enormous powers which the new forms of economic agency and technique give to the individual who can wield them, enable him to crush competitors. The process has been repeated over and over within the past few years in various fields. The only way in which a semblance of competition has been maintained in railroad business has been by appeal to the courts. This is an appeal to maintain individualism by checking individualism, and as might be expected from such a contradictory procedure, has accomplished little. Nor can it be maintained that the evils may be obviated, as Spencer holds, by private restraints on excessive competition. As already pointed out, if one of a body of competitors is unscrupulous, the rest are necessarily at a disadvantage. Under present conditions individualism cannot guarantee, and in many cases cannot permit, just distribution and a true organic society.

The other school of individualists is not disturbed by inequality of goods. It frankly accedes to the logic of unrestrained competition. It stakes its case upon the importance for social welfare of the exceptionally gifted few. It is important to have their services. It can have them only on terms which they set, as they will not work unless there is sufficient motive. It is, on this view, perfectly just that all the enormous increase of wealth due to modern methods should go to the few leaders, for their ability has produced it all. "The able minority of men who direct the labor of the majority are the true producers of that amount of wealth by which the annual total output, in any given community, exceeds what would have been produced by the laborers if left to their own devices, whether working as isolated units or in small self-organized groups, and controlled by no knowledge or faculties but such as are possessed in common by any one who can handle a spade or lay one brick upon another."[5]

Either from the standpoint of natural rights or from that of utilitarianism it is proper, according to this school, that all the increasing wealth of society, now and in all future

5. Mallock, *Socialism*.

time, should go to the few. For, on the one view, it belongs to the few since they have produced it; and, on the other, it must be given them if society is to have their services. It is possible they may not claim it all for their exclusive possession. They may be pleased to distribute some of it in gifts. But this is for them to say. The logical method for carrying out this programme would require an absolute abandonment by the people as a whole, or by their representatives, or the courts, of any attempt to control economic conditions. The courts would be limited to enforcing contracts and would cease to recognize considerations of public interest except in so far as these were accepted by the able minority. All such legislation as imposes any check upon the freedom of the individual is mischievous. Under this head would presumably come regulation of child labor, of hours, of sanitary conditions, of charges by railroads, gas companies, and other public service corporations. Graded income or inheritance taxes are also to be condemned from this standpoint. It should in fairness be added that while its upholders do not allege as their main argument that individualism is for the interest of the many, they hold, nevertheless, that the many are really better off under individualism than under socialism. For since all the increase in wealth is due to the able few whom individualism produces, and since some of this increase, in cases where the few compete for the custom or labor of the many, may fall to the share of the many or else be given them outright by the more generous, it appears that the only hope for the many lies through the few.

The general naturalistic theory has been discussed in Chapter 18. Here it is only necessary to point out that it is a misreading of evolution to suppose unregulated competition to be its highest category of progress, and that it is a misinterpretation of ethics to assume that might is right. With the dawn of higher forms of life, cooperation and sympathy prove stronger forces for progress than ruthless competition. The "struggle" for any existence that has a claim to moral recognition must be a struggle for more than physical existence or survival of force. It must be a struggle for a *moral* existence, an existence of rational and social beings on terms of mutual sympathy and service as well as of full individuality. Any claim for an economic process, if it is to be a moral claim, must make its appeal on moral grounds and to moral beings. If it recognizes only a few as having worth, then it can appeal only to these. These few have no moral right to complain if the many, whom they do not recognize, refuse to recognize them.

Summary of the Ethics of Individualism.—Individualism provides well for production of quantity and kinds required of goods and services; for activity and formal freedom. Under present conditions of organization and modern methods it cannot be made to serve a democratic conception of justice, but inevitably passes over into a struggle for preeminence, in which the strong and less scrupulous will have the advantage. It can be treated as just only if justice is defined as what is according to contract (formal freedom); or if the welfare of certain classes or individual members of society is regarded as of subordinate importance; or, finally, if it is held that this welfare is to be obtained only incidentally, as gift, not directly through social action. The criticism on individualism is then that under a collective system like that of the present, it does scant justice to most individuals. It leaves the many out from all active participation in progress or morality.[6]

Literature

Individualism and Socialism are discussed in the works of Hadley, Veblen, Hobson, Spencer, Marx, George, already cited; cf. also Menger, *The Right to the Whole Produce of Labor*, 1899; Ely, *Socialism*, 1894; Bosanquet, Individualism and Socialism, in *The Civilization of Christendom*, 1893; Fite, "The Theory of Democracy," *International Journal of Ethics*, XXVIII (1907), pp. 1–18; Huxley, "Administrative Nihilism," in *Critiques and Addresses*; Godwin's *Political Justice*, 1793, raised many of the fundamental questions. Recent representative Individualistic works are: Spencer, *Social Statics*, *The Man Versus the State*, various essays in Vol. III of *Essays*; Sumner, *What Social Classes Owe to Each Other*, 1883; Donisthorpe, *Individualism*, 1889; Harris, *Inequality and Progress*, 1897; Mallock, *Socialism*,

6. Above, p. 422.

1907. On Socialism: *Fabian Essays in Socialism,* edited by Shaw, London, 1889, New York, 1891; Spargo, *Socialism,* 1906; Marx and Engels, *The Communist Manifesto,* Eng. tr.; Reeve, *The Cost of Competition,* 1906; Rae, *Contemporary Socialism,* 1891; Hunter, *Socialists at Work,* 1908; Wells, *New Worlds for Old,* 1907.

---

§ 4. *The Theory of Public Agency and Control*

The various theories of public direction, including socialism in the technical sense, are primarily interested in the just distribution of goods. It is not so much "How many goods can be produced?" as "Who is to get them?" Individualism was chiefly concerned in increasing public wealth, assuming (in the case of the democratic individualists) that all would get the benefit. Socialism is more concerned that the producing persons shall not be sacrificed, and that each member shall benefit by the result. Public agency and control might assert itself (1) as a method of production, (2) as a method of distribution of goods and returns, (3) as a method of property. It is important to note at the outset that all civilized peoples have some degree of social direction in each of these fields. (1) Practically all peoples collect taxes, coin money, carry mails, protect life and property, and supply such elementary demands as those for water and drainage, through State or municipal agency instead of leaving it to private initiative. And in every one of the instances the work was formerly done privately. (2) Under distribution, all progressive peoples give education through the State. Further, the benefits of the mail service are distributed not in proportion to receipts, but on other principles based on social welfare. (3) As a method of property-holding, all civilized peoples hold certain goods for common use, and in the United States, after a period in which it has been the policy to distribute for little or no compensation public lands, public franchises, and public goods of all kinds, the public policy is now not only to retain large tracts for forest reserve, but to construct irrigation plants, and to provide public parks, playgrounds, and other forms of property to be used for common advantage. Just as the individualist does not necessarily carry his doctrine to the extreme of dispensing with all social agency, at least in the matters of public protection and public health, so the socialist does not necessarily wish to abolish private property or private enterprise. We have, then, to consider briefly the ethical aspects of public agency for production, public control over distribution, public holding of wealth.

§ 5. *Society as Agency of Production*

The advantage claimed for society as an agent of production is not primarily greater efficiency, although it is claimed that the present method is enormously wasteful except where there already is private monopoly. Nor is it in the social service rendered by providing great variety of goods, and of the kinds most wanted. It is rather (1) that in the case of public service enterprises, such as transportation or lighting, fairness to the various shippers, localities, and other users can be secured only through public control or operation. These services are as indispensable to modern life as air or navigation. Only by public agency can discrimination be avoided. (2) That the prizes to be gained are here so enormous that bribery and corruption are inevitable under private management. (3) That the profits arising from the growth of the community belong to the community, and can only be secured if the community owns and operates such agencies of public service as transportation, communication, and in cities water supply and lighting. (4) That the method of individualistic production is reckless of child life and in general of the health of workmen. Great Britain is already fearing a deterioration in physical stature and capacity. (5) The motive of self-interest, relied upon and fostered by individualism, is anti-social. How can morality be expected to improve when the fundamental agency and method of business and industry is contradictory to morality? (6) More complete socialism maintains that, under modern capitalism, a disproportionate share is sure to fall to the capitalist, and, more than this, to the great capitalist. Modern production is complex and expensive. It requires an enormous plant; the capitalist, not the workman, has the tools, and can therefore charge what he pleases. The small capitalist cannot undertake competition with the great capitalist, for the latter can undersell him until he drives him from business, and can then recoup himself by greater gains. Hence the only way to secure fair distribution is through social ownership of the tools and materials for production.

Private Interests and Public Welfare.—Touching these points it may be said that the public conscience is rapidly coming to a decision upon the first five. (1) The public has been exploited, the officials of government have been bribed, and individual members of society discriminated against. The process of competition always involves *vae victis*, but the particular factor which makes this not only hard but unjust, is that in all these cases we have a quasi-public agency (monopoly, franchise, State-aided corporation) used to give private advantage. This must be remedied either by public ownership or public control, unless the ethics of the struggle for existence is accepted. The corruption which has prevailed under (2) must be met either by public ownership or control, or by so reducing the value of such franchises as to leave "nothing in it" for the "grafter" and his cooperators. Vice—gambling, excessive use of drugs and liquors, prostitution—is no doubt injurious to its victims, and when leagued with public officials and yielding enormous corruption funds to debauch politics, it is a public evil as well. But its victims are limited, and its appearance not attractive to the great majority. The exploitation and corruption practiced by the more generally successful and "respectable" members of society, is far more insidious and wide-reaching. It demoralizes not individuals only, but the standards of society. As to (3) there is no doubt as to the rights of the matter. Gains due to social growth should be socially shared, not appropriated by a few. The only question is as to the best method of securing these gains. European States and cities have gone much farther than the United States along the line of public agency, and, while there is still dispute as to the balance of advantage in certain cases, there is a growing sentiment that the more intelligent and upright the community, the more it can wisely undertake. The moral principle is that the public must have its due. Whether it pays certain agents a salary as its own officials, or a commission in the form of a moderate dividend, is not so important.[1] But to pay a man or a small group of promoters a million dollars to supply water or lighting or transportation, seems no more moral than to pay such a salary to a mayor or counsel or superintendent of schools. Taxpayers would probably denounce such salaries as robbery. Such franchises as have for the most part been given in American cities have been licenses to collect high taxes from the citizens for the benefit of a few, and do not differ in principle from paying excessive salaries, except as the element of risk enters. What is needed at present in the United States is a larger number of experiments in various methods of agency to see which type results in least corruption, fairest distribution, and best service.

Conditions of Labor.—On the fourth point, the necessity of public control to regulate child labor, the labor of women, sanitary conditions, and the use of dangerous machinery, the public conscience is also awakening. Decisions of the courts on the constitutionality of regulating women's labor have been somewhat at variance. But the recently announced decision[2] of the United States Supreme Court in the "Oregon case" seems likely to be decisive of the principle that women may be treated as a class. Freedom of contract cannot be regarded as interfering with the right to establish reasonable precautions for women's health. Woman may be protected "from the greed as well as from the passion of man." The immorality of child labor under modern conditions is also becoming clear. For the public to see child life stunted physically, mentally, and morally by premature labor under the exhausting, deadening, and often demoralizing conditions of modern industry and business, is for the public to consent to wickedness. It cannot leave this matter to the conscience of individual manufacturers and parents, for the conscientious manufacturer is at a disadvantage, and it might with as much morality consent to a parent's starving or poisoning

1. Boston has an ingenious method of dividing profits. The company which supplies gas must lower the price of gas in proportion as it increases its rate of dividends.
2. February 24, 1908.

his child as to his injuring it in less violent manner. For a society pretending to be moral to permit little children to be used up or stunted under any plea of cheap production or support of parents, is not above the moral level of those peoples which practice infanticide to prevent economic stress. Indeed, in the case of a country which boasts of its wealth, there is far less justification than for the savage. In the case of provision against accident due to dangerous machinery, the ethical principle is also clear. To throw all the burden of the accidents incident to modern production upon the families of the laborers is entirely unjust. To impose it upon the conscientious manufacturer is no better, for it places him at a disadvantage. This is a necessary—except so far as it can be minimized by safety devices—part of the modern machine process. It ought to be paid for either by all manufacturers, who would then shift it to the consumers in the price of the goods, or by the public as a whole in some form of insurance. European countries have gone much farther than the United States in this direction. The theory that the employer is exempt if a fellow workman contributes in any way to the accident has been applied in the United States in such a way as to free employers, and thus the public, from any share in the burden of a large part of accidents—except as these entail poverty and bring the victim and his family into the dependent class.

Moreover, it is only by public action that fair conditions of labor can be secured in many trades and under many employers. For the single workman has not the slightest chance to make conditions, and the union has no effective means to support its position unless it represents a highly skilled trade and controls completely the supply of labor. It may go without saying that violence is wrong. But it is often ignored that for a *prosperous society to leave the laborer no remedy but violence for an intolerable condition is just as wrong.*

Motives.—(5) On the question of motives the collectivist theory is probably over-sanguine as to the gain to be effected by external means. It is difficult to believe that any change in methods would eliminate selfishness. There is abundant exercise of selfishness in political democracy, and even in families. Further, if it should be settled on other grounds that competition in certain cases performs a social service, it would then be possible for a man to compete with a desire to serve the public, just as truly as it would be possible to compete for selfish motives. That a process causes pain incidentally does not necessarily pervert the motive of the surgeon or parent. It does, of course, throw the burden of proof upon the advocate of the process. Rivalry need not mean enmity if the rivals are on an equal footing and play fair.

Exploitation of Labor.—(6) The question whether all capitalistic production first exploits the laboring class, and then tends to absorb or drive out of business the small capitalist, is not so easy of decision. It seems to be easy to make a plausible statement for each side by statistical evidence. There seems little doubt that the general standard of living for laborers is rising. On the other hand, the number of enormous fortunes seems to rise much faster, and there is an appalling amount of poverty in the great cities. This is sometimes attributed to thriftlessness or to excessively large families. A careful study of an English agricultural community, where the conditions seemed at least as good as the average, showed that a family could not have over two children without sinking below the line of adequate food, shelter, and clothing, to say nothing of medical attendance or other comforts. In the United States there has been such a supply of land available that the stress has not been so intense. Just what the situation will be if the country becomes thickly settled cannot be foretold. Professor J. B. Clark shows that the tendency in a static society would be to give the laborer more and more nearly his share—provided there is free competition for his services. The difficulty is that society is not static and that a laborer cannot shift at will from trade to trade and from place to place.

That sometimes capital exploits labor is merely to say that the buyer sometimes gets the advantage. That capital usually has the advantage in its greater resources may be admitted, but that it *invariably must* seems an unwarranted deduction. The multiplication of wants widens continually the number of occupations and thus increases the competition for the service of the more skilled. In such cases some, at least, of the sellers should be in a position to make a fair bargain. Indeed, recent socialists do not advocate any such complete assumption by society of all production as is presented in some of the socialistic Utopias. Their principle is "that the State must undertake the production and distribution of social wealth wherever private enterprise is dangerous or less efficient than public enterprise."[3]

It is for those who do not believe in public control to prove that in the great enterprises for the production of the necessaries of life, for transportation, banking, mining, and the like, private enterprise is not dangerous. The conduct of many—not all—of these enterprises in recent years, not only in their economic aspects, but in their recklessness of human life, health, and morality, is what makes socialism a practical question. If it is adopted, it will not be for any academic or *a priori* reasons. It will be because private enterprise fails to serve the public, and its injustice becomes intolerable. If business enterprise, as sometimes threatens, seeks to subordinate political and social institutions, including legislatures and courts, to economic interests, the choice must be between public control and public ownership. And if, whether by the inherent nature of legal doctrine and procedure, or by the superior shrewdness of capital in evading regulation, control is made to appear ineffective, the social conscience will demand ownership. To subordinate the State to commercial interests is as immoral as to make the economic interest supreme in the individual.

As regards the relations between capital and labor, it argues an undeveloped state of society that we have no machinery for determining controversy as to what is a fair wage. In the long run, and on the whole, supply and demand may give an approximately fair adjustment, but our present method of fighting it out in doubtful cases is barbaric. The issue is decided often by violence or the no less unmoral motive of pressing want, instead of by the moral test of what is fair. And the great third interest, the consumer, or the public at large, is not represented at all. New Zealand, Canada, and some of the states in the United States have made beginnings. The President undoubtedly commanded general support in his position during the coal strike, when he main-

3. Spargo, *Socialism*, pp. 220–27.

tained that the public was morally bound to take some part in the struggle.

Must not society be lacking in resources if its only resource is to permit exploitation, on the one hand, or carry on all industry and business itself, upon the other? To lose the flexibility, variety, and keenness of interest secured by individual or associated enterprise, would certainly be an evil. Early business was conducted largely by kinship organizations. The pendulum has doubtless reached the other extreme in turning over to groups, organized on a purely commercial basis, operations that could be more equitably managed by city or state agency. Most favor public agency in the case of schools. Railroads, gas companies, and other monopolies are still subject to controversy. But that an ideally organized society should permit associations and grouping of a great many kinds as agencies for carrying on its work seems a platform not to be abandoned until proved hopeless.

Collective Agency is Not Necessarily Social. — The socialist is inclined to think that if the agency of production were the government or the whole organized society this would give a genuine social agency of control. This by no means follows. Party government and city government in the United States have shown the fallacy of this. But even apart from the possibility of a corrupt boss there is still a wide gap between the collective and the socialized agency. For until the members of society have reached a sufficiently high level of intelligence and character to exercise voluntary control, and to cooperate wisely and efficiently, there must be some central directing agency. And such an agency will be morally external to a large number. It doesn't matter so much what name this agent is called by—i.e., whether he is "capitalist," or "government,"—so long as the control is external. In general, individuals are still without the mutual confidence and public intelligence which would enable them really to socialize the mechanically collective process.

§ 6. *Theories of Just Distribution*

Socialism as theory of distribution does not necessarily imply public operation of production. By graded taxation the proceeds of production might be taken by society and either held, used, or distributed on some supposedly more equitable basis. To give point to any inquiry as to the justice of a proposed distribution, it would be desirable to know what is the present distribution. Unfortunately, no figures are accepted by all students. Spahr's *Present Distribution of Wealth in the United States* estimates that seven-eighths of the families in the United States own only one-eighth of the wealth, and that one per cent own more than the remaining ninety-nine per cent. This has been challenged, but any estimate made by the economists shows such enormous disproportion as to make it incredible that the present distribution can be regarded as just on any definition of justice other than "according to the principles of contract and competition." Suppose, then, the question is raised, How can we make a just distribution?

Criteria Proposed.—The simplest, and at the same time most mechanical and abstract, method would be to divide all goods equally. This would be to ignore all moral and other differences, as indeed is practically done in the suffrage. If all men are accounted equal in the State, why not in wealth? It may be admitted that, if society were to distribute, it would have to do it on some system which could be objectively administered. To divide wealth according to merit, or according to efforts, or according to needs, would be a far more moral method. But it is difficult to see how, in the case of material goods or their money equivalent, such a division could be made by any being not omniscient as well as absolutely just. If we are to consider distribution as administered by society, we seem reduced to the alternative of the present system or a system of equality.

1. The Individualistic Theory.—It is indeed supposed by some that the individualistic or competitive system distributes on a moral basis: viz., according to merit. This claim would have to meet the following criticisms:

(1) The first abstraction which this individualistic principle of reward usually makes is that it gives a man credit for all he achieves, or charges him with all his failures, without recognizing the threefold origin of these achievements or failures. Heredity, society, personal choice, have each had some share in

the result. But, in considering the ethics of competition upon this maxim, there is evidently no attempt to discriminate between these several sources. The man born with industrial genius, presented by society with the knowledge of all that has been done in the past, and equipped by society with all the methods and tools society can devise, certainly has an advantage over the man of moderate talents and no education. To claim that the first should be justly rewarded for his superiority would imply that the reception of one gift constitutes a just claim for another.

(2) Secondly, the theory as applied to our present system is guilty of a further abstraction in assuming that the chief, if not the only, way to deserve reward is by individualistic shrewdness and energy.

(3) It measures desert by service rendered without taking any account of motive or even of intent. The captain of industry performs an important service to society; therefore, it is argued, he should be rewarded accordingly, quite irrespective of the question whether he was aiming at social welfare or at selfish gain. It may even be plausibly argued that to reward men financially for good motives would be bribing men to be honest. It is true that financial rewards will not make good citizens, but this is irrelevant. The point is that whatever other reasons,—expediency, difficulty of estimating intent and motive,—may be urged for abstracting from everything but the result, the one reason which cannot be urged is, such abstraction is just. A person has rights only because he is a social person. But to call a man a social person because he incidentally produces useful results, is to say that purpose and will are negligible elements of personality.[4]

2. *Equal Division.*—The system of equal division is liable to the following criticism. In their economic services men are not equal. They are unequal not merely in talent and ability; not merely in the value of their work; they are unequal in their disposition. To treat idle and industrious, useless and useful, slow and quick alike is not equality, but inequality. It is to be guilty of as palpable an abstraction as to say that all men are equally free because they are not subject to physical constraint. Real equality will try to treat like conditions alike, and unlike character, efforts, or services differently.

There is, moreover, a psychological objection which would weigh against an equal division even if such were

4. Tufts, *Philosophical Review*, XV, p. 370 f.

regarded as just. The average man perhaps prefers an economic order in which there are prizes and blanks to an order in which every man draws out the same. He prefers an exciting game to a sure but tame return of his investment. He may call for a "square deal," but we must remember that a "square deal" in the great American game from which the metaphor is taken is not designed to make the game less one of chance. It is designed to give full scope to luck and nerve. A game in which every player was sure to win, but also sure to win just what he had put in, would be equitable, but it would not be a game. An equal distribution might rob life of its excitement and its passion. Possibly the very strain of the process develops some elements of character which it would be unfortunate to lose.

Is there no alternative possible for society except an equality which is external only, and therefore unequal, or an inequality which charges a man with all the accrued benefits or evils of his ancestry? Must we either recognize no moral differences in men, or else be more merciless than the old orthodox doctrine of hereditary or imputed guilt? The theological doctrine merely made a man suffer for his ancestors' sins; the doctrine of unlimited individualism would damn him not only for his ancestors' sins and defects, but for the injustice suffered by his ancestors at the hands of others. The analysis of the sources of a man's ability may give a clue to a third possibility, and it is along this line that the social conscience of to-day is feeling its way.

3. *A Working Programme.* — A man's power is due (1) to physical heredity; (2) to social heredity, including care, education, and the stock of inventions, information, and institutions which enables him to be more efficient than the savage; and finally (3) to his own efforts. Individualism may properly claim this third factor. It is just to treat men unequally so far as their efforts are unequal. It is socially desirable to give as much incentive as possible to the full development of every one's powers. But the *very same reason demands that in the first two respects we treat men as equally as possible.* For it is for the good of the social body to get the most out of its members, and it can get the most out of them only by giving them the best start possible. In physi-

cal heredity the greater part is, as yet, wholly outside control, but there is an important factor which is in the sphere of moral action, namely, the physical condition of the parents, particularly of the mother. Conditions of food, labor, and housing should be such that every child may be physically well born. In the various elements included under social heredity society has a freer hand. Not a *free* hand, for physical and mental incapacity limit the amount of social accumulation which can be communicated, but we are only beginning to appreciate how much of the deficiency formerly acquiesced in as hopeless may be prevented or remedied by proper food, hygiene, and medical care. *Completely* equal education, likewise, cannot be given; not in kind, for not all children have like interests and society does not want to train all for the same task; nor in quantity, for some will have neither the ability nor the disposition to do the more advanced work. But as, little by little, labor becomes in larger degree scientific, the ratio of opportunities for better trained men will increase, and as education becomes less exclusively academic, and more an active preparation for all kinds of work, the interests of larger and larger numbers of children will be awakened. Such a programme as this is one of the meanings of the phrase *"equal opportunity,"* which voices the demand widely felt for some larger conception of economic and social justice than now obtains. It would make formal freedom, formal "equality" before the law, less an empty mockery by giving to every child some of the power and knowledge which are the necessary conditions of real freedom.

Society has already gone a long way along the line of giving an equal share in education. It is moving rapidly toward broader conceptions of education for all occupations —farming, mechanics, arts, trade, business—as well as for the "learned professions." It is making a beginning toward giving children (see the Report of the New York Tenement House Commission) a chance to be born and grow up with at least a living minimum of light and air. Libraries and dispensaries and public health officials are bringing the science and literature of the world in increasing measure into the lives of all. When by the better organization of the courts the poor man has real, and not merely formal equality before the law, and thereby justice itself is made more accessible to all, another long step will be taken toward a juster order. How far society can go is yet to be solved. But is it not at least a working hypothesis for experiment, that society should try to give to all its members the gains due to the social progress of the past? How far the maxim of equal opportunity will logically lead it is impossible to say. Fortunately, the moral problem is to work out new ideals, not merely to administer old ones. Other possibilities of larger justice are noticed under § 8 below.

§ 7. *Ownership and Use of Property*

The public wealth may be controlled and used in four ways: It may be (1) Privately owned and used; (2) Privately owned and publicly used; (3) Publicly held, but privately used; (4) Publicly held and commonly used. The individualist would have all wealth, or as much as possible, under one of the first two forms. The tendency in the United States until very recently has been to divest the public of all ownership. The socialist, while favoring private ownership and use of the more strictly personal articles, favors the public holding of much which is now privately owned —notably the land, or the instruments of production—as versus the holding of these by private or corporate persons. Or, again, it may be maintained that while individuals should be allowed to accumulate as much property as they can, they should not be allowed to transmit it entirely to their heirs.

Value of Private Property.—The individualist may properly point to the psychological and historical significance of private property, which has been stated in a preceding chapter (p. 438). He may say that the evils there mentioned as attendant upon private property do not belong to the property in itself, but to the exaggerated love of it. He may admit that the present emphasis of attention upon the ownership of wealth, rather than upon intellectual or aesthetic or social interests, is not the highest type of human endeavor. But he urges that the positive values of property are such that the present policy of placing no check upon property should be maintained. In addition to the indirect social value through the power and freedom given to its owners, it may be claimed that the countless educational, charitable, and philanthropic agencies sustained by voluntary gifts from private property, are both the best method of accomplishing certain socially valuable work, and have an important reflex value in promoting the active social interest of those who carry them on. Nor is the force of this entirely broken by the counter claim that this would justify keeping half the population in poverty in order to give the other half the satisfaction of charity. No system short of absolute communism can abolish the need of friendly help.

Defects and Dangers in the Present System. —The first question which arises is: If property is so valuable morally, how many are profiting by it under the present system, and how many are without its beneficent effects? Is the number of property-owners increasing or diminishing? In one of the morally most valuable forms of property, the number of those who profit is certainly decreasing relatively: *viz.,* in the owning of homes. The building of private residences has practically ceased in New York and many other cities except for the very rich. With the increasing value of land the owning of homes is bound to become more and more rare. Only the large capitalist can put up the apartment house. In the ownership of shops and industries the number of owners has relatively decreased, that of clerks has increased. The wage-workers in cities are largely propertyless. The management of industries through corporations while theoretically affording opportunity for property has yet, as Judge Grosscup has pointed out forcibly, been such as to discourage the small investor, and to prompt to the consumption of wages as fast as received. The objection to individualism on this ground would then be as before, that it is not individual enough.

An objection of contrary character is that the possession of property releases its owner from any necessity of active effort or service to the public. It may therefore injure character on both its individual and its social side. Probably the absolute number of those who refrain from any social service because of their property is not very large, and it may be questioned whether the particular persons would be socially very valuable under any system if they are now oblivious to all the moral arguments for such activity and service.

A more serious objection to the individualistic policy is the enormous power allowed to the holders of great properties. It has been estimated that a trust fund recently created for two grandchildren will exceed five billion dollars when handed over. It is easily possible that some of the private fortunes now held may, if undisturbed, amount to far more than the above within another generation. Moreover, the power of such a fortune is not limited to its own absolute purchasing value. By the presence of its owners upon directorates of industrial, transportation, banking, and insurance corporations the resources of many other owners are controlled. A pressure may be exerted upon political affairs compared with which actual contributions to campaign funds are of slight importance. The older theory in America was that the injury to the private character of the owners of wealth would negative the possible dangers to the public, since possession of large wealth would lead to relaxation of energy, or even to dissipation. It was assumed that the father acquired the fortune, the son spent it, and thus scattered it among the many, and the grandson began again at the bottom of the ladder. Now that this theory is no longer tenable, society will be obliged to ask how much power may safely be left to any individual.

It must be recognized that the present management of such natural resources as forests under the régime of private property has been extremely wasteful and threatens serious injury to the United States. Individual owners cannot be expected to consider the welfare of the country at large, or of future generations; hence the water power is impaired and the timber supply of the future threatened.

Finally it must be remembered that many of the present evils and inequities in ownership are not due necessarily to a system of private property, but rather to special privileges possessed by classes of individuals. These may be survivals of past conquests of arms as in Europe, or derived by special legislation, or due to a perfectly unconscious attitude of public morals which carries over to a new situation the customs of an early day. Mill's famous indictment of present conditions is not in all respects so applicable to America as to the older countries of Europe, but it has too much truth to be omitted in any ethical consideration.

If the choice were to be made between communism with all its chances, and the present state of society with all its sufferings and injustices, if the institution of private property necessarily carried with it, as a consequence, that the produce of labor should be apportioned as we now see it, almost in an inverse ratio to the labor,—the largest portions to those who have not worked at all, the next largest to those whose work is almost nominal, and so in descending scale, the remuneration dwindling as the work grows harder and more disagreeable, until the most fatiguing and exhausting bodily labor cannot count with certainty on being able to earn even the necessaries of life,—if this, or communism, were the alternative, all the difficulties, great or small, of communism would be but as dust in the balance. But to make the comparison applicable, we must compare communism at its best with the régime of individual property, not as it is, but as it might be made. The principle of private property has never yet had a fair trial in any country. (*Political Economy*, Book II, ch. i.)

§ 8. *Present Tendencies*

Individualistic Foundations.—The general tendency up to very recent time in the United States has been decidedly individualistic, both in the policy concerning the method of holding property, and in the legal balance between vested property rights and the social welfare. Public lands were granted on easy terms to homesteaders; mines as well as soil were practically free to the prospector; school fund lands were in most cases sold for a song instead of being kept for the public. So general has been the attitude that all wealth ought to be in private hands that it has been difficult to convict men who have fraudulently obtained vast tracts of public land. The magnitude of the operation has given "respectability" to the beneficiaries. The taxing power has done little to maintain adjustment. In this, as in many other respects,

the policy of the United States has been far more individualistic than that of Great Britain. The latter has graded income and inheritance taxes. In the United States, on the
other hand, the Federal taxation bears more heavily on the
poor as they are the large body of consumers,—not, of
course, in the sense that the individual poor man pays more
than the individual rich man, but in the sense that a million
of dollars owned by a thousand men pays more than a million owned by one man. Legally, the Constitution of the
United States and certain of its amendments gave private
rights extraordinary protection, especially when contracts
were construed to mean charters, as well as private contracts.
The public welfare was conceived to reside almost solely in
private rights.[5]

Increased Recognition of Public Welfare.—Recent policy and legal decisions show a decided change. Reserves of
forest lands have been established. Water-supplies, parks,
and many other kinds of property have been changed from
private to public ownership. The question as to mines has
been raised. Graded inheritance taxes have been established
in some states, and the question of graded income taxes is
likely to be more generally considered unless some other
form of taxation based on the social values given to land,
or franchises, or other forms of property seems more equitable. The Supreme Court in recent decisions "has read into
the constitution two sweeping exceptions to the inviolability
of property rights."[6] One is that of public use. "Whenever the
owner of a property devotes it to a use in which the public
has an interest, he in effect grants to the public an interest
in such use, and must to the extent of that use submit to be
controlled by the public for the common good so long as he
maintains the use." The second exception is that of the police
power which in 1906 (204 U. S., 311, 318) was declared to
extend "to so dealing with the conditions which exist in the
state as to bring out of them the greatest welfare of its people." The application of this broad principle is still in an un-

5. Cf. J. A. Smith, *The Spirit of American Government*, 1907.
6. I have followed in this paragraph the discussion of Professor
Munroe Smith, *Van Norden Magazine*, February, 1908. For a
full history see E. Freund, *The Police Power*, 1904.

certain condition, but there can be no question that it recognizes a changed situation. When people are living in such interdependence as in the collective life of to-day, it is no longer possible to locate public welfare in any such preponderating degree in private rights as was justified under the conditions of a new country a century ago. Says Professor Smith:

On the fundamental question of the relation of public policy to private property rights the [Supreme] Court has abandoned the individualist views with which the founders of the constitution were imbued; and in its doctrines of the public use and the police power it has distinctly accepted what may be termed, in the literal and proper sense of the word, the socialist view. In so doing, it has unquestionably expressed the dominant opinion of the American people. The American people does not accept the collectivist theory; it believes in private property; but it recognizes that rights of property must yield, in cases of conflict, to the superior rights of society at large.

If some of the means set forth above for securing juster distribution were adopted, the first step toward Mill's demand[7] would be met. If the community should reap the return for its own growth, if taxation should be so arranged as to fall most heavily on those best able to pay rather than on those who are most honest or least able to evade, it would seem rational to hold that society will find a way to continue the four forms of control now existing, making such shifts as changing conditions require.

Some of these shiftings are already evident and give promise of greater justice without loss of any of the benefits accruing from private property.

Social Justice through Economic, Social, and Scientific Progress.—Not all moral advance comes "with observation," or by political agency. The economic process is providing in certain lines a substitute for property. Science and invention, which are themselves a fine illustration of the balance and interaction between individual and social intelligence, individual effort and social cooperation, are making possible in many ways a state of society in which men have at once greater freedom and greater power through association,

7. Above, p. 495.

greater individual development and greater socialization of interests, less private property but greater private use and enjoyment of what is common.

The substitute for property provided by the economic process itself is permanence or security of support. If the person can count definitely upon a future, this is equivalent to the security of property. And through the organization of modern industry supplemented by insurance and pensions, either state, institutional, or in corporations, or in mutual benefit associations, there has been on the whole, a great increase of security, although it is still unfortunately true that the wage-worker may in most cases be dismissed at any moment, and has virtually no contract, or even any well-assured confidence of continued employment.

It is a mutual cooperation of economic, social, and scientific factors which has brought about a great increase of individual use and enjoyment through public ownership. This *has placed many of the things which make life worth living within the enjoyment of all*, and at the same time given a far better service to the users than the old method of private ownership. *In this change lies, perhaps, the greatest advance of justice* in the economic sphere, and a great promise for the future. There was a time when if a man would sit down on a piece of ground and enjoy a fine landscape, he must own it. If he would have a plot where his children might play, he must own it. If he would travel, he must carry his own lantern, and furnish his own protection from thieves. If he would have water, he must sink his own well. If he would send a letter, he must own or hire a messenger. If he would read a book, he must not merely own the book, but own or hire the author or copyist. If he would educate his children, he must own or hire the tutor. We have learned that public parks, public lighting and water works, public libraries, and public schools, are better than private provision.

The objection which comes from the individualist to this programme is that it does too much for the individual. It is better, urges individualism, to stimulate the individual's activity and leave his wants largely unsatisfied than to satisfy all his wants at the expense of his activity. But this assumes that what is done through public agencies is done for the people and not by the people. A democracy may do for itself what an aristocracy may not do for a dependent class. The greatest demoralization at the present time is not to those who have not, but to those who appropriate gains due to associated activity, complacently supposing that they have themselves created all that they enjoy.

Another Great Advance is the Change in What Makes Up the Chief Values of Life.—In early times the values of life were largely found in food, clothing, personal ornaments, bodily comfort, sex gratifications. Enjoyment of these involved exclusive possession and therefore property. But with the advance of civilization an increasing proportion of life's values falls in the mental realm of sharable goods.

Satisfaction in knowledge, in art, in association, in freedom, is not diminished, but increased when it is shared. The educated man may have no more property than the illiterate. He has access to a whole system of social values. He has freedom; he has a more genuinely independent type of power than accrues from the mere possession of things. The society of the future will find a part of its justice in so adjusting its economic system that all may enter as fully as possible into this more social world.

Methods of Social Selection.—Finally, recognizing all the value of the competitive process in the past as a method of selecting ability, it must be regarded as crude and wasteful. It is like the method of blind trial and error which obtains in the animal world. The method of ideas, of conscious use of means to secure ends, is the more effective and the more rational. Society now is gaining the scientific equipment which may allow the substitution of the more effective and less wasteful method. It should discover and educate capacity instead of giving merely a precarious encouragement to certain special types.

§ 9. *Three Special Problems*

Three special problems may be noticed about which moral judgment is as yet uncertain: The open versus the closed shop, the capitalization of corporations, and the "unearned increment."

1. The Open versus the Closed Shop.—In certain industries in which the workmen are well organized they have
made contracts with employers which provide that only
union men shall be employed. Such a shop is called a closed
shop, in distinction from an "open shop" in which non-union
men may be employed in part or altogether. The psychological motive for the demand for the closed shop is natural
enough: the union has succeeded in gaining certain advantages in hours or wages or both; this has required some expense and perhaps some risk. It is natural to feel that those
who get the advantage should share the expense and effort,
and failing this, should not be admitted to the shop. If the
argument stopped here it would be insufficient for a moral
justification for two reasons. First, joining a union involves
much more than payment of dues. It means control by the
union in ways which may interfere with obligations to family, or even to the social order. Hence, to exclude a fellow
workman from the opportunity to work because he—perhaps
for conscientious reasons—would not belong to the union,
could not be justified unless the union could make it appear
that it was maintaining a social and not merely a group interest. Second, in some cases unions have sought to limit
output. In so far as this is done not for reasons of health
but to raise prices, the union is opposing the interest of consumers. Here again the union must exhibit a social justification if it is to gain social approval.

On the other hand it may be noted that the individualist
of the second sort—who believes in the competitive struggle
as a moral process—has no ground on which to declare for
"open shop." Exactly the same principle which would permit
combination in capital and place no limit on competitive
pressure, provided it is all done through free contracts, can
raise no objection against combinations of laborers making
the best contracts possible. When a syndicate of capitalists
has made a highly favorable contract or successfully under-
written a large issue of stock, it is not customary under the
principle of "open shop" to give a share in the contract to
all who ask for it, or to let the whole public in "on the ground
floor." Nor are capitalists accustomed to leave a part of the
market to be supplied by some competitor for fear such competitor may suffer if he does not have business. When the

capitalist argues for the open shop upon the ground of freedom and democracy, it seems like the case of the mote and the beam.

An analogy with a political problem may aid: Has a nation the right to exclude (or tax heavily) goods or persons from other countries? May it maintain a "closed shop"? The policy of the American colonists and of the United States has varied. The Puritans maintained a "closed shop" on religious lines. They came to this country to maintain a certain religion and polity. They expelled several men who did not agree with them. The United States excludes Chinese laborers, and imposes a tariff which in many cases is intended to be prohibitive against the products of other countries. This is done avowedly to protect the laborer, and in so far as it is effective it closes the shop. The maxim "This is a white man's country" is a similar "closed shop" utterance. On moral grounds the non-union man is in the same category as the man of alien race or country. What, if anything, can justify a nation or smaller group from excluding others from its benefits? Clearly the only conditions are (1) that the group or nation is existing for some morally justifiable end, which (2) would be endangered by the admission of the outsiders. A colony established to work out religious or political liberty would be justified in excluding a multitude who sought to enter it and then subvert these principles. If a union is working for a morally valuable end, e.g., a certain standard of living which is morally desirable, and if this were threatened by the admission of non-union men, the closed shop would seem to be justified. If the purpose were merely to secure certain advantages to a small group, and if the open shop would not lower the standard but merely extend its range of benefits, it is hard to see why the closed shop is not a selfish principle—though no more selfish than the grounds on which the tariff is usually advocated.

2. *The Capitalization of Corporations*, especially of public service corporations, is a matter on which there is a difference of policy in different states, owing probably to uncertainty as to the morality of the principles involved. The two theories held are: (a) Companies should issue capital stock only on the basis of money paid in; dividends then represent a return on actual investment. (b) Companies may

issue whatever stock they please, or whatever they expect
their income will enable them to pay dividends upon; dividends will then represent return for valuable privileges, or
for some utility to be marketed. In behalf of this latter view
it may be claimed that if the company pays dividends the
investors have nothing to complain of, and if it sells its
products or transportation at market rates, the consumer
has nothing to complain of.

So far as the relations between corporation and investor
are concerned, the issues are simple. If the stocks are issued
with no expectation that they will give any return, merely
to "sell," it is pure dishonesty, of the same type which under
cruder conditions sold spavined horses or made counterfeit
money, and now assumes the more vulgar type of dealing in
"green goods." The fact that fictitious capital can be publicly
advertised, gives it a financial but not a moral advantage.
This, however, would have such decided limitations, credu-
lous as human nature is, that if fictitious capital paid no
dividends it would soon have no market. Hence, for the far-
seeing promoter, the pressure is toward making some at least
of the fictitious capital pay dividends. What is the principle
in this case? If we are dealing with a new and untried mode
of production or public service, the case is simply that of
any speculation. If a proposed product has a possible utility,
but at the same time involves so much risk that in the long
run only half of such enterprises will succeed, society may
consider it worth offering a profit equal to fifty per cent in
order to pay for the risk. If, on the other hand, the income
is to derive from valuable public franchises, or from the
growth of the community and its necessities, the case is different. Here there is little, if any, risk for which it is fair
for society to pay. The excessive capital beyond the cost is
designed to disguise the rate of profit, and therefore conceal
from the community the cost of the goods or service. If the
public demands cheaper rates it is told that the company is
now paying only a fair dividend upon its stock.[8] The usual
method of capitalizing many enterprises of a quasi-public
sort is to issue bonds to cover the cost of construction or

8. As in the case of gas in New York City, where the court has
   decided that the public cannot refuse to pay interest on the
   value of the franchise—its own gift.

plant, and then one or more series of stocks which are known as "velvet." In part these stocks may represent a work of organization which is a legitimate public service, but in many cases they represent devices for transferring public wealth to private property. Enormous sums have been taken from the public in this manner. The element which makes this method particularly obnoxious is that the quasi-public corporations are given a monopoly by the community and then take advantage of this to capitalize indefinitely the necessities of a growing community. In this case the conception of public service is lost sight of in the "dazzling possibility of public exploitation."[9]

Few methods of extorting wealth have equaled this. In some cases bribery of public officials has added an item of expense to be collected later from the public. When the various forms of public service or protected industry were first projected there was risk involved. It was necessary to offer inducements to capital to engage in them. It was desirable to have railroads, gas, water, express service. But as the factor of risk has been eliminated, the public tires of paying double prices, and a "fair" return must be estimated on the basis of actual rather than fictitious capital. The public has come to have a clear idea as to the morality of such practices as have been employed in letting contracts for public buildings at prices far above market value. The New York City courthouse and Pennsylvania capitol offer familiar examples. Does it differ materially from such practices when a company charges the public an excessive price for transportation or lighting, and when State or municipal authorities authorize by franchise or monopoly such excessive charges? Probably the conscience of the next century, if not of the next generation, will fail to see the superior moral quality of the latter procedure.

3. *The "Unearned Increment."*—This term is applied most frequently to the increase in land value or franchise value which is due, not to the owner, but to the growth of the community. A tract of land is bought at a price fixed by its value as farm land. A city grows up. The owner of the land may have been active in the building up of industry, but he may not. An increase of values follows, which is due

9. Cf. Hadley, *Economics*, p. 159.

to the growth of the community. Shall the owner have it all, or shall the community have it all, or shall there be a division? The growth in value of a franchise for gas, electric lighting, transportation, presents the same problem. It is not usually recognized, however, that the same principle is found in every increase of value due to increasing demand. The logical basis for distinction would seem to be that in some cases increase of demand calls out competition, and the price is lowered; the public thus receives its share in lower cost. In other cases, notably those first mentioned, there can be no competition, the price is therefore not often lowered unless by legislative action, and the whole benefit goes to the owner of land or franchise. As regards land, the case is much stronger in Europe, for land titles were originally gained there largely by seizure, whereas in America private titles have been largely through purchase.

Individualism, according as it argues from the platform of natural rights or from that of social welfare, would claim either that individuals should have all the increase because they have a right to all they can get under a system of free contracts, or that it is for the social welfare to allow them all they can get since private property is public wealth. From the standpoint of natural rights the reply would seem to be unanswerable: the community gives the increased value; it belongs to the community. From the standpoint of social welfare the answer is not so simple. It might, for example, be socially desirable to encourage the owners of farming land by leaving to them the increase in value due to the growth of the country, whereas city land-owners might need no such inducement. Investors in a new form of public service corporation might need greater inducements than would be fair to those in enterprises well established. But, although details are complex, the social conscience is working toward this general principle: the community should share in the values which it produces. If it cannot do this by cheaper goods and better service, it must by graded taxation, by ownership, or by some other means. The British government has already considered a measure for ascertaining the land values in Scotland as a preliminary step toward adjustment of this question.

---

*Professor Seager's Programme of Social
Legislation with Special Reference to Wage-Earners*

In the conviction that in the field of social legislation the United States is behind the more progressive countries of Europe, Professor Henry R. Seager, of Columbia University, presented the following *Outline* for discussion at a meeting of the American Association for Labor Legislation, December 30, 1907. It is reproduced with his consent as giving concrete expression to several of the principles advocated in the foregoing chapters.

The ends to be aimed at in any programme of social legislation are:

I. To protect wage-earners in the continued enjoyment of standards of living to which they are already accustomed.

II. To assist them to attain to higher standards of living.

I. Measures to protect prevailing standards of living.

The principal contingencies which threaten standards of living already acquired are: (1) industrial accidents; (2) illness; (3) invalidity and old age; (4) premature death; (5) unemployment. These contingencies are not in practice adequately provided against by wage-earners themselves. In consequence the losses they entail, in the absence of any social provision against them, fall with crushing force on the families which suffer from them, and only too often reduce such families from a position of independence and self-respect to one of humiliating and efficiency-destroying social dependency. The following remedies for the evils resulting from this situation are suggested.

(1) Employers' liability laws fail to provide adequate indemnity to the victims of industrial accidents because in a large proportion of cases no legal blame attaches to the em-

ployer and because litigation under them is costly and uncertain in its outcome. Adequate indemnification must be sought along the line of workmen's compensation for all industrial accidents at the expense of the employer (the British system) or of compulsory accident insurance (the German system). The former seems to accord better with American ideas and traditions.

(2) The principle of workmen's compensation may be extended to include indemnity for loss of wages due to trade diseases. Provision against illness not directly traceable to the employment must be sought either in compulsory illness insurance or in subsidized and state-directed sick-insurance clubs. Trade unions may assume the functions of such clubs in organized trades. The latter plan seems better suited to present American conditions than compulsory illness insurance.

(3) Provision against invalidity and old age may be through compulsory old age insurance, or through state old age pensions. The latter, though more costly, are believed to be better suited to American conditions, when hedged about by proper restrictions, than compulsory old age insurance with the elaborate administrative machinery which it entails.

(4) Premature death may be provided against by an extension of the machinery for caring for the victims of industrial accident and of illness to provide for their families when accident or illness results fatally.

(5) Provision against losses due to unemployment is attended with great difficulties because unemployment is so frequently the consequence of incapacity or of disinclination for continuous labor. The most promising plan for providing against this evil appears to be through subsidizing and supervising trade unions which pay out-of-work benefits to stimulate this side of their activity. Public employment bureaus and industrial colonies for the unemployed may also help to alleviate the evil of unemployment.

Adequate social provision against these five contingencies along the lines suggested, would, it is believed, go a long way towards solving the problem of social dependency. If these concessions were made to the demands of social justice, a more drastic policy towards social dependents than public opinion will now sanction might be inaugurated with good prospect of confining social dependency to the physically, mentally, and morally defective.

II. *Measures to elevate standards of living.*

The primary conditions essential to rising standards of living are energy and enterprise on the part of wage-earners and opportunities to make energy and enterprise count in the form of higher earnings. The principal contributions which social legislation may make to advancing standards of living in the United States are believed to be: (1) measures serving to encourage saving for future needs on the part of wage-earners by providing safe investments for savings; (2) measures protecting wage-earners from the debilitating effects of an unregulated competition; (3) measures serving to bring within the reach of all opportunities for industrial training. Standards of living will also be advanced, of course, by nearly all measures calculated to promote the general well-being, such as tax and tariff-reform legislation, laws safeguarding the national domain, the public regulation of corporations, especially those with monopolistic powers, etc., but these are not usually classed under the head of social legislation.

(1) The greatest present need under this head is for a postal savings bank like those of European countries. The advantages of a postal savings bank over privately managed banks are the wider distribution of places of deposit, post-offices being located in every section of the country, and the greater confidence depositors would feel in such a bank. Once established the postal savings bank might enter the insurance field, as has the British postal savings bank, not as a rival of privately managed insurance companies, but to bring to every wage-earner the opportunity to secure safe insurance. Next to providing itself opportunities for safe investment and insurance, the government has an important duty to perform in supervising the business of privately managed savings banks and insurance companies. Notwithstanding the progress made in recent years in the United States in

this field, there is still something left for social legislation to accomplish.

(2) If energy and enterprise are to be kept at a maximum, wage-earners must be protected from exhausting toil under unhealthful conditions. Skilled wage-earners can usually protect themselves through trade unions, but unskilled workers, women and children, require legal protection. Under this head belong, therefore, the familiar types of protective labor laws. The following may be specified:

(a) Laws prohibiting the employment of children below fourteen in all gainful pursuits. Such laws should be uniform throughout the United States and rigidly enforced by means of employment certificates based on convincing evidence of age and physical examination to determine fitness. As provision for free public education is made more adequate to present needs the minimum age may be advanced perhaps to sixteen.

(b) Laws limiting the hours of labor of young persons over fourteen. Protection here should extend to eighteen, at least in factory employments, and employment certificates should be required of all under that age.

(c) Laws limiting the hours of labor of women. In the regulation of women's work in the United States the principal needs are uniformity and machinery for efficient enforcement. The last is facilitated by the plan of specifying in the law the working period for the protected classes, and American courts must be brought to see the reasonableness (administratively) of such prescriptions. The nine-hour day and prohibition of night work set a high enough standard until greater uniformity and more efficient enforcement shall have been secured.

(d) Prescriptions in regard to sanitation and safety appliances. General prescriptions in regard to ventilation, etc., need to be made more exact, and much more attention needs to be given to the special regulation of dangerous trades, the existence of which has been largely ignored thus far in American legislation.

(3) The chief reason for restricting the labor of children and young persons is to permit the physical and mental development of childhood and youth to proceed unhampered

and to ripen into strong, vigorous, and efficient manhood and womanhood. To attain this end, it is necessary to provide not only for wholesome living conditions and general free public education, but also for special industrial training for older children superior to the training afforded in modern factories and workshops. The apprenticeship system now fails as a method of industrial training, even in those few trades which retain the forms of apprenticeship. There is urgent social need for comprehensive provision for industrial training as a part of the public school system, not to take the place of the training now given to children under fourteen, but to hold those between fourteen and sixteen in school. As this need is supplied the period of compulsory school attendance may gradually be extended up to the sixteenth year. The guiding principle of such industrial training should be that it is the function of free public education in the United States not only to prepare children to lead useful, well-rounded and happy lives, but to command the earnings without which such lives are impossible.

The above programme of social legislation is urged as a step towards realizing that canon of social justice which demands for all equal industrial opportunities. It is believed that it will also help to raise the standard of citizenship in the country by making both wage-earners and employers more intelligent, more efficient, and more truly democratic. Thus it will serve to prepare the way for such further industrial reorganization as may be found desirable.

26. THE FAMILY

The family in its moral aspects has one end, the common good of all its members, but this has three aspects. (1) Marriage converts an attachment between man and woman, either of passion or of friendship, into a deliberate, intimate, permanent, responsible union for a common end of mutual good. It is this common end, a good of a higher, broader, fuller sort than either could attain in isolation, which lifts passion from the impulsive or selfish to the moral plane; it is the peculiar intimacy and the peculiar demands for common sympathy and cooperation, which give it greater depth and reach than ordinary friendship. (2) The family is the great social agency for the care and training of the race. (3) This function reacts upon the character of the parents. Tenderness, sympathy, self-sacrifice, steadiness of purpose, responsibility, and activity, are all demanded and usually evoked by the children. A brief sketch of the development of the family and of its psychological basis, will prepare the way for a consideration of its present problems.

§ 1. Historical Antecedents of the Modern Family

The division of the sexes appeals to the biologist as an agency for securing greater variability, and so greater possibility of adaptation and progress. It has also to the sociologist the value of giving greater variety in function, and so a much richer society than could exist without it. Morally, the realization of these values, and the further effects upon character noted above, depend greatly upon the terms under which the marriage union is formed and maintained. The number of parties to the union, the mode of forming it, its stability, and the relations of husband and wife, parents and children, while in the family relation, have shown in western civilization a tendency toward certain lines of progress, although the movement has been irregular and has been interrupted by certain halts or even reversions.

The Maternal Type.—The early family, certainly in many parts of the world, was formed when a man left his father and mother to "cleave unto his wife," that is, when the woman remained in her own group and the man came from his group to live with her. This tended to give the woman continued protection—and also continued control—by her own relatives, and made the children belong to the mother's clan. As recent ethnologists seem inclined to agree, this does not mean a matriarchal family. The woman's father and brothers, rather than the woman, are in the last analysis the authority. At the same time, at a stage when physical force is so large a factor, this type of family undoubtedly favors the woman's condition as compared with the next to be mentioned.

The Paternal Type.—When the woman leaves her own group to live in the house of her husband, it means a possible loss of backing and position for her. But it means a great gain for the influence which insures the wife's fidelity, the father's authority over the children and interest in them, and finally the permanence of the family. The power of the husband and father reached its extreme among western peoples in the patriarchate at Rome, which allowed him the right of life and death. At its best the patriarchal type of family fostered the dignity and power of a ruler and owner, the sense of honor which watched jealously over self and wife and children to keep the name unsullied; finally the respective attitudes of protector and protected enhanced the charm of each for the other. At its worst it meant domineering brutality, and either the weakness of abject submission or the misery of hopeless injustice.

Along with this building up of "father right" came variations in the mode of gaining a wife. When the man takes a wife instead of going to his wife, he may either capture her, or purchase her, or serve for her. In any of these cases, she may become to a certain extent his property as well as his wife. This does not necessarily imply a feeling of humiliation. The Kafir women profess great contempt for a system in which a woman is not worth buying. But it evidently favors a commercial theory of the whole relation. The bride's consent may sometimes be a necessary part of the transaction, but it is not always.

Effects of Father Right.—This family of "father right" is also likely to encourage a theory that the man should have greater freedom in marriage than the woman. In the lowest types of civilization we often find the marital relations very loose from our point of view, although, as was noted in Chapter 2, these peoples usually make up for this in the rigidity of the rules as to who may marry or have marriage relations. With some advance in civilization and with the father right, we are very apt to find polygamy permitted to chiefs or those who can afford it, even though the average man may have but one wife. In certain cases the wives may be an economic advantage rather than a burden. It goes along with a family in which father and children are of first importance that a wife may even be glad to have her servant bear the children if they may only be reckoned as hers. The husband has thus greater freedom—for polyandry seems to have been rare among civilized peoples except under stress of poverty. The greater freedom of the husband is likely to appear also in the matter of divorce. Among many savage peoples divorce is easy for both parties if there is mutual consent, but with the families in which father right prevails it is almost always easier for the man. The ancient Hebrew might divorce his wife for any cause he pleased, but there is no mention of a similar right on her part, and it doubtless did not occur to the lawgiver. The code of Hammurabi allows the man to put away the mother of his children by giving her and her children suitable maintenance, or a childless wife by returning the bride price, but a wife who has acted foolishly or extravagantly may be divorced without compensation or kept as a slave. The woman may also claim a divorce "if she has been economical and has no vice and her husband has gone out and greatly belittled her." But if she fails to prove her claim and appears to be a gadder-about, "they shall throw that woman into the water." India and China have the patriarchal family, and the Brahmans added the obligation of the widow never to remarry. Greater freedom of divorce on the part of the husband is also attended by a very different standard for marital faithfulness. For the unfaithful husband there is frequently no penalty or a slight one; for the wife it is frequently death.

The Roman Family. — The modern family in western civilization is the product of three main forces: the Roman law, the Teutonic custom, and the Christian Church. Early Roman law had recognized the extreme power of the husband and father. Wife and children were in his "hand." All women must be in the *tutela* of some man. The woman, according to the three early forms of marriage, passed completely from the power and hand of her father into that of her husband. At the same time she was the only wife, and divorce was rare. But by the closing years of the Republic a new method of marriage, permitting the woman to remain in the *manus* of her father, had come into vogue, and with it an easy theory of divorce. Satirists have charged great degeneracy in morals as a result, but Hobhouse thinks that upon the whole the Roman matron would seem to have retained the position of her husband's companion, counselor, and friend, which she had held in those more austere times when marriage brought her legally under his dominion.[1]

The Germanic Family. — The Germanic peoples recognized an almost unlimited power of the husband. The passion for liberty, which Caesar remarked as prevalent among them, did not seem to require any large measure of freedom for their women. In fact, they, like other peoples, might be said to have satisfied the two principles of freedom and control by allotting all the freedom to the men and all, or nearly all, the control to the women. Hobhouse thus summarizes the conditions:

The power of the husband was strongly developed; he might expose the infant children, chastise his wife, dispose of her person. He could not put her to death, but if she was unfaithful, he was, with the consent of the relations, judge and executioner. The wife was acquired by purchase from her own relatives without reference to her own desires, and by purchase passed out of her family. She did not inherit in early times at all, though at a later period she acquired that right in the absence of male heirs.

1. Hobhouse, *Morals in Evolution*, Vol. I, p. 216.

She was in perpetual ward, subject, in short, to the Chinese rule of the three obediences, to which must be added, as feudal powers developed, the rule of the king or other feudal superior. And the guardianship or *mundium* was frankly regarded in early law rather as a source of profit to the guardian than as a means of defense to the ward, and for this reason it fetched a price in the market, and was, in fact, salable far down in the Middle Ages. Lastly, the German wife, though respected, had not the certainty enjoyed by the early Roman Matron of reigning alone in the household. It is true that polygamy was rare in the early German tribes, but this, as we have seen, is universally the case where the numbers of the sexes are equal. Polygamy was allowed, and was practiced by the chiefs.

Two Lines of Church Influence.—The influence of the church on marriage and family life was in two conflicting lines. On the one hand, the homage and adoration given to Mary and to the saints, tended to exalt and refine the conception of woman. Marriage was, moreover, treated as a "sacrament," a holy mystery, symbolic of the relation of Christ and the church. The priestly benediction gave religious sacredness from the beginning; gradually a marriage liturgy sprang up which added to the solemnity of the event, and finally the whole ceremony was made an ecclesiastical instead of a secular function.[2] The whole institution was undoubtedly raised to a more serious and significant position. But, on the other hand, an ascetic stream of influence had pursued a similar course, deepening and widening as it flowed. Although from the beginning those "forbidding to marry" had been denounced, it had nearly always been held that the celibate life was a higher privilege. If marriage was a sacrament, it was nevertheless held that marriage made a man unfit to perform the sacraments. Woman was regarded as the cause of the original sin. Marriage was from this standpoint a concession to human weakness. "The generality of men and women must marry or they will do worse; therefore, marriage must be made easy; but the very pure hold aloof from it as from a defilement. The law that springs from this source is not pleasant to read."[3] It must, however,

2. Howard, *History of Matrimonial Institutions*, Vol. I, ch. vii.
3. Pollock and Maitland, *History of English Law*, Vol. II, p. 383, quoted in Howard, Vol. I, pp. 325–26.

be noted that, although celibacy by a selective process tended to remove continually the finer, more aspiring men and women, and prevent them from leaving any descendants, it had one important value for woman. The convent was at once a refuge, and a door to activity. "The career open to the inmates of convents was greater than any other ever thrown open to women in the course of modern European history."[4]

Two important contributions to the justice of the marriage relation, and therefore to the better theory of the family, are in any case to be set down to the credit of the church. The first was that the consent of the parties was the only thing necessary to constitute a valid marriage. "Here the church had not only to combat old tradition and the authority of the parents, but also the seignorial power of the feudal lord, and it must be accounted to it for righteousness that it emancipated the woman of the servile as well as of the free classes in relation to the most important event of her life."[5] The other was that in maintaining as it did the indissolubility of the sacramental marriage, it held that its violation was as bad for the husband as for the wife. The older theories had looked at infidelity either as an injury to the husband's property, or as introducing uncertainty as to the parenthood of children, and this survives in Dr. Johnson's dictum of a "boundless" difference. The feelings of the wife, or even of the husband, aside from his concern for his property and children, do not seem to have been considered.

The church thus modified the Germanic and Roman traditions, but never entirely abolished them, because she was divided within herself as to the real place of family life. Protestantism, in its revolt from Rome, opposed both its theories of marriage. On the one hand, the Reformers held that marriage is not a sacrament, but a civil contract, admitting of divorce. On the other hand, they regarded marriage as the most desirable state, and abolished the celibacy of the clergy. The "subjection of women," especially of married women, has, however, remained as the legal theory until very recently. In England it was the theory in Blackstone's time that "The very being or legal existence of the woman

4. Eckenstein, *Woman under Monasticism*, p. 478.
5. Hobhouse, *Morals in Evolution*, Vol. I, p. 218.

is suspended during the marriage, or at least is incorporated and consolidated into that of the husband, under whose wing, protection, and cover, she performs everything." According to the old law, he might give her "moderate correction." "But with us in the politer reign of Charles II., this power of correction began to be doubted." It was not until 1882, however, that a married woman in England gained control of her property. In the United States the old injustice of the common law has been gradually remedied by statutes until substantial equality in relation to property and children has been secured.

§ 2. The Psychological Basis of the Family

The psychology of family life may be conveniently considered under two heads: that of the husband and wife, and that of parents and children, brothers and sisters.

1. The complex sentiment, love, which is found in the most perfect family life, is on the one hand (1) a feeling or emotion; on the other (2) a purpose, a will. Both these are modified and strengthened by (3) parenthood and (4) social and religious influences.

(1) *The Emotional and Instinctive Basis.*—As feeling or emotion love may have two roots. A mental sympathy, based on kindred tastes and interests, is sometimes present at the outset, but in any case it is likely to develop under the favoring conditions of a common life, particularly if there are either children or a common work. But it is well known that this is not all. A friend is one thing; a lover another. The intimacy involved requires not only the more easily described and superficial attraction of mind for mind; it demands also a deeper congeniality of the whole person, incapable of precise formulation, manifesting itself in the subtler emotional attitudes of instinctive reaction. This instinctive, as contrasted with the more reflective, attraction is frequently described as one of opposites or contrasting dispositions and physical characteristics. But this is nothing that enters into the feeling as a conscious factor. The only explanation which we can give in the present condition of

science is the biological one. From the biological point of view it was a most successful venture when Nature, by some happy variation, developed two sexes with slightly different characters and made their union necessary to the continuance of life in certain species. By uniting in every new individual the qualities of two parents, the chances of variation are greatly increased, and variation is the method of progress. To keep the same variety of fruit the horticulturist buds or grafts; to get new varieties he plants seed. The extraordinary progress combined with continuity of type, which has been exhibited in the plant and animal world, has been effected, in part at least, through the agency of sex. This long process has developed certain principles of selection which are instinctive. Whether they are the best possible or not, they represent a certain adjustment which has secured such progress as has been attained, and such adaptation to environment as exists, and it would be unwise, if it were not impossible, to disregard them. Marriages of convenience are certainly questionable from the biological standpoint.

But the instinctive basis is not in and of itself sufficient to guarantee a happy family life. If man were living wholly a life of instinct, he might trust instinct as a guide in establishing his family. But since he is living an intellectual and social life as well, intellectual and social factors must enter. The instinctive basis of selection was fixed by conditions which contemplated only a more or less limited period of attachment, with care of the young for a few years. Modern society requires the husband and wife to contemplate lifelong companionship, and a care for children which implies capacity in the father to provide for a great range of advantages, and in the mother to be intellectual and moral guide and friend until maturity. To trust the security of these increased demands to instinct is to invite failure. Instinct must be guided by reason if perfect friendship and mutual supplementation in the whole range of interests are to be added to the intenser, but less certain, attraction.

(2) *The Common Will.*—But whether based on instinct or intellectual sympathy, no feeling or emotion by itself is an adequate moral basis for the life together of a man and a woman. What was said on p. 229, as to the moral worth-

lessness of any *mere* feeling abstracted from will, applies
here. Love or affection, in the only sense in which it makes
a moral basis of the family, is not the "affection" of psychological language—the pleasant or unpleasant tone of consciousness; it is the resolute purpose in each to seek the other's good, or rather to seek a *common* good which can be
attained only through a common life involving mutual self-
sacrifice. It is the good will of Kant specifically directed toward creating a common good. It is the formation of a small
"kingdom of ends" in which each treats the other "as end,"
never as means only; in which each is "both sovereign and
subject"; in which the common will, thus created, enhances
the person of each and gives it higher moral dignity and
worth. And, as in the case of all purpose which has moral
value, there is such a common good as the actual result. The
disposition and character of both husband and wife are developed and supplemented. The male is biologically the more
variable and motor. He has usually greater initiative and
strength. Economic and industrial life accentuates these
tendencies. But alone he is apt to become rough or hard, to
lack the feeling in which the charm and value of life are
experienced. On the other hand, the woman, partly by instinct, it may be, but certainly by vocation, is largely occupied with the variety of cares on which human health, comfort, and morality depend. She tends to become narrow,
unless supplemented by man. The value of emotion and feeling in relation to this process of mutual aid and enlargement,
as in general, is, as Aristotle pointed out, to perfect the will.
It gives warmth and vitality to what would otherwise be in
any case partial and might easily become insincere. There
was a profound truth which underlay the old psychology in
which "the heart" meant at once character and passion.

(3) *The Influence of Parenthood.*—Nature takes one
step at a time. If all the possible consequences of family life
had to be definitely forecasted, valued, and chosen at the outset, many would shrink. But this would be because there
is as yet no capacity to appreciate new values before the actual experience of them. "Every promise of the soul has innumerable fulfillments; each of its joys ripens into a new
want." Parental affection is not usually present until there

are real children to evoke it. At the outset the mutual love of husband and wife is enough. But as the first, more instinctive and emotional factors lose relatively, the deeper union of will and sympathy needs community of interest if it is to become permanent and complete. Such community of interest is often found in sharing a business or a profession, but under present industrial organization this is not possible as a general rule. The most general and effective object of common interest is the children of the family. As pointed out by John Fiske, the mere keeping of the parents together by the prolongation of infancy in the human species has had great moral influence. Present civilization does not merely demand that the parents cooperate eight or ten years for the child's physical support. There has been a second epoch in the prolongation. The parents now must cooperate until the children are through school and college, and in business or homes of their own. And the superiority of children over the other common interests is that in a different form the parents repeat the process which first took them out of their individual lives to unite for mutual helpfulness. If the parents treat the children not merely as sources of gratification or pride, but as persons, with lives of their own to live, with capacities to develop, the personality of the parent is enlarged. The affection between husband and wife is enriched by the new relationship it has created.

(4) *Social and Religious Factors.*—The relations of husband and wife, parent and child, are the most intimate of personal relations, but they are none the less relations of social interest. In fact, just because they are so intimate, society is the more deeply concerned. Or, to put it from the individual's standpoint, just because the parties are undertaking a profoundly personal step, they must take it as members of a moral order. The act of establishing the family signifies, indeed, the entrance into fuller participation in the social life; it is the assuming of ties which make the parties in a new and deeper sense organic parts of humanity. This social and cosmic meaning is appropriately symbolized by the civil and religious ceremony. In its control over the marriage contract, and in its prescriptions as to the care and education of the children, society continues to show its in-

terest. All this lends added value and strength to the emotional and intellectual bases.

2. *Parent and Child.*—The other relationships in the family, those of parents and children, brothers and sisters, need no elaborate analysis. The love of parents for children, like that of man and woman, has an instinctive basis. Those species which have cared for their offspring have had a great advantage in the struggle for existence. Nature has selected them, and is constantly dropping the strains of any race or set which cares more for power, or wealth, or learning than for children. Tenderness, courage, responsibility, activity, patience, forethought, personal virtue—these are constantly evoked not by the needs of children in general, but by the needs of our own children. The instinctive response, however, is soon broadened in outlook and deepened in meaning. Intellectual activity is stimulated by the needs of providing for the physical welfare, and, still more, by the necessity of planning for the unfolding mind. The interchange of question and answer which forces the parent to think his whole world anew, and which with the allied interchange of imitation and suggestion produces a give and take between all members of the family, is constantly making for fluidity and flexibility, for tolerance and catholicity. In the thoughtful parent these educative influences are still further enriched by the problem of moral training. For in each family, as in the race, the need of eliciting and directing right conduct in the young is one of the most important agencies in bringing home to the elders the significance of custom and authority, of right and wrong. It is natural enough, from one standpoint, to think of childhood as an imperfect state, looking forward for its completeness and getting its value because of its rich promise. But the biologist tells us that the child is nearer the line of progress than the more developed, but also more rigidly set, man. And the lover of children is confident that if any age of humanity exists by its own right, and "pays as it goes," it is childhood. It is not only meet, but a joy, that the fathers labor for the children. Many, if not most, of the objects for which men and women strive and drudge seem less satisfactory when obtained; because we have meanwhile outgrown the desire. Children afford an

object of affection which is constantly unfolding new powers, and opening new reaches of personality.[6] Conversely, an authority which is also tender, patient, sympathetic, is the best medium to develop in the child self-control. The necessity of mutual forbearance where there are several children, of sharing fairly, of learning to give and take, is the best possible method of training for membership in the larger society. In fact, from the point of view of the social organism as a whole, the family has two functions; as a smaller group, it affords an opportunity for eliciting the qualities of affection and character which cannot be displayed at all in the larger group; and, in the second place, it is a training for future members of the larger group in those qualities of disposition and character which are essential to citizenship.[7]

§ 3. General Elements of Strain In Family Relations

Difference in Temperament.—While there are intrinsic qualities of men and women that bring them together for family life, and, while there is in most cases a strong reenforcement afforded by the presence of children, there are certain characteristics which tend just as inevitably to produce tension, and those forces of tension are strengthened at the present time by certain economic, educational, and cultural conditions. The differences between men and women may be at the basis of their instinctive attraction for each other; they certainly have possibilities of friction as well. A fundamental difference already noted is that the male is more variable, the female more true to the type. Biologically

6. Helen Bosanquet, *The Family*, p. 313: " 'They must hinder your work very much,' I said to a mother busy about the kitchen, with a two-year-old clinging to her skirt. 'I'd never get through my work without them,' was the instant rejoinder, and in it lay the answer to much of our sentimental commiseration of hard-worked mothers. It may be hard to carry on the drudgery of daily life with the little ones clamoring around; it is ten times harder without, for sheer lack of something to make it worth while."

7. Bosanquet, *The Family*, Part II, ch. x.

at least, the *varium et mutabile* is applied by the poet to the wrong sex. Applied to the mind and disposition, this means probably not only a greater variation of capacity and temper as a whole,—more geniuses and also more at the other extreme than among women,—but also a greater average mobility.

Differences Accentuated by Occupation.—From the early occupations of hunting and fishing, to the modern greater range of occupations, any native mobility in man has found stimulation and scope, as compared with the energies of women which have less distinct differentiation and a more limited contact with the work of others. And there is another industrial difference closely connected with this, which has been pointed out by Ellis,[8] and Thomas.[9] Primitive man hunted and fought. Much of primitive industry, the prototype, so far as it existed, of the industrial activity of the modern world, was carried on by woman. Industrial progress has been signalized by the splitting off of one phase of woman's work after another, and by the organization and expansion of this at the hands of man. Man's work has thus become more specialized and scientific; woman's has remained more detailed, complex, and diffused. Her work in the family of ordering the household, caring for the children, securing the health and comfort of all its members, necessarily involves personal adjustment; hence it resists system. As a result of the differentiation man has gained in greater and greater degree a scientific and objective standard for his work; woman neither has nor can have—at least in the sphere of personal relations—the advantage of a standard. Business has its ratings in the quantity of sales or the ratio of net profits. The professions and skilled trades have their own tests of achievement. A scientist makes his discovery, a lawyer wins his case, an architect builds his bridge, the mechanic his machine; he knows whether he has done a good piece of work, and respects himself accordingly. He can appeal from the man next to him to the judgment of his profession. Conversely, the standard of the trade or profes-

8. Ellis, *Man and Woman.*
9. W. I. Thomas, *Sex and Society.*

sion helps to lift the individual's work. It is a constant stimulus, as well as support. A woman's work in the family has no such professional stimulus, or professional vindication. If the family is lenient, the work is not held up to a high level. On the other hand, it must make its appeal to the persons immediately concerned, and if they do not respond, the woman feels that she has failed to do something really worth while. If her work is not valued, she feels that it is not valuable. For there is no demonstrative proof of a successful home any more than there is of a good work of art. It is easy enough to point out reasons why the picture or the home should please and satisfy, but if the work itself is not convincing, no demonstration that similar works have satisfied is of any avail.

The way in which men and women come into contact with others is another element in the case. Man comes into contact with others for the most part in an abstract way. He deals not with men, women, and children, but with employers or employed, with customers or clients, or patients. He doesn't have to stand them in all their varied phases, or enter into those intimate relations which involve strain of adjustment in its fullest extent. Moreover, business or professional manner and etiquette come in to relieve the necessity of personal effort. The "professional manner" serves the same function in dealing with others, which habit plays in the individual life; it takes the place of continual readjustment of attention. When a man is forced to lay this aside and deal in any serious situation as "a human being," he feels a far greater strain. The woman's task is less in extension, but great in intension. It obliges her to deal with the children, at any rate, as wholes, and a "whole" child is a good deal of a strain. If she does not see the whole of the husband, it is quite likely that the part not brought home—the professional or business part of him—is the most alert, intelligent, and interesting phase. The constant close-at-hand personal relations, unrelieved by the abstract impersonal attitude and the generalizing activity which it invites, constitute an element of strain which few men understand, and which probably few could endure and possess their souls. The present division of labor seems, therefore, to make the man excessively abstract, the woman excessively personal, instead of supplementing to some extent the weak side of each.

Difference in Attitude toward the Family.—As if these differences in attitude based on disposition and occupation were not enough, we have a thoroughgoing difference in the attitude of men and women toward the very institution which invites them. The man is ready enough to assent to the importance of the family for the race, but his family means not an interference with other ambitions, but usually an aid to their fulfillment. His family is one interest among several, and is very likely subordinate in his thought to his profession or his business. In early ages to rove or conquer, in modern life to master nature and control her resources or his fellowmen—this has been the insistent instinct which urges even the long-tossed Ulysses from Ithaca and from Penelope again upon the deep. Woman, on the other hand, if she enters a family, usually abandons any other ambition and forgets any acquired art or skill of her previous occupation. To be the mistress of a home may be precisely what she would choose as a vocation. But there is usually no alternative if she is to have a home at all. It is not a question of a family in addition to a vocation, but of a family *as* a vocation. Hence woman must regard family life not merely as *a* good; it must be *the* good, and usually the exclusive good.

If, then, a woman has accepted the family as the supreme good, it is naturally hard to be in perfect sympathy with the man's standard of family life as secondary. Of course a completer vision may find that a division of labor, a difference of function, may carry with it a difference in standards of value; the mastery of nature and the maintenance of the family may be neither an absolute good in itself, but each a necessity to life and progress. But neither man nor woman is always equal to this view, and to the full sympathy for the relative value of the other's standpoint. Where it cuts closest is in the attitude toward breach of faith in the family tie. Men have severe codes for the man who cheats at cards or forges a signature, but treat much more leniently, or entirely ignore, the gravest offenses against the family. These latter do not seem to form a barrier to political, business, or social success (among men). Women have a severe standard for family sanctity, especially for their own sex. But it would probably be difficult to convince most women that it is a more heinous offense to secrete a card, or even with Nora in *The Doll's House*, to forge a name, than to be unfaithful. It is not meant that the average man or woman approves either form of wrongdoing, but that there is a difference of emphasis evidenced in the public attitude. In view of all these differences in nature, occupation, and social standard it may be said that however well husband and wife may love each other, few understand each other completely. Perhaps most men do not understand women at all. Corresponding to the "psychologist's fallacy," whose evils have been depicted by James, there is a "masculine fallacy" and a "feminine fallacy."

Difference in Age.—The difference in age between parents and children brings certain inevitable hindrances to complete understanding. The most thoroughgoing is that parent and children really stand concretely for the two factors of continuity and individual variation which confront each other in so many forms. The parent has found his place in the social system, and is both steadied and to some extent made rigid by the social tradition. The child, though to some extent imitating and adopting this tradition, has as yet little reasoned adherence to it. The impulses and expanding life do not find full expression in the set ways already open, and occasionally break out new channels. The conservatism of the parent may be a wiser and more social, or merely a more hardened and narrow, mode of conduct; some of the child's variations may be irrational and pernicious to himself and society; others may promise a larger reasonableness, a more generous social order—but meanwhile certain features of the conflict between reason and impulse, order and change, are constantly appearing. Differences in valuation are also inevitable and can be bridged only by an intelligent sympathy. It is easy to consider this or that to be of slight importance to the child when it is really his whole world for the time. Even if he does "get over it," the effect on the disposition may remain, and affect the temper or emotional life, even though not consciously remembered. Probably, also, most parents do not realize how early a crude but sometimes even passionate sense for "fairness" develops, or how different the relative setting of an act appears if judged from the motives actually operative with the child, and not from those which might produce such an act in a "grown-up." Most parents and children love each other; few reach a complete understanding.

§ 4. Special Conditions Which Give Rise to Present Problems

In addition to the more general conditions of family life, there are certain conditions at present operative which give rise to special problems, or rather emphasize certain aspects of the permanent problems. The family is quite analogous to political society. There needs to be constant readjustment between order and progress, between the control of the society and the freedom of the individual. The earlier bonds of custom or force have to be exchanged in point after point for a more voluntary and moral order. In the words of Kant, heteronomy must steadily give place to autonomy, subordination of rank or status to division of labor with equality in dignity. The elements of strain in the family life at present may fairly be expected to give rise ultimately to a better constitution of its relations. The special conditions are partly economic, partly educational and political, but the general process is a part of the larger growth of modern civilization with the increasing development of individuality and desire for freedom. It is sometimes treated as if it affected only the woman or the children; in reality it affects the man as well, though in less degree, as his was not the subordinate position.

The Economic Factors. — The "industrial revolution" transferred production from home to factory. The household is no longer as a rule an industrial unit. Spinning, weaving, tailoring, shoemaking, soap-making, iron- and wood-working, and other trades have gone to factories. Men, young unmarried women, and to some extent married women also, have gone with them. Children have lost association with one parent, and in some cases with both. The concentration of industry and business leads to cities. Under present means of transportation this means apartments instead of houses, it means less freedom, more strain, for both mother and children, and possible deteriorating effects upon the race which as yet are quite outside any calculation. But leaving this uncertain field of effects upon child life, we notice certain potent effects upon men and women.

It might be a difficult question to decide the exact gains and losses for family life due to the absence of the man from home during the day. On the one hand, too constant association is a source of friction; on the other, there is likely to result some loss of sympathy, and where the working-day is long, an almost absolute loss of contact with children. If children are the great natural agencies for cultivating tenderness and affection, it is certainly unfortunate that fathers should be deprived of this education. The effect of the industrial revolution upon women has been widely noted. First of all, the opening of an increasing number of occupations to women has rendered them economically more independent. They are not forced to the alternative of marriage or dependence upon relatives. If already married, even although they may have lost touch to some extent with their former occupation, they do not feel the same compulsion to endure intolerable conditions in the home rather than again attempt self-support. An incidental effect of the entrance of women upon organized occupations, with definite hours and impersonal standards, is to bring out more strongly by contrast the "belated" condition of domestic work. It is difficult to obtain skilled workers for an occupation requiring nearly double the standard number of hours, isolation instead of companionship during work, close personal contact with an employer, a measure of control over conduct outside of the hours on duty, and finally the social inferiority implied by an occupation which has in it survivals of the status of the old-time servant. Indeed, the mistress of the house, if she "does her own work," doesn't altogether like her situation. There is now no one general occupation which all men are expected to master irrespective of native tastes and abilities. If every

male were obliged to make not only his own clothing, including head- and foot-wear, but that of his whole family, un-
assisted, or with practically unskilled labor, there would
probably be as much misfit clothing as there is now unsatisfactory home-making, and possibly there would be an increase of irritability and "nervousness" on the one side and
of criticism or desertion on the other, which would increase
the present strain upon the divorce courts. To an increasing
number of women, the position of being "jack-at-all-trades
and master-of-none" is irritating. The conviction that there
is a great waste of effort without satisfactory results is more
wearing than the actual doing of the work.

For the minority of women who do not "keep house,"
or who can be relieved entirely of domestic work by experts,
the industrial revolution has a different series of possibilities.
If there is a decided talent which has received adequate cultivation, there may be an opportunity for its exercise without
serious interference with family life, but the chances are
against it. If the woman cannot leave her home for the entire day, or if her husband regards a gainful occupation on
her part as a reflection upon his ability to "support the family," she is practically shut out from any occupation. If she
has children and has an intelligent as well as an emotional
interest in their welfare, there is an unlimited field for scientific development. But if she has no regular useful occupation, she is not leading a normal life. Her husband very
likely cannot understand why she should not, in the words
of Veblen, perform "vicarious leisure" for him, and be satisfied therewith. If she is satisfied, so much the worse. Whether
she is satisfied or not, she is certainly not likely to grow
mentally or morally in such an existence, and the family
life will not be helped by stagnation or frivolity.

In certain classes of society there is one economic feature which is probably responsible for many petty annoy-
ances and in some cases for real degradation of spirit. When
the family was an industrial unit, when exchange was
largely in barter, it was natural to think of the woman as a
joint agent in production. When the production moved to
factories and the wage or the wealth was paid to the man
and could be kept in his pocket or his check-book, it became

easy for him to think of himself as "supporting" the family, to permit himself to be "asked" for money for household expenses or even for the wife's personal expenses, and to consider money used in these ways as "gifts" to his wife or children. Women have more or less resistingly acquiesced in this humiliating conception, which is fatal to a real moral relation as well as to happiness. It is as absurd a conception as it would be to consider the receiving teller in a bank as supporting the bank, or the manager of a factory as supporting all the workmen. The end of the family is not economic profit, but mutual aid, and the continuance and progress of the race. A division of labor does not give superiority and inferiority. When one considers which party incurs the greater risks, and which works with greater singleness and sincerity for the family, it must pass as one of the extraordinary superstitions that the theory of economic dependence should have gained vogue.

Cultural and Political Factors. —Educational, cultural, and political movements reenforce the growing sense of individuality. Educational and cultural advance strengthens the demand that woman's life shall have as serious a purpose as man's, and that in carrying on her work, whether in the family or without, she may have some share in the grasp of mind, the discipline of character, and the freedom of spirit which come from the scientific spirit, and from the intelligent, efficient organization of work by scientific methods. Political democracy draws increasing attention to personal dignity, irrespective of rank or wealth. Increasing legal rights have been granted to women until in most points they are now equal before the law, although the important exception of suffrage still remains for the most part. Under these conditions it is increasingly difficult to maintain a family union on any other basis than that of equal freedom, equal responsibilities, equal dignity and authority. It will probably be found that most of the tension now especially felt in family life—aside from those cases of maladaptation liable to occur under any system—results either from lack of recognition of this equality, or from the more general economic conditions which society as a whole, rather than any particular family, must meet and change.

§ 5. Unsettled Problems: (1) Economic

The family as an economic unit includes the relation of its members to society both as producers and as consumers.

The Family and Production.—We have noted the industrial changes which have seemed to draw the issue sharply between the home and outside occupations. We have seen that the present organization of industry, business, and the professions has separated most of the occupations from the family, so that woman must choose between family and a specific occupation, but cannot ordinarily combine the two. We have said that in requiring all its women to do the same thing the family seems to exclude them from individual pursuits adapted to their talents, and to exclude them likewise from the whole scientific and technical proficiency of modern life. Is this an inevitable dilemma? Those who think it is divide into two parties, which accept respectively the opposite horns. The one party infers that the social division of labor must be: man to carry on all occupations outside the family, woman to work always within the family. The other party infers that the family life must give way to the industrial tendency.

(1) The "domestic theory," or as Mrs. Bosanquet styles it, the "pseudo-domestic" theory, is held sincerely by many earnest friends of the family in both sexes. They feel strongly the fundamental necessity of family life. They believe further that they are not seeking to subordinate woman to the necessities of the race, but rather to give her a unique position of dignity and affection. In outside occupations she must usually be at a disadvantage in competition with men, because of her physical constitution which Nature has specialized for a different function. In the family she "reigns supreme." With most women life is not satisfied, experience is not full, complete consciousness of sex and individuality is not attained, until they have dared to enter upon the full family relations. Let these be preserved not merely for the race, but especially for woman's own sake. Further, it is urged, when woman enters competitive occupations outside the home, she lowers the scale of wages. This makes it harder

for men to support families, and therefore more reluctant to establish them. Riehl urges that not only should married women remain at home; unmarried women should play the part of "aunt" in some one's household—he says *alte Tante*, but it is not necessary to load the theory too heavily with the adjective.

(2) The other horn of the dilemma is accepted by many writers, especially among socialists. These writers assume that the family necessarily involves not only an exclusively domestic life for all women, but also their economic dependence. They believe this dependence to be not merely a survival of barbarism, but an actual immorality in its exchange of sex attraction for economic support. Hence they would abandon the family or greatly modify it. It must no longer be "coercive"; it will be coercive under present conditions.

Fallacies in the Dilemma.—Each of these positions involves a fallacy which releases us from the necessity of choosing between them. The root of the fallacy in each case is the conception that the economic status determines the moral end, whereas the moral end ought to determine the economic status.

The fallacy of the pseudo-domestic theory lies in supposing that the home must continue its old economic form or be destroyed. What is essential to the family is that man and wife, parents and children, should live in such close and intimate relation that they may be mutually helpful. But it is not essential that present methods of house construction, domestic service, and the whole industrial side of home life be maintained immutable. There is one fundamental division of labor between men and women. The woman who takes marriage at its full scope accepts this. "The lines which it follows are drawn not so much by the woman's inability to work for her family in the outside world—she constantly does so when the death or illness of her husband throws the double burden upon her; but from the obvious fact that the man is incapable of the more domestic duties incident upon the rearing of children."[10] But this does not involve the total

10. Helen Bosanquet, *The Family*, p. 272.

life of a woman, nor does it imply that to be a good wife and
mother every woman must under all possible advances of
industry continue to be cook, seamstress, housemaid, and
the rest. True it is that if a woman steps out of her profession
or trade for five, ten, twenty years, it is in many cases difficult to reenter. But there are some occupations where total
absence is not necessary. There are others where her added
experience ought to be an asset instead of a handicap. A
mother who has been well trained ought to be a far more
effective teacher in her wholesome and intelligent influence.
She ought to be a more efficient manager or worker in the
great variety of civic and social enterprises of both paid and
unpaid character. There is no doubt that the present educational and social order is suffering because deprived of the
competent service which many married women might render,
just as women in their turn are suffering for want of congenial occupation, suited to their capacities and individual
tastes. A growing freedom in economic pursuit would improve the home, not injure it. For nothing that interferes
with normal development is likely to prove beneficial to the
family's highest interest.

The fallacy of those who would abolish the family to
emancipate woman from economic dependence is in supposing that because the woman is not engaged in a gainful occupation she is therefore being supported by the man for
his own pleasure. This is to adopt the absurd assumptions of
the very condition they denounce. This theory at most, applies to a marriage which is conceived from an entirely selfish and commercial point of view. If a man marries for his
own pleasure and is willing to pay a cash price; if a woman
marries for cash or support and is willing to pay the price,
there is no doubt as to the proper term for such a transaction. The result is not a family in the moral sense, and no
ceremonies or legal forms can make it moral. A family in the
moral sense exists for a common good, not for selfish use
of others. To secure this common good each member contributes a part. If both husband and wife carry on gainful
occupations, well; if one is occupied outside the home and
the other within, well also. If there are children, the woman
is likely to have the far more difficult and wearing half of

the common labor. Which plan is followed, i.e., whether the woman works outside or within the home, ought to depend on which plan is better on the whole for all concerned, and this will depend largely on the woman's own ability and tastes, and upon the number and age of the children. But the economic relation is not the essential thing. The essential thing is that the economic be held entirely subordinate to the moral conception, before marriage and after.

The Family as Consumer.—The relation of the family as consumer to society and to the economic process at large involves also an important moral problem. For while production has been taken from the home, the selective influence of the family over production through its direction of consumption has proportionally increased. And in this field the woman of the family is and should be the controlling factor. As yet only the internal aspects have been considered. Most women regard it as their duty to buy economically, to secure healthful food, and make their funds go as far as possible. But the moral responsibility does not stop here. The consumer may have an influence in helping to secure better conditions of production, such as sanitary workshops, reasonable hours, decent wages, by a "white label." But this is chiefly valuable in forming public opinion to demand workrooms free from disease and legal abolition of sweatshops and child labor. The greater field for the consumers' control is in determining the kind of goods that shall be produced. What foods shall be produced, what books written, what plays presented, what clothing made, what houses and what furnishing shall be provided—all this may be largely determined by the consumers. And the value of simplicity, utility, and genuineness, is not limited to the effects upon the family which consumes. The workman who makes fraudulent goods can hardly help being injured. The economic waste involved in the production of what satisfies no permanent or real want is a serious indictment of our present civilization. It was said, under the subject of the economic process, that it was an ethically desirable end to have increase of goods, and of the kind wanted. We may now add a third end: it is important that society should learn to want the kinds of goods which give happiness and not merely crude gratification. Men often need most what they want least. Not only the happiness of life but its progress, its unfolding of new capacities and interests, is determined largely by the direction of the consumption. Woman is here the influential factor.

If there were no other reason for the better and wider education of woman than the desirability of more intelligent consumption, society would have ample ground to demand it.

§ 6. Unsettled Problems: (2) Political

The family may be regarded as a political unit, first in its implication of some control of the members by the common end, and in the second place in its relation to the authority of the State.

1. Authority within the Family.—If the political character of the family were kept clearly in mind, the internal relations of the members of the family would be on a far more moral basis and there would be less reason for friction or personal clashes. If there is a group of persons which is to act as a unity, there must be some leadership and control. In many cases there will be a common conviction as to the fittest person to lead or direct, but where the group is a permanent one with frequent occasions for divergent interests, unity has been maintained either by force or by some agency regarded by the people as embodying their common will. In the earliest forms of society this, as we have seen, was not clearly distinguished from personal and individual command. But as the conception of the political worked free from that of the personal agent, it could be recognized more and more that the ruler was not the man—not Henry or William,—but the King or the Parliament, as representing the nation. Then government became a more consciously moral act. Obedience was not humiliating, because the members were sovereign as well as subject. It was not heteronomy but autonomy. In the family the personal relation is so close that this easily overshadows the fact that there is also a family relation of a political sort. The man in the patriarchal family, and since, has exercised, or has had the legal right to exercise authority. And with the legal theory of inequality to support him it is not strange that he should often have conceived that obedience was due to him as a person, and not to him as, in certain cases, best representing the joint purpose of the family, just as in other cases the woman best represents this same purpose.

Equality or Inequality.—But even when there had been recognition of a more than personal attitude the question would at once arise, are the members of a family to be considered as of equal or unequal importance? The answer until recently has been unequivocal. In spite of such apparent exceptions as chivalry, and the court paid to beauty or wit, or the honor accorded to individual wives and mothers, woman has seldom been taken seriously in the laws and institutions of society. Opportunities for education and full participation in the thought and life of civilization are very recent. Public school education for girls is scarcely a century old. College education for women, in a general sense, is of the present generation. But the conviction has steadily gained that democracy cannot treat half the race as inferior in dignity, or exclude it from the comradeship of life. Under primitive society a man was primarily a member of a group or caste, and only secondarily a person. A woman has been in this situation as regards her sex. She is now asserting a claim to be considered primarily as a person, rather than as a woman. This general movement, like the economic movement, has seemed to affect the attitude of unmarried women, and to a less degree, of men, toward marriage, and to involve an instability of the family tie. The question is then this: does the family necessarily involve inequality, or can it be maintained on a basis of equality? Or to put the same thing from another angle: if the family and the modern movement toward equality are at variance, which ought to give way?

The "pseudo-domestic" theory on this point is suggested by its general position on the economic relations of the family as already stated. It believes that the family must be maintained as a distinct sphere of life, coordinate in importance for social welfare with the intellectual, artistic, and economic spheres. It holds, further, that the family can be maintained in this position only if it be kept as a unique controlling influence in woman's life, isolated from other spheres. This of course involves an exclusion of woman from a portion of the intellectual and political life, and therefore an inferiority of development, even if there is not an inferiority of capacity. Some of this school have maintained that in America the rapid advance in education and intelligence among women has rendered them so superior to the average man who has to leave school for business at an early age that they are unwilling to marry. A German alliterative definition of woman's "sphere" has been found in "the four K's"—Kirche, Kinder, Küche, und Kleider.

If the permanence of the family rests on the maintenance of a relation of inferiority, it is indeed in a perilous state. All the social and political forces are making toward equality, and from the moral standpoint it is impossible successfully to deny Mill's classic statement, "The only school of genuine moral sentiment is society between equals." But some of the advocates of equality have accepted the same fallacious separation between the family and modern culture. They have assumed that the family life must continue to be unscientific in its methods, and meagre in its interests. Some women—like some men—undoubtedly place a higher value on book learning, musical and dramatic entertainment, and other by-products of modern civilization than on the elemental human sympathies and powers which these should serve to enrich. It is too easily granted that the opportunity and duty of woman as wife and mother are limited to a purely unscientific provision for physical wants to the exclusion of scientific methods, intellectual comradeship, and effective grappling with moral problems.

Isolation Not the Solution.—The solution for the present unrest is therefore to be found not in forcing the separation between the family on the one hand and the intellectual, political, and other aspects of civilization on the other, but in a mutual permeation. They think very lightly of the elemental strength of sex and parental instincts who suppose that these are to be overslaughed in any great portion of the race by cultural interests. And it is to ignore the history of political progress to suppose that organic relations founded on equality and democracy are less stable than those resting on superiority and subordination. The fact is that there is no part of life so much in need of all that modern science can give, and no field for intellectual penetration and technological organization so great as the family. Correlative with its control over economic processes through its position as consumer, is its influence over social, educational, and political life, through its relation to the children who are constantly renewing the structure. To fulfill the possibilities and even the duties of family life under modern conditions requires both scientific training and civic activity. Provisions for health and instruction and proper social life in school, provisions for parks and good municipal housekeeping, for public health and public morals,—these demand the intelligent interest of the parent and have in most cases their natural motive in the family necessities. A theory of the family which would limit the parent, especially the mother, to "the home" needs first to define the limits of "the home." To measure its responsibilities by the limit of the street door is as absurd as to suppose that the sphere of justice is limited by the walls of the courtroom. A broader education for women is certainly justified by precisely this larger meaning of the care of children and of the family interests. The things of greatest importance to human life have scarcely been touched as yet by science. We know more about astrophysics than about health and disease; more about waste in steam power than about waste in foods, or in education; more about classical archaeology than about the actual causes of poverty, alcoholism, prostitution, and childlessness, the chief enemies of home life. In the light of the actual possibilities and needs of family life two positions seem equally absurd: the one that family life can be preserved best by isolating it, and particularly its women, from culture; the other, that it does not afford an opportunity for a full life. Neither of these errors can be corrected apart from the other. It is in the mutual permeation and interaction of the respective spheres of family and cultural life, not in their isolation, that the family is to be strengthened. Here, as in the economic field, no one family can succeed entirely by itself. The problem is largely a social one. But every family which is free and yet united, which shows comradeship as well as mutual devotion, is forcing the issue and preparing the way for the more perfect family of the future.

2. *Authority over the Family: Divorce.*—The strains which have been noticed in the foregoing paragraphs have centered public attention on the outward symptoms of unrest and maladaptation. Current discussions of family problems are likely to turn largely upon the increase of divorce. For the reasons which have been given there has doubtless been increasing tendency to seek divorce, and this may continue until more stable conditions are reached. Now that the authority of the church is less implicitly accepted, individuals are thrown back upon their own voluntary controls, and whether marriages are arranged by parents as in France, or formed almost solely on the initiative and unguided will of the parties as in America, the result is much the same. Two classes of persons seek divorce. Those of individualistic temperament, who have formed the marriage for selfish ends or in frivolous moments, are likely to find its constraints irksome when the expected happiness fails to be realized and the charm of novelty is past. This is simply one type of immoral conduct which may be somewhat checked by public opinion or legal restraint, but can be overcome only by a more serious and social attitude toward all life. The other class finds in the bond itself, under certain conditions, a seemingly fatal obstacle to the very purpose which it was designed to promote: unfaithfulness, cruelty, habitual intoxication, and other less coarse, but equally effective modes of behavior may be destructive of the common life and morally injurious to the children. Or alienation of spirit may leave external companionship empty of moral unity and value, if not positively opposed to self-respect. This class is evidently actuated by sincere motives. How far society may be justified in permitting dissolution of the family under these conditions, and how far it may properly insist on some personal sacrifice for the sake of larger social ends is simply another form of the problem which we considered in the economic field—the antithesis between individual rights and public welfare. The solution in each case cannot be reached by any external rule. It will be found only in the gradual

socializing of the individual on the one hand, and in the correlative development of society to the point where it respects all its members and makes greater freedom possible for them on the other. Meanwhile it must not be overlooked that the very conception of permanence in the union, upheld by the state, is itself effective toward thoughtful and well-considered action after as well as before marriage. Some causes of friction may be removed, some tendencies to alienation may be suppressed, if the situation is resolutely faced from the standpoint of a larger social interest rather than from that of momentary or private concern.

General Law of Social Health.—Divorce is a symptom rather than a disease. The main reliance in cases of family pathology, as for the diseases of the industrial and economic system, is along the lines which modern science is pursuing in the field of medicine. It is isolating certain specific organisms which invade the system under favorable circumstances and disturb its equilibrium. But it finds that the best, and in fact the only ultimate protection against disease is in the general "resisting power" of the living process. This power may be temporarily aided by stimulation or surgery, but the ultimate source of its renewal is found in the steady rebuilding of new structures to replace the old stagnation; the retention of broken-down tissues means weakness and danger. The social organism does not escape this law. Science will succeed in pointing out the specific causes for many of the moral evils from which we suffer. Poverty, crime, social injustice, breaking down of the family, political corruption, are not all to be accepted simply as "evils" or "wickedness" in general. In many cases their amount may be greatly reduced when we understand their specific causes and apply a specific remedy. But the great reliance is upon the primal forces which have brought mankind so far along the line of advance. The constant remaking of values in the search for the genuinely satisfying, the constant forming, criticizing, and reshaping of ideals, the reverence for a larger law of life and a more than individual moral order, the outgoing of sympathy and love, the demand for justice—all these are the forces which have built our present social system, and these must continually reshape it into more adequate expressions of genuine moral life if it is to continue unimpaired or in greater vigor.

We do not know in any full sense whence the life of the spirit comes, and we cannot, while standing upon the platform of ethics, predict its future. But if our study has shown anything, it is that the moral *is* a life, not a something ready-made and complete once for all. It is instinct with movement and struggle, and it is precisely the new and serious situations which call out new vigor and lift it to higher levels. Ethical science tracing this process of growth, has as its aim not to create life—for the life is present already, —but to discover its laws and principles. And this should aid in making its further advance stronger, freer, and more assured because more intelligent.

Literature

On the early history of the Family, see the works cited at close of ch. 2; also Starcke, *The Primitive Family*, 1889; Westermarck, *The History of Human Marriage*, 1901; Howard, *A History of Matrimonial Institutions*, 3 vols., 1904. On present problems: H. Bosanquet, *The Family*, 1906; Parsons, *The Family*, 1906; Bryce, "Marriage and Divorce in Roman and in English Law," in *Studies in History and Jurisprudence*, 1901; Ellis, *Man and Woman*; Thomas, *Sex and Society*, 1907; Bebel, *Woman Under Socialism*; Riehl, *Die Familie*.

FIRST EDITION PAGINATION KEY

Between the 1908 publication by Henry Holt and Co. of the first edition of *Ethics* and the appearance of the second, greatly revised edition in 1932, numerous scholarly studies of the work were made, all using the 1908 pagination for reference. The list below shows how the first edition pagination is related to that of the present edition. The first number refers to the page of the 1908 edition; the number after the colon represents the pages of the present edition on which the corresponding text is found.

89:87–88	129:121–22	169:157–58	209:193–94
90:88	130:122–23	170:158–59	210:194–95
91:89	131:123–24	171:160	211:195–96
92:89–90	132:124–25	172:160–61	212:197
93:90–91	133:125–26	173:161–62	213:197–98
94:91–92	134:126	174:162–63	214:198–99
95:92–93	135:126–27	175:163–64	215:199–
96:93–94	136:127–28	176:164–65	200
97:94–95	137:128–29	177:165–66	216:200–201
98:95	138:129–30	178:166	217:201–2
99:95–96	139:130–31	179:166–67	218:202
100:96–97	140:131–32	180:167–68	219:202–3
101:97–98	141:132–33	181:168–69	220:203–4
102:98–99	142:134	182:169–70	221:204–5
103:99–100	143:134–35	183:170–71	222:205–6
104:100–101	144:135–36	184:171	223:206
105:101–2	145:136–37	185:171–72	224:207
106:102	146:137–38	186:172–73	225:207–8
107:102–3	147:138–39	187:173–74	226:208–9
108:103–4	148:139–40	188:174–75	227:209–10
109:104–5	149:140–41	189:175–76	228:210–11
110:105	150:141	190:176–77	229:211–12
111:106	151:141–42	191:177	230:212–13
112:106–7	152:142–43	192:177–78	231:213
113:107–8	153:143–44	193:178–79	232:213–14
114:108–9	154:144–45	194:179–80	233:214–15
115:109–10	155:145–46	195:180–81	234:215–16
116:110–11	156:146–47	196:181–82	235:216–17
117:111	157:147–48	197:182–83	236:217–18
118:111–12	158:148–49	198:183	237:218–19
119:112–13	159:149	199:185	238:219
120:113–14	160:149–50	200:186	239:219–20
121:114–15	161:150–51	201:187	240:221
122:115–16	162:151–52	202:187–88	241:221–22
123:116–17	163:152–53	203:188–89	242:222–23
124:117–18	164:153–54	204:189–90	243:223–24
125:118–19	165:154–55	205:190–91	244:224–25
126:119	166:155	206:191–92	245:225–26
127:119–20	167:155–56	207:192	246:226
128:120–21	168:156–57	208:192–93	247:226–27

248:227–28	288:262–63	328:297	367:330–31
249:228–29	289:263–64	329:297–98	368:331–32
250:229–30	290:264–65	330:298–99	369:332–33
251:230–31	291:265–66	331:299–	370:333–34
252:231–32	292:266–67	300	371:334
253:232	293:267–68	332:300–301	372:334–35
254:232–33	294:268	333:301–2	373:335–36
255:233–34	295:268–69	334:302	374:336–37
256:234–35	296:269–70	335:302–3	375:337–38
257:235–36	297:270–71	336:303–4	376:338–39
258:236–37	298:271–72	337:305	377:339–40
259:237–38	299:272–73	338:305–6	378:340–41
260:238–39	300:273	339:306–7	379:341
261:239–40	301:273–74	340:307–8	380:341–42
262:240	302:274–75	341:308–9	381:342–43
263:241	303:275–76	342:309–10	382:343–44
264:241–42	304:276–77	343:310	383:344–45
265:242–43	305:277	344:310–11	384:345–46
266:243–44	306:278	345:311–12	385:346
267:244–45	307:278–79	346:312–13	386:346–47
268:245–46	308:279–80	347:313–14	387:347–48
269:246–47	309:280–81	348:314–15	388:348–49
270:247–48	310:281–82	349:315–16	389:349–50
271:248	311:282–83	350:316	390:350–51
272:248–49	312:283	351:316–17	391:351–52
273:249–50	313:283–84	352:317–18	392:352–53
274:250–51	314:284–85	353:318–19	393:353
275:251–52	315:285–86	354:319–20	394:353–54
276:252–53	316:286–87	355:320–21	395:354–55
277:253–54	317:287–88	356:321–22	396:355–56
278:254	318:288–89	357:322	397:356–57
279:254–55	319:289–90	358:322–23	398:357–58
280:255–56	320:290	359:323–24 .	399:359
281:256–57	321:290–91	360:324–25	400:359–60
282:257–58	322:291–92	361:325–26	401:360–61
283:258–59	323:292–93	362:326–27	402:361–62
284:259–60	324:293–94	363:327	403:362–63
285:260	325:294–95	364:328	404:363–64
286:261	326:295–96	365:328–29	405:364
287:261–62	327:296–97	366:329–30	406:364–65

407:365–66	447:400–401	488:436–37	529:473
408:366–67	448:401–2	489:437–38	530:473–74
409:367–68	449:402	490:438–39	531:474–75
410:368–69	450:402–3	491:439–40	532:475–76
411:369	451:404	492:440–41	533:476–77
412:369–70	452:404–5	493:441	534:477–78
413:370–71	453:405–6	494:441–42	535:478–79
414:371–72	454:406–7	495:442–43	536:480
415:372–73	455:407–8	496:443–44	537:480–81
416:373–74	456:408–9	497:444–45	538:481–82
417:374–75	457:409–10	498:445–46	539:482–83
418:375	458:410	499:446–47	540:483–84
419:375–76	459:410–11	500:447	541:484–85
420:376–77	460:411–12	501:447–48	542:485
421:377–78	461:412–13	502:448–49	543:485–86
422:378–79	462:413–14	503:449–50	544:486–87
423:379–80	463:414–15	504:450–51	545:487–88
424:380	464:415–16	505:451–52	546:488–89
425:381	465:416–17	506:452–53	547:489
426:382	466:417	507:453–54	548:489–90
427:383	467:417–18	508:454–55	549:490–91
428:383–84	468:418–19	509:455	550:491–92
429:384–85	469:419–20	510:455–56	551:492–93
430:385–86	470:420–21	511:456–57	552:493–94
431:386–87	471:421–22	512:457–58	553:494–95
432:387–88	472:422–23	513:458–59	554:495–96
433:388–89	473:423	514:460	555:496
434:389	474:423–24	515:460–61	556:496–97
435:389–90	475:424–25	516:461–62	557:497–98
436:390–91	476:425–26	517:462–63	558:498–99
437:391–92	477:426–27	518:463–64	559:499–
438:392–93	478:427–28	519:464	500
439:393–94	479:428–29	520:464–65 .	560:500–501
440:394–95	480:429–30	521:465–66	561:501–2
441:395	481:430	522:466–67	562:502
442:395–96	482:430–31	523:468	563:502–3
443:396–97	483:431–32	524:468–69	564:503–4
444:397–98	484:432–33	525:469–70	565:504
445:398–99	485:433–34	526:470–71	566:505–6
446:399–	486:435	527:471–72	567:506–7
400	487:435–36	528:472–73	568:507–8

569:508–9	579:516–17	589:525–26	599:533–34
570:509	580:517–18	590:526–27	600:534–35
571:510	581:518–19	591:527	601:535–36
572:510–11	582:519–20	592:527–28	602:536–37
573:511–12	·583:520–21	593:528–29	603:537–38
574:512–13	584:521	594:529–30	604:538–39
575:513–14	585:521–22	595:530–31	605:539–40
576:514–15	586:522–23	596:531–32	606:540
577:515	587:523–24	597:532–33	
578:515–16	588:524–25	598:533	

TEXTUAL APPARATUS
INDEX

TEXTUAL COMMENTARY

The professional paths of the two authors of *Ethics* crossed initially when John Dewey, upon his return to the University of Michigan in 1889 after one year at the University of Minnesota, made his first appointment to the staff in philosophy at Michigan—James Hayden Tufts. This early association between Dewey and Tufts at Michigan occurred during the years Dewey was developing his ethical theory, which he discussed in his first work on the subject, *Outlines of a Critical Theory of Ethics*.[1]

The year the *Outlines* appeared, 1891, Tufts resigned from the University of Michigan in order to take advanced studies at the University of Freiburg. When Tufts returned from his studies abroad, he accepted a post at the newly formed University of Chicago. Upon learning in 1894 that President William Rainey Harper was seeking a person to head the department of philosophy, Tufts warmly recommended Dewey.[2] Dewey accepted Harper's offer of the chairmanship, but before he left Michigan, his second book in ethics—*The Study of Ethics: A Syllabus*[3]—was published. During the ten subsequent years that Dewey spent at the University of Chicago, he and Tufts became good friends and worked closely together, developing independently as well as jointly many of the ideas later presented in their *Ethics*.

When Dewey resigned from the University of Chicago in 1904, he went on an extended trip to Europe with his family,

---

1. John Dewey, *Outlines of a Critical Theory of Ethics* (Ann Arbor, Mich.: Register Publishing Co., 1891); *The Early Works of John Dewey, 1882–1898*, ed. Jo Ann Boydston (Carbondale: Southern Illinois University Press, 1967–1972), 3:237–388.
2. James H. Tufts to William Rainey Harper, memorandum of 1894, Presidents' Papers, 1889–1925, Special Collections, The Joseph Regenstein Library, University of Chicago, Chicago, Ill.
3. Dewey, *The Study of Ethics: A Syllabus* (Ann Arbor, Mich.: Register Publishing Co., 1894); *Early Works* 4:218–362.

returning to the United States to take up his new post at
Columbia University in February of the following year. Thereafter, up until the *Ethics* was published in 1908, most of the
authors' collaboration was necessarily by correspondence.
But it is apparent that the general character and structure
of the book were well established even before Dewey left
Chicago: only three months after he returned from Europe to
start teaching at Columbia University, he wrote Frank
Manny in May 1905, "I think (or I hope) our Ethics will be
out about February or March of next year. It is not likely to
be done before."[4] Because of the demands of Dewey's new
post, and probably in part because of the authors' geographi-
cal separation, it was not until 9 December 1907 that Dewey
and Tufts signed a publishing agreement with Henry Holt
and Company for the *Ethics*, with manuscript promised for
May 1908.[5]

Ethics was published by Holt as a volume in its distinguished American Science Series that had been initiated
in 1879.[6] By 1908, works by a number of such outstanding
scholars as Ira Remsen, President of The Johns Hopkins University,[7] Henry Carter Adams, the University of Michigan
economist,[8] and William James,[9] had already appeared in this
series.[10] The Dewey and Tufts work was in fact one of the
last in the series; however, most series volumes were popular
textbooks and, like the *Ethics*, were reprinted a number of
times.

But soon after the *Ethics* was published, and immedi-

4. Dewey to Manny, Frank A. Manny Papers, University of Michigan
   Historical Collections, Ann Arbor, Mich.
5. James H. Tufts Papers, Special Collections, Morris Library,
   Southern Illinois University at Carbondale.
6. The *Publishers' Weekly* announcement of the American Science
   Series said it would be "one of the most important lines of textbooks and general manuals yet published in this country." *Publishers' Weekly* 16 (October 1879): 506.
7. Ira Remsen, *An Introduction to the Study of Chemistry*, American Science Series, Briefer Course (New York: Henry Holt and
   Co., 1886).
8. Henry C. Adams, *The Science of Finance*, American Science
   Series (New York: Henry Holt and Co., 1898).
9. William James, *Psychology*, American Science Series, Briefer
   Course (New York: Henry Holt and Co., 1892).
10. A complete list of volumes in the series, including two published
    after the *Ethics*, appeared in each impression of the Dewey and
    Tufts work.

ately after the appearance of the first of what was to be a number of favorable reviews,[11] Dewey was not at all sure the book would sell well. He wrote to Tufts in October of 1908:

When I was at Holts I saw the number of books ordered from various institutions—Averages pretty small, Univ. of Mich. 5 for example—probably library reference copies. I think in a year of [sic] two some of the lecture course people may decide they can use the book as a text. . . . The difficulties in the way of getting the book to the "general reader" are great—book stores *do not* carry anything advertised as a text, and the inertia to be overcome in the case of any one text are [sic] very great. I don't quite see the way out yet—I'm glad they have begun advertising.[12]

Whether as a result of this advertising, or of the four enthusiastic reviews that appeared before the end of 1908, Dewey was able to say to Tufts in a letter of 16 January 1909:

I saw Burnett the other day—He says the actual sales to date are between 12 and 1300; introduced in about 30 colleges, the largest single order from the Univ. of Washington on the Pacific Coast! He expects that after this year it will average about 3000 for a few years.[13]

Numerous approving reviews appeared throughout 1909 and one as late as 1910. Recognizing that *Ethics* was published as a textbook, the reviews often mentioned, as did the *Nation*, that the authors "have lifted their volume above the level of textbooks" (5 November 1908, p. 438). E. B. McGilvary said in the *Psychological Bulletin* that "the book is not merely a text-book. It is too original to be just that. It

---

11. The first review was in the *Boston Evening Transcript*, 24 October 1908, part 3, p. 7; it was followed by: *Nation*, 5 November 1908, p. 438; *Journal of Philosophy, Psychology and Scientific Methods* 5 (1908): 636–39 (Norman Wilde); *Outlook* 90 (1908): 595–96; *Economic Bulletin* 1 (1908): 335–36 (Charles Abram Ellwood); *American Journal of Psychology* 20 (1909): 151 (Evander Bradley McGilvary); *Psychological Bulletin* 6 (1909): 14–22 (Evander Bradley McGilvary); *American Journal of Theology* 13 (1909): 140–43 (Arthur Oncken Lovejoy); *Educational Review* 37 (1909): 210; ibid.: 413–16 (Walter Taylor Marvin); *Dial* 46 (1909): 146; *American Journal of Sociology* 14 (1909): 687–90 (Guy Allen Tawney); *Philosophical Review* 18 (1909): 221–29 (William Caldwell); *School Review* 17 (1909): 204–6 (Irving Elgar Miller); *Survey* 22 (1909): 217–18 (Frank Addison Manny); *Science* n.s. 30 (1909): 89–92 (Frank Thilly); *Independent* 67 (1909): 310; *Monist* 20 (1910): 478.
12. Dewey to Tufts, 28 (?) October 1908, Tufts Papers.
13. Dewey to Tufts, 16 January 1909, Tufts Papers.

deserves to rank among the systematic treatises which every advanced student of the science must reckon with" (p. 14). And Arthur O. Lovejoy said in the *American Journal of Theology* (13:1909) what gives the book

a real distinction amid the multitude of ethical textbooks is the fact that it makes the study of ethics appear practical, vital, pertinent to affairs, capable of contributing to the settlement of problems that contemporary mankind is really in doubt about. This is not only a great virtue but also a curiously rare one, in this class of books (p. 140).

Reviewers also noted that this work that was "not merely a text-book" would appeal to a wide audience. The *Boston Evening Transcript* pronounced it "an excellent book, sufficiently readable to be pleasant to the layman as well as to the professional moralist." McGilvary said, "Even the 'general reader' . . . will be repaid by making more than a casual acquaintance with the volume." Irving Miller wrote in *School Review* that "it ought to have a wide reading among all classes of citizens interested in the moral problems of our social, industrial, economic, and political life."

Aware that the book was included in a series labeled "American Science," a number of reviewers also emphasized the authors' scientific approach to the study of ethics. Charles A. Ellwood, writing in the *Economic Bulletin* (1:1909), said the book's method

illustrates the close dependence which is coming to exist between modern scientific ethics and the other social sciences. . . . An ethics consciously developed upon the basis of psychology and the social sciences, with a minimum of metaphysics, has long been a desideratum; and we have it in this book (pp. 335–36).

The *Monist* reviewer pointed out (20:1910), "This volume is a by no means unimportant member of Holt's American Science Series and brings within the scope of junior students the accumulated results of the science of morals up to the present day" (p. 478). All in all, the descriptive adjectives applied to the work ranged from "fruitful," "original," "powerful" to the *Independent's* (67:1909) "vivid and convincing, bold and innovative" (p. 310).

Dewey and Tufts probably delivered the manuscript for

Ethics ahead of the May 1908 deadline; the work was registered for copyright (A208523) in June of 1908 and Library of Congress copyright records indicate that two copies were received 3 August 1908. This first edition was kept in print up.to the time a revised second edition appeared in 1932.

Although the exact number of impressions of the first edition of *Ethics* cannot now be determined, the evidence suggests a total of at least twenty-five. From 1908 through 1913, printing dates appeared on the title page. Copies with no title-page date but with impression numbers on the copyright page have also been located; the numbers are "9", "10", and "11". That these are later impression numbers rather than printing dates is substantiated by the existence of multiple copies with 1909 and 1910 on the title page itself, as well as by the increasing amount of worn and broken type in the text pages of copies with impression numbers but without date. Printing dates (but no impression numbers) appeared on the copyright page from December 1923 to March 1929. Copies have been found with the following dates: December, 1923; June, 1924; February, 1925; February, 1926; October, 1926; March, 1929. One undated impression was made after March 1929. The frequency and regularity of dated printings, both early and late, and evidence in the bindings and front matter support a hypothesis that the book was reprinted at least once a year, and twice in some years (1909, and possibly 1913, and 1916), for a total of at least twenty-five impressions.

The "American Science Series" identification was stamped on the book's spine through the ninth printing (and on one copy located of the tenth) after which it was dropped, as was also the publisher's Chicago address on the Series advertising page. The Series advertising page was, however, included throughout the work's publishing history. Although one copy of the tenth printing has "American Science Series" stamped on the spine, two other copies, identical in every other way, have been found, suggesting that two bindings of the tenth impression (1915?) were made. Similarly, two copies of the eleventh printing (1916?) have the same large trim size and the same copyright page as in preceding print-

ings; one of these is the British issue discussed below. Two
other copies of the eleventh printing have been found with
a smaller trim size, one of which carries for the first time in
the book's printing history a "Printed in the U.S.A." notice
on the copyright page. These differences among copies of
the eleventh printing suggest, as for the previous printing,
two separate bindings; however, no textual differences exist
among these four copies.

After the first impression, "London: George Bell and
Sons" appeared on the title page below the "New York /
Henry Holt and Company" line. Only one copy has been
located with the order reversed: "London / G. Bell & Sons,
Limited / New York: Henry Holt and Company." Even
though the Bell name did not appear in the 1908 impression,
Ethics was probably distributed in England from the outset: Dewey wrote to Tufts late in October 1908, "I hope we
will get a good Hibbert Journal notice. The English reviews
are all attended to by the English agents which accounts for
their absence from Holt's list."[14] The incomplete publishing
records for this work have only one reference to the British
issue, a notation: "12/31/1910 . . . plus 200 sheets to England @.07."[15]

Even though it is not possible to identify each impression by both ordinal number and by year of printing, the
years of each impression with text changes can be determined with reasonable certainty. The edition has therefore
been designated as "E" and the last two digits of the impression year have been used to identify impressions discussed
here—E08, E09^a, E09^b, E13, E29, E29+.

Neither of the copyright deposit copies of the 1908
Ethics is extant. To prepare the present edition, therefore,
three copies of the book with 1908 on the title page were
collated on the Hinman machine and found to be invariant.
To eliminate the possibility that an undated printing with
"Copyright, 1908 / by Henry Holt and Company" on the copyright page might have preceded copies dated 1908, a copy
of this undated impression was also machine-compared with

14. Dewey to Tufts, 28 (?) October 1908, Tufts Papers.
15. Archives of Henry Holt and Company, Princeton University,
    Princeton, N. J.

a 1908 dated copy; that collation revealed a number of substantive and accidental differences between the two. Machine collation of that undated copy against the last dated copy, March, 1929, established that the undated impression was subsequent to the March, 1929 impression: identical substantive and accidental differences appear, but the undated impression shows additional wear on the plates and several more instances of broken type. This undated printing has been labeled E29+.

The 1908 first impression has served as copy-text for the present edition. Machine collation of the Dewey sections of E08 and E29 revealed twenty-two substantive differences and fifteen differences in accidentals between the texts of these two impressions, indicating that relatively few changes were made in the plates during the more than twenty-one years of reprinting the *Ethics*. In the Tufts sections, only five substantive variants and seven accidental variants occurred. Sight collation established that after the E08 impression, twenty-five substantive and nineteen accidental changes —chiefly corrections—were made for the second printing (E09^a) as were three corrections in the index; one major substantive correction and two in notes were made for the third printing (E09^b).[16] No further changes occurred in the text itself; however, in the 1913 impression (E13), the page number "286" was dropped and not restored in any impression thereafter, and in E16, the eleventh impression (1916?), the comma after "happiness" (274n.12) disappeared, not to be restored. In effect, then, after 1909, except for these two omissions caused by wear or damage to the plates, the only changes in the book were those in front matter, binding, and size described above.

16. That this was probably a third impression rather than a second state of the second impression is substantiated by the partial records in the expense and ledger books of the Archives of Henry Holt and Company at Princeton. The authors' contract with Holt (Tufts Papers) stipulated payment of royalties of 10% on the first 1,000 copies sold. By December 1908, 1,359 copies had been sold, with 12.5% royalty paid on the first 359 copies of the second thousand copies. No figures appear for the June 1909 payment, but the December 1909 payment was on 1,296 copies, all at the rate of 15%, indicating that by the time the (unrecorded) June payment was made, sales had gone over 2,000. These early printings were about 1,000 copies each.

At least two persons found errors in the 1908 first impression of *Ethics*. In his review published in January 1909, Evander Bradley McGilvary called attention to the following erroneous readings: 36.33, "bound" for "bond"; 115.30, "Erinnys" for "Erinnyes"; 119.18, "Philip" for "Alexander"; 235.7, transposition of "motive" and "intention"; 356.2, "of" for "or". Also in January of 1909, Dewey wrote to Tufts, "I had a letter from I. E. Miller the other day speaking of the book. Said he would send you a list of misprints."[17]

The reading that McGilvary presumed to be an error at 36.33, "bound" for "bond", was in fact a correct reading and was not changed in any printing. Curiously, even though the rest of the items were errors, the only one ever corrected was the transposition of "motive" and "intention". Of I. E. Miller's list, nothing is known; however, a number of both substantive and accidental changes made for E09ᵃ were simple corrections. In the Dewey sections of the work, substantive corrections made in E09ᵃ were: 210.32, "is" for "of"; 214.22, "depends" for "depended"; 218.39, *"an overt"* for *"a overt"*; 296.32, "agent's disposition" for "disposition agent"; 378.19, "one" deleted after "Every"; 419.37, "gives" for "give"; 429.25, "emphasize" for "emphasizes". Four additional substantive changes that little affect meaning were: 258.8, "only" was moved to follow "bad"; 266.18, "do" was deleted before "conduce"; 292.8, "equally" was changed to "just"; 356.11, "may" was substituted for "might". Nine other substantive changes in E09ᵃ that significantly alter meaning were: the three word changes at 5.36–37 to rewrite the sentence; the transposition of "motive" and "intention" at 235.7; "however" moved at 276.25; "such" changed to "common" at 277.2; "nor" substituted for "and" at 296.32; "an ideal embodied" substituted for "and was embodied" at 365.4; "general" substituted for "another" at 366.15. In the Tufts sections, E09ᵃ added a footnote number and a footnote at 87.17, changed "term" to "turn" at 129.31, "an essentially" to "as essentially" at 181.34, "word" to "work" at 480.22, and "had" to "has" at 532.9.

The changes in accidentals made for E09ᵃ were corrections, clarifications, or necessary alterations caused by changes in substantives. They were: the deletion of two commas at 3.8, a change with substantive implications; the change of a comma to a semicolon and the reverse at 196.2 to correct two bibliographical listings in the literature section; addition of quotation marks around "what" at 221.23 to set it off as parallel with other terms in the same passage; the correction of a question mark to a period at 287.5; the addition of an apostrophe when "disposition agent" was corrected to "agent's disposition" at 296.32; one comma deleted to clarify meaning at 415.35; and the addition of a footnote number at 371.32. In the Tufts sections, the following accidental changes were made for E09[a]: comma to period at 33.13, deletion of comma at 52.14, comma to semicolon at 115.35, capitalization of "state" at 120.12 and 120.14, addition of quotation marks at 120.36, period to colon at 125.4, and changing "and" from roman to italic at 452n.2, correcting an erroneously listed book title.

One substantive error not noticed before the second printing was the omission of a full line from the Bentham quotation at 234.5–6, a printer's error easily explained by the repetition of the word "apparently" within the sentence; the effect of the omission, however, was to attribute to Bentham exactly the opposite of what he had said. The missing part of the sentence was supplied in E09[b] by resetting twelve lines of type, leaving the page two lines longer than the facing one, an anomaly that appeared in all later printings. Also in E09[b], two erroneous references in notes at 233n.1 and 234n.4–5 were corrected.

Whether McGilvary or I. E. Miller called the authors' attention to the need for changes in the second and third printings, or whether they discovered errors through their own reading and use of the text is not important; aside from necessary corrections, the changes go beyond the kind that might be instituted by an editor since they substantially alter meaning at several points. Each of the changes described above (except for dropped type) has therefore been considered to have authority and all have been accepted as emendations of the copy-text for the present edition. A number of additional corrections in the text have been made here for the first time.

A new, heavily revised edition of *Ethics* appeared in

1932; in a "Preface to the 1932 Edition" the authors' first sentence was, "It is a fair question whether to call this edition of 1932 a revision or a new book. . . . About two-thirds of the present edition has been newly written, and frequent changes in detail will be found in the remainder" (p. iii). Because of the extensiveness of the revision, and because the second edition appeared twenty-four years after the first, the two editions of *Ethics* are treated in the Collected Works of John Dewey as two completely separate works, each with its own publishing history, and each included in the Works in its proper chronological setting.

TEXTUAL NOTES

165.22   come] The inadvertent omission of the verb here was
          corrected in the 1932 revision of the *Ethics*; on the
          authority of that edition, it has also been supplied in the
          present text.

241.31–242.2   "Strictly . . . pleasure."] Despite the quotation
          marks, the sentence attributed to Bentham is a para-
          phrase of the same material that Dewey quoted at length
          and accurately in his *Outlines of a Critical Theory of
          Ethics, Early Works of John Dewey*, 3:262n.1–263n.21.

284.27–44   A man . . . uniformity] Because Dewey set this
          material off as an extract, references to the Kant origi-
          nal appear in the Correction of Quotations. Dewey's
          quotation marks, however, distinguish the direct quote
          from the paraphrase.

286.20–21   "Each . . . one"] J. S. Mill's reference to "Bentham's
          dictum, 'Everybody to count for one, nobody for more
          than one'" (*Dissertations and Discussions*, 1874,
          3:388.22–23) is apparently Dewey's source for this
          phrase. It has not been found in Bentham's works, and
          J. M. Robson, editor of *The Collected Edition of the
          Works of J. S. Mill*, cites the analogues on which Mill
          probably based his quotation (Vol. 10, p. 515).

322.7   disobedience] The sense of the quoted sentence makes
          clear that Dewey intended to use Bain's word, "disobedi-
          ence," rather than "obedience." It is curious to note,
          however, that in his syllabus, *The Study of Ethics*,
          quoting exactly the same passage, Dewey used "his
          obedience" rather than "disobedience." In *The Study of
          Ethics, Early Works of John Dewey*, 4:330, Bain's read-
          ing has also been restored.

386.10–11   counties] The progression from "parishes" up to
          "nations," with each step a higher governmental unit,
          indicates that "countries" is a typographical error for
          "counties."

EMENDATIONS LIST

All emendations in both substantives and accidentals introduced into the copy-text are recorded in the list that follows, with the exception of the changes in formal matters described below. The reading to the left of the square bracket is from the present edition; the bracket is followed by an abbreviation for the source of the emendation's first appearance. After the source abbreviation comes a semicolon, followed by the copy-text reading.

A number of formal, or mechanical, changes have been made throughout:

1. Book and journal titles have been put in italic type; articles and sections of books have been put in quotation marks.

2. The form of documentation has been made consistent and complete: "op. cit." has been eliminated and "ibid." is used only when a title is repeated within a single entry; section numbers are arabic, volume numbers are upper-case roman with following periods removed, and chapter numbers are lower-case roman; abbreviations have been regularized; book titles have been supplied and expanded where necessary.

3. The following spellings have been editorially altered to the characteristic Dewey forms, given to the left of the bracket:

centre] center 16.15, 297.35, 375.13; (-s) 322.18, 349.32, 404.4
cooperate] coöperate 224.20–21, 407.16, 425.13; (-ion) 16.2, 276.12–13, 276.23, 277.1, 386.15–16; (-ive) 276.23, 285.31–32, 299.37, 405.29, 428.35
coordinated] coördinated 312.1
engrained] ingrained 327.4
fibre] fiber 231.13
labeled] labelled 296.27
meagre] meager 385.32
mold] mould 321.25

preeminently] preëminently 369.26, 372.15–16
reenforce] reënforce 259.24–25, 288.7–8, 325.21, 362n.1;   (-ment)
      204.31, 248.6, 259.31;   (-ed) 286.28–29, 316.15;
      (-ing) 327.25;   (-s) 330.28
self-defense] self-defence 15.7
self-enclosed] self-inclosed 4.19
Shakespere's] Shakspere's 215.24
skillful] skilful 187.14, 192.30

3.8	typical$_\Lambda$] E09$^\text{a}$; ～,
3.8	social$_\Lambda$] E09$^\text{a}$; ～,
5.36	political state] E09$^\text{a}$; political
5.36–37	economic order] E09$^\text{a}$; economic
5.37	the family] E09$^\text{a}$; and that of the family
8n.1	§ 320 ff.] W; $_\Lambda$～
11.26	"attitude."] W; $_\Lambda$～·$_\Lambda$
11.39	σεμνά] W; σέμνα
14.22	desire,] W; ～$_\Lambda$
17.14	aspects:] W; ～.
18.19	4th] W; 3rd
18.25	1885;] W; ～,
18.29	1882.] W; ～;
18.31	by] W; in part by
18.36	*Ethics:*] W; ～,
18.38	1888] W; 1887
18.40	1901] W; 1900
18.41	1901] W; 1902
19.7	Vol. I, Part I, 1887] W; 2 vols., 1881–92
19.17–18	University . . . Publications] W; [*ital.*]
19.19	*Self-Realization*] W; *Self-realization*
19.20	Publications in Philosophy, I,] W; Publications: *Philosophy*, I.,
19.21–22	Articles on Economic Theory] W; Article *Economic Theory*
19.22	*Dictionary.*] W; *Dict.*
186.3–4	Plato . . . *Protagoras*] W; Plato, dialogues entitled *Republic, Laws, Protagoras*
186.5	*finibus*] W; *Finibus*
186.5	*officiis*] W; *Officiis*
186.6	*Discourses*] W; *Conversations*
186.8	*Ethics;*] W; ～,
186.9	Concerning] W; *concerning*
186.13	*Fundamental Principles*] W; *Foundations*
186.14	*Positive Philosophy*] W; Course of Positive Philosophy
186.19	the Introduction to this volume] W; ch. i. of Part I
188.16	factor.] W; ～,
191.20	Vol. I,] W; [*not present*]
194.29	present] W; presents

195.38   *Ethics*:] W;   ∼,
196.2   Vol. I_Λ;] W;   Vol. I.;   E09ª;   Vol. I.,
196.2   *Theory*,] E09ª;   ∼;
198.5   consistent,] W;   ∼;
198.40   advance,] W;   ∼;
199.1   selfishness:] W;   ∼;
199.8   reflection_Λ] W;   ∼,
202.32   administration] W;   admistration
203.34   supernatural,] W;   ∼_Λ
206.21   ¹ch. 1] W;   ch. i. of Part I.
206.24   "Introduction,"] W;· [*not present*]
208n.4   Hegel,] W;   Hegel's_Λ
208n.4   § 150] W;   _Λ150
208n.6–7 § 258 (pp. 240–41)] W;   _Λ258 (p. 241)
208n.8   Hegel, *Werke*, Vol.] W;   *Werke*, Book
209.2   ἐμπειρικός] W; ἐμπειρικōς
210.32   side is] E09ª;   side of
213.14   (1)] W;   [*not present*]
214.22   depends] E09ª;   depended
214.30   will,] W;   ∼;
215.31   (1_Λ)] W;   _Λ1.Λ
218.39   *an overt*] E09ª;   *a overt*
220.15 *et seq.*   *Ethics* (1901),] W;   *Ethics*,
221.23   "what,"] E09ª;   _Λ∼,_Λ
222.16   Kant,] W;   ∼:
222.26; 223.16, 39; 313.31   *Theory of Ethics*,] W;   *Ibid.*,
224.33   achievement] W;   achievment
232n.1   James,] W;   [*not present*]
233n.1   Bentham,] W;   [*not present*]
233n.1   xi] E09ᵇ;   ii
234.5–6   which . . . such as are] E09ᵇ;   [*not present*]
234n.3   Bentham, *Principles of Morals and Legislation*,] W;
          Ibid.,
234n.4–5 Bentham, . . . 28] W;   *Ibid.*, §§ 27 and 28 E09ᵇ;
          Ibid., §§ 17 and 18
235.7   on . . . motive] E09ª;   on motive not upon intention
235n.3   "he is thoughtful of,"] W;   _Λ∼,_Λ
235n.4   "considerate of,"] W;   _Λ∼,_Λ
235n.4   "regardful of,"] W;   _Λ∼,_Λ
235n.4   "mindful of,"] W;   _Λ∼,_Λ
235n.4   "attentive to,"] W;   _Λ∼,_Λ
236.22   appeals] W;   appeal
236.23   stirs] W;   stir
237n.7   203–4] W;   199–200
237n.14   all-important] W;   ∼_Λ∼
240.12 *et seq.*   *Progress* (1891)] W;   *Progress*
240.13–14 "Introduction,"] W;   [*not present*]
240.18   Lectures] W;   chs.

240.22   further] W;   farther
240.24   203] W;   200
242n.6   third . . . from] W;   third, and fourth from
242n.7   ch. xiii.] W;   ch. xiii.; and the last from ch. ii
243.28   philanthropic] W;   philanthrophic
243n.2   p. 42] W;   pp. 42
244.19   that∧] W;   ∼,
245.31   light] W;   lights
246.22–23   *Judgment*; . . . *Happiness*.] W;   *Judgment*.
246.31–32   "supposing . . . satisfaction"] W;   ∧∼ . . . ∼∧
250.5   Capreæ] W;   Capræ
251.16   are regarded] W;   regarded
252.14   *vice-versa*] W;   ∼∧∼
255.25   VI] W;   III
255.33   others." "Human] W;   ∼.∧ ∧∼
258.8   bad only] E09ᵃ;   only bad
260.7   Book II.] W;   Book II., Branch iv.
260.10   §§ 14–17] W;   § 14–17
260.21; 357.32   *Ethical Principles*] W;   *Principles of Ethics*
260.22   *Lectures on the Ethics*] W;   *The Ethics*
260.22–23   Mr. *Herbert Spencer*,] W;   *Herbert Spencer*∧
260.25   901] W;   903
261.16   *Ethics* [1877],] W;   *Ethics*,
262n.1   Green,] W;   [*not present*]
263n.1   Green, *Prolegomena to Ethics*,] W;   *Ibid*.,
264n.7   Kant,] W;   Abbott's *Kant's*
264n.8; 267n.5;   Mill,] W;   [*not present*]
268n.1; 269n.1
266.2   *Principles*, ch. xvii] W;   *Ibid*., ch. xix
266.6   *Principles*,] W;   *Ibid*.,
266.18   conduce] E09ᵃ;   do conduce
267n.5,6   Mill, *Early Essays*,] W;   *Ibid*.,
268n.1   1873, pp. 143–44] W;   1884, p. 143
272n.6–7   Essay on Bentham, p. 362] W;   *Op. cit*., p. 356
276.24–25   be confessed, however,] E09ᵃ;   be, however, confessed
277.2   common] E09ᵃ;   such
278.2   LIFE:] W;   ∼;
278n.5   ix, 2] W;   ch. ix
279.20   *intueor*:] W;   ∼;
279.29   The] W;   the
281.20   insoluble∧"] W;   ∼."
281.20; 282.20   *Theory of Ethics*,] W;   Abbott's *Kant*,
281.21   p. 36).] W;   ∼.)
283.17, 22–23   *Theory of Ethics*,] W;   *Op. cit*.,
283.26   deed,] W;   ∼;
284.22   nature.∧] W;   ∼."
284.26   exist."] W;   ∼.∧
286n.1   Kant,] W;   *Kant's*

287.5   reason.] E09^a;   ~?
290n.1; 303.37–38   Human] W;   the Human
292.8   just] E09^a;   equally
293.13   follow;] W;   ~:
296.32   agent's disposition] E09^a;   disposition agent
296.32   nor] E09^a;   and
299.3   Essay on Bentham] W;   [ital.]
303.30   on the Ethics] W;   on Ethics
303.39–40   A Review . . . Evolution] W;   Review of Evolutional
             Ethics
304.7–8   Essay on . . . Judgment] W;   [ital.]
304.15   chs. i$_\wedge$–ii$_\wedge$] W;   chs. i.–iii.
306n.1   Arnold,] W;   [not present]
306n.1   "Preface."] W; $_\wedge$preface.$_\wedge$
311.12 $_\wedge$II.$_\wedge$] W;   (2$_\wedge$)
313.10   Theory] W;   Kant's Theory
314.16   Theory of Ethics] W;   Kant's Theory
314.34–35   affections, leads] W;   ~$_\wedge$ ~
316.23   Theory of Ethics] W;   Abbott
317.32   sake:] W;   ~;
319.29   quotation] W;   quotations
319n.4–5   'when . . . another.' "] W; $_\wedge$~ . . . ~.$_\wedge$"
320.15   (c)] W;   (3)
*322.7   disobedience] W;   obedience
322.31 $_\wedge$the reasons . . . , "the] W;   "~ . . . , $_\wedge$~
323.9   remains,$_\wedge$] W;   ~,"
324.29–30   Principles of Ethics, Vol. I,] W;   Ibid.,
324.37; 325.8   Spencer, Principles of Ethics, Vol. I,] W;   Ibid.,
326.24   4] W;   3
327.39   Morality Independent of] W;   Morals, without
329.13   place] W;   plece
341n.5   James,] W;   [not present]
345.12   perfecting.] W;   ~,
346n.1; 370n.2   Psychology] W;   Principles of Psychology
356.2   or happiness] W;   of happiness
356.11   may have] E09^a;   might have
357.18–19   Polity, Vol. I, "Introductory Principles,"] W;   Politics,
             Introduction,
357.19   Vol. II] W;   Part II.,
357.24–25   the Bees] W;   Bees
357.36   Field] W;   Heart
365.4   an ideal embodied] E09^a;   and was embodied
365.36   Negative . . . negative] W;   Negative Phase:—Self-
             control. A negative
366.15   general] E09^a;   another
368.28   Courage^s] W;   ~$_\wedge$
370n.3   Second Series] W;   Vol. II.,
371.32   Senses.—(1) In] W;   Senses.^{1}—In E09^a;   Senses.$_\wedge$—In

375.29   Greeks] W;   Greek
378.19   Every] E09ᵃ;   Every one
380.16   *Spencer,*] W;   ∼∧
380.19   VIII∧–IX∧] W;   VII.–IX.
380.22   Book] W;   Part
380.23   Book III∧,] W;   Book II.,
380.27   *Methods of Ethics* (1901)] W;   [*not present*]
382.4   Bergemann] W;   Bergmann
382.8   Leslie, *Essays*] W;   Ritchie, *Studies*
382.8–9; 403.8   1879; 2d ed., 1888] W;   1888
382.15   1821] W;   1820
382.17–18   (1902, 1905)] W;   Vol. I., ∧1902, Vol. II., 1905∧
385n.1   Hobhouse, *Morals in Evolution*] W;   [*not present*]
385n.3   Green,] W;   [*not present*]
*386.10–11   counties] W;   countries
386.36   possibilities] W;   posibilities
402.36   1796] W;   1798
402.37   1895] W;   1893
403.7   Leslie] W;   Stephen
403.16   Lallemand] W;   L'Allemand
403.17   1898–99] W;   1898
405.10   Modes] W;   1. Contract Rights.—Modes
405.19–20   upon. . . . —Rights of] W;   upon. (1) Contract
          rights. Rights of
410n.5   *Morals in Evolution,*] W;   *op. cit.,*
411n.1   §§ 873–74] W;   873
411n.7   *History of English Law,*] W;   *op. cit.,*
411n.8   Westermarck, . . . I,] W;   *op. cit.,*
411n.9   "cause"] W;   ∧∼∧
411n.9   "to blame"] W;   ∧∼∧
412n.1–2   *History* . . . p. 30] W;   *op. cit.,* II., p. 469; I., 30
412n.4   *of England*] W;   *in England*
412n.7; 414n.2   *Origin* . . . I,] W;   [*not present*]
414.18   results∧] W;   ∼;
415.35   consequences∧] E09ᵃ;   ∼,
416n.1   *History* . . . *Law,*] W;   [*not present*]
419.37   gives] E09ᵃ;   give
420n.1   Emerson,] W;   [*not present*]
424n.6   *Lectures*] W;   *Essays*
429.25   emphasize] E09ᵃ;   emphasizes
433.36   1895] W;   1888
433.38   1891] W;   1901
434.3   1872] W;   1882
434.7   1869] W;   1859
434.8   *Between*] W;   *between*
434.11   Addams,] W;   [*not present*]
434.12   *Progress:*] W;   ∼,
434.15   pp. 361–79] W;   p. 361

EMENDATIONS IN TUFTS SECTIONS

In the list that follows appear all changes and corrections made in the first-impression copy-text of the Tufts sections of *Ethics*, except the expansion of authors' names and of titles in footnotes, with symbols identifying the first appearance of the emended reading.

The same formal changes in documentation and in the form of titles made in the Dewey sections have been made here. In addition, the following spellings have been editorially regularized to the characteristic Tufts usage appearing before the bracket:

centre] center 37.9, 37.14, 59.24, 66.38, 91.23; (-s) 153.30, 174.5
cooperate] coöperate 163.3, 487.28, 519.13, 519.15; (-tion) 31.16,
　　41.9, 45.32, 46.2, 46.10, 46.13–14, 46.16, 46.32, 47.10,
　　48.5, 48.26, 48.27, 52.12, 52.25, 83.36, 120.18, 435.23–
　　24, 439.36, 454.14, 463.4, 477.34, 497.37, 498.15;
　　(-tive) 446.29, 453.19
cooperation] co-operation 78.13
coordinate] coördinate 141.25, 535.38
entrench] intrench 175.7
fibre] fiber 177.20
fulfill] fulfil 157.5
meagre] meager 536.22
preeminent] preëminent 87.24; (-ly) 157.20; (-ence) 137.35,
　　478.12
preeminent] pre-eminent 127n.3
ready-made] ready made 540.7
reenforce] reënforce 60.9–10, 529.19; (-ment) 45.26, 83.2,
　　147.1–2, 521.20–21; (-d) 55.32, 474.10–11
reenforced] reinforced 38.33, 66.25
reenter] reënter 532.6
reestablishment] reëstablishment 151.9
Shakespere] Shakspere 145.7, 182.8
skillful] skilful 77.16
theatre] theater 154.23

22.7　　　1897] W;　1902
22.10　　　1906] W;　1907

22.11	Bergemann] W; Bergmann
22.15	1892] W; 1759
24n.1	Moellendorff, *Aristoteles*] W; Möllendorf, *Aristotle*
29n.20	McLennan] W; MacLennan
32.38	responsibility] W; Responsibility
33.13	this.] Eo9^a; ∼,
33.33	group] W; Group
34.17	*saraad*] W; *saraal*
35.19	unites] W; units
38n.1	*Colonus.*] W; *Colonus*, vv. 186 f.
39.23	*Organizations . . . Marriage*] W; *Organization and Group Marriages*
39.26	1870] W; 1871
39.29	Mindeleff in 15th] W; Mendeleff in 19th
39.36–37	Fustel de Coulanges] W; Coulanges
39.37	1874] W; 1873
39.41	Starcke] W; Starke
40.7	Thomas, "Sex and] W; Thomas, *Relation of Sex to*
45n.1	*Aid: A Factor of*] W; *Aid*∧ *a Factor in*
52.14	sphere∧] Eo9^a; ∼,
52.35	Savage] W; the Savage
52.36	1902] W; 1892
52.37–38	*Aid: A Factor of*] W; *Aid, a Factor in*
52.38	*Sociology*] W; *Society*
53.3	1905] W; 1906
53.6	*Origins*] W; *Origin*
57.6	approval] W; Approval
59n.1	*in*] W; *of*
68n.2	1906] W; 1905
72.36	*Kafir*] W; *Kaffir*
72.38	1906–07] W; 1907–
73.1–2	3 vols., 1905–08] W; 2 vols., 1905
73.7	1888,] W; 1888;
73.8	*Entwickelungsgeschichte*] W; *Entwicklungsgeschichte*
73.9	1884,] W; 1884∧
73.10	1895] W; 1899
81.34	life,"] W; ∼",
87.17	powers.^{5} . . . ^{5}Kant, . . . View."] W; ∼."^{1} . . . ^{1}Kant, *Idea of a Universal Cosmopolitical History* Eo9^a; powers."
88.28–29	"Idea . . . View"] W; *The Idea of a Universal Cosmopolitical History*
88.30	1871;] W; 1871, 1882–87;
88.34	1896] W; 1895
88.36	*um's*] W; *ums*
95.18	first-born] W; ∼∧∼
98n.2	Genung, *The*] W; Genung, *Job, The*
99n.1	*Life*] W; *in Life*

100n.1	16;] W; 16,
101n.11	35;] W; 35,
101n.11	19;] W; 19,
105.15	*Israel*] W; *the Old Testament*
105.16	1898–99] W; 1899
105.24	1892–99] W; 1899
105.24	1873] W; 1891
105.27	Hastings's] W; Hastings'
115.30	Erinyes] W; Erinnys
115.35	discredited;] Eo9ᵃ; ∼,
116.9	union,"] W; ∼",
117.24	convention,"] W; ∼",
117.37	nature,"] W; ∼",
119.18	Alexander] W; Philip
120.12, 14	State] Eo9ᵃ; state
120.36	"in . . . attained"] Eo9ᵃ; ∧∼∧
123.5	thing:] Eo9ᵃ; ∼.
125.4	judges:] Eo9ᵃ; ∼.
125.30	Or] W; Of
126.6	Eudaimonism] W; Eudaemonism
126.31	mean."] W; ∼".
127n.22	iii, 29–34] W; vi–viii
129.31	turn] Eo9ᵃ; term
130n.1	*Ethics*, Book X∧, vii, 8.] W; *Ethics*, X., vii.
131.38	evildoers] W; evil doers
133.6–7	1901–5);] W; 1900–05),
133.8	*Sceptics*);] W; ∼),
133.8	Windelband;] W; ∼,
133.14–15	4 vols., 1899–1907] W; 3 vols., 1896
133.17–18	Conception] W; *Theory*
133.18	Wilamowitz-Moellendorff] W; Wilamovitz-Möllendorf
133.18–19	*Aristoteles*] W; *Aristotle*
133.19	1893] W; 1900
133.23	1856.] W; 1856–75.
133.28	1872,] W; 1872;
133.29	*Sokrates*] W; *Socrates*
148.5	restriction] W; restrictions
158.27–28	*English Utilitarians*] W; *Utilitarians*
158.40	1894] W; 1895
159.2	1887] W; 1877
159.7	1898–1900,] W; 1900;
159.9	1894–98] W; 1894
159.10	1897–98] W; 1897
159.13	1899] W; 1901
159.17	1895,] W; 1895;
159.18	*Between*] W; *of*
159.20–21	*Nineteenth Century Literature*, 1901–05] W; *the Literature of the Nineteenth Century*, 1905

159.22   1896] W; 1895
159.23   Culturentwickelung] W; Culturentwicklung
*165.22   come such] W; such
176.32   become] W; becomes
178n.15   them.] W; ~:
181.34   as essentially] E09ᵃ; an essentially
452n.2   reprinted by Taylor] W; reprinted
452n.2   Charities and] E09ᵃ; Charities and
452n.22–23   10. Inability . . . wages.] W; [not present]
452n.24   11] W; 10
459.6   Volkswirtschaftslehre] W; Staatswirtschaftslehre
459.10   Cooke-Taylor] W; Taylor
459.17   1906] W; 1907
462.38   Methods_Λ] W; ~.
467.16   to] W; toward
478.28   Socialism] W; Socialism and Social Reform
478.31–32   Critiques and Addresses] W; Essays
479.2   1889] W; 1890
480.22   work] E09ᵃ; word
488.37   is] W; it
489n.1   XV] W; xiv
496n.3   Van Norden] W; Van Norden's
496n.4   1904] W; 1905
501.23   religious] W; religous
503.2   "velvet."] W; "~._Λ
515n.1   Eckenstein] W; Eckstein
526.33   transferred] W; tranferred
532.9   has] E09ᵃ; had
540.23   1907] W; 1906
540.24   Under] W; and

I. Copy-text List.

The following are the editorially established forms of possible compounds which were hyphenated at the ends of lines in the copy-text.

14.1	ready-made	349.25	so-called
94.1	non-moral	375.32	non-existent
109.12	subject-matter	425.5	law-making
109.23	all-controlling	449.21	overcharged
127.23	ongoing	480.33	play-grounds
129.23	preexistence	481.31	anti-social
177.31	cooperation	482.22	cooperators
339.7	anti-social	510.11	cooperation

II. Critical-text List.

In transcriptions from the present edition, no line-end hyphens in ambiguously broken possible compounds are to be retained except the following:

13.36	middle-ground	349.5	breaking-point
104.32	peace-makers	364.1	whole-hearted
127n.2	high-mindedness	371.4	ostrich-like
148.32	money-lender	378.24	all-exhaustive
176.35	high-minded	410.6	quasi-physical
215.34	truth-telling	424.1	ballot-box
216.19	non-progressive	473.15	wage-workers
241.4	subject-matter	507.28	post-offices
265.25	semi-social	517.28	life-long
265.26	semi-social	527.36	old-time
296.26	pigeon-holes		

CORRECTION OF DEWEY'S QUOTATIONS

Dewey represented source material in varying ways, from memorial paraphrase to verbatim copy, sometimes citing his source fully, in others mentioning only authors' names, and, in still others, omitting documentation altogether.

To prepare the critical text, all material inside quotation marks, except that obviously being emphasized or restated, has been searched out and the documentation has been verified and emended when necessary. Steps regularly used to emend documentation are described in Textual Principles and Procedures (*Middle Works of Dewey*, 1:358), but Dewey's substantive variations from the original in his quotations have been considered important enough to warrant a special list.

All quotations have been retained within the texts as they were first published, except for corrections required by special circumstances and noted in the Emendations List. Substantive changes that restore original readings in case of possible compositorial or typographical errors are similarly noted as "W" emendations. The variable form of quotation suggests that Dewey, like many scholars of the period, was unconcerned about precision in matters of form, but many of the changes in cited materials may have arisen in the printing process. For example, comparing Dewey's quotations with the originals reveals that some journals house-styled the quoted materials as well as Dewey's own. In the present edition, therefore, the spelling and capitalization of the source have been reproduced, except in concept words where Dewey changed the form of the source.

Dewey's most frequent alteration in quoted material was changing or omitting punctuation. He also often failed to use ellipses or to separate quotations to show that material had been left out. No citation of the Dewey material or of the original appears here if the changes were only omitted or changed punctuation. In the case of Dewey's failure to use ellipses, omitted short phrases are listed; if, however, a line or more has been left out, an ellipsis in brackets calls attention to the omission. When a substantive difference between Dewey's material and its source has been caused by the context in which the quotation appears, that difference is not recorded.

Italics in source material have been treated as accidentals. When Dewey omitted those italics, the omission is not noted, though Dewey's added italics are listed. If changed or omitted accidentals have substantive implications, as in the capitalization or failure to capitalize concept words, the quotation is noted.

The form of listing the quotations, from Dewey as well as from his source, is designed to assist the reader in determining whether Dewey had the book open before him or was relying on his memory. Notations in this section follow the formula: page-line numbers from the present text, followed by the text condensed to first and last words or such as make for sufficient clarity, followed by a bracket. After the bracket comes the necessary correction, whether of one word or a longer passage, as required. Finally, in parentheses, the author's surname and shortened source-title from the Checklist of Dewey's References are followed by a comma and the page-line reference to the source.

10.12	reserved] reserved only (Bacon, *Advancement,* 421.39)
10.13	the Angels] Angels (Bacon, *Advancement,* 421.39)
10.20	A life] the life (Plato, *Apology,* 335.29)
10.20–21	unexamined, uncriticized] which is unexamined_Λ (Plato, *Apology,* 335.30)
10.21	worthy of man] worth living (Plato, *Apology,* 335.30)
190.32	reading] or reading (Spencer, *Ethics,* 1:5.6)
190.33	morality] Morality (Spencer, *Ethics,* 1:5.7)
191.8	of the] of (Spencer, *Ethics,* 1:5.36)
191.13	But if] If (Spencer, *Ethics,* 1:6.10)
191.15	indifferent. Again] indifferent. [. . .] Again (Spencer, *Ethics,* 1:6.12–16)
191.18	while] while taking (Spencer, *Ethics,* 1:6.19)
191.19	one] one or other (Spencer, *Ethics,* 1:6.20)
193.2	nature] Nature (Goldsmith, *Vicar,* 49.29)

208.7   *state of feeling*]   [*rom.*]   (Spencer, *Ethics*, 1:46.12)
208.9   *to . . . beings*]   [*rom.*]   (Spencer, *Ethics*, 1:46.14)
208.9   an]   an inexpugnable   (Spencer, *Ethics*, 1:46.14)
208.20   The individual]   he   (Hegel, *Philosophy*, 240.33)
208.21   the State. His]   it. [. . .] His   (Hegel, *Philosophy*, 241.1–3)
211.9   one. If motives]   *one.* [. . .] If they   (Bentham, *Principles*, 1:169.26–170.14)
211.14–15   If this law determines]   The law in that case determines   (Kant, *Critique*, 153.21–22)
211.17   principle]   maxim   (Kant, *Critique*, 153.23)
215.24   right or wrong]   either good or bad   (Shakespeare, *Hamlet*, 2.2.255)
217.33   *opinions*]   [*rom.*]   (Mill, "Bentham," 339.28)
217.33   *method*]   [*rom.*]   (Mill, "Bentham," 339.29)
217.35   *detail*]   [*rom.*]   (Mill, "Bentham," 340.1)
221.32   out]   even out   (Kant, *Critique*, 9.1)
221.33   called Good]   called good   (Kant, *Critique*, 9.2)
222.3   individually]   undoubtedly   (Kant, *Critique*, 9.5)
222.9   Good Will]   good will   (Kant, *Critique*, 9.13)
222.10   mind. Moderation]   mind. [. . .] Moderation   (Kant, *Critique*, 9.13–24)
222.10   ²of]   in   (Kant, *Critique*, 9.25)
222.15   bad. The]   bad, and the   (Kant, *Critique*, 10.3)
222.15   villain]   villain not only   (Kant, *Critique*, 10.3)
222.16   both]   far   (Kant, *Critique*, 10.4)
222.16   and]   but also directly makes him   (Kant, *Critique*, 10.4)
223.17   Good Will]   good will   (Kant, *Critique*, 10.7)
223.18–19   *not . . . end*]   [*rom.*]   (Kant, *Critique*, 10.8–9)
223.24   Good Will]   good will   (Kant, *Critique*, 10.17)
223.25   assuming]   summoning   (Kant, *Critique*, 10.18)
223.27   fruitfulness]   usefulness   (Kant, *Critique*, 10.20)
223.34   *object of desire*]   [*rom.*]   (Kant, *Critique*, 16.9)
223.35   effect]   effects   (Kant, *Critique*, 16.11)
223.36   the actions an]   to actions any   (Kant, *Critique*, 16.12)
223.38   Will,]   *will*ₐ   (Kant, *Critique*, 16.15)
225n.5   assuming all the]   summoning of all   (Kant, *Critique*, 10.18)
227.32   inspiring]   improving   (Bentham, *Principles*, 1:178.4)
228.2   *intention*]   [*rom.*]   (Mill, *Utilitarianism* [1864], 27n.21)
228.3   *what*]   [*rom.*]   (Mill, *Utilitarianism* [1864], 27n.21)
228.4   made]   makes   (Mill, *Utilitarianism* [1864], 27n.22)
228.4   when]   if   (Mill, *Utilitarianism* [1864], 27n.22)
228.12   *when*]   if   (Mill, *Utilitarianism* [1864], 27n.22)
228.1   *it . . . act*]   [*rom.*]   (Mill, *Utilitarianism* [1864], 27n.22–23)

232.17   acting] of acting (James, *Psychology*, 2:562.13)
233.21   *agent*] [*rom.*] (Mill, *Utilitarianism* [1864], 27n.24)
233.26   which can] that can properly (Bentham, *Principles*, 1:218.7–8)
234.15–16   *and . . . motives*] [*rom.*] (Bentham, *Principles*, 1:237.11)
242.7   interests are] interest is (Bentham, *Principles*, 1:3.5)
242.10   the only] only (Bentham, *Principles*, 1:2n.1)
242.12   Only . . . do the] When thus interpreted, the (Bentham, *Principles*, 1:6.14)
242.12–13   words . . . have] words *ought*, and *right* and *wrong*, and others of that stamp, have (Bentham, *Principles*, 1:6.15–16)
242.13   an intelligent . . . actions;] a meaning: (Bentham, *Principles*, 1:6.16)
242.14   otherwise∧] when otherwise, (Bentham, *Principles*, 1:6.16–17)
242.14   not] none (Bentham, *Principles*, 1:6.17)
242.29   happiness] Happiness (Bain, *Moral Science*, 27.25)
242.30   procedures] pursuit (Bain, *Moral Science*, 27.25)
242.32   judgments] judgment (Bain, *Moral Science*, 27.27)
243.1–2   it. In] it; [. . .] In (Mill, "Utilitarianism," 3:348.24–26)
243.2   proof that] evidence (Mill, "Utilitarianism," 3:348.27)
243.18   else] other (Carlyle, *Sartor Resartus*, 153.16)
243.23   honesty] an Honesty (Carlyle, *Past and Present*, 25.30–31)
244.9–10   *point . . . do*] [*rom.*] (Bentham, *Principles*, 1:1.9–10)
244.22   *shall*] [*rom.*] (Bentham, *Principles*, 1:1.11)
246.4   itself] itself as such (Hazlitt, "Bentham," 7.5)
246.5   *idea*] [*rom.*] (Hazlitt, "Bentham," 7.6)
246.31   aroused or created] excited (Green, *Prolegomena*, 168.41)
250.5   pillar or] column, of (Stephen, *Ethics*, 44.26)
250.8   mystics,] mystics, cynics, (Stephen, *Ethics*, 44.29)
252.21–22   balance . . . good] balance, if it be on the side of pleasure, will give the *good* (Bentham, *Principles*, 1:52.9–10)
255.16   man wills] man, then, wishes for (Aristotle, *Ethics*, 73.17)
255.16   intent,] wish; (Aristotle, *Ethics*, 73.18)
255.17   desires] wishes for (Aristotle, *Ethics*, 73.18)
255.17   anything] anything whatever (Aristotle, *Ethics*, 73.19)
255.17–20   just as . . . correctly] just as [. . .] correctly (Aristotle, *Ethics*, 73.19–24)

255.21   right about pleasure] right (Aristotle, *Ethics*, 40.2)
255.22   man is apt] man (Aristotle, *Ethics*, 40.2)
255.25   principle] principles (Aristotle, *Ethics*, 205.4–5)
261.11–12 is the Utilitarian] forms the utilitarian (Mill, "Utilitarianism," 3:323.12)
261.14   Utilitarianism] utilitarianism (Mill, "Utilitarianism," 3:323.15)
261.20   produces] will produce (Sidgwick, *Methods*, 379.18)
261.20ᵢ   *on the whole*] [*rom.*] (Sidgwick, *Methods*, 379.19)
261.24   ₐUniversalistic hedonism.ₐ] "Universalistic Hedonism." (Sidgwick, *Methods*, 379.22)
261.26   principle] theory (Bain, *Emotions*, 303.2)
261.28   interests to the] interest to that (Bain, *Emotions*, 303.4)
264.10   wants,] Charles wishes (Kant, *Critique*, 116.12)
264.10   want too] wish also (Kant, *Critique*, 116.12)
264.11   namely] viz. (Kant, *Critique*, 116.12)
264.24   obtainable] attainable (Mill, "Utilitarianism," 3:349.5)
265.37   on] in (Bentham, *Principles*, 2:238.24)
265.40   and] or (Bentham, *Principles*, 2:238.28)
266.1   motives of amity] motives of love of amity (Bentham, *Principles*, 2:238.29–30)
266.4   Dictates of Utility] dictates of utility (Bentham, *Principles*, 1:202.10)
267.15   Self-culture,] self-education; (Mill, *Early Essays*, 357.9–10)
268.31–32 *he . . . body*] [*rom.*] (Mill, "Utilitarianism," 3:343.29–30)
269.5–6   from without] by the power of society (Mill, "Utilitarianism," 3:347.19)
269.6   to be] for them to be (Mill, "Utilitarianism," 3:347.20–21)
269.8   *bear*] [*rom.*] (Mill, "Utilitarianism," 3:347.30)
269.8   line] plan (Mill, "Utilitarianism," 3:347.31)
270.6   happiness of] happiness or (as, speaking practically, it may be called) the interest of (Mill, "Utilitarianism," 3:323.23–25)
272n.3   in check] under government (Mill, "Bentham," 1:362.19)
274n.4   thoughtₐ] thoughts, (Eliot, *Romola*, 516.19)
278n.3   amount] extent (Aristotle, *Ethics*, 55.18)
278n.3   aimₐ] object, (Aristotle, *Ethics*, 55.19)
278n.4   manner—this is] manner, is (Aristotle, *Ethics*, 55.20)
278n.4–5 any one can easily do.] everybody can do, and is by no means easy; (Aristotle, *Ethics*, 55.20–21)

281.19   of determining] to determine   (Kant, *Critique*, 36.4)
281.19   certainly] certainly and universally   (Kant, *Critique*, 36.4)
281.20   insoluble] completely   insoluble   (Kant,   *Critique*, 36.5–6)
283.7   trouble] difficulty   (Kant, *Critique*, 19.18)
283.11–12 personally] presently   (Kant, *Critique*, 19.23)
283.14   no such thing as a]   no   (Kant, *Critique*, 19.25)
283.14–15 promise. . . . or,] promises [. . .] or∧   (Kant, *Critique*, 19.25–28)
283.16   one] me   (Kant, *Critique*, 19.28)
283.16   one's] my   (Kant, *Critique*, 19.28)
283.16–17 coin . . . opportunity] coin   (Kant, *Critique*, 19.29)
283.22   universal law of nature]   *Universal Law of Nature*   (Kant, *Critique*, 39.8)
284.22   nature. We] nature. [. . .] Now we   (Kant, *Critique*, 39.15–20)
284.23   by which] of which   (Kant, *Critique*, 39.21)
284.24   feeling . . . nature] feeling   whose   special   nature   (Kant, *Critique*, 39.22)
284.25   maintenance] improvement   (Kant, *Critique*, 39.22–23)
284.27–34 (2∧) A man who has a certain talent . . . serve for all] ∧3.∧ A third finds in himself a talent [. . .] serve him, and have been given him, for all   (Kant, *Critique*, 40.27–41.8)
284.35–44 (3∧) A prosperous man . . . uniformity.] ∧4.∧ A fourth, who is in prosperity [. . .] he desires.   (Kant, *Critique*, 41.9–28)
298.18–19 It is no small] Nor is it a small   (Locke, *Essay on Human Understanding*, 1:80.2)
298.19   another] another, to have the authority   (Locke, *Essay on Human Understanding*, 1:80.3)
299.14   act] art   (Mill, "Utilitarianism," 3:333.29)
299.17   already] ready   (Mill, "Utilitarianism," 3:333.32)
300.34   *self-suggested*] [*rom.*]   (Grote, *Plato*, 1:252.7)
306.20   with] as to   (Arnold, *Last Essays*, xvi.16)
306.21   however we may∧] how we will, (Arnold, *Last Essays*, xvi.17)
306.23   over men] in man   (Arnold, *Last Essays*, xvi.19)
313.8   prove that] make us believe that   (Kant, *Critique*, 13.27)
313.9   so] has so   (Kant, *Critique*, 13.27)
313.29   *The idea*] *the concept*   (Kant, *Critique*, 154.7)
313.30   *law, but*] *law (of which it seems as if it must be the foundation), but*   (Kant, *Critique*, 154.8–9)
315.26   Then . . . enjoin] Then do with disdain, that which

thy duty commands. (Schiller, *Works*, 1:146.15–16)

316.3 by knowledge∧] with knowledge, (Emerson, "Worship," 240.22–23)

316.5 spontaneous. When] spontaneous. [. . .] When (Emerson, "Spiritual Laws," 133.22–26)

316.20 man] ·man as (Kant, *Critique*, 128.20)

316.21 with a sense of] with mental dissatisfaction by the consciousness of (Kant, *Critique*, 128.20–21)

316.22–23 as morally . . . character] as in the main basis of his character, at least in some degree, morally good (Kant, *Critique*, 128.22–23)

319.33 *ought* to] ought, as far as depends upon the legislator, to (Bentham, *Principles*, 1:41.10–11)

321.33 action] actions (Bain, *Emotions*, 286.10)

322.9 his] the (Bain, *Emotions*, 315.12)

322.24 added on and] added, and the conscience is then a triple compound, and (Bain, *Emotions*, 316.3–4)

322.25 action] actions in question (Bain, *Emotions*, 316.4)

322.26–27 *protective . . . sympathies*] protective of the general interests of those who have engaged our sympathies (Bain, *Emotions*, 316.28–29)

322.29 *an . . . interests*] [*rom.*] (Bain, *Emotions*, 316.31)

322.31–32 *the character . . . transformed*] [*rom.*] (Bain, *Emotions*, 318.25–26)

324.27 *necessary . . . results*] [*rom.*] (Spencer, *Ethics*, 1:120.23)

337n.5 individual] citizen (Spencer, *Ethics*, 1:169.22)

340n.7 service. In] service. [. . .] In (Stephen, *Ethics*, 241.16–19)

341.9 seat; it is] seat, is (James, *Psychology*, 1:320.26)

341.10 *them*] [*rom.*] (James, *Psychology*, 1:320.26)

341.14 true] true that (James, *Psychology*, 1:320.33)

341.18–19 lust∧ and] lusts, and (James, *Psychology*, 1:320.39)

341n.1 pain as your pain at all] pain so far as it is your pain (Stephen, *Ethics*, 241.20)

341n.1 to some] by some (Stephen, *Ethics*, 241.21)

341n.2 consequences] consequence (Stephen, *Ethics*, 241.21)

367n.3 *extraordinary excitement*] [*rom.*] (Hazlitt, "Bentham," 13.19–20)

384.5 No savage is free] The savage is nowhere free (Lubbock, *Origin of Civilisation*, 486.18–19)

384.7 apparently] often (Lubbock, *Origin of Civilisation*, 486.20)

385.11–12 *and . . . organization*] and are therefore the care of society as a whole rather [than] of any partial group organization (Hobhouse, *Morals*, 368.11–13)

385.19   person of]   persons of   (Green, *Prolegomena*, 262.35)

401.18   of a life of excessive]   of excessive   (Marshall, *Economics*, 4.5)

411.19   the sow]   whilst the sow   (Westermarck, *Origin and Development*, 1:257.20)

416n.2–3   Formulation . . . the twin-sister]   formalism is the twin-born sister   (Pollock and Maitland, *English Law*, 2:561.13–14)

CHECKLIST OF DEWEY'S REFERENCES

All titles and authors' names both in the text and in the Literature listings have been verified and appear in the list that follows, corrected and expanded to conform accurately and consistently to the original works. All corrections appear in the Emendations List.

This section gives full publication information for each work cited. When Dewey gave page numbers for a quotation, the edition from which he quoted was identified exactly by locating the reference. Similarly, the books in Dewey's personal library have been used to verify his citations of a particular edition. For other references, both by Dewey and by Tufts, the edition listed here is the one from among the various editions possibly available to them that were their most likely sources by reason of place or date of publication, or on the evidence from correspondence and other materials, and their general accessibility during the period.

Abelard, Peter. *Opera*. Edited by Victor Cousin. 2 vols. in 4. Paris: A. Durand, 1849–59.

Adams, George Burton. *Civilization During the Middle Ages, Especially in Relation to Modern Civilization*. New York: Charles Scribner's Sons, 1894.

Adams, Thomas Sewell, and Sumner, Helen L. *Labor Problems: A Text Book*. Edited by Richard T. Ely. London: Macmillan and Co., 1905.

Addams, Jane. *Democracy and Social Ethics*. The Citizen's Library of Economics, Politics, and Sociology. Edited by Richard T. Ely. New York: Macmillan Co., 1902.

———. *Newer Ideals of Peace*. The Citizen's Library of Economics, Politics, and Sociology. Edited by Richard T. Ely. New York: Macmillan Co., 1906, 1907.

———, et al. *Philanthropy and Social Progress: Seven Essays*. New York: Thomas Y. Crowell Co., 1893.

Aeschylus. *The Tragedies of Aeschylus*. Translated by E. H. Plumtree. New York: George Routledge and Sons, [n.d.].

Albee, Ernest. *A History of English Utilitarianism*. New York: Macmillan Co., 1902.

Alexander, Samuel. *Moral Order and Progress: An Analysis of Ethical Conceptions*. London: Trübner and Co., 1889. [2d ed. London: Kegan Paul, Trench, Trübner, and Co., 1891.]

American and English Decisions in Equity. Annual. First Series. 10 vols. Philadelphia: M. Murphy, 1895–1905.

Angell, James Rowland. *Psychology: An Introductory Study of the Structure and Function of Human Consciousness*. New York: Henry Holt and Co., 1904.

Annual Report of the Commissioners of Taxes and Assessments. New York, 1907.

Aristophanes. *The Comedies of Aristophanes*. Bohn's Classical Library. Translated by William James Hickie. 2 vols. London: George Bell and Sons, 1901–2.

Aristotle. *The Nicomachean Ethics of Aristotle*. 2d ed. Translated by F. H. Peters. London: Kegan Paul, Trench and Co., 1884.

———. *The Politics of Aristotle*. Translated by J. E. C. Welldon. London: Macmillan and Co., 1883.

Arnold, Matthew. *Culture and Anarchy, An Essay in Political and Social Criticism*. New York: Macmillan Co., 1902.

———. *Last Essays on Church and Religion*. London: Smith, Elder and Co., 1877.

Ashley, Sir William James. *An Introduction to English Economic History and Theory*. 2d ed. 2 vols. London: Longmans, Green, and Co., 1892–93.

Aurelius Antoninus, Marcus. *Meditations of Marcus Aurelius*. Translated by John Jackson. Oxford: Clarendon Press, 1906.

———. *The Thoughts of the Emperor Marcus Antoninus Aurelius*. Translated by George Long. Boston: Little, Brown and Co., 1899.

Austin, John. *Lectures on Jurisprudence; or, The Philosophy of Positive Law*. 2 vols. London: John Murray, 1869. [4th ed., rev. Edited by Robert Campbell. 2 vols. London: John Murray, 1873.]

Bacon, Francis. *Advancement of Learning*. In *The Works of Francis Bacon*, edited by James Spedding, Robert Leslie Ellis, and Douglas Denon Heath, 3:253–492. 14 vols. Vols. 1–8: new ed. London: Longmans and Co., 1857–90.

———. *New Atlantis*. In *Works*, 3:119–66. 1876.

Bagehot, Walter. *Physics and Politics*. International Scientific Series, vol. 2. New York: D. Appleton and Co., 1890.

Bain, Alexander. *The Emotions and the Will*. London: John W. Parker and Son, 1859.

———. *Moral Science: A Compendium of Ethics*. New York: D. Appleton and Co., 1882.

Baldwin, James Mark, ed. *Dictionary of Philosophy and Psychology*. 3 vols. in 4. New York: Macmillan Co., 1901–5.
———. *Social and Ethical Interpretations in Mental Development: A Study in Social Psychology*. 3d ed., rev. and enl. New York: Macmillan Co., 1902.
Barton, George Aaron. *A Sketch of Semitic Origins, Social and Religious*. New York: Macmillan Co., 1902.
Bebel, August. *Woman Under Socialism*. 33d ed. Translated by Daniel De Leon. New York: New York Labor News, 1904.
Benn, Alfred William. *The Philosophy of Greece Considered in Relation to the Character and History of Its People*. London: G. Richards, 1898.
Bentham, Jeremy. *An Introduction to the Principles of Morals and Legislation*. New ed. 2 vols. London: Printed for W. Pickering, 1823.
———. "Fragment on Government; or, A Comment on the Commentaries." In *The Works of Jeremy Bentham*, edited by John Bowring, 1:221–95. Edinburgh: William Tait, 1843.
Bergemann, Paul. *Ethik als Kulturphilosophie*. Leipzig: J. Hoffman, 1904.
Beyschalg, Willibald. *New Testament Theology*. Translated by Rev. Neil Buchanan. 2 vols. Edinburgh: T. and T. Clark, 1895.
Bonar, James. *The Intellectual Virtues*. New York: Macmillan Co., 1894.
———. *Philosophy and Political Economy in Some of Their Historical Relations*. Library of Philosophy. Edited by J. H. Muirhead. New York: Macmillan Co., 1893.
Bosanquet, Bernard, ed. *Aspects of the Social Problem*. New York: Macmillan Co., 1895.
———. *Civilization of Christendom and Other Studies*. The Ethical Library. New York: Macmillan Co., 1893. ["The Antithesis Between Individualism and Socialism Philosophically Considered," pp. 304–57.]
———. *The Philosophical Theory of the State*. New York: Macmillan Co., 1899.
———. *Psychology of the Moral Self*. New York: Macmillan Co., 1897.
Bosanquet, Helen. *The Family*. New York: Macmillan Co., 1906.
———. *The Standard of Life*. New York: Macmillan Co., 1898.
Bowne, Borden P. *The Principles of Ethics*. New York: Harper and Bros., 1892.
Bradley, Andrew Cecil. "Aristotle's Conception of the State." In *Hellenica: A Collection of Essays on Greek Poetry, Philosophy, History and Religion*, pp. 181–243. Edited by Evelyn Abbott. New York: Longmans, Green, and Co., 1880.
Bradley, Francis Herbert. *Ethical Studies*. London: H. S. King and Co., 1876. ["Why Should I Be Moral?", pp. 53–77.]

Brandes, George Morris Cohen. *Main Currents in Nineteenth Century Literature*. Translated by Diana White and Mary Morison. 6 vols. [Vols. 1, 2, and 5 by both; 3, 4, and 6 by Morison.] London: W. Heineman, 1901–5.

Brooks, John Graham. *The Social Unrest: Studies in Labor and Socialist and Labor Movements*. New York: Macmillan Co., 1903.

Brown, Thomas. *Lectures on the Philosophy of the Human Mind*. 4 vols. London: Longman, Hurst, Rees, Orme, and Brown, 1820.

Bruce, William Straton. *The Ethics of the Old Testament*. Edinburgh: T. and T. Clark, 1895.

Bryant, Sophie. *Short Studies in Character*. The Ethical Library, vol. 2. Edited by J. H. Muirhead. New York: Macmillan Co., 1894.

Bryce, James Bryce, viscount. *The Holy Roman Empire*. New ed., rev. and enl. New York: Macmillan Co., 1904.

———. *Studies in History and Jurisprudence*. 2 vols. Oxford: Clarendon Press, 1901. ["Marriage and Divorce in Roman and in English Law," 2:782–859.]

Bücher, Karl. *Arbeit und Rythmus*. 3d ed., enl. Tübingen: H. Laupp, 1901.

———. *Industrial Evolution*. 3d ed. Translated by S. Morley Wickett. New York: Henry Holt and Co., 1901.

Budde, Karl Ferdinand Reinhart. *Religion of Israel to the Exile*. American Lectures on the History of Religions, 4th series, 1898–99. New York: G. P. Putnam's Sons, 1899.

Burckhardt, Jakob Christoph. *The Civilisation of the Renaissance in Italy*. Half Guinea International Library. Translated by S. G. C. Middlemore. London: Swan Sonnenschein and Co., 1892.

Burnet, John. "Law and Nature in Greek Ethics." *International Journal of Ethics* 7(1897):328–33.

Burns, Robert. *The Complete Poetical Works of Robert Burns*. New York: Thomas Y. Crowell Co., 1900.

Butler, Joseph. *Fifteen Sermons*. London: Longman, Brown, Green, and Longmans, 1856.

Caesar. *Caesar's Gallic War*. Allen and Greenough's edition. Re-edited by James B. Greenough, Benjamin L. D'Ooge, and M. Grant Daniell. Boston: Ginn and Co., 1898.

Caird, Edward. *The Critical Philosophy of Immanuel Kant*. 2 vols. Glasgow: James Maclehose and Sons, 1889.

———. *The Evolution of Theology in the Greek Philosophers*. 2 vols. Glasgow: James Maclehose and Sons, 1904.

———. *The Social Philosophy and Religion of Comte*. New York: Macmillan Co., 1885.

Calderwood, Henry. *Handbook of Moral Philosophy*. 14th ed. London: Macmillan and Co., 1888.

──────. "The Relation of Intuitionism to the Ethical Doctrine of Self-Realization." *Philosophical Review* 5(1896):337–51.

Carlyle, Thomas. *The Works of Thomas Carlyle*. Centenary Edition. 31 vols. London: Chapman and Hall, 1898–1907. [*Sartor Resartus: The Life and Opinions of Herr Teufelsdröch*, vol. 1, 1897; *On Heroes, Hero-Worship and the Heroic in History*, vol. 5, 1904; *Past and Present*, vol. 10, 1899; *Latter-Day Pamphlets*, vol. 20, 1907; *Critical and Miscellaneous Essays*, vol. 27, 1905.]

Carriere, Moriz. *Die Kunst im Zusammenhang der Culturentwickelung und die Ideale der Menschheit*. 3d ed., rev. 5 vols. Leipzig: F. A. Brockhaus, 1877–86.

Cherry, Richard Robert. *Lectures on the Growth of Criminal Law in Ancient Communities*. New York: Macmillan Co., 1890.

Cicero, Marcus Tullius. *De finibus bonorum et malorum libri V.* 3d ed., rev. Edited by Johan Nicolai Madvig. Copenhagen: Glydendal, 1876.

──────. *De legibus libri tres*. Edited by W. D. Pearman. Cambridge: J. Hall and Son, 1881.

──────. *De natura deorum libri tres*. Edited by J. H. Swanson. 3 vols. Cambridge: University Press, 1883–91.

──────. *De officiis libri tres*. 7th ed. Edited by Hubert Ashton Holden. Cambridge: University Press, 1891.

Clark, John Bates. *Essentials of Economic Theory as Applied to Modern Problems of Industry and Public Policy*. New York: Macmillan Co., 1907.

Clifford, William Kingdon. *Lectures and Essays*. 2d ed. Edited by Leslie Stephen and Sir Frederick Pollock. New York: Macmillan Co., 1886. ["On the Scientific Basis of Morals," pp. 287–99.]

Comte, Auguste. *Cours de philosophie positive*. 6 vols. Paris: Bachelier, 1830–42.

──────. *The Positive Philosophy of Auguste Comte*. Translated by Harriet Martineau. 2 vols. London: Trübner and Co., 1875. [Translation and abridgement of *Cours de philosophie positive*.]

──────. *System of Positive Polity*. Translated by John Henry Bridges et al. 4 vols. London: Longmans, Green, and Co., 1875–77.

Cone, Orello. *Paul: the Man, the Missionary, and the Teacher*. New York: Macmillan Co., 1898.

──────. *Rich and Poor in the New Testament: A Study of the Primitive Christian Doctrine of Earthly Possessions*. New York: Macmillan Co., 1902.

Cooke-Taylor, Richard Whately. *The Modern Factory System*. London: Kegan Paul, Trench, Trübner and Co., 1891.

Cooley, Charles Horton. *Human Nature and the Social Order*. New York: Charles Scribner's Sons, 1902.

Crawley, Alfred Ernest. *The Mystic Rose: A Study of Primitive Marriage and of Primitive Thought in Its Bearings on Marriage*. New York: Macmillan Co., 1902.

Cunningham, William. *An Essay on Western Civilization in Its Economic Aspects*. Cambridge Historical Series, edited by G. W. Prothero, 2 vols. Cambridge: University Press, 1898–1900.

———. *The Growth of English Industry and Commerce*. 3 vols. [Vol. 1, 3d ed.] Cambridge: University Press, 1896–1903.

Darwin, Charles Robert. *The Descent of Man*. 2 vols. New York: D. Appleton and Co., 1871.

Denis, Jacques François. *Histoire des théories et des idées morales dans l'antiquité*. 2d ed. 2 vols. Paris: E. Thorin, 1879.

Dewey, John. *Logical Conditions of a Scientific Treatment of Morality*. Chicago: University of Chicago Press, 1903. [*Middle Works* 3:3–39.]

———. *Outlines of a Critical Theory of Ethics*. Ann Arbor: Register Publishing Co., 1891. [*Early Works* 3:237–388.]

———. *The School and Society*. Chicago: University of Chicago Press, 1900. [*Middle Works* 1:1–237.]

———. *The Study of Ethics: A Syllabus*. Ann Arbor: Register Publishing Co., 1894. [*Early Works* 4:219–362.]

———. "The Evolutionary Method as Applied to Morality." I. Its Scientific Necessity, *Philosophical Review* 11(1902):107–24; II. Its Significance for Conduct, *Philosophical Review* 11(1902):353–71. [*Middle Works* 2:3–38.]

———. "Interpretation of Savage Mind." *Psychological Review* 9 (1902):217–30. [*Middle Works* 2:39–52.]

———. "Moral Theory and Practice." *International Journal of Ethics* 1(1891):186–203. [*Early Works* 3:103–9.]

———. "Self-Realization as the Moral Ideal." *Philosophical Review* 2(1893):652–64. [*Early Works* 4:42–53.]

Dicey, Albert Venn. *Lectures on the Relation Between Law and Public Opinion in England During the Nineteenth Century*. New York: Macmillan Co., 1905.

Dickinson, Goldsworthy Lowes. *The Meaning of Good: A Dialogue*. New York: McClure, Phillips and Co., 1906.

Dinsmore, Charles Allen. *Atonement in Literature and Life*. Boston: Houghton Mifflin Co., 1906.

Donisthorpe, Wordsworth. *Individualism: A System of Politics*. New York: Macmillan Co., 1889.

Doring, August. *Die Lehre des Sokrates als sociales Reformsystem: Neuer Versuch zur Lösung des Problems der Sokratischen Philosophie*. Munich: C. H. Beck, 1895.

Dorsey, James Owen. "Omaha Sociology." In *Third Annual Report of the Bureau of Ethnology to the Secretary of the Smithsonian Institution 1881–'82*, pp. 205–370. Washington: Government Printing Office, 1884.

———. "A Study of Siouan Cults." In *Eleventh Annual Report of the Bureau of Ethnology to the Secretary of the Smithsonian Institution 1889–'90*, pp. 361–544. Washington: Government Printing Office, 1894.

Draper, John William. *History of the Intellectual Development of Europe.* Rev. ed. 2 vols. New York: Harper and Bros., 1876.

Dunning, William Archibald. *A History of Political Theories Ancient and Medieval.* New York: Macmillan Co., 1902.

———. *A History of Political Theories from Luther to Montesquieu.* New York: Macmillan Co., 1905.

Durkheim, Émile. *De la division du travail social: Étude sur l'organisation des sociétés supérieures.* Paris: F. Alcan, 1893.

Eastman, Charles Alexander. *Indian Boyhood.* New York: McClure, Phillips and Co., 1902.

Eckenstein, Lina. *Woman Under Monasticism: Chapters on Saint-Lore and Convent Life Between A.D. 500 and A.D. 1500.* Cambridge: University Press, 1896.

Eddy, Arthur J. *The Law of Combinations Embracing Monopolies, Trusts, and Combinations of Labor and Capital.* 2 vols. Chicago: Callaghan and Co., 1901.

Eicken, Heinrich von. *Geschichte und System der mittelalterlichen Weltanschauung.* Stuttgart: J. G. Cotta, 1887.

Eliot, George. *Romola.* Novels of George Eliot, vol. 5. New York: Harper and Bros., 1872.

Ellis, Havelock. *Man and Woman: A Study of Secondary Sexual Characters.* The Contemporary Science Series. Edited by Havelock Ellis, vol. 24. New York: Charles Scribner's Sons, 1894.

Ely, Richard T. *The Labor Movement in America.* New York: Thomas Y. Crowell Co., 1886.

———. *Socialism: An Examination of Its Nature, Its Strength and Its Weakness, with Suggestions for Social Reform.* Library of Economics and Politics, edited by Richard T. Ely, no. 3. New York: Thomas Y. Crowell Co., 1894.

Emerson, Ralph Waldo. "Compensation." In *Essays: First Series. The Complete Works of Ralph Waldo Emerson,* vol. 2. Boston: Houghton Mifflin Co., 1903.

———. "Domestic Life." In *Society and Solitude. Works,* vol. 7. 1904.

———. "Man the Reformer." In *Nature: Addresses and Lectures. Works,* vol. 1. 1903.

———. "Spiritual Laws." In *Essays: First Series. Works,* vol. 2. 1903.

———. "Worship." In *Conduct of Life. Works,* vol. 6. 1904.

Encyclopedia Biblica. Edited by Thomas Kelly Cheyne and John Sutherland Black. 4 vols. New York: Macmillan Co., 1899–1903.

Epictetus. *The Discourses of Epictetus*. Translated by George Long. 2 vols. London: George Bell and Sons, 1903.

Erdmann, Johann Eduard. *A History of Philosophy*. 2d ed. Translated by Williston S. Hough. 3 vols. London: Swan Sonnenschein and Co., 1892–97.

Euripides. *The Tragedies of Euripides in English Verse*. Edited and translated by Arthur S. Way. 3 vols. New York: Macmillan Co., 1894–98.

Fagan, J. O. "Confessions of a Railroad Signalman." *Atlantic Monthly* 101(1908):80–87, 225–32, 497–505, 684–92, 805–15; 102 (1908):109–20.

Falckenberg, Richard Friedrich Otto. *History of Modern Philosophy from Nicolas of Cusa to the Present Time*. Translated by Andrew Campbell Armstrong, Jr. New York: Henry Holt and Co., 1893.

Farnell, Lewis Richard. *The Cults of the Greek States*. 4 vols. Oxford: Clarendon Press, 1899–1907.

Fewkes, Jesse Walter. "Hopi Katcinas." In *Twenty-First Annual Report of the Bureau of Ethnology to the Secretary of the Smithsonian Institution 1899–1900*, pp. 13–126. Washington: Government Printing Office, 1903.

———. "Tusayan Katcinas." In *Fifteenth Annual Report of the Bureau of Ethnology to the Secretary of the Smithsonian Institution 1893–'94*, pp. 245–313. Washington: Government Printing Office, 1897.

Fichte, Johann Gottlieb. *The Popular Works of Johann Gottlieb Fichte*. The English and Foreign Philosophical Library. 4th ed. Translated by William Smith. 2 vols. London: Trübner and Co., 1889. ["Characteristics of the Present Age," 2:1–288.]

———. *The Science of Rights*. Translated by A. E. Kroeger. Philadelphia: J. B. Lippincott and Co., 1869.

Fisher, George Park. *History of the Christian Church*. New York: Charles Scribner's Sons, 1887.

Fiske, John. *Outlines of Cosmic Philosophy*. 4 vols. Boston: Houghton Mifflin Co., 1903.

———. *Through Nature to God*. Boston: Houghton Mifflin Co., 1899. ["The Cosmic Roots of Love and Self-Sacrifice," pp. 57–130.]

Fison, Lorimer, and Howitt, Alfred William. *Kamilaroi and Kurnai*. Melbourne: G. Robertson, 1880.

Fite, Warner. *An Introductory Study of Ethics*. New York: Longmans, Green, and Co., 1903.

———. "The Theory of Democracy." *International Journal of Ethics* 18(1907):1–18.

Fletcher, Alice C. "The Hako: A Pawnee Ceremony." In *Twenty-Second Annual Report of the Bureau of Ethnology to the Secretary of the Smithsonian Institution 1900–1901*. 2 parts.

2:1–368. Washington: Government Printing Office, 1904.

Francke, Kuno. *Social Forces in German Literature: A Study in the History of Civilization*. New York: Henry Holt and Co., 1896. [Beginning with 4th edition the title was changed to *A History of German Literature as Determined by Social Forces*.]

Frazer, Sir James George. *The Golden Bough: A Study in Magic and Religion*. 2d ed., rev. and enl. 3 vols. New York: Macmillan Co., 1900.

Freund, Ernst. *The Police Power: Public Policy and Constitutional Rights*. Chicago: Callaghan and Co., 1904.

Fustel de Coulanges, Numa Denis. *The Ancient City: A Study on the Religion, Laws, and Institutions of Greece and Rome*. Translated by Willard Small. Boston: Lee and Shepard, 1874.

Genung, John Franklin. *The Epic of the Inner Life: Being the Book of Job*. Boston: Houghton Mifflin Co., 1900.

George, Henry. *Progress and Poverty: An Inquiry into the Cause of Industrial Depressions, and of Increase of Want with Increase of Wealth—The Remedy*. Author's ed. San Francisco: W. M. Hinton and Co., 1879.

Giddings, Franklin Henry. *Democracy and Empire: With Studies of Their Psychological, Economic, and Moral Foundations*. New York: Macmillan Co., 1901. ["The Costs of Progress," pp. 67–96.]

———. *Inductive Sociology: A Syllabus of Methods, Analyses and Classifications, and Provisionally Formulated Laws*. New York: Macmillan Co., 1901.

———. *The Principles of Sociology: An Analysis of the Phenomena of Association and of Social Organization*. 3d ed. New York: Macmillan Co., 1896.

Gizyeki, Georg von. *A Student's Manual of Ethical Philosophy*. Translated by Stanton Coit. London: Swan Sonnenschein and Co., 1889.

Godwin, William. *Godwin's "Political Justice": A Reprint of the Essay on "Property" from the Original Edition*. Edited by Henry Stephens Salt. 1890. Social Science Series, vol. 11. St. Clair Shores, Michigan: Scholarly Press, [1969?].

Goldsmith, Oliver. *The Vicar of Wakefield*. Edited by Mary A. Jordan. New York: Longmans, Green, and Co., 1898.

Gomperz, Theodor. *Greek Thinkers: A History of Ancient Philosophy*. Authorized ed. 3 vols. (Vol. 1 translated by Laurie Magnus, 1901; vols. 2 and 3 translated by George Godfrey Berry, 1905.) London: John Murray, 1901–5.

Gray, John Henry. *China: A History of the Laws, Manners, and Customs of the People*. Edited by William Gow Gregor. 2 vols. London: Macmillan and Co., 1878.

Green, Thomas Hill. *Lectures on the Principles of Political Obligation*. Reprinted from Green's Philosophical Works, vol. 2

(*Works of Thomas Hill Green*. Edited by R. L. Nettleship. 3 vols. 1885–88). London: Longmans, Green, and Co., 1895.

———. *Prolegomena to Ethics*. Edited by A. C. Bradley. Oxford: Clarendon Press, 1883.

Grosse, Ernst. *Die Formen der Familie und die Formen der Wirthschaft*. Freiburg and Leipzig: J. C. B. Mohr (P. Siebeck), 1896.

Grote, George. *Plato and Other Companions of Sokrates*. 3d ed. 3 vols. London: John Murray, 1875. [4 vols. London: John Murray, 1888.]

———. *A History of Greece: From the Earliest Period to the Close of the Generation Contemporary with Alexander the Great*. 4th ed. 10 vols. London: John Murray, 1872.

Grote, John. *An Examination of the Utilitarian Philosophy*. Cambridge: Deighton, Bell, and Co., 1870.

Gummere, Francis Barton. *The Beginnings of Poetry*. New York: Macmillan Co., 1901.

Guyau, Jean Marie. *A Sketch of Morality Independent of Obligation or Sanction*. 2d ed. Translated by G. Kapteyn. London: Watts and Co., 1898.

Hadley, Arthur Twining. *Economics: An Account of the Relations Between Private Property and Public Welfare*. New York: G. P. Putnam's Sons, 1896.

———. *The Relations Between Freedom and Responsibility in the Evolution of Democratic Government*. New York: Charles Scribner's Sons, 1903.

———. "Constitutional Position of Property in America." *Independent* 64(1908):834–38.

Halévy, Élie. *La Formation du Radicalisme Philosophique*. 3 vols. Paris: F. Alcan, 1901–4.

Hall, Arthur Cleveland. *Crime in Its Relations to Social Progress*. New York: Columbia University Press, 1901.

Hammurabi, King of Babylonia. *The Oldest Code of Laws in the World*. Translated by C. H. W. Johns. Edinburgh: T. and T. Clark, 1903.

Hardy, Edmund. *Der Begriff der Physis in der griechischen Philosophie*. Vol. 1. Berlin: Weidmann, 1884. [No more published.]

Harnack, Adolf von. *What Is Christianity?* 2d ed., rev. Translated by Thomas Bailey Saunders. New York: G. P. Putnam's Sons, 1901.

Harris, George. *Inequality and Progress*. Boston: Houghton Mifflin Co., 1897.

———. *Moral Evolution*. Boston: Houghton Mifflin Co., 1896.

Harrison, Jane Ellen. *Prolegomena to the Study of the Greek Religion*. Cambridge: University Press, 1903.

Hastings, James et al., eds. *A Dictionary of the Bible*. 5 vols. New York: Charles Scribner's Sons, 1898–1904.

Hazlitt, William. "Jeremy Bentham." In *The Spirit of the Age; or, Contemporary Portraits*. The World's Classics, vol. 57. *The Works of William Hazlitt*, 4:1–16. London: Henry Froude, 1904.

Hearn, Lafcadio. *Japan: An Attempt at Interpretation*. New York: Macmillan Co., 1904.

Hearn, William Edward. *The Aryan Household, Its Structure and Development: An Introduction to Comparative Jurisprudence*. London: Longmans, Green, and Co., 1879.

Hegel, Georg Wilhelm Friedrich. *Lectures on the Philosophy of History*. Bohn's Philosophical Library. Translated from the 3d German ed. by John Sibree. London: George Bell and Sons, 1881.

———. *Philosophy of Right*. Translated by S. W. Dyde. London: George Bell and Sons, 1896.

———. *Ueber die wissenschaftlichen Behandlungsarten des Naturrechts*. Vol. 1 of Werke. 2d ed. Edited by Phillip Marheineke et al. 8 vols. Berlin: Duncker and Humblot, 1845.

Held, Adolf. *Zwei Bücher zur socialen Geschichte Englands*. Leipzig: Duncker and Humblot, 1881.

Henderson, Charles Richmond. *Social Elements, Institutions, Characters, Progress*. New York: Charles Scribner's Sons, 1898.

Hensel, Paul. "Problems of Ethics." Translated by J. H. Woods. In *Congress of Arts and Science: Universal Exposition, St. Louis, 1904*, edited by Howard J. Rogers, 1:403–14. Boston: Houghton Mifflin Co., 1905.

Hirn, Yrjö. *The Origins of Art: A Psychological and Sociological Inquiry*. New York: Macmillan Co., 1900.

Hobbes, Thomas. *Leviathan*. 3d ed. London: George Routledge and Sons, 1887.

Hobhouse, Leonard Trelawney. *Morals in Evolution: A Study in Comparative Ethics*. 2 vols. New York: Henry Holt and Co., 1906.

Hobson, John Atkinson. *The Evolution of Modern Capitalism: A Study of Machine Production*. The Contemporary Science Series, edited by H. Ellis, vol. 25. New York: Charles Scribner's Sons, 1894.

———. *The Social Problem: Life and Work*. London: J. Nisbet and Co., 1901.

Höffding, Harald. *Ethik*. Translated from *Etik*, Copenhagen, 1887, by F. Bendixen. Leipzig: Reisland, 1888.

———. *A History of Modern Philosophy: A Sketch of the History of Philosophy from the Close of the Renaissance to Our Own Day*. Translated by B. Ethel Meyer. 2 vols. London: Macmillan and Co., 1900.

———. *Outlines of Psychology*. Translated by Mary E. Lowndes. London: Macmillan and Co., 1891.

————. "The Principles of Welfare." *Monist* 1(1891):525–51.

Hollander, Jacob Harry, and Barnett, George Ernest, eds. *Studies in American Trades Unionism.* New York: Henry Holt and Co., 1906.

Holmes, Oliver Wendell, Jr. *The Common Law.* Boston: Little, Brown and Co., 1881.

Homer. *The Odyssey of Homer.* Translated by George Herbert Palmer. Boston: Houghton Mifflin Co., 1891.

Howard, George Elliot. *A History of Matrimonial Institutions Chiefly in England and the United States.* 3 vols. Chicago: University of Chicago Press, Callaghan and Co., 1904.

Howitt, Alfred William. *The Native Tribes of South-East Australia.* London: Macmillan and Co., 1904.

Hume, David. *A Treatise of Human Nature.* Edited by T. H. Green and T. H. Grose. 2 vols. London: Longmans, Green, and Co., 1898.

————. "An Inquiry Concerning the Principles of Morals." In *Essays: Moral, Political, and Literary,* edited by T. H. Green and T. H. Grose, 2:169–287. London: Longmans, Green, and Co., 1889.

Hunter, Robert. *Socialists at Work.* New York: Macmillan Co., 1908.

Hutcheson, Francis. *A System of Moral Philosophy.* 2 vols. 1775. Reprint (2 vols. in 1). Reprints of Economic Classics. New York: Augustus M. Kelly, 1968.

Huxley, Thomas Henry. *Critiques and Addresses.* New York: Macmillan Co., 1890. ["Administrative Nihilism," pp. 3–32.]

Ihering, Rudolph von. *Der Kampf um's Recht.* 15th ed. Vienna: Manz, 1903.

————. *Der Zweck im Recht.* 3d rev. ed. Leipzig: Breitkopf and Härtel, 1893.

Illinois Supreme Court Reports. *A. R. Barnes & Co., et al. Appellees,* v. *The Chicago Typographical Union No. 16 et al. Appellants.* 232(Feb. 1908):424–40.

Illinois Supreme Court Reports. *John O'Brien* v. *The People ex rel. Kellogg Switchboard and Supply Co.* 216(Oct. 1905): 354–76.

James, William. *The Principles of Psychology.* 2 vols. New York: Henry Holt and Co., 1893.

————. "The Moral Philosopher and the Moral Life." *International Journal of Ethics* 1(1891):330–54.

Janet, Paul Alexandre René. *Histoire de la science politique dans ses rapports avec la morale.* 3d ed. 2 vols. Paris: F. Alcan, 1887.

————. *The Theory of Morals.* Translated by Mary Chapman. Edinburgh: T. and T. Clark, 1884.

Jevons, Frank Byron. *An Introduction to the History of Religion.* 2d ed., rev. London: Methuen and Co., 1902.

Jewish Encyclopedia. Edited by Isidore Singer et al. 12 vols. New York: Funk and Wagnalls Co., 1901–6.

Jodl, Friedrich. *Geschichte der Ethik in der neueren Philosophie.* 2 vols. Stuttgart: Cotta, 1882–89.

Kant, Immanuel. *Critique of Practical Reason and Other Works on the Theory of Ethics.* 4th rev. ed. Translated by Thomas Kingsmill Abbott. London: Longmans, Green, and Co., 1889.

———. *Fundamental Principles of the Metaphysics of Ethics.* 3d ed. Translated by Thomas Kingsmill Abbott. London: Longmans, Green, and Co., 1907.

———. *Kant's Principles of Politics, Including His Essay on Perpetual Peace.* Edited and translated by William Hastie. Edinburgh: T. and T. Clark, 1891. ["Idea of a Universal History from a Cosmopolitical Point of View," pp. 1–29.]

———. *The Philosophy of Law: An Exposition of the Fundamental Principles of Jurisprudence as the Science of Right.* Translated by William Hastie. Edinburgh: T. and T. Clark, 1887.

Kelly, Florence. *Some Ethical Gains Through Legislation.* The Citizen's Library of Economics, Politics, and Sociology, edited by Richard T. Ely. New York: Macmillan Co., 1905.

Kidd, Dudley. *The Essential Kafir.* London: A. and C. Black, 1904.

———. *Savage Childhood: A Study of Kafir Children.* London: A. and C. Black, 1906.

Köstlin, Karl Reinhold von. *Geschichte der Ethik.* Vol. 1, pt. 1. Tübingen: H. Laupp, 1887. [No more published.]

Kovalevsky, Maxime. *Tableau des origines et de l'évolution de la famille et de la propriété.* Stockholm: Samson and Wallin, 1890.

Krauss, Friedrich Salomon. *Sitte und Brauch der Südslaven.* Vienna: A. Holder, 1885.

Kropotkin, Petr Aleksiêvich. *Mutual Aid: A Factor of Evolution.* New York: McClure, Phillips and Co., 1902.

Ladd, George Trumbull. *Philosophy of Conduct: A Treatise of the Facts, Principles, and Ideals of Ethics.* New York: Charles Scribner's Sons, 1902.

Lallemand, Léon. *Histoire de la charité.* 4 vols. in 5. Paris: A. Picard, 1902–12. [Vols. 1–3, 1902–6; vol. 4, 1910–12.]

Lankester, Sir Edwin Ray. *The Kingdom of Man.* London: A. Constable and Co., 1907.

Lecky, William Edward Hartpole. *History of European Morals: From Augustus to Charlemagne.* 3d ed., rev. 2 vols. New York: D. Appleton and Co., 1879.

Leslie, Thomas Edward Cliffe. *Essays in Political and Moral Philosophy.* Dublin: Hodges, Foster, and Figgis, 1879.

———. *Essays in Political Economy.* 2d ed. Edited by J. K. Ingram and C. F. Bastable. Dublin: Hodges, Figgis and Co., 1888.

Lioy, Diodato. *The Philosophy of Right*. Translated by William Hastie. 2 vols. London: Kegan Paul, Trench, Trübner, and Co., 1891.

Loch, Charles Stewart. "Charity and Charities." *The Encyclopædia Britannica*. 10th edition. 1902–3.

Locke, John. *Essay on Human Understanding*. *The Works of John Locke*, vols. 1–3. 1823. Reprint, Berlin: Scientia Verlag Aalen, 1963.

Lubbock, Sir John, the Right Honorable Lord Avebury. *The Origin of Civilisation and the Primitive Condition of Man: Mental and Social Condition of Savages*. 6th ed. London: Longmans, Green, and Co., 1902.

Lucretius Carus, Titus. *T. Lucreti Cari de rerum natura libri sex*. 4th ed., rev. Translated by Hugh A. J. Munro. 3 vols. London: George Bell and Sons, 1898–1900.

Lyall, Sir Alfred Comyn. *Asiatic Studies, Religious and Social*. 2d ed. London: John Murray, 1882.

McGilvary, Evander Bradley. "The Consciousness of Obligation." *Philosophical Review* 11(1902):333–52.

Mackenzie, John Stuart. *An Introduction to Social Philosophy*. Glasgow: James Maclehose and Sons, 1890.

———. *A Manual of Ethics*. The University Tutorial Series. 4th ed. London: University Correspondence College Press, 1900.

———. "Moral Science and the Moral Life." *International Journal of Ethics* 4(1894):160–73.

———. "Self-Assertion and Self-Denial." *International Journal of Ethics* 5(1895):273–95.

McLennan, John Ferguson. *Studies in Ancient History: Comprising a Reprint of Primitive Marriage*. New ed. London: Macmillan and Co., 1886.

Maine, Sir Henry Sumner. *Ancient Law: Its Connection with the Early History of Society, and Its Relation to Modern Ideas*. London: John Murray, 1861. [10th ed., 1885.]

———. *Ancient Law*. Introduction and notes by Sir Frederick Pollock. London: John Murray, 1906.

———. *Dissertations on Early Law and Custom*. Author's ed. New York: Henry Holt and Co., 1886.

———. *Lectures on the Early History of Institutions*. New York: Henry Holt and Co., 1888.

Mallock, William Hurrell. *Socialism*. New York: The National Civic Federation, 1907.

Mandeville, Bernard. *The Fable of the Bees*. Edinburgh: Mundell and Sons, 1806.

Marett, Robert R. "Is Taboo a Negative Magic?" In *Anthropological Essays Presented to Edward Burnett Tylor*, edited by W. H. R. Rivers, R. R. Marett, and Northcote W. Thomas, pp. 219–34. Oxford: Clarendon Press, 1907.

Marshall, Alfred. *Principles of Economics*. Vol. 1. 4th ed. London: Macmillan and Co., 1898. [No more published to September 1919.]

Marti, Karl. *The Religion of the Old Testament: Its Place among the Religions of the Nearer East.* Crown Theological Library, vol. 19. Edited by Rev. William Douglas Morrison. Translated by Rev. Gustav Adolph Bienemann. New York: G. P. Putnam's Sons, 1907.

Martineau, James. *Types of Ethical Theory.* 2 vols. Oxford: Clarendon Press, 1885. [3d ed., rev. 2 vols. in 1. New York: Macmillan Co., 1891.]

Marx, Karl, and Engels, Frederick. *Manifesto of the Communist Party.* Authorized English translation. Edited by Frederick Engels. Chicago: C. H. Kerr and Co., 1902.

Matthews, Shailer. *The Social Teaching of Jesus: An Essay in Christian Sociology.* New York: Macmillan Co., 1897.

Maurice, John Frederick Denison. *The Conscience.* London: Macmillan and Co., 1868.

Mead, George H. "The Philosophical Basis of Ethics." *International Journal of Ethics* 18(1908):311–23.

Menger, Anton. *The Right to the Whole Produce of Labor.* Translated by M. E. Tanner. London: Macmillan and Co., 1899.

Merz, John Theodore. *A History of European Thought in the Nineteenth Century.* [Vol. 1, 2d unaltered ed., 1904; vol. 2, 1903.] Edinburgh: William Blackwood and Sons, 1903–4.

Mezes, Sidney Edward. *Ethics: Descriptive and Explanatory.* New York: Macmillan Co., 1901.

Mill, James. *Analysis of the Phenomena of the Human Mind.* New ed. Edited by John Stuart Mill. 2 vols. London: Longmans, Green, Reader and Dyer, 1869.

Mill, John Stuart. *Autobiography.* London: Longmans, Green, Reader and Dyer, 1873.

———. *Considerations on Representative Government.* London: Parker, Son, and Bourn, 1861.

———. *Dissertations and Discussions: Political, Philosophical, and Historical.* 2 vols. London: John W. Parker and Son, 1859. ["Bentham," 1:330–91.]

———. *Dissertations and Discussions: Political, Philosophical, and Historical.* 4 vols. New York: Henry Holt and Co., 1874. ["Utilitarianism," 3:300–391.]

———. *Early Essays.* Selected from the original sources by J. W. M. Gibbs. London: George Bell and Sons, 1897.

———. *On Liberty.* New York: Henry Holt and Co., 1859.

———. *Principles of Political Economy.* The New Science Library, vols. 12–13. New York: J. A. Hill and Co., 1904.

———. *The Subjection of Women.* Philadelphia: J. B. Lippincott and Co., 1869.

———. *Utilitarianism.* Reprinted from "Fraser's Magazine." 2d ed. London: Longman, Green, Longman, Roberts, and Green, 1864.

Milton, John. *The Tenure of Kings and Magistrates.* In *The Prose Works of John Milton*, edited by J. A. St. John, 2:1–47. Bohn's Standard Library. 5 vols. London: George Bell and Sons, 1875–83.

Mindeleff, Cosmos. "The Repair of Casa Grande Ruin, Arizona, in 1891." In *Fifteenth Annual Report of the Bureau of Ethnology to the Secretary of the Smithsonian Institution 1893–'94*, pp. 315–49. Washington: Government Printing Office, 1897.

Mitchell, John. *Organized Labor: Its Problems, Purposes and Ideals and the Present and Future of American Wage Earners.* Philadelphia: American Book and Bible House, 1903.

Moore, George Edward. *Principia Ethica.* Cambridge: University Press, 1903.

Morgan, Lewis Henry. *Ancient Society: or, Researches in the Lines of Human Progress from Savagery, through Barbarism to Civilization.* New York: Henry Holt and Co., 1877.

———. *Houses and House-Life of the American Aborigines.* Contributions to North American Ethnology, vol. 4. Washington: Government Printing Office, 1881.

———. *League of the Ho-dé-no-sau-nee, or Iroquois.* Rochester, N. Y.: Sage and Brothers, 1851.

———. *Systems of Consanguinity and Affinity of the Human Family.* Smithsonian Contributions to Knowledge, vol. 17. Washington: Smithsonian Institution, 1870.

Muirhead, John Henry. *The Elements of Ethics: An Introduction to Moral Philosophy.* New York: Charles Scribner's Sons, 1892.

Mulford, Elisha. *The Nation: The Foundations of Civil Order and Political Life in the United States.* New York: Hurd and Houghton, 1872.

Murray, John Clark. *An Introduction to Ethics.* Boston: De Wolfe Fiske and Co., 1891.

Newman, William Lambert. *Introduction to the Politics. The Politics of Aristotle*, vol. 1. Edited by W. L. Newman. Oxford: Cambridge University Press, 1887–1902.

New York Supplement. *Rogers et al. v. Evarts et al.* 17(11 Feb.–24 Mar. 1892):264–70. St. Paul: West Publishing Co., 1892.

Nicholl, Sir George. *History of the English Poor Law, in Connection with the State of the Country and the Condition of the People.* New ed., rev. 2 vols. New York: G. P. Putnam's Sons, 1898–99.

Nietzsche, Friederich Wilhelm. "The Antichrist: An Essay towards a Criticism of Christianity." Translated by Thomas Common. In *Works*, edited by Alexander Tille, 11:233–351. New York: Macmillan Co., 1896.

———. *Beyond Good and Evil: Prelude to a Philosophy of the Future*. Authorised translation by Helen Zimmern. Edinburgh: T. N. Foulis, 1907.

———. *Der Wille zur Macht: Versuch einer Umwerthung aller Werthe*. Leipzig: C. G. Naumann, 1901.

Nitobé, Inazo Ota. *Bushido, The Soul of Japan: An Exposition of Japanese Thought*. 10th rev. and enl. ed. New York: G. P. Putnam's Sons, 1905.

Paley, William. *The Principles of Moral and Political Philosophy*. 2 vols. in 1. Boston: N. H. Whitaker, 1828.

Palmer, George Herbert. *The Field of Ethics*. Boston: Houghton Mifflin Co., 1901.

———. *The Nature of Goodness*. Boston: Houghton Mifflin Co., 1903.

Parsons, Elsie Clews. *The Family: An Ethnological and Historical Outline*. New York: G. P. Putnam's Sons, 1906.

Pater, Walter Horatio. *Marius the Epicurean: His Sensations and Ideas*. 2d ed. London: Macmillan and Co., 1885.

Paulsen, Friedrich. *System der Ethik*. 2 vols. in 1. Berlin: Besser, 1889. [5th rev. ed. 2 vols. Berlin: W. Hertz, 1900.]

———. *A System of Ethics*. Edited and translated by Frank Thilly. New York: Charles Scribner's Sons, 1899.

Peake, Arthur Samuel. *The Problem of Suffering in the Old Testament*. London: Robert Bryant, 1904.

Pfleiderer, Otto. *Paulinism: A Contribution to the History of Primitive Christian Theology*. Translated by E. Peters. 2 vols. London: Theological Translation Fund Library, 1873.

———. *Primitive Christianity: Its Writings and Teachings in Their Historical Connections*. Theological Translation Library, vol. 22. Edited by William Douglas Morrison. Translated by William Montgomery. London: Williams and Norgate, 1906.

Plato. *The Dialogues of Plato*. Translated by Benjamin Jowett. 4 vols. Boston: Jefferson Press, 1871. [*Protagoras*, 1:97–162; *Apology*, 1:303–39; *Crito*, 1:341–59; *Republic*, 2:1–452; *Gorgias*, 3:1–119; *Theaetetus*, 3:301–419; *Laws*, 4:1–480.]

———. *The Republic of Plato*. Golden Treasury Series. Translated by John Llewelyn Davies and James Vaughan. New York: Macmillan Co., 1897.

Pöhlmann, Robert von. *Geschichte des antiken Kommunismus und Sozialismus*. 2 vols. Munich: C. H. Beck, 1893–1901.

Pollock, Sir Frederick. *The Expansion of the Common Law*. London: Stevens and Sons, 1904.

———. *Oxford Lectures and Other Discourses*. 1890. Essay Index Reprint Series. Freeport, N. Y.: Books for Libraries Press, 1972.

————, and Maitland, Frederic William. *The History of English Law Before the Time of Edward I.* 2 vols. Cambridge: University Press, 1895. [2d ed., 1899.]

Post, Albert Hermann. *Die Grundlagen des Rechts und die Grundzüge seiner Entwickelungsgeschichte.* Oldenburg: Schulze (A. Schwartz), 1884.

————. *Grundriss der ethnologischen Jurisprudenz.* 2 vols. Oldenburg: Schulze, 1894–95.

Powell, John Wesley. "On the Evolution of Language." In *First Annual Report of the Bureau of Ethnology to the Secretary of the Smithsonian Institution 1879–'80*, pp. 1–16. Washington: Government Printing Office, 1881.

————. "Sketch of the Mythology of the North American Indians." In *First Annual Report of the Bureau of Ethnology to the Secretary of the Smithsonian Institution 1879–'80*, pp. 17–56. Washington: Government Printing Office, 1881.

————. "Wyandot Government: A Short Study of Tribal Society." In *First Annual Report of the Bureau of Ethnology to the Secretary of the Smithsonian Institution 1879–'80*, pp. 57–86. Washington: Government Printing Office, 1881.

Pratt, James Bissett. *The Psychology of Religious Belief.* New York: Macmillan Co., 1907.

Rae, John. *Contemporary Socialism.* Half Guinea International Library. 2d ed., rev. and enl. London: Swan Sonnenschein and Co., 1891.

Rambaud, Alfred Nicolas. *Histoire de la civilisation française.* 2 vols. [Vol. 1, 7th ed., 1898; vol. 2, 6th ed., 1897.] Paris: A. Colin, 1897–98.

Rand, Benjamin. *Bibliography of Philosophy, Psychology, and Cognate Subjects.* Vol. 3, Parts 1 and 2, of *Dictionary of Philosophy and Psychology*, edited by James Mark Baldwin. New York: Macmillan Co., 1905.

Rashdall, Hastings. *The Theory of Good and Evil: A Treatise on Moral Philosophy.* Oxford: Clarendon Press, 1907.

————. *The Universities of Europe in the Middle Ages.* 2 vols. in 3. Oxford: Clarendon Press, 1895.

Ratzel, Friedrich. *The History of Mankind.* Translated from the 2d German edition by Arthur John Burler. 2 vols. London: Macmillan and Co., 1896–98.

Reeve, Sidney Aaron. *The Cost of Competition: An Effort at the Understanding of Familiar Facts.* New York: McClure, Phillips and Co., 1906.

Reinach, Salomon. *Cultes, mythes et religions.* 3 vols. Paris: E. Leroux, 1905–8.

Rickaby, Joseph John, S.J. *Moral Philosophy; or, Ethics and Natural Law.* English Manuals of Catholic Philosophy. New York: Benziger Brothers, 1888.

—. *Political and Moral Essays.* New York: Benziger Brothers, 1902.

Riehl, Wilhelm Heinrich. *Die Naturgeschichte des Volkes als Grundlage einer deutschen Sozial-Politik.* 4 vols. Stuttgart: Cotta, 1892–99. [Vol. 3, *Die Familie,* 11th ed., 1897.]

Ritchie, David George. *Darwin and Hegel.* London: Swan Sonnenschein and Co., 1893.

—. *Natural Rights: A Criticism of Some Political and Ethical Conceptions.* London: Swan Sonnenschein and Co., 1895.

—. *Philosophical Studies.* Edited by Robert Latta. London: Macmillan and Co., 1905.

—. *The Principles of State Interference: Four Essays on the Political Philosophy of Mr. Herbert Spencer, J. S. Mill, and T. H. Green.* London: Swan Sonnenschein and Co., 1891.

—. "On the Meaning of 'Motive'." *International Journal of Ethics* 4(1894):236–38.

—. "On the Meaning of the Term 'Motive,' and on the Ethical Significance of Motives." *International Journal of Ethics* 4(1893):89–94.

Rivers, William H. R. "On the Origin of the Classificatory System of Relationships." In *Anthropological Essays Presented to Edward Burnett Tylor,* edited by W. H. R. Rivers, R. R. Marett, and Northcote W. Thomas, pp. 309–23. Oxford: Clarendon Press, 1907.

Robbins, Hayes. "The Personal Factor in the Labor Problem." *Atlantic Monthly* 99(1907):729–36.

Robertson, John Mackinnon. *A Short History of Free Thought.* 2d ed., rewritten and enl. 2 vols. London: Swan Sonnenschein and Co., 1899.

Robinson, James Harvey, and Beard, Charles A. *The Development of Modern Europe: An Introduction to the Study of Current History.* 2 vols. Boston: Ginn and Co., 1907–8.

La Rochefoucauld, François VI, duc de. *Maxims and Moral Reflections.* New York: D. Appleton and Co., 1899.

Rohde, Erwin. *Psyche: Seelencult und unsterblichkeitsglaube der Griechen.* 2 parts. Freiburg in Breisgau and Leipzig: J. C. B. Mohr, 1894.

Ross, Edward Alsworth. *Foundations of Sociology.* The Citizen's Library of Economics, Politics, and Sociology. New York: Macmillan Co., 1905.

—. *Sin and Society: An Analysis of Latter-Day Iniquity.* Boston: Houghton Mifflin Co., 1907.

Rousseau, Jean Jacques. *The Social Contract.* Translated by Henry J. Tozer. London: Swan Sonnenschein and Co., 1895.

Royce, Josiah. *Nature, Man, and the Moral Order.* The World and the Individual, second series. New York: Macmillan Co., 1901.

————. *Studies of Good and Evil: A Series of Essays Upon Problems of Philosophy and of Life*. New York: D. Appleton and Co., 1898. ["The Problem of Job," pp. 1–28.]

Runze, Georg. *Praktische Ethik*. Ethik: Encyklopädische Skizzen u. Literaturangaben, vol. 1. Berlin: Carl Duncker, 1891. [No more published.]

Santayana, George. *The Life of Reason*. 5 vols. New York: Charles Scribner's Sons, 1905–6.

Schiller, Johann Christoph Friedrich von. *Schiller's Complete Works*. Edited, revised and translated by Charles J. Hempel. 2 vols. Philadelphia: I. Kohler and F. Leypoldt, 1863.

Schmidt, Leopold Valentine. *Die Ethik der alten Griechen*. 2 vols. Berlin: W. Hertz, 1882.

Schmoller, Gustav Friedrich von. *Grundriss der allgemeinen Volkswirtschaftslehre*. 2 vols. Leipzig: Duncker and Humblot, 1900–1904.

Schoolcraft, Henry Rowe. *Information Respecting the History, Conditions and Prospects of the Indian Tribes of the United States*. Ethnological Researches, Respecting the Red Man of America. 6 vols. Philadelphia: Lippincott, Grambo and Co., 1851–57.

Schultz, Hermann. *Old Testament Theology: The Religion of Revelation in Its Pre-Christian Stage of Development*. Translated from the 4th German edition by Rev. James Alexander Paterson. 2 vols. Edinburgh: T. and T. Clark, 1892.

Schurman, Jacob Gould. *The Ethical Import of Darwinism*. New York: Charles Scribner's Sons, 1887. [Another printing, 1888.]

————. "The Consciousness of Moral Obligation." *Philosophical Review* 3(1894):641–54.

Schurtz, Heinrich. *Altersklassen und Männerbünde*. Berlin: G. Reimer, 1902.

————. *Urgeschichte der Kultur*. Leipzig and Vienna: Bibliographisches Institut, 1900.

Seebohm, Frederic. *Tribal Custom in Anglo-Saxon Law*. London: Longmans, Green, and Co., 1902.

————. *The Tribal System in Wales: Being Part of an Inquiry into the Structure and Methods of Tribal Society*. London: Longmans, Green, and Co., 1895.

Selby-Bigge, Sir Lewis Amherst, ed. *British Moralists: Being Selections from Writers Principally of the Eighteenth Century*. 2 vols. Oxford: Clarendon Press, 1897.

Seth, James. *A Study of Ethical Principles*. 6th ed., rev. New York: Charles Scribner's Sons, 1902.

————. "The Evolution of Morality." *Mind* 14(1889):27–49.

Shaftesbury, Anthony Ashley Cooper, 3d Earl of. *Characteristics of Men, Manners, Opinions, Times, etc*. Edited by John M. Robertson. 2 vols. London: G. Richards, 1900.

————. "An Inquiry Concerning Virtue or Merit." In *Character-istics*, 1:225–338. London: G. Richards, 1900.

Shakespeare, William. *Hamlet*. 11th ed. London: J. M. Dent and Co., 1905.

Sharp, Frank Chapman. "An Analysis of the Idea of Obligation." *International Journal of Ethics* 2(1892):500–513.

————. "An Analysis of the Moral Judgment." In *Studies in Philosophy and Psychology*, edited by James Hayden Tufts et al., pp. 101–35. Boston: Houghton Mifflin Co., 1906.

Shaw, George Bernard, ed. *Fabian Essays in Socialism*. London: n.p., 1889. [American edition. Edited by H. G. Wilshire. New York: Humboldt Publishing Co., 1891.]

Sidgwick, Henry. *The Elements of Politics*. London: Macmillan and Co., 1891.

————. *Lectures on the Ethics of T. H. Green, Mr. Herbert Spencer, and J. Martineau*. London: Macmillan and Co., 1902.

————. *The Methods of Ethics*. London: Macmillan and Co., 1874. [2d ed., 1877; 6th ed., 1901.]

————. *Outlines of the History of Ethics, for English Readers*. 3d ed. London: Macmillan and Co., 1892.

————. *Practical Ethics: A Collection of Addresses and Essays*. London: Swan Sonnenschein and Co., 1898. ["Public Morality," pp. 52–82.]

Simcox, Edith J. *Natural Law: An Essay in Ethics*. The English and Foreign Philosophical Library, vol. 4. London: Trübner and Co., 1877.

Simmel, Georg. "The Sociology of Secrecy and of Secret Societies." *American Journal of Sociology* 11(1906):441–98.

Simmons, Duane B. "Notes on Land Tenure and Local Institutions in Old Japan." Edited by John H. Wigmore. *Transactions of the Asiatic Society of Japan* 19(1891):37–270.

Skeat, Walter William, of the Malay Civil Service. *Malay Magic: Being an Introduction to the Folklore and Popular Religion of the Malay Peninsula*. London: Macmillan and Co., 1900.

Small, Albion Woodbury. *General Sociology: An Exposition of the Main Development in Sociological Theory from Spencer to Ratzenhofer*. Chicago: University of Chicago Press, 1905.

————. *The Significance of Sociology for Ethics*. Chicago: University of Chicago Press, 1902.

Smith, Adam. *The Theory of Moral Sentiments*. New ed. London: George Bell and Sons, 1892.

Smith, Arthur Henderson. *Chinese Characteristics*. 2d ed., rev. New York: Fleming H. Revell Co., 1894.

————. *Village Life in China: A Study in Sociology*. New York: Fleming H. Revell Co., 1899.

Smith, Henry Preserved. *Old Testament History*. The International Theological Library. New York: Charles Scribner's Sons, 1903.

Smith, James Allen. *The Spirit of American Government: A Study of the Constitution*. The Citizen's Library of Economics, Politics, and Sociology, edited by Richard T. Ely. New York: Macmillan Co., 1907.

Smith, Munroe. "Judge-made Constitutional Law." *Van Norden Magazine*, February 1908, pp. 25–32.

Smith, William Robertson. *Kinship and Marriage in Early Arabia*. Cambridge: University Press, 1885.

———. *Lectures on the Religion of the Semites*. First Series, The Fundamental Institutions. Burnett Lectures 1888–89. New ed., rev. London: A. and C. Black, 1894.

———. *The Prophets of Israel and Their Place in History to the Close of the Eighth Century B.C. Eight Lectures*. New ed. London: A. and C. Black, 1895.

Sophocles. *The Tragedies of Sophocles*. Translated by E. H. Plumtree. New York: George Routledge and Sons, [1881?]. [*Oedipus at Colonos*, 57–125; *Antigone*, 127–77; *Philoctetes*, 341–97.]

Sorley, William Ritchie. *On the Ethics of Naturalism*. London: William Blackwood and Sons, 1885.

———. *Recent Tendencies in Ethics: Three Lectures to Clergy, given at Cambridge*. London: William Blackwood and Sons, 1904.

Spahr, Charles B. *An Essay on the Present Distribution of Wealth in the United States*. Library of Economics and Politics, edited by Richard T. Ely, number 12. New York: Thomas Y. Crowell Co., 1896.

Spargo, John. *Socialism: A Summary and Interpretation of Socialist Principles*. New York: Macmillan Co., 1906.

Spencer, Herbert. *The Data of Ethics*. New York: D. Appleton and Co., 1879.

———. *Essays: Scientific, Political, and Speculative*. Library ed. 3 vols. New York: D. Appleton and Co., 1891.

———. *The Man Versus the State*. London: Williams and Norgate, 1892.

———. *The Principles of Ethics*. 2 vols. New York: D. Appleton and Co., 1892–93.

———. *The Principles of Psychology*. 2 vols. New York: D. Appleton and Co., 1872–73.

———. *The Principles of Sociology*. 3 vols. London: Williams and Norgate, 1876–96. [3 vols. in 4. New York: D. Appleton and Co., 1880–97.]

———. *Social Statics*. Abridged and rev. New York: D. Appleton and Co., 1897.

Spencer, Sir Walter Baldwin, and Gillen, Francis James. *The

Native Tribes of Central Australia. London: Macmillan and Co., 1899.

———. *The Northern Tribes of Central Australia.* London: Macmillan and Co., 1904.

Spinoza, Benedict de. *Ethic.* Translated by William Hale White. London: Trübner and Co., Ludgate Hill, 1883.

Starcke, Carl Nicolai. *The Primitive Family in Its Origin and Development.* The International Scientific Series. American ed., vol. 65. New York: D. Appleton and Co., 1889.

Stein, Ludwig. *Die sociale Frage im Licht der Philosophie.* Stuttgart: F. Enke, 1897.

Steinmetz, Sebald Rudolf. *Ethnologische Studien zur ersten Entwicklung der Strafe.* 2 vols. Leipzig: O. Harrassowitz, 1894.

Steinthal, Heymann. *Allgemeine Ethik.* Berlin: G. Reimer, 1885.

Stephen, Sir James Fitzjames, Bart. *A History of the Criminal Law of England.* 3 vols. London: Macmillan and Co., 1883.

———. *Liberty, Equality, Fraternity.* London: Smith, Elder and Co., 1873.

Stephen, Leslie. *The English Utilitarians.* 3 vols. New York: G. P. Putnam's Sons, 1900.

———. *History of English Thought in the Eighteenth Century.* 3d ed. 2 vols. New York: G. P. Putnam's Sons, 1902.

———. *The Science of Ethics.* London: Smith, Elder and Co., 1882.

———. *Social Rights and Duties: Addresses to Ethical Societies.* The Ethical Library. 2 vols. London: Swan Sonnenschein and Co., 1896.

Stevenson, James. "Ceremonial of Hasjelti Dailjis and Mythical Sand Painting of the Navajo Indians." In *Eighth Annual Report of the Bureau of Ethnology to the Secretary of the Smithsonian Institution 1886–'87*, pp. 229–85. Washington: Government Printing Office, 1891.

Stevenson, Matilda Coxe. "The Zuñi Indians: Their Mythology, Esoteric Fraternities, and Ceremonies." In *Twenty-Third Annual Report of the Bureau of Ethnology to the Secretary of the Smithsonian Institution 1901–'02*, pp. 3–608. Washington: Government Printing Office, 1904.

Stuart, Henry Waldgrave. *The Logic of Self-Realization.* University of California Publications in Philosophy, vol. 1, no. 9, pp. 175–205. Berkeley: University Press, 1904.

———. "Valuation as a Logical Process." *Studies in Logical Theory* by John Dewey et al. The Decennial Publications, second series, vol. 11. Chicago: University of Chicago Press, 1903.

Sturt, Henry. "Duty." *International Journal of Ethics* 7(1897): 334–45.

Sumner, William Graham. *Folkways: A Study of the Sociological*

Importance of Usages, Manners, Customs, Mores, and Morals. Boston: Ginn and Co., 1906.

————. *What Social Classes Owe to Each Other.* New York: Harper and Bros., 1883.

Sutherland, Alexander. *The Origin and Growth of Moral Instinct.* 2 vols. London: Longmans, Green, and Co., 1898.

Tarde, Gabriel de. *Les lois de l'imitation: étude sociologique.* 2d ed., rev. and enl. Paris: F. Alcan, 1895.

Taylor, Alfred Edward. *The Problem of Conduct: A Study in the Phenomenology of Ethics.* London: Macmillan and Co., 1901.

————. "Self-Realization.—A Criticism." *International Journal of Ethics* 6(1896):356–71.

Taylor, Graham Romeyn. "The Chicago Industrial Exhibit." *Charities and the Commons* 18(1907):39–45.

Taylor, Henry Osborn. *Ancient Ideals: A Study of Intellectual and Spiritual Growth from Early Times to the Establishment of Christianity.* 2 vols. New York: Macmillan Co., 1900.

Thilly, Frank. *Introduction to Ethics.* New York: Charles Scribner's Sons, 1900.

Thomas, Northcote Whitridge. *Kinship Organisations and Group Marriage in Australia. Cambridge Archaeological and Ethnological Series.* Cambridge: University Press, 1906.

————, ed. *The Native Races of the British Empire.* 4 vols. London: A. Constable and Co., 1906–7. [No more published.]

Thomas, William Isaac. *Sex and Society: Studies in the Social Psychology of Sex.* Chicago: University of Chicago Press, 1907. ["Sex and Primitive Social Control," pp. 55–94.]

Thomas Aquinas, Saint. *Aquinas Ethicus; or, The Moral Teaching of St. Thomas.* Translated by Joseph John Rickaby. 2 vols. London: Burns and Oates, 1896. [On t.-p. of vol. 2, "Second Edition."]

Tolstoi, Lev Nikolaevich. *What Is Art?* Translated by Aylmer Maude. London: G. Richards, 1904.

Toynbee, Arnold. *Lectures on the Industrial Revolution of the 18th Century in England: Popular Addresses, Notes, and Other Fragments.* 3d ed. London: Longmans, Green, and Co., 1890.

Traill, Henry Duff, ed. *Social England.* 6 vols. London: Cassell and Co., 1894–98.

Tufts, James Hayden. *The Individual and His Relation to Society as Reflected in the British Ethics of the Eighteenth Century.* [Vol. 1, no. 6, *University of Chicago Contributions to Philosophy.*] New York: Macmillan Co., 1904.

————. "On Moral Evolution." In *Studies in Philosophy and Psychology,* edited by J. H. Tufts et al., pp. 3–39. Boston: Houghton Mifflin Co., 1906.

――――. "Some Contributions of Psychology to the Conception of Justice." *Philosophical Review* 15(1906):361–79.

――――, and Thompson, Helen B. *The Individual and His Relation to Society as Reflected in British Ethics. Part 1. The Individual in Relation to Law and Institutions.* [*University of Chicago Contributions to Philosophy*, no. 5, 1896.] Chicago: University of Chicago Press, 1898.

Tylor, Edward B. *Primitive Culture: Researches into the Development of Mythology, Philosophy, Religion, Language, Art, and Culture.* 4th ed., rev. 2 vols. London: John Murray, 1903.

Ueberweg, Friedrich. *History of Philosophy, from Thales to the Present Time.* Translated by George Sylvester Morris. 2 vols. New York: Charles Scribner's Sons, 1892.

Uhlhorn, Gerhard. *Christian Charity in the Ancient Church.* Translated. New York: Charles Scribner's Sons, 1883.

United States Reports. *Bacon v. Walker. Error to the Supreme Court of the State of Idaho.* 204(1907):311–20.

Veblen, Thorstein. *The Theory of Business Enterprise.* New York: Charles Scribner's Sons, 1904.

――――. *The Theory of the Leisure Class.* New York: Macmillan Co., 1899.

Voigt, Moritz. *Das jus naturale, aequum et bonum, und jus gentium der Römer.* 4 vols. Leipzig: Voigt and Gunther, 1856–76. [Vol. 1. *Die Lehre vom jus naturale, aequum et bonum, und jus gentium der Römer,* 1856.]

Waitz, Theodor. *Anthropologie der Naturvölker.* 6 vols. Leipzig: F. Fleischer, 1859–72.

Wallace, William. *Epicureanism.* New York: Pott, Young, and Co., 1880.

――――. *Lectures and Essays on Natural Theology and Ethics.* Edited by Edward Caird. Oxford: Clarendon Press, 1898.

Watson, John. *Hedonistic Theories from Aristippus to Spencer.* New York: Macmillan Co., 1895.

Webb, Sidney James, Baron Passfield, and Webb, Beatrice Potter, Baroness Passfield. *The History of Trade Unionism.* London: Longmans, Green, and Co., 1894.

――――. *Industrial Democracy.* New ed. London: Longmans, Green, and Co., 1902.

――――. *Problems of Modern Industry.* London: Longmans, Green, and Co., 1898.

Webster, Hutton. *Primitive Secret Societies: A Study in Early Politics and Religion.* New York: Macmillan Co., 1908.

Wells, Herbert George. *New Worlds for Old.* New York: Macmillan Co., 1907.

Wendt, Hans Hinrich. *The Teaching of Jesus.* Translated by Rev. John Wilson. 2 vols. Edinburgh: T. and T. Clark, 1892–99. [On t.-p. of vol. 2: Second English Edition.]

Westermarck, Edward Alexander. *The History of Human Marriage.* 3d ed. 3 vols. London: Macmillan and Co., 1901.

――――. *The Origin and Development of the Moral Ideas.* 2 vols. London: Macmillan and Co., 1906–8.

――――. "The Influence of Magic on Social Relationships." *Sociological Papers* 2(1906):141–74.

Whewell, William. *The Elements of Morality, Including Polity.* New York: Harper and Bros., 1856.

――――. *Lectures on the History of Moral Philosophy in England.* New ed. Cambridge: University Press, 1862.

Wilamowitz-Moellendorff, Ulrich von. *Aristoteles und Athen.* 2 vols. Berlin: Weidmann, 1893.

Williams, Cora May. *A Review of the Systems of Ethics Founded on the Theory of Evolution.* New York: Macmillan Co., 1893.

Willoughby, Wester Woodbury. *An Examination of the Nature of the State: A Study in Political Philosophy.* New York: Macmillan Co., 1896.

――――. *Social Justice: A Critical Essay.* New York: Macmillan Co., 1900.

Wilson, John Matthias, and Fowler, Thomas. *The Principles of Morals.* 2 vols. [Vol. 1 by Wilson and Fowler, 1886; vol. 2 by Fowler, 1887.] Oxford: Clarendon Press, 1886–87.

Wilson, Woodrow. *The State: Elements of Historical and Practical Politics.* Rev. ed. Boston: D. C. Heath and Co., 1899.

Windelband, Wilhelm. *History of Ancient Philosophy.* Translated by Herbert Ernest Cushman. New York: Charles Scribner's Sons, 1899.

――――. *A History of Philosophy with Especial Reference to the Formation and Development of Its Problems and Conceptions.* 2d ed., rev. and enl. Translated by James Hayden Tufts. London: Macmillan and Co., 1901.

Woods, Robert Archey. "Democracy, A New Unfolding of Human Power." In *Studies in Philosophy and Psychology,* edited by James Hayden Tufts et al., pp. 71–100. Boston: Houghton Mifflin Co., 1906.

Wundt, Wilhelm Max. *Ethik: Eine Untersuchung der Thatsachen und Gesetze des sittlichen Lebens.* Stuttgart: F. Enke, 1886. [3d rev. ed. 2 vols. 1903.]

――――. *Ethics: An Investigation of the Facts and Laws of the Moral Life.* 3 vols. (Vol. 1. *Introduction: The Facts of the Moral Life.* Translated by Julia Henrietta Gulliver and Edward Bradford Titchener. 1897. Vol. 2. *Ethical Systems.* Translated by Margaret Floy Washburn. 1897. Vol. 3. *The Principles of Morality and the Departments of the Moral Life.* Translated by Washburn. 1901.) London: Swan Sonnenschein and Co., 1897–1901.

Xenophon. *The Anabasis; or, Expedition of Cyrus.* Translated by Rev. John Selby Watson. Boston: W. Small, 1893.

————. *The Memorabilia of Socrates.* Pocket Literal Translation of the Classics. Translated by Rev. John Selby Watson. Philadelphia: David McKay Co., 1899.

Zeller, Eduard. *Aristotle and the Earlier Peripatetics.* Translated by B. F. C. Costelloe and J. H. Muirhead. London: Longmans, Green, and Co., 1897.

————. *Plato and the Older Academy.* New ed. Translated by Sarah Frances Alleyne and Alfred Goodwin. London: Longmans, Green, and Co., 1888.

————. *Socrates and the Socratic Schools.* 3d ed., rev. Translated by Oswald J. Reichel. London: Longmans, Green, and Co., 1885.

————. *The Stoics, Epicureans and Sceptics.* New ed., rev. Translated by Oswald J. Reichel. London: Longmans, Green, and Co., 1880.

Ziegler, Theobald. *Die geistigen und socialen Strömungen des neunzehnten Jahrhunderts.* Berlin: G. Bondi, 1899.

INDEX